The Continuity of Mind

OXFORD PSYCHOLOGY SERIES

Editors

Mark D'Esposito   Daniel Schacter
Jon Driver   Anne Treisman
Trevor Robbins   Lawrence Weiskrantz

The Continuity of Mind

Michael Spivey

OXFORD
UNIVERSITY PRESS

2007

OXFORD
UNIVERSITY PRESS

Oxford University Press, Inc., publishes works that further
Oxford University's objective of excellence
in research, scholarship, and education.

Oxford New York
Auckland   Cape Town   Dar es Salaam   Hong Kong   Karachi
Kuala Lumpur   Madrid   Melbourne   Mexico City   Nairobi
New Delhi   Shanghai   Taipei   Toronto

With offices in
Argentina   Austria   Brazil   Chile   Czech Republic   France   Greece
Guatemala   Hungary   Italy   Japan   Poland   Portugal   Singapore
South Korea   Switzerland   Thailand   Turkey   Ukraine   Vietnam

Published by Oxford University Press, Inc.
198 Madison Avenue, New York, New York 10016

www.oup.com

Library of Congress Cataloging-in-Publication Data
Spivey, J. M.
  The continuity of mind / by Michael Spivey.
    p. cm. — (Oxford psychology series; no. 40)
  ISBN-13 978-0-19-517078-8
  ISBN 0-19-517078-4
  1. Cognition. I. Title. II. Series.
  BF311.S6695 2006
  153—dc22   2006005937

9 8 7 6 5 4 3 2 1

Printed in the United States of America
on acid-free paper

For Gramma Donna

Foreword

This book marks a major step forward in cognitive science, an effective way of thinking about minds and brains that isn't just another computer metaphor. Many of us have been looking for such a step, but where would it come from? One promising possibility was dynamical systems theory, which indeed is basic to Michael Spivey's argument here. Until now, however, dynamical systems have had little to say about genuinely cognitive achievements such as language, categorization, or thought. Neural nets have been another promising possibility (one that also plays a role here), but most of them are still essentially step-by-step computer models indifferent to the properties of real neurons that live in real time. On the empirical side there have been many ingenious new methods and exciting new findings in recent years, but until now no coherent theory has emerged to hold them all together. How could any theory deal with so much complexity?

Here's how. First, any such theory will have to establish its own units of analysis. What could those units be? They can't just be *responses*: The early behaviorists took responses as far as they would go, which wasn't very far. It also won't do to start with *information*, the vehicle that made cognitive psychology possible a generation ago. Of course, it's still true that brains process information, but saying so is no longer revolutionary or even very helpful. Nor can the basic units be *single neurons*: that soon leads to "grandmother cells," implausible for many reasons. Spivey's proposal here—a seriously expanded version of dynamical systems theory with many original twists—is based instead on trajectories through the state space of the human brain. His insistence that those trajectories must be continuous has led him to new insights over a surprisingly broad range of cognitive phenomena.

But what is a state space? What sorts of things move through state spaces? What does it mean to assert that those movements are continuous? Taking the last question first, "continuity" means that movements away from a given brain state are always to an adjacent state and always take real time, a time during which much can happen. Speech perception provides a convenient example. Although a spoken word is not fully defined until its last syllable ends, the process of understanding it starts much earlier. *Candle* and *candy*, for example, both begin with *can*. Spivey's ingenious eye movement studies show that a listener presented with one of these words will actively consider both those possibilities at first, making a commitment only later as more information arrives. The moral here is that word representations—indeed, all mental representations—are probabilistic and overlapping rather than sharply bounded. The brain is "hungry" for information, always using whatever it has and looking for more.

These characteristics have implications for the theory's units of analysis. A representation capable of overlapping widely and probabilistically with other representations must involve a large number of neurons, some of which are active at a given moment while others are not. Such collections of neurons are *distributed representations* or *population codes*. Their interwoven patterns of activation are what produce the effects we observe.

Important as they are, population codes are not the ultimate units of analysis. To provide a richer description of the brain's activity, Spivey uses a *multidimensional state space*. Each brain neuron corresponds to one dimension of that space, which thus has a billion or so dimensions. At any given moment, the total state of brain activity corresponds to a single point in the space. Changes in that activity over time then produce *trajectories* through the space. Regions of the space to which many trajectories go (and where they sort of stay) are called *attractor basins*. In many contexts a given attractor basin corresponds to a fully developed percept—to a word understood, a face recognized, a stable perceived version of the Necker cube. The attractors are thus very important, but Spivey is even more interested in the trajectories themselves. The basic units of his thinking are events, not states.

The Continuity of Mind is not an easy book, but its organization is clear. After the introduction (chapter 1), Spivey devotes three chapters to intellectual tools that the rest of the argument will require. The first of these, chapter 2, reviews the logic of state space representations. Chapter 3 surveys such diverse but relevant paradigms as reaction time, MEG, ERP, EEG, single-cell recording, repetitive rhythmic motor tasks, 3D motion capture, and especially eye movements. Eye tracking is Spivey's favorite paradigm, not only because he has worked on it so effectively himself but also because it is surprisingly good at revealing rapid mental activity that occurs outside of consciousness. Then comes the third conceptual-tool chapter, chapter 4, which is specifically designed "to gently walk the reader through some of the mathematics of a few simple demonstrations of dynamical systems." It does help.

With these conceptual tools in hand, Spivey sets out to show how his continuity assumption addresses the major issues of contemporary cognitive science. The first of those issues is modularity à la Fodor, which he is at pains to reject. (If we must have metaphors, the brain is not so much a Swiss army knife with separate blades as a woven plaid of interlinked threads.) Then six more issues get chapters of their own: categories, language, vision, motor action, problem solving, and memory (mostly external memory). Each of these chapters builds on references from the relevant literature to present an array of stimulating new insights.

In keeping with his commitment to events rather than stable states, Spivey's last chapter is not a review of what has been covered but an account of what may come next. Here, he has the mind/body problem in his sights. The present book has focused primarily on trajectories through a *neuronal* state space, but there's a bigger space on the horizon, a "fully ecological dynamic account of perception cognition and action." When dualism is finally overthrown, we will be able to see that the mind is made of "the same stuff" as the environment. Well, maybe so, maybe not. One thing is already clear: Cognitive science is on a new trajectory, and it's moving fast. Hold on to your hats!

—Ulric Neisser

Acknowledgments

I want each sequential change of mind in its true, knotted, clotted,
viny multifariousness, with all of the colorful streamers of
intelligence still taped on and flapping in the wind.
—Nicholson Baker

There are many people whom I should thank for helping me get to where I could write this book. The first people I want to thank are my family. My mother, father, and sister always tolerated and even encouraged my nerdy pursuits like computer programming and fantasy role-playing games—without which I probably would have ended up a Bohemian artist living on welfare. Steve and Sheryl Knowlton provided years of intellectual stimulation, patience, and support. I thank my wife, Melinda Tyler, for being just enough smarter than me to inspire me to work harder. Last but not least, among my family, I am grateful to little Samuel Rex Spivey for sleeping soundly in his baby sling while I write this.

The next people to thank are my intellectual family. It is perhaps egregious to actually list all the personal instructors, advisors, and colleagues whose guidance I think played key roles in developing the way I have come to think about the mind. However, when I look at the list of names, it is blatantly obvious that basically *anyone* who had this particular combination of intellectual guides (and in the particular order that I had them) would develop the viewpoint that I describe in this book. Therefore, egregious or not, their names deserve listing, as they are—in aggregate form—arguably more responsible for this book than I am. That's right—both the success and the failures of this book are more their fault than mine.

During my college years at UC Santa Cruz, particularly inspirational professors for me were Dom Massaro, Bruce Bridgeman, Ray Gibbs, and Alan Kawamoto. I also benefited from important older brother graduate students such as Brian Fisher, Ken Nemire, and Bill Farrar. During graduate school at

University of Rochester, my advisors Mike Tanenhaus and Mary Hayhoe and another older brother, Ken McRae, taught me invaluable lessons and kept me on the right track. I am also grateful to Kyunghee Koh for tricking me into falling in love with MATLAB, and to Tony Movshon for helping further my enthusiasm for computational modeling. And although I never took a course with him or collaborated with him, Jay McClelland has provided me with crucial encouragement and behind-the-scenes support in many ways and for many years.

Over the past nine years at Cornell University, I have been the lucky recipient of some incredible nurturance from my entire department, but particularly deserving of mention is the intellectual support provided by Barbara Finlay, David Field, Shimon Edelman, Ulric Neisser, and of course, the ghost of J. J. Gibson, who often walks the halls of these floors and these minds. Ulric Neisser gave me particularly helpful advice on how to make this book more encouraging and less combative (and I even managed to follow some of it). Some of the arguments in this book have also benefited from discussions with Eric Dietrich and Ken Kurtz at nearby SUNY Binghamton. Recently, I had the wonderful good fortune to serve several times on Guy Van Orden's NSF grant review panel on Perception, Action, and Cognition, where I was richly educated by the grant proposals themselves and especially by the many intense panel discussions of research and theory. I am extremely grateful to the entire panel (with its rolling membership from spring 2002 to fall 2004) and to Guy for giving me that amazing growth experience.

Essentially, I think a certain weighted combination of all of these minds, into one mind, would have written this book almost exactly as I have. And perhaps that is a valid description of what has, in fact, taken place.

I would also like to thank all of my many collaborators over the years (especially Julie Sedivy, John Trueswell, Kathy Eberhard, Viorica Marian, Daniel Richardson, and Rick Dale) whose intellectual influences induced important changes in my academic development.

This book in your hands has benefited from innumerable suggested revisions from Ulric Neisser, Daniel Richardson, Rick Dale, and many anonymous reviewers (such as Larry Barsalou, Jeff Elman, Mary Hayhoe, Art Markman, Guy Van Orden, Bob McMurray and several others whom I didn't quite manage to confidently suss out). Also, Cabot Nunlist, Jeremy Kipling, and Adam November all provided helpful early explorations into the visual search simulations in chapter 8. The incomparable Nick Hindy helped immensely with line editing and tracking down the full citations on almost 1,400 references.

I am extremely grateful to Robert and Helen Appel for their generous gift of the Appel Fellowship, which assisted greatly in providing me with time away from university duties so that a large part of this book could be written. In the summers of 2003 and 2004, at the Max Planck Institute for Psychological Research in Munich, Wolfgang Prinz and his team (Günther Knoblich, Marc Grosjean, Edmund Wascher, Peter Keller, Matthias Weigelt, Nathalie Sebanz, and many others like Maggie Shiffrar and Bruno Repp) similarly helped me with time, money, inspiration, and Bavarian beer for working on this book. This book consumed quite a bit of all four of those precious commodities.

Finally, I wish to thank my Oxford University Press editor, Catharine Carlin, for her incredible patience and for knowing just what to say to me to trigger the necessary commitment of time and energy for writing a first book.

Contents

The Continuity of Mind

1

Toward a Continuity Psychology

The older dualism between sensation and idea is repeated in the
current dualism of peripheral and central structures and functions;
the older dualism of body and soul finds a distinct echo in the
current dualism of stimulus and response.
—John Dewey (1896)

The Continuity of Mind

In an attempt to raise awareness of the benefits of emphasizing *continuous* processing, and therefore of continuous representation as well, this book ties together selected findings from neuroscience, cognitive neuroscience, cognitive psychology, ecological psychology, psycholinguistics, neural network theory, and dynamical systems theory. Without slavishly adhering to the dominant tenets of any one of those areas of research, I will build a case for a perspective on mental life in which the human mind/brain typically construes the world via partially overlapping fuzzy gray areas that are drawn out over time, a thesis that I fondly refer to as "the continuity of mind." In the service of action and communication, these continuous and often probabilistic representations are frequently collapsed into relatively discrete, rigid, nonoverlapping response categories. Each hand usually grasps only one object at a time. Each footstep is usually in only one particular direction at a time, not multiple directions. When you talk, your mouth usually utters only one sound at a time. The external discreteness of these actions and utterances is commonly misinterpreted as evidence for the internal discreteness of the mental representations that led to them. Thus, according to the continuity of mind thesis, the bottleneck that converts fuzzy, graded, probabilistic mental activity into discrete easily labeled units is *not* the transition from perception to cognition—contra cognitive psychology. Rather, that conversion does not take place until the transition from motor planning to motor execution. Everything up to and including that point is still distributed and probabilistic.

3

(And sometimes even the motor execution still has some multifarious gradations in it as well.)

Although this main thesis may already seem agreeable to some contemporary psychologists, not all of them may realize that it is fundamentally inconsistent with the symbolic-computation approach to cognition that traditional cognitive psychology still assumes, implicitly if not explicitly. Moreover, a wide range of other cognitive scientists, from philosophy, linguistics, and computer science, as well as other circles in psychology, have yet to seriously consider (or in some cases already strongly oppose) this perspective on the format of representation employed by the human mind. I contend that cognitive psychology's traditional information-processing approach (borrowed from the early days of computing theory), as well as certain tendencies within the more recent connectionist approach (often using strictly feedforward neural networks), place too much emphasis on easily labeled static representations that are claimed to be computed at intermittently stable periods of time. Rather than focusing on those intermittent moments when the brain's pattern of activity may be brushing up next to an identifiable *discrete* mental state representation, the continuity of mind thesis focuses on the continuous trajectory that the mind travels through the set of possible brain states—the entire *thread of thought*, if you will, rather than just the stitches that are visible on the surface of the hem.

The pattern of exposition throughout this book will be to describe a range of methodologies and findings that point to some innovative ways to observe and simulate the genuine gradedness of those mental states over time—not merely take them for granted. The continuity framework offered here draws much of its inspiration from related theoretical frameworks that preceded it, especially ecological and dynamical approaches to psychology (e.g., Gibson, 1979; Kelso, 1995; Neisser, 1976; Port, 2002; Thelen & Smith, 1996; Turvey & Carello, 1995; van Gelder, 1998; Van Orden, Holden, & Turvey, 2003). However, at the same time, this book is intended to work largely within the terminology and constraints of the dominant methodological and theoretical toolbox of contemporary cognitive psychology. For example, I will continue to use words like *representation* and *mental state*, despite their unpopularity in current dynamical and ecological approaches to cognition. However, in the process of using these traditional conceptual tools for exploring and describing the continuous nature of cognitive processing and representation, it will become clear that some new conceptual tools (and eventually a whole new toolbox) will be necessary to deal with the emerging landscape of data.

As you work your way through this book, you should expect to gradually lose some of the baggage associated with the term *representation* along the way. It need not refer to an internal mental entity that symbolizes some external object or event to an attentive central executive. Because *representation* appears unlikely to fade in use, I suggest that instead of fighting the use of the word, we can merely allow it to naturally shed that albatross of *symbolizing* something.

The word can simply continue to refer to a kind of mediating stand-in (see Markman & Dietrich, 2000), in between sensory stimulation and physical action, which is implemented largely by neuronal assemblies. However, the crucially important alteration to this stand-in function, to be touched on time and time again throughout this book, is that it is not composed of "mediating *states*" (Dietrich & Markman, 2003) but instead of something like "mediating *processes.*" As the neuronal assemblies that implement most of this stand-in function never settle into truly stable states, we should not expect the mathematical description of the mediation process to settle into stable states. Therefore, my continued use of the term *representation* refers exclusively to internal mental processing that is continuous in time, is contiguous in state space, and whose function is to mediate between sensory stimulation and physical action.

The overall goal of my endeavor here is to punctuate and perturb the current instability in the metatheoretical system of cognitive science—the inconsistency between recent phenomena in the field and the accepted ways the field has for talking about phenomena in general—thereby helping enable the impending massive reorganization that the cognitive sciences so desperately need. This book is intended to map an escape route out of traditional cognitive psychology, with some hints and pointers for where to go next and build.

For those who already share this continuous, dynamical perspective on the mind, the studies described herein will hopefully provide a greater appreciation for the relationship between our multifarious, probabilistic, distributed brain states and our illusory phenomenological sense of being in one discrete unitary state of mind at a time. For those who already oppose this perspective on the mind, the many examples littered throughout this book will hopefully pose constructive challenges (some more difficult than others) for their theories to tackle. For those of you who have not already made up your minds, good for you.

These first two chapters provide a brief, easy-to-read tour through the motivation and explication of what mental representations might look like if they were indeed continuous, partially active, and partially overlapping patterns. The first thing the reader will notice is that they begin to look less like what *representation* was originally intended to mean. The reason I continue to use the term is largely to ease the intellectual transition from cognitive psychology's traditional information-processing framework to a dynamical-systems framework. I submit the notion of a trajectory through state space (a temporally drawn-out pattern of multiple "representations" being simultaneously partially active) as a replacement for the traditional notion of a *static symbolic* representation. To bring this notion to life, this chapter soon draws an analogy to the concept of a wave function in quantum mechanics, which attempts to describe the state of a system before it has been observed. Although there are explicit quantum mechanical accounts of brain states and consciousness (Goswami, 1990; Lockwood et al., 1996; Penrose, 1994; Zohar, 1995; but see Schrödinger, 1944; Scott, 1996), the continuity approach to cognition does not depend on them. The appeal to quantum mechanics at this point is purely for expository purposes, with the goal of drawing an analogy between distributed representational brain states (that are partially consistent with multiple discrete mental states at once) and quantum mechanical superposition. Based on reactions from my colleagues, the reader will most probably either like or hate my use of this analogy. An intermediate reaction is rare.

This notion of a wave function is then connected to the way populations of neurons in the brain cooperate to represent individual perceptions. It does not seem to be the case that thoughts, ideas, concepts, categories, words, objects, or even faces are represented by solitary, individual neurons in the brain. Individual neurons appear to represent minute pieces of words, objects, and so forth. Large groups of neurons collectively represent entire words and objects. These coordinated groups of neurons are variously referred to as population codes, population vectors, cell assemblies, and cell ensembles, to name a few. For simplicity, I stick with the term *population code*. The discussion of population codes is then connected to quantitative descriptions of probabilistic representations, along with a brief treatment of the history of probability theory. After addressing the relationship between probability theory and fuzzy logic, this chapter walks the reader through two experiential demonstrations of continuous dynamical transitions through probabilistic mental states. The chapter finishes with some discussion of the conceptual reformulation that will be necessary to make sense of continuous processing and continuous representations in the mind.

The next chapter is devoted to offering some concrete (although vastly oversimplified) examples of distributed brain states and probabilistic mental states, in an attempt to make this thesis not only visualizable but indeed intuitively compelling. These examples will take us slightly (only slightly) in the direction of the conclusion favored by Churchland and Churchland (1998), that discrete nameable mental states, of the kind typically espoused by folk psychology, simply do not exist. Rather than thinking in terms of an inventory of discrete mental operands on which a central executive can perform logical operations, a continuity psychology (drawing prodigiously from ecological psychology, dynamical systems theory, and computational neuroscience) will need to think in terms of a continuous and often recurrent trajectory through a state space. Although different types of mental trajectories may be segregated into different classes for descriptive convenience, it must be recognized that the full metric range of the state space is always available to the system, in principle, and this is precisely what allows unexpected (sometimes called "productive" or "creative") organized behavior to emerge.

The third chapter reviews some concrete experimental methods that help provide a window into the continuous-time processes of the mind/brain. The fourth chapter offers some formal treatment of dynamical systems in general and describes not exactly a model but a "simulation arena" for implementing and demonstrating the complex temporal dynamics arising from biased competition (e.g., Desimone & Duncan, 1995) between idealized stable states in a localist attractor network. Chapter 5 then outlines cognitive psychology's obsession with naming apparent discontinuities in representation and process, discusses the treatment of the overall cognitive architecture of the mind, and addresses some of the consequences that the continuous dynamical approach has for psychology. Later chapters will then review the literature, and focus on a series of experiments and idealized neural network simulations, providing compelling evidence for continuous, graded, partially overlapping representations in the mind/brain during categorization (chapter 6), language comprehension (chapter 7), visual attention (chapter 8), action (chapter 9), and reasoning (chapter 10). Finally, in the last few chapters, this book concludes by addressing some of the broader implications that a dynamical psychology has for the cognitive science notions of modularity and of representation, as well as for our own personal understandings of social interaction, consciousness, and our intellectual lives in general.

Flowing Stimulus Array, Flowing Mind

In a nutshell, the message of this book is that the human mind is constantly in motion. It does not receive individual stimuli and compute individual interpretations of them. And yet, for several decades now, the dominant frameworks of psychology have taken for granted that the mind's job is to compute individual interpretations of individual stimuli. After all, how else could we recognize what a stimulus is, if we did not activate some internal stable representation of it?

Before I get to what a temporally dynamic internal representation might be, let me first note—as J. J. Gibson (1950) did—that, in the normal everyday world, individual stimuli simply do not exist. If it is the case that individuated stimuli do not normally exist in our sensory input, then it can hardly be said that they have individuated representations devoted to them. For a given stimulus to truly be an independent entity, activating its own independent symbolic representation, it would need to be spatially and temporally separate from all other stimuli. Look around you right now. See if there are any objects that from your current perspective, are not intersecting or abutting the contours of another (potential) object. Probably not. Now move some objects around in a natural way. Take a sip from a cup, or move some paper from one place to another. As the objects move, the changes in your field of view are largely continuous through time, saccadic eye movements notwithstanding. The changes aren't freeze-frames of the object being in one location at one point in time and then suddenly in another distant location at another point in time. (Of course, it is possible to present individual objects in spatial and temporal isolation in a dark laboratory, but if that never really happens in real life, how generalizable will those lab results be?)

Now, listen to the ambient sound in your environment. Just like the visual objects abutting and occluding one another, there are several different sounds that are overlaying one another at any one point in time. All of the sounds have a temporal duration over which they may change in complexity, pitch, volume, and so on. Just like the field of view in an interactive visual environment, the changes in your acoustic environment are largely continuous through time as well. Even the sounds that seem most "object-like," spoken words, usually abut one another in time, rarely separated from one another by even a millisecond of silence.

What this means is that the "flowing array of stimulus energy," as Gibson called it, is never presegmented into easily defined independent chunks, or stimuli—even though we feel as though we perceive it that way. Now, if the environmental stimulation impinging on our sensory systems is almost always partially overlapping in space and continuous through time, why would the mind work in a staccato fashion of entertaining one discrete stable nonoverlapping representational state for a period of time, and then instantaneously flipping to entertain a different discrete stable nonoverlapping representational state for another period of time? Why would the mind work like a computer? This book is aimed—like some other recent books (e.g., Kelso, 1995; Port & van Gelder, 1995; see also Fodor, 2000)—at responding to that question with the following answer: "It doesn't."

The New Dualism

The computer metaphor for the mind was really just the latest in a historical series of stage-based accounts of cognition. Whether the stages are the body-and-soul of dualism, or the stimulus-and-response of behaviorism, or the stimulus-and-interpretation of cognitive psychology, it may just be the idealized discrete separation of different functions that is most responsible for leading the endeavor astray. In the middle of the seventeenth century, René Descartes proposed that the mind worked by way of immaterial forces that were separate from the physical forces of our material world, and that the mind communicated with the brain via the pineal gland. Aside from the occasional personal belief in a soul, this kind of magical thinking is no longer prevalent in science. However, the same breed of dichotomous treatment of the mind as separate from the body is still quite common in the cognitive sciences—just with slightly less ethereal mechanisms being assumed.

In the middle of the twentieth century, cognitive psychology in particular, and the cognitive sciences in general, came under the spell of a new form of dualism—one fueled at least partially by our history of computing theory and artificial intelligence. Since the 1950s, when computing theory was just beginning, psychologists have likened the mind to a computer. Indeed, as other scientists have noted, humankind has made a habit of conceiving of the mind as working much like whatever happens to be the latest technological advancement. For hundreds of years, philosophers and psychologists have written about the mind working like an hourglass, or like a clock, or like the printing press, or like a telephone switchboard, and now like a computer. Is there any reason to think this penchant for mechanical analogies is right this time?

The worrisome dualism encouraged by this mind-as-computer analogy is that it implies that the human brain is somehow functioning under very different rules, or patterns of organization, than the rest of the body and indeed, the rest of the natural world. Of course, this attitude existed well before the computer, as evidenced by Kant's (1785/1996) claim that human intelligence followed "laws, which being independent of nature, are not empirical but have their ground in reason alone." Imbuing the human brain with the power of discrete symbolic computation places it in a category by itself in nature, with all the continuous and probabilistic phenomena exhibited by the peripheral nervous system, and everything else in the natural world, placed in a different category. It becomes a "mind versus the rest of the world" attitude. But no mind is an island unto itself.

Contemporary psychology risks becoming a mockery of itself by its addiction to hypothesizing discrete discontinuities of this sort. This is precisely what Dewey (1896), from whom a quote begins this introductory chapter, was trying to curtail in his critique of the reflex arc concept. The reflex arc concept was a relatively new idea at that time, framing the questions of psychology in terms of causal arcs between (1) a sensory stimulus stage, (2) a central (mental) activity stage, and (3) an action/response stage. Essentially, studying the causal arcs between 1 and 2 *or* between 2 and 3 were to be considered legitimate scientific enterprises in and of themselves. In contrast, treating the progression of the three components as one continuous process that naturally loops back on itself was what Dewey was attempting to encourage. Actions take place over time and they continuously alter the stimulus environment, which in turn continuously alters mental activity, which is continuously expressing and revising its inclinations to action.

Behaviorism's unhelpful but long-standing solution after Dewey (1896) was to hamfistedly eliminate the second (mental) stage. After a few decades of behaviorism, the cognitive revolution, as they liked to call it, essentially resurrected that second stage and all but erased the third one (action). (At this level of description, the theoretical alteration from behaviorism to cognitivism appears minute enough that one wonders if it truly warrants being called a "revolution," see Leahey, 1992.) Essentially, cognitive psychology replaced behaviorism's emphasis on stimulus and response with an emphasis on stimulus and interpretation. These incremental adjustments to the linear treatment of the three stages reminds me of when I find myself trying to solve a toy puzzle using parametric variations of the same losing strategy, rather than trying a completely different strategy. Most of cognitive science and psychology has missed the whole point of *not* studying these stages as a linear sequence of separable components, but instead studying them as one continuous inseparable loop. Is it any wonder that our progress is plateauing once again?

Curiously, Dewey's (1896) reference to an "older dualism between sensation and idea" doesn't actually sound that old to contemporary ears. In many ways, the cognitive psychology that began with Newell, Shaw, and Simon (1958), Chomsky (1957), and Neisser (1967) among others reinvigorated the notion that sensation and perception could be part of a separate preliminary (in every sense of the word) component of mental activity, with cognition (i.e., the computation of ideas and reasoning) being a subsequent and more psychologically relevant component. Perception was just perception. But cognition was "the mind." In fact, since around the time of Neisser's (1967) *Cognitive Psychology* (see also Pylyshyn, 1984), Dewey's terms *stimulus* and *central activity* have gradually become incorporated into the central nervous system as the *discontinuous* modular suites of "perception" and "cognition". So when Dewey says, "the older dualism between sensation and idea," I have to say I feel a little bit of déjà vu.

Meet Schrödinger's Cat

Perhaps what is needed instead is a breaking down of these idealized distinctions between putative stages, a reconceptualization of mental activity as continuous in time and graded in format. To illustrate my claim that mental representations are fundamentally continuous, graded, and partially overlapping (before overt behavior converts them into discrete actions), I draw an analogy to a celebrity from popular physics: Schrödinger's cat. First, for the uninitiated, allow me to explain this feline's rise to fame. When quantum physics was gaining respectability and suggesting that the duality of light being both a wave and a particle was mathematically acceptable, there were a number of critics. Erwin Schrödinger (1935), a quantum physicist himself, became one of those critics. In his discomfort with quantum physics' claim that a particle could be simultaneously in multiple spatial locations, Schrödinger designed a thought experiment that he expected would prove quantum physics wrong. In a typical version of this thought experiment, one places a cat inside a box that also contains a chunk of mildly radioactive material, a Geiger counter, and a vial of poison gas. According to its quantum mechanical properties, this particular chunk of radioactive material is 50% likely to emit one radioactive particle per hour. If and when the Geiger counter detects this emitted radioactive particle, it triggers a device that breaks the vial of poison gas and thus kills the cat. After an hour has passed from the time you began this experiment, you might naturally conclude that there is a 50% chance that the cat is dead and a 50% chance that the cat is alive. Quantum physics would disagree with you. Quantum physics, because it allows that particle to have been emitted and not emitted at the same time, suggests that—before you look inside the box—the cat is both dead and alive.[1] Schrödinger expected the absurdity of this claim to invalidate the popular interpretation of quantum physics once and for all. How could a cat possibly be both dead and alive at the same time?! However, to his shock and dismay, this thought experiment was *not* generally taken as proof that quantum physics must be wrong. Indeed, most quantum physicists of the time saw no absurdity in the prediction at all! As far as they were concerned, Schrödinger had beautifully demonstrated how quantum duality at the subatomic level could, under the right circumstances, be recapitulated at the macroscopic level. His cat became a popular icon for how wonderful and powerful quantum physics can be.[2]

Population Codes in the Brain

What does a confused cat have to do with the human mind/brain? The analogy I wish to draw from Schrödinger's cat to the human mind/brain is in the understanding that being *in multiple states at once* is a condition in which one can be. In fact, one might argue that it is basically impossible for the human brain to ever be in one single, entirely stable state—except for death, of course. If it were, it would not be able to gravitate out of such a state without external input. But even when the brain is cut off from all external input, during sleep or sensory deprivation, it continues to travel from one brief nearly stable state to the next: we dream, or we hallucinate, or we experience a "stream of consciousness."

When we look at how the brain encodes information, we see that it is a lot like the wave function that characterizes the multifarious state Schrödinger's cat is in. The majority of neurons studied in mammalian brains send their signals in the form of relatively discrete all-or-none action potentials, brief but intense depolarizations (1–10 milliseconds) of their electrochemical membrane potentials. However, it does not appear to be the case that the firing of individual neurons is used to signal the presence of things like objects, words, and concepts (see Damasio & Damasio, 1994; Hebb, 1949; Pouget, Dayan, & Zemel, 2000; Rose, 1996; see also Barlow, 1972). For some time now, neuroscientists have been able to record the activity of many neurons at once in various regions of the nonhuman primate brain and have generally been finding that *populations of neurons* participate together to embody a representation. For example, in the 1970s, David Sparks and colleagues showed that the neural signal that tells the eye muscles to move the eyes in a particular direction is made up of many neurons, in the superior colliculus of the macaque monkey, each of which represents a different direction of eye movement. It is the *distribution of activity* across this population of neurons that determines the direction of the eye movement, not just the activation of those neurons that specifically code for the actual direction the eyes wind up going in (Sparks, Holland, & Guthrie, 1976). In the 1980s, Georgopoulos and colleagues found similar evidence for population codes of arm movements in the motor cortex of the macaque (Georgopoulos et al., 1982). Moreover, it appears that population codes are used not only for representing and producing motor *output* (e.g., eye and arm movements) but also for representing perceptual *input.*

For example, in the 1990s, Wilson and McNaughton (1993) demonstrated that ensembles of cells in the rat hippocampus cooperate to encode the animal's knowledge of what environment it is in. And Tanaka (1996, 1997) showed that visual objects (faces included; see Gauthier & Lokothetis, 2000; Perret, Oram, & Ashbridge, 1998) are represented by populations of cells within the inferotemporal region of visual cortex in the macaque.[3]

One of the things that makes population codes (i.e., distributed representations) robust and powerful is that under noisy or degraded stimulus conditions or following physical injury, they will often still be able to approximate the original input signal: *graceful degradation* (Rumelhart & McClelland, 1986a). For example, imagine that a particular set of 100 neurons participate in the representation of your grandmother's face, such that when you look at her, the ideal, perfect recognition would happen if those 100 neurons were at their appropriate activation levels (firing rates). If she laughs and covers her mouth, then some of those 100 neurons will reduce in activation because the parts of her face to which they especially respond are occluded. Nonetheless, if 80 of those 100 neurons are still doing what they are supposed to do, that population code for grandmother (with its 80% "confidence") will still be by far the most coherent code available in the brain. In contrast, if you had only one neuron devoted to recognizing grandmother, this "grandmother cell" (Lettvin, 1995) may not be able to do its job when grandmother covers her mouth, turns her head, or makes a funny face. You'd suddenly fail to recognize her!

What this means is that with population codes, we are *always* dealing with internal representations that have what you might call percentages of confidence (or probabilities, loosely) associated with them. The image on your retina of your grandmother will almost never be the same at any two points in time. Therefore, the input to those 100 neurons (your grandmother population code) will never be exactly perfect to turn them all on. This population code will be in a nearly stable state. What often happens then is that the connections between the members of this population code will pass the activity back and forth and increase the percentage of them that are active. This *pattern completion* process (e.g., Grossberg, 1980) will gradually increase the population code's "confidence," and thus its probability of producing an associated behavior—such as pushing air out of your lungs to vibrate your vocal chords while articulating parts of your mouth to make the sound, "Grandma!" Importantly, that discrete behavior—saying one particular word and not any other words—is often interpreted by the people around you as indicating that your internal representation for grandmother is 100% "confident." The continuity of mind thesis posits that your representation is *not* 100% confident and can *never* be 100% confident.

Although the process of pattern completion will increase the total activation (or probability) of a representation over time, its associated action will be produced long before the representation ever reaches maximum activation (or probability 1.0). This action (even something as benign as moving your eyes to a chair, near Grandma, that you plan to sit in) then inevitably changes the sensory array, so that the original input to that population code is now crucially altered, and a new pattern completion process must begin—gravitating the system toward a new and different probabilistic mental representation.

Versions of Probability

If we accept this account of population codes as probabilistic representations of multiple unitary concepts (see Zemel, Dayan, & Pouget, 1998), for example, 0.8 Grandma, 0.02 Kathryn Hepburn, 0.01 Mother Teresa, and hundreds of other representations with very low confidence, that together add up to 1.0, then we begin to see how the mind is indeed like Schrödinger's cat: in multiple identifiable states at once. However, we must acknowledge that this is using a particular connotation of *probability*, a term which has taken on many senses in the last couple of centuries. Because a form of probabilism is infused in a great deal of the theoretical treatment throughout this book, the following section will describe some of the different interpretations of probability, cover some of its history, and also jog your memory with just a touch of math.

In the eighteenth and nineteenth centuries, a great many philosophers, mathematicians, economists, and physicists (as well life insurance statisticians!) were employing the tools of probability to essentially make predictions about future events. Much of early probability theory was actually developed in the interest of using death statistics (i.e., mortality tables) to determine profitable life insurance coverage and premiums. Crucially, the dominant meaning of probability at the time was one of describing the likelihood (as a value between 0 and 1) that a future event will end up discretely in one state or another. Thomas Bayes formulated an extremely influential theorem that instructs exactly how to do this (Bayes, 1763/1958).

Let's walk though an example. Imagine that you just lost all your money at the roulette table of a new casino. Let's assume you usually at least break even at roulette (95% of the time), so you're now suspicious—for the first time in your life—that the wheel might be rigged. Bayes's theorem lets you pit the likelihood of your rare event against the general likelihood of casinos cheating, to calculate the probability that this particular casino just cheated you. For the sake of argument, assume that based on crime reports, 1 out of 100 casinos rig their roulette tables to cheat gamblers out of their money. Understanding equation (1) is easier than you might think.

$$P(C \mid L) = \frac{P(C)\,P(L \mid C)}{P(C)\,P(L \mid C) + P(notC)\,P(L \mid notC)}. \qquad (1.1)$$

Let $P(C \mid L)$ be read as "the probability of this casino cheating, C, given that you just lost all your money, L." For the numerator, we multiply the base rate, or prior probability, of C (i.e., 1/100) by the probability of your losing if the casino cheated, $P(L \mid C)$; let's assume that would be 1.0. In the denominator, that same product, $P(C)\ P(L \mid C)$, must be added to the probability of the casino being fair, $P(notC)$, multiplied by the probability of your losing at a fair casino, $P(L \mid notC)$. This is necessary to normalize your suspicion against the alternative possibility: that you just got unlucky. Dividing the numerator $(0.01 * 1)$ by the denominator $(0.01 * 1 + 0.99 * 0.05)$, results in $P(C \mid L) = 0.168$. Certainly a much higher likelihood than the base rate of 1 in 100, but not quite enough confidence to warrant contacting the police. Perhaps if it happens to you three times in a row at that same casino, then it might be time for an investigation . . . or then again, maybe you've just lost your touch.

Probability theory also allows us to compute the probability of *combinations* of events. For example, the probability of a flipped coin coming up heads twice in a row is computed by simply *multiplying the probability of the first event with the probability of the second event*: $0.5 * 0.5 = 0.25$. (Of course, this only really works when the probabilities are independent of one another.) The probability of that casino *not* cheating, even though you've lost at roulette three times in a row there, could be calculated as $(1 - 0.168) * (1 - 0.168) * (1 - 0.168) = 0.576$. Thus, it would appear that Bayesian theorists can make some pretty sophisticated predictions, not only of individual events but also of combined events.

However, the Bayesian interpretation of those mathematical results is not accepted by everyone. A frequentist's view of probability would emphasize that although the 0.25 probability of flipping two heads in a pair of coin flips tells us to expect about 25 heads-heads out of 100 pairs of coin flips, probability can say nothing about which face of the coin is actually up on any one flip. We must rely on observation to tell us that. In the strict frequentist account of probability, there is no discussion of the degrees to which an individual event is *likely* to be in one state or another—and certainly no acknowledgment of the degrees to which an individual event is *in one state and another at the same time!*

The way I would like to encourage the reader to think of probability in the mind is a far cry from the frequentist's interpretation and even subtly different from the Bayesian interpretation. The continuity of mind thesis holds that simultaneously partially active mental representations can be treated as summing to 1.0 and thus may represent the probability of their individual associated actions being elicited. In this view, it is the fact that the body's effectors (limbs, hands, eyes, speech apparatus, etc.) can each typically only do one action at a time, which causes the multifarious amalgam of mental states to warp itself over time toward largely approximating only one mental state just long enough to produce that mental state's associated action. Thus, when relating these multiple graded mental states to possible actions, the thesis looks decidedly probabilistic, but when examining the mental states for their own sake, the thesis might be best compared to fuzzy logic.

Following some initial work by logicians on elements of a formal logic that allowed for "vague" truth values, Lotfi Zadeh introduced the notion of fuzzy logic (Zadeh, 1975; see also Massaro, 1997). In fuzzy logic, the truth value of a proposition (such as "Donald is rich") has a range between 0 and 1. Moreover, the truth value of a conjunction of propositions (such as "Donald is rich and I am poor") is equal to *the truth value of one proposition multiplied by the truth value of the other proposition.* Sound familiar? The mathematics of fuzzy logic and the mathematics of probability are essentially the same. It is the interpretation that differs. Fuzzy logic takes the mathematical results of traditional probability statistics and accepts them at face value as "the (multifarious) state of the system," not as "a prediction of the possible discrete states the system might be in." This is precisely what quantum physics does with its mathematical description of the probability that Schrödinger's cat is dead and the probability that it is alive. It accepts the math as a *conjunctive description* of the world, not as a *disjunctive prediction* about it.

"Warping" the Probabilities

You can begin to see the tension here between the notions of probability and fuzzy logic. I will perhaps add to that tension when I note here that the "probabilistic" activations of mental representations discussed throughout this book often do not adhere to the mathematics of Bayesian probability theory (see chapter 4 for details). From this perspective, my use of the term *probability* may seem somewhat glib. The conjunctive description of mental contents provided by fuzzy logic is converted into a disjunctive prediction, via probabilities, of the motor responses being recorded by the psychological experimenter. The way in which *probability* truly does apply here is in the stipulation that these fuzzy logical activations of mental states are treated as "the probability that the mind will activate a motor action that is associated with a particular perceptual category." However, because their activations change continuously, these partially active mental representations should not really be interpreted as "the mind computing the probability of a given stimulus belonging to a particular category." At a very deep level, this claim is actually quite shocking, if not preposterous. It amounts to saying that A and B (below) are true, but C is *not always true.*

A. There are Bayesian probabilistic relationships between external states in the environment.
B. There are Bayesian probabilistic relationships between mental states in the mind and motor actions in that environment.
*C. There are Bayesian probabilistic relationships between external states in the environment and mental states in the mind.

What could be so special about that transition from stimulus to percept (statement C) that it dares defy the mathematics of Bayesian probability?

In fact, a considerable amount of research in a subfield that calls itself Bayesian perception adheres rather strongly to statement C (e.g., Kersten, 1991; Knill, 1998; see also Rao, Olshausen, & Lewicki, 2002). Bayesian approaches to perception usually acknowledge the gradedness of internal mental states; however, they still tend to treat them as static in time. The temporal dynamics of cognition is largely ignored by the Bayesian approach to perception. Thus, although an experiment in Bayesian perception can often demonstrate an accurate mathematical prediction (in the form of some probabilities) about the overt categories into which an observer will place her percepts, it usually demonstrates nothing about the temporally extended process by which the sensory input eventually led to a particular categorical response. In the context of having considered the pattern completion process exhibited by neural population codes and by attractor dynamics, this two-step process of *stimulus* and then *probability* is reminiscent of the two-step "stimulus and then response" attitude criticized by Dewey (1896).

There are properties inherent to dynamical systems that are often responsible for the mind not quite adhering to probability theory. There is a kind of momentum that the mind develops as it travels through the state space, causing it to warp and exaggerate its deterministic influences. The mind has a tendency to gravitate closer to the nearest attractor (mental state) than warranted. That is, dynamical systems often settle toward stable states, with one attractor being almost, but not perfectly, satisfied (i.e., its "interpretation" of the input being somewhere near 1.0 probability)—even when the input is unresolvably ambiguous. As mentioned earlier, this pattern completion process takes place over a period of time (whether it be a few hundred milliseconds or a few seconds). One must look inside this pattern completion process to find evidence of probabilistic mental states. Too often, researchers examine the final result of a mental process, such as the category or accuracy of the solicited overt motor response. Although informative for characterizing the hypothesized representations that putatively get computed, this mindset largely neglects the process of settling toward those representations and the fact that many amalgams of representations are often considered along the way. The continuity of mind thesis is not particularly aimed at discounting the expository usefulness of those idealized discrete representations of pure mental states. Rather, it is aimed at bringing to the reader's attention the fact that "getting there is half the fun."

Nonlinear Attraction, Stability, and Instability in Visual Perception

Figure 1.1 shows a cartoon example of a two-dimensional perspective on a vector landscape for the high-dimensional state space of a dynamical system. This is a way to visualize the temporal dynamics of a system's state as it would traverse through its state space. Pick a location anywhere on that

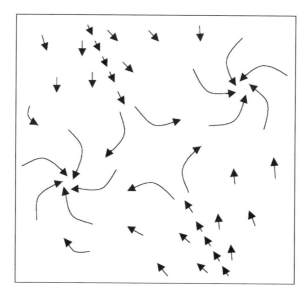

Figure 1.1. A schematic example of a vector landscape for a dynamical system with two attractor basins.

two-dimensional map (recognizing that it would actually correspond to a location in the high-dimensional state space of the dynamical system itself), and put your finger on the location. There are arrows nearby that (with a little interpolation) give an indication of what direction the system would move in. Longer arrows imply stronger attraction and hence faster movement. Move your finger in the direction of the attraction, and check the direction of the arrows near your finger's new location. Continue moving your finger so, and you'll simulate the continuous trajectory of a dynamical system as it moves through its state space. Note that the two attractor basins are spiral-shaped, such that the system would take a while to settle motionlessly into the point attractor, tending to make smaller and smaller orbits almost indefinitely. Thus the vector landscape itself is likely to change shape (due to new sensory input and/or planned motor output) before the state of the system actually becomes static.

Figure 1.2 shows a different kind of rendition of a similar state space manifold. The energy landscape in figure 1.2 shows the two attractor basins as actual bowls in the surface. The vertical axis is treated as energy, and the dynamics will always push the state of the system toward a reduction in energy. Imagine placing a marble on the mesh surface of figure 1.2, and envision where it would roll. Thus would be the trajectory of the system over time.

Any time there is more than one attractor in a dynamical system, it is considered a *nonlinear* dynamical system. With more attractors comes greater potential for any given trajectory to meander quite nonlinearly in its high-dimensional state space. What is crucial to defining a dynamical system is its

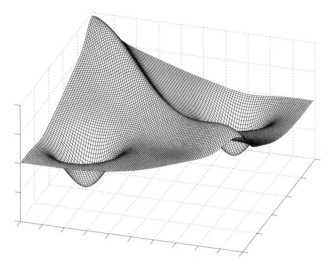

Figure 1.2. An energy landscape similar to the vector landscape in figure 1.1.

balance of stability and instability (e.g., Glendinning, 1994; Spencer & Schöner, 2003; Ward, 2002; see also Bak, 1994).[4] Nonlinear attraction is how a system achieves relative stability, as it travels from unstable point to unstable point in state space to gradually settle into the basin of a point attractor. However, too much stability can be a bad thing. If the system settles all the way into the point attractor—rather than just orbiting its basin[5]—then the system is stuck there until external perturbation dislodges it. In thermodynamics, this kind of true stability is affectionately referred to as heat death.

One easy way to undo a relatively stable state in a dynamical neural system, and reachieve instability, is through fatigue. If a neural population code is continuously stimulated for a significant amount of time, one can naturally expect that the refractory periods of the individual neurons will accumulate in number and duration until it becomes quite difficult to substantially excite that population code for some time. This has been demonstrated in neural firings rates in monkeys (e.g., Baylis & Rolls, 1987; Carandini, 2000; Maffei, Fiorentini, & Bisti, 1973; Sekuler & Pantle, 1967), in human neuroimaging (e.g., Noguchi, Inui, & Kakigi, 2004; Thompson-Schill, D'Esposito, & Kan, 1999), and in neural network simulations (e.g., Huber & O'Reilly, 2003; Kawamoto & Anderson, 1985). This fatigue of the population code results in the reduction of its attraction strength in the state space, and other nearby attractors (population codes) will now be able to pull the system toward them. Such neural fatigue is a common explanation for a wide range of perceptual alternations and illusions, including the following experiential demonstration. It has long been suggested that the perspective alternations of the Necker cube (figure 1.3) are due to fatigue, or satiation, of neural representations (e.g., Orbach, Ehrlich, & Heath, 1963; see also Köhler & Wallach, 1944).

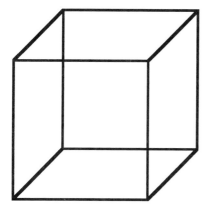

Figure 1.3. The Necker cube. At first glance, it appears to be a wireframe box with one particular perspective, for example, viewed from slightly above it. However, after staring at it for a few seconds, the perspective will change to one in which the box is being viewed from slightly underneath it. See text for discussion of these perspective reversals.

When looking at this wire frame cube, the lower square will often appear to be the front (or closer) panel of the cube, as if your head is slightly above the cube and you are looking down at it. However, after staring at it for several seconds, your percept will switch to having the upper square appear to be the front panel, as if your head is slightly below the cube and you are looking up at it. A few seconds later, the percept will switch back for a little while. As the perspective with the upper square appearing in front is a somewhat unusual one (requiring the cube to be suspended in air or resting on a glass shelf), it is perhaps not surprising that this percept usually lasts for a slightly shorter period than the more canonical one (see Wallach & Slaughter, 1988). Over time, this oscillation between perspectives of the Necker cube tends to increase in rate. Thus, if you were to report when the perspective reverses over time, the graph of those reversals would look something like figure 1.4.

The bistable pattern of Necker cube perspectives has been described as a dynamical system in which two attractors compete against one another

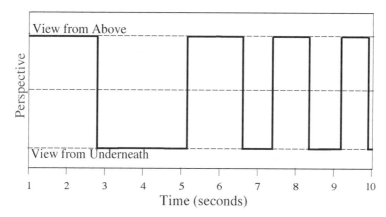

Figure 1.4. An example time course plot of reported perspective reversals during viewing of the Necker cube.

(DeMaris, 2000; Kawamoto & Anderson, 1985; Kelso, 1995; see also Hock, Kelso, & Schöner, 1993, and van Leeuwen, Steyvers, & Nooter, 1997, for similar dynamical treatment of bistable visual input). The perceptual alternations observed with the Necker cube (as well as other ambiguous figures, such as the classic vase/faces silhouette and the Schröder stairs) are consistent with a dynamical systems account of a nonlinear trajectory settling into one attractor basin and then into the other, and back, and so on. However, flipping back and forth between two relatively stable states is something that a logical symbolic (computerlike) system can do as well. What a logical symbolic system cannot do is visit intermediate gradations between the two identifiable states, as a dynamical system naturally does. Therefore, the important observation to note regarding the perceptual alternations of the Necker cube is not simply that they bounce back and forth but that they take a nonzero amount of time to do so. The transition from one identifiable percept to the other is not instantaneous. Based on numerous informal phenomenological reports, when a stable Necker cube perspective begins to transition to the alternative perspective, it seems to take somewhere around half a second for that current percept to finally give way and be replaced by the alternative percept. If this is the case, then the actual perceptual state is not quite accurately described by the instantaneous transitions plotted in figure 1.4. The discrete step-function quality of the data may be more an artifact of the constraints of the experimental task, for example, "press this button or that one, not both," than a true indication of the internal mental state of the observer. (For similar circumstances of *response discreteness* being misinterpreted as *mental discreteness*, see the discussion of categorical perception in chapter 6.) Rather than discretely jumping from one perspective to the next with a step function, perhaps it would be more accurate to plot the Necker cube perspectives as transitioning with a sigmoid function (i.e., an S-shaped curve). See figure 1.5.

In fact, some observers report being able to perceive some visual properties of the intermediate conditions *during the transition*. The perceptual transition is often described as the back panel moving closer in depth and the front panel moving away in depth, until they are at the same depth plane, and the image looks something like a wire frame mobile that is collapsed. The two panels continue their movement, crossing each other, and eventually take each other's previous places. And, believe it or not, there is even one introspective report of the percept "getting stuck" in one of those intermediate conditions for a couple of seconds!

This account is based on introspective reports, of course, and therefore should be taken with a grain of salt. But then, so is the original measure of the Necker cube's perspective reversals, as exemplified in figure 1.4. The only difference is that the introspective report for the data in figure 1.4 is methodologically constrained to a two-alternative forced choice. That is, the observer is explicitly instructed to press one button when one perspective comes into view, and then press another button when the other perspective comes into view. Pressing both buttons at once is not an option. This requirement of

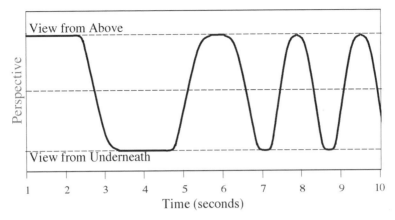

Figure 1.5. A hypothetical time course plot of the actual perceptual state during viewing of the Necker cube. The flat horizontal portions of this oscillating curve are, in dynamical systems terminology, the stable states, where the system is nestled in one of the attractor basins in the state space. The diagonal and curved portions characterize the periods of time when the system is unstable and not inside either attractor basin, but is in the process of being attracted to one of them.

discrete, categorical responses is quite common in cognitive psychology. In contrast, if we allow observers to (at least attempt to) provide more than just a selection of one of two categories, then we have a chance at obtaining a measure of the continuous probabilistic character of mental activity. Throughout this book, there are many different examples of ways to measure and observe, with considerable experimental rigor, that continuous probabilistic character of mind. Consider the sigmoid curves in figure 1.5 our first data visualization (of many to come) of what I call the continuity of mind.

Another compelling data visualization of the continuous manner in which a percept gradually comes into view can be found in neurophysiology research. Recordings from multiple neurons in the inferotemporal cortex of the macaque monkey suggest that it takes a few hundred milliseconds for the right population of cells to achieve their appropriate firing rates for fully identifying a fixated object or face (Rolls & Tovee, 1995; see also Perrett, Oram, & Ashbridge, 1998). The cumulative information (in bits) provided by an inferotemporal neuron in the service of recognizing a face or object accrues continuously (though nonlinearly) over the course of about 350+ milliseconds (see figure 1.6). About 80 milliseconds after the presentation of the visual stimulus, these cells begin firing, and during the first 70 milliseconds of firing, about 50% of the total information to be encoded is already accumulated. Thus, very quickly the network is able to project itself into the right general "neighborhood" in its state space. (This allows some coarse visual discriminations to actually be made with 100 milliseconds or less of stimulus presentation

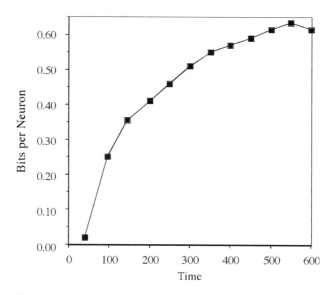

Figure 1.6. Average cumulative information accrued over milliseconds by inferotemporal cells representing objects and faces (adapted from Rolls & Tovee, 1995).

time; see Potter, 1976, 1993; Van Rullen & Thorpe, 2001.) However, over the next 200+ milliseconds, the process of object or face recognition is still *in progress*, during which the remaining 50% of the information to be represented by the distributed population code is gradually accumulated.

Admittedly, 350 milliseconds for a population code to be in transit on the way toward achieving its potentially stable state might not seem like a lot of time. The stable states depicted for the Necker cube in figure 1.5 certainly take up a substantial amount of the total time. Are the transition periods perhaps just interesting curiosities, and the important observation is that a stable state is eventually reached, and it is *that* on which logical mental computations are performed? I think not. Throughout the course of this book, I hope to convince you that the transitions are the important observations, not the seemingly stable states. It is my hypothesis that in more complex visual (as well as auditory, olfactory, etc.) environments, the proportion of time spent in these unstable regions of state space—that is, in the process of traveling toward an attractor basin, but not in one yet—is actually much greater than the proportion of time spent in relatively stable (or, more precisely, metastable) orbit-prone regions of state space.

This gradual accrual of the information comprising a population code (figure 1.6) has powerful consequences for how we conceptualize what the brain is doing when we go about our business of naturally perceiving the world around us. Consider how your eyes move around a complex scene like the one in front of you right now. Your eyes rest, with the two foveas fixating a particular location in the visual field, for about 200–300 milliseconds on average (e.g., Rayner, 1998). They then make a fast, ballistic jump (lasting a few dozen milliseconds or so) away from that location to fixate another location in the visual field. After resting there for another 200–300 milliseconds, they jump yet again to another location. Each new fixation brings a new word, object, or object part, into the high-resolution view of your foveas for little more than a quarter of a second. Now, if it takes almost half a second for the appropriate population code to get fully settled in recognizing a fixated object, but your eyes normally move to a new object every quarter of a second, how can the brain achieve a genuinely stable state for any object recognition event?

Perhaps a stable state is not necessary. Perhaps the relevant neural networks in the brain need only approach an attractor basin in their state space closely enough so that it is unambiguously the most coherent of the many partially active population codes, and then that attractor's associated motor actions and anticipated perceptions go on to carry out their own activation processes. From this perspective, the image of a mental trajectory is now decidedly different from one in which the state of the system lands in one attractor in state space, to consider one thought or percept, and then it lands in another attractor to consider another thought or percept. Rather, the image is one in which the neural system continuously traverses intermediate regions of its state space and occasionally briefly brushes up near an attractor basin just long enough to bring that attractor's associated percepts and actions into prominence. The emphasis is on the journey, not the destinations.

Thinking of objects (or words) as living in a high-dimensional space is a little bit like shooting pool, if you treat the cue ball as the current state of the system, and the object ball (the one you're aiming at) as the next upcoming attractor. A good pool player thinks not only about how to sink the object ball but also about where the cue ball will go after that. Where the state of the system goes after brushing up next to the current attractor is incredibly important. The process of recognizing the *next* word or object does not begin from some neutral central location in state space. It begins from where the system last left off. In a dynamical neural system, the mind travels a continuous trajectory in this state space; it cannot teleport itself to neutral locations in the state space in between recognition events, the way a computer can instantaneously flip its states to some context-free unbiased baseline. Therefore, precisely where in state space the previous word/object left the system has a powerful influence on the trajectory it takes to get to the location in state space corresponding to recognition of the next word/object. Hence, one should expect "priming" effects from the previous word/object on the recognition of the current word/object. And of course, as every cognitive psychologist knows, the literature is rife with reports of words priming one another (e.g., Lukatela, Lukatela, & Turvey, 1993; Neely, 1977; see also Trueswell & Kim, 1998) and reports of objects priming one another (e.g., Cooper, Beiderman, & Hummel, 1992; Gauthier & Tarr, 1997; see also Dill & Edelman, 2001).

Nonlinear Attraction, Stability, and Instability in Language Processing

If you are one those people who feel as though they can catch a glimpse of what the Necker cube looks like—sort of—during the time course of its transition from one perspective to the other, then you have witnessed, firsthand, the continuity of mind. However, if such a glimpse eludes you, fear not. I have a second experiential demonstration of the neural fatigue of a population code that just might work for you. In much the same way that staring at a bistable visual image and perceiving it in one of its two possible perspectives for several seconds essentially overexposes the population of neurons that represents that percept, one can induce the same kind of effect in language. Look at the word in figure 1.7. This is a familiar, easy-to-recognize word. On looking at it, you feel as though your mind achieves a stable interpretation of its meaning. However, if you overexpose the system to this input, you can actually fatigue that meaning to the point that it no longer produces a stable state but instead a clearly introspectively unstable one. Fixate the word in figure 1.7 and read it out loud to yourself, about once per second, for one minute. Each time you say the word, run a kind of mental inventory check on what the word is making you think of at that point in time.

For most people, most of the time, the meaning of the word seems to disappear after many repetitions. The word will begin to look and sound like an unfamiliar nonsense word or perhaps a word from a foreign language. Sometimes you can notice the gradualness with which the original meaning fades. Moreover, one can also occasionally become aware of strange associations that arise, which are indicative of more than just a loss of the original meaning but instead a gradual transition of the system into unusual regions of state space. That is, as the neurons comprising the population code for the meaning of giraffe begin to fatigue, other slightly related populations codes become relatively more prominent. For example, as the meaning "a very-long-necked orange quadruped from Africa" dwindles, you might find yourself making peculiar observations, such as the fact that the *g* is ambiguous with respect to its pronunciation (e.g., as in *giant* and *gimlet*). Or similar sounding words may come to mind, such as *raffle*, *draft*, or even *rafter* (if you speak fast and the syllables exchange order). Or perhaps, you'll think of names, like

giraffe

Figure 1.7. To demonstrate semantic satiation, look at this word and read it out loud to yourself, about once per second, for a minute. As the repetitions continue, the meaning of the word will seem to fade.

Al Jaffe, a cartoonist for *Mad* magazine, or Daniel Jurafsky, a well-respected computational linguist and recent MacArthur Fellow. One colleague even said that the word began to sound like a pretentious French-derived adjective, as in "he's *so* giraffe," meaning something like *gauche* or *jejune*. This odd stream of consciousness, occurring as the original meaning diminishes, should not be surprising if one conceives of word meanings as living in a high-dimensional state space. With each dimension being represented by the activation of its corresponding neuron in the network, reducing the coherence of the population code for the word *giraffe* unavoidably means increasing the coherence of other population codes in nearby regions of state space. As the system gravitates away from the *giraffe* attractor basin, it cannot help but travel somewhat near others. Figure 1.8 is a simplified caricature of a hypothetical two-dimensional perspective through this high-dimensional space that would allow one to watch the trajectory of the system exhibiting fatigue of the *giraffe* attractor and therefore meandering slightly near some other attractors.

This bizarre phenomenon has actually been well studied for decades and is commonly referred to as semantic satiation (e.g., Jakobovits, 1967; Smith & Klein, 1990; see also Tuller, Ding, & Kelso, 1997). Although early theories about semantic satiation treated the effect as though it was a discrete loss of meaning that took place at a particular point in time (e.g., Mason, 1941; Severance & Washburn, 1907), Lambert and Jakobovits (1960) demonstrated

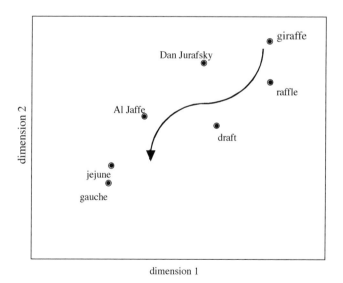

Figure 1.8. During semantic satiation, the meaning of a word diminishes, and similar associations can come to mind. This schematic two-dimensional state-space depicts a hypothetical trajectory away from the satiated word, *giraffe*, and skimming near other words/concepts in the space.

the gradual nature of this reduction in meaning over time. Using Osgood, Suci, and Tannenbaum's (1957) semantic differential measure, which projects the meaning of a word into a several-dimensional space, Lambert and Jakobovits had participants provide responses for locating the word in that space after longer periods of word repetition. As semantic satiation accrued over more repetitions, the resulting projections of word meanings in the semantic differential space indicated a gradual and continuous movement toward but not all the way into the null origin of the space.

Osgood et al.'s (1957) three to six dimensions for representing the meanings of words was an important breakthrough, but it was still quite different from the high-dimensional state space of a neural network. Their dimensions were based on rather abstract concepts, such as good/bad, active/passive, and potent/impotent, for which participants simply provided metacognitive ratings for any one word (e.g., on a scale of $+3$ to -3, how good/bad, active/passive, and potent/impotent is a giraffe?). Moreover, the physical mechanisms by which these abstract dimensions might be instantiated were not forthcoming. In fact, precisely because the actual space in which these words live is high-dimensional, which is merely approximated by Osgood et al.'s abstract dimensions, *almost any* set of concepts that are sufficiently different from one another could probably serve as the basis vectors for a several-dimensional projection of that high-dimensional neural space (e.g., Edelman, 1998, 1999). For example, if one had participants report how similar any word is to a peanut, an airplane, and a horse, one could probably produce a three-dimensional mock-up that would exhibit important clusterings of abstract concepts such animate/ inanimate, natural/artifact, and so on. But it's probably not the case that the principal dimensions on which our brains encode the world are *peanutness*, *airplaneness*, and *horseness*.

Nonetheless, Osgood et al.'s (1957) insight that word representation should be carried out in a metric space, where graded similarity is easily embodied as the distance between representations, was important—yet was quickly swept under the rug as the computer metaphor of the mind took hold in the 1960s. In cognitive psychology, the dominant account of word representation became symbolic entries for words (like in a dictionary), with their relationships to one another encoded by logical rules and/or sharing of an integral number of discrete semantic features. Essentially, if one could easily imagine coding the representation scheme in the popular programming language of the time (LISP), then it was considered a legitimate representation scheme. Coding a high-dimensional metric space, with each word being a continuous vector in that space, was not what LISP was best at doing. However, now that symbolic programming is nowhere near as dominant as it was in the 1960s and 1970s, and numerical computation has become quite popular, perhaps it is not surprising that high-dimensional geometric accounts of word representation are becoming accepted again (e.g., Landauer & Dumais, 1997; Lund & Burgess, 1996; Schutze, 1993).

Deprogramming the Cognitive Psychologist

The change in styles of programming languages from symbolic to numerical is only one of many transitions that have recently taken place to help set the stage for what promises to be the next paradigm shift in psychology and the cognitive sciences. For example, connectionism, though not quite becoming the dominant paradigm in psychology, managed to make the concept of distributed representations an acceptable notion (e.g., Clark, 1993; Elman et al., 1996; O'Reilly, Munakata, & McClelland, 2000; Rogers & McClelland, 2004; Rumelhart & McClelland, 1986a; but see Dietrich & Markman, 2003; Fodor & Pylyshyn, 1995; Marcus, 2001). One could argue that much of the connectionist literature has devoted slightly too much of its attention to trajectories through synaptic-weight-space as an account of learning and not enough to trajectories through activation-space as an account of real-time processing. Nonetheless, the step to having knowledge live as partially overlapping distributed representations in the high-dimensional state space of a network has been a crucial departure from cognitive psychology's traditional symbolic computation approach.

Moreover, improvements in continuous and semi-continuous measures of cognitive processing have helped open the door to visualizing the continuous dynamics of mental activity. For example, speech shadowing (repeating continuous speech as quickly and accurately as possible) provided important insights into language processing (e.g., Marslen-Wilson, 1973, 1975). Recordings of electrical potentials from the scalp (e.g., Hillyard & Kutas, 1983) as well as from the peripheral muscles (e.g., Tuller, Kelso, & Harris, 1982) have provided continuous measures of a wide range of perceptual, cognitive, and motor processes. Recording from multiple neurons at once (e.g., Georgopoulos et al., 1982), recording from neurons in awake behaving animals (e.g., Motter, 1993), and microstimulating neurons in awake behaving animals (e.g., Gold & Shadlen, 2000) has provided concrete examples of the distributed probabilistic states in which neural systems spend much of their time. Eye tracking has provided real-time semi-continuous measures of language and vision (e.g., Rayner, 1998; Tanenhaus et al., 1995). These relatively recent advancements in methodologies (as well as many others; see chapter 3) have made it possible to catch glimpses of the graded states that the mind travels through on its way to produce discrete actions.

Another development in the cognitive and neural sciences that assists in placing us at the brink of a significant movement away from traditional cognitive psychology is that of dynamical systems theory. As a field of its own, dynamical systems theory has advanced a great deal in both sophistication as well as popularity since the days of Hamilton, Boltzmann, and Poincare. For example, recent treatments of dynamical systems theory benefit considerably from computer simulations (Polking, 1995; Scheinerman, 1995; Strogatz, 1994). Most relevant to the cognitive sciences, dynamical systems theory is being successfully applied to a wide range of human behaviors, such as categorization (Anderson et al., 1977), language (Tabor & Tanenhaus, 1999), visual perception (Grossberg, 1980), motor movement (Kelso, 1995), as well as music perception (Large & Palmer, 2002), and developmental processes (Thelen & Smith, 1994). I genuinely suspect at this point that these advances of dynamical systems in various subfields of psychology spell doom for the computer metaphor of the mind.

As should be evident by now, the purpose of this book is to deprogram the cognitive psychologist in us all. We all have a tendency to want to draw a circle around a set of phenomena and label that set with a name like *perception* and perhaps label another set of phenomena with the name *cognition*. Even within those circles, we feel the need to draw smaller circles of things like "word recognition," as if it was completely unrelated to "object recognition." We all have a tendency to want to draw boxes around presumed transformations of information (e.g., combining spoken sounds over time to map onto words representations, or combining visual features and surfaces to map onto object representations), and call them *processors* or *modules*. We have these tendencies because without these overidealized categorical separations and discrete labels, we feel at a loss for how to talk about these phenomena. But how do I refer to a process that combines spoken sounds *and* visual features over time to map onto possible motor actions? The vocabulary of traditional cognitive psychology is simply not built for it. In contrast, the intersection of dynamical systems theory, neural network modeling, and ecological psychology, a nexus that I refer to as continuity psychology, is developing not only the vocabulary but also the conceptual and mathematical tools for it.

As we watch traditional cognitive psychology giving way to continuity psychology, one is tempted to ask, as Douglas Hintzman (1993) did, "Was the cognitive revolution a mistake?" And I think the answer is clearly "no"—but not because it got anything right about the mind. The cognitive revolution of the 1960s was the right thing to do at the time because, in opposing the antimentalism of the behaviorist tradition, it provided the necessary realization that the mind has sufficient complexity of processing to make it required reading, as it were. Psychology could no longer focus solely on the stimulus and the response, ignoring the complex nested dynamical processes that take place in between. The first-order associationism of the 1940s simply wasn't powerful enough to fit the data (Lashley, 1951; see also Chomsky, 1959). Unfortunately, where cognitive psychology in particular and cognitive science in general went wrong was in its marriage to the computer metaphor of the mind. Box-and-arrow diagrams, borrowed from computer engineering, ran amok in the scientific journals, and serial digital processes were used as the square pegs to be forced into the round holes of cognition. The mind was treated as an independent system, somehow composed of multiple internal independent subsystems.

However, in the past few decades, evidence from ecological psychology, neuroscience, and real-time methodologies in cognitive psychology has cast doubt on this serial digital computational perspective on the mind. Rather than the mind being composed of independent systems for perception, cognition, and action, the entire process is perhaps better conceived of as a continuous loop through perceptionlike processes, partially overlapping with cognitionlike processes, and actionlike processes, producing continuous changes in the environment, which in turn, continuously influence the perceptionlike processes (see Neisser, 1976). In this large feedback loop, the brain itself is more of an interdependent subsystem *contributing to mind* than a system *comprising mind*. It carries out more of a subprocess than a process.

Given the tumultuous history of psychology and its relatively late application of mathematical techniques from dynamical systems theory, one could argue that the symbolic-computation approach to cognition, spanning from the 1960s to the 1990s, was a necessary first approximation at characterizing mental activity—a first approximation that has run its course and served its purpose. For the new psychology on the horizon, perhaps we are ready to discard the metaphor of the mind as a computer, because its drawbacks now outweigh its advances, and replace it with a treatment of the mind as a natural continuous dynamical event—whose decidedly nonmetaphorical substrate consists of the brain and body and the environment with which they interact.

2

Some Conceptual Tools for Tracking Continuous Mental Trajectories

I can best illustrate this conception of nervous action by picturing the brain as the surface of a lake. The prevailing breeze carries small ripples in its direction, the basic polarity of the system. Varying gusts set up crossing systems of waves, which do not destroy the first ripples, but modify their form, a second level in the system of space coordinates. A tossing log with its own period of submersion sends out periodic bursts of ripples, a temporal rhythm. The bow wave of a speeding boat momentarily sweeps over the surface, seems to obliterate the smaller waves yet leaves them unchanged by its passing, the transient effect of a strong stimulus.
—Karl Lashley (1951)

Timing Is Everything

Time is continuous. We are generally forced to talk about it in discrete quanta, be it billions of years in astronomy, millions of years in geology and in evolution, centuries in history, decades in sociology, years in economics, days in our personal lives, seconds in cognitive psychology, milliseconds in cognitive neuroscience, microseconds in chemistry, nano- and picoseconds in computer engineering, and femto- and attoseconds in physics. These discrete labels that carve up time into delineated chunks are certainly useful descriptive conveniences. However, it would be foolish to think that they are real. That is, it seems highly unlikely that naturally organized systems of multiple interacting units, such as a brain, a society, or a planet, would function in lockstep to the pace of some systemwide counter using a particular temporal quanta, such that each new second, or millisecond, or attosecond signaled an instantaneous *and simultaneous* updating of the discrete state of each and every unit in the system. This is not a straw man I'm building. This is the kind of lockstep synchronization that would genuinely be necessary for the brain to function like a digital computer.

If, at the spatial scale of neurons and behavior, time truly is continuous, that is, not decomposable into discrete quanta, then changes in a system's state (or even its units' states) over time must also be continuous. Thus, claiming that a system was in a particular "state," X, at a particular point in time, really boils down to saying that the *average* of the system's states during that *period of time* was **X**. This kind of coarse averaging measurement is often a practical necessity in science, but should not be mistaken as genuine evidence for the system actually resting in a discrete stable state.

Real time does not function like a digital computer's clock. It does not move forward and then stop to be counted, and then move forward again only to stop again. At the level of human behavior, real time does not have an objective functional unit. The system of temporal units that we have settled on—based on one second equaling 9,192,631,770 periods of radiation from the cesium-133 atom—is relatively arbitrary. Historically speaking, one rotation of the Earth around the sun, which is almost naturally carved up into 365 day units—leap years notwithstanding—is arguably a rather terracentric basis for setting the clock of the universe, is it not? We could just as easily have developed a system that treated the equivalent of 1.37 femtoseconds as a unit of time, given it its own funny name, and built the rest of the time scale system around multiples of that unit. In any case, for pragmatic day-to-day concerns of humans, there are still many time scale systems that could have been devised to fit into Earth's solar and lunar cycles, and it is simply a series of disconnected scientific endeavors over centuries (some based on the metric system and others not) that have meandered onto the one we now use planetwide. Time itself has no idea, nor does it care, what method we use for pretending to carve it up. It just keeps flowing continuously.[1]

If, for the purposes of analyzing physical processes at the molar scale, time is best described as continuous and unhesitating, then it is perhaps difficult to imagine that the time-dependent trajectories of the mind, through the brain's state space, could be any different. The firing rates of all the billions of neurons in the brain do not and could not all remain simultaneously constant for any significant period of time. What this means is that there is no point in time during which the mind is not changing. There is simply no such thing as a static internal representation, as required by the computer metaphor of the mind.

Trajectories in Neural State Space

This practice of treating time as though it was comprised of discrete independent units is at the heart of why a somewhat unexpected clash of mindsets exists between connectionist modelers and dynamical systems theorists of cognition (see van Gelder, 1998). One of the reasons dynamical cognition theorists criticize connectionist modelers is precisely because most artificial neural networks (including the simulations in this book) treat the updating of all the neuronal activations as though they took place in lockstep to the beat of some arbitrary and nondecomposable temporal quanta (but see Pearlmutter, 1989, 1995; Williams & Zipser, 1989). In contrast, a differential equation from dynamical systems theory describes a truly continuous trajectory existing in a state space with time included as a continuous dimension. For example, the basic dynamical system is described by the following simple equation:

$$\partial X / \partial t = f(X), \tag{2.1}$$

where X is the vector of coordinates describing the system's location in its state space, and t is time. The derivative of the vector X is proportional to the change in time as a result of the function f. Nowhere in this equation is there reference to *steps* in time or in space. There is only flow.

Although such mathematical accounts are indeed elegant and probably closer to the truth about temporal dynamics, they are at times criticized for being descriptions of the phenomena rather than explanations. Understanding *why* a brain does something equivalent to following a particular trajectory in state space could perhaps be aided by simulations in an architecture that resembles actual neural assemblies, rather than one that merely provides a metaphor of their temporal dynamics. Thus we arrive at the compensatory strengths and weaknesses of dynamical systems theory and of artificial neural networks. Dynamical systems theory accommodates the genuine continuity of time and state space but says little about neurophysiology. Neural network simulations provide some approximated account of the actual neural hardware that carries out these functions, but they chop their time, and therefore their state space, into segmented periods and regions of artificial stasis.

Such computer simulations of state space trajectories over time are sometimes called iterated maps, because with each discrete iteration in time the simulation plots a new point in space to describe the state of the system. With neural network models that proceed in lockstep, it is as though the state of the system doesn't *move* through its state space but rather *teleports* from one specific location to another, resting statically in each location for the duration of the temporal quantum. The answer that most connectionist modelers give in response to this criticism—and the one that I give in response as well when I use neural networks—is that, as long as the time steps are small, the loss of some temporal contiguity is a minor simplification that allows several benefits in explication and visualization. Essentially, this amounts to advocating the approximation of continuous dynamical systems by discrete dynamical systems. In employing any model, one must choose where the oversimplifications will be permitted, and where the crucial mechanisms will be more precisely implemented.

Importantly, once the decision to use artificial neural networks has been made, there is still a choice to be made about temporal resolution. This choice is crucial for simulating perceptual/cognitive phenomena. For example, a significant proportion of connectionist models of cognition have focused on the temporally static spatial resolution of "stored" exemplars and categories of individuated stimuli in the state space of the network (e.g., the feedforward networks of Browne, 2002; Kruschke, 1990; Rosenblatt, 1967; Rumelhart & Todd, 1993) rather than on the temporal dynamics of the internal processing of input (e.g., the recurrent attractor networks of Anderson et al., 1977; Grossberg, 1980; Hinton, Plaut, & Shallice, 1993; McClelland & Elman, 1986; McRae, deSa, & Seidenberg, 1997). As indicated by the demonstrations offered in chapter 1 and the many experimental results described in chapters 6–9, it will become clear that even when an individual stimulus input is artificially isolated for presentation to the sensory systems, a temporally dynamic perceptual/cognitive process ensues such that the brain travels continuously through its state space, gravitating toward multiple semi-stable attractor basins. This temporally dynamic process is arguably best modeled by recurrent attractor networks (rather than by feedforward networks) because they combine the benefits of semi-continuous processing (rather than one time step per one stimulus) with approximate neural plausibility.

In chapter 1, the concepts of a neural population code and of an attractor basin were used almost interchangeably. However, the link between the two was not quite fully mapped out. Chapter 2 is designed to do exactly that. That said, keep in mind that the use of a high-dimensional state space, and the mathematical insight from dynamical systems theory, are for *modeling* how the mind works. The emergence of mind takes place in the medium of patterns of activation across neuronal cell assemblies in conjunction with the interaction of their attached sensors (eyes, ears, etc.) and effectors (hands, speech apparatus, etc.) with the environment in which they are embedded. Make no mistake about it, *that* is the stuff of which human minds are made: brains, bodies, and environments. Trajectories through high-dimensional state spaces are merely convenient ways for scientists to describe, visualize, and model what is going on in those brains, bodies, and environments.

The reason for using a metaphor to approach one's object of study is the same as that for using any model. When the *target* domain, for example, the mind, is too complex to understand in its full detail, we can import a richer understanding of other similar and somewhat simpler source domains, for example, dynamical systems theory and attractor networks, to provide descriptions and explanations of how the mind might function. Done properly, this requires a cyclic interplay between empirical predictions made by the metaphor/model, and results of those empirical tests being used to improve the metaphor/model (for more details, see chapter 4).

To conceptualize thought as a trajectory through state space, first visualize in front of you a very high-dimensional space. Let's say, one for each neuron—at least a few billion dimensions. All right, perhaps that is more difficult than it sounds. It's usually easier to cheat a little and visualize a large three-dimensional space and just tell yourself that it has more dimensions than that. If each neuron is treated as a dimension of the system's state space, then any pattern of activation that is exhibited by the neural network corresponds to a location in that high-dimensional state space. That is, the firing rates of all the neurons (averaged over some short, sliding temporal window) can stand as the coordinates of that location in the state space. A number of researchers have encouraged a focus on this kind of geometric framework for representing brain states (e.g., Aleksander, 1973; Anderson et al., 1977; Braitenberg, 1977; Churchland, 1986; Churchland & Sejnowski, 1992; Edelman, 1999, 2002; Pasupathy & Connor, 2002; see also Kiss, 1972; Osgood, Suci, & Tennenbaum, 1957; Shepard, 1962).

The demonstrations included in this chapter are intended to provide simplified visual examples of distributed brain states and probabilistic mental states over time. As the cognitive and neural sciences gradually let go of the computer metaphor of the mind, where a central executive performs logical operations on discrete mental entities, a continuity framework (inspired by ecological psychology, dynamical systems theory, and computational neuroscience) can replace that abstracted metaphor with the concrete and neurally plausible notion of a continuous trajectory through a neuronal state space.

Probabilistic Versus Pure Mental States

One can think of the set of possible *brain states* as a high-dimensional space with as many dimensions as you have neurons. If you could know the activity level of each neuron, that would provide you with the coordinates in that high-dimensional space that correspond to that brain state's location in the space. Similar brain states will be in nearby locations in that space. *Mental states*, by contrast, can be thought of as a subset of particular locations in that brain state space that have been visited frequently enough and are familiar enough to be easily labeled by the scientist/observer with linguistic identifiers that describe that mental state (such as the mental state of being hungry, or of recognizing Grandma, or perhaps of grasping the continuity of mind thesis).[2] You can think of this as the folk psychology in the machine.

The important point to be made by the continuity of mind thesis is that these specific locations in state space which seem to have easily labeled identities, these "pure mental states," can only ever be *approximated* by the actual neural system for which this state space is a metaphor. That is not to say those pure mental states are irrelevant or nonexistent. They do exist, as possible locations in the neural system's state space. They just never *happen*. The neural population codes get sufficiently activated (i.e., the system approaches close enough to a frequently visited and identifiable attractor basin) to fool everyone—including the self—into thinking that the pure mental state has been perfectly instantiated. However, for this dynamical system comprised of billions of neurons to perfectly instantiate a pure discrete logical symbolic state, such as *I am hungry*, in exactly the same way every time that state is computed would require more precision than the system is capable of achieving.

One counterargument that a rule-and-symbol theorist might launch at this account is that rather than the mental state being a mathematically unachievable attractor point, as assumed in this description, perhaps it is the entire attractor basin, which includes many locations in a nearby region of space (e.g., a delimited contiguous manifold). For example, a neural subsystem could enter one of its attractor basins, travel around within that basin, and send its output to a second neural subsystem in a sufficiently coarse format that the receiving subsystem is unable to distinguish among the subtle changes in the exact neural activation patterns resulting from changes in location within that basin. The second subsystem could only discern that the first subsystem is somewhere in that attractor basin and thus would be forced to treat the entire set of locations within the basin as belonging completely and indiscriminately to one discrete symbolic category (see the discussion of symbolic dynamics in chapter 4, and the discussion of categorical perception in chapter 6). This arrangement can seem an intuitively pleasing hybrid notion of continuous distributed patterns at a lower (perceptual?) level of the system and discrete symbolic entities at a higher (cognitive?) level of the system.

However, two related problems quickly arise with this hybrid framework: One is perhaps technical, whereas the other is arguably a deal-breaker. The first problem is in deciding precisely where to put the discrete threshold defining the inside and outside of the attractor basin. This arbitrary threshold problem is one of the major bugbears of symbolic dynamics, because a tiny misplacement of a threshold can cause massive inconsistencies in the system's behavior over time (Bollt et al., 2000). Essentially, a "receiving" subsystem that computes symbols based on the (even slightly misplaced) threshold crossings of a "sending" continuous dynamical subsystem can wind up frequently and drastically misinterpreting the actual behavior of the subsystem.

The second, and probably more fatal problem with the hybrid dynamic-to-symbolic cognition idea concerns the temporal continuousness of real-world sensory stimulation. The continuous input that characterizes most ecologically valid cognitive phenomena generally will not allow the system to languish in an attractor basin for any significant amount of time. For example, by the time a listener has understood a particular word in a spoken utterance, and thus traveled to the appropriate attractor basin in her state space, a new word is already being delivered in the speech stream that will impose its own influences on the listener's movement through her state space (see chapter 7). Corresponding observations hold for visual perception in a moving observer (Gibson, 1950). In most natural human behaviors, an incremental achievement of understanding is not meditated on for even a second. New sensory stimulation, new imagined stimulation, new motor movement, and/or new imagined movement are continuously in play. Thus, in naturalistic circumstances, the amount of time spent in an attractor basin is likely to be far outweighed by the amount time spent traveling toward attractor basins.

One promising solution to these problems with symbolic dynamics is to forgo using strict thresholds and instead measure the system's current distances to its many point attractors. Thus, rather than merely reporting a single attractor partition containment, as in symbolic dynamics, reporting instead the profile of proximities to all the attractors, a kind of *fuzzy* symbolic dynamics. In such a framework, we go from talking about pure mental states, which are discrete logical, perfectly repeatable symbols, to probabilistic mental states, which are fuzzy, graded, partially overlapping distributed patterns. Although this format of description clearly uses labeled symbols (albeit fuzzy ones), they are purely for expository ease in scientific communication. It is not to be claimed that some part of the system itself actually uses them.

That said, these probabilistic mental states may nonetheless appear to satisfy, to some degree, at least one of the demands of classical computational cognition: an *internal mediating state* between sensory input and motor output (e.g., Dietrich & Markman, 2003; see also Fodor & Pylyshyn, 1981, 1995; Marcus, 2001; Markman & Dietrich, 2000). However, if the brain is a dynamical system, that is, best defined by its changes in state rather than by the states themselves, then the mediating representational system we are talking about is, oddly enough, one that does not generate mediating representational states, in the usual sense. The mediating representational space instantiated by the brain—in between sensory input and motor output—is one that generates a continuously dynamic trajectory and never really stops long enough to be in a logical state per se. Strictly speaking, a state requires stasis. When we talk about states in a continuous dynamical systems framework, we're really referring to artificial freeze-frames of time for the purpose of analysis, not because the states actually behave like real states. Perhaps a fruitful step toward compromise between classical computational cognition and dynamical cognition would be to speak of internal mediating *processes*, rather than internal mediating states.

Visualizing a Probabilistic Mental State

Despite my eschewing of mental states in favor of a mental trajectory, in this next section, I start out discussing and offering visualizations of how a brain might instantiate a probabilistic mental state. Once the concept of a probabilistic mental state is clear, the discussion and the visualizations will turn to the state space trajectory that results from stringing together a continuous series of probabilistic mental states in real time. I will walk through an example of how the brain's pattern completion processes deal with ambiguous input, traveling through many brain states and occasionally getting close to particular mental states.

The toy demonstration begins now. Imagine you go for an after dinner stroll through your neighborhood, and the sun goes down before you get home. A few blocks from your home, you notice an animal approaching you in the street from some distance. At that instant, before you have determined exactly how to respond to the situation, your brain will be exhibiting a pattern of activity that is partially consistent with a number of alternative states of mind. Figure 2.1 is a cartoon version of that brain state—if you had only 14 neurons, instead of about 100 billion.

In the idealized brain state in figure 2.1, a few neurons are excited near their maximum firing rate, several neurons are moderately above their resting

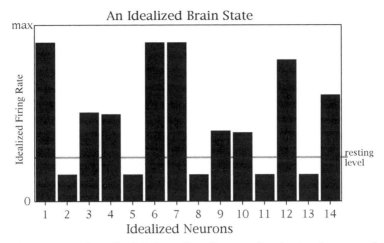

Figure 2.1. A hypothetical time slice of averaged activation for a set of 14 neurons.

level of tonic activation, and several neurons are conspicuously inhibited below their resting level. (As these are firing rates and not action potentials, this state is obviously averaged over a few dozen milliseconds.) Although this pattern of neural activation can be treated as a discrete location in the space of possible *brain* states, it does not correspond to a discrete, pure *mental* state. That is, I have devised this demonstration such that the pattern of neural activity in figure 2.1 corresponds to a brain state that is partially consistent with two different identifiable mental states.

Figures 2.2 and 2.3 show what the pattern of neural activity would need to be to perfectly instantiate the pure mental states, "I see a cat" and "I see

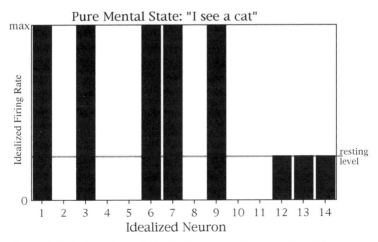

Figure 2.2. A hypothetical idealized pattern of neuronal activity corresponding to a discrete mental state.

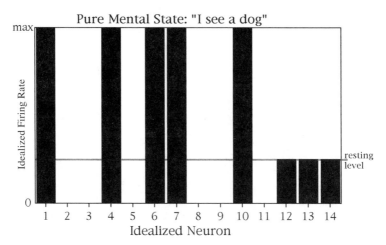

Figure 2.3. A hypothetical idealized pattern of neuronal activity corresponding to another discrete mental state.

a dog," respectively. In figure 2.2, one can see that neurons 1, 3, 6, 7, and 9 comprise the population code for the mental state of "I see a cat." Partially overlapping with this, in figure 2.3, it becomes clear that neurons 1, 4, 6, 7, and 10 comprise the population code for the mental state of "I see a dog." Due to the complexity of multiple sensory inputs, nonlinear dynamics in neural processing, and noise in neural activity, these kinds of pure mental states are practically unattainable, but they are regularly approximated by the brain's actual pattern of activity.

Figure 2.4 shows the same pattern of neural activity as in figure 2.1 but with idealized interpretations for what each neuron represents. Thus, if we pretend that we know what each neuron is coding for, we can folk psychologize that the brain has perceived a living object that has four legs and a tail. The brain is telling the body to walk, not run, and to dilate the pupils of the eyes because it is dark—and also perhaps because it is rather curious about the four-legged creature that is approaching. Interestingly, this brain is not quite sure if the animal is small or medium-sized, but—due to some partial hints of recognition—it is beginning to suspect that the animal's label begins with either the letter *c* or the letter *d*.

Of course, there are thousands of other relevant features one could add to this array. For the purposes of depicting it graphically, I have vastly oversimplified the features that might define the situation. Even more important than that oversimplification is the oversimplification implied here about what neurons can encode. Just as we probably do not have grandmother cells (see chapter 1), we also probably do not have "has four legs" cells, or "starts with the letter *d*" cells. Individual neurons usually represent far tinier details than those depicted in figure 2.4. The term *microfeatures* has been used to refer to the properties of the sensory input to which individual neurons respond

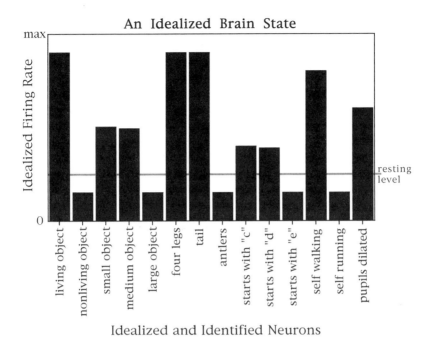

Figure 2.4. An "interpreted" version of the neurons from figure 2.1.

(Hinton, 1981). Often, these individual microfeatures are not easily deciphered, either in artificial neural networks or in biological neural networks.

Now, despite my acknowledgment of the egregious oversimplifications in these graphical demonstrations, I am going to commit one more. I am about to convert the pattern of activity across those 14 neurons into individual numbers indicating how closely the pattern resembles each of a handful of pure mental states (such as those in the labels of figures 2.2 and 2.3). Each pure mental state is a specific location in the 14-dimensional hypercube that constitutes this brain's state space. Figures 2.2 and 2.3 specify locations in state space that belong to the two particular pure mental states to which this neural pattern (in figure 2.4) is closest. In fact, the neural pattern is almost equally close to the two of them. Figure 2.5 shows the same brain state again, but presented in terms of a kind of normalized proximity to eight different pure mental states. Essentially, one can think of figure 2.5 as representing the same information as figure 2.4, but in the language of mental states rather than the language of neural firing rates. In a sense, the brain state we are dealing with here currently instantiates the pure mental states of "I see a dog" and "I see a cat" with fuzzy truth values of 0.34 and 0.35, respectively. This brain is approaching multiple pure mental states at once—or more precisely, it is in a probabilistic mental state.

Within this framework, a brain state is a concrete physical thing: It is the pattern of neural activation across the entire brain at a given point in time

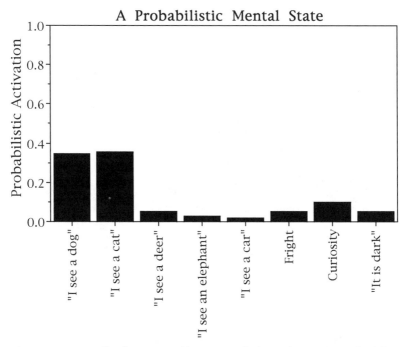

Figure 2.5. Normalized proximity (the inverse of relative distance) to eight different "pure mental states."

(or averaged across a short period of time). A probabilistic mental state is exactly that same thing, but represented in the form of its proximity to idealized pure (identifiable) mental states instead of activity levels of individual neurons—and thus a probabilistic mental state refers to a concrete physical thing as well. In contrast, a *pure* mental state refers to an ideal pattern of neural activation that—due to the complex and noisy dynamics of a brain with billions of neurons and trillions of synapses—is never actually instantiated. A pure discrete (i.e., symbolic) mental state is an abstract concept. It is a useful construct for theory development, but an actual physical instantiation of it never comes into being. Nonetheless, the labels attached to pure mental states are extremely helpful in understanding probabilistic mental states. Without the descriptive conveniences of the labels along the abscissa in figure 2.5, a probabilistic mental state would be essentially uninterpretable.

Visualizing Trajectories Through State Space

The important thing about brain states, or probabilistic mental states, is that they change over time. As it more and more closely approximates a pure mental state via pattern completion, the brain can be visualized as traveling through its state space (a bit like a meteor in a solar system) toward a particular region that will actualize some motor output (or simulated motor behavior, such as motor imagery or an internal monologue). This notion of a trajectory through a state space is at the heart of the continuity of mind thesis. It allows one to conceive of the intermediate regions in state space that are visited *on the way toward* an attractor basin that approximates some interpretable pure mental state. Contrary to what traditional cognitive psychology and philosophy of mind would lead you to believe, those intermediate regions are where we spend most of our mental life—not in the easily labeled pure mental states.

Although this informal description of trajectories and attractor basins may seem intuitive enough, it can be quite difficult to actually depict them when the dimensionality of the state space is very high. A common mathematical way to visualize these trajectories and attractor basins in high-dimensional spaces is principal component analysis (PCA). In PCA, a low-dimensional perspective of the high-dimensional space is depicted, using orthogonal dimensions that cut through the space in ways that maximize the variance of the data points in the original space. Think of the array of stars you see in the night sky. This is a two-dimensional perspective (with nary a depth cue) on a three-dimensional space. Looked at from another solar system, a completely different set of constellations would be apparent. PCA can find the two- or three-dimensional perspective that best reveals the separate clusters of frequently visited locations (attractor basins) in the high-dimensional state space, as well as the pathway traveled by a system (semi-) continuously gravitating toward one or more of those attractor basins (e.g., Elman, 1991; Pearlmutter, 1989; Tabor & Tanenhaus, 1999).

Much simpler than PCA, ternary diagrams (sometimes called chemographic representations) provide a relatively easy example of visualizing data in fewer than the original number of dimensions. For example, if we were using three factors to define the state of a brain, we might depict this brain-state-in-a-box as a location in a three-dimensional cube (e.g., Anderson et al., 1977). When there are three dimensions to a state space, but they need to be depicted in two dimensions on a piece of paper, the values of the three factors can be normalized to sum to 1.0. This projects them onto the triangular plane connecting coordinates [1, 0, 0], [0, 1, 0], and [0, 0, 1] of the three-dimensional state space. In figure 2.6, these three corners of the triangular plane are labeled as the pure mental states, where only one of the three factors has greater than zero activation.

If you rotate this isosceles triangle so that you're facing it head-on, you can depict the normalized state of this three-dimensional system in just two dimensions; see figure 2.7. In this ternary diagram, the trajectory of the system's state over time can be plotted with numbers indicating time steps to reveal changes in velocity (see Tabor, 1995). The system in figure 2.7 starts out around coordinates [0.41, 0.26, 0.33], for the pure mental states 1, 2, and 3, respectively. It initially gravitates toward Pure Mental State 2, and away from

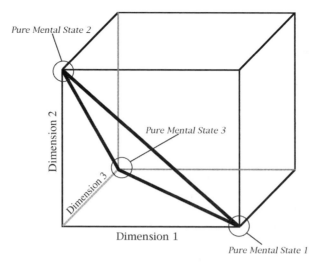

Figure 2.6. Defining a ternary diagram inside the 3D cube.

Pure Mental State 3. Then the system slows down in a somewhat equi-based region of the state space, near a location called a *saddle point,* and then turns its trajectory to Pure Mental State 1, toward which it gravitates precipitously.

In fact, this same technique can be used to concretely visualize *four* spatial dimensions! A quaternary diagram represents, in three dimensions, the normalized coordinates of a four-dimensional state space; see figure 2.8. And in general, with a greater number of attractors in the state space, trajectories will tend to be more nonlinear. Of course, in more realistic complex systems, such

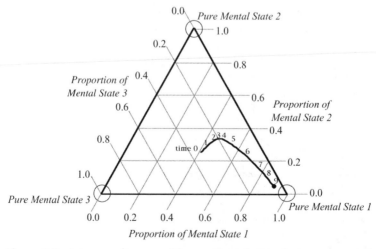

Figure 2.7. A ternary diagram with pure mental states in its corners and a time-dependent trajectory.

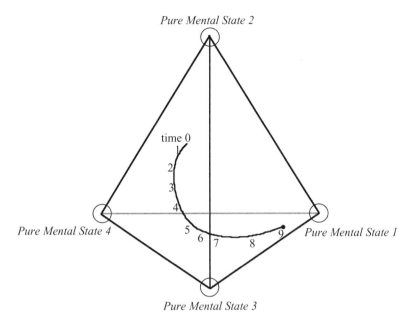

Figure 2.8. A quaternary diagram with pure mental states in its corners and a three-dimensional trajectory.

as biological neural networks, there are far greater than four dimensions, and the stable locations in the state space may not always be in the corners of the space, as idealized in these last three figures. Moreover, the stable states, or point attractors, may not be equidistant from one another either, as depicted here. Some population codes are nearby one another in the high-dimensional state space of the brain, whereas others are quite distant from each other.

Visualizing a Probabilistic Mental State Changing Over Time

What I hope to make clear in these visualizations is that the many references to attractor basins and continuous trajectories in state space that crop up in so many discussions of dynamical cognition are in fact grounded in quite concrete, tangible, visualizable, and mechanistic assumptions. They are not vague abstract theoretical constructs or hand-wavy buzzwords. They correspond to very real physical implementations.

Let us return now to the idealized probabilistic mental state illustrated for encountering that mysterious animal during your evening stroll through the neighborhood. Figure 2.5 is repeated here, for convenience, as figure 2.9— with the added notation that it is but the first time step among many. Because that pattern of neural activation is closer to the mental state of curiosity than

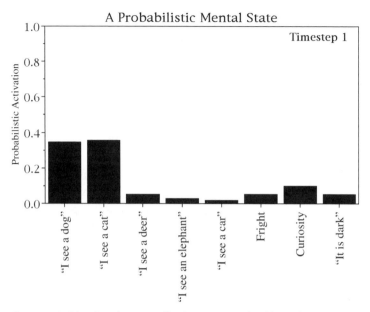

Figure 2.9. Treating the normalized proximity plot (from figure 2.5) as the first of several time steps.

to the mental state of fright (i.e., figure 2.9 shows you being twice as curious as you are afraid), let's say you stick around long enough to find out what the animal really is. During this idealized freeze-frame, your mind is like Schrödinger's cat: in multiple states at once (i.e., especially "I see a cat" and "I see a dog"). As the discrimination is being made, the probabilistic activation of the mental states "I see a cat" and "I see a dog" will rise and compete, while the probabilities of the other mental states will drop commensurately.

For example, in time step 2 (figure 2.10), the probabilistic activations have changed somewhat. A very simple algorithm was used, in this example, to carry out these changes in activations—or equivalently, the trajectory through mental state space that this system follows. The probabilistic activations in figure 2.9 were each squared, and then they were all renormalized, that is, each was divided by the total sum. This settling algorithm is called squared normalization. Note that in this particular settling algorithm, it is guaranteed that the probability value that starts out higher will be the eventual winner. It is only a matter of time. After all, time is what it's all about. However, there are more complex versions of this kind of normalization-based settling algorithm that do occasionally allow an initially lower probability representation to eventually usurp an initially higher probability representation (see chapter 4).

Time step 3, figure 2.11, is achieved by applying squared normalization again—but this time to the values of time step 2 (figure 2.10). Note how quickly the two mental states of "I see a cat" and "I see a dog" have taken over the probability space, with the system moving toward those locations in space

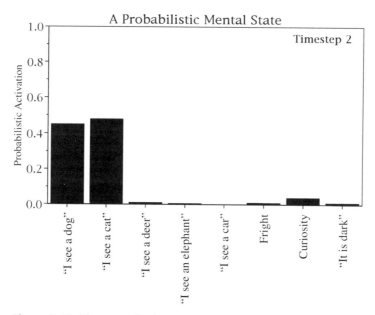

Figure 2.10. The normalized proximity pattern gravitates toward some pure mental states and away from others.

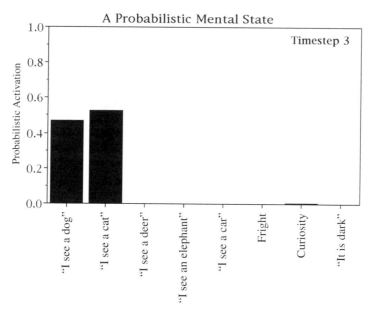

Figure 2.11. By time step 3, proximity to the other mental states is already negligible.

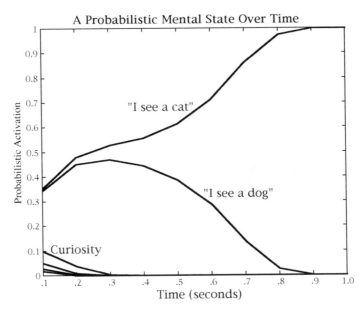

Figure 2.12. Ten time steps of the normalized proximity pattern settling into a "pure mental state."

and away from the other mental states. This probabilistic mental state, depicted as a pattern of activations associated with several pure mental states, is "what the mind is thinking" at that period in time.

Eventually, these two nearly equi-probable mental states will have to diverge, and the system will gravitate toward one and away from the other. This bifurcation begins to take place around time step 4. Figure 2.12 shows a line graph of the mental states changing activation as a function of time. In this rendition, we can pretend that each time step corresponds to a tenth of a second. Thus, much like the progressive activation of a population code, as discussed in chapter 1, recognition of an object is a gradual process that occurs over the course of several hundred milliseconds. Importantly, there is no punctate instant in time along this trajectory at which one can point and say, "That is when recognition occurred; and one millisecond before then, it had not."

Although figure 2.12 shows the mental state of "I see a cat" achieving 1.0 probability at 900 milliseconds, this should be regarded as an artifact of the decontextualized toy simulation. To make the simulation easy to analyze, I presented a single stimulus input just once and then allowed the system to settle into a stable "interpretation" state without any actual motor output being activated. Under realistic circumstances, changing perceptual input and continuous motor output would generally prevent the system from ever achieving 1.0 activation for any mental state. If one mental state has achieved around, let's say, 0.8 probability, then that should provide the organism with enough confidence to execute a particular unique motor action associated with that mental state (a little bit like the collapsing of the quantum wave that determines Schrödinger's cat to be either dead or alive). Then the system is able to gravitate toward other attractor basins as new input arrives and new behavioral goals emerge.

In simplifying the simulation, a number of artificialities have been imposed on the stimulus array, the representations, and especially on the timeline itself. In real life, there is no objective starting point for the timeline, as idealized in figure 2.12. In real life, we are very rarely in situations where we have nothing at all on our minds, and then suddenly a stimulus impinges on our minds, instigating a new trajectory through mental space. It is not even the case that a stimulus instigates a new trajectory. There is only one trajectory, and it is constantly getting diverted, sometimes smoothly and sometimes abruptly, by incoming stimuli and by expectations based on previous stimuli.

Not only would it be wrong to think of a trajectory belonging to or being instigated by a stimulus, but as Gibson suggested, the very concept of a *stimulus* may be misleading. In our everyday normal lives, we do not get exposed to stimuli one at a time, each demanding its own individual response. Instead, we continuously interact with a flowing train of multimodal perceptual arrays containing objects, agents, and events. Indeed, one might argue that the only reason to carve up the environment into stimuli at all is in the attempt to quantize the flowing stream into time steps, so that we cognitive scientists can record the sequence of perceptual arrays that most recently preceded a given behavior. These idealized time steps, or freeze-frames, along the extent of the flowing stream of perceptual input might best be called environmental instances rather than stimuli. And at all times, we must remind ourselves that these idealized environmental instances belong to and are contextualized by a temporally contiguous stream of environmental stimulation.

Therefore, just as unrealistic as the *start* of the timeline in figure 2.12 is, so is the *end* of that timeline. In the simulation that produced the curves in figure 2.12, the system received no new input while it was settling and produced no output whatsoever. It simply gravitated to a stable corner (attractor basin) in its state space. In real life, new input is constantly arriving, and we are often producing continuous motor output. Thus, by the time your brain state has approached a location in state space that is predominantly consistent with only one pure mental state, such as "I see a cat," changes in the environment and your own behavior will alter the brain state such that it travels back into unlabeled regions in state space, preparing for another near-settling event where it gets just close enough to a pure mental state to elicit an associated behavior and then veers off yet again. This is at the very core of the continuity of mind thesis: It means that the vast majority of the mind's time is spent *in between* identifiable mental states rather than *in* them.

Importantly, replacing the concept of stimulus-and-response, or perception-and-action for that matter, with the concept of a continuous trajectory in mental state space highlights the fatal flaw that behaviorism and cognitivism shared—despite their apparent opposition. Although the cognitive revolution criticized behaviorism for ignoring the intermediate processes between stimulus and response, they nonetheless embraced stimulus and response as the start and finish of a temporally bounded linear process. Therein lies the error, because most responses immediately become stimuli (i.e., we are *perceiving* our own actions *while we are executing them*). The process is not temporally bounded. It has no start and no finish. Even preparation of a response can often influence the internal processing of the incoming stimulus stream (see Duhamel, Colby, & Goldberg, 1992; Hommel et al., 2001). Thus, as the continuous dynamic closed loop of sensory input and motor output makes infeasible a true discrimination of stimulus from response, so does the embedded continuous dynamic closed loop of perceptual processing and action preparation make infeasible a true discrimination of perception from action (see Jordan, 1999).

Contemporary Ecological and Dynamical Systems Psychology

The largely happy marriage of ecological psychology and dynamical systems theory has had considerable success at producing elegant mathematical accounts and successful predictions of experimental data in rhythmic and coordinated motor movements and in motor learning (e.g., Beek & Van Wieringen, 1994; Kelso, 1995; Newell, Liu, & Mayer-Kress, 2002; Pressing, 1999). However, comparatively little of this framework has been applied to the favorite topics of cognitive psychologists, for example, categorization, language, attention, and so on (but see Beer, 2000; Elman et al., 1996; Port & van Gelder, 1995; Spivey & Dale, 2004; Thelen & Smith, 1994; Tuller, Case, Ding, & Kelso, 1994). The goal of this book is to encourage the field and rally the troops, as it were, to move our science in this direction. By absorbing ecological psychology's emphasis on continuous and ecologically valid experimental tasks, as well as dynamical systems theory's emphasis on continuous trajectories in state space, the kinds of studies described throughout this book will benefit from more parsimonious theoretical accounts than cognitive psychology's symbolic, stage-based, information-processing approach could ever have offered.

Ecological psychology has a long history of arguing for the continuous flow of visual information having a continuous determination of motor output (Gibson, 1966, 1979; Turvey, 1977; see also Warren, 1998). This perspective stands in stark contrast to the information-processing framework, which assumes that external stimuli arrive at the senses in static snapshots, which then get processed through multiple internal stages, with each stage having to wait until the previous stage is complete before it can begin its processing. Throughout this book, you will find a multitude of experimental demonstrations of perceptual, cognitive, and motor processes that are simply not accommodated by the linear stage–like account encouraged by the digital computer metaphor of the mind. The majority of such examples that I have amassed are especially relevant to three of the most prominent topics in cognitive psychology: categorization (chapter 6), psycholinguistics (chapter 7), and visual cognition (chapters 8 and 11). However, I should give credit where credit is due. It is still the case that the area where much of the initial ground-work has already been laid for dynamical systems approaches to the mind is in studies of motor movement (chapter 9).

Significant advances in the development of a dynamical systems frame-work for motor action have been made by researchers such as Kelso (1995), Kugler and Turvey (1987), and Schöner (2002), to name just a few. Much of the work has focused on coordinated rhythmic actions, where instead of attractors in state space, behavior is described via coordination dynamics equations and manifolds in phase space. (Phase space usually involves dimen-sions that refer to *patterns of change* in state space, such as relative phase between two oscillators or the juxtaposition of previous and current loca-tions, rather than to *raw locations* in state space.) For example, Kelso (1984) demonstrated that when human subjects rhythmically move their hands in *antiphase* (one hand flexing one set of muscles while the other flexes an oppo-site set, and then both reversing) and the speed (frequency of cycles, with a fixed amplitude) is gradually increased, they tend to involuntarily transition to *in-phase* cycles (with the hands flexing corresponding sets of muscles at the same time). The phase space defining this phenomenon contains attractor basins, toward which the system will gravitate, as well as repellors, away from which the system will gravitate. As cycle frequency increases, and the hands are moving back and forth faster and faster, the relative strengths of the antiphase and in-phase attractor basins gradually change. At some point, the antiphase attractor basin actually becomes an unstable region in the phase space, a repellor instead of an attractor, and the system then moves toward the nearest stable attractor basin: the in-phase attractor. A coordination dynamics treat-ment of changes in the phase space manifold that defines these attractor basins and repellors (Haken, Kelso, & Bunz, 1985; Kelso, 1995) provides an account of a wide range of data from perturbed and coordinated movements of fingers (Kelso, 1981), hands (Kelso, 1984), arms and legs (Kelso & Jeka, 1992), hands with speech (Kelso, Tuller, & Harris, 1983), hands with external sounds (Kelso, Del-Colle, & Schöner, 1990), and even, as demonstrated by Schmidt, Carello, and Turvey (1990), across multiple people! For more details, see chapter 9.

Thus, according to this general framework, and despite the limited scope of the visualizations throughout this chapter, the genuine trajectory that instantiates mind is more than just the visited regions of neural state space as defined by the networks of the brain. The causal relationship between a sensory receptor and a cortical neuron is arguably not qualitatively different from the causal relationship between a cortical neuron and a muscle, or even between an external object and a sensory receptor. After all, causal law is causal law. This is what Turvey and Shaw (1999) mean when they refer to the "animal-environment mutuality and reciprocity." The animal and its environment form a system. Change in one produces change in the other, and the loop of circular causality continues over time. The animal subsystem and the environment subsystem are sufficiently coupled that it would be impossible for one to be following laws that the other does not also follow. Thus, one might perhaps include all of those parameters (neural activation patterns, muscular-skeletal kinematics, and even external objects) as dimensions in the state space that defines mind (see chapter 11). In this view, the relevant definition of mind becomes a trajectory through the full animal–environment state space, not just the brain's state space. And when two animals (such as myself and my friend Steve) are in sufficient spatial proximity to each other that an external object (even something as mundane as a ball) is in the immediate environment of both animals, then those two minds are sharing a few dimensions of their respective state spaces. They become a system, describable by a single unified (and recurrent) trajectory—as the ball gets tossed back and forth for hours on end.

3

Some Experimental Tools for Tracking Continuous Mental Trajectories

If behavior does not consist of responses, what does it consist of?
—J. J. Gibson

The Purple Perils

In the late 1960s, James J. Gibson ran a seminar on Thursday afternoons in which heady, pregnant questions like the one in the epigraph were regularly discussed. The sometimes lengthy handouts for these meetings were dittoed on a mimeograph, hence earning the nickname "the purple perils." Some of the purple perils found their way into an edited volume (Reed & Jones, 1982), and others can be easily found on the Internet. In the case of this particular excerpt, Gibson was trying to get the students and faculty involved in the seminar to think hard about the fact that if natural environmental stimulation does not arrive at the organism's sensors in discrete packets of stimuli, then motor output is unlikely to depart the organism's effectors in discrete packets of responses. But what then do we call this continuous motor output that is so often dynamically coupled in time (at short and/or long time scales) with the sensory input?

Despite Gibson's eloquent warnings, and despite cognitive psychology's overarching opposition to behaviorism's stimulus-response mantra, cognitive psychologists have, for decades now, blithely gone about their business designing experiments that present discrete stimuli and collect discrete responses. Indeed, it is quite ironic that, during the cognitive revolution, while cognitive psychology was rejecting behaviorism's *theoretical* emphasis on stimulus and response, the *methodological* emphasis on stimulus and response remained status quo. Gibson's ecological psychology (1979; see also Brunswick, 1955) would suggest that this methodology of stimuli and responses, not the theory, is actually the more detrimental habit.

Cognitive psychology has found it all too easy to survive on the tacit assumption that these isolated "responses," from one experimental trial to the next unrelated experimental trial, are somehow unaltered indicators of internal mental states. The field's allegiance to an internal symbolic computation stage, composed of discrete internal states, arises not from experimental techniques that unmistakably tap some unaltered rendition of the cognitive stage's internal representation, and certainly not from any neurophysiological evidence, but predominantly from off-line measures of overt metacognitive responses in artificially constrained tasks. In contrast, what I will argue throughout this book is that mental activity does not consist of a series of discrete internal states. Instead, the mind continuously traverses its state space, traveling from one attractor basin to another, and spending a considerable amount of time in transit in between those basins. An attractor basin to which the mind gets particularly close will occasionally be responsible for an observable outcome–based response (e.g., pressing one button instead of another, reaching for one object instead of another). However, all of the attractors to which the mind gets even slightly near will have graded subtle influences on the manner in which the continuous action is carried out on the way toward its outcome (e.g., pressing that button somewhat late and with less force, reaching in a curved motion slightly toward other objects before settling on the correct object and grasping it). Measuring the dynamic properties of those continuous actions will reveal far more about how the mind works than simply tabulating the final outcomes of those actions.

Moreover, the kinds of questionnaires and other outcome-based metacognitive tasks that populate much of cognitive psychology rely far too much on the subjects' intuitions about hypothetical situations. With so much time to develop explicit strategies for the task and subvocalized linguistic labels for the various response alternatives, is it any wonder that people's response patterns make them look as though their minds are succinctly transitioning from one discrete state to another? Asking someone to give a verbal protocol on what they think they would think in some hypothetical categorization or reasoning task is about as useful as asking them what they think their reaction time would be in some hypothetical visual search task. Quite some time ago, social psychologists documented the degree to which people's self-reports of cognitive phenomena and objective measures of those same cognitive phenomena can be wildly discrepant (e.g., Nisbett & Wilson, 1977). Much of social psychology then seemed to decide that "what people *think* they think" (whether accurate or not) was what that subfield cared about anyway—so the discrepancy was not a problem. I can only hope that cognitive psychology does not also continue down that path.

On the Continuity of Your Measure

Consider what happens when a human subject is presented a stimulus in a typical cognitive psychology experiment and asked to provide some form of verbal or button-press report on how she perceived it or what she concluded from it. She may take several hundred milliseconds, or even several seconds, before producing an answer. What goes on in her mind during those hundreds and hundreds of milliseconds of deliberation? That is the kind of question that can help tease apart many competing theories in the cognitive sciences. However, in that typical cognitive psychology experiment, with solely an off-line outcome-based measure, you will never know the answer to that question.

In this chapter, I briefly discuss some of the limitations of traditional psychophysical and cognitive psychology methods, focusing particularly on their emphasis on discrete categories of metacognitive responses to individual decontextualized stimuli. Additionally, criticisms are levied against the standard format of experimentation in problem-solving research, concepts and categories research, and even neuroimaging, for not addressing the temporal dynamics of the continuous uptake of real-time stimulus input. (For example, even visual displays that are presented all at once usually get perused piecemeal by a series of eye fixations.) The fundamental weakness of some of the major experimental techniques in cognitive psychology and cognitive neuroscience is that they ignore much of the time course of processing and the gradual accumulation of partial information, focusing instead on the outcome of a cognitive process rather than the dynamic properties of that process.

At the core of this issue is the concept of time scales. Every state transition (except perhaps some at the subatomic level) has a time scale at which the full transition can be seen as gradual (see figure 3.1C). At larger time scales, this transition will appear instantaneous (figures 3.1A and B), and at smaller time scales, it won't really look like a transition between two states (figure 3.1D). Analyzing your chosen phenomenon at the right time scale, where the system can be observed as spending a substantial portion of its time in those intermediate values between states, is crucial for understanding the forces or mechanisms that bring about the system's change of state. Figure 3.1 uses the logistic function—a symmetric sigmoid curve prevalent throughout nature in physics, chemistry, and biology—as a mathematical metaphor aimed at elucidating the importance of finding the proper scale at which one's *x*-axis can reveal the gradedness of the state transition in question. The logistic function implements qualitative-looking behavior from a purely quantitative process. The curve from this continuous nonlinear equation can be easily misconstrued as evidence for a genuinely discrete step-function process, if observed at too coarse a time scale (figures 3.1A and B). Only at the proper time scale can the smooth continuity of the state transition be brought into stark relief (figure 3.1C). I submit that the time scale of hundreds of milliseconds is a special scale at which the process of cognition, as revealed by perception-action cycles, becomes most transparent. Therefore, experimental measures that function at this time scale may enjoy a privileged status in the goal of understanding cognition.

Measures that ignore temporal dynamics at this time scale run the risk of falsely depicting cognition as consisting solely of discrete symbolic states—when

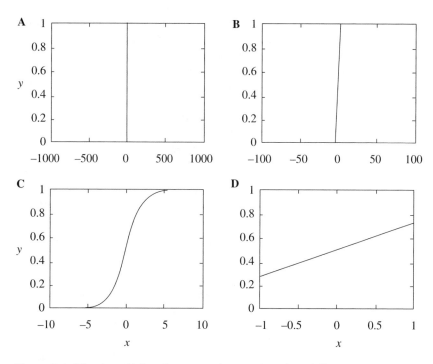

Figure 3.1. The sigmoid function, $y = 1/(1 + e^{-x})$, at four different scales. If x was time, and each integer increment of x equaled 10 milliseconds, then panel A would correspond to a $\pm$ 10 seconds time scale, panel B would correspond to a $\pm$ 1 second time scale, panel C would correspond to a $\pm$ 100 milliseconds time scale, and panel D would correspond to a $\pm$ 10 milliseconds time scale.

in fact those symbolic states may actually be better understood as graded fuzzy attractor basins, which the system flirts with long enough to produce some identifiable motor output, while it pursues a continuous trajectory through its state space. If your measure only provides the outcome of a deliberative cognitive process, such as a forced choice between predesigned alternatives, then of course it cannot help but make cognition look as though it is made of those succinct categories. Card-sorting tasks, in categorization or problem-solving research, are particularly disappointing in that they allow participants to spend several minutes exploring combinations of judgments, undoing them, and then constructing new decisions—and none of the intermediate partial card arrangements that were temporarily considered ever become part of the data set! Even if your measure is a rating between 1 and 7, it will still crucially fail to show whether there was a single confident selection of a number or a gradual nonlinear process partly considering multiple numbers and then settling on one number. And then there are measures that include ongoing processing as well as final outcomes, but they average or sum the activity over a substantial time course, thus eliminating any chance of identifying the temporal dynamics of the process. For example, the behemoth of cognitive neuroscience, functional magnetic resonance imaging (fMRI), frequently integrates over an entire second or more to produce one image of brain activity for one trial.[1] This poses interesting methodological challenges for fMRI researchers who wish to conduct an in-depth examination of the cognitive processing of temporally dynamic input, such as a sentence (e.g., Fiebach, Vos, & Friederici, 2004) or visual motion (e.g., Heeger et al., 1999). Another popular experimental measure that integrates over too large a period of time, and thus loses any temporal resolution for discovering interesting nonlinear state transitions in cognition on the way toward the participant's final overt response, is whole-sentence reading times. As a participant reads a sentence over the course of a second or two or three, an incredible dance of lexical, semantic, syntactic, and contextual factors is undulating from word to word to word. And whole-sentence reading time tasks ignore all of that, thus failing to provide any indication of *when* during those few seconds the dance may have involved a particularly impressive pirouette or perhaps instead been briefly tripped up by its own feet.

My comments here are not intended to discourage researchers from ever using these methodologies. I often use many of them myself, as pilot studies and as additional experiments to accompany more online measures. Rather than summarily proscribing the use of all off-line measures, or measures that integrate over entire seconds or more, I instead recommend a conscientious combination of temporally dynamic measures of ongoing processing along with simple nondynamic measures. The existing literature of results based on off-line outcome-based measures is by no means to be discarded or ignored. Quite the opposite—the challenge of a dynamical systems approach is to account for the discrete-seeming findings from those methodologies as well as the continuous findings that are typically revealed by temporally dynamic methodologies.

The following sections briefly review a variety of experimental methods that—unlike accuracy measures, off-line rating tasks, and so on—pay attention to one or another aspect of the temporal dynamics of perceptual/cognitive processing. To varying degrees and for varying purposes, they provide a window into the continuous-time processes of the mind/brain (for an excellent in-depth review of many of these methods, see Kutas & Federmeier, 1998). I have distributed the methods into three rough divisions, mostly just to make the list more manageable. At one extreme, there are outcome-based measures with time-delimited tasks (from traditional experimental psychology), such as reaction times and speeded responses. At the other extreme, there are continuous measures with continuous tasks (from dynamical systems approaches to perception, cognition, and action), such as bimanual coordination and postural sway. In between these extremes, one can find a number of semi-continuous measures with time-delimited tasks. This middle ground set of methodologies serves a number of purposes that should interest cognitive psychologists: (1) many of these measures can be easily applied to established experimental tasks, (2) these measures often involve less metacognitive control over the particular output being recorded (therefore, less room for strategic effects), and (3) many of these measures can easily be applied to normal everyday kinds of tasks, for improved ecological validity.

Outcome-Based Measures With Delimited Tasks

Let's start with traditional experimental psychology. Since Donders's (1868/ 1969) subtractive method and, more recently, Sternberg's (1969) additive factor method, button-press reaction times have been widely perceived as an effective measurement for determining the identity, sequence, and duration of intermediate cognitive subprocesses that occur on the way toward producing an overt motor output as a response to an individual stimulus. This goal of picking apart the intervening processes between an early sensory event and a motor output event is generally in line with the goal of this book. Unfortunately, the overarching assumption with these subtractive and additive methods has been that the subprocesses to be identified are independent sequential stages, like the mechanisms of a clock or the components of a computer. As the cognitive sciences are gradually learning, the brain's subcomponents are richly interdependent on one another and anything but sequential in their bidirectional cascades of information flow. Likewise, the mind itself is perhaps best described as an emergent property of a complex nonlinear brain, attached to two-dimensional sensory surfaces and three-dimensional effectors, and embedded in a complex dynamic environment—with bidirectional cascades of information flow between these larger subcomponents as well. Therefore, using reaction-time tasks to isolate individuated serial cognitive stages of processing—which aren't there—is unlikely to prove fruitful (see Van Orden & Holden, 2002). Nonetheless, button-press reaction times can still be a generally useful measure of the overall time course of processing, for the purposes of exploring certain questions regarding the timing of information integration in language processing (chapter 7), in visual search (chapter 8), in the role of motor representations in cognition (chapter 9), and for studying long-distance correlations in overall task performance (Van Orden, Holden, & Turvey, 2003), to name just a few. In many tasks, reaction times can be conceived of as the time taken by the system to settle enough into a particular attractor basin to execute its associated motor output. Without recording reaction times in these tasks, one would merely have a tabulation of the proportion of trials on which one or another button was pressed, and no evidence whatsoever for whether one or another of the button-pressing decisions involved a slow and difficult settling process or a quick and easy one. Reaction times provide a respectable amount of evidence regarding the temporal dynamics of perceptual/cognitive processing. We just need to be careful about interpreting them in ways that involve implausible assumptions about feedforward box-and-arrow cognitive architectures.

An important advance in the use of reaction times is in analyzing their distributions, not just the means across conditions. Mounting evidence indicates that simply comparing mean reaction times violates the assumptions of our tools of statistical inference and can miss important subtleties in performance. It is extremely rare for the distribution of reaction times in a perceptual/cognitive task to actually have a normal, Gaussian distribution. Yet a normal distribution is what t-tests and analyses of variance, cognitive psychology's favorite statistics, assume the data exhibit for the statistical inference to be valid. A growing body of literature is finding that analyzing reaction-time distributions and their moments (skewness, kurtosis, etc.) can be considerably more informative for teasing apart specific competing models of cognition (e.g., Ratcliff, 1979, 2002; Van Zandt, 2000, 2002). However, it looks as though the debate between continuous versus discrete processing may not be resolvable via distributional analyses of reaction times (e.g., Meyer et al., 1988; Miller, 1982; Ratcliff, 1988).

Reaction times are also recently being analyzed not in terms of their indications regarding the cognitive processes involved in a single stimulus-recognition event, but instead in terms of their indications of overall task performance over the course of an entire experiment (Gilden, 2001; Van Orden, Holden, & Turvey, 2003; Ward, 2002). Long-range correlated structure in a time series of reaction times can provide hints about the fractal nature of interactions between the subsystems that comprise cognition and can point toward changes in the attractor landscape over the course of hours in a task. However, because this type of analysis treats the overall experiment (not discrete individual trials) as the focus of interest, it fits slightly better in the "continuous measures with continuous tasks" section, where it will be discussed in more detail.

One particularly special improvement on the basic reaction-time methodology is the speed–accuracy trade-off (SAT) method (e.g., Dosher, 1976; McElree & Griffith, 1995, 1998; Reed, 1973), because it provides evidence for what is going on before a response decision has reached a fully confident stable state. Whereas reaction times are merely able to demonstrate that the culmination of a response decision took a longer or shorter period of time, the SAT method can plot evidence for the internal salience or activation of that response option at 50 milliseconds after stimulus presentation, or 100 milliseconds, or 150, and so on. As a rule of thumb, whenever you transition from comparing values on a bar graph (such as reaction times) to plotting points on a smooth-looking curve (such as d-prime over time), you can bet you're making important improvements in your ability to analyze the temporal dynamics of the system in question.

In the SAT method, signal detection theory (Green & Swets, 1966) is used to compute a measure of d-prime (sensitivity to a stimulus property, independent of the participant's response bias for saying yes or no in the detection task). The detection task can be anything from searching for a visual target amid distractors, to reporting on whether a test probe item was present in a memorized list, to determining the grammaticality of a sentence as a function of its final word. In some blocks of trials, the participant is given only a couple hundred milliseconds to produce the response, and their d-prime for those trials is generally near 0 (at chance performance). Late responses are followed by a truly nasty buzzing sound that is intended to prevent the participant from being late with their response on subsequent trials—and it is surprisingly effective. In other blocks of trials, they are given several hundred milliseconds to produce their response, and although they often feel like they are still guessing, their d-primes are usually in the 1–2 range, reliably above chance. Other blocks of trials have even later response deadlines, and participants are able to make reasonably deliberated confident responses that asymptote around a d-prime of 3–4. Figure 3.2 depicts some representative hypothetical data from an SAT task, where the different response deadlines are 300 milliseconds after stimulus presentation and 500, 700, 900, 1,200, 1,800, and 3,000 milliseconds after stimulus presentation. Real results regularly look approximately like those in figure 3.2, demonstrating a gradual accumulation of perceptual/cognitive evidence, as it were, for the correct yes/no response. (Note the general similarity between figure 3.2 and figure 1.6.) In terms of the conceptual framework laid out in the previous chapter, this task is roughly equivalent to interrupting the dynamical system's continuous trajectory through the state space and forcing it to elicit the response associated with the closest attractor. Noise in this closest attractor estimate produces imperfect d-prime values, and plotting them at each time slice can be construed as measuring the relative Euclidean proximity between the state of the interrupted system and the correct attractor versus the incorrect attractor.

One pragmatic drawback of the SAT methodology is that it requires many hundreds of trials from each participant. Participants often have to visit the lab for multiple sessions for the experimenter to collect enough data. And of

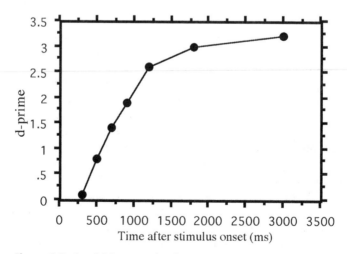

Figure 3.2. Sensitivity to a stimulus property rising over time in a hypothetical speed–accuracy trade-off task.

course, as with most of these outcome-based measures with delimited tasks, SAT involves a somewhat ecologically invalid interruption of real-time cognitive processing to elicit a forced-choice metacognitive judgment.[2] Nonetheless, SAT provides a unique and important record of gradually rising d-prime (sensitivity) functions over time that appear to be sampling a continuous dynamic process.

Perhaps ironically, the SAT method is often used not just to document the time course of processing within a given process but also to explore possible discrete stage-based distinctions between two or more putatively independent continuous processes, such as the accrual of syntactic evidence and the accrual of semantic evidence. However, as we will see with event-related potentials (ERPs), one has to be careful with extrapolating SAT curves to their zero-crossing (e.g., finding that the curve in figure 3.2 would hit zero d-prime at about 250 milliseconds poststimulus) and treating that point in time as a discrete instance at which some cognitive processing module "becomes operative." The fact that very different interpretations for syntax and semantics result from using this way of thinking with SAT and with ERP methodologies suggests that something is wrong with that way of thinking. For example, results with the SAT methodology suggest that syntactic information becomes operative a couple hundred milliseconds before semantic information (McElree & Griffith, 1995, 1998), whereas with very similar kinds of stimuli in an ERP methodology, results suggest that semantic information is processed a couple hundred milliseconds before syntactic information (Hagoort, 2003; Osterhout & Holcomb, 1992). It is not clear that there is a way to adjudicate between these two claims. Perhaps they are, in a sense, both wrong because they assume there are separate modules for syntax and semantics and are asking which one "turns on" first. If there are not separate independent modules for these subtly different (and arguably partially overlapping) formats of information (see chapters 5 and 7), then asking which one turns on first is clearly an ill-formed question.

An intriguing new method that is slightly similar to SAT, because it involves interrupting ongoing task processing at specified points in time, is transcranial magnetic stimulation (TMS). However, the interruption doesn't merely request a premature button-press, it directly interferes with the brain! TMS emits a 100-microsecond pulse of a magnetic field (of about 1–2 Tesla) directly over the scalp near the cortical region of interest. This single pulse of TMS induces high-frequency synchronized neural activity in that localized region of cortical surface for a few milliseconds, followed by a substantial refractory period across that entire population of neurons, effectively disrupting any task-related patterns of neural activity in that area for perhaps a hundred milliseconds or so in total.[3] This temporary disruption of organized neural processing in localized regions of cortex has been referred to as a virtual lesion (Walsh & Rushworth, 1999). There are two basic ways to use these temporary virtual lesions for understanding cognition. One can explore the interactive role that a cortical area plays in performing some perceptual/cognitive task by disrupting activation in that area when the task is being performed, and one can also explore the precise timing of that area's participation in the task by delivering the TMS at different latencies after stimulus presentation (see Walsh & Pascual-Leone, 2003, for an excellent review). For example, Schluter and colleagues (1998) found that a visual choice reaction time task was most disrupted when a single TMS pulse was applied to premotor cortex around 100 milliseconds after the stimulus or to primary motor cortex around 300 milliseconds after the stimulus. It is almost as if TMS allows you to chase down the wave of information as it travels from cortical region to cortical region and thus track the sequence of perceptual/cognitive events.

Speaking of events, let us now move on to ERPs. ERPs provide a continuous record of brain activity during exposure to stimuli that often do not require any metacognitive deliberate judgment or response. In this way, they are somewhat less outcome-based than the other methodologies discussed so far. Unfortunately, rather than fully embracing the temporal continuity of this measure of neural activity (sometimes sampled at greater than 1,000 Hz), most of the literature has taken to testing for specific discrete wave peaks at particular time slices, as though those peaks were the responses they are measuring. For example, a conspicuously positive wave component around 300 milliseconds poststimulus (dubbed the P300) appears to be indicative of an unexpected or low-probability event (Donchin et al., 1988). A conspicuously negative wave component around 400 milliseconds poststimulus (N400) appears to be the result of detecting a semantic anomaly (Kutas & Hillyard, 1980). And a conspicuously positive wave component around 600 milliseconds poststimulus (you guessed it, the P600) is correlated with *syntactic* anomaly, or ungrammaticality (Hagoort, 2003; Osterhout & Holcomb, 1992). Positive and negative components[4] in the 100 and 200 range are typically attributed to early sensory processing (Mangun & Hillyard, 1988). As researchers continue to pick apart smaller and smaller wavelike pieces of this continuous pattern of neural activity, they have localized some of these waves to the left or right hemispheres or the frontal, parietal, or occipital lobes (e.g., Baas, Kenemans, & Mangun, 2002; Swick, Kutas, & Neville, 1994), they have pointed to P300s somehow occurring earlier or later than 300 milliseconds (e.g., Kim, Kim, & Kwon, 2001), and they have expanded the list of wave components to include separate listings for the N20, P30, P45, N60, N140, P150, P180, P250, N250, P350, P450, and more (e.g., DeFrance et al., 1997; Josiassen et al., 1990). As the fractionation of this continuous wave pattern escalates, proliferating a potentially infinite number of putatively separate components, it should eventually become clear that these wave peaks are not discrete emissions of perceptual and cognitive modules that become operative at their specific points in time, as some ERP practitioners seem to advocate. Instead, a conspicuous wave component might be better understood as signifying a period of time when populations of neurons in coarsely defined (but not necessarily modular) regions of the brain are ramping up their activity in the service of integrating and resolving conflicting signals from multiple information sources, for example, a mismatch between perceptual anticipations and afferent sensory input (see Eimer, 1998; Kutas & Hillyard, 1984; Picton et al., 2000; Rugg & Coles, 1995). In fact, when event-related electroencephalography (EEG) wave forms are studied via time-series analysis, based on symbolic dynamics, the results provide independent statistical motivation not only for some of the usual ERP components but also for additional patterns that are not detected by the traditional ERP analysis technique (see beim Graben et al., 2000).[5]

Magnetoencephalography (MEG) has a great deal in common with ERPs. In fact, the two methods can be combined to cross-validate their respective data sets (Hopf et al., 2002). Because the magnetic field emitted by neural activity is interfered with much less by electrolytes in the cerebrospinal fluid, MEG provides a substantial improvement, over ERPs, in spatial resolution. Nonetheless, MEG's spatial resolution still doesn't hold a candle to that of fMRI. However, for the purposes of combining both spatial resolution (for cortical localization of function) and temporal resolution (for attribution of these functions to different aspects of dynamic stimulation), MEG may very well be the sharpest tool in the shed (Hari & Antervo, 1982; Noguchi et al., 2004; Rogers, 1994). Both MEG and ERPs share a practical methodological drawback with the SAT method: These experiments will often require hundreds of trials per condition per participant, which leads to long experimental sessions and only relatively simple experimental designs. It doesn't help that an MEG facility is about as expensive as an fMRI facility, costing millions of dollars. In contrast, an ERP lab can get up and running for a mere $100,000 or so. Pocket change. But what this all boils down to is that by placing a premium on fine temporal resolution, one appears forced to sacrifice spatial resolution, because the electrical or magnetic signal leaking out of someone's head is so noisy.

As it turns out, there is a solution to the problem of all that confounded noise in the electrical (ERP) or magnetic (MEG) fields that manage to pass through the dura and the skull and finally get recorded by a headful of scalp electrodes. Just get the skull and dura out of the way! One slightly grisly method, known as optical imaging (of intrinsic neural signals or of voltage-sensitive dyes), does exactly that—literally (see Grinvald, 1984, 1992).[6] With nonhuman animals, one can remove a portion of skull, peel back the dura, point a camera system at the exposed cortical surface, and thereby get a continuous record of what populations of cells are active during the presentation of various auditory or visual stimuli to the immobilized animal (e.g., Jancke et al., 2004; Nelken et al., 2004; Sengpiel et al., 1998). However, it is common for this continuous signal to get averaged over a substantial window of time to get robust topographical images of regions of activation. Depolarizing neurons will reflect more light by about 0.5% of the total illumination, compared to inactive neurons. So your camera better be fairly sensitive.

A related methodology, similarly unimpeded by skull and dura, is single-cell electrophysiology. Direct electrical recording from neurons has been around a bit longer than optical imaging and allows measurement from areas further beneath the surface of the brain. It involves inserting an electrode into a neuron (or at least sidling it up next to one) and recording the action potentials it emits. Like optical imaging, this is not for the faint of heart. In fact, it's not really intended for healthy humans at all—which tends to put a damper on using it to study language or complex cognition (but see Engel et al., 2005; Ojemann et al., 1988, for recordings of neurons in brain surgery patients). The vast majority of neural recording studies have been conducted in the service of examining the early stages of visual perception in nonhuman primates (for reviews, see Palmeri & Gauthier, 2004; Parker & Newsome, 1998), and a fair bit of the findings have been corroborated with neuroimaging in humans (e.g., Engel et al., 1994; Heeger et al., 1999). Even better, multicell recording allows the researcher to compute an estimate of a neural population code and its dynamics (e.g., Georgopoulos, 1995; Rolls & Tovee, 1995; Zemel, Dayan, & Pouget 1998). One can even mathematically interpret the population code's activation pattern in terms of probability density functions of different continuous-valued sensory properties (Barber, Clark, & Anderson, 2003), a little bit like the highly idealized probabilistic mental states depicted in chapter 2.

The tradition in visual neuroscience for some time was to present individual stimuli, from trial to trial, to an anesthetized monkey and record from cells in appropriate areas (Gilbert, 1983; Lennie, 1980). Averaged firing rates could then be plotted as a function of some stimulus dimension to determine the selectivity of that cell for that stimulus dimension. For example, figure 3.3 shows a hypothetical example of a cell that is highly selective for a narrow range of this stimulus dimension (circles) and another cell that is not particularly

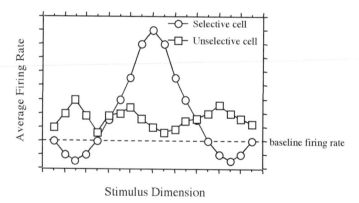

Figure 3.3. Hypothetical firing rates of two neurons, averaged over a second, showing one cell to be selective for a delimited range of the stimulus dimension and the other unselective. In this case, the stimulus dimension could be anything from the orientation of a visually presented bar to the frequency of an auditorily presented tone.

selective with this stimulus dimension (squares). Although there are dynamic analyses that compare the initial burst phase of a neural spike pattern to the overall average firing rate (e.g., Kim & McCormick, 1998), there is still a tendency for visual neuroscientists to average over a sizable window of time, thus rendering their measure somewhat less continuous and somewhat more outcome-based, as in figure 3.3.

Not until the 1990s did recording from awake behaving animals become at all common (e.g., Gallant, Connor, & Van Essen, 1998; Motter, 1993; but see Lynch et al., 1977). (See chapter 5 for a discussion of the theoretical consequences of this methodological transition.) Gallant et al.'s (1998) work even breaks out of the trial-by-trial delimited-task mindset and actually fits more with the continuous measure with a continuous task approach described in the next section. In their experiment, the monkey was allowed to view natural scenes and move his eyes around naturally. By tracking the eye movements and recording from cells in visual cortex at the same time, they found that free-viewing conditions caused these visual cells to behave quite differently than during controlled viewing conditions—further bolstering the growing distinction between the antiquated concept of classical feedforward receptive fields and what appear to be nonclassical receptive fields that receive input from lateral connections and/or feedback projections (e.g., Allman, Miezen, & McGuinness, 1985; Rao & Ballard, 1997; Spillman & Werner, 1996). Given findings like this, one cannot help but analogously wonder whether less constrained ongoing continuous behavior in the cognitive psychologist's lab might cause mental processes to behave quite differently than they do during traditional trial-by-trial outcome-based time-delimited tasks.

Continuous Measures With Continuous Tasks

Much of the argumentation here has been to advocate continuous measures of the perceptual/cognitive consequences of an individual stimulus presentation. However, a major weakness of most experimental methods in the cognitive and neural sciences—including many of those discussed throughout this book (especially the categorization experiments in chapter 6)—is the tendency to present the participant with an artificially extracted time slice of what would normally be a temporally extended dynamic stimulus array. To properly address the temporal continuity of perception, action, and cognition, more cognitive experimentation in the future will need to not only use more continuous response measures but also use continuous (and ecologically valid) dynamic sensory stimulation. There are two possible solutions to this concern: (1) use tasks that do not simply involve an isolated stimulus followed by a discrete response, for example, rhythmic tasks or motor measures during extended periods of task performance; or (2) dynamical analyses of the processes occurring over the long-term course of an entire experiment, for example, spectral analyses of long-distance correlations across many trials.

This leads us to discovering *another* time scale at which—with the appropriate analysis techniques—we can observe dynamic properties in overall task performance.

As hinted at earlier when discussing reaction times, even just examining a cognitive psychologist's data in terms of the time series over an hour or so of data collection—rather than trial by trial—can treat the pattern of button-press latencies as a somewhat continuous measure and can treat the overall cognitive performance as a somewhat continuous task (Van Orden et al., 2003). At this larger time scale, one is no longer investigating the cognitive architecture of a particular mental faculty, such as word recognition or object recognition, but is instead exploring *what kind of system* cognition is in general. Is it a discrete stage-based system with component-dominant dynamics, like a Turing machine? Or is it a more continuous distributed system with interaction-dominant dynamics, like a biological organism?

When a time series of response latencies, for any of a variety of experimental tasks, is subjected to Fourier analysis, the amount of energy in the various frequencies (the power spectrum in log/log coordinates) scales downward linearly with a slope corresponding roughly to 1/freq ($1/f$) (e.g., Gilden, 2001; Van Orden et al., 2003; Ward, 2002). Thus, amid the seemingly random fluctuations in response time from trial to trial—once the effects of experimental manipulations are extracted from the data—there actually remains a reliable pattern of long-distance correlations (those robust low frequencies in the power spectra) that are not easily accounted for by modular systems of multiple independent autoregression-based estimators or component-dominant dynamics (see Van Orden, Holden, & Turvey, 2005; Wagenmakers, Farrell, & Ratcliff, 2005). This $1/f$ noise, or pink noise (because it's subtly more correlated than white noise), is also observed in an endless cornucopia of complex dynamical natural processes in physics (Bak, 1996; Mandelbrot, 1999), chemistry (Sasai, Ohmine, & Ramaswamy, 1992), biology (Hausdorff & Peng, 1996; Musha, 1985), vision (Billock, de Guzman, & Kelso, 2001), music, and language (Voss & Clarke, 1975). $1/f$ noise is seen as a signature data pattern for complex dynamic systems that self-organize in fractal time. If cognition is such a system, then we'd better start analyzing it as such.

Another way to analyze the self-organizing dynamics of perception and action is through rhythmic patterns of coordinated motor behavior (see Kelso, 1995). The majority of this book will focus on attractors in state space, as it is often the most appropriate format of description for nonrepetitive cognitive processes, but the majority of the psychological literature so far on dynamical systems actually focuses on attractors in phase space for coordination dynamics. Although the two are sometimes treated almost synonymously, a point in *state* space usually describes a system in terms of values of instantaneous state parameters (such as neuronal firing rates or the positions of the limbs), whereas a point in *phase* space often describes a system in terms of periodic change in those state parameters (such as frequency or relative phase of limb displacements). Both formats of description are crucial aspects of the application of dynamical systems theory to the mind, and the successes of one should instill optimism for successes of the other.

Rhythmic motor behavior is precisely where continuous measures with continuous tasks excel at revealing limit cycles (repeated loops) in state space as systematic patterns in the mind, sometimes plotted as static locations in phase space. As mentioned briefly in the previous chapter, one such limit cycle is the coordinated rhythmic movement between two limbs. Give this a try: Put your hands on a table, palms down, and then fold your fingers and thumb under, extending only your index fingers. Now, your rhythmic coordination mission, should you choose to accept it, is to move both index fingers leftward in unison and then rightward in unison, and back again, repeated at about 1 Hz (one cycle per second). Gradually ramp up the frequency of this oscillatory behavior, until you're flicking your fingers left and right about as fast as you can. Did you manage to maintain the leftward-in-unison and rightward-in-unison phase relationship between those two fingers? In most experiments, as people increase the rate of finger oscillation, they involuntarily slip into an inward-in-unison and outward-in-unison phase relationship. You probably did that, too. Essentially, as the oscillation frequency increases, there appears to be a powerful attractor in phase space that pulls your fingers' movements toward a phase pattern that flexes and extends pairs of corresponding hand muscles at the same time. Myriad extensions of this experimental design, with different limbs (and even across two people), have provided powerful insight into understanding perception and action in terms of self-organizing attractor manifolds in phase space (e.g., Kelso & Jeka, 1992; Schmidt, Carello, & Turvey, 1990). See chapter 9 for a more in-depth discussion of rhythmic coordination tasks.

Repetitive tapping tasks (e.g., Fitts, 1954) provide another continuous measure with a continuous task that can provide information regarding the overall constraints of the motor system. However, isochronous finger-tapping tasks (e.g., Franek et al., 1987), where the participant must tap a finger in synchrony with some external sensory input, can provide information regarding the dynamic coupling of sensory and motor processes and thus more readily point to a dynamical analysis of cognition. As a participant is exposed to a rhythmic stimulation pattern of auditory tones or visual flashes, he or she can get accustomed to the frequency of the stimulation and tap nearly synchronously with the sensory input. Some form of cognitive oscillatory process that predicts each next tone or flash (see Pressing, 1999) may be involved in this behavior because each tap often anticipates the actual external stimulus. If each tap was actually a response to the perceived tone or flash, then it would unavoidably *follow* that tone or flash by at least a few hundred milliseconds— as that is about how long sensory transduction and motor execution would take. However, it is commonly observed in these kinds of tasks that participants' taps actually *precede* the sensory input by a few dozen milliseconds or more (e.g., Müller et al., 1999). Further examination of the types of stimulation that best entrain this kind of cyclic motor output can uncover a richer understanding of the relationships between perceptual subsystems and action subsystems. For example, complex metrically structured rhythms can induce finger tapping that is synchronized at varying metrical levels (Large, Fink, & Kelso, 2002; Toiviainen & Snyder, 2003). Moreover, rhythmic *auditory* events appear to be better than rhythmic *visual* events at inducing isochronous finger tapping (Repp, 2003a; Repp & Penel, 2004).

Although finger-tapping tasks typically just record the timing of the cyclic taps and not the dynamics of the finger movement toward or away from contact, there are other measures that do record the truly continuous movement of the body. Postural sway, as measured by the force applied to different regions of a metal plate on which the participant is standing, can be recorded continuously over time and thus provides a measure of rhythmic movements in state space and in phase space (Riley, Balasubramaniam, & Turvey, 1999). During a variety of tasks, postural sway can be measured without interrupting task performance, without requiring any metacognitive report regarding task performance, and without any strategic influences on the measure being recorded (Stoffregen et al., 2000). Intriguingly, it turns out that postural sway— though seemingly irrelevant to linguistic and visual tasks—actually provides an informative window to the dynamical perception-action processes of visual perception (Warren, Kay, & Yilmaz, 1996) and of language use (Shockley, Santana, & Fowler, 2003). For example, Shockley and colleagues showed that when two conversants coordinate over a puzzle task, their postural sway coordinates as well. When the same two persons converse with other people, their respective postural sways do not get entrained with one another. See chapter 9 for a more in-depth discussion of postural sway tasks.

Another continuous implicit measure of perceptual/cognitive processing, which doesn't necessarily require any motor output, is EEG. In contrast to ERPs, EEG does not assume any special start or stop time with regard to the sensory input.[7] Therefore, it is ideal for continuous rhythmic tasks, such as repetitive visual tasks or repetitive linguistic tasks, or even just listening to music (Fitzgibbon et al., 2004). Different perceptual/cognitive tasks can show their effects at different frequency ranges in the EEG signal: alpha (10 Hz), beta (20 Hz), and gamma (40 Hz) bands. Although continuous EEG involves laboratory constraints similar to ERPs, which can somewhat reduce the ecological validity of the perceptual circumstances, the collection of an unbroken signal of neural activity during the ongoing performance of a cyclic task is an extremely precious source of information for the dynamical perspective on cognition (e.g., Babiloni et al., 2003; Wallenstein, Nash, & Kelso, 1995).

Semi-Continuous Measures With Delimited Tasks

Many of our everyday perceptual/cognitive activities are not particularly rhythmic or repetitive. Although the cognitive and motor dynamics involved in writing a check and putting it in an envelope, or getting in your car and starting the engine, can be well described by a relatively continuous trajectory through a (cognitive and/or motor) state space, that trajectory is not especially cyclic and thus does not easily lend itself to a description in phase space (but see Jirsa & Kelso, 2005). Because reaction time and ERP wave components may focus a little too much on artificially discretized outcome measures, and rhythmic coordination tasks and continuous EEG waves may focus a little too much on repetitive tasks, this final section tries to carve out a middle ground of methodologies that involve delimited nonrepetitive tasks and nearly continuous implicit measures of cognitive processing during those tasks.

For example, a continuous record of arm movement during a reaching task, such as with an Optotrak 3D motion capture system, can be incredibly informative about the cognitive processes involved in that task. By video-recording reflective markers along the joints of the arm and hand, patients with damage to the ventral portion of the visual system (who suffer from visual form agnosia and thus cannot identify objects) can be observed to execute reaching movements and preparatory handshapes for grasping those objects that exhibit perfectly normal temporal dynamics (Milner & Goodale, 1995). This suggests that the intact dorsal portion of their visual system is silently recognizing the object and sending appropriate motor commands to the arm and hand in real time—despite the fact that the patient cannot verbally identify the object. As further evidence for this dissociation, when nonbrain-damaged participants reach for a target object and it shifts location, the arm can smoothly adjust its trajectory midflight, even when the participant cannot see her arm and even when she claims not to have consciously perceived the target object shifting its location (Goodale, Pélisson, & Prablanc, 1986). Results like these point to a relatively automatic perception-action loop, in the dorsal visual stream, that doesn't necessarily require visuomotor feedback or even conscious awareness. The real-time interplay between these dorsal and ventral visual streams, as well as between reaching and grasping commands, in the service of acting on one's environment (or even just imagining objects and actions in one's environment), is a busy topic of study (e.g., Jacob & Jeannerod, 2003; Jeannerod, 1996; Servos & Goodale, 1995).

In addition to recording overt limb movements in real time with a 3D motion capture system, one can also record subtle muscle activity that may not even result in limb movement at all. Electromyography (EMG) follows the same principle as EEG, in that it simply records changes in the electric field that reaches the surface electrodes—except that these surface electrodes are placed on the skin of the arms, hands, or face.[8] As muscles under the skin contract, tiny electrical discharges are detectable even when it's a minor contraction that is not strong enough to physically move that limb, finger, or facial feature. Thus, EMG can provide an implicit measure of muscle groups that are partially active, but not so much that overt movement is executed (Fridlund & Cacioppo, 1986). This would be consistent with the trajectory in mental state space getting close to a particular attractor basin, but not close enough to actually elicit its corresponding motor movement. For example, EMG activity of particular regions of the face can provide evidence of subtle, partial activation of emotional states that remain undetectable by visual observation of those regions of the face or by participants' introspective reports (Cacioppo et al., 1988). Continuous EMG records of the hand muscles can also be informative about partial activation of multiple action commands in a response competition task. Coles and colleagues (1985) measured EMG activity of participants' two response hands as they gripped choice-response handles and found that potentially confusing stimuli elicited partial muscle activity in the incorrect response hand even on trials where the correct overt response was the one that got executed. See chapter 9 for more in-depth discussion of these and related experiments.

Two additional implicit measures of cognitive processing that have also been quite popular and informative are heart rate and galvanic skin response (GSR; changes in electrical conductivity of the skin due to sweat gland activity). Their latency to react is not immediate, but it is usually less than a second. For example, one can actually detect heart rate briefly slowing, or delaying a pulmonary contraction, during the inhibition of a motor response (Jennings, 1992). Moreover, as evidence for the implicit nature of these measures, prosopagnosic patients, who are specifically unable to recognize faces, actually show a normal increase in skin conductance when viewing familiar faces, despite the fact that they claim not to recognize them (Tranel & Damasio, 1988). Measures of heart rate and of GSR have been combined with measures of pupil dilation (Kahneman et al., 1969), and all three generally increase concomitantly with the intensity of cognitive effort involved in a task. Pupil diameter begins to expand in response to increases in cognitive load (or complexity of a task) a few hundred milliseconds after the critical change in sensory input, and this dilation peaks a little more than a second after the sensory change (Beatty, 1982). Pupillary dilation has proven to be informative for studying cognitive load in auditory processing (Bradshaw, 1968), visual processing (Pratt, 1970; Verney, Granholm, & Dionisio, 2001), memory (Karatekin, 2004), word recognition (Ben-Nun, 1986), and sentence processing (Just & Carpenter, 1993; Schluroff, 1982, 1986). All three of those measures, however, reveal only general activity of the sympathetic and parasympathetic autonomic systems. For example, heart rate, GSR, and pupillary dilation will generally increase about equally for emotions of happiness, anger, fear, and so on. For an experimenter to get a handle on *what* the participant is thinking about, not just *how intensely* she's thinking about it, a more selective measure is needed.

Eye Tracking and Mouse Tracking

The outcome-based measures reviewed earlier in this chapter are certainly useful and have provided a considerable database of evidence that continues to constrain theorization in cognitive science. Although they overlook the interim temporal dynamics, they nonetheless provide a crucial measure of where the dynamics ended up. And sophisticated analyses of the distributions (and other large-scale dynamic patterns) in such data also provide valuable evidence for adjudicating between specific theories of task performance, as well as between general frameworks of cognitive processing. Moreover, analyses of the phase space manifolds resulting from rhythmic dynamic motor patterns have provided a strong mathematical foundation for the burgeoning field of dynamical cognitive science. However, because the focus of this book is primarily on state space dynamics rather than phase space dynamics, experimental methods that provide glimpses into state space trajectories exhibited by the mind during perceptual/cognitive tasks are of utmost importance. A great deal of the experimental evidence marshaled throughout this book comes from tracking people's eye movements and their computer mouse movements to provide some form of semi-continuous visualization of their mental trajectory, so I grant these measures their own section here.

Eye movements have a long history of being used as an unusually informative measure of perceptual-cognitive processing in a wide range of tasks (see Richardson & Spivey, 2004).[9] The methodology of eye tracking has advanced considerably over the years, from the days of attaching devices to the eyeball itself (Delabarre, 1898; Huey, 1898; see also Yarbus, 1967), to reflection-based static photographic techniques (Diefendorf & Dodge, 1908; Tinker, 1928), to motion-picture recordings (Buswell, 1935), to electronic laser-reflection systems (Rayner, 1978), and most recently to computerized headband-mounted infrared optical methods (e.g., Ballard, Hayhoe, & Pelz, 1995; Land & Lee, 1994; Tanenhaus et al., 1995). In contemporary cognitive psychology, eye tracking has produced important experimental findings in reading, visual search, and scene perception (see Rayner, 1998, for an excellent review). Eye movement methods have also been at the cutting edge of research in visual memory (e.g., Ballard et al., 1995; Richardson & Spivey, 2000), change blindness (Hollingworth & Henderson, 2002; O'Regan et al., 2000), visual imagery (e.g., Brandt & Stark, 1997; de'Sperati, 2003; Laeng & Teodorescu, 2002; Spivey & Geng, 2001), spoken language production (e.g., Griffin & Bock, 2000), spoken language comprehension (Tanenhaus et al., 1995), speech perception (McMurray et al., 2003), categorization (Nederhouser & Spivey, 2004; Rehder & Hoffman, 2005), problem solving (Hegarty, 1992; Knoblich, Öllinger, & Spivey, 2005; Rozenblit, Spivey, & Wojslawowicz, 2002), chess (Reingold & Charness, 2005), driving (Crundall, 2005), and even video games (Underwood, 2005).

Many of the disadvantages of outcome-based measures, such as reaction time, are avoided when using eye movement data as a measure of cognitive processing. Saccadic eye movements (sudden jumps from fixating one object to fixating another) naturally occur three to four times per second, so eye movement data provide a semi-continuous record of regions of the display that are briefly considered relevant for carrying out whatever experimental task is at hand. Critically, this record provides data during the course of cognitive processing, not merely after processing is complete, as with reaction times and off-line judgment tasks. Saccades take about 200 milliseconds to program once the target has been selected (Matin, Shao, & Boff, 1993; Saslow, 1967), so they are a nearly immediate measure of cognitive processing, compared to many of those discussed in the chapter.

Perhaps most important, eye movements exhibit a unique sensitivity to partially active representations that may not be detected by other experimental methods. Only a small amount of spatial attention is required to trigger a saccade (Kowler et al., 1995). Essentially, if one thinks of it in terms of thresholds for executing motor movement, eye movements have an exceptionally low threshold for being triggered, compared to other motor movements. Because they are extremely fast, quickly corrected, and metabolically cheap, there is little cost if the eyes fixate a region of a display that turns out to be irrelevant for the eventually chosen action. A mere 300 milliseconds have been wasted, and reorienting the eyes to a more relevant location requires very little energy. Therefore, briefly partially active representations—that might never elicit reaching, speaking, or even internal monologue activity, because they fade before reaching those thresholds—can nonetheless occasionally trigger an eye movement that betrays this otherwise undetectable momentary consideration of that region of the visual display as being potentially relevant for interpretation and/or action. Consider, for example, a task with two alternative responses, and the stimulus in question is slightly ambiguous with respect to the two possible responses. In the state space of the participant's mind, these response alternatives can function as attractor basins, and her mental processing of that slightly ambiguous stimulus is equivalent to a trajectory in that state space that temporarily flirts with both attractors, until finally settling into one of them, to select a response. Figure 3.4 depicts an idealized rendition of this state space and that mental trajectory. The rather lenient—nay, downright promiscuous—thresholds for saccadic eye movements (dashed circles) are crossed as early as halfway through the trajectory's traversal. Thus, the eyes would fixate both response alternatives in this case before settling on the chosen one. In contrast, the more conservative threshold for overt response selection, such as pressing a button (solid circles), is crossed much later in time.

This early and quite sensitive semi-continuous measure of cognitive processing can also frequently be used in ways that do not interrupt task processing with requests for metacognitive reports or other overt responses that may alter what would otherwise be normal uninterrupted processing of the task. Thus, in addition to providing evidence for partially active representations throughout the course of an experimental trial, and not just after it, eye tracking also allows for a certain degree of ecological validity in task performance, as the responses it collects are ones that are naturally happening anyway. Figure 3.5 shows a hypothetical—but typical—scan path (based on a study reported by Eberhard et al., 1995) from an individual trial in which the participant was instructed to "put the king of hearts that's below the jack of diamonds above the queen of spades." The eye position starts at the central cross and jumps to the king of clubs soon after hearing "king." After hearing "of

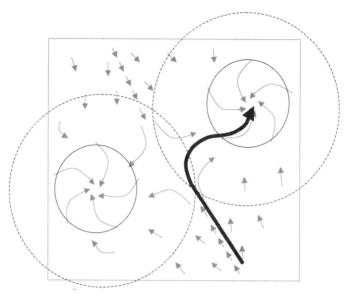

Figure 3.4. An idealized vector field with two attractor basins divided by a ridge, or saddle point (gray arrows show direction and velocity of attraction). The mental trajectory (black arrow) crosses the threshold for executing a saccade (dashed circles) well before it crosses the threshold for an overt button-press response (solid circles).

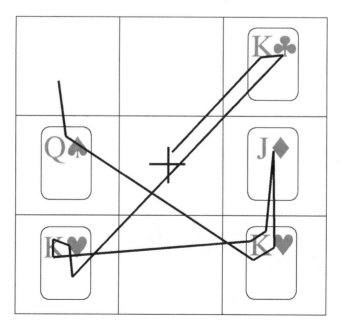

Figure 3.5. Example scan path (starting at the central cross) while hearing, "Put the king of hearts that's below the jack of diamonds above the queen of spades."

hearts," the eyes saccade down to the distractor king of hearts and flit around there until "that's below the jack of diamonds," causes them to fixate the target king of hearts. After a quick check of that jack of diamonds, and once "queen of spades" is heard, the eyes finally move up to the upper left corner of the display to beginning planning the manual action.

These scan paths can be analyzed in a multitude of ways, most of which require the visual display to be segmented into different regions of theoretical interest—although fixation patterns on a blank screen can actually be informative under the right circumstances (Altmann & Kamide, 2004; Spivey & Geng, 2001). Importantly, without some form of linking hypothesis between fixations of certain regions and particular cognitive processes (e.g., Tanenhaus et al., 2000), the full accumulated scan path from any given trial will often be difficult to interpret (see Viviani, 1990). With specific predictions for a preponderance of attention in certain areas under certain stimulus conditions, one can produce interpretable results from examining the mean durations of fixations in various display regions or comparing the sum total of all fixation durations in different regions (total gaze duration). Total gaze duration can then be converted into percentage of total time spent fixating different display regions.[10] When this proportion of time spent fixating each possible object is calculated for each time slice and plotted as a function of time, one can see something equivalent to an object salience map changing dynamically. Figure 3.6 shows hypothetical data from a collection of trials like those in figure 3.5. Note how during the first 500 milliseconds on the graph—immediately following the onset of "king"—all three kings (circles, squares, and triangles) tend to get fixated for a while. Keep in mind that in studies like these, participants won't begin reaching toward one of those incorrect kings, their eyes will just investigate them briefly. As the distinguishing information is gradually delivered, only the target king of hearts (circles) continues to be fixated. Then, the jack

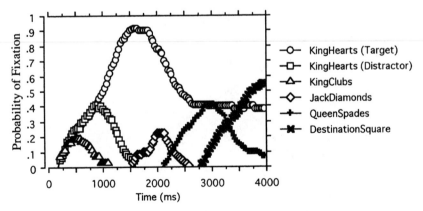

Figure 3.6. Hypothetical data showing the proportion of trials in which various cards were being fixated at each (33 ms) time slice during a sentence like, "Put the king of hearts that's below the jack of diamonds above the queen of hearts." See text for description.

of diamonds is briefly fixated in some trials (diamonds). Eventually, as the last prepositional phrase is being heard, the queen starts getting fixated (+'s), and the target king begins losing some of its salience at that point in time. Finally, the empty square above the queen (x's) begins to attract attention.

There are, of course, methodological concerns related to using eye tracking. It should be acknowledged that visual attention is not always coincident with eye position. Ever since Posner, Snyder, and Davidson (1980) demonstrated that participants' covert visual attention can be effectively dissociated from the point of ocular fixation (when explicitly instructed to not move their eyes), there have been cognitive psychologists who question whether eye movements are really indicative of cognitive processes at all (Anderson, Bothell, & Douglass, 2004). That said, it would be a rather unusual claim to propose that movement of the eyes is purely random and not causally related to cognitive neural processes. Even under extreme cases of unpredictable visual search circumstances where variation in absolute eye position appears to exhibit noise consistent with a random walk process, saccade amplitudes exhibit long-range temporal correlations, $1/f$ noise (Aks, Zelinksy, & Sprott, 2002). In fact, a great deal of behavioral and neuroscience research has shown a very close coupling between movement of visual attention and movement of the eyes. Not only do the eyes generally follow where attention leads, with a typical latency of about 50 milliseconds (see Henderson, 1993, and Hoffman, 1998, for reviews), but many of the same regions of frontal and parietal cortex that are involved in planning and executing eye movements are also implicated in covert visual attention (see Corbetta, 1998, and Corbetta & Shulman, 1999, for reviews).

Another concern with eye movement data is the averaging that goes into making graphs like that in figure 3.6. It is all too easy to produce smooth curves from averaging many discrete but slightly asynchronous saccadic transitions. In fact that's precisely how these eye position curves become smooth. The logic behind it is that dynamically changing activation levels of internal mental representations are constantly in flux, and occasionally one of them exceeds some relatively low threshold for executing a discrete saccadic eye movement. By measuring many eye movement patterns under the same conditions, one can extract the graded patterns of activation that produced those saccades. This linking hypothesis between the smooth averaged curves and the gradually accruing activations of mental representations admittedly requires something of a leap of faith. However, the alternative explanation—that the mind is discretely jumping to one unitary interpretation and executing its corresponding eye movement, then discretely jumping to a different unitary interpretation and executing its eye movement—can be somewhat difficult to defend. In most of these eye tracking experiments, one occasionally observes an oscillatory eye movement pattern where participants initially fixate object A (for example, some candy when instructed to "pick up the candy"), then fixate object B (such as a candle, because the first few phonemes are about the same in *candy* and *candle*), and then fixate object A again, finally making an overt response that corresponds with object A, such as grasping the candy or pressing a button that has its label. In a formal logical system that follows rules to flip from one discrete mental state to another, it is not at all clear why such a system would not have executed its overt response during the *first* instance of fixating object A.

A methodological solution to the averaging concern would be to use a motor output that is not saccadic, not quite so ballistic. Recall Goodale et al.'s (1986) evidence for smooth continuous adjustment of arm movement trajectories during a reaching task. Might an individual reaching movement, for example, toward the candy, be slightly curved toward the candle? Spivey, Grosjean, and Knoblich (2005) designed a computerized version of these displays, with candle/candy, tower/towel, and so on (where a spoken instruction, such as "click the candle," is temporarily ambiguous for the first couple hundred milliseconds of the target word), and with candy/nickel, ladle/dolphin, and so on (where the target word is not temporarily ambiguous with respect to the visible alternatives). Participants mouse-clicked a start button, then the display showed up, and then the prerecorded spoken instruction was delivered. By recording the trajectory of the computer mouse's cursor, sampled at 60 Hz, we have a nearly continuous measure of where in space the spoken instruction has "pushed" the participant's motor output and the degree to which the two images on the computer screen have "pulled" that movement toward themselves.[11]

Figure 3.7 shows an actual individual mouse movement trajectory when the participant was instructed to "click the ladle," with a display containing a ladle and a dolphin. In this control condition, the trajectory is relatively straight, moving directly to the ladle with a reasonably constant velocity. It is as though there was only ever one significant attractor basin available to pull the state of this system. In contrast, when the two objects have similar sounding names, competition between the objects/attractors is quite evident in the trajectory. Figure 3.8 plots an actual—and quite typical—individual mouse movement trajectory when the participant was instructed to "click the beetle," with a display containing a beetle and a beaker. Note how the mouse trajectory moves upward, equidistant from the beetle and beaker, slows down briefly (circles overlaying one another), and then finally curves over to the beetle. Although it is not common, there is occasionally a trial in which the mouse trajectory exhibits some overt vacillation between the competing objects, not unlike the oscillatory eye movement pattern already mentioned. Figure 3.9 shows the mouse cursor moving somewhat toward the correct object (carrot), then somewhat toward the competitor object (carriage), then turning again to finally settle on the correct object. This suggests perhaps some stochasticity in the continuous motor command and/or significant real-time fluctuation in the shape of the attractor manifold.

The mouse trajectory in figure 3.8 (beetle versus beaker), moving toward the midpoint between two attractor basins, slowing on the saddle point briefly, then finally sliding down one of the basins, is quite reminiscent of the idealized attractor manifold and mental trajectory in figure 3.4.[12] One could

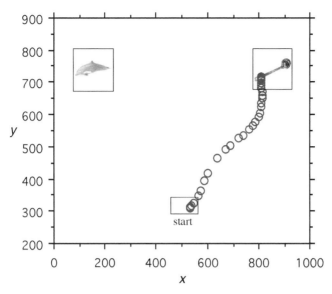

Figure 3.7. Mouse movement trajectory (in pixels) for "Click the ladle," with a dolphin as the neutral distractor.

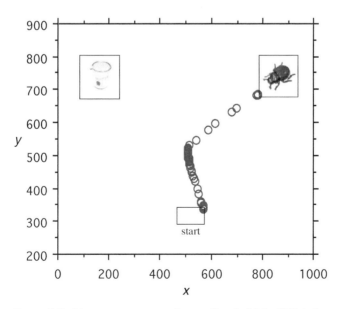

Figure 3.8. Mouse movement trajectory (in pixels) for "Click the beetle," with a beaker as the cohort competitor. (Note the similarity with the mental trajectory in figure 3.4.)

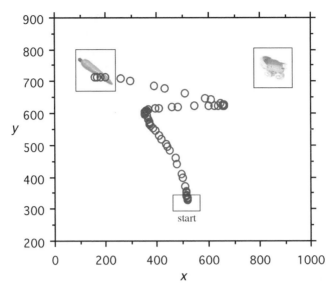

Figure 3.9. Mouse-movement trajectory (in pixels) for "Click the carrot," with a carriage as the cohort competitor.

interpret this similarity, between a mental trajectory in a high-dimensional state space and a movement trajectory in a two-dimensional space, as an illustrative metaphor for understanding how dynamic competition between two partially active action-goals takes place. However, if someone were compelled by the situated cognition framework in the larger cognitive sciences (e.g., Greeno, 1989; Gupta, 1992; Hutchins, 1995; Kirsh, 1995; Schwarz, 1998), they might be tempted to describe this correspondence between mental trajectories and motor trajectories not metaphorically at all but indeed quite concretely. In principle, one can conceive of the experimental task constraints as forcing the participant to emit her continuously changing high-dimensional internal state onto a physical workspace that has only two dimensions. In such a circumstance, the mouse movement trajectory would be posing, quite literally, as an external two-dimensional projection of the person's internal high-dimensional cognitive dynamics. That is, the real-time cognitive process of spoken word recognition imposes a continuous influence on the shape of the visuospatial salience map in the parietal cortex that determines where attention is directed (e.g., Desimone & Duncan, 1995; Itti & Koch, 2001), which in turn imposes a continuous influence on the dynamic field of neuronal population codes for motor preparation in primary motor cortex (e.g., Bastian, Schöner, & Riehle, 2003; Erlhagen & Schöner, 2002; Georgopoulos, 1995), which in turn directs motor output in a fashion that reveals the continuous evolution of the movement command (e.g., Paninski et al., 2004).

There are two reasons why this computer mouse trajectory methodology provides a richer signal than eye movements of the continuous process of real-time spoken language comprehension influencing motor output. First, it samples this process about 60 times per second (depending on the software), instead of 3–4 times per second (as with saccades). Second, with some minor and subtle exceptions (Doyle & Walker, 2001; Gaveau et al., 2003; Theeuwes, Olivers, & Chizk, 2005), saccadic eye movements are ballistic and straight, unable to adjust or curve in midflight. In contrast, skeletal motor movements with the hands and arms are often able to curve substantially in midflight (Goodale et al., 1986; Tipper, Howard, & Jackson, 1997), and can thereby expose graded spatial attraction effects that might not be detected with other methods. And it certainly doesn't hurt that recording computer mouse trajectories requires equipment that is far less expensive than eye tracking. Nonetheless, eye movements usually precede arm movements, and thus provide a more immediate index of cognitive processes than arm movements. Therefore, computer mouse trajectories are best seen not as a replacement for any other method but instead as an important complementary data source for revealing the continuous flow of mental activity to motor activity (e.g., Coles et al., 1985; see also McClelland, 1979). (For some further discussion of the measurement of computer mouse movements, see chapter 9.)

Though This Be Dynamic, Yet There Is Method in It

The previous chapter focused on a conceptual framework for understanding the continuity of mind, that is, the spatiotemporal continuousness with which a mental state traverses its neural state space. Dovetailing with this purpose, the current chapter has focused on a variety of experimental measures for empirically examining the continuity of mind. The next chapter will focus on explicit mathematically implemented and temporally dynamic models of the continuity of mind. In all of these cases, the role of real-time perceptual-motor representations looms large in cognitive processing.

It could be argued that the reason motor output is as illuminating of cognition as it is—be it a hesitant button-press, a curved mouse movement, a vacillatory eye movement pattern, or rhythmic fingers dancing on the edge of chaos—is precisely because so much of cognition is carried out by perceptual-motor simulations (e.g., Hesslow, 2002; Jeannerod, 2003; Pecher, Zeelenberg, & Barsalou, 2003; Solomon & Barsalou, 2004). Much (if not all) of cognition is fundamentally composed of combinations of dynamic perceptual-motor simulations or complex preparedness for situated action (see Barsalou, 2003). There is no internal encapsulated "mind in an ivory tower" that independently conducts these simulations. It is the senses themselves, the motor systems themselves, and an emergent cognition self-organizing amid the two, that carry out these simulations. And this is why measuring the output of those motor systems in a number of different time-dependent manners provides rich evidence for the activity of these simulations. According to the framework of dynamic embodied cognition, motor output is not merely an emitted signal from the process of cognition, it is *part* of cognition. We aren't using the experimentally recorded behavior to make an *inference* about a cognitive process, that behavior *is part of* the cognitive process.

Indulge me while I recount a little anecdote that epitomizes, for me, the intimate role that the body plays in cognition. One day, I had spent much of the morning and afternoon mulling over in my head different versions of a few sentences for a manuscript I was working on. I was somewhat frustrated with trying to find the right wording. Later, while sitting in the audience for a visiting speaker's lecture, the phrasing for those sentences suddenly fell into place. I quickly grabbed a pen and the back of an envelope, and scribbled them down just legibly enough that as long as I transcribed them onto my computer within 24 hours, I could probably decipher the chicken scratchings. Then, a brief, inexplicable, unidentifiable motoric urge came over me. For about half a second, I felt a dire need to carry out some unspecified motor movement that would safely preserve these precious sentences that I had finally, after several hours, found a way to arrange that was likable. Then the feeling was gone. I folded the envelope, tucked it in my pocket, and then continued to ignore the visiting speaker's words while my mind uncontrollably wandered to try to explore what that weird urge had been. By running some kind of mental inventory of my body, asking what limbs had wanted to move, I gradually localized it to my left arm. I am right-handed, so this seemed slightly odd. Then I felt the remnants of the motoric urge continue to localize themselves further, down my arm to my left hand. I wiggled those fingers, and two of them seemed to want to wiggle more than the others. My thumb and middle finger seemed somehow potentiated for action. But why? Then it hit me: My thumb and middle finger had wanted to press the Command and S keys on my keyboard to *save* those prized sentences! My left thumb and middle finger had participated in my powerful desire to preserve those much-pondered phrasings. That, for me, is the embodiment of cognition.

Nevertheless, as the debate rages between continuous distributed embodied cognition (e.g., Barsalou, 1999; Coles et al., 1985; McClelland & Rogers, 2003; Port & van Gelder, 1995) and discrete symbolic amodal cognition (e.g., Anderson & Lebiere, 1998; Dietrich & Markman, 2003; Fodor & Pylyshyn, 1995; Miller, 1988), one could imagine that a pacifist with good intentions and an annoying penchant for physics analogies might suggest that the mind is like light. Depending on how you measure it, it can come out looking like it's made of particles (symbols) or of waves (distributed patterns). Thus, to claim that the mind's true fundamental medium of processing is solely symbolic particles or solely continuous waves may be wrong-minded.

But we should be wary of walking on the paving of those good intentions, out of concern for where that road leads. I have a suspicion that this analogy doesn't quite hold up. First, it is not entirely clear that every physicist is satisfied by and accepting of the conventional account of the dual nature of light. Second, and more important, it can be argued that the experimental methodologies that have been producing evidence for particlelike symbolic mental representations are seriously flawed. Borrowed from the psychophysics of 100 years ago, off-line measures of forced-choice responses have dominated cognitive psychology since its inception in the 1960s. Participants are presented with a static temporally bounded stimulus and instructed to select among a set of possible discrete nonoverlapping responses to it. Experiments like these couldn't detect a continuous representation (in time and/or in feature space) if it was staring them in the face! Or even if it bit them somewhere! We should not be surprised at all that when an experimental participant is forced to choose a single temporally discrete mutually exclusive response alternative, they tend to produce output that looks indicative of a single temporally discrete mutually exclusive mental state. (For concrete examples, see the sections on categorical perception in chapter 6.) What cognitive psychology needs are experimental designs and measures that at least give the organism in question a chance to exhibit evidence for continuous graded blends of multiple mental states. If there is indeed a continuous uninterrupted flow of patterns of activation (or state space trajectories) from perception to cognition to action (Cacioppo et al., 1988; Coles et al., 1985; Eriksen & Schultz, 1979; McClelland, 1979; see also Balota & Abrams, 1995; Gold & Shadlen, 2000), then continuous measures of motor output can actually provide an impressively accurate index of real-time perceptual and cognitive processing.

As we come to the end of this tour through several continuous and semi-continuous measures of motor output, that focus on dynamic properties of action rather than merely the outcome of an action, we can at last revisit Gibson's question that began this chapter. What does behavior consist of? It cannot consist of "responses," because a response is but a small, late-in-the-game aspect of the many properties of motor output that one can examine, and its emphasis on the final result of an action misses out on a great deal of information that can often disentangle competing theories of cognition. In naturalistic behavior (especially rhythmic actions like walking or playing a musical instrument), motor output does not always have identifiable start times and stop times. Therefore, pointing to the part of that behavior that is "the response" is impossible. What behavior actually consists of, and therefore what experimental psychologists should probably be measuring, is continuous action—not responses. As any scientist (or vinyl audiophile) will tell you, if you want to understand what is going on in a continuous process, the highest-fidelity signal will come from a continuous measure of that process.

4

Some Simulation Tools for Tracking Continuous Mental Trajectories

We know, from the pre-Socratic period of Greek philosophy, the expression panta rhei: all states of things are incorporated in a stream of motion and change. Nothing stays the same, and when we want to study certain process phenomena, we are compelled to regard them as stages of change, as parts of a dynamic process.
—Jan Eberg

Nothing *is*, everything is *becoming*.
—Heraclitus

How Can Blind Men Build a Sculpture of the Mind?

Dynamical systems accounts of mind are often perceived as foreign objects in the body of psychology. They are poorly understood, and if their descriptions aren't annoyingly vague, then their math is daunting. Perhaps most problematic is the simple fact that for some scientists, it simply conflicts with introspection to claim that the mind does not think one discrete "thing" and then think another discrete "thing."

The purpose of this chapter is to gently walk the reader through some of the mathematics of a few simple demonstrations of dynamical systems to prove that it's really not that daunting after all. I promise. As for any private intuition that one's mind "stands still during each thought," it will be up to the rest of the book (especially chapters 6–8) to convince such a reader to trust experimental data over his or her subjective self-reflections.

But before getting to those data, let's examine the theory. To properly cash out the claim that the mind is a continuous dynamical system, rather than a digital computer, we will need to design idealized model simulations of the theory and its explicit implementation. Persuasive prose and trendy buzzwords are simply not enough.

As it turns out, it is dangerously easy to string together a handful of axiomatic claims about how some aspect of mind works and call this collection of stipulations a theory—only to later discover that they are self-contradictory when functionally integrated. Rather than permitting oneself to wax philosophical about a laundry list of cognitive assertions that may turn out to be inconsistent with one another if actually put into operation, a number of researchers have argued strongly for the development of mathematical and/or computational implementations of theories about cognition (e.g., Broadbent, 1987; Hintzman, 1991; Seidenberg, 1993; Smolensky, 1988a; see also Newell, Shaw, & Simon, 1958). Hintzman (1991) has pointed to a perfect example of the kinds of pitfalls that one can encounter when theorizing without simulating. His example comes from research by sociobiologists making claims about gender differences in sexual promiscuity. Based on survey results from equal sized populations of men and women on how frequently they have heterosexual, two-person one-night stands, the researchers concluded (by statistically generalizing their sample results to the entire population) that men have more one-night stands than do women. That is what the questionnaires revealed. At first glance, this kind of result doesn't really surprise us. It corresponds well with our intuitions and cultural prejudices concerning men and women. And acquiring some scientific corroboration of those intuitions is perhaps self-edifying. There's just one problem. In the context of men and women having heterosexual, two-person dates, it is *mathematically impossible* for the average number of one-night stands conducted by men to be any different from the average number of one-night stands conducted by women! It simply cannot happen. Every time a man is having a one-night stand, as defined by the questionnaire, so is a woman. (The distributions could be skewed in one or the other of the groups, but the arithmetic means have to be the same.) Thus, our intuitive theory of dating makes a prediction that is completely illogical and mathematically invalid. Had the researchers conducting this survey bothered to construct even the simplest mathematical account of their theory, they would have realized that the prediction they thought their theory made was fundamentally ill-formed.

Implementing one's theory is like building a machine that embodies the axioms of the theory, rather than merely listing those axioms and claiming that they work together. The machine has to work for the theory to be considered sound. Indeed, it is a common experience for a simulation programmer to start out thinking that the theory she is trying to implement provides all the components that will be necessary to build a working system, only to find, after some initial pilot simulations, that the theory leaves out one or more parameters or processes that are absolutely essential to allowing the rest of the components to work together. Verbal descriptions of theories tend to be like that. They look good on paper, but they often do not stand up to the demands of actual implementation.

A somewhat cutesy but nonetheless illustrative example that I use with my students, comes from the Steven Spielberg film *Close Encounters of the Third Kind* (1977). In this film, Richard Dreyfuss's character (as well as several other people throughout the country) is apparently psychically receiving from extraterrestrials images of some mountain. He and the other receivers independently become obsessed with depicting this mountain. They paint it and sketch it compulsively. Then, at one point, Dreyfuss's character is inspired with the idea of sculpting, rather than painting, his channeled vision of the mountain in 3D (starting out with mashed potatoes and ending up using garbage, potting soil, plants, etc.). What he thereby discovers is that there is a plateau (actually a UFO landing pad) on the backside of the mountain, which the other receivers had failed to ascertain. This discovery of a new idea, resulting from building a richer, more detailed model of one's obsession, has much in common with what happens when one builds a simulated implementation of a theory. While attempting to implement a simulation of a theory, one often discovers novel system properties and novel system behaviors that the theory actually entailed all along and that can then be empirically tested for in the laboratory.

Each of the experimental measures discussed in chapter 3 is like a microscope providing a particular two-dimensional perspective, or sketch, of the full three-dimensional structure of perception and cognition. These two-dimensional peeks into the actual system of interest provide useful pictures of its function, but they lack the full volumetric feeling provided by a simulation. The two-dimensional images provided by a few experimental measures can occasionally neglect to reveal a striking anomaly hidden in the back of the data structure, such as a plateau or even a UFO landing pad. With an approximated simulation, one can get the full volumetric feeling of observing the entire system in action and sometimes deduce those anomalies. But of course, we must always remind ourselves that it is still just an approximated hypothetical model of the actual system of interest.

Not unlike the allegory about the blind men and the elephant (where they each touch a different part of the elephant and generalize attributes of that part to the whole animal), trusting only one of those experimental measures can give one a peculiar and probably skewed impression of the mind. The full solution, which the original elephant allegory fails to provide, is that perhaps the blind men should collaborate in sculpting a full 3D model of the elephant. Further empirical exploration of the actual animal could then test the generalizations they had to make in simulating the elephant, and a duly revised sculpture would then offer new and better generalizations to test. This cyclic process of "fit data," "predict new data," "empirically test predictions," "refit data," and so on, is precisely what the juxtaposition of chapters 3 and 4 is all about (and what will be seen in much of chapters 6–10): the marriage of experimentation and simulation.

Qualitative Transitions

In taking us away from simulations of mind that are based on logical rules and discrete symbols (e.g., Anderson, 1983; Marcus, 2001; Pylyshyn, 1984), and moving us toward simulations of mind that are more continuous and dynamical, let us first explore how continuous systems can behave in ways that could easily be mistaken as discretely symbolic and formally logical

(Dietrich & Markman, 2003). One of the key phenomena in dynamical systems that allows them to approximate symbol-like processes is qualitative transitions, such as bifurcations and phase transitions. Qualitative transitions are seen in sigmoid curves (often called s-curves) all over nature. Sigmoid curves like the one in figure 4.1 simultaneously exhibit the apparent *suddenness* of a qualitative transition from one stable state to another, as well as the actual *smoothness* of that transition itself. The transition is not instantaneous; it has a nontrivial time course to it. In this time course one can find clues as to how analog, continuous processes can often appear digital and discrete. During the range of values along the horizontal axis where the hypothetical quantity of some generic substance is no longer in state A but also neither in state B, the state must be described as a form of graded titration of states A and B.

The logistic function, figure 4.2, is an elegant symmetric model of a generic s-curve-shaped process.[1] The logistic function is used in physics for subatomic particle identification and event classification, in chemistry for saturation processes, in biology for species population dynamics; the list goes on. In statistics, to convert a log-likelihood ratio of two alternatives into a probability, one uses the logistic equation. In neuroscience, the logistic function is used to approximate the average firing rate of a neuron (e.g., Britten et al., 1992) as well as the probability of a neuron carrying out a single action potential (e.g., Burnod & Korn, 1989). The logistic function is also used in connectionist simulations of a neuronlike unit summing its linear inputs and then squashing that value to a range between 0 and 1 (see Rumelhart & McClelland, 1986a). And sigmoidal curves are routinely observed in "microgenetic" studies of children in the process of transitioning from one developmental stage to the next (see Siegler & Crowley, 1991).

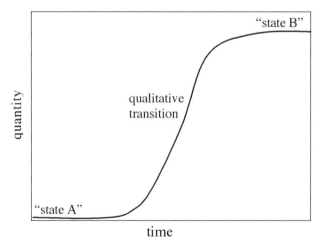

Figure 4.1. A qualitative transition from one steady state to another.

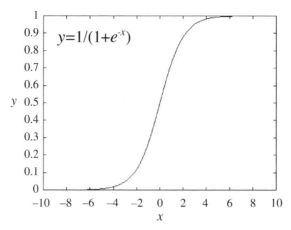

Figure 4.2. The logistic function as a mathematical model of a state transition.

Sigmoidlike curves in empirical data, and logistic functions fitting those curves, are ubiquitous throughout science. And yet traditional cognitive psychology has preferred to overidealize the qualitative transitions demonstrated by sigmoid curves like this into discrete, logical, set-theoretic step functions that categorically delineate one cognitive representation from another. In a step function, like that in figure 4.3, the transition between category A and category B is instantaneous. That is, the boundary between these two categories is treated as discrete, and no gray area is acknowledged to exist between them (as in figure 4.1).

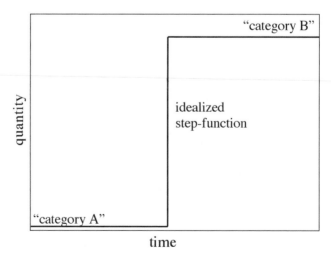

Figure 4.3. The kind of state transition required by discrete models of the mind.

A Playground for Dynamics: The Logistic Map

The purpose of the following demonstration is twofold. First, it is intended to walk the reader through the logistic map in a fashion that will perhaps make clear why this simple little (yet deceptively powerful) iterated equation still garners so much excitement and interest in the mathematical field of dynamical systems. Second, in my own experience with reading about the logistic map, it was rare that it was presented in a manner that made the math and the graphs easy to understand. I hope that I have achieved a more easily understood presentation in the following few pages, thereby perhaps convincing some cognitive psychologists that the mathematics and data visualizations of dynamical systems theory are not as opaque as they may have thought.

The derivative of the logistic function in figure 4.2 is solved as $y * (1 - y)$. Thus, the derivative is at its highest, 0.25, when $x = 0$ (and the curve's slope is at its steepest). The derivative approaches a steady 0 when $x < -5$ or $x > 5$ (where the curve is quite flat). In the back-propagation learning algorithm for connectionist networks (Rumelhart, Hinton, & Williams, 1982), which depends on the logistic function for computing the activation of output units and hidden units, this derivative, $y * (1 - y)$, is used to scale the degree to which a unit's error term (desired output minus actual output, multiplied by the presynaptic unit's activation) is allowed to change its incoming synaptic weights. Thus, a connectionist unit that is near 0 or near 1.0 in its activation will actually be allowed to make only very minor changes to its incoming synaptic weights, as the $y * (1 - y)$ scaling factor for weight changes will be near 0. Moreover, when the network's learning rate (η typically around 0.1) is included in this weight-change scaling factor, $\eta * y * (1 - y)$, the actual weight changes implemented become minuscule.[2]

The interesting thing about this scaled derivative of the logistic function, $\eta * y * (1 - y)$, is that it is exactly equivalent to the logistic map (equation 4.1), an iterative equation first developed in the mid-nineteenth century by Belgian mathematician Pierre Verhulst for modeling population dynamics. This unassuming, simple equation has a long history of revealing insight into the multifarious time-dependent behavior that can result from a system whose output becomes its next input, that is, a recurrent system. The logistic map is now treated as the quintessential example of a complex dynamical system whose temporal dynamics can transition from being characterized by stable states to being characterized by metastable states and eventually to chaotic behavior (e.g., Davies, 1999; Killeen, 1989). The logistic map is an iterated simulation of a continuous dynamical system in which the value of y at time t is inserted back into the equation to produce the value of y at time $t + 1$, which is then inserted into the equation again to produce the next value of y, and so on.

$$y_{t+1} = \eta * y_t * (1 - y_t) \tag{4.1}$$

As long as the growth factor, η is between 0 and 4, y will have a minimum of 0 and a maximum of 1. The logistic map shows how a species population will

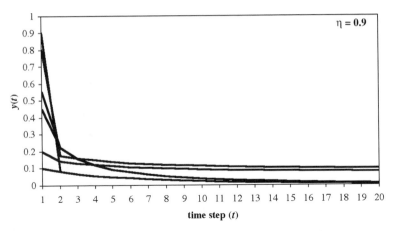

Figure 4.4. Six runs of the logistic map: values of y over time, when $\eta = 0.9$.

increase at a rate proportional to its current population, but continued expansion will be limited by the environment's food resources, thus eventually balancing the species into a relatively stable population number. For example, when $\eta = 0.9$, the value of y will gradually approach 0 no matter what its initial value is (figure 4.4). When $\eta = 2.9$, the value of y will gradually approach about 0.65—again, no matter what its initial value is (figure 4.5). When $\eta = 3.4$, the value of y, no matter where it starts between 0 and 1, will eventually oscillate between 0.84215 and 0.45196 indefinitely (figure 4.6). Thus, somewhere between $\eta = 2.9$ and $\eta = 3.4$, this dynamical system's single attractor has bifurcated into two attractors. As η increases further, those attractors bifurcate again and again. For example, when $\eta = 3.55$ (figure 4.7), no matter what its initial conditions, the system eventually settles into a

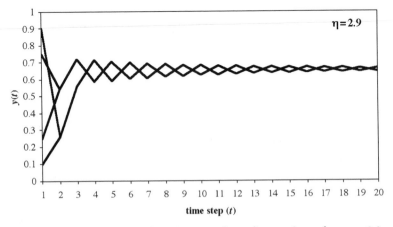

Figure 4.5. Four runs of the logistic map: values of y over time, when $\eta = 2.9$.

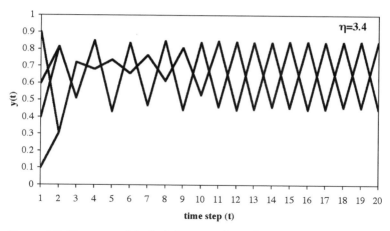

Figure 4.6. Four runs of the logistic map: values of y over time, when $\eta = 3.4$.

metastable pattern with eight distinct and perfectly repeated attractors: 0.8874, 0.3548, 0.8127, 0.5405, 0.8817, 0.3703, 0.8278, and 0.5060.

One particularly illustrative way to visualize this period doubling behavior, where attractors split themselves into two, is by graphing a scatter plot of multiple y values for every value of η (Feigenbaum, 1978). In the bifurcation plot in figure 4.8, each value of η, at 0.01 increments, has plotted (as tiny dots) the last 40 values of y from a 2,000-iteration run (i.e., the 1,961st through the 2,000th time steps of y). The upper panel is the full bifurcation plot for $0 < \eta < 4$, and the lower panel is a zoom-in for $2.9 < \eta < 3.75$. Notice in the upper panel of figure 4.8 that with values of η that are < 3, those 40 y values all land right on top of each other. When $3 < \eta < 3.448$, 20 of the y values land on top of each other in one spot and the other 20 land on top of each

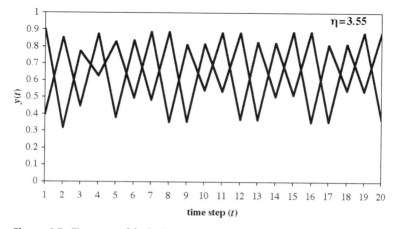

Figure 4.7. Two runs of the logistic map: values of y over time, when $\eta = 3.55$.

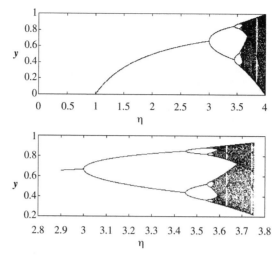

Figure 4.8. Scatterplot of multiple *y* values of the logistic map for each value of η.

other in another spot. When η = 3.449, those two points each split, or bifurcate, into two more—making four distinct attractors (distinguishable at the fourth decimal place of *y*). With slightly higher values of η, those four attractors then bifurcate into 8, and so on, until around 32 attractors, where the distinctness becomes difficult to discern (figure 4.8, lower panel). When η > 3.57, the clustering of 40 *y* values is generally much less apparent. What this amounts to is that in both panels of figure 4.8, the punctate *y* values at a particular value of η (forming clear black lines amid a white background) are highly specific point attractors, and the somewhat loosely clustered *y* values (looking a bit like curving dark contours within the black mass) indicate more graded and fuzzy attractor basins.

A particularly interesting phenomenon happens at this transition region between order and chaos, about 3.6 < η < 3.86, as the system exhibits quasi-periodicity (or a type of pattern called intermittency, which is equivalent to the 1/*f* noise discussed in chapter 3, see Manneville, 1980), where very subtle variations in the control parameter, η, can make the difference between strictly periodic behavior and fully chaotic behavior. This intermittency behavior is the hallmark of a system at the edge between stable predictable order and genuinely unpredictable (though still deterministic) chaos. For example, note the gaps amid the chaos (those vertical white bands amid the black mass in both panels of figure 4.8). When 3.829 < η < 3.857 (figure 4.8, upper panel), the system is not chaotic at all. In fact, it is quite ordered with three attractors: around 0.15, 0.50, and 0.96. (Similar periodic regions emerge from the chaos around η = 3.63 and η = 3.74; figure 4.8, lower panel.) As η increases barely beyond 3.857, each of those three attractors bifurcates, making the system period six. Then those bifurcate, and the system quickly becomes chaotic again. In fact, when $3.86 < \eta < 4$, the trajectory of y over time becomes so chaotic and unpredictable that despite the equation being completely deterministic, it can legitimately be used as a random number generator (Ulam & Von Neumann, 1947).

Finally, another hallmark property of self-organizing recurrent systems, like the logistic map, is fractal structure. Note the self-similar (i.e., fractal) nature of how the shape of each tiny bifurcation resembles the shape of the larger ones. At different spatial scales, across multiple orders of magnitude, the logistic map exhibits the same general layout of curvilinear bifurcations leading to similar curvilinear bifurcations as a function of the parameter η. Fractal structure like this can be seen all over nature by looking at multiple spatial scales of coastlines, mountain ranges, trees, even the human vascular system.

A Proving Ground for Dynamics: Attractors, Networks, and Attractor Networks

If a simple equation like the logistic map can produce behavior as complex as that just described, imagine what can result from dynamical equations with a few more parameters or artificial neural network models that often involve several parameters. Imagine the complexity of behavior that might result from a human brain with billions of neurons and trillions of synapses.

Many of those involved in the dynamical approach to perception, action, and cognition see the goals of the field as fundamentally continuous with the goals of the physical sciences (see Turvey & Carello, 1995; van Gelder, 1999; Ward, 2002): to develop compact universal descriptions of the behavior of systems—usually in the form of dynamical equations. This approach typically entails discovering principled single-valued functions that refer to collective variables, and fitting those functions to a broad but cohesive set of related behaviors (Thelen, 1995; Turvey & Carello, 1995). For example, in furthering Gibson's (1979) mission to define psychology's domain of interest as the coupled subsystems of organism and environment (rather than just the brain), Turvey and colleagues (e.g., Barac-Cikoja & Turvey, 1991, 1993; Fitzpatrick, Carello, & Turvey, 1994; Pagano & Turvey, 1993) have reported a number of rich descriptions of haptic (specifically, dynamic touch) perception in which the perceived size or length of unseen objects is accounted for by equations based solely on parameters derived from the dimensions of the objects and limbs themselves—no explicit reference to internal muscular, sensory, or cognitive parameters is required. The same general approach of discovering collective variables that can serve as single-valued functions of behavior is also evident in the work of Kelso and colleagues on interlimb rhythmic coordination (e.g., Haken, Kelso, & Bunz, 1985; Kelso, 1995; Kelso, Scholz, & Shöner, 1986). These two bodies of work are discussed in some detail in chapter 9, on the dynamics of motor movement.

Dynamical systems equations that define attractors in particular locations of a state space or of a phase space are probably best treated as complementary to dynamical neural network simulations, rather than adversarial to them (see Bechtel & Abrahamsen, 2002; Horgan & Tienson, 1996; Smith & Samuelson, 2003). However, dynamical equations are occasionally offered as the *only* appropriate level of description for perception, action, and cognition, accompanied by the suggestion that descriptions at the level of neurons or neural assemblies is unlikely to prove fruitful. This kind of claim is often made on the grounds that what's good enough for physics should be good enough for psychology. To take a simple example, consider Newton's law of universal gravitation for the force of attraction between two bodies: $F = G(m_1 m_2 / r^2)$. Combined with an acceleration function, this simple equation can describe the highly complex motions of a congregation of multiple objects orbiting one another. Arguably, this kind of equation-based account for complex phenomena has been good enough for physics for hundreds of years. So, what makes psychology think it needs something better than what physics has subsisted on for so long?

The problem is that as of yet, physics has come up with no coherent agreed-on understanding of what gravity is made up of and what causes it to work the way it does. Physicists are stuck with the equations at that particular descriptive level. Contrary to popular belief, they are not actually content with that good enough state of affairs. Indeed, a genuine understanding of what gravity really is could in principle resolve some of the glaring conflicts between Newtonian gravity and Einstein's special relativity. The fundamental problem is that the rich *description*, and even relatively accurate prediction, provided by the equations still does not *explain how* gravity exerts its attraction.[3] With only a descriptive account—such that gravity is understood merely as a constant that is required to make the equation work, with no clear linking hypothesis between the behavior (motion) and the substrate (gravity)—the opportunities to find connections to potentially related phenomena, resolve theoretical and empirical conflicts, and thus build a more broadly applicable theory, are severely limited.

To finally bring this poor belabored physics analogy to its conclusion and put it out of your misery, in the case of the cognitive and neural sciences, we actually *do* know something about the substrate that contributes to human behavior. Physics may not have found its graviton yet, but psychology has found its brain. Primate neurophysiology, human neuroanatomy, and cognitive neuroscience provide a wealth of knowledge for constraining theoretical accounts of "how minds happen." Therefore, there is no justification for avoiding the link between mind and brain. (Note that I did not say "the explaining away of mind by brain," as body and environment are also crucial; see chapter 11.) Computational neuroscience in general (e.g., Dayan & Abbott, 2005; O'Reilly & Munakata, 2000; Trappenberg, 2002), and attractor networks in particular (e.g., Amit, 1989) offer a way to bridge the gap between the abstract concepts of attractor spaces and the concrete physical material of brains that are inside bodies that are inside environments.

One very popular artificial neural network that functions as a dynamical system is the simple recurrent network (e.g., Christiansen & Chater, 1999; Cleeremans, Servan-Schreiber, & McClelland, 1989; Elman, 1990, 1991; Rodriguez, Wiles, & Elman, 1999). This network architecture has much in common with traditional three-layer feedforward back-propagation connectionist networks (for reviews, see Bechtel & Abrahamson, 2002; Rogers & McClelland, 2004; Rumelhart & McClelland, 1986a). The labeled input nodes get their activations set by the experimenter, each unlabeled hidden node in the middle layer calculates its activation as a weighted sum of the input nodes (and then squashed by the logistic function), and the labeled output nodes calculate their activations as a weighted sum of the hidden node activations (also then squashed by the logistic function). Distributed patterns of activation in the hidden layer function a bit like the neuronal population codes discussed in chapter 1, except the nodes are not connected to each other. The simple recurrent network, however, has two very important alterations on that scheme. See figure 4.9. First, instead of the output layer's target activation being an arbitrary pattern to be associated with the input pattern, in a simple recurrent network, the output activation pattern is usually treated as a prediction of the next input pattern. This allows the network to use the "supervised" back-propagation learning algorithm without really needing an explicit "teaching signal." That is, instead of having a hypothetical teacher provide the network with an example of the desired output activation pattern with which to compute an error term by comparing the teaching signal with its actual output, the network need simply "listen" to the next input and compare that to its prediction. By using prediction-based learning, the system can internalize the structure of a time-dependent signal by *eavesdropping* on it, without requiring any explicit negative evidence from the signal source at all (see Spivey-Knowlton & Saffran, 1995). The second alteration that a simple recurrent network (SRN) involves is the adding of a context layer of units that is connected to the hidden layer, which copies the hidden layer activations and loops them back into the hidden layer as reentrant feedback on the next time step. This allows the network to base its predictions on a weighted combination of the

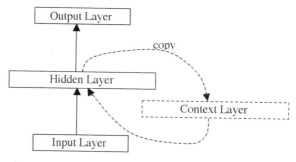

Figure 4.9. The basic architecture of the simple recurrent network (Elman, 1990).

past few time steps. (In contrast to the usual tactic of dimensionality reduction in most feedforward connectionist networks, SRNs usually have more hidden nodes than input nodes, as they must encode multiple time steps' worth of information.)

By examining the regions visited in the hidden layer's state space (with hierarchical cluster analysis, Elman, 1990, or with principal component analysis, Elman, 1991), one can observe how the network's internalization of a sequence of inputs, such as a sentence, consists of a trajectory moving from one attractor basin to another to another, and so on. Strictly speaking, however, it is not so much a continuous trajectory as a series of "teleportations" in state space, each triggered by an input pattern (and modulated by the context layer's influence on the hidden layer). The hidden layer does not spend any time in the intermediate regions between the locations that it visits in state space; it just blinks out from one location and reappears in another (in the form of a newly calculated activation pattern). Each input pattern triggers *one* projection into state space, and the system stays there until the next input pattern projects the system into a new location in its state space (but see Pearlmutter, 1995, and Tabor, Juliano, & Tanenhaus, 1997, for iterations of processing that take place *in between* input-induced projections into state space). Thus the SRN's temporal dynamics are somewhat coarse and staccato when compared to the ideal of a continuous trajectory through state space and time. Nonetheless, because an SRN is focused on temporal patterns, it displays a useful kind of dynamics as long as input continues to be fed into it.

The amalgam of information in the context layer, accumulated over several time steps, has been referred to as a kind of gestalt (St. John, 1992). However, if you look at the math of the context nodes combining with the hidden nodes' feedforward input, and then being copied back onto the context layer, it's not actually more than the sum of its parts at all. In fact, it is *exactly* the sum of its parts. The place where true gestalten become relevant is when a not-so-simple recurrent network (such as a Hopfield net) is allowed to settle toward an attractor over the course of several time steps, irrespective of external input, as in the case of *fully* recurrent networks. When the state of the system is allowed to gravitate in its dynamic field, as it were, toward an internalization of the input that does *not* actually match a veridical version of the sensory input (as in the case of pattern completion, see chapter 1), then the system's encoding of the sensory input can genuinely be referred to as constructing a gestalt (see Köhler, 1922/1938).

Although the temporal dynamics of an SRN's input processing is comprised of rather large jumps in state space, its changes in weight space during learning are certainly sufficiently small to allow for the mapping of a relatively continuous trajectory through the energy landscape of the weight space. This allows one to depict the gradient descent of the network's synaptic connectivity from a state exhibiting poor predictions to a state exhibiting good predictions. Thus, although they may not be ideal for simulating the temporal dynamics of pattern completion kinds of phenomena during real-time processing, SRNs are perfect for simulating the continuous perceptual and cognitive changes that take place over the time scale of learning (Elman et al., 1996).

When I teach my undergraduates to program an SRN from scratch in MATLAB, I am fond of telling them, "There's nothing simple about a simple recurrent network." It is probably the most difficult assignment in the course. But in truth, compared to fully recurrent networks, SRNs *are* rather simple. Fully recurrent networks introduce a host of complex details concerning the (synchronous or asynchronous) activation update schedule (see Amit, 1989), how far to propagate error with the learning algorithm (see Beer, 1995; Pearlmutter, 1989, 1995), whether to use averaged firing rates as activation values or to use spiking neurons (see Maass, Natschläger, & Markram, 2002), and how to interpret the psychological relevance of their activation patterns over time (Zemel & Mozer, 2001). However, the most relevant property exhibited by fully recurrent networks, for the purposes here, is that they spread their activation throughout the network over the course of multiple time steps even after the designated input pattern has ceased being presented. Thus they are perfect for simulating and examining the temporal dynamics of a pattern completion process during real-time processing.

A Hopfield network (Hopfield, 1982) is a fully and symmetrically interconnected set of neuronlike units with no designation of input or output layers (see figure 4.10). An external source of input sets the initial activation values for all the units, and then the synaptic weights pass the activation all around (via a random activation update schedule using a binary linear activation threshold) until the network settles into a stable state. Hinton et al. (1993)

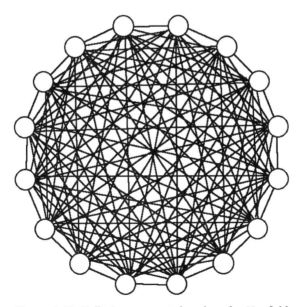

Figure 4.10. Fully interconnected nodes of a Hopfield network.

have used a Hopfield network as part of their neural network simulations of different forms of dyslexia. Similarly, McRae, de Sa, and Seidenberg (1997; see also McRae et al., 1999) used a Hopfield network to simulate semantic priming effects in psycholinguistic experiments. An important feature that fully recurrent networks exhibit—and one that is not shared by SRNs—is the fact that one can measure reaction times from the system by simply recording how many time steps it takes to reach a specified level of stability. Calculating such reaction times from feedforward networks is possible, but less straightforward, typically involving additional parameters for determining cascaded activation flow (see Cohen, Dunbar, & McClelland, 1990). How long the network takes to settle into its various attractor basins for a range of different initial input vectors will often correspond well with how long a human subject takes to respond to a range of different laboratory stimuli (e.g., Hinton et al., 1993; Masson, 1991; McRae et al., 1997; see also Usher & McClelland, 2001).

Closely related to the Hopfield net is the Boltzmann machine. The Boltzmann machine was named after the physicist who developed the entropy equations that describe the diffusion of heat through a metal plate from a single heat transference contact point. (Interestingly, variants of these same entropy equations have been used in information theory for several decades now; Shannon & Weaver, 1949.) As with a Hopfield net, a Boltzmann machine is fully interconnected; however, some nodes can be designated as input, output, or hidden. Moreover, the activation threshold is stochastic rather than linear, such that the summed input to a node is converted into the probability that the node will be in a 0 activation state or a 1.0 activation state. Kawamoto (1993; see also Cottrell, 1989) used a Boltzmann machine to simulate the nonlinear state space trajectories that a written word recognition network follows in the process of settling on a unique interpretation of an ambiguous word like *rose*, as a verb or a noun, or like *bug*, as referring to an insect or a spy device (see chapter 7).

A number of other types of attractorlike networks have been developed to study perceptual/cognitive phenomena like pattern completion (Grossberg, 1980), categorical perception (Anderson et al., 1977), visual masking (Turvey, 1973), memory (Little & Shaw, 1975), to name just a few. The many different attractor network types have their individual strengths for certain applications and weaknesses for others (see Amit, 1989). Many of the attractor networks mentioned so far rely on distributed representations, such that the mental representations of interest are instantiated by diffuse patterns of activation across multiple nodes in the network, for example, the feature nodes that comprise a concept (McRae et al., 1997).

There is another type of attractorlike network that usually has more limited connectivity than Hopfield nets or Boltzmann machines, and it is often referred to as a localist attractor network. A localist attractor network, as I will broadly and inclusively treat it, can include multiple levels of representation (e.g., lexical, phonemic, and subphonemic, or scenes, objects, and object parts), but the different levels will typically be treated by somewhat separate vectors of network nodes. Within the lexical vector, for example, individual nodes will be devoted to individual words, whereas within the subphonemic vector, individual nodes will be devoted to individual phonetic features. Thus, the "representations of interest" within the subphonemic layer of the network will still correspond to individual nodes. This makes the behavior of localist attractor networks considerably easier to interpret and track over time than that of distributed attractor networks; moreover, they are much less likely to exhibit spurious or inappropriate attractors (Zemel & Mozer, 2001). I will loosely include a number of spreading-activation networks in this category of localist attractor networks. For example, spreading-activation types of models, such as interactive-activation (Grainger & Jacobs, 1998, 1999; McClelland & Rumelhart, 1981; McClelland & Elman, 1986; Rumelhart & McClelland, 1982; see also Dell, 1986, for a similar kind of network), use nodes whose content is easily identified, thus allowing the network's state to be easily described at any moment in time. Notably, such networks spend a great deal of their time in intermediate, multifariously interpretable, regions of their state space, on the way *toward* some uniquely identifiable state in which only a perfectly consistent set of nodes is active—much like what was argued for how the mind works in chapters 1 and 2. One drawback of most localist attractor network simulations of perception and cognition is that the setting of synaptic weights and other parameters is often carried out "by hand" rather than by using a principled arrangement of weights or a learning algorithm (but see Zemel & Mozer, 2001). This makes them less useful for simulating dynamics over developmental time. However, the focus of this book is on temporal dynamics of real-time processing, at the scale of seconds and milliseconds, so this weakness of localist attractor networks is somewhat less relevant to the present purposes.

A Demonstration Arena for Probabilistic Dynamic Competition: Normalized Recurrence

Compared to distributed attractor networks, localist attractor networks are one step further abstracted from the real neurophysiology, because they overidealize mental representations as instantiated by individual nodes. This makes them a somewhat shorter bridge between psychology and neuroscience—thus requiring longer leaps of inference between the two. But in some ways, simpler is better when it comes to modeling the mind because as one's model gets too large and unwieldy, it risks becoming as opaque as the subject it is intended to reveal. Indeed, some network modelers have resorted to running experiments on their elaborate, convoluted networks in the same manner that psychologists run experiments on humans, as their sole method of figuring out how the model works! In any case, building the theory bridge between mind and brain clearly requires multiple partially overlapping frameworks (e.g., computational neuroscience, localist attractor networks, parallel distributed processing networks, and dynamical systems; see Spencer & Thelen, 2003) that can maintain connections to one another and stand as a contiguous fabric of mutually consistent simulations that will allow future generations to safely walk between psychology and neuroscience without having to take too many risky speculative leaps.

In the following pages, I describe a localist attractor network architecture (normalized recurrence) that—because of its extreme simplicity—I do not call a model per se. This competition algorithm exhibits a kind of temporal dynamics, resulting from continuous and recurrent information integration, that resembles the temporal dynamics observed in categorization experiments (chapter 6), language comprehension experiments (chapter 7), and visual search experiments (chapter 8), but it does not make any explicit architectural or representational claims about the mind. It simulates process, not content. Its only assumptions are the following: (1) that disparate information sources in perception and cognition are continuously integrated (rather than temporarily encapsulated from one another by stages or modules), and thus must share a common format of representation (perhaps neural population codes—for which the localist nodes are a kind of shorthand); and (2) that reentrant neural projections facilitate a recurrence in information flow that allows partially integrated information to bias the initial processing of incoming afferent sensory input.

The equations for this competition algorithm are simple enough, and there are few enough parameters, that it serves as a useful introduction to implemented dynamical simulations of perceptual/cognitive processes that readers can write themselves in MATLAB, for example, in just a few lines of code. MATLAB code for several example simulations reported throughout this book is included in the appendix.

Normalized recurrence can be treated as a localist attractor network that allows disparate formats of information to be combined in the form of probabilities with which their various biases would support a set of enumerated outputs (McRae, Spivey-Knowlton, & Tanenhaus, 1998; Spivey et al., 2002a; Spivey & Tanenhaus, 1998; Tanenhaus, Spivey-Knowlton, & Hanna, 2000). Those outputs can be a set of perceptual interpretations, cognitive decisions, or motor actions. One can think of them as attractors that have been plucked out of their high-dimensional state space and converted into the dimensions of a lower dimensional "attractor space" (not unlike figure 2.5 in chapter 2). The pattern of probabilistic activations across the output layer of the normalized recurrence network can be treated as a location in that attractor space. See figure 4.11. This unfairly treats all the attractors as equidistant from one another (which is unlikely to be true about the brain); however, this drawback is often outweighed by the expository benefits of normalized recurrence. Think of it as if one has taken a distributed system's current coordinates in state space and computed the proximity to all relevant point attractors (or neural population codes) in the state space. Normalize these proximity values, so that they sum to 1.0, and you have the profile of a probabilistic mental state—as described in chapter 2.

Output (Integration) Layer

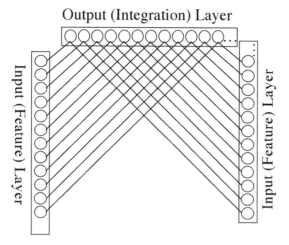

Figure 4.11. Basic architecture of the normalized recurrence localist attractor network.

Normalized recurrence is intended at a level abstraction significantly removed from the real dynamics of actual neurons and synapses. Although it is helpful to depict it in the connectionist style of circles for units and connecting lines for synapses, it is not even as neurophysiologically plausible as the typical connectionist network. It does not employ distributed representations, and it does not have any learning algorithm at all. The system's focus on real-time dynamics is consistent with this book's emphasis on perceptual/cognitive processing time scales rather than developmental time scales (e.g., Elman et al., 1996; Thelen & Smith, 1994). The synaptic weights, if they need to be varied, must be set by hand, as is done in interactive activation types of networks (e.g., Burton, 1994; Dell, 1986; Grainger & Jacobs, 1999; McClelland & Rumelhart, 1981; Page, 2000; Rumelhart & McClelland, 1982; van Heuven et al., 2001; see also McClelland & Elman, 1986). Perhaps what most glaringly deviates from neurophysiological plausibility in normalized recurrence, as will be seen, is the use of multiplicative feedback from the output layer to the individual input layers. Although multiplicative synapses have been reported in the electrophysiology literature (see Bugmann, 1992), they do not appear to be the norm.

Probabilism in Normalized Recurrence

The most important aspect of this generic simulation system is its probabilism. Probabilistic representations, such as those used in the fuzzy logical model of perception (Massaro, 1989), allow the enhancement of activation of behaviorally relevant information to be complementary and commensurate with the suppression of activation of behaviorally irrelevant information (see also

Rumelhart, 1970). In fact, even if enhancement and suppression were somehow two independent mechanisms in perception/cognition (e.g., Gernsbacher, 1990; Posner & Cohen, 1984), an *assessment of the probabilities* of the possible behavioral outputs (as well as any associated internal representations) at any one point in time would necessarily have enhancement and suppression result in a zero-sum game. It is exactly this assessment of probabilities that provides the starting point for motivating the design of normalized recurrence.

One of the primary reasons to use probabilistic activation values is that they eschew any notion of processing resources, something that has been criticized as a fast and loose wild card for cognitive psychologists for decades (see Allport, 1989; Morrison, 1984; Navon, 1984; Palmer, 1995). There are several problems with the notion of processing resources or processing capacity. The notion was first invoked to account for the results of dual-task paradigms, where simultaneous performance on two easy tasks (i.e., tasks that require few processing resources) is not compromised, but simultaneous performance on two hard tasks (i.e., tasks that require many processing resources) *is* compromised. Clearly, the definition of a hard task and the definition of a task whose performance is compromised in a dual-task paradigm becomes a circular argument very quickly. (Besides, these kinds of results are accommodated by a probabilistic activation scheme, e.g., see the visual search simulations in chapter 8.)

This perspective owes much to the traditional bottleneck theories of information processing (Broadbent, 1958; Treisman, 1964), where it was assumed that early perceptual processes superficially encoded the entire stimulus input. At a later (more cognitive) stage, attention with its limited processing capacity filtered the inputs to allow complex information processing to be performed on only a (manageable) restricted set of the input. Since then, this perspective has received increased critical scrutiny (e.g., Allport, 1989).

One of the biggest problems introduced by the notion of processing resources is the assumption that when the system as a whole is not being severely taxed, there are extra, unused resources waiting to be deployed. This implies that there is a storehouse in the brain from which these processing resources are doled out, and where the system's capacity, or "metabolic budget," is constantly tabulated. To my knowledge, no such storehouse, or accounting executive, has ever been convincingly localized in the brain.

Further support for probabilism and against unbounded or raw activation values is seen in recent neurophysiological data and modeling suggesting that normalized activations are in fact an appropriate format for representing the firing rates of neurons in the primary visual cortex of the macaque monkey (Carandini & Heeger, 1994). Basically, when a neuron is receiving a fixed amount of afferent excitatory input, its firing rate is high if few of its neighboring neurons are also active, and its firing rate is low if many of its neighboring neurons are also active. Whether this is due to intracortical inhibition (Carandini, Heeger, & Movshon, 1997) or to synaptic depression from the thalamus (Carandini, Heeger, & Senn, 2002), it winds up being equivalent to a linear summation procedure followed by a normalization procedure.

Thus, theoretical and experimental observations are consistent with a perspective in which the notion of limited processing capacity, at all levels of analysis in the perceptual/cognitive system, is best explained (or perhaps explained away) by normalized activations. Note, however, that just because these activations are normalized does not mean that the mind is computing the probability of a given stimulus belonging to a particular category. That would require a great deal more adherence to Bayesian probability theory than mere normalization to a sum of 1.0. The sense in which normalized recurrence treats these activations of the output layer as probabilities is in the claim that they represent "the probability that the mind will trigger a motor action that is associated with a particular stimulus category." That is directly stipulated in how the normalized activations of the output layer are mapped onto proportions of the available responses in human data.

Localist Representations in Normalized Recurrence

Once raw amounts of stimulus salience have been replaced by probabilistic values of stimulus salience, there still remains the problem of how to instantiate these probabilities. It seems unavoidable that the way the brain instantiates any complex concept, word, or object is in the form of distributed patterns of activation (e.g., Hinton, McClelland, & Rumelhart, 1986) or sparse "population codes" (e.g., Georgopoulos, 1995; Olshausen & Field, 2004; Pouget et al., 2000; Young & Yamane, 1992; see also chapters 1 and 2). However, this does not mean that the only way to simulate such mental entities is in terms of many interconnected nodes encoding microfeatures (Hinton, 1981). For example, there is little or no difference, in principle, between 9 out of the 10 microfeatures for a concept being digitally activated and having a single *localist* node for that concept set at 0.9 activation (see Hopfield, 1984). In fact, some findings in the psycholinguistics of word recognition are consistent with the idea that lexical representations may indeed be reasonably treated as "functionally unitized" or localist in format (e.g., Bowers, 2002; Stone & Van Orden, 1989). These different levels of description should be seen as complementary, not mutually exclusive (Smolensky, 1988a).

One place where localist representations have proven quite useful is in Dell's (1986) spreading activation model of sentence production. In this model, phonological features, syllables, words, and syntactic categories are all given idealized representations as individual nodes. With explicitly represented nodes for each of these levels of description, Dell's model exhibits the same patterns of speech errors that are seen in human data, including *anticipation* and *perseveration* of phonemes, phoneme clusters, syllables, and morphemes (Dell & Reich, 1981).

One of the practical benefits of modeling with localist representations is that the state of the system at any one point in time is typically quite transparent, as opposed to the patterns of activation in a fully distributed representation, which can often be quite difficult to interpret (Hinton et al., 1986). For example, if a system with localist representation is at a bifurcation point between two mutually exclusive states, this will generally be quite apparent, in that the nodes representing those two states will have high and nearly equal activations. In a system with distributed representations, it is difficult enough to identify diffuse patterns of activations with their attractor basins, but identifying the state of the system (at time *t*) when it is at a *bifurcation point between attractors* is even more daunting.

Additionally, when the model's architecture forces these localist probabilistic perceptual representations to correspond to particular response categories, it provides a powerful task-specific constraint on processing. Response categories that are not allowed by the task or are not availed by the organism cannot have their associated perceptual representations instantiated by this system. This architectural constraint enforces a rather strict (perhaps too strict) form of embodiment and situatedness of cognition (e.g., Ballard, Hayhoe, Pook, & Rao, 1997; Glenberg, 1997; Greeno, 1998; Harnad, 1993). That is, the model cannot conceive of things on which it cannot potentially act. Nonetheless, with enough perceptual inputs brought to bear on a given set of possible response categories, some quite complex emergent properties can become apparent in this mapping of perception to action. Thus, in this framework, cognition may be viewed not as a separate set of static symbols and rules that this model dares to ignore but as the complex dynamic processing that emerges between perception and action, grounded in (and parasitic on) the representational formats of both (see Barsalou, 1999; Jones & Smith, 1993).

Integration in Normalized Recurrence

At this point, having committed to probabilistic and localist representations, perhaps it would help to offer some concrete examples of this notion of probabilistic salience values of localist representations. Take, for example, the various factors that might go into choosing a beer at a restaurant. For simplicity, let's examine only the beer's flavor and affordability (we will ignore beer foam decay rates for now, but see Dale et al., 1999; Leike, 2002). In terms of flavor, one might have normalized salience values like that in figure 4.12a. In terms of affordability, one might have normalized salience values like that in figure 4.12b. Note that these two feature vectors (which can act as input layers for a normalized recurrence simulation) are somewhat at odds with one another. The flavor vector is biased toward Franziskaner and Guinness, and against Sam Adams and Pabst Blue Ribbon. In contrast, the affordability vector (based on prices in the United States) is biased toward Pabst Blue Ribbon and Sam Adams and against Guinness and Franziskaner. If money were of no concern, then the flavor vector could be used as the sole determinant of the beer selection. However, if money were the sole concern, then the affordability vector would be used to determine beer selection. But usually *both* money and

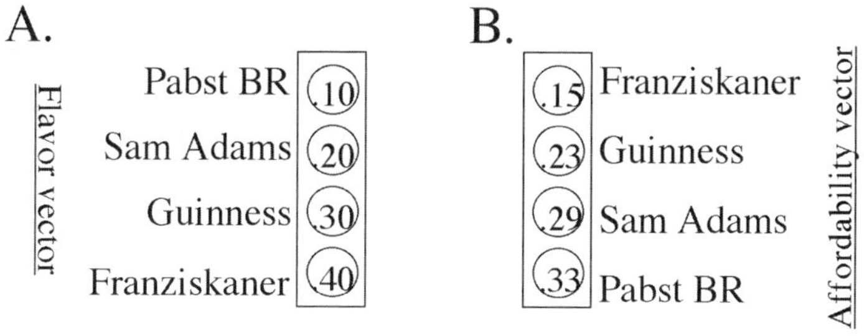

A.

Flavor vector

Pabst BR ⑩
Sam Adams ⑳
Guinness ㉚
Franziskaner ㊵

B.

⑮ Franziskaner
㉓ Guinness
㉙ Sam Adams
㉝ Pabst BR

Affordability vector

Figure 4.12. Values for feature vectors in a toy simulation.

enjoyment are of significant concern. So how does one integrate these competing biases?

Once an activation regime (probabilistic) and a representational medium (localist) have been chosen, it still remains to be determined exactly how the different sources of information are to be integrated. Because they are designed as vectors of equal size, one obvious solution would be to combine them in a pointwise fashion. Because they are a little bit like actual probabilities, one might consider multiplying them (i.e., a dot-product) and renormalizing them in a fashion similar to Bayes's theorem (see Massaro, 1989). However, if the eventual goal is to simulate temporal dynamics, by applying the operation iteratively with some form of recurrence, it takes only a few exploratory pilot simulations to demonstrate that this general approach settles onto a single alternative extremely quickly—usually within two or three iterations. Such a narrow range of attractor settling times would certainly not provide sufficient temporal resolution for approximating real-time data, such as reaction times. Perhaps a better solution would be to simply sum the two vectors.

Vector sum methods have been employed for a wide range of psychological phenomena. For example, Kinchla (1974) used Gaussian (i.e., normally distributed) noise with a vector sum to simulate accuracy data in visual search, and N. Anderson (1964; see also Anderson, 1996) summed differentially weighted vectors to simulate performance in a sequential number averaging task. In Kinchla's model, which was derived from signal detection theory (Green & Swets, 1966), the weights that were applied to the vector always summed to 1.0 (making it a weighted average). This allowed the model's outputs, for example "target present" versus "target absent" in Kinchla's case, to be a probabilistic pair of values that could be fed into a Gaussian random decision rule.

Although the inputs to this kind of one-step integration method can be made to change over time, the integration method itself does not provide anything in the way of temporal dynamics. A vector sum model, in which mutually exclusive representations compete with one another over time, can provide exactly the kind of temporal dynamics necessary for reaction time data, but it needs some additional components to get those dynamics. There are many ways for representations to compete with one another. They could each gradually accumulate their evidence and independently race against one another toward their respective criteria, as in Ratcliff's (1981, 1985) diffusion model, a random walk process that integrates principles from signal detection theory, usually with the goal of simulating reaction times. Or activation can be continuously fed forward through a series of hierarchical processing levels that allows the system to combine and accumulate information for simulating accuracy (and d-prime) at different points in time, as in McClelland's (1979) cascade model. Similarly, with an architecture like that in figure 4.11, the activations of the representations can be computed in a feedforward fashion as localist nodes that then, within a processing level, produce autofacilitation and exert mutual inhibition until one node reaches some criterion level of supremacy, with the number of competition cycles mapping onto reaction time (Spivey-Knowlton, 1994).

These kinds of algorithms, however, assume that the feature (input) vectors do not change over time during competition; only the integration vector changes. By contrast, in the interactive-activation model (McClelland & Rumelhart, 1981; Rumelhart & McClelland, 1982), a bank of inputs (i.e., letters) activates a bank of higher-level representations (i.e., words), which then feedback to further activate the input bank. This cyclic recurrence in information transfer allows converging biases from both levels of representation to eventually settle on a coherent encoding of the input. Importantly, in the case of the normalized recurrence arrangement, simple additive feedback from the output layer to the input layers would not be sufficient to eventually propel the network into a unique attractor basin (with all the nodes in each vector near 0 activation, except for one of them near 1.0 activation). A multiplicative feedback rule (in which the amount of activation added to an input node is the product of the corresponding integration node's activation and the amount of activation most recently passed to it by that input node) allows the averaged biases that have resulted at the integration vector to "reward" the corresponding input nodes commensurately with how responsible they were for producing those averaged biases in the first place. After sending this feedback to all the input nodes, the next thing to do is renormalize the feature vectors, so that they sum to 1.0 again, as the next competition cycle (time step) begins. This regime of operations within a cycle—normalize input (feature) layer, compute weighted average at output (integration) layer, send feedback to input later—typically yields settling times in the range of dozens of iterations; a temporal resolution that should be sufficient for approximating reaction times.

Combining the model characteristics discussed thus far yields a generic computational architecture that exhibits probabilistic activations of localist representations and employs a vector sum (on the feedforward step) for integration, with multiplicative recurrence (on the feedback step) for temporal dynamics. In normalized recurrence, representations compete with one another over time. This provides simulations of reaction times, eye movement patterns, as well as accuracy data at specified temporal intervals.

The Algorithm

Normalized recurrence (McRae et al., 1998; Spivey-Knowlton, 1996; Spivey et al., 2002a; Spivey & Tanenhaus, 1998; Tanenhaus et al., 2000) is a computational architecture that bears similarities with McClelland and Rumelhart's (1981) interactive-activation architecture, except that there are multiple input vectors, which I call constraint vectors, and the recurrence is restricted to feedback from the integration vector to the individual constraint vectors. That is, the c input constraints, shown as feature vectors (F_c) do not have direct cross-talk with one another (see figure 4.11), but the feedback from the integration vector (I) produces an *indirect* cross-talk between constraints.

Rather than squeezing it all into one long, ugly equation, it is perhaps more easily grasped as a series of small steps to be carried out within one iteration. Normalized recurrence allows representations to (implicitly) compete with one another by dividing each individual feature-vector activation by the sum of that vector (equation 4.2). This forces the elements within that vector to share the limited resources of the probability space.

$$F_c(\text{norm}) = F_c/\Sigma F_c \qquad (4.2)$$

The integration vector (I) is simply recomputed at each cycle as the weighted sum of the constraint vectors (equation 4.3). The weights (w_c) can be set to each equal 1.0 (Spivey-Knowlton, 1996), they can be set to each equal $1/c$ (Spivey & Tanenhaus, 1998), or they can be independently estimated by curve-fitting off-line norming data (with $\Sigma w_c = 1.0$), and then those same weights can be used to simulate real-time data (McRae et al., 1998).

$$I = \Sigma w_c F_c(\text{norm}) \qquad (4.3)$$

This weighted sum is then normalized in the integration vector (equation 4.4, a simpler version of the softmax activation function; see Bridle, 1990), as was done in the constraint vectors, to result in approximated probabilities of each possible response category. Of course, if the weights sum to 1, equation 4.4 is actually unnecessary because multiplying constraint vectors that sum to 1 by weights that sum to 1 would automatically result in an integration vector that sums to 1. However, in some circumstances, you might want the weights of the input vectors to each equal 1.0 (Spivey-Knowlton, 1996), in which case the normalization exacted by equation 4.4 is crucial.

$$I(\text{norm}) = I/\Sigma I \qquad (4.4)$$

The feedback from the integration vector back to each constraint vector is equal to the activation of each integration vector element multiplied by the weighted input it received up that particular pathway, added to the current activation of the corresponding element in a constraint vector (equation 4.5). Over the course of many iterations, this feedback process allows the emerging interpretation resulting from the (weighted) average of the c feature vectors to gradually coerce each individual feature vector (even those that are biased quite differently from the average) to warp its activation pattern into a form that supports the developing consensus. Thus, as the integration vector is approaching a moderately confident singular interpretation of the input, noise or ambiguity in one feature vector can be resolved, or pattern completed, by certainties in the other feature vectors.

$$F_c = F_c(\text{norm}) + Iw_c F_c \qquad (4.5)$$

The cycle (of equations 4.2–4.5) then repeats. Without needing to impose a logistic function (e.g., the equation in figure 4.2) on the output activations, normalized recurrence naturally approximates a sigmoidal function over time, with converging biases among the various constraints leading the integration vector to settle toward a single highest probability representation. For example, given the beer preference vectors in figure 4.12, conducting a normalized recurrence simulation of the beer choice decision-making process is trivial. If the weights assigned to flavor and affordability are equal (i.e., 0.5 for each), then the integration layer exceeds 0.95 activation for Franziskaner, naturally, on the 24th iteration. (See code in the appendix.) However, as the vector weights trade off, for different financial or gustatory refinement circumstances, such that affordability becomes more valued than flavor, one can observe the model settle in favor of Guinness or Sam Adams. In fact, if affordability is given a weight of 0.75 and flavor thus given a weight of 0.25, as might be the case for a starving undergraduate, the model will actually settle in favor of Pabst Blue Ribbon, believe it or not. Figure 4.13 shows the integration- and feature-vector activation plots over time for this unfortunate circumstance. Not unlike the discussion of Schrödinger's cat in chapter 1, at any one time slice in the integration vector's activation pattern here, the idealized freeze-frame of the system can be described as being in multiple partial states at once: partly wanting Pabst, partly wanting Sam Adams and Guinness, and wistfully wishing it could afford Franziskaner. Note how the integration vector shows both Pabst and Sam Adams rising in tandem for the first several iterations. Note also how the flavor vector's activation of Sam Adams takes the lead for a period of time, peaking at the 19th iteration, only to have its hopes dashed as the emerging consensus for Pabst coerces even the flavor vector to coincide with the choice. That is, the network eventually convinces itself that it prefers the taste of Pabst—because that is all it can afford. Figure 4.14, in the form of a two-dimensional window on the integration vector, plotting the Pabst node activation by the Sam Adams node activation time step after time step, shows the nonlinear trajectory through representational state space that the model traverses as it decides on Pabst. This perspective on the activations reveals the simulation's mental state starting out almost equidistant from the Pabst attractor (bottom right corner) and the Sam Adams (top left corner),

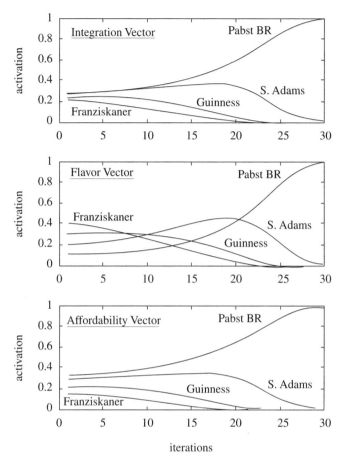

Figure 4.13. Activation curves from normalized recurrence settling on a beer choice.

but then eventually turning and quickly gravitating into the Pabst attractor. It is as if the poor undergraduate could almost taste the Sam Adams as his hand reached for the Pabst Blue Ribbon.

Of course, this competition algorithm on its own will happily cycle indefinitely, well after one integration node reaches asymptote at 1.0 activation and all the others have dropped to 0 activation. Therefore, some kind of criterion must be set for when the model is to stop competition and treat the normalized activation pattern exhibited by the output layer as the distributed interpretation of the input, and as the probability density function corresponding to the response categories available for execution. This criterion can be a fixed activation value of 0.95, or perhaps 0.75 for low-threshold motor outputs such as eye movements (Spivey-Knowlton, 1996), or it can be a dynamic criterion that starts at 1.0 and is gradually reduced by some small amount each time step (McRae et al., 1998; Spivey & Tanenhaus, 1998). Alternatively, the model can be interrupted at various time intervals and tested on its accuracy (Spivey et al., 2002a). Finally, the dynamic criterion can be made stochastic so that there is some variation from trial to trial in how long competition is allowed to take place, and selection of an interpretation can be a random choice, weighted by the activation values (see the simulation of eye movements during spoken word recognition in chapter 7). This criterion setting issue can sometimes be thorny (see Proctor, 1986, and Ratcliff, 1987), but with normalized recurrence, the basic pattern of results is rarely substantially different as long as the criterion is between about 0.5 and 0.95.

The key strength of normalized recurrence is its transparency. At any point in time, the model can be stopped, and its activation patterns are as easily interpreted as the idealized bar graphs of probabilistic mental states in chapter 2. Another strength of the normalized recurrence competition algorithm is its generalizability. In fact, it has already provided quantitative accounts of human data from a range of perceptual/cognitive phenomena. It has been used to simulate semantic and discourse context effects in reading times of syntactically ambiguous sentences (McRae et al., 1998; Spivey & Tanenhaus, 1998), reaction times in visual search (Spivey-Knowlton, 1996),

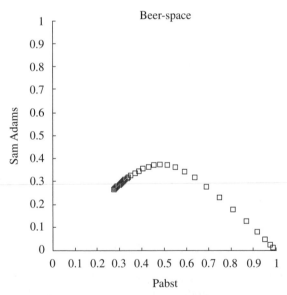

Figure 4.14. A trajectory in part of the localist attractor network's state space, simply plotted as the simultaneous activation of the Pabst node and the Sam Adams node over 30 time steps. This nonlinear trajectory, starting from almost equally preferring Pabst Blue Ribbon and Sam Adams, eventually settles solidly and unambiguously on Pabst Blue Ribbon.

and d-prime sensitivity values for speeded grammaticality judgments in a speed–accuracy trade-off task (Spivey et al., 2002a). The broad applicability of this algorithm suggests that it may be appealing to some fundamental characteristics of how the mind continuously integrates information (at a relatively abstract level of description, of course), in terms of encoding system internal representations as probabilities, and the interactive exchange of these probabilities between subsystems via recurrent feedback.

Exploratory Simulations

In a series of simulations designed purely to explore the temporal dynamics of normalized recurrence, four random feature vectors combined their support for six competing response categories. Initial input activations were randomly set between 0 and 1 for each input node, and vectors were simply summed at the integration layer (i.e., all weights equaled 1.0). The model was allowed to cycle all the way to the end of its pattern completion process (i.e., there was no criterion set), and the activations of all six integration nodes were recorded over time. In the vast majority of such simulations, the initially most active integration node takes up the entire probability space relatively quickly. See figure 4.15.

However, pattern completion with normalized recurrence is not always that easy. Occasionally, two response categories will end up in a time-consuming tug of war over the probability space. Figure 4.16 shows a run of the model in which the initially most active integration node (starting at 0.24679) *did* end

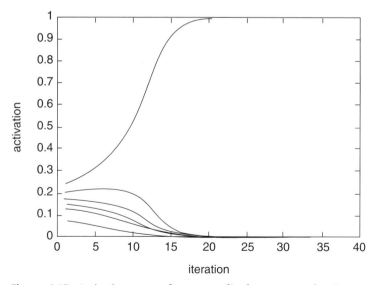

Figure 4.15. Activation curves from normalized recurrence showing an easy pattern completion.

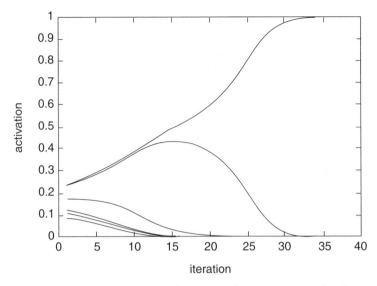

Figure 4.16. Activation curves from normalizes recurrence showing a difficult settling process.

up owning the entire probability space, but the initially second most active integration node (starting at 0.24004) postponed that result by putting up a prolonged competition until the eventual bifurcation point much later. In dynamical systems theory, which describes systems in terms of how they change, this tug of war between the two mutually exclusive representations happens when the system is in a region nearly perfectly equidistant between two point attractors. This region is a kind of plateau in the state space, called a saddle point, where the system has little energy and can, for a while, move only very slowly toward one or the other attractor. However, once it reaches the edge between the saddle point and one of the attractor basins (almost like a cliff in the state space), the system very quickly gravitates toward that nearest point attractor—much like pattern-completing a population code.

In addition to quantitative simulations helping one avoid mathematically impossible theoretical predictions, as noted early on in this chapter, simulations can also allow one to observe mathematically possible results that intuitions about the theory might tell us are impossible. For example, given the relatively simple equations involved in the normalized recurrence competition algorithm (equations 4.2–5), an intuitive assumption might be that whichever response category (integration node) starts out with the highest activation will eventually be the winning response category. In fact, most of the time, that *is* the case. But our intuitions are not always correct.

Once in a great while, these exploratory simulations came up with a result in which the initially most active integration node gave way to the initially second most active integration node, which then took over the probability space. Figure 4.17 shows just such a result. One of the integration nodes

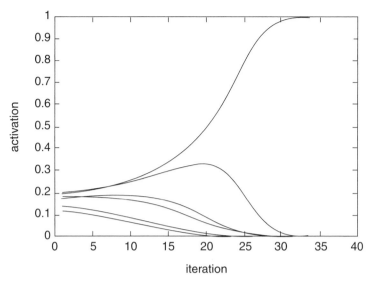

Figure 4.17. Activation curves from normalized recurrence showing a usurpation event.

started with an activation of 0.19469, whereas another integration node started with an activation of 0.19462. However, by the 10th iteration, those activation curves crossed one another, and the initially second most active integration node eventually won the competition. This is what has been called a gang effect (e.g., Zemel & Mozer, 2001), in which the arrangement and varying strengths of the different attractors in the state space elicit a nonlinear trajectory that causes the system to settle *not* into the attractor with the shortest Euclidean distance from the starting point, but instead to settle into a different attractor. It is as if the other attractors gang up against the initially closest attractor, causing it to lose the competition.

On examination, it is clear that what allows normalized recurrence to exhibit this nonmonotonic behavior is actually quite simple. Occasionally, an integration node will have all but one of its supporting input nodes highly active, with the remaining input node very close to zero probability. The initial average of these inputs may still be higher than the averaged input to any other integration node. However, to own the entire probability space (at the end of competition), *all* of an integration node's supporters must be at 1.0 themselves. And because the feedback in normalized recurrence is multiplicative, a supporting input that is very close to zero probability will almost never be coerced into reaching 1.0.

These exploratory simulations clearly demonstrate that one's intuitions about a theory can often be faulty, and a computational implementation can occasionally reveal unknown capabilities in the theory. With quantitative implementations of our theories, particularly ones that are at least generally consistent with the basic principles of neuroscience, the science of the mind can prevent intuitive interpretations of theories from leading us astray and can point us toward some fundamental principles of perception, action, and cognition (see Seidenberg, 1993). Moreover, with the help of research in neuroscience and cognitive neuroscience, implemented simulations provide a way to imagine "peeking inside" and catching a glimpse of the graded, fuzzy, partially overlapping representations that underlie our more easily observable (and sometimes misleading) discrete motor outputs, and discrete theoretical claims.

From One Section to Another

In the previous section, the beautiful curves in figures 4.13–4.17 are evocative in their illustration of the smooth, continuous, and nonlinear interplay that takes place between probabilistic representations that are competing against one another as the system settles into an attractor. However, realistic natural cognition involves the system getting out of attractor basins as well. Not only is environmental stimulation usually continuously streaming into our sensory subsystems, but a neural population code itself will fatigue (or adapt), causing its attractor status to convert into a repellor status (recall the Necker cube discussion in chapter 1). Thus, as soon as one attractor basin is being confidently approached, changes in the sensory input (as well as changes in the system's internal parameters) are propelling the system to new and different regions of state space in the direction of another attractor basin. This continuous trajectory that constitutes mental activity compels cognitive scientists to explore experimental measures that are sensitive to this continuous process (see chapter 3), as well as theoretical frameworks that are consistent with its consequences (see chapter 5).

To address transitions from one attractor toward another, presenting *sequences* of individuated nonoverlapping stimuli to the input layer of an attractor network over time is a step in the right direction, but it is perhaps not enough. Even qualitative transitions over time in sensory streams are usually fundamentally continuous despite their apparent suddenness. Sensory input flows; it does not come in packages (e.g., Gibson, 1950). For example, when we listen to our native language being spoken, we feel as though the words are clearly separated by gaps of silence, when in fact they typically are not. In contrast, when listening to a language we barely know, we find it quite hard to segment one word from another. Similarly, artificial mini-languages, such as that designed by Saffran, Newport, and Aslin (1996), can be constructed to have no pauses between words. When one first listens to this speech stream, it sounds like a seamless flow of one syllable after another. However, the temporal statistics of the syllables reliably converge on a few triplets of syllables behaving like words in the mini-language, and people's guesses about these words (after a mere 20 minutes of exposure) are significantly above chance. Moreover, after many months of hearing these speech streams and knowing the words extremely well, the experimenters and their colleagues developed a compelling (albeit, illusory) phenomenological impression that there were pauses between the artificial words. Obviously, in such circumstances, it is not the speech stream that has changed; it is the listener. The speech stream is still a continuous flow of evenly timed syllable after syllable after syllable. Perhaps our attractor simulations of perception, cognition, and action should maintain this relative continuity of sensory input flow (e.g., as opposed to presenting one word/object at a time) and allow the nonlinear attractor dynamics intrinsic to the system to impose the apparent segmentation that leads to things like constituent structure.

Even in this case, however, the subcomponents (e.g., syllables) of the elements of interest (e.g., words) are still being presented to the system as individuated nonoverlapping stimuli. The finer time scale provides a better approximation of continuity, but it merely pushes the problem further down. What if one's interest was syllables and phonotactics? One interesting solution is to blend, somewhat, the patterns corresponding to temporally adjacent inputs. For example, McClelland and Elman's (1986) TRACE model of speech perception used patterns of afferent input that corresponded to the mixture of phonemic features that happens when the transition from one phoneme to another exhibits coarticulation. Coarticulation occurs when the shape and positioning of the tongue and mouth during production of one phoneme must change dramatically to produce a subsequent very different phoneme. The result is that the articulation of the subsequent phoneme is slightly skewed in the direction of the previous phoneme. An attractor network whose inputs are blended in a manner similar to this—or perhaps even just interleaving each time step of temporally discrete input with a time step of blended input—might more readily exhibit the spatiotemporal continuity inherent to sensory input, cognitive processing, and motor output.

That said, there are still those who would take issue with this assumed ubiquity of the spatiotemporal continuity of cognitive processing (e.g., Anderson, 1983; Dietrich & Markman, 2003; Marcus, 2001). In principle, it is conceivable that a part of the mind is blind to the details of the continuous metric state space devoted to perception and action, and all it actually receives is a series of symbolic outputs corresponding to instantaneous boundary crossings of the trajectory leaving one section of state space and entering another. If cognition thus treats the continuous (and often recurrent) flowing trajectory of perception and action more as a series of discretely labeled and nonmetric teleportations from one section to another, then *cognitive* psychology would indeed require a completely different format of experimental inquiry and theoretical analysis from the rest of perception and action.

Symbolic Dynamics?

It may sound like just another oxymoron—among the likes of "military intelligence," "compassionate conservatives," and "business ethics"—but "symbolic dynamics" is a legitimate field of inquiry in the mathematics of dynamical systems theory. In fact, symbolic dynamics have even been employed to study what happens as the logistic map (figure 4.8) transitions from an ordered regime to a chaotic regime (Bonanno & Menconi, 2002). In symbolic dynamics (see, Bollt et al., 2000; Crutchfield, 1994; Devaney, 2003; Robinson, 1998), a discretely delineated and internally contiguous region of state or phase space can be assigned a symbol that is categorically different from the symbol assigned to a neighboring (and abutting) delineated region of state or phase space (see also Casey, 1996; Cleeremans et al., 1989). As the continuous trajectory of the system's state moves into one region, the corresponding symbol is emitted, and when the trajectory then leaves that region and enters a different one, a new symbol is emitted. Figure 4.18 shows a vector landscape with two attractors (as in figure 1.1), and it has had symbolic thresholds (dashed lines) added to delineate each discrete region from its neighboring discrete regions. It is as if fences have been put up throughout the state space, and fence sitting is not allowed. As the system continuously changes state, moving through this vector landscape and eventually settling into one of the attractors, a new symbol is emitted each time the trajectory crosses a threshold. Thus, the thick solid line representing a continuous trajectory from location m to location n would produce the symbol sequence, BQY. The other possible symbol sequences allowed by this landscape (assuming one starts in A or B) are BQX, BRY, BPX, AQY, AQX, ARY, and APX. The attractor dynamics of this continuous vector field do not allow trajectories that would produce any other

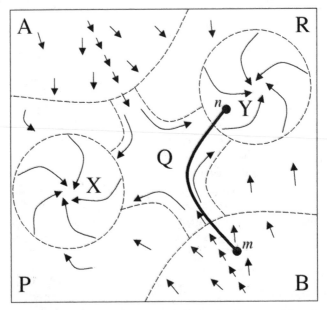

Figure 4.18. A simplified vector field that has been partitioned into discretely labeled regions.

sequences of symbols. Crucially, the system receiving the symbols emitted from this process has no direct information at all about the continuous dynamics of the original system's trajectory inside any delineated regions, much like classical claims regarding categorical perception (see chapter 6).

Interestingly, although the receiving system does not have access to the continuous dynamics within the original system, it is nonetheless capable of reconstructing an approximation of those continuous dynamics if it has a continuous state space of its own to work with (Takens, 1981). For example, if you take the famous Lorenz attractor as the original system (i.e., a sort of semi-recurring figure-eight pattern bent at the middle in a 3D space) and sample from it a single value corresponding to the trajectory's projection onto a randomly chosen vector in that space, you get a time series of numbers that waver around one narrow range of values and then quickly transition to wavering around another narrow range of values. A recurrent network with one input node, three hidden nodes, and one output node, using a prediction-based learning algorithm, can learn to mimic this one-dimensional time series. More important, when you plot a 3D graph of the hidden node activations over time, the network's trajectory looks just like the Lorenz attractor (Andrews, 2003). It can even work if symbolic thresholds are imposed on that one-dimensional time series and fed into the network as localist binary input vectors. Score one for symbolic communication, perhaps. But in the end, all this is not actually that surprising when one recognizes the simple fact that symbolic states are really nothing more than a special case within the space of possible continuous dynamic structures. A continuous metric state space logically subsumes the set of symbols that exist inside it.

The notion of regions of state space with symbolic meanings assigned to them may sound a bit similar to the way the notion of attractor basin has been treated so far. Although the discretely delineated regions of symbolic dynamics can share some commonalities with attractor basins, one critical difference is that in symbolic dynamics, a genuinely categorical threshold has been imposed (by someone or something) that determines when the system instantaneously enters or leaves a region. Exact placement of these thresholds, even with statistically sophisticated methods, can become a difficult process with dire consequences for imprecision (Bollt et al., 2000). With complex trajectories through the state space, ungrammatical or incoherent symbol strings can sometimes be emitted, thus producing a dramatic misrepresentation of the system's dynamics. This frailty of symbolic dynamics can be loosely likened to an electoral college system that carves up its voting body into subgroups, discretizing each subgroup's majority vote and then calculating a majority preference among the subgroups. Such a process can produce a peculiar error in democracy, where the subgroup majority preference calculation favors one symbolic result and the truer "one element one vote" calculation favors another.

In contrast, with attractor basins—even very steep and deep ones—the transition from "outside" to "inside" (or vice versa) is always genuinely continuous in its actual mathematical form. Thus, to the extent that attractor basins are similar to symbols, they might perhaps be loosely thought of as fuzzy symbols. In fact, because normalized recurrence uses probabilistic localist representations, it could be described as exhibiting a kind of *fuzzy* symbolic dynamics. Note, however, that I am not suggesting that some fuzzy logic–based module in the mind receives these emitted fuzzy symbols and tracks their competition to select among potential interpretations or motor actions. The purpose of converting the true continuous dynamics of a high-dimensional state space into a fuzzy symbolic dynamics of a low-dimensional state space is solely for the purpose of allowing the scientist/observer to more easily describe, understand, and communicate the behavior of the system. The neural system itself, which is of course being very abstractly simulated by a localist attractor network, need not include any discrete symbolics at all in its dynamical processes.

Chapters 6 to 9, in particular, will illustrate a number of experimental demonstrations of perceptual/cognitive phenomena in categorization, language, vision, and action that appear to still be using the continuous parameters of the system's trajectory through its state space, rather than relying solely on symbols extracted from those dynamics. Besides, if there were a higher cognition part of the brain that truly performed symbolic dynamics on its continuous input, it would only have to convert those symbols right back into continuous state space trajectory coordinates over time for the motor system, which we know works that way (see chapter 9). Rather than the discretization of a continuous metric state space taking place in between perception and motor planning (the "categorical bottleneck," as it were), I submit instead that—to the extent that it takes place at all—it takes place *after* motor planning: during action itself. Our eyes fixate only one object at a time (and stay almost still for a few hundred milliseconds). Each hand typically grasps only one object at a time (although grasping and lifting is often performed in a remarkably fluid continuous motion). Our speech apparatus usually produces only one sound at a time (even then, sequential phonemes often exhibit coarticulation, where features of one phoneme are partially present during production of the other). The upshot of all this is that when you look at the dynamical perception-action loop, there does not appear to be any objective evidence for discrete symbolic internal representations anywhere (and even the apparent observations of discrete motor actions are not really perfect examples of discrete logical categories).

If there is a fundamental truth to symbolic mental representations being emitted from the continuous dynamical state space of perceptual areas of the brain and then being received and processed by cognitive areas of the brain that function in a logical rule-based manner and then being converted back into a continuous dynamic state space format for motor areas of the brain, then I will eat my hat. But if there is a more reasonable sounding account of how genuinely discrete logical symbols can exist inside a neural system that so regularly reveals itself as representing information via population codes (see Barber, Clark, & Anderson, 2003; Georgopoulos et al., 1982; Zemel,

Dayan, & Pouget, 1998), then it seems likely that it will come from the field of symbolic dynamics. To avoid the risk of concluding that distributed and continuously dynamic representations cannot possibly implement human cognition (in the same way that some apocryphal scientists concluded that bumble bees cannot possibly fly), the interdependence between algorithmic and implementational accounts of the mind should encourage researchers who advance symbolic accounts of mind (e.g., Dietrich & Markman, 2003; Marcus, 2001; Pinker & Ullman, 2002) to develop realistic neurophysiological accounts of how discrete symbols emerge from neural-like processes. Until then, imposing symbolic partitions onto continuous cognitive dynamics might be best likened to telling a geologist that her research should take into account national boundaries.

The Limitations of Existence Proofs

This chapter began with a call to arms based on the importance of developing explicit implemented models of one's theories. I have tried to make it clear that with simulations like these, scientists of the mind can extrapolate their data points to an imagined full account of the phenomena they study (like the blind men collaborating to sculpt a model elephant, rather than simply professing their individual impressions). Of course, there are many strategic ways to model existing data, and the true test of a model is its ability to naturally accommodate new data. This imagined full account then makes clear unambiguous predictions (which is more than can usually be said for unimplemented verbal descriptions of theories) that can be tested experimentally, thus providing further constraining information for revision of the model.

However, this prediction issue for quantitative models is often seen as walking a thin line. In certain circumstances, a verbal theory can make those empirical predictions by itself, without ever having to be mathematically or computationally implemented. Moreover, if the simulation comes up with a prediction that you didn't initially expect or predict from your theory, that may suggest that you have a poor understanding of how your model works. Thus, there is a catch-22: If the model offers no unexpected predictions, then it can get accused of providing nothing more than the theory already does, but if it offers surprising predictions, then it can get accused of being a black box with no informativeness about the process in question. What is missed by that attitude is the fact that theorists often have poor understandings of exactly how their own theories work (as clearly established by the sociobiologists early in this chapter)! A mathematical or computational implementation of a theory will often come up with what seems like a novel prediction from the theory, not so much because the model is poorly understood but because the theory was poorly understood in the first place.

Thus, it is still arguable that the first and most important result of witnessing a theory being implemented in a simulation or in an equation is the simple demonstration that this version of the model is internally consistent enough to at least function without breaking down or contradicting itself. When the functioning model successfully fits some existing empirical data, the model thus stands as an existence proof that this kind of theory can account for this particular sample of data and therefore is a viable (though certainly not the only possible) explanation of the given phenomena. However, when there are parameters in the model that can be freely set to whatever values are necessary, fitting existing data is often all too easy (see Roberts & Pashler, 2000)—perhaps not as easy as an aspiring taxi driver writing his own name, as Roberts and Pashler (2000) analogized, but still very easy. If a model cannot fit its target data, or if the taxi driver is unable to write his own name, then neither of them should be allowed on the road.

As it turns out, several criteria have been noted as important for model evaluation and selection. In their treatment of a collection of articles on written word recognition models, Jacobs and Grainger (1994) list the following: (1) descriptive adequacy (i.e., how well does the model fit the data it was designed to fit?), (2) generality (i.e., how broad is the dataset the model was designed to fit?), (3) simplicity (i.e., how many free parameters are involved in the model?), (4) falsifiability (i.e., are there hypothetical patterns of data that the model cannot fit?), (5) explanatory adequacy (i.e., does the model naturally account for new data, or does it require additional ad hoc assumptions/mechanisms?), and (6) neurobiological plausibility (i.e., is the model consistent with what is known about how neural systems work?). (See also Cutting's 2000 discussion of model flexibility as measured by cross-validation.)

Pitt, Myung, and Zhang (2002; see also Pitt & Myung, 2002) offer a method based on minimum description length (Rissanen, 1978) for combining such factors into a quantitative algorithm for producing ratings of competing psychological models. The upshot is that *generalizability* (a sort of combination of Jacobs and Grainger's 1994 "generality," and "explanatory adequacy," along with a "simplicity" component) is perhaps the most important ability for a successful model to exhibit. That is, a model that fits lots of existing data and, without significant adjustment, also fits new data, is a good model. This should not be surprising. But what is perhaps surprising is that it is the simpler models that tend to do better at generalizing to new data. Highly complex models frequently run the risk of overfitting the existing data, thus making it quite difficult for them to generalize to new data.

It has been argued that in psychology, descriptive adequacy—rather than generalizability—too often winds up being the only criterion used to advocate a particular model (Pitt, Myung, & Zhang, 2000; Roberts & Pashler, 2000). And the parameter setting conducted to achieve that descriptive adequacy is often not principled enough. Mapping the entire space of possible results from the full range of parameter values is important to know whether the model predicts a sufficiently narrow range of results. A model that can predict anything, even nonsensical data, doesn't really help anybody's theory (see Cutting et al., 1992). Of course, it is often the case that some combinations of parameter values are patently inconsistent with the theory being promoted by the model. In fact, with a model that is sufficiently generic to allow itself to instantiate versions of the competing theories, via the relevant parameter values, one can make controlled comparisons of theoretical accounts. For example, if one theory claims that *all* information sources are immediately combined to produce an interpretation of some stimulus array (all source weights > 0), and a competing theory claims that certain information sources initially *do not* contribute to the interpretation (certain source weights equal 0 for an initial period of time), this can be implemented as two versions of the model simply by setting those parameters appropriately and comparing their respective results to existing and future empirical data. May the best model win. Exactly this kind of procedure has in fact been carried out with normalized recurrence (see McRae et al., 1998). For psychological modeling to do more than precisely explicate a theory and provide existence proofs but to actually adjudicate among competing theories, opposing theorists may need to eventually agree on relatively generic modeling frameworks, such as symbolic dynamics, and convert their theories into parameter value ranges that correspond to their respective theories (see Dale & Spivey, 2005).

5

Constructive Feedback for Modularity

The limits of modularity are also likely to be the limits of what we are going to be able to understand about the mind, given anything like the theoretical apparatus currently available.
—Jerry Fodor

When the independent displacement of particles in a distribution brings about reciprocal influences, the relations within such a distribution are no longer summative. In this case, one displacement can and will determine other displacements—and we now have a "physical *system.*" With increasing mutual dependence among the parts, we reach systems where no displacement or change of state is without its influence throughout the entire system.
—Wolfgang Köhler (translated by Willis Ellis)

On Paradigm Shifts and State Transitions

As early as the 1920s, Wolfgang Köhler had noticed that the continuous dynamical mathematics that were just starting to be explored in physics and chemistry might actually be relevant to understanding how the brain works. Dynamical systems theory was a nascent theoretical apparatus that was suddenly solving problems that had been vexing those scientists for decades. This theoretical apparatus, however, was largely ignored in psychology during the behaviorist years, and it continued to be suppressed throughout the cognitive revolution. Perhaps it is only now, in the twenty-first century, that dynamical systems theories designed specifically for handling nonmodular phenomena with long-range interactions—a theoretical apparatus that Köhler (1922/1938) tried to promulgate and Fodor (1983) lamented wasn't available—can finally get a fair chance to prove their value for studying the mind.

In that cognitive revolution of the 1960s, it is curious what changed and what didn't change in how we study the mind. As behaviorism was giving way, the field was once again allowing itself to refer to internal mental events, but the two-step feedforward reflex arc common to behaviorism remained, just with a new name: "stimulus → response" was merely replaced with "stimulus → interpretation." In 1967, Ulric Neisser's book, *Cognitive Psychology*, marshaled contemporary experimental evidence from a wide range of psychologists showing that internal mental constructs could indeed be measured in the laboratory and described in a theoretically rigorous fashion. This book changed psychology by legitimating and popularizing the information-processing approach to cognition. It was the swift metatheoretical kick to the head that the field needed to finally relinquish its obsession with behaviorism (another movement that made its own seminal contributions before outliving its usefulness) and the prohibition of the postulation of mental constructs. Many important advances in our understanding of the mind resulted from this information-processing movement. However, almost 40 years later, psychology and the cognitive sciences may be in need of another metatheoretical kick to the head.[1] This time, though, it looks as though that kick may not be quite so swift. The cognitive sciences may require more than one book to galvanize such a paradigm shift. The book in your hands stands on the shoulders of similar works produced by dynamically minded perceptual-cognitive theorists such as Thelen and Smith (1994), Kelso (1995), Port and van Gelder (1995), Elman et al. (1996), A. Clark (1997), J. Prinz (2002), and Ward (2002). In the way that Neisser's *Cognitive Psychology* helped identify the commonalities and channel the efforts of experimental psychologists, psycholinguists, philosophers of mind, linguists, and artificial intelligence researchers, *The Continuity of Mind*, along with these related books, aims to identify the commonalities and channel the efforts of dynamical systems theorists, connectionists, ecological psychologists, cognitive neuroscientists, and computational neuroscientists. The experimental findings and line of argumentation that permeate this book are intended to increase the probability further still that a gradual state transition can occur in the cognitive sciences, such that old-fashioned, no-longer-workable metaphors for describing mental activity in terms of rules and symbols get properly backgrounded in favor of more fluid and dynamic concepts of intermediating mental activity that is distributed both in time and in representational space. However, to do this, there are some roadblocks that we need to get out of the way first. Modularity is one of those roadblocks.

A Philosopher's Evidence

In arguing for modularity, it has been popular among philosophers of mind to note that one's knowledge that a visual illusion is illusory is not sufficient to eliminate the illusory percept (Fodor, 1983). For example, I can honestly tell you that the two horizontal lines in the Müller-Lyer illusion (figure 5.1) are of equal length. Yet that knowledge is not enough to make the illusion go away. The line with outward-fanning wings still appears longer than the line with inward-fanning wings. Regardless of the perceptual mechanism for this illusion, the fact that it seems impervious to higher level knowledge is often taken as empirical evidence for the absence of top-down influences on perceptual modules. Note, however, that you wouldn't really want top-down influences to

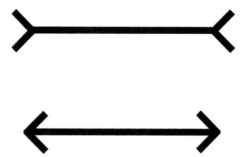

Figure 5.1. In the Müller-Lyer illusion the horizontal bar with outward-fanning lines appears longer than the one with inward-fanning lines. But the top-down knowledge that it is an illusion does not eliminate the perceptual effect.

be so strong that they completely overturn a perceptual representation (illusory or veridical), because then you would risk perceiving only what you *want* to perceive and not what's really out there. Instead, the top-down influences that are suggested by the ubiquitous feedback projections seen in the neuroanatomy should, at best, be capable of *subtly modifying* perceptual representations—not summarily rewriting them.

It could very well be that the Müller-Lyer illusion is indeed quantitatively milder after one is informed that the two lines are actually the same length. It may just be difficult to introspectively discern (or test without response bias) the reduction in illusion magnitude that takes place. Other visual illusions may lend themselves more readily to quantitative measures of their magnitude without response bias. Figure 5.2 shows the tilt aftereffect, first discovered by Gibson (1933). In this illusion, you start out by looking at one of the tilted gratings in the upper row for a full minute. Let your eyes roam around the middle of the grating, rather than holding your gaze fixed and motionless, so that you avoid forming a brightness-contrast afterimage. When the minute is up, move your eyes to one of the vertical gratings in the lower row. It will appear not quite vertical, but instead tilted slightly counterclockwise. One can measure the magnitude of this illusion by having the observer rotate the grating until it is perceived as perfectly vertical. Observers typically set the grating a couple degrees clockwise, indicating that their visual illusion involved the vertical grating appearing tilted about two degrees counterclockwise.

What's crucial for the argument here is that this visual illusion has been demonstrated to be subtly but reliably modulated by top-down influences. Rather than fixating directly on a grating, if you instead keep your gaze inside the center circle of the upper row for a full minute and then move your eyes to the lower circle, you will get mild tilt aftereffects (of equal magnitude) for both the left and right vertical gratings in your peripheral vision. But what if you direct your visuospatial attention during that minute of adaptation

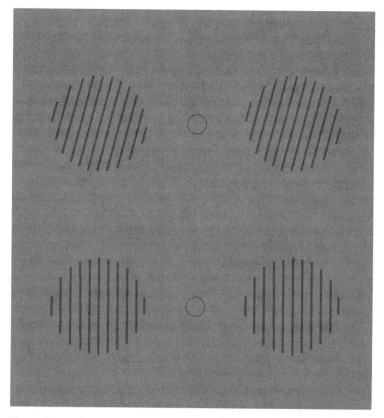

Figure 5.2. Visuospatial attention can modulate the strength of the tilt aftereffect (see text for details).

toward only one of the upper gratings—say, the left-hand grating—while keeping your eyes inside the upper circle? It may feel awkward to have your attention on the upper left-hand grating while maintaining eye fixation on the upper circle, and you may notice your attention wandering a bit during that minute. If you keep pushing your attention, but not your eyes, toward that left-hand grating, when you finally move your eyes down to the lower circle, you may notice that the left-hand grating (on that lower row) appears slightly *more* tilted counter-clockwise than the right-hand grating. The experimental data showed that the illusion was about 25% greater on the attended side than on the unattended side (Spivey & Spirn, 2000; see also Chaudhuri, 1990; Durgin, 2002; and Shulman, 1992, for similar attentional influences on different illusions).

Although it is not the same thing as higher level knowledge, this voluntary manipulation of endogenous spatial attention is clearly something that initiates within association cortex, as it is instigated by an experimenter instruction and mediated by a decision to comply. Therefore, the visual cortical area in which the tilt aftereffect illusion takes place—most likely, primary visual cortex (Bednar & Miikkulainen, 2000; Blakemore & Campbell, 1969)—is clearly being subtly influenced by feedback signals from association cortex (e.g., Brefczynski & DeYoe, 1999; Dragoi, Sharma, & Sur, 2000; Lamme & Roelfsema, 2000). Although the synaptic projections that send feedback signals to the perceptual systems are not capable of completely overriding the local pattern of information in visual cortex, they are clearly capable of subtly modulating it. Thus, contrary to the philosopher's introspections, even visual illusions are not impervious to top-down influences.

Modularity Versus Distribularity

Of course, it will take more than an illusion to vanquish this wily foe that people refer to as modularity. There are at least two definitions of the term *module*—one used by cognitive scientists and one used by neuroscientists. The use of the same technical term for importantly different concepts is often at the root of scientific debates and confusions, and the modularity debate in the cognitive and neural sciences is no exception. Cognitive scientists tend to rely on Fodor's (1983) definition of modularity, which depends heavily on the computer metaphor of the mind. Fodor claimed that sensory input systems were linear feedforward encapsulated information processors whose internal workings were already becoming well understood via standard reductive scientific means. Interestingly, he suggested that high-level cognitive processes were probably interactive, nonmodular, and as such were unlikely to ever be understood by science as he knows it. I am actually inclined to agree with him on that point, but with the following proviso: Given the evidence for interaction among perceptual systems, which I will recount in this chapter, I would add that the perceptual systems themselves will also never be understood by science as Fodor knows it. The new theoretical apparatus that can allow science to get a handle on richly interactive autocatalytic processes—and which has been successfully employed in chemistry and biology but has barely had a chance to scratch the surface so far in psychology (see Turvey, 2004)—is complex dynamical systems theory. This most definitely is not science as Fodor knows it. Complex dynamical systems theory acknowledges the fact that many systems of interest are *open* systems and therefore cannot be fully analyzed via encapsulated reductionism, because some of the parameters that drive an open system's behavior are not internal to the system. We could be talking at the level of a phonological module embedded within the language system (e.g., Elman & McClelland, 1988; Magnuson et al., 2003; Pitt & McQueen, 1998), a vision module embedded within a brain (see Churchland, Ramachandran, & Sejnowski, 1994; Zeki, 1993), a brain embedded within a body (Barsalou, 1999; Varela, Thompson, & Rosch, 1992), or an organism embedded within an environment (Gibson, 1979; Shaw & Turvey, 1999). In each case, the accumulating data suggest that the system of interest is not encapsulated from its larger embedding system and is therefore not a Fodorian module.

In contrast to Fodor's definition, when real neuroscientists use the word *module*, they start with portions of neural tissue that have anatomical separations from nearby portions of tissue or have morphological differences from one another in cell shapes. If these different anatomical areas also appear to have different selectivities to properties of environmental stimulation, then they may apply the label *module*. However, it is generally the case that any pair of neural modules that are connected by a synaptic projection share their signal transmissions *bidirectionally* (see Felleman & Van Essen, 1991). This neuroanatomical fact is quite problematic for Fodor's original version of modularity. Information encapsulation goes out the window when module A is sending feedforward signals to module B, and at the same time module B is sending feedback signals right back to module A. For example, the vast majority of neural projections connecting the lateral geniculate nucleus (LGN) and primary visual cortex are feedback synapses (Churchland & Sejnowski, 1992; see also Webb et al., 2002). Thus, despite most perception textbooks describing early vision as involving LGN sending visual signals to the primary visual cortex, it appears that the bulk of what that bundle of neural fibers is doing is allowing primary visual cortex to tell LGN what to do!

It is, of course, true that not every cortical region is directly connected to every other cortical region. This is part of why full equipotentiality (the extreme opposite of modularity) is also not an accurate description of the brain. However, most cortical regions have at least indirect connections with just about any other cortical region through one or two relays (Palm, 1982). This makes the relationships among neural subsystems in cortex a bit like a small-world network (Kleinberg, 2000; Watts & Strogatz, 1998), with no more than a couple degrees of separation between any two perceptual/cognitive processes (Sporns et al., 2004). Importantly, this kind of soft modularity—in which separate anatomical regions are roughly specialized for one or another perceptual/cognitive function but share some of their processes continuously—does not need to be innately specified but can instead emerge as a result of learning (Elman et al., 1996; Karmiloff-Smith, 1992). For example, visual motion perception is substantially influenced by color information early in a child's development (Dobkins & Anderson, 2002), but over the years the two information sources become somewhat more independent of one another (Zeki, 1993; but see Treue & Martinez-Trujillo, 1999). Moreover, the topographical layout of the somatosensory homunculus can get significantly reorganized after amputation of a hand (Farne et al., 2002; see also Merzenich et al., 1984). And neural network simulations readily demonstrate how separate modules with only subtle and abstract computational differences can, over the course of learning, *become* specialized for nonoverlapping cognitive aspects of the sensory input (Jacobs, Jordan, & Barto, 1991).

Somewhere in between cognitive scientists and real neuroscientists, cognitive neuroscientists who use case studies of patients with brain damage, as well as neuroimaging techniques, appear to be developing some form of third, hybrid version of the term *module* that is not quite naive enough to assume true information encapsulation, but nonetheless places great emphasis on functional specificity, such that a cortical module is often treated as though it has one and only one perceptual/cognitive job. A common method for putatively revealing such independent processes is double dissociation. In a double dissociation design, brain damage in one region causes impaired performance on task A but normal performance on task B, whereas brain damage in a different region causes normal performance on task A and impaired performance on task B. Such a result is routinely interpreted as evidence for the two different brain regions being independently devoted to the two different tasks. It is, however, problematic to interpret this kind of result as evidence for independent processes, because neural networks and other complex dynamical systems can readily produce double dissociations even when their physical architecture is essentially monolithic and unsegmented (Chater & Ganis, 1991; Plaut, 1995; Van Orden, Jansen op de Haar, & Bosman, 1997). Similarly, reports of category-specific deficits (such as being unable to name fruits and vegetables), which are often used as evidence in favor of stage-based modular accounts of cognition (Hillis & Caramazza, 1991), do not result only from localized damage to some module putatively devoted to that skill. They can also arise from widespread neural degeneration (such as that caused by Alzheimer's disease), and in neural network simulations, focal lesions and broadly distributed mild damage can each elicit category-specific deficits in the network's performance (Devlin et al., 1998). Essentially, each cortical area's "separate job" is likely to be partially overlapping with some other jobs, because the cascaded bidirectional connections between different regions indicate that they unavoidably share each other's responsibilities to some extent. These modules must know at least a little bit about how each of their neighbors carry out their tasks.

In fact, when one module is damaged or altered somehow, other modules that don't normally perform much of that module's job are often able to take up the slack in a matter of weeks or months. For example, when a monkey's visual motion perception areas (MT and MST) are permanently ablated, the monkey is unable to perform visual motion perception tasks, but much of this deficit lasts only a few weeks or so (e.g., Newsome & Paré, 1988; Pasternak & Merigan, 1994; Rudolph & Pasternak, 1999). With training, other visual areas can quickly learn to perform many of the motion perception abilities previously performed by MT and MST. Moreover, in the ferret, when visual nerve fibers from the thalamus are redirected to auditory cortex (instead of visual cortex) during early development (Pallas & Sur, 1993), auditory cortex neurons develop visual receptive fields that are quite similar to what is normally seen in the visual cortex, exhibiting selectivity for different spatial frequencies (von Melchner, Pallas, & Sur, 2000) and for different orientations (Sharma, Angelucci, & Sur, 2000). In fact, a cortical map can even develop a patterned structure that was never present in that species in the first place. For example, a frog has a separate visual tectum for each of its eyes, but when a third eye is surgically implanted in its forehead during early development, one of the tecti will learn to accommodate the incoming synapses from that supernumerary eye. With that extra optic nerve being directed toward one of those tecti, the frog will develop systematic ocular dominance columns (stripe-shaped regions devoted to one or the other eye) on that tectum, as the two eyes learn to share space on that one topographic map (Constantine-Paton & Law, 1978; Law & Constantine-Paton, 1981). Frogs don't have ocular dominance columns, but the brain of the laboratory-designed three-eyed frog learns how to make them anyway. What these three quick examples show is that cortical areas do not necessarily need to innately know the structure of the sensory input that they are going to have to deal with as they develop. The structure is in the statistics of the environmental stimulation, and over the course of learning, that structure operates on and molds the connectivity of the cortical area receiving it—not the other way around.

The playful term *distribularity*, informally coined by Barbara Finlay (see discussion of this kind of concept in Kingsbury & Finlay, 2001), refers to a sort of middle ground between fully distributed processing that is equipotential throughout the brain (e.g., Lashley, 1950) and fully modular processing that involves one encapsulated module per mental faculty (e.g., Fodor, 1983). According to distribularity, there is anatomical modularity in the sense that real neuroscientists use. However, the real-time processing of each of these neural modules (as well as their development) is not independent of the others. Their population codes and their analog computations are shared substantially between one another (see Haxby et al., 2001).

This chapter will not be debunking the version of modularity defined by real neuroscientists. That version is more or less inarguable, given concrete anatomical and neurophysiological evidence. The version of modularity that this chapter will be debunking is Fodor's (1983) information-encapsulation version that still manages to permeate and implicitly motivate theory development in much of present-day cognitive science. By replacing Fodorian modularity with a notion of distribularity, where anatomically distinct and partially specialized neural subsystems continuously exchange a substantial portion of their activity patterns, we will keep our theories closer to the neurophysiological and behavioral facts on the ground.

Fuzzy Borders in State Space

This partial specialization of neural subsystems endorsed by a distribularity framework may initially seem like a difficult property to instill in a mathematical description where neuronal activations across the entire brain are envisioned to form a *single* very high-dimensional state space. The way one can imagine a graded (nondiscrete) independence between functionally specialized brain regions in this framework is to consider how one cortical area might be described by a particular hyperplane in the global state space, and another cortical area would have a different hyperplane. If the two brain areas

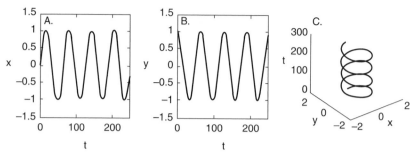

Figure 5.3. A sine wave and an uncorrelated cosine wave (A and B) shown together in time (C).

are richly interactive, then the activations in their respective hyperplanes will be significantly correlated (or anticorrelated). If, however, the two brain areas in question are independent of one another, then their respective activation patterns will not be especially correlated with one another. Nonetheless, the global state space (i.e., the full set of conjoined hyperplanes, correlated and uncorrelated) will still be a valid and informative monolithic format of description of the system's states over time. In terms of this global state space description, the correlational patterns in activity would result in regions of the global state space that the trajectory tends not to visit and fuzzy borders that it tends not to cross.

For a highly simplified example, consider two different one-dimensional systems and their conjoint description. One subprocessor produces a sine wave over time, and the other subprocessor produces a cosine wave over time. They can reasonably be described in terms of two separate state spaces since they are completely uncorrelated (figures 5.3A and B), but they can also be described in terms of one conjoined state space (figure 5.3C). The circular spiral over time, in figure 5.3C, shows how the values of x and of y spend equal time in their ranges of relative values. Thus the conjoined state space description, although not required (because x and y are uncorrelated), is nonetheless an informative depiction of the data. Now, if x and y happen to be positively correlated (figure 5.4) or negatively correlated (figure 5.5), we observe a

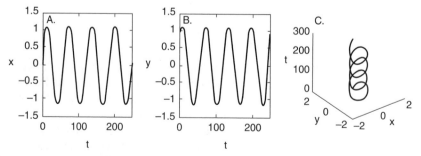

Figure 5.4. A sine wave and a positively correlated cosine wave (A and B) shown together in time (C).

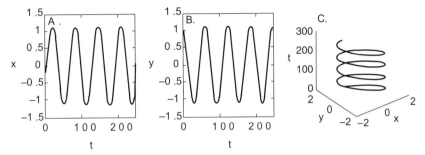

Figure 5.5. A sine wave and a negatively correlated cosine wave (A and B) shown together in time (C).

decidedly elliptical rather than circular spiral over time. That is, only a restricted range of relative values of x and y are ever visited. In such cases, not only is it informative to analyze the conjoined state space, indeed it is crucial—as analyzing either subspace by itself will prevent one from detecting the relationship.

In fact, it is very much this kind of logic that led Haxby and colleagues (2001; see also Hanson, Matsuka, & Haxby, 2004) to perform correlational analyses on fMRI activity across a variety of brain regions during face recognition. They found that even when they excluded data from the fusiform face area, a region hypothesized to be the face recognition module (Epstein & Kanwisher, 1998), the pattern of low-level activity across the remaining regions within the ventral temporal cortex carried enough information to discriminate between various faces and five different categories of man-made objects. They concluded that face and object recognition involves partly overlapping representations that are distributed across multiple cortical regions in ventral temporal cortex—not independent representations that are localized solely to individual regions. Thus, the relevant state space for describing the temporal dynamics of something like face recognition includes not just dimensions derived from the fusiform face area, but also dimensions from a variety of other brain areas. That is, the face recognition state space, within which a trajectory would define the process of recognizing a face, is a much more global state space than a localized one.

The "Outer Space" of the Mind

Some readers may be finding this "continuous trajectory through a global state space" story somewhat objectionable. But in fact, it is actually mathematically uncontestable that mental content can be described in terms of a location in a high-dimensional state space, as described in chapter 4. This is not hypothesis; it is fact. Whether or not you like this form of description, it is mathematically true that if you treat the averaged activation of each neuron in the brain as a dimension in state space, then any given freeze-frame of the brain's state will be a location in that global state space. Crucially, if the sliding temporal window for computing that average activation is more than just a few milliseconds wide, then a sequence of multiple such freeze-frames will look like a remarkably smooth trajectory through that state space.

One might counter that the neurons studied by most neuroscientists appear to send their signals in the form of one-millisecond action potentials, rather than graded potentials. Thus, the fundamental quanta of the mind are temporally and informationally discrete. However, the brain's neurons are not all in lockstep to the ticking of a single clock.[2] The transition from one millisecond to another is not characterized by a transition from one set of neurons being in midspike to another set of neurons being in midspike. In fact, even an individual action potential, lasting about 1 millisecond, does not instantaneously jump to +25 millivolts and hold steady there for the full 1,000 microseconds, and then jump back to –60 millivolts. An action potential is a gradual fluctuation of electrochemical differential, starting from about –60 millivolts at resting level, through a 100-microsecond rising phase up to about –45 millivolts, peaking at +25 millivolts about halfway through, and then going through a repolarization phase for several hundred microseconds, and eventually into a hyperpolarization phase where it's around –70 millivolts for a whole other millisecond. Thus, if you were to take a frozen microsecond of the brain's neuronal activity, that microsecond would show most neurons at resting level, some neurons in hyperpolarization phase, fewer neurons in depolarization phase, fewer still in rising phase, and (depending on how you define *peak*) the fewest neurons would be at their ever-so-briefly visited peak of electrical potential. With this wildly staggered array of nonaligned time frames, holding a stable bit-vector pattern of activation to function as a discrete conceptual symbol would be impossible.

This is why, in addition to examining very short bursts of spikes for their individual timing (Bohte, 2004; Softky, 1996) and relative latency (Maass, 1997), many neuroscientists average over larger chunks of a few dozen milliseconds when calculating the activation of a neuron in terms of its average firing rate (Shadlen & Newsome, 1994; see Fairhall et al., 2001, for some discussion of rate coding, burst coding, and individual spike coding). A sliding window for averaging this firing rate would thus describe transitions from one briefly semi-stable population code to another in a manner that unavoidably involved instantiating patterns of activity that were partial blends in between the previous population code and the upcoming population code—and probably exhibiting some similarity with other nonvisited population codes as well. In terms of a state space that encompassed these population codes in the form of attractor basins, the result would be a trajectory that visits one attractor basin and, on its way to another, vaguely flirts with several others in the "outer space" of the mind.

When you listen to someone talking to you, you may feel as though you fully understand one word and then suddenly fully understand the next word, and so on, like a sequence of discrete linguistic symbols. And when your eyes scan around a complex scene, you may feel as though you fully recognize one object and then suddenly fully recognize the next object, and so on, like a sequence of logical entries on an inventory list. However, in both cases, the psychological and neurophysiological evidence recounted throughout this book clearly demonstrate that your mind is doing most of its work in between those seemingly discrete recognition events. When someone is talking to you, your mind is partly understanding each incoming word as a mélange of potential words, and by the time it settles on a unique word that it thinks it has heard, the next word is already coming in, launching the mind into another blended dynamic comprehension process. The same is true for when your eyes are scanning a complex scene. The key question is whether this description opens up new conceptualizations of human data and experimental methodologies that are not readily available with discrete symbolic descriptive formats. It is particularly the goal of chapters 6–9 to convince you that the answer to that question is an emphatic *yes*.

The format of a high-dimensional state space is sufficiently flexible that it can even be used to describe an idealized version of a discretely symbolic cognition. For example, the mathematics of symbolic dynamics (see chapters 4 and 10) is designed to take a continuous trajectory in a metric state space, or phase space, record when that trajectory enters specified volumetric regions, and emit (to another system) symbol labels that belong to those regions. Alternatively, a discrete symbolic cognition would involve the trajectory, essentially teleporting from corner to corner in the state space—much as a digital computer does in its flip-flopping of CPU states.[3] Either of these symbolic frameworks would allow separate neural subsystems to share only limited (and discretely computable) information with one another, as Fodor's modularity hypothesis predicted. Thus, they would exhibit *component-dominant dynamics*, such that the various subsystems' internal processing dynamics provide the key information about how the overall system works. A lexical system would wait until it received enough input and performed enough internal computations to reach a stable state before it passed the result of its computations on to a semantic system. The same would hold for phonology and the lexicon, syntax and semantics, syntax and discourse, and even for language and vision in general.

However, if these various subsystems involved in different aspects of perception, cognition, and action were all to cascade continuous updates of their respective patterns of activation to one another, they would be sufficiently nonmodular to no longer exhibit component-dominant dynamics and would instead exhibit *interaction-dominant dynamics*. That is, as the temporal granularity of the information transmission between subsystems gets finer (see Miller, 1982), the behavior of such a system will unavoidably conform less and less to the modularity hypothesis.[4] Cascaded integration of multiple information sources tends to produce multifarious patterns of activation that are unstable and do not straightforwardly map onto unique coherent motor outputs.

What is needed, then, is a process by which the initially multifarious pattern can settle into a unitary stable pattern at least long enough to produce motor output. As suggested in chapter 4, competition between population codes may be this very process (e.g., Keysers & Perett, 2002). Crucially, as argued in chapter 3, to report compelling evidence for this neural competition process, one needs experimental methods that can provide a glimpse of the partial activation of the competing alternatives *before one of them wins* (see Enns & Di Lollo, 2002). Cascading interactive systems such as this, composed of richly intermeshed subsystems, are better understood by analyzing how the components interact and produce emergent patterns between them (e.g., Van Orden, Moreno, & Holden, 2003), than by dividing and conquering the individual components themselves. The next few pages will review a wide variety of cross-modal interactions in perception and cognition, showing that the mind exhibits interaction-dominant dynamics rather than component-dominant dynamics, thus ruling out Fodor's (1983) version of the modularity hypothesis.

Transcortical Interactions

There are quite a few examples of perceptual systems interacting in ways that Fodorian modularity assumed would be impossible. In the brief treatment in this section, I start with some examples of visual features interacting with one another, which caused problems for traditional views of visual perception being composed of separate channels for independent feature extraction. I then move on to a wide array of perceptual interactions across vision, touch, audition, and speech. Although minuscule in comparison to the actual body of literature, this section should provide sufficient sampling of the data to make the case that Fodorian modularity is severely evidentially challenged. For extensive reviews of cross-modal interactions, see Marks (1978), Welch and Warren (1986), Stein and Meredith (1993), Calvert (2001), and Spence and Driver (2004).

Despite early claims of encapsulated modules within visual cortex being devoted to nonoverlapping visual features, such as luminance, color, orientation, motion, and depth (Cavanagh, 1988; Lennie, 1980; Livingstone & Hubel, 1988), interactions between visual subsystems have been cropping up in the literature with increasing regularity. For example, a simultaneous version of the tilt aftereffect, called the tilt illusion (figure 5.6), is stronger when the surrounding tilted inducing annulus is of similar color and luminance to that of the vertical test grating in the middle (Clifford et al., 2003; see also McCollough, 1965, for related phenomena). Because the tilt illusion is believed to take place in primary visual cortex, this suggests that the separate channels for color, luminance, and orientation aren't that separate after all. In fact, recent evidence shows that there are cells in primary visual cortex that are selective for specific *combinations* of color, luminance, and orientation (Johnson, Hawken, & Shapley, 2001).

Figure 5.6. With simultaneous tilt contrast (or the tilt illusion), the central vertical grating looks tilted a couple degrees in the direction opposite that of the surrounding grating.

Similar findings are seen with color, surface segmentation, and motion perception. When visually segmenting a group of dots of one color from a background of dots of another color, the distribution of motion directions among the dots substantially affects performance (Møller & Hurlbert, 1997), indicating that color and motion processing are more interactive than once thought (see also Ruppertsberg, Wuerger, & Bertamini, 2003). Moreover, binocular disparity and surface transparency combine to produce depth information that reliably influences whether local motion signals are pooled into a single coherent movement direction (Trueswell & Hayhoe, 1993). Such immediate interactions between color, depth, and motion would not take place if these different visual features were processed by encapsulated modules that completed their jobs on their own and then shunted the finished results to a later cognitive stage.

Indeed, the neurophysiology suggests that intrinsic lateral connections within primary visual cortex may be responsible for simultaneous contextual influences of the kind just described (Stettler et al., 2002). These intrinsic lateral connections within primary visual cortex are denser than the feedback projections going into primary visual cortex and are more limited to regions of similar orientation specificities. Hence, the lateral connections are likely to be responsible for the cross-featural interactions, as well as for contour integration effects (Field, Hayes, & Hess, 1993), whereas the feedback projections are likely to be responsible for attentional modulation of those lateral processes (e.g., Gandhi, Heeger, & Boynton 1999; Ito & Gilbert, 1999; Lamme & Roelfsema, 2000; Motter, 1993).

Although these interactions among features *within vision* compromise traditional modular accounts of visual perception, perhaps what is more fundamental to debunking the modularity mindset in general is evidence for interactions *across entirely different perceptual modalities*. For example, although visual cortex is not active during most tactile tasks (Sadato et al., 1996), it is active during tactile discrimination of orientation (Sathian et al., 1997). Disrupting visual cortical processing via transcranial magnetic stimulation interferes with tactile discrimination of orientation (Zangaladze et al., 1999). Thus, visual imagery appears to be more than just associated with tactile processing, it plays a functional role in how tactile input is used to discriminate orientations. In fact, blind Braille readers exhibit activation of visual cortex during a variety of tactile tasks (Buchel et al., 1998; Sadato et al., 1996). Indeed, the many topographical maps in visual cortex are well suited for the spatial resolution necessary for Braille reading.

As it happens, Braille reading is not the only language-related task that involves cross-modal interactions. The visual input received during skilled silent lip reading elicits conspicuous activation of auditory cortex (Calvert et al., 1997). That is, even though no significant auditory input is being received, the lip reader's brain nonetheless sort of "hears" what is being said. And, of course, the McGurk effect is perhaps the most famous example of interaction between visual and linguistic processes. When you see a televised face repeatedly saying "ga-ga," but the audio stream from the speakers actually delivers "ba-ba" in synchrony with the movements of the mouth, you have a compelling percept of hearing "da-da" (McGurk & MacDonald, 1976). Basically, the acoustic-phonetic properties of the speech stream support a "ba-ba" percept, but the visual input, with the lips not touching during the consonant, rule out that percept. The next best match for those acoustic-phonetic properties is "da-da," which would not require the visual evidence of a bilabial stop, so "da-da" is the percept. If you close your eyes, the speech stream begins to sound like "ba-ba," but when you reopen your eyes, it returns to sounding like "da-da." Some of the extensions on that work are discussed in chapter 6.

Just as visual input can modulate an auditory percept, so can auditory input modulate a visual percept. For example, when a single flash of light is accompanied by two beeps, it is often perceived as two flashes of light (Shams, Kamitani, & Shimojo, 2000). When a leftward-moving circle and a rightward-moving circle are animated on a computer screen, the type of sound emitted when they pass through each other will influence how this event is perceived (Sekuler, Sekuler, & Lau, 1997). If the observer hears a *whoosh* sound just as the circles pass through each other, they will appear to travel past one another on slightly different depth planes. However, if the observer hears a *boing*, with exactly the same visual input, the two circles will appear to bounce off of each other and reverse their respective directions.

Visual and auditory inputs do not only affect the *way* each other is perceived, they also can affect the *location* from which the other event is perceived to originate. The basic trick of ventriloquism relies on people's tendency to attribute the location of visual motion as the source of a simultaneous auditory signal. This is why professional ventriloquists turn their head toward the dummy and hold themselves still while it talks. This way, the dummy's face is the only thing moving while the audience hears its voice. The ventriloquism effect has been studied quite extensively in perceptual psychology (e.g., Bertelson & Radeau, 1981; Howard & Templeton, 1966; Vroomen, Bertelson, & de Gelder, 2001), where it is generally found that the illusion reduces in magnitude with greater temporal asynchrony and greater spatial separation—and also with greater mismatch between visual and acoustic features (see Fisher & Pylyshyn, 1994).

One way to conceptualize how visual, auditory, and tactile signals are spatially integrated is in terms of a two-dimensional supramodal map of attentional salience. A universal map of external space, perhaps in parietal cortex, would explain how visual, auditory, and tactile cues succeed in orienting spatial attention for each other (Driver & Spence, 1998; Eimer, Van Velzen, & Driver, 2002). For example, when a brief tactile input is applied to the hand, a visual stimulus presented in the same general area a few hundred milliseconds thereafter is responded to faster than the same visual stimulus in a different (noncued) location. As long as the task allows the eyes to move around naturally, this cross-modal cuing of spatial attention seems to work in all pairwise combinations across vision, audition, and touch.[5] In fact, these cross-modal attentional influences even exhibit a kind of rebound effect, known as inhibition of return (Posner & Cohen, 1984). Several hundred milliseconds after spatial attention has been applied to a location, the salience of (or sensitivity to) that location goes *below* baseline for at least a few hundred milliseconds. Thus, if an auditory cue is presented in one location, and 100 milliseconds later a tactile stimulus is presented in the same location, participants will be faster to respond to that tactile stimulus. But if the delay between the two stimuli is 800 milliseconds instead of 100, participants will be conspicuously *slower* than baseline to respond to the tactile stimulus (Spence et al., 2000). Figure 5.7 is a schematic visual depiction of what a salience map might look like during the dynamic transition from increased attention at a cued location to conspicuously *decreased* attention (inhibition of return) soon thereafter. This illustration also includes a mild inhibitory surround (the small troughs on the spatial left and right of the salience peak) that circumscribes the attended region (see Cutzu & Tsotsos, 2003; Mounts, 2000).

Importantly, the merging of these different sensory inputs is not carried out solely by a feedforward integration process. The supramodal salience map appears to send feedback signals returning to the unimodal maps. For example, when an auditory cue involuntarily pulls visual attention to a particular location in space, this modulation of visual processing is detectable as increased activity in extrastriate visual cortex (McDonald & Ward, 2000; see also Eimer & Schröger, 1998; Hillyard et al., 1984). With the help of figure 5.8, one can think of it this way: Visual salience maps in visual cortical areas (e.g., Itti & Koch, 2001; Parkhurst, Law, & Niebur, 2002) combine with auditory salience maps in auditory areas and the inferior colliculus (e.g., King, 1999) to make supramodal salience maps in the posterior parietal cortex (Behrmann, Geng, & Shomstein, 2004) and the superior colliculus (King et al., 1988; Meredith, 2002; see also Knudsen & Knudsen, 1989), some of which then send polysensory feedback to the unimodal sensory systems (as shown by the bidirectional arrows in figure 5.8). A similar kind of arrangement can be envisioned for integrating (and feeding back) visual and tactile inputs as well (Macaluso, Frith, & Driver, 2000; Spence, McDonald, & Driver, 2004).

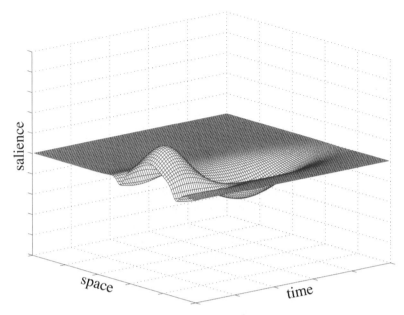

Figure 5.7. Part of a salience map over time, depicting the temporal dynamics of attentional facilitation at a cued location, flanked by some lateral inhibition, and followed by inhibition of return. Only one spatial dimension is depicted so that time and salience can also be graphed.

In figure 5.8, the salience maps are depicted as two-dimensional topographically arranged layers of neurons, where the height dimension indicates the increased sensitivity exhibited by a local group of neurons when their input is partially attended (or salient). The supramodal salience map continuously

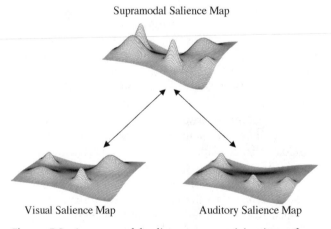

Figure 5.8. A supramodal salience map receiving input from and sending feedback to unimodal salience maps.

updates its pattern as a combination of the salience maps that feed into it. Thus, although this visual salience map has a conspicuously large peak on the far right portion of its surface, the auditory salience map has no such peak in that location, so the supramodal salience map does not exhibit a particularly competitive salience peak in that location. Note, however, that the feedback is likely to eventually induce some nonzero activation in that location in the auditory salience map. This may explain how the ventriloquism effect is so compelling. But in the freeze-frame of figure 5.8, the somewhat modest peak in the far left portion of the surface in both unimodal maps is what becomes the highest salience peak when combined at the supramodal map. This highest peak would likely be the target of the first saccade and would also strongly influence a continuous reaching movement. Thus, feedforward integration, coupled with recurrent feedback, allows different perceptual domains to influence one another in a manner that resolutely violates the modularity hypothesis.

Natural Interactive Tasks Reveal Natural Interactive Processing

There is a reason why the modularity hypothesis reigned supreme for as long as it did. There is a history—in both vision research and language research, actually—of perceptual-cognitive processing appearing quite modular when it is measured in highly restricted laboratory tasks that allow precise, real-time measures. Then, when improved methods allow those same real-time measures to be collected during more natural goal-oriented tasks, all of sudden perceptual-cognitive processing begins to appear more interactive. For example, in vision research, single-cell recordings with immobilized and anesthetized animals tended to produce evidence consistent with modular linear systems accounts of hierarchical receptive field structures (e.g., Livingstone & Hubel, 1988; Movshon, Thompson, & Tolhurst, 1978). However, when awake behaving monkeys are trained to perform goal-oriented perceptual-motor tasks while electrodes are busy recording from neurons in visual cortex, we see that visual neurons are influenced by a number of factors outside the scope of the classical receptive field (e.g., Gallant, Connor, & Van Essen, 1998; Motter, 1993). (See chapters 3 and 8 for more details.)

Similarly, in language research, when undergraduate experimental participants had to read isolated sentences on a computer screen in the dark while their head was held motionless so that a table-mounted eye tracker could record their eye movements, the millisecond timing of this measure tended to produce evidence for syntax being modular and independent of semantics and other contextual factors (e.g., Ferreira & Clifton, 1986; Rayner, Carlson, & Frazier, 1983; see chapter 7 for more details). In contrast, experiments with awake behaving undergraduates involved in rich contexts and goal-oriented tasks produced evidence consistent with the idea that syntax, semantics, and pragmatics interact fluidly (e.g., Bransford & Johnson, 1972; Clark & Carlson, 1982). Unfortunately, most of the psycholinguistic experiments from the 1970s and 1980s that exhibited this level of ecological validity did not involve online measures of performance with any substantial temporal resolution. Natural contexts and real-time measures seemed to be mutually exclusive properties for the experimental methods available to psycholinguistics at that time.

Interestingly, in the cases of both vision and language, head-mounted eye tracking has figured prominently in the mission to find ways to combine naturalistic task performance with real-time measures of perception and cognition (Ballard, Hayhoe, & Pelz, 1995; Gallant et al., 1998; Land & Lee, 1994; Tanenhaus et al., 1995). For example, by recording participants' eye movements while they carried out spoken instructions to move real objects around on a table, Tanenhaus and colleagues (1995) were able to do more than show that language was interactive or that vision was interactive. They showed that at a very fine time scale, vision and language interact with each other. Even partway through hearing a single word, the visual context can modulate the activations of potential lexical representations in real time (see chapter 7). Perhaps not surprisingly, demonstrating that visual context could "tell language what to do" didn't go over very well with parts of the psycholinguistic community. There was considerable resistance from those who had grown to think of their area of study as separate from visual perception—indeed, separate from the rest of cognition. However, when we presented these findings to vision researchers instead, they found them interesting, if perhaps a bit trivial. "Of course, vision would be important enough to boss language around! Those psycholinguists really should pay more attention to visual processes."

Ironically, this set of attitudes from the two fields reversed symmetrically when we later produced evidence for linguistic context modulating real-time visual processes. When the target identity for a visual conjunction search task is presented verbally over headphones (e.g., "Is there a red vertical?"), such that one hears one visual feature before hearing the next while viewing the display, the search is conducted more efficiently than if the target identity speech file is presented entirely before the display is presented (Reali et al., in press; Spivey et al., 2001). When we presented these findings to the psycholinguistic community, they found them interesting, if perhaps a bit trivial. "Of course, language would be important enough to boss vision around! Those vision researchers really should pay more attention to linguistic processes." And this time, the vision community resists. No one likes to be told that their favorite perceptual-cognitive faculty can be "told what to do" by some other perceptual-cognitive faculty.

The lesson is this: As real-time measures are developed that allow natural complex interactive behavior on the part of the experimental participant, natural complex interactive behavior is what will be observed among the perceptual-cognitive subsystems involved. When this general methodology is applied to syntax and semantics or to color and motion, the subsystems involved exhibit richly interactive functioning. When this general methodology is applied to language and vision together, the subsystems involved exhibit richly interactive functioning. Finally, when this general methodology is applied to the brain and its environment, once again the subsystems involved exhibit richly interactive functioning.

A New Theoretical Apparatus

The traditional theoretical apparatus of component-dominant dynamics cannot provide a good description of how the brain fluidly interacts with the world. Instead, interaction-dominant dynamics provide a more useful account, as demonstrated well by the relative timing between eye movements and cognitive processes. As indicated in chapter 1 (and illustrated numerous times in chapter 6, 7, 8, and 12), the brain does not achieve a stable percept, then make an eye movement, then achieve another stable percept, then make another eye movement, and so on. The eyes often move during the process of attempting to achieve a stable percept. This means that before perception can finish settling into a stable state, oculomotor output changes the perceptual input by placing new and different visual information on the foveas. Think of it this way: An initial eye fixation *causes* certain dynamical perceptual processes to be set in motion, which then (before they become stable) *cause* a new eye movement, which then allows different environmental properties to *cause* different dynamics in the perceptual process, which then *cause* yet another eye movement, and so on (see Findlay & Gilchrist, 2003; Gold & Shadlen, 2000; van der Heijden, 1996b; see also Spivey, Richardson, & Fitneva, 2004). Thus, visual perception is simultaneously the result of the environment's sensory input (caused by physical surfaces reflecting light onto the retinas) and of its own oculomotor output (caused by intermediate products of perception's analog computations). Because eye movements operate at a slightly faster time scale than does perceptual recognition, the perception–action cycle in this case becomes an autocatalytic causal loop—for which distinguishing the chicken from the egg becomes moot. Such a loop is called *impredicative* (Poincare, 1906; see also Russell, 1906) because it is composed of elements that can only be defined with reference to the larger system of which they are members (see Rosen, 2000). With impredicative systems, there can be no context-independent definition of each element, followed by a linear, feedforward, component-wise integration of those elements to build the larger system. Interactive self-organizing systems—such as avalanches and earthquakes (Bak, 1996), the Belousov-Zhabotinski reaction in chemistry (see Prigogine & Stengers, 1984), artificial neural networks that both evolve and learn (Beer, 1996), the human brain (Chialvo, 2004), and cognitive performance in general (Turvey, 2004; Van Orden, Holden, & Turvey, 2003)—are impredicative systems. Such systems are impossible to describe via modular component-dominant dynamics in particular and via simple reductionism in general.

As the quote at the beginning of this chapter indicates, in *The Modularity of Mind* (1983), Fodor warned us of the problems posed by fully interactive systems. Compared to modular systems, they are extremely difficult to analyze. In fact, Fodor all but said that perceptual systems had better be modular or we have no chance of ever understanding them. Perhaps, then, it is no wonder that some scientists still dig their heels in today in their attempt to maintain a modular characterization of perception. But Fodor also went further. He suggested that central systems, such as reasoning and problem solving, were *not* modular because they require such complex integration of information from varied sources. Thus, it becomes supremely ironic that as the modularity of perceptual input systems has gradually been dismissed over the past 20 years, the place where modularity enthusiasts have gone is to higher level cognition (such as lie detection modules, theory of mind modules, and mathematics modules)—precisely the place where Fodor claimed modules could not be found.

But when it comes down to it, the facts on the ground are the facts on the ground. We can lament the fact that perception and cognition are not modular—and therefore require far more complex measures, analyses, and models than previously used—but we cannot ignore it. What so many feared all along appears to be true: A new theoretical apparatus for studying the mind is indeed required after all. And a continuous nonlinear trajectory through a high-dimensional state space just might be that theoretical apparatus.

No Things in the Mind

Having armed yourself now with some appreciation for the methodological tools (chapter 3) and computational techniques (chapter 4) that reveal continuous mental dynamics, and now recounting some of the ways in which these dynamics interact between functional subsystems of the mind (this chapter), you should be prepared to withstand the upcoming onslaught of distributed dynamic cognitive phenomena in categorization (chapter 6), language (chapter 7), vision (chapter 8), action (chapter 9), and even reasoning (chapter 10). You will find throughout this book that I tend to mix my metaphors between dynamical systems and information processing terminologies. I will use terms like *mental trajectory* and even *dynamical representations*. For some die-hard dynamicists, this will undoubtedly be highly objectionable. Perhaps for some die-hard classical theorists, it will sound mealy mouthed. But for the growing numbers of disillusioned cognitive psychologists, these mixed metaphors will provide a much-needed bridge for making the trek from their training in the information processing framework toward a framework that is more amenable to the continuity of mind. In this new framework, there are no independent static objects in the mind; every mental entity is promiscuous in its content and continuous in its dynamics.

When we look at the vast array of perceptual-cognitive abilities that the human brain brandishes, it is often tempting to conclude that each ability has its own individual processor, a box for every job. However, much of the evidence described in this chapter and throughout this book points to a very different characterization. If our perceptual-cognitive abilities are not independent functions that only share their information with one another when their processing jobs are completed, but instead are interactive processes that distribute their duties across one another continuously, then it seems unlikely that these abilities are individually selected for in our evolutionary history (see Bechtel, 2003). If there are no such boxes in the head, then the evolution of mental faculties is likely to be a far more complex and interactive process than simply mapping each environmental pressure onto its own personalized evolved mental function. For example, Cosmides and Tooby's (1994) Swiss army knife metaphor for the collection of discrete cognitive abilities that evolution has bequeathed to us does not jive well at all with the kinds of richly interactive processing described in this chapter. Rather than a linearly combined collection of independent mechanisms, as implied by the Swiss army knife metaphor, perhaps Kingsbury and Finlay's (2001) woven plaid metaphor is more appropriate. In a woven plaid, there are identifiable patches that superficially look segmented from one another, a bit like a quilt. However, quite unlike a quilt, the substructure (and the construction) of a plaid's patches reveal complex and rich interdependencies among regions—as recounted throughout this chapter. Thus the field of evolutionary psychology would be wise to pay a visit to its theory pawn shop and trade in Cosmides and Tooby's Swiss army knife for Kingsbury and Finlay's woven plaid.

Just as there are no truly individuated tools in the mind, there are also no truly individuated units of mental activity in the mind either. When the information-processing theorist zooms in on one of those patches in the woven plaid, to look for the computational units that it processes, he will be disappointed. Although introspection about our own cognitive experience may tempt us to conclude that we think in sequences of individual symbolic units, mountains of evidence in the next five chapters strongly suggest otherwise. When real-time measures are applied to naturalistic tasks, not only do we observe more interaction between domains than previously suspected (this chapter), we also observe more gradedness in the temporal dynamics of the representations than previously suspected (chapters 6–10).

The key metatheoretical shift being proposed in this book is simple: Mental content does not consist of objects but of events. Individual representations are not temporally static *things* in the mind that can be found, grasped, and inspected, like a homunculus fondling a glass figurine on his bookshelf. Representations are *processes* in and of themselves, sparsely distributed patterns of neural activation that change nonlinearly over the course of several hundred milliseconds, and then blend right into the next one. Likewise, individual cognitive faculties (language, vision, memory, reasoning, etc.) are also not spatially and temporally separated things in the mind, but are processes that emerge from the time-dependent interaction of multiple neural subsystems. Importantly, I contend that this seemingly innocent shift in descriptive format—from objects to events, from things to processes—has radical consequences for just about every conventional theory in the cognitive sciences. If the process of spoken word recognition takes visual context into account immediately, then is it really fair to refer to it as "spoken word recognition?" The process in question is clearly doing more than just recognizing spoken words. Or when visual search takes into account concurrent linguistic input immediately, is it really fair to summarily label this process "visual search?"

This is not the first time that someone has argued that it is misleading to apply a linguistic label to a putative mental process (e.g., word recognition, working memory, visual imagery) and draw discrete demarcations in space and time for its separation from other mental processes. However, it was perhaps easy, during the cognitive revolution, to dismiss such claims on the grounds that the discrete modular engineering approach allows for theoretically explicit and mathematically rigorous accounts of the mind. Simply saying that we shouldn't oversimplify a richly interconnected dynamic biological system like the brain by describing it in terms of computationally tractable encapsulated subsystems leaves open the question of how we do describe it then! In the past decade or so, the mathematics of dynamical systems, along with a focus on real-time experimental measures, have produced a number of successful inroads toward providing precisely this theoretically explicit and mathematically rigorous description of how the dynamic mind works. Therefore, I think the cognitive and neural sciences actually are finally at a point where one can responsibly claim again that inventing linguistic labels for discrete mental processes dangerously oversimplifies what's really going on. This time we can work conscientiously, rigorously, and successfully toward an account of mind that leans significantly less on such computational idealizations while nonetheless maintaining scientific respectability.

6

Temporal Dynamics in Categorization

Is it always permissible to speak of the extension of a concept, of a class? And if not, how do we recognize the exceptional cases? Can we always infer from the extension of one concept's coinciding with that of a second, that every object which falls under the first concept also falls under the second? These are the questions raised by Mr. Russell's communication.
—Gottlob Frege

I think categorization is a sin.
—Dave Mustaine

Categorize Not, Lest Ye Be Categorized

Categorization, or categorization-like processing, is one of the most important functions in all of mental activity (see Harnad, 1987). If you search a psychological literature database for the combined set of articles on either the subject of categorization or the subject of categories, you will find more articles than if you search for the subjects of word recognition, object recognition, or visual attention. The mental skill of knowing what featural differences between things in the world can be more or less ignored and what featural differences warrant treating two things differently is crucial to interacting with the world successfully and safely. But the different ways the mind might implement this skill of categorization have been the topic of intense debate for many decades.

This chapter starts out with a textbook example (literally) of how one of these ways can break down rather spectacularly. Formal logical frameworks for categorization have a history rooted in set theory, where categories have discrete, crisply defined boundaries between one another, with no fuzzy graded overlap between them. Although the majority of this chapter will point to the gray areas that lie in between putative categories and that are particularly visible when one examines the continuous real-time process of perception and cognition, it is nonetheless useful to begin with a famous criticism of formal logic that essentially beats it at its own game. This classic bug in the software of formal logic is known as Russell's paradox.

As a foundation of logic and mathematics, *set theory* is a key component of how one might begin to formalize a treatment of categorization. For example, the set of apples contains all apples as true unmitigated members, and it excludes all nonapples (e.g., Asian pears, oranges, hammers, toenail clippings, etc.) as complete nonmembers. See figure 6.1A. Crucially, there is no gray area between true/membership and false/nonmembership (not even for Asian pears, whose shape and texture are remarkably similar to apples; they are treated as equally lacking in applehood as toenail clippings). The set of apples can be represented as a subset of the set of fruits, as well as a superset of the set of red delicious apples. As such, set theory provides a robust format of hierarchical knowledge representation. One of the strengths of traditional set theory—as well as what led to its downfall—is its ability to represent internal recursion. Sets can refer to and contain themselves. Figure 6.1B shows the *set of all sets*, which contains a great many sets, including the set of apples, as well as the set of all sets, because being a set qualifies it to be a member of itself. Being a member of itself makes it a somewhat odd kind of set, and this is perhaps slightly mind-bending for the uninitiated, but it's nothing compared to what comes next. As noted by Bertrand Russell (1903), included in this set of all sets (which happens to be a member of itself), is an easily constructed subset called the set of all sets that are not members of themselves (figure 6.1C). This set notably does not include the set of all sets (notice the absence of the tiny Venn diagram in the lower right region, when comparing set C to set B). However, the set of all sets that are not members of themselves does include the set of apples. As a "set of apples" is not the same as an "apple," the set of apples does not include itself as a member of itself. Thus, it qualifies for membership in set C. But what happens when you ask whether the set of all sets that are not members of themselves includes itself as a member?

Basically the world comes crashing in on set theory at that point. If the set of all sets that are not members of themselves includes itself as a member,

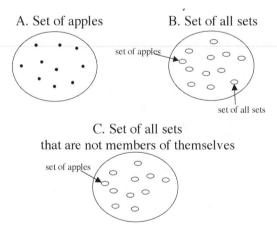

Figure 6.1. Russell's paradox: Set C must and must not contain itself.

it thereby disqualifies itself from being a member, by its very own definition. But if it excludes itself from being a member of itself, then it thus qualifies as a set that is not a member of itself, and should, by its definition, be included as a member. Thus, the framework of traditional set theory allows a self-contradiction, making itself internally inconsistent. It's like they say: Unable to assign a binary membership value if you *do*, unable to assign a binary membership value if you *don't*.

As it turns out, Russell's paradox is not an across-the-board damning of all possible set theories. It damns only a subset of all set theories. There are ways to revive many combinations of set theoretical axioms as long as one removes a powerful functionality from the theory: One must prohibit sets from making reference to themselves. Russell's type theory as well as the Zermelo-Fränkel set theory do exactly this. Nonetheless, Russell's famous critique of basic set theory was enough to make Gottlob Frege (1903/1964, whose quote begins this chapter) gradually distance himself from his previous works on logic and mathematics. This paradox is also frequently used as a motivating example in many introductory descriptions of fuzzy set theory and fuzzy logic.

Fuzzy set theory can maintain the functionality of self-reference and internal recursion because it adds the functionality of allowing graded, instead of binary, truth values (Zadeh, 1965). Fuzzy set theory assigns *degrees* of membership, typically on a scale from 0 to 1. A red delicious apple might get a 0.95 membership to the set of apples, a Granny Smith might get a 0.9, a mostly eaten golden delicious apple core might get a 0.7, and an Asian pear (also called a nashi) might get a 0.25 because it resembles an apple's appearance and texture. Fuzzy set theory does not catastrophically break down when a paradox occurs, precisely because it allows these gray areas between true/membership and false/nonmembership. When a particular set membership appears to be equally true and false, one can simply assign it a value of 0.5 true and 0.5 false. The set of all sets that are not members of themselves can simply include itself with 0.5 membership. Granted, this is a rather uninformative state to be in, but at least the system is not forcing itself to violate any of its own axioms. Maybe being unable to assign a binary truth value doesn't damn a theory after all (Fine, 1975; Hyde, 1997; Williamson, 1994; but see Fodor & Lepore, 1996). In fact, fuzzy logic (along with other multiple-valued logics) has been enjoying a great deal of popularity in electrical engineering applications. Fuzzy control systems can be found in circuits for everything from toasters to vacuum cleaners to elevators to trains—even in the antilock braking system of many cars!

That said, fuzzy, graded treatments of categories in the mind have been slow to gain appreciation in certain areas of cognitive science (e.g., Dietrich & Markman, 2003; Fodor, 1998; Haack, 1979; Jones, 1982; Osherson & Smith, 1981, 1982; but see Epstein, 1982; Lakoff, 1987; Love, Medin, & Gureckis, 2004; Massaro, 1989; Rogers & McClelland, 2004; Rosch, 1973). Despite Russell's proven crippling of (the sometimes called naive version of) set theory a century ago, basic set theoretic symbol-minded treatments of concepts and categorization still run rampant in cognitive psychology (but see Sloman, 1998). It is almost as though the profound intuitiveness of traditional set theoretical frameworks is justification enough to ignore Russell's proof.

But there is another logical paradox that is more regularly brought up in philosophical and psychological discussions of the battle between crisp atomic concepts and fuzzy vague concepts: the Sorites paradox. This paradox comes in many forms, but one of the more colorful versions (and one that hits close to home for a lot of men!) is the question of when a man's head can be said to be bald. If a full head of hair is in the neighborhood of 100,000 hairs, then is a man with only 99,999 hairs bald? Clearly not. But what if you keep plucking hair after hair from this poor man's head, and asking whether he is bald each time? Is he bald at 70,000 hairs? No. 50,000 hairs? Perhaps not. When you pluck the 90,000th hair, and he has only 10,000 hairs remaining, is he finally bald? If so, does that mean he was *not bald* when he had 10,001 hairs? At what individual instance of single-hair plucking did he abruptly become bald?[1] The point of the Sorites paradox is to demonstrate that the line at which a false proposition like "the man is bald" discretely becomes true is impossible to draw. At every pair of adjacent values, for example, 10,367 and 10,368 hairs, it seems woefully arbitrary to say the distinction between "bald" and "not bald" lies there and nowhere else. (This clearly harkens back to the concerns about threshold setting in symbolic dynamics discussed in chapter 4; see Bollt et al., 2001). Once again, a solution that has been proposed for this paradox is to introduce degrees of truth, or fuzzy set theory (Machina, 1976).

Part of the reason that concepts like baldness must be vague and fuzzy is probably because they are actually collective variables rather than the atomic concepts that the linguistic labels imply. The property of being bald is perhaps an unevenly weighted combination of hair thinness in different regions of the scalp. A man with a short-cropped Mohawk haircut may actually have less total hair volume than a man with midstage male pattern baldness. But it is the latter man who will get called bald, isn't it? Moreover, the use of the label *bald* for a man might also vary depending on different contextual circumstances, such as how attractive his facial structure is, how much you like his personality, and how old he is. For example, the hair thinness threshold for being bald could very well be slightly higher for men in their 70s than for men in their 30s. (At age 75, a man with half a head of hair is doing pretty well.) If so, this would mean that the concept of being bald somehow includes measures of age, and perhaps attractiveness, as well as other variables. This distributed collection of variables that converge to produce the label *bald* is clearly not at all the nondecomposable atomic concept of the type that so many philosophers have argued must exist. I will argue in this chapter that perhaps no concept can be truly atomic (i.e., nondecomposable into constituent subcomponents). After all, not even atoms are atomic. Philosophers just thought they were at one time.

And Yet, We Cannot Help But Categorize

When we introspect and when we communicate, we tend to naturally, automatically, and implicitly impose categories on the things around us, even events that are actually quite continuous. Sometimes our categorizations are transparently mere heuristics, used for ease in communicating, such as referring to Baby Boomers, Generation X, Generation Y, and Generation D, when we know full well that these labels are not empirically based on nonoverlapping distributions of birthdates and mutually exclusive affiliations with separate periods of popular culture. But other times, the parceling of continua into individual chunks that we carry out is genuinely opaque to self-reflection. For example, when you look at a real rainbow, you are exposing your retinas to an approximately evenly distributed continuum of wavelengths. Yet you perceive it as composed of separated bands of different colors with slightly different widths. This humanly visible range of wavelengths (from about 400 to 700 nanometers) is a tiny portion of the spectrum of radiation wavelengths in the universe, from gamma rays (around 0.001 nanometer) to AM radio (around a trillion nanometers) and beyond. But even this tiny range seems to be carved up into several distinct groupings within our perceptual experience. This little example of our carving up of rainbows, despite their actual continuity, is emblematic of how biological (as well as cultural) evolution has instilled the tendency to pigeonhole related experiences in such a way that differences within a group are downplayed and differences between groups are exaggerated. It also stands as a helpful reminder of how profoundly subjective perception is!

Decades ago, it was suspected that people who grew up with languages that grouped the color spectrum into different linguistic categories—for example, using one word for both green and blue, or for blue and black, or in some languages, one word for all three—also *perceived* colors in those different categories (Whorf, 1956). These cultures do of course communicate via a different set of color names, but psychophysical color perception experiments tend to show that regardless of language or culture, color is more or less perceived in basically the same way by humans worldwide (Berlin & Kay, 1969; Heider, 1972; but see also Roberson, Davies, & Davidoff, 2000; Kay & Kempton, 1984)—excluding, of course, those people with fewer (or more) than the typical three retinal color receptors, such as dichromats (and tetrachromats). Thus, when a native monolingual Tamahumara speaker (who uses the same color word for blue and for green) looks at a rainbow, she sees pretty close to the same chromatic array that a native monolingual English speaker sees. The wavelength continuum is perceptually segregated into more or less the same set of *almost* discretely separated bands of color. (It seems noteworthy, does it not, that those boundaries between the color bands appear somewhat fuzzy and graded?)

This color categorization is due largely to low-level opponent-process color perception mechanisms in the retina and lateral geniculate nucleus

(Boynton, 1960; Lennie, 1984). It is not due to some contemplative culturally and linguistically determined thought process that converts perceptual continua into cognitive and linguistic categories. However, there are other aspects of our perceptual experience that are perhaps somewhere in between these extremes of purely biologically determined and purely socially determined (see Gumperz & Levinson, 1996). For example, Japanese and English use different sets of grammatical groupings for referring to objects and to substances, and the way children learn to categorize and differentiate simple objects and substances appears to differ in the two cultures (Imai & Genter, 1997). (See also Boroditsky, 2001, for effects of Mandarin and English spatial metaphors for time.)

Whether due to innate biological mechanisms or to cultural/linguistic influences (or, more typically, a combination of the two), the ability to categorize perceptual experiences, instead of treating each individual stimulus array as independent of every other stimulus array, is a fundamental cognitive ability of the utmost importance for defining and understanding the human mind (see Harnad, 1987). Categorization is among the most studied mental faculties, and thus is at the core, of cognitive psychology.

What I will demonstrate to the reader in this chapter is that categorization is not a Kantian mental faculty that performs computations on discrete symbolic variables (Dietrich & Markman, 2003; Marcus, 2001) with logical rules (e.g., Nosofsky & Palmeri, 1998). Rather, this crucial cognitive skill is a natural result of a dynamical system that has developed graded attractor basins in state space (e.g., Anderson et al., 1977; see also Damper & Harnad, 2000). Before a novel stimulus array can stake claim to its own attractor, thus having its own personal representational identity, it will first have a chance to settle into one or more of the existing attractors, thus being treated as a member of that attractor's category.[2] In this framework, settling into or toward an existing attractor basin is tantamount to being categorized, just probabilistically so.

Temporal Dynamics

In the following two sections, the discussion will focus on two informal demonstrations of categorization in continuous time and in continuous feature space. As a dynamical systems account would naturally predict, categorization tasks often show quite different results from speeded responses than from nonspeeded responses (e.g., Lamberts, 1995, 1998, 2000; Lin & Murphy, 1997; Nosofsky & Alfonso-Reese, 1999; see also Brownell & Caramazza, 1978; Medin & Smith, 1981). Essentially, a speeded response forces an unsettled trajectory to select among multiple nearby attractors in an unsystematic fashion (e.g., perhaps stochastically). The results can allow one to infer partial activation of multiple competing interpretations of the stimulus array. Unfortunately, as noted by Lamberts (2000), it is still somewhat new and unusual for categorization studies to give consideration to temporal dynamics.

The bulk of the literature over the past few decades has focused almost exclusively on the outcome of categorization rather than the process. This tradition ignores the fact that by examining the continuous time course of an online categorization event, one can tease apart various theoretical accounts that would never have been rigorously tested by outcome-based off-line experimental measures.

For example, one theoretical account of the process of categorization, which is generally consistent with Lamberts's (2000) information accumulation theory, can be idealistically demonstrated by a normalized recurrence simulation. Figure 6.2 shows the diagram of a very simple normalized recurrence architecture used to approximate the changing patterns of activation during the categorization of different animals into the classes of fish, mammal, bird, and reptile. As the normalized recurrence competition algorithm works (see chapter 4 for details), these five feature vectors (framed circles) each normalize so that they sum to 1.0 and then are combined at the integration layer (framed ovals), erasing any previous activation values at that layer. In this simulation, there are no differential weights for the five feature vectors;

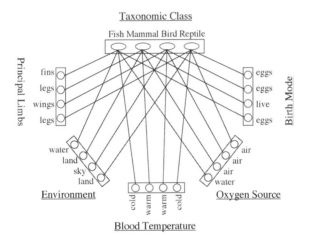

Figure 6.2. Schematic diagram of a normalized recurrence simulation of the temporal dynamics of categorization. The repeated node labels in some of the feature vectors (circles) are necessary because each integration node (ovals) must have its own unique feature node. This allows the feature vectors to function as probability distributions in their support for the appropriate taxonomic class. For example, after the initial feature vector normalization step, a "live" birth mode vector would pass 1.0 activation to the mammal node and 0 activation to the other taxonomic class nodes, whereas an "eggs" birth mode vector would send 0.333 activation to the fish, bird, and reptile nodes, and 0 activation to the mammal node.

they simply sum together at the integration vector. The integration layer then divides each node's activation by the vector's sum activation (always 5.0 in this case, thus making the integration vector simply an average of the five feature vectors). Then cumulative feedback is sent by adding to each feature node the product of itself and its corresponding integration node. The next time step begins with the feature nodes normalizing themselves (dividing each node by the vector's sum), and the integration and feedback take place again. These four calculations are computed within each time step, and the network continues until a criterion node activation (often 0.95) is reached by an integration node. The cyclic recurrent flow of activation between the integration vector and the feature vectors allows strong and selective biases within certain feature vectors to coerce weak and uncertain biases in others, until the system gradually settles into a stable state (see appendix for the relevant MATLAB code).

For this simple animal categorization simulation, feature vectors were entered for nine example animals. For the toucan, the nodes for wings, sky, warm, air, and eggs were set at 1.0 activation. For the goldfish, the nodes for fins, water, cold, water, and eggs were set at 1.0 activation. For the lizard, the nodes for legs, land, cold, air, and eggs were set at 1.0 activation. For the cat, the nodes for legs, land, warm, air, and live were set at 1.0 activation. For the turtle, the nodes for legs, water, cold, air, and eggs were set at 1.0 activation. For the penguin, the nodes for wings, water&land, warm, air, and eggs were set at 1.0 activation. For the seal, fins, water&land, warm, air, and live were set at 1.0 activation. For the whale, the nodes for fins, water, warm, air, and live were set at 1.0 activation. For the platypus, the nodes for legs, water&land, warm, air, and eggs were set at 1.0 activation. This localist attractor network easily categorizes animals that are typical exemplars of their taxonomic class, such as toucan, goldfish, and cat (see figures 6.3 and 6.4). However, with animals that are unusual members of their class, the network undergoes a long, drawn-out competition—not unlike the long reaction times described by Rosch, Simpson, and Miller (1976) and Smith (1978)—due to the animal's partial match with multiple taxonomic classes.[3]

Figure 6.3 presents two-dimensional perspectives on the representational state space of the taxonomic class vector for all nine simulations. In each case, 30 circles plot the activation of one relevant node by the activation of another relevant node time step after time step. When these circles are far apart, it shows that the state space trajectory was moving quickly at the time, and when the circles are close to one another, it shows that the state space trajectory was moving slowly. Figure 6.4 plots the activations for all four nodes in the taxonomic class vector (along the y-axis) over time (along the x-axis). Note how the simulations for seal, whale, penguin, turtle, and platypus exhibit late rises to asymptote for the correct classification, and even then those asymptotes are substantially below 1.0. In the end, the model concludes that a whale is 0.6 a mammal and 0.4 a fish. And in fact, during its first few time steps of processing, the model briefly conceives of a whale as *slightly more a fish than a mammal.* A similar crossing of curves is seen with turtle.

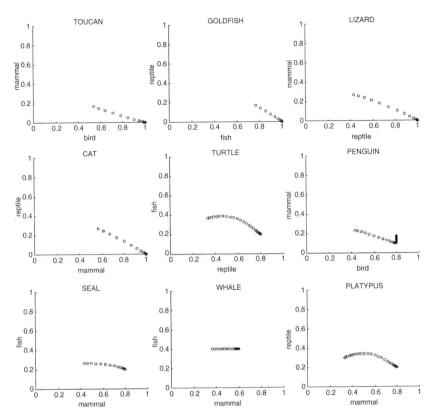

Figure 6.3. Trajectories through representational state space, seen through a variety of two-dimensional windows on the four-dimensional taxonomic class vector (axes vary across panels). Note how all simulations start somewhere in between the two relevant attractors (at top left and bottom right corners) and move in the direction of one of them.

Keep in mind that this simulation is really just an existence proof of one way a graded temporal dynamics could be realized in a dynamical system. Even if these predictions were to fit human data perfectly, that still wouldn't prove that the way that normalized recurrence produces these curves is the same way human brains produce their curves. But could these curves really be anything at all like what a human mind does when it categorizes animals anyway? During the early moments of settling on a categorization for an animal, do people simultaneously partially consider multiple categories? Do those partially active representations compete over time for a cognitive trajectory to settle into eliciting a unique motor output?

Comparing speeded instinctive responses to slow contemplative responses (e.g., Lin & Murphy, 1997) is a good start for measuring this kind of time

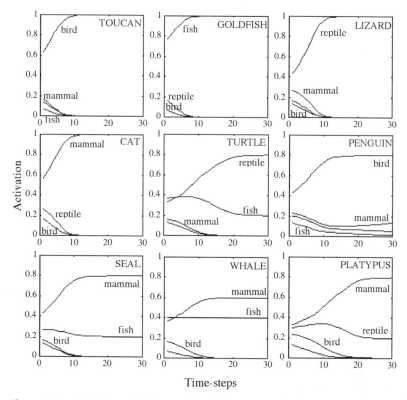

Figure 6.4. Activation of all four nodes of the taxonomic class vector over time, for all nine simulations.

course question, but a (semi-)continuous many-samples measure of which responses are accruing activation and approaching threshold (such as many of those methods discussed in chapter 3) is substantially more revealing. For example, because eye movements occur about three to four times per second and are largely unaffected by deliberative strategies, they can provide a stream of multiple honest proto-responses over the course of the couple seconds it takes to produce a single overt verbal or manual response.

Nederhouser and Spivey (2004) recorded the eye movements of 17 participants while they categorized small plastic toy animals (about 2 inches × 3 inches) into either of two bins. Participants were first shown a set of animals (half from one taxonomic class, half from another), and then were presented each animal one at a time. Nederhouser and Spivey found that animals that are atypical members of their taxonomic classes, like turtle, penguin, seal, and whale, took longer to categorize than more typical animals (see Glass & Meany, 1978; Rips, Shoben, & Smith, 1973), and they also elicited quite a bit of vacillation in eye movements between the two category bins. Crucially, when one looks again at the records of eye position over time, one can plot fixation

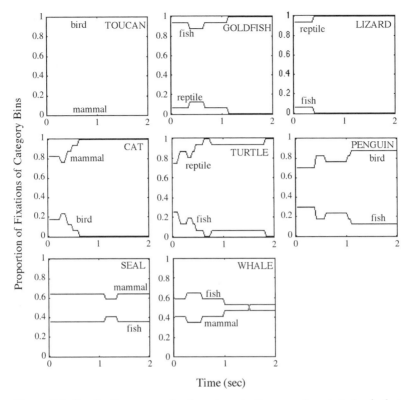

Figure 6.5. Eye fixation curves for the categorization experiment. Animals that are atypical examples of their taxonomic class elicited considerable vacillation in eye movements during the early moments of categorization.

curves based on the proportion of fixations at each time slice (figure 6.5) that resemble somewhat the activation curves from the network simulations (figure 6.4). The curves in figure 6.5 show, for each 33-millisecond time slice, the proportion of trials in which the subjects were fixating the correct category bin or the incorrect category bin, following their first saccade away from the toy animal that was placed in front of them. (Similar kinds of findings, but with continuous mouse movements, are reported by Dale, Kehoe, & Spivey, in press.) Note how in the case of penguin, seal, and whale, some subjects continued to fixate the incorrect bin for the full two seconds shown; in some cases, they even placed the whale in the bin of fish!

The present eye movement data (figure 6.5) do not include the platypus in figure 6.4. Do you have any idea how hard it is to find a small plastic toy platypus?! Anyway, a wide range of additional interesting animals, such as the eel, the ostrich, the bat (perhaps even adding more taxonomic classes), can be the focus of future, more richly fleshed out simulations and experiments. Of course, if some of our participants had trouble correctly classifying the whale, one can probably expect the underappreciated and misunderstood platypus to elicit even more noisy and confused responses from many participants.

This comparison of pilot simulation and pilot data provides a glimpse into the beginning stages of how a research project can pursue a recurrent interplay between model prediction and experimentation in studying the temporal dynamics of real-time categorization. The demonstration is intended to illustrate how one can begin to visualize the fuzzy graded representations that change over time during categorization, both in a localist attractor network and in a semi-continuous record of cognitive processing. And perhaps some of the more static, formal approaches to concepts and categorization might have trouble accommodating such evidence that during a categorization event, the mind spends so much of its time in graded, rather than discrete, mental states.

Categorical Perception: Vision

One common objection to the claim that mental representations are fuzzy and multifarious—at any point in time—is that under certain experimental circumstances, one can demonstrate that perceivers appear to uniformly categorize certain perceptual inputs and lose access to the continuous information that originally constituted the stimulus array (especially with speech; see Liberman et al., 1957). Clearly, addressing this categorical perception phenomenon is thus of paramount importance in advancing and defending the continuity of mind thesis.

In a categorical identification task, a stimulus feature is "stretched out" into a continuum. For example, one could present human participants with many color patches over and over from a green to blue portion of the color spectrum, say, 540 to 480 nanometers in 5-nanometer increments, and ask them to identify each patch as either green or blue. In principle, one might perhaps expect participants to respond to this continuum in a continuous fashion. That is, a green that is near the blue region, say 520 nanometers, might get identified as green only 60% of the time and as blue the other 40%, and vice versa for 500 nanometers. Figure 6.6 shows a pretend version of this hypothetical continuous perception. However, what is actually found with such continua, in most circumstances, is that all stimuli in one portion of the continuum are identified with nearly 100% consistency as belonging to one category and all stimuli in the remaining portion of the continuum are identified with nearly 100% consistency as belonging to the other category. Figure 6.7 shows a schematic version of the kind of data that are typically observed in such experiments.

Following work in the speech domain (Liberman et al., 1957), Bornstein and Korda (1984, 1985; see also Pilling et al., 2003; Roberson & Davidoff, 2000) gave participants a discrimination task instead of the identification task. True categorical perception requires that the graded distinctions between

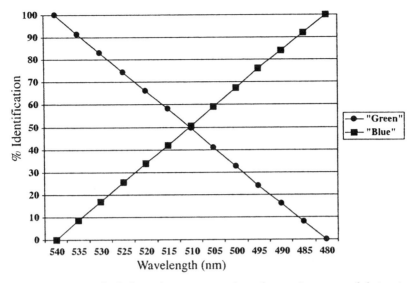

Figure 6.6. Hypothetical continuous perception of a continuous modulation in wavelength.

a pair of within-category stimuli from the continuum are lost to the processing system and unable to affect responses. Consistent with this, Bornstein and Korda showed that a pair of hues that just barely straddled across the category boundary between green and blue were more easily discriminated than a pair

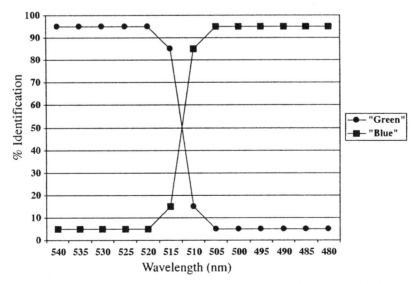

Figure 6.7. Hypothetical categorical perception of a continuous modulation of wavelength.

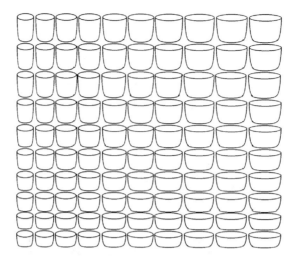

Figure 6.8. A two-dimensional continuum of height (along the vertical axis) and width (along the horizontal axis) for cups and bowls.

of hues (with the same distance from one another in nanometers) from within either category. However, they also found that reaction times were longer for same judgments of nonmatching hues within the same hue category than for same judgments of identical hues. Thus, something about the difference between two slightly different but same category hues is obviously still affecting processing, at least enough to influence the time course of discrimination.

In this next illustration of human data and model simulation, I briefly describe some experiments on the categorical perception of cups and bowls. These experiments have much in common with work by Labov (1973), Oden (1981), and Newell and Bülthoff (2002). The primary feature that distinguishes a cup from a bowl is aspect ratio: width divided by height. All other features being equal, a cup is typically taller than it is wide, and a bowl is typically wider than it is tall. Figure 6.8 shows a two-dimensional continuum between a typical cup (upper left) and a typical bowl (lower right). This matrix was constructed by starting with the stimulus in the lower left corner and increasing its height by increments of 10% (upward in the matrix) and increasing its width by increments of 10% (rightward in the matrix). Thus, the stimuli along each diagonal going from lower left to upper right all have the same aspect ratio—they differ only in size.

In the first of this pair of experiments, 20 participants were shown each of these stimuli one at a time on an otherwise blank computer screen and asked to identify each one as either a cup or a bowl. Averaging across stimuli with the same aspect ratio, figure 6.9 shows the percentage of people's bowl judgments (filled circles) along this cup/bowl continuum. Just as in other categorical perception phenomena (e.g., Beale & Keil, 1995; Cutting & Rosner, 1974; Eimas &

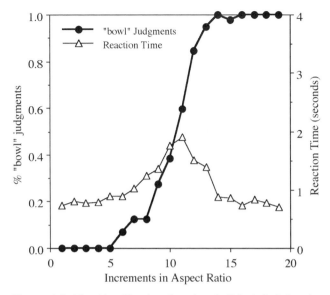

Figure 6.9. The identification function (solid circles) for the categorical response task with the cup–bowl continuum looks similar to the idealized categorical step function in figure 6.7. However, note that the reaction times (open triangles) show some sensitivity to particularly ambiguous shapes.

Corbit, 1973; Livingston, Andrews, & Harnad, 1998; Newell & Bülthoff, 2002; Sailor & Shoben, 1996) people's judgments reveal a striking nonlinearity in their responses to a continuous linear manipulation of the stimulus. Near the middle of the cup/bowl continuum (an aspect ratio of approximately 1.2), subjects almost discretely switched from consistent cup judgments to consistent bowl judgments.

Interestingly, people's reaction times (open triangles) near this boundary point were longer than those near the extremes of the continuum (see also Pisoni & Tash, 1974, for similar slowed reaction times with speech stimuli). These slowed reaction times are naturally predicted by a dynamical systems account in which the mental representations associated with the two sanctioned response categories, cup and bowl, compete against each other over the course of several hundred milliseconds. These two competing attractors (or neural population codes), with stimulus-triggered trajectories that start out either equidistant from the two attractors or closer to one than the other, might look something like the vector landscape in figure 6.10. Longer trajectories to cross the verbal response threshold correspond to longer reaction times.

To get quantitative and somewhat more explicit with this dynamical systems account, an idealized simulation with normalized recurrence was conducted to show how probabilistic representations of cup and bowl can go

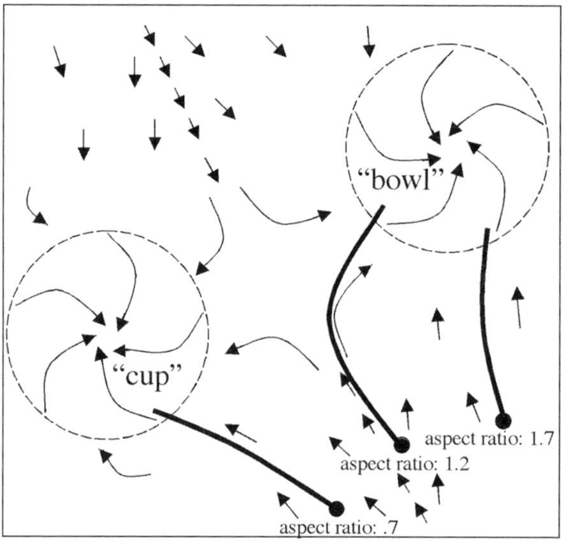

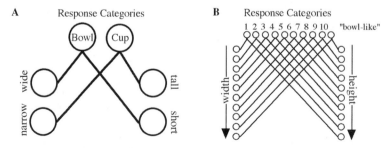

Figure 6.10. A hypothetical attractor landscape in which different visual objects from figure 6.8 have different distances from the cup attractor and the bowl attractor. When the mental trajectory finally crosses an attractor's threshold, that cup or bowl button gets pressed.

through a pattern completion process over time to settle on a unitary response category. Figure 6.11A shows the architecture of this network. As described in chapter 4, normalized recurrence is a competition algorithm implemented as a localist attractor network that merges probabilistic representations of different perceptual inputs into an integrated representation that corresponds to some response category. The probabilities of the different response categories at this integration layer then send feedback to the perceptual inputs, biasing them slightly toward supporting the most active (or most probable) response category. This feedforward integration and feedback biasing cycle repeats

Figure 6.11. A: a normalized recurrence simulation of a categorical response task; B: a normalized recurrence simulation of a rating task.

until one response category reaches a threshold (at which point it triggers its associated behavior, such as pressing the cup button).

Because this model necessarily converts its inputs into probabilities of individual perceptual representations (so that they can use a common currency for integration), it operates at a level of description above the actual population codes of the brain. A single localist node with a probabilistic activation of 0.8 is analogous to 800 of the 1,000 neurons in a distributed population code being active (see Zemel & Mozer, 2001). Thus, we can think of the population code as "functionally unitized" (Stone & Van Orden, 1989)—such that despite being composed of hundreds of interconnected subunits, it behaves roughly like a coherent whole.

By entering input values corresponding to the matrix indices (and inverse matrix indices)[4] of the various stimuli in figure 6.8, the network in figure 6.11A forces the *Cup* and *Bowl* response categories to compete against each other over time—just as two mutually exclusive population codes would compete against one another for the privilege of executing their associated actions. The weight for each feature vector was 1.0. With a gradually decreasing threshold (a dynamic criterion that starts at 1.0 and is reduced by 0.01 after each time step), the model will eventually stop cycling, with one response category substantially higher in probability than the other. Using the probabilistic activation value of the response category node for *Bowl* as an indicator of the percentage of bowl judgments, the figure 6.11A version of this model mimics the human data rather well (compare figure 6.9 with figure 6.12). Additionally, the number of

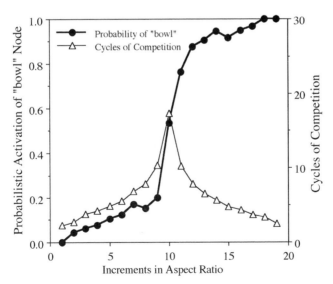

Figure 6.12. Simulation results of the categorical response task from normalized recurrence. The localist attractor network from figure 6.11A mimics the human data in figure 6.9.

competition cycles that the model takes to reach this nearly settled state also mimics the human data. What this simulation demonstrates is that a perceptual processing system that is exposed to graded information yet is forced to pigeonhole the input into one of two binary response categories, can do so via a competitive pattern completion process *without immediately dismissing the graded information in the original signal.*

When examining the experimental task on which this simulation is based, the following question naturally arises: Does the fact that this task *requires* a discretized response (i.e., a forced choice between *either* cup *or* bowl) discourage the participant from acting on gradations in the stimulus?[5] What if, in a different version of the experiment, the same stimuli from the cup/bowl continuum were presented, but the task was to rate how bowl-like the stimulus was, on a scale from 1 to 10 (see Massaro & Cohen, 1983, for a similar task with speech stimuli)? The perceptual input is the same, but the rules for the behavioral output have changed.

This arrangement is easily implemented in normalized recurrence by changing the number of integration nodes to accommodate the number of possible responses in the rating task. With 10 integration nodes, one for each numerical response, the network then has its feature vectors offer their evidence in the form of probabilistic support for any of those 10 response options, hence, 10 nodes in each feature vector as well. Essentially, the constraints on the possible responses in turn impose constraints on the possible perceptions. This next simulation used the normalized recurrence architecture in figure 6.11B, in which the possible response categories are the numbers 1 through 10, indicating how bowl-like the stimulus is. The activation input to this version of the network was a Gaussian distribution centered on the input node corresponding to the stimulus's row (for width) and column (for shortness) in the matrix.[6] When the activation of any one response category reached the dynamic criterion, competition stopped. At that point, the activation function across all 10 response categories of the integration layer constituted a probability distribution. A bowl-like rating was then randomly sampled from this probability distribution, such that the most active node was usually what response category got executed, but occasionally a less active response category would get selected for discrete output. This stochastic simulation was run 20 times for each stimulus, and the results were averaged into the curves seen in figure 6.13. These simulation results stand as the theory's quantitative prediction of what would happen if the cup/bowl categorical-response task (whose human data are shown in figure 6.9) were converted into a cup/bowl rating task.

So logically, the next phase of this recurrent interplay between modeling and experimentation would be to empirically test this quantitative prediction. When 20 human participants are given a range between 1 and 10 to respond with, would they produce responses similar to those produced in the simulation? Or would they behave categorically, shying away from using intermediate values, and tending instead to pigeonhole the stimuli as 1s and 2s

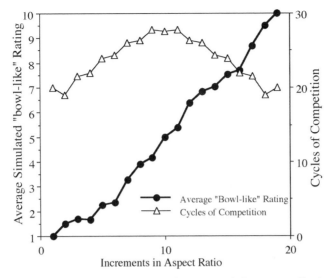

Figure 6.13. Simulation results of a rating task from normalized recurrence. The localist attractor network from figure 6.11B produces a predicted pattern for human data.

(obvious cups), and 9s and 10s (obvious bowls)? Figure 6.14 shows exactly the straight diagonal line (filled circles) that one would predict if the gradations in the stimuli were in fact preserved and still accessible during perception. Thus, at least in this little example of cups and bowls, it looks as though it is not the case that gradations in the stimuli are truly inaccessible to the perceiver. Perhaps it is more accurate to say that it is the behavioral task, rather than the perceiver, to which gradations in the stimuli can sometimes be inaccessible.

Categorical Perception: Speech

Probably the most well-known example of categorical perception comes from research on how people process speech (Aslin, Jusczyk, & Pisoni, 1998; Liberman et al., 1961; see also Kluender, Diehl, & Killeen, 1987; Kuhl & Miller, 1975, for similar research with quail and chinchilla). This work is perhaps most famous for popularizing the notion that "speech is special" (Liberman, 1982). Continua between pairs of phonemes can be constructed with speech synthesis equipment, such that realistic-sounding intermediate increments in between the two phonemes can be presented to human participants. For example, there is one phonetic feature that plays a large role in distinguishing the sound *bah* from the sound *pah*. This particular phonetic feature, called voice onset time (VOT), is the time between the opening of the lips (releasing air from the mouth) and the vibration of the vocal chords. If the VOT is around 10 milliseconds, the sound will be perceived as *bah*. If the VOT is

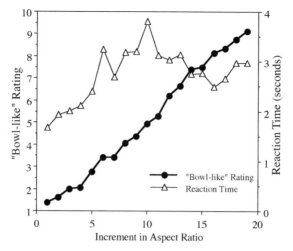

Figure 6.14. The identification function (solid circles) for the rating task with the cup–bowl continuum looks similar to the idealized continuous perception function in figure 6.6. Both ratings and reaction times (open triangles) adhere moderately closely to the normalized recurrence simulation in figure 6.13.

increased to around 50 milliseconds, the sound will be perceived as *pah*. That extra 40 milliseconds is enough to completely change your perception. In the context of the discussions of probabilistic representations, attractors in state space, and neural population codes, the obvious question now is the following: What happens when the VOT is 20 milliseconds? Or 30? Or 40?

Liberman et al. (1961) demonstrated that when listeners are presented a series of sounds along a continuum of VOT (with *bah* at one extreme and *pah* at the other), everything under about 30 milliseconds VOT is consistently reported as sounding like *bah*, and everything above about 30 milliseconds VOT is consistently reported as sounding like *pah*. Only around 30 milliseconds VOT are the identifications near 50/50 *bah/pah*. Figure 6.15 shows a schematic rendition of this kind of data in the percentage of *pah* judgments (filled circles, mapping to the left-hand *y*-axis). If the graded information of VOT were being used in this task, one might expect to see a straight diagonal line in this graph going directly from the bottom left corner to the top right corner.

Additionally, and perhaps more important, listeners are unable to discriminate between stimuli within a category, such as a *bah* with 10 milliseconds VOT and a *bah* with 20 milliseconds VOT. However, when the stimuli span the category boundary, such as a sound with 25 milliseconds VOT and one with 35 milliseconds VOT, discrimination is well above chance performance. Thus, the graded information within a category appears to be absent from the internal perceptual representation (Liberman et al., 1961; see also Dorman, 1974; Molfese, 1987; Simos et al., 1998; Steinschneider et al., 1995).

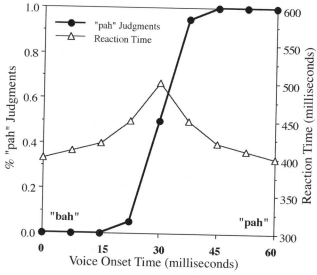

Figure 6.15. An idealized pattern of data from a categorical speech perception task.

Nonetheless, there are a couple of hints suggesting that the graded information in the stimulus is not completely discarded. Pisoni and Tash (1974) showed that when listeners are attempting to identify a sound that is on or near the boundary between these categories (somewhere between 20 and 40 milliseconds VOT), they take a longer time to make the identification, even though they rather systematically make the same identification almost every time. See the reaction times (open triangles, mapping to the right-hand *y*-axis) in figure 6.15. It is as though the two possible categories are partially represented simultaneously, like two mutually exclusive population codes that are each trying to achieve pattern completion and must compete against each other to do so. If they are nearly equal in their activation (or confidence), they will compete for a while before one reaches a probability high enough to trigger its associated response, thus delaying the identification. Converted into the language of attractor basins, this idea is the same as that depicted by the vector landscape in figure 6.10. Simply replace the aspect ratios with VOTs, and the cup and bowl labels with bah and pah labels.

Another hint that graded information is actually still available in categorical speech perception comes from work by Massaro (1987, 1999), on extending what is often called the McGurk effect (McGurk & MacDonald, 1976; see also Munhall & Vatikiotis-Bateson, 1998, and chapter 5). In addition to being exquisitely sensitive to a wide variety and timing of acoustic contexts (Holt, 2005; Mann & Repp, 1980), speech perception is also sensitive to visual contexts. In the McGurk effect, the visual perception of a speaker's dynamic mouth shape has a powerful and immediate influence on the listener's speech perception of the phoneme being spoken. In Massaro's experimental framework, he presents to listeners a bah/dah continuum, where the place of articulation (what parts of the mouth constrict airflow during the sound) is varied in steps by digitally altering the speech waveform. That by itself tends to produce the standard categorical perception effect, as though the gradations in the stimuli are completely discarded by the perceiver. But Massaro couples this auditory bah/dah continuum with a computerized face, whose lips can be adjusted in steps along a *visual* bah/dah continuum (basically, by increasing the aperture between the lips). When these graded visual and auditory information sources are combined for perceiving the syllable, results are consistent with an algorithm in which the probabilistic biases in each information source are *preserved*, not discretized, and a weighted combination of those graded biases determines categorization. Massaro calls his algorithm the fuzzy logical model of perception.

Consistent with more temporally dynamic approaches to categorization (e.g., Anderson et al., 1977; Cree, McRae, & McNorgan, 1999; Dailey et al., 2002; Lamberts, 2000; McRae et al., 1997; Tuller et al., 1994), one might expect even categorical speech perception to not only be underlyingly comprised of graded patterns of activation (or fuzzy truth values) but also exhibit these gradations when the categorization process is measured in a fashion more continuous-in-time than simple outcome-based measures that record which identification the participant eventually reports at the end of the experimental trial. McMurray and Spivey (1999) tested exactly that by recording participants' eye movements while they performed the standard categorical identification task, with sounds from a bah/pah VOT continuum, by mouse clicking /ba/ and /pa/ icons on a computer screen. Thus, in addition to the record of which icon participants ultimately clicked, there was also a record of when the eyes moved away from the central fixation dot and toward one or another of the response icons while making the categorization. With stimuli near the categorical boundary, the eye movement record clearly showed participants conspicuously vacillating their attention between the /ba/ and /pa/ icons. Figure 6.16 shows two schematic depictions of the eye fixations over time during the speech categorization process for a clear *pah* stimulus (panel A) and for a stimulus that was near the category boundary but was nonetheless identified (by mouse clicks) as a /pa/ 95% of the time (panel B). The eye position records depicted here came only from trials in which the /pa/ icon was indeed clicked at the end of the trial. Despite the identification outcome being identical in this subset of trials (all categorized as /pa/), the pattern of eye movements reveals substantially more time spent fixating the /ba/ icon (dashed area in panel B) when the speech stimulus was near the VOT category boundary; thus indicating a clear effect of perceptual gradations in the speech input.

In fact, these temporary phonemic ambiguities, as tested with VOT continua and eye movement records, exhibit their effects not just in phoneme identification tasks but also in spoken word recognition tasks (McMurray, Tanenhaus, & Aslin, 2002; McMurray et al., 2003). For example, within-category

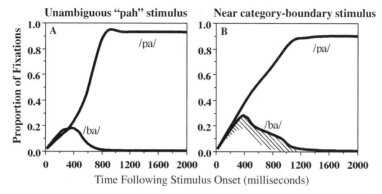

Figure 6.16. Schematic, smoothed, data patterns of eyes fixating on the /ba/ and /pa/ icons over the course of two seconds. Hashmarked region in panel B indicates the amount of increased fixations of /ba/ (compared to panel A) with a borderline speech token.

variation of VOT does not affect the final outcome of recognizing *bear* versus *pear*, however it does affect the eye movement records of participants looking at and mouse clicking the corresponding images on the computer screen (McMurray et al., 2002). More effects at the level of spoken word recognition will be discussed in further detail in chapter 7.

A particularly compelling way to visualize these eye movement data for the phoneme identification task is to convert them into identification functions (like that in figure 6.15) for early, intermediate, and late periods of time during the identification process. Figure 6.17 shows a schematic example,

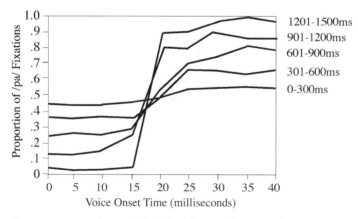

Figure 6.17. Versions of the identification function, based on time spent fixating the /pa/ or /ba/ icon, during early, intermediate, and late periods of time after stimulus presentation but before the mouse click response.

based on McMurray and Spivey's (1999) results, of the proportion of time the eyes spent fixating the /pa/ icon (normalized by the total amount of time spent on either /pa/ or /ba/ icons). The later period of the identification process (1,201–1,500 ms) reveals an eye movement identification function that looks just like the typical discrete categorical identification function produced by button-press responses (e.g., figure 6.15). However, the earlier periods of the identification process (i.e., 0–300 ms, 301–600 ms, and even 601–900 ms), produce eye movement identification functions that look significantly more probabilistic and graded. Thus, if the identification function is to be interpreted as a kind of signature of the internal pattern of activation favoring the perception of *bah* or *pah*, this signature looks decidedly more continuous than discrete during those early moments in time.

As in the previous explorations of categorization in this chapter, the natural next step is to simulate these graded temporal dynamics in categorical speech perception with a localist attractor network to better visualize the continuous change taking place in the patterns of activation corresponding to mutually exclusive categorylike representations. Figure 6.18 illustrates the architecture of a normalized recurrence simulation that integrates a speech vector (that pits *bah*-like sounds against *pah*-like sounds) and a visual vector (that compares fixation probabilities to a /ba/ icon, a /pa/ icon, and the central fixation dot). The speech vector is given a pattern of input corresponding to a speech sound somewhere along the VOT continuum. For example, a rather unambiguous *pah* sound might get a starting activation of [0.1 0 0.9] for those three nodes, whereas a borderline *bah* sound might get [0.6 0 0.4]. The visual vector always starts at [0.33 0.33 0.33], treating each visual object as equally worthy of attracting an eye movement. These two vectors simply sum

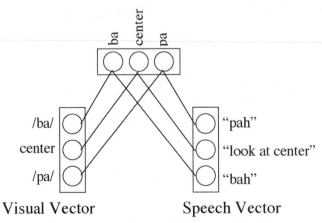

Figure 6.18. A normalized recurrence network for simulating eye movements to visual icons in a categorical speech perception task.

(unweighted) at the integration layer, which then normalizes itself and sends feedback to the feature vectors.

In this simulation, one can sample the proportion of fixations from the visual vector and thus watch the simulated eye movement patterns move away from fixating the central dot and toward one or the other response icon. Figure 6.19 shows the activation curves over time for the /pa/ visual node and the /ba/ visual node. Panel A plots these curves for a rather clear *pah* speech input [0.2 0 0.8], and panel B plots these curves for a *pah* speech input that is near the category boundary [0.4 0 0.6]. These activation curves from the visual vector mimic the proportion of fixations at each time slice in the results of McMurray and colleagues (1999, 2003); compare figure 6.19 with figure 6.16.

When this simulation is run for all 11 speech tokens along the VOT continuum, it is possible to calculate the proportion of time the model spends fixating the /pa/ icon versus the /ba/ icon, and thus plot a categorical identification function. Crucially, this can be done for early periods of time during the network's settling process, as well as for intermediate and late periods of time— just as was done in figure 6.17. The resulting graph is shown in figure 6.20. Note the similarity between figures 6.17 and 6.20. In both cases, the identification function starts out rather unbiased and gradually approaches the classic step function profile by continuously increasing one half of the curve and decreasing the other half of the curve over time.

This gradual expansion of the identification function over time to eventually achieve the famous step function profile suggests that over the course of several hundred milliseconds while hearing and identifying a speech sound, the relevant phoneme representations are actually rather continuous and analog, not particularly categorical and binary. Recall the discussion of the Necker cube, object recognition, and the temporal dynamics of neural population codes in chapter 1. It was argued there that if it takes several hundred milliseconds to fully activate a population code to achieve a maximally confident object recognition event, but

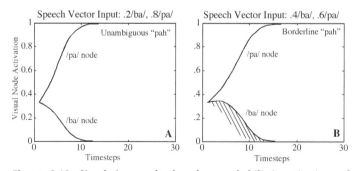

Figure 6.19. Simulation results, based on probabilistic activations of the visual nodes, approximating the human data pattern in figure 6.16. Hashmarked region in panel B indicates the amount of increased visual attention on /ba/ (compared to panel A) with a borderline speech token.

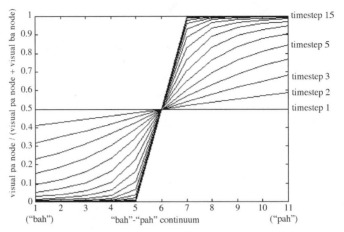

Figure 6.20. Simulation results of the identification function from normalized recurrence during early, intermediate, and late periods of time after stimulus presentation (compare to figure 6.17).

eye movements to other objects occur every few hundred milliseconds, then maximally confident or categorical recognition events must be rather rare. Instead, recognition probably operates with nondiscrete, partially active "good-enough representations" (see Ferreira, Bailey, & Ferraro, 2002). The same logic applies here with respect to these findings for categorical speech perception. If it takes upward of 800 milliseconds for a clear unambiguous *pah* speech sound to be completely and confidently identified as that phoneme and no other, and until then multiple phoneme representations are simultaneously partially active, this raises serious questions for how people manage to recognize natural flowing speech, where each new phoneme is uttered less than 100 milliseconds after the previous one. At this fast rate of sensory input and that slow speed of identification, spoken word recognition and spoken sentence comprehension must be operating (like object recognition during eye movements) with only partially active moderately confident patterns of neural population code activity—not logical categorical symbolic representations.

Action, Not Cognition, Categorizes Perception

The goal of this chapter has been to pinpoint one aspect of categorization phenomena, their temporal dynamics, and demonstrate how this aspect suggests that, as implied by Russell's paradox and the Sorites paradox, pure logical categories simply do not exist in the mind. This is not to say that categorization doesn't happen. On the contrary, categorization is a ubiquitous cognitive process whereby broadly multifarious, diffuse, and continuous perceptual information is whittled, funneled, shaped, and coerced over hundreds of milliseconds into a pattern that is just close enough to discrete that it can facilitate the execution of a relatively unitary motor action, such as grasping a particular object or producing a particular spoken word. Crucially, during the time course of that process, new perceptual input is already nudging the system toward other regions of state space, so that even that moment of being just close enough to a discrete internal representation is quite short-lived indeed.

In a dynamical framework such as this, there is no need to postulate some internal cognitive bottleneck that transmogrifies the distributed patterns of neural activation that constitute representation in perceptual areas of the brain into a handful of crisply defined formal symbols that live in some heretofore unidentified area of the brain. After all, those crisply defined symbols would only have to be "untransmogrified" right back into the distributed patterns of neural activation that constitute representations in motor areas of the brain!

Even if a computational representationalist (e.g., Dietrich & Markman, 2003) was to concede that truly static representations may not exist, and instead recruit representations whose phasic properties are stable (such as a limit cycle, where the system's state repeatedly orbits a point repellor) to serve as the symbols to be operated on by the system's rules and algorithms, problems for interpretation of data like those presented in this chapter still remain. Because the gradations of the system's specific location in state space are clearly "leaking out" in eye movement patterns and reaction times, the symbolization that computationalism claims is taking place for cognition appears to play a rather epiphenomenal role in the flow of information from sensory input to motor output. It is as if the perfect discretization of graded representations into formal logical category memberships is being done only for some inescapably subjective cognition/consciousness module that is actually not needed to explain natural online behavior. Although the individual participants may find themselves unable to produce a verbal protocol that can do justice to the gradual process of getting from an ambiguous segment of speech input to a discrete action of clicking one icon or the other, this should be seen as a limitation of language and memory rather than a limitation of the original internal representations.

The place where unitary crisply-delimited categories exist, if anywhere, is at the level of our intersubjective agreement on what individual words to use when we refer to these fuzzy groups of things, such as apples, mammals, and bowls. A dozen people might grasp an apple with a dozen subtly different reaching trajectories and hand shapes, but we, as observers of these varied motor outputs, will generally refer to each of them as "an apple-grasping event." Likewise, when an experimental participant is presented with two slightly different-sounding (but within-category) speech sounds, she might produce a variety of different intermediate motor behaviors (such as eye movements) before finally selecting her interpretations, but those final overt reports will be generally agreed on by observers as belonging to the same categorical response alternative. (Unfortunately, cognitive psychologists will too often blithely record *only* these final outcomes of the categorical identification process and thus mistakenly conclude that subtle continuous differences in phonetic fea-ture variables do not affect perception at all.)

These unitary labels that observers wind up agreeing on are best treated as descriptive conveniences that indeed attempt to function as discrete logical sets, for the purpose of scientific communication, but do so only as long as the overt actions and speech acts of the linguistic community continue to corre-late perfectly with them. The fact is, exceptions abound. It is quite rare for any theoretical construct, and its corresponding label, to have perfect agreement in its use in the scientific community of the cognitive sciences. More impor-tant, these descriptive conveniences are only observable as actions, not as internal mental entities. The hints at fuzzy internal representations and multi-farious activations of population codes, shown in this chapter and throughout this book, indicate that those internal mental entities that one infers from observing motor output (or electrophysiological measures) in the laboratory are far from discrete logical unitary cognitive objects. On the contrary, they are better described as graded attractor basins in a continuous metric state space, for which linguistic labels may be loosely applied but for which precise boundaries may not be drawn.

A dynamical and ecological approach to cognition treats categories not as static things in the head that are accessed when queried, but instead as dynamic flexible patterns, or complex structures in state space that can be used not just for these somewhat artificial laboratory classification tasks but also for on-the-fly conceptualizations and real-time applications of knowl-edge in the service of realistic goal-oriented action (e.g., Barsalou 1991; Markman & Ross, 2003). A very basic fundamental implication that this con-tinuous perspective has for our intellectual lives is that nothing in the mind is logically true or logically false. Likewise, nothing in the mind is discretely included or discretely excluded from any potential set. When dealing with fuzzy truth values and with probabilities, there are no pure 1s and no pure 0s.[7] By the time some internal representation has reached a probabilistic threshold for triggering one of its associated actions, other perceptual inputs (even just witnessing the action oneself is carrying out) have changed the state space manifold enough that the system will never settle into a perfectly stable state. That is to say, the continuity of mind is not merely a brief curiosity that can be observed with sophisticated real-time measurements, it is the modus operandi of thought. This suggests that one cannot fully trust what people (including oneself) *say* they think, or in some cases even how they *act*. Both of those behaviors unfairly discretize what a person is really thinking. Action and communication—particularly communication (this book included!)— necessarily overidealize and exaggerate the discreteness of people's internal representations, typically settling on the closest response category to what was originally intended. The continuity of mind provides an explanation for why it is often the case that the response category that truly accurately repre-sents the thoughts one wishes to act on or convey—for example, a choice of wording—*simply does not exist*.

7

Temporal Dynamics in
Language Comprehension

Language is a virus.
—William Burroughs

With Humankind Its Only Reservoir?

The casual observation that humans use linguistic communication more complexly and more ubiquitously than any other animal species has, for many centuries, motivated the speculation that there might be something uniquely innate about the human brain that is specifically programmed for developing and acquiring language. This is the large time scale arena of *language evolution*. The debate over this hypothesis has been especially heated in the past half-century (e.g., Bates & Dick, 2002; Chomsky, 1957; Christiansen & Kirby, 2003; MacWhinney, 1999; Marcus, 2001; Pinker, 1994, 1999; Seidenberg, 1997; Wexler & Culicover, 1980). Teaching language to nonhuman primates is quite slow, effortful, and culminates in somewhat less than impressive results (Seidenberg & Pettito, 1987; but see Savage-Rumbaugh, 1987), so it seems reasonably clear enough that there must be *something* innately different about humans, compared to other animals, that allows them to learn language so easily. However, for some time now, a number of researchers have suggested that what might have evolved to be innate in humans, and gets coopted for their language learning, is actually something rather low-level and generic (not at all solely devoted to language in particular), such as an exceptional statistical sensitivity to hierarchical structure in *any* time-dependent signal (e.g., Christiansen & Dale, 2004; Elman et al., 1996; Seidenberg, 1997; Tallal et al., 1993; see also Lashley, 1951). And just to prove that progress is occasionally made in the cognitive sciences, recent theoretical proposals from some usual proponents of pure linguistic nativism have at last begun to capitulate on this point (Hauser, Chomsky, & Fitch, 2002; Marcus, Vouloumanos, & Sag, 2003).

In this domain-general framework of language innateness, where the hypothesized genetic predisposition is for finding structure in time (Elman, 1990), rather than for finding specific linguistic triggers in one's speech input (Wexler & Culicover, 1980), the onus of how to evolve a human communication system over centuries and millennia is shifted significantly toward the social and cultural environment, not solely on the shoulders of the genes.

Regardless of the degree to which its evolution was biological (passed down by reproduction of genes) or cultural (passed down by societal transmission of memes; see Bonner, 1980; Dawkins, 1976), language truly does seem to act like a virus whose favorite host is humanity—as suggested by William Burroughs in the epigraph that starts this chapter. Many thousands of years ago, it propagated itself from generation to generation, spreading across the globe and infecting practically every living human being. In fact, the evolution of language, over a time scale of thousands of generations, has been modeled with some of the same kinds of algorithms as those used to model the spreading of actual viruses (Nowak, Plotkin, & Jansen, 2000). These dynamic simulations of the evolution of language can guide our understanding of what computational constraints led to the human species developing complex syntax-rich language and other animal species not doing so (Nowak, Komarova, & Niyogi, 2002; see also Batali, 1998; Cangelosi & Parisi, 1998, 2002; Christiansen & Dale, 2003; Christiansen & Kirby, 2003; Oliphant, 1999).

Finer and Finer Time Scales

The evolution of language in the human species is but one time scale for examining the temporal dynamics of language. Let's zoom in on these dynamics by a couple orders of magnitude, to the time scale of decades and centuries. Now we're in the arena of research on language change. Here, one finds that subtle alterations in a language that take place over dozens of years have in fact been referred to in the scientific literature as "grammatical viruses" (Slobin, 1997). For example, it is not only sappy soft-rock songwriters trying to squeeze out a rhyme who come up with ungrammatical sentences like "I'll never say goodbye to you and I." (The correct form would be "you and me.") Regular everyday speakers of English make this kind of pronoun case error all the time. Perhaps in 100 years it won't even be considered grammatically incorrect anymore. Similarly, people say "I could care less," when they're actually trying to imply that they already care very little. The original form "I couldn't care less," clearly stating that one cares the least amount physically possible, seems to be falling victim to a grammatical virus that blithely omits the negation of the modal verb *could*.[1]

Though the synchronic account of a language limits itself to describing the grammar-and-lexicon as though it were a static entity at some particular time slice, the diachronic account of a language tracks the changes that take place in that grammar-and-lexicon over the course of decades and centuries.

For example, Tabor (1995) calculated the frequencies of the construction "be going to," as in "Daniel is going to the West Coast," in eight English texts ranging from the years 1590 to 1970, and found a continuous nonlinear transition from this construction being used solely to describe motion in space toward instead being used predominantly to mark the future tense, as in "Daniel is going to move to the West Coast."[2] The key observation from these data, and in Tabor's connectionist simulation of their trajectory in state space, is the following: As a language diachronically changes its grammar-and-lexicon over many decades, any given synchronic account of that grammar-and-lexicon, at any given time slice, will necessarily have a number of constructions that are *in flux* and must therefore be described in a statistical or analog fashion, rather than in terms of a set of formal all-or-none rules (Tabor, 1995; see also Cooper, 1999; Hare & Elman, 1995).

Indeed, one of the reasons that the Chomskian position was so resistant to the standard gradual natural selection account of language evolution (e.g., Pinker & Bloom, 1990) is that it essentially requires—much like continuous diachronic language change—that there be periods of time in which the synchronic account of a language will involve graded probabilistic contingencies (not logical rules) governing the relationships between syntactic categories. Nowhere in any of the many different Chomskian accounts of syntactic competence is there a significant role for graded or probabilistic contingencies.

Let us continue this time scale telescoping. Zooming in a few more orders of magnitude, to the time scale of dozens of days and weeks, you will again see a similar continuity in the temporal dynamics of language. Now we're in the arena of research on language acquisition. Dynamic approaches to understanding how an individual human child learns her native language have recently been making substantial progress (Christiansen & Chater, 2001; Elman et al., 1996; MacWhinney, 1999; Thelen & Smith, 1994; see also Culicover & Nowak, 2003). Although there are impressive nonlinearities in children's development of language (e.g., the "vocabulary spurt" [e.g., Goldfield & Reznick, 1990; Nazzi & Bertoncini, 2003]; and the overgeneralization of the "-ed" past tense onto irregular verbs [e.g., Marcus et al., 1992; Rumelhart & McClelland, 1986b; Pinker & Prince, 1988; Plunkett & Marchman, 1996; see also Joanisse & Seidenberg, 1999, and Ramscar, 2002]), these nonlinearities are very rarely step functions where language abilities appear to suddenly incorporate a previously unused but now consistently executed rule (but see "fast mapping," Dollaghan, 1985; Markson & Bloom, 1997; Wilkinson, Dube, & McIlvane, 1996; see also Brown, Hulme, & Dalloz, 1996, for a neural network–inspired account of such one-trial learning). Rather, the majority of a child's development of his or her overall linguistic ability appears to be largely characterized by sigmoidal curves (like the logistic function, sometimes steep, sometimes shallow) of continuous improvement in vocabulary and grammar (Elman et al., 1996). Much of this continuity in learning dynamics is captured well by connectionist simulations of language acquisition, and given proper in-depth treatment in other sources (e.g., Christiansen, Allen, & Seidenberg, 1998;

Cleeremans, Servan-Schrieber, & McClelland, 1989; Elman, 1990; Hanson & Negishi, 2002; Rohde & Plaut, 1999; see also Tabor, 2002).

Finally, zoom in one more time on these temporal dynamics, but this time by about six orders of magnitude, to the time scale of seconds. Now we're in the arena of real-time language processing. This chapter will walk you through a series of experimental demonstrations of how real-time language comprehension takes place not just "incrementally," as the field of sentence processing is fond of saying, but in a genuinely *continuous* fashion, without breaks, without stops and starts. As phonemes, words, and sentences flow into a listener's ears, this stream of input is continuously processed into an evolving estimate of the communicative message and of plans for motor action. The leitmotif running throughout this book, of continuous cognitive dynamics at the time scale of hundreds of milliseconds, is perhaps most clearly illustrated by these findings in online language processing.

Some Some Back Back Ground Ground

In his prescient 1973 article in the journal *Nature*, William Marslen-Wilson reported evidence supporting an equal footing for grammar (syntax) and meaning (semantics), standing in sharp contrast to the "syntax as sovereign" view that was popular in linguistics at the time. In his experiment, he had participants listen to a spoken passage and repeat everything they heard as quickly and continuously as possible. This is called close speech-shadowing, where he had people shadowing approximately 250 milliseconds behind the speech input, about a single syllable of lag (see also Chistovich, 1960). This paradigm was among the first online measures of language processing. Up until then, the more popular measures were of memory for sentences, queried well after presentation (e.g., Anderson & Bower, 1971, 1972; Barclay, 1973).

Interestingly, 20 years before Marslen-Wilson's research, my mother tells me she and her brother used to play this speech-shadowing game as children, to see who could echo the radio the longest before screwing up. But actually, screwing up is the interesting part. What Marslen-Wilson found was that when people make mistakes in the speech-shadowing task, their speech errors are still grammatical and semantically appropriate with what they've been saying so far.[3] These extremely fast syntactically and semantically accurate "mistakes" suggest that syntax and semantics are being simultaneously and continuously processed in the streaming incoming speech, and moreover that a significant component of language comprehension may involve some degree of prediction of what words and constructions are coming next. These predictions may be incorrect about the exact words that come next, but they will nonetheless conform to the syntactic and semantic constraints on what words are acceptable to come next. In fact, this phenomenon has much in common with what a simple recurrent network (SRN) does: Its output is a prediction of the next input (Elman, 1990, 1991). In a way, speech-shadowing turns people into SRNs for the duration of the task. Of course, in this case, they are syllable-by-syllable SRNs that manage to encode not only phonotactics but also syntax and semantics—not exactly a trivial modeling project.

This perspective on language comprehension as a continuous interactive process (e.g., Marslen-Wilson, 1973, 1975; Rumelhart, 1977) has gone through its share of trials and tribulations since the 1970s. A continuous interactive account of real-time language comprehension posed some profound challenges for the existing theoretical attempts to map a sentence's surface structure onto its putative deep structure (e.g., Miller & McKean, 1964; Valian & Wales, 1976). If processing were this continuous in language, that is, as fine-grained as syllable by syllable, then dozens of temporary ambiguities in syntactic structure would be arising with the uptake of each new word in the speech stream! Moreover, if processing were this interactive in language, that is, syntax and semantics interweaving their constraints simultaneously, then the purely structural (devoid of semantics) accounts of linguistic competence that were popular at the time would have some serious explaining to do. The response to the challenge posed by Marslen-Wilson's (1973, 1975) findings was twofold: (1) attack the apparent continuousness of processing in language comprehension, and (2) attack the syntactic/semantic interactivity implied by the results. Little did anyone realize it, but these two responses were actually on a collision course with one another.

A number of experiments, especially using a slightly unnatural phoneme-monitoring task, produced evidence suggesting that more comprehension processes were in operation at the *end* of a sentential clause than elsewhere in the clause. These kinds of findings were treated as evidence for a clausal processing theory in which comprehension was not smoothly continuous at all, but instead words were collected over time and stored in a kind of memory buffer, without their meaning or structure being computed just yet. Only when a clause was complete did genuine comprehension processes begin to work on those stored words (e.g., Bever & Hurtig, 1975; Dunlap & Hurtig, 1981; Townsend & Bever, 1978; but see Tyler & Marslen-Wilson, 1977; Whaley, 1979). This attack on the continuous aspect of Marslen-Wilson's framework led to the clausal processing theory being perceived as a useful way to continue the mission handed to psycholinguists by the field of linguistics to find the relationship between surface structure and deep structure, to discover the algorithms by which observable linguistic performance arises from the true underlying, albeit invisible, linguistic competence.

Continuous but not Interactive?

Then came along the attack on the interactive aspect of Marslen-Wilson's framework. Following up on Kimball's (1973) "seven principles of surface structure parsing in natural language," Lyn Frazier and Janet Fodor (1978) proposed a set of syntactic structuring heuristics for real-time sentence processing that were intended to account for how certain types of sentences are routinely misparsed and thus misunderstood. Frazier and colleagues argued that a syntactic parsing module in the mind automatically attaches each new incoming word to the developing syntactic tree structure in such a way that minimizes the number of branching nodes in the structure. With sentences like that in 7.1 (taken from Bever, 1970), which contain temporary syntactic ambiguities, the particular tree-structuring format that Frazier employed posited fewer branching nodes if the verb *raced* was integrated as part of the sentence's verb phrase rather than as a relative clause inside the noun phrase. Thus, the parsing heuristic that was postulated, "minimal attachment," claimed that a reader/listener will build the syntactic structure consistent with the horse *doing the racing* (rather than being raced by someone), and this would essentially lead the language comprehension system "down the garden path" to a parse that will not work with the second verb in the sentence. The result— powerfully apparent when one first encounters this sentence—is that by the end of the sentence, the verb *fell* has nowhere to attach, no way to be grammatically integrated into the sentence.[4]

(7.1) The horse raced past the barn fell.

The sentence in 7.1 is indeed perfectly grammatical, as long as you take "raced past the barn" as a relative clause describing which horse is being referred to. Another way to write it would be, "The horse that was raced past the barn fell." The "that was" part is optional in English, and no commas are required (I promise). These kinds of reduced relative clause structures actually show up all over newspapers and spoken news reports as well.

Throughout the 1980s, Frazier and colleagues recorded students' eye movements while they read a variety of syntactically ambiguous sentences like that in 7.1, and concluded two things. (1) *Sentence processing is not interactive* because contextual factors did not appear to be able to prevent the all-important syntactic heuristics from leading the comprehension process down the garden path and producing very long reading times (e.g., Ferreira & Clifton, 1986; Rayner, Carlson, & Frazier, 1983). (2) *Sentence processing is continuous*, at least at a word-by-word grain, because the effects of the syntactic heuristics are detectable in the eye movement data (as increases in reading times) the moment the reader fixates the critical word that disambiguates the sentence, regardless of where any clause boundaries are (Frazier, 1998; Frazier & Clifton, 1989; Frazier & Rayner, 1987). Thus, by developing measures with fine temporal resolution, to identify an early period of time during processing when syntax might appear to be sovereign, the researchers who were attempting to discount the interactive component of Marslen-Wilson's framework managed to soundly discredit the clausal processing theory. This work constituted more than a decade of research in which the field characterized language comprehension as an incremental word-by-word (not clause-by-clause) process in which syntax alone was processed in an early stage of the system, and then semantics and other contextual constraints were consulted in a later stage of the system, in the occasional event that the early syntactic parsing decisions happened to produce problems.

The Field Led Down the Garden Path Recovered

With the field of sentence processing pretty much in agreement about the continuousness of the uptake of linguistic input during real-time comprehension, the battle continued to be fought over the modularity versus the interactivity of syntax and semantics. Does the process of language comprehension really begin solely with syntactic heuristics, and semantics and other contextual constraints merely wait in the wings, off stage, in case they're suddenly needed for an improvised cameo?

Citing a wide range of contemporary findings in sentence processing, MacDonald, Pearlmutter, and Seidenberg (1994) argued that what look like syntactic heuristics actually arise out of a combination of lexical and semantic biases. For example, sentence 7.2 (from Tanenhaus & Trueswell, 1995) has the very same syntactic structure as sentence 7.1, and yet it does not seem to induce a garden path effect.

(7.2) The landmine buried in the sand exploded.

If syntactic heuristics were the sole determinant of online initial parsing decisions during reading, then sentence 7.2 should be just as flummoxing as sentence 7.1. However, it appears that verbs (like *raced* and *buried*) have graded preferences for particular argument structures, and these preferences appear to guide parsing immediately (e.g., Ford, Bresnan, & Kaplan, 1982; Mitchell & Holmes, 1985; Pollard & Sag, 1994; Trueswell, Tanenhaus, & Kello, 1993; see also Kako & Wagner, 2001, for related findings). The verb *raced* is frequently used in an intransitive form (lacking a direct object). And because horses are semantically appropriate subjects of a racing event, the lexical and semantic biases in 7.1 encourage the reader to pursue the main clause interpretation of the sentence (in which the horse is doing the racing)—which turns out to be wrong. In contrast, since the verb *buried* is strongly transitive (requiring a direct object), and a landmine is a semantically appropriate direct object of a burying event, the reader is encouraged to pursue the relative clause interpretation—which turns out to be correct.

When the syntax of a sentence is temporarily ambiguous, multiple sources of information (lexical, semantic, pragmatic) combine simultaneously to bias the comprehender toward one or another parse (MacDonald et al., 1994; Tanenhaus & Trueswell, 1995; see also Bates & MacWhinney, 1989).[5] However, it is only in very rare and perfectly balanced situations that one can get *one source* of contextual constraint to single-handedly sway the resolution process its way. In most situations, the remaining unexamined constraints will just happen to converge reasonably strongly toward one or another syntactic parse. Therefore, the presence or absence of the single contextual constraint of interest will have relatively little effect on parsing. (Of course this does not mean that when a single contextual bias fails to overpower the collection of other linguistic constraints, the contextual bias in question is not being processed at that point in time—it was merely outvoted.) Thus, it is perhaps not surprising that so many studies had difficulty finding immediate effects of this or that kind of individual contextual bias on syntactic ambiguity resolution (e.g., Britt et al., 1992; Ferreira & Clifton, 1986; Mitchell, Corley, & Garnham, 1992; Rayner et al., 1983). When the various other constraints (e.g., lexical and semantic) are controlled and balanced in each stimulus item, then a single contextual constraint (e.g., discourse context) will reliably exhibit an immediate influence on the resolution of a syntactic ambiguity (e.g., Altmann & Steedman, 1988; Altmann, Garnham, & Henstra, 1994; Farrar & Kawamoto, 1993; Spivey-Knowlton, Trueswell, & Tanenhuas, 1993; Spivey & Tanenhuas, 1998; van Berkum, Brown, & Hagoort, 1999; see also McRae, Spivey-Knowlton, & Tanenhaus, 1998; Spivey-Knowlton & Sedivy, 1995; Trueswell & Kim, 1998; Trueswell, Tanenhaus, & Garnsey, 1994).

The majority of psycholinguists are beginning to accept this continuous, interactive, multiple-constraints account of sentence processing. However, the jury is still out on exactly how these different information sources combine and settle on one alternative of a syntactic ambiguity (e.g., Jurafsky, 1996, 2002; MacDonald et al., 1994; McRae et al., 1998; Stevenson, 1994; Tabor & Tanenhaus, 1999; Tanenhaus, Spivey-Knowlton, & Hanna, 2000; van Gompel et al., 2005; van Gompel, Pickering, & Traxler, 2001; see also Binder, Duffy, & Rayner, 2001). Spivey and Tanenhaus (1998) introduced a quantitatively explicit dynamic simulation (described in the next section) of how these different constraints might combine to have the syntactic alternatives compete against one another in time. In this framework, nearly equal competition between the syntactic alternatives results in long reading times, whereas highly unequal competition results in fast reading times. Thus, if the various informational constraints in the early portion of a sentence unanimously push the reader toward a syntactic parse that will eventually turn out to be untenable (e.g., sentence 7.1), reading times in this early region will be fast and reading times in the later disambiguating region can be very slow. In contrast, if those informational constraints in the early portion of the sentence just barely favor the correct parse (e.g., sentence 7.2), one should expect to see moderately slow reading times due to competition in that early region, and fast reading times in the later region (McRae et al., 1998; see also Green & Mitchell, 2006).

However, there are also circumstances in which the contextual bias toward the correct parse can be so strong that it eliminates any detectable processing difficulty. For example, in context 7.3a, a single actress is introduced into the discourse context. So when the target sentence (7.4a) starts with "The actress," it is clear to whom the phrase is referring. As a result, parsing the syntactically ambiguous verb *selected* as the main verb (with the actress *doing the selecting*) might be slightly preferred from the standpoint of contextual pragmatics. In such a case, the local structural, lexical, and semantic biases might push the reader the rest of the way toward the main clause parse (i.e., toward a garden path). Compare this to context 7.3b, where two actresses are introduced into the discourse context. When sentence 7.4a starts with "The actress," it is not at all clear which actress is being referred to. Therefore, from a contextual pragmatics standpoint, it makes sense to use the syntactically ambiguous verb *selected* as a relative clause that distinguishes the actress being referred to from the other one. Hence, the reader should not be led down the garden path.[6]

(7.3) *Context*
      a. An actress and the producer's niece were auditioning
         for a play. The director chose the actress but not the niece.
         (One-referent context)
      b. Two actresses were auditioning for a play. The director
         chose one of the actresses but not the other. (Two-referent
         context)

(7.4) *Target Sentence*
      a. The actress selected by the director believed that her
         performance was perfect. (Ambiguous reduced relative)
      b. The actress who was selected by the director believed that
         her performance was perfect. (Unambiguous full relative)

By tracking readers' eye movements and examining an early measure of processing (first-pass reading times), Spivey and Tanenhaus (1998) found that in the one-referent context (7.3a), people exhibited a 25% increase in reading time for the by-phrase, for example, "by the director," of the syntactically ambiguous sentence (7.4a) compared to the unambiguous control sentence (7.4b). This is exactly the garden path effect predicted when the various available constraints initially converge toward the main clause alternative. In contrast, in the two-referent context, readers showed no difference in first-pass reading times between the syntactically ambiguous and unambiguous sentences. Discourse context had eliminated, indeed prevented, the garden path. (For similar findings with visual contexts and spoken target sentences, see Snedeker & Trueswell, 2004; Spivey et al., 2002b; Tanenhaus et al., 1995; Trueswell, Sekerina, & Logrip, 1999).

Localist Attractor Simulations of Syntactic Ambiguity Resolution

The quantitatively explicit dynamic simulation that Spivey and Tanenhaus (1998) provided for these findings employs a version of the normalized recurrence localist attractor network (see also chapters 4, 6, and 8). This kind of network idealizes its representations (such as the relative clause and the main clause) as individual nodes to make it easy to follow their relative activations over time, not because it is thought that the representations are actually that unitary. The actual representation of a relative clause in the mind of a language user is certainly more accurately conceptualized as a pattern of activation across many subunits that correspond to micro-featural components of the representation. An account that failed to acknowledge this underlying description of the actual biological material that implements such representations would be woefully neurophysiologically implausible and incapable of dealing with the graded subtleties and partially overlapping meanings and structures that characterize language processing in real time. In normalized recurrence, these graded subtleties and partially overlapping meanings and structures are transparently exhibited as simultaneous parallel activation of mutually exclusive localist representation nodes.

Figure 7.1A shows a schematic of this localist attractor network, with four constraints that are relevant at the point of syntactic ambiguity (e.g., the verb *selected*). The lexical bias constraint is based on the frequency with which each individual verb is used in a past participle form, favoring the reduced relative alternative, versus a simple past tense form, favoring the main clause alternative (see Francis & Kucera, 1982). The main clause (or subject-verb-object) bias is based on the frequency with which any sentence initial noun phrase, followed by a verb + -ed, turns out to be a main clause (92% of the time) versus a reduced relative clause (8% of the time) (Tabossi et al., 1994; see also Bever, 1970). The parafoveal "by" bias is based on evidence from eye tracking reading studies revealing that the word to the right of the currently fixated word is often processed as well at the same time (e.g., Rayner, 1998). And in a corpus analysis, McRae et al. (1998) found that 20% of sentences with a sentence-initial noun phrase followed by a verb + -ed, and then followed by the word *by*, turn out to be main clauses, whereas 80% of them turn out to be relative clauses. Finally, the referential context bias was estimated as two-thirds support for the main clause (with one-third support for the reduced relative) when it was a one-referent context, and two-thirds support for the reduced relative (with one-third support for the main clause) when it was a two-referent context.

In normalized recurrence, these different biases are each normalized to sum to 1.0 in their relative support for the two syntactic alternatives, and then these constraints are combined in a weighted average to produce activations for the syntactic alternatives. As long as the integration weights sum to 1.0, the activations of the alternatives will do the same. Then the probabilistic activations of the syntactic alternatives are multiplied pointwise by the activations of the constraint nodes, and the products are added to their respective constraint node activations. As the constraint nodes are renormalized to sum to 1.0, thus begins another time step of competition (see chapter 4 for normalized recurrence equations).

Competition in this model (or processing difficulty over and above normal reading times) continues until the maximum activation of either syntactic alternative reaches a dynamic criterion. This criterion is called dynamic because it changes over time; starting at 1.0 and decreasing by 0.01 each

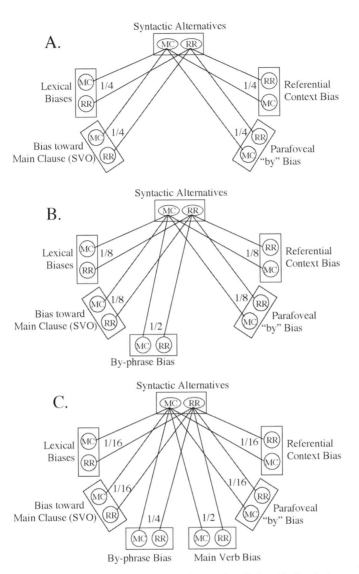

Figure 7.1. Schematic of Spivey and Tanenhaus's (1998) simulation (see text for details).

time step. This means that if the constraints are especially balanced for a particular sentence, the model won't fixate that region of the sentence indefinitely. Rather, it will give up on the competition process at some point in time, with each syntactic alternative still being moderately active, and those activation levels will be the starting point for when the reader's eyes move to the next sentence region and the model gets a new constraint added. For simulating the amount of processing difficulty at the by-phrase, the model adds a constraint that is biased seven-eighths toward the reduced relative and one-eighth toward the main clause (see figure 7.1B). For simulating the amount of processing difficulty at the main verb, the model adds a constraint that is biased 1.0 toward the reduced relative and 0 toward the main clause (see figure 7.1B).[7]

In similar work by McRae et al.'s (1998), the values of the weights were set based on a best-fit metric for simulating off-line gated sentence completions, and then those same weights were used for prediction of online reading times. For simplicity, in this simulation, the weight assigned to each constraint is simply based on Bayesian priors, that is, each constraint's weight is $1/n$, with n being the number of constraints. So that the weights always sum to 1.0, when a new constraint is added (due to the reader's eyes moving to new regions of the sentence with new content), the new constraint is given a weight of 0.5, and the previous constraints share the remaining 0.5 weight equally.

Figure 7.2 shows a pair of simulations with a hypothetical verb that has a 0.75 bias toward the past participle reduced relative (RR) and a 0.25 bias toward the simple past main clause (MC).[8] In the one-referent context (figure 7.2A), the model spends time steps 1 through 19 settling on the MC alternative at the ambiguous verb. Then, as the eyes would have moved on to the by-phrase, this constraint is included, and the model spends time steps 20 through 59 settling still *slightly toward* (i.e., 60/40) the MC alternative before reaching its dynamic criterion. Finally, when the eyes then move to the main verb, and this constraint is added to the model, it spends time steps 60 through 72 settling on the RR alternative.

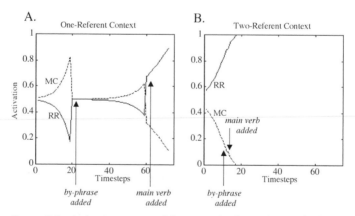

Figure 7.2. Activation curves of the syntactic alternatives in the localist attractor network simulation. Note how, in the one-referent context, the Main Clause (MC) alternative (dotted line) slowly accrues activation during the verb region of the ambiguous sentence, as well as during the by-phrase region of the ambiguous sentence. The system finally recovers from this garden path during the main verb region. In contrast, in the two-referent context, the Reduced Relative (RR) alternative wins the competition quickly.

Something completely different happens when the model simulates the competition between syntactic alternatives that would take place in the same sentence but in a two-referent context. In the two-referent context (figure 7.2B), the model spends time steps 1 through 12 settling on the RR alternative at the ambiguous verb, then time steps 13 through 16 settling on the RR alternative at the by-phrase, and only time step 17 settling on the RR alternative at the main verb. Thus, whereas in the one-referent context, the simulation exhibits substantial competition, producing slow-downs in reading time that correspond to garden path phenomena, in the two-referent context, the simulation exhibits little or no such competition (see Spivey & Tanenhaus, 1998).

Additional evidence for graded activation of multiple syntactic alternatives, and for a time-consuming competition process, comes from speeded sentence completions. Borrowing the logic from McElree and Griffith's (1995, 1998) use of the speed–accuracy trade-off method (see chapter 3), Spivey et al. (2002a) gave experimental participants sentence fragments (presented visually one word at a time) that they were instructed to complete as grammatical sentences with the first thing that came to mind. The critical sentence fragments in this experiment were syntactically ambiguous as to whether they would continue as an MC (e.g., "*The manager sent* . . . two clerks to the other branch office.") or as a RR clause (e.g., "*The manager sent* . . . to the other branch office decided to quit."). Each verb was coupled with a typical agent/subject of that event (e.g., The doctor cured . . .) and with a typical patient of that verb (e.g., The patient cured . . .). In some conditions, these participants had a mere 300 milliseconds (after seeing the third word in the fragment) to begin their completion of the sentence, and in other conditions they had 600, 900, or 1,200 milliseconds.

The first thing to know about any kind of sentence completion task with MC/RR ambiguities is that the majority of completions will be in the form of a main clause, simply because the MC form is about 10 times more frequent than the RR form with this kind of sentence structure (Tabossi et al., 1994). For example, even something as seemingly obvious as "The patient cured" will often get completed as "The patient cured himself" or "The patient cured his mother's cancer" instead of as a RR, such as "The patient cured by the doctor was elated." (This is likely due to the fact that *cured* is rarely used in a past participle construction.) Nonetheless, at the response deadline of 300 milliseconds, the reduced relative alternative had not yet completely lost the competition and was still active enough to occasionally trigger its response (figure 7.3D). See averaged results from four example sentences, with their typical agents and typical patients, in figure 7.3.

To more rigorously cash out this claim that partially active and temporally dynamic representations underlie these sentence completions in the face of syntactic ambiguity, a normalized recurrence simulation was conducted for each of the 16 sentences from the experiment with its typical agent and with its typical patient. This localist attractor network resembled that in figure 7.1A, in that it included a general MC bias and a lexical bias (for the verb's frequency

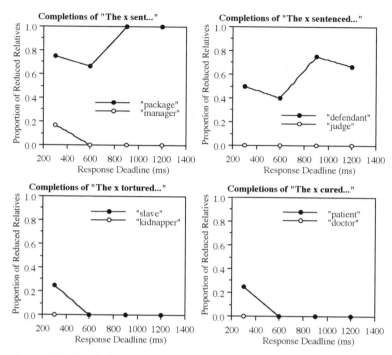

Figure 7.3. Speeded sentence completions with typical agents and typical patients (Spivey et al., 2002a).

as a simple past tense and as a past participle). However, instead of the referential context bias, there was a semantic fit bias (based on ratings of how typical it is for each noun to be an agent of the verb and a patient of the verb), and there was no parafoveal bias of course. Treating each time step in the model as equivalent to 10 milliseconds, the simulations produced activation curves that nicely mimicked most of the sentence completion curves. Figure 7.4 shows the simulations corresponding to the four example sentences in figure 7.3.

These simulations (and their fit to the human data) illustrate how, if multiple constraints converge toward relatively balanced support for both the MC and RR alternatives, then a single constraint (such as discourse context or semantic fit) can dramatically sway the syntactic ambiguity resolution process toward its preferred alternative. Crucially, the gradual activation curves in figures 7.2–4 suggest that the slowed reading times resulting from a syntactic garden path need not be due to an acknowledged and verbally reportable misconstrual of the sentence that requires deliberative reasoning (or a syntactic reanalysis module) to recover from it. Instead, partially active misinterpretations of a sentence can slow down comprehension merely by causing the system to linger in nameless intermediate regions of its state space, in between the two syntactically permissible versions of the sentence.[9] This shift in the literature from a stage-based account of syntactic garden pathing to a continuous dynamical

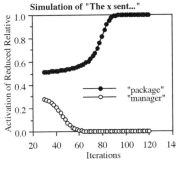
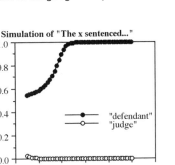
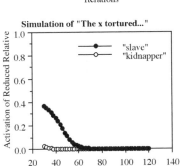
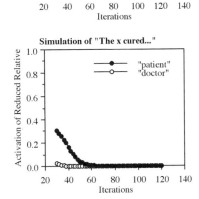

Figure 7.4. Normalized recurrence simulations of speeded sentence completions (compare to figure 7.3).

account is emblematic of the metatheoretical transition taking place in many areas of psycholinguistics and cognitive psychology.

More Time Scale Zooming: Lexical Ambiguity Resolution

Let's zoom in on language another order of magnitude, from the time scale of seconds to the time scale of hundreds of milliseconds. Now instead of talking about sentence processing, we're talking about word recognition. As with syntactic parsing, the best circumstances under which one can test the degree to which multiple information sources combine continuously and immediately (instead of being applied in a serial stage-like fashion) is when the input is temporarily ambiguous.

In general, the continuous processing of an incoming linguistic signal is fraught with temporary ambiguities that often require contextual mediation for their resolution. For example, concurrent with the research on syntactic ambiguity resolution discussed in the previous sections, research in psycholinguistics has spent many years testing whether discourse and syntactic context can constrain the initial processing of an ambiguous word like *bank* (as a financial institution or a river embankment). Initial findings were consistent with a stage-based account in which word recognition took place in an encapsulated module that only used immediate phonemic or orthographic input, and context was consulted only at a later stage (Swinney, 1979; Tanenhaus, Leiman, & Seidenberg, 1979).

Tanenhaus et al. (1979) presented participants with sentences that ended with words that were ambiguous between being a noun or a verb (e.g., *watch*, *rose*, *fly*, etc.). Shortly after the ambiguous word (0, 200, or 600 milliseconds after), a word was visually presented for the subject to read aloud as quickly as possible. This target word was related to either the noun sense of the ambiguous word or the verb sense (or unrelated, as a control condition). When the syntactic context of the sentence was consistent with only the verb sense, for example, "I will watch," and the target word showed up 200 or 600 milliseconds after *watch*, participants were faster to name a target word like *eyes* than a target word like *time*. Essentially, the syntactic context had made the verb sense of *watch* salient enough that it primed words like *eyes* and not words like *time*. The reverse happened when the syntactic context was consistent with only the noun sense, for example, "He wore a watch."

But something very different happened when the target word was presented 0 milliseconds after the ambiguous word. When the target word was presented immediately after the ambiguous word, Tanenhaus et al. (1979) found priming for *both* senses of the word. This kind of result was interpreted as evidence for a brief initial stage of processing in word recognition that performed its computations on the linguistic input in a manner that was uninfluenced by context (see also Swinney, 1979).

However, recent findings have suggested that more strongly constraining contexts can indeed bias lexical access immediately (Fitneva & Spivey, 2004; Tabossi, Colombo, & Job, 1987; Vu, Kellas, & Paul, 1998). If the context strongly biases the features associated with one of the ambiguous word's senses (regardless of whether it is the dominant, more frequent sense or the subordinate, less frequent sense), then there does not appear to be much effect from the contextually disfavored meaning. For example, when the contexts are rated in advance for how strongly or weakly constraining they are, strong contexts, such as passage 7.5, result in initial priming for only the contextually supported meaning (e.g., flower) of the ambiguous noun *bulb*, and weak contexts, such as passage 7.6, result in initial priming for *both* senses (e.g., coal and explosive) of the ambiguous noun *mine* (Martin et al., 1999; but see Rayner, Binder, & Duffy, 1999).

(7.5) The gardener dug a hole. She inserted the *bulb* carefully into the soil.

(7.6) The scout patrolled the area. He reported the *mine* to the commander.

These effects are sometimes described as though context selectively ushered access to one of the word's meanings and categorically prevented access to the other. But this way of conceptualizing context's influence on word recognition is probably dangerously oversimplified. It could very well be that by using box-and-arrow types of metaphors borrowed from the information-processing framework, the debate becomes unresolvable and descends into methodological nitpicking of one another's experimental designs (Kambe, Rayner, & Duffy, 2001; Vu & Kellas, 1999). The problem is this: The discrete stage-based way of thinking can pretty much only predict one or the other set of findings, either early context effects, or delayed context effects. When the literature is full of both kinds of findings, the only way to accommodate them all at the same time may be to relinquish the stage-based account and instead adopt a framework that allows graded partial influences (in time and in state space) of contextual variables on afferent sensory input, that is, a dynamical systems perspective.

Kawamoto (1993) described a Boltzmann machine simulation of lexical ambiguity resolution that concretely demonstrated how an ambiguous word can induce an internal state in the system that is in between two attractors that correspond to the word's two senses. Settling into one of those attractors is a time-dependent process that depends on the relative frequency of the two senses and on the previous contextual bias affecting where in state space that system was located right before receiving the ambiguous word as input. At no point in this kind of system can one actually ask whether a particular lexical meaning has been accessed or not. On exposure to the ambiguous word, depending on both context and frequency, the system will be in a state that is near one attractor or the other, or about equally near both.

If the system's state is about equally near both attractors, and far from unrelated attractors, then the system will exhibit long reading times for that word (as seen in the data of Rayner et al., 1999) because the two attractors compete with about equal efficacy for pulling the system toward themselves, and the system will also briefly exhibit priming for both meanings of the ambiguous word (Swinney, 1979; Tanenhaus et al., 1979). However, if a strong context or a strong frequency imbalance (or combination thereof) starts the system out in a location that is especially close to one of the attractors and far from the other, then on exposure to the ambiguous word, the system will quickly settle into the nearby attractor, exhibiting fast reading times and priming for only the nearby meaning (Vu et al., 1998).

Figure 7.5 provides an idealized depiction to help clarify this process for stimuli like passages 7.5 and 7.6. This cartoon formulation borrows heavily from images of state space trajectories exhibited by simple recurrent networks processing sentences, when their high-dimensional state spaces are viewed from a two-dimensional perspective via principal component analysis (see Elman, 1991; Tabor & Tanenhaus, 1999). After reading "The gardener dug a hole. Then she inserted the—," the system is naturally projected into a region of state space that has a rather narrowly clustered set of attractors that share a substantial portion of their semantic features (e.g., *flower, seed, bulb, roots*). Therefore, when the ambiguous word *bulb* is presented, the system has only a

A.

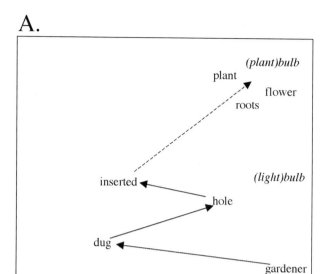

(plant)bulb
plant
flower
roots

(light)bulb
inserted
hole
dug
gardener

B.

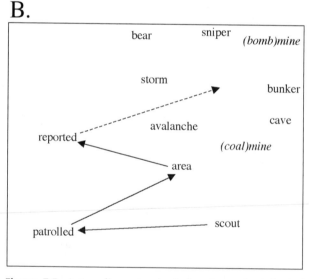

bear   sniper   *(bomb)mine*

storm   bunker

avalanche   cave

reported   *(coal)mine*

area

patrolled   scout

Figure 7.5. A two-dimensional window into a hypothetical state-space exhibiting strong (A) and weak (B) context effects in lexical ambiguity resolution. The dashed line shows the system's predictive trajectory immediately prior to receiving the ambiguous word, (e.g., "bulb" or "mine"). In panel A, the predictive trajectory is close to one sense of *bulb* and far away from the other. In panel B, the predictive trajectory is equidistant from both senses of *mine*.

very short distance to travel to settle into that attractor (figure 7.5A). Moreover, if a probe word were introduced to measure semantic priming, it would show strong priming for associates of (*plant*)*bulb*, to which the system is already extremely close in state space, and little or no priming for associates of (*light*)*bulb* or for unrelated words that are all quite far away in state space.

In contrast, after reading "The scout patrolled the area. He reported the—," there is quite a variety of concepts that could be acceptable direct objects of that verb in that context (e.g., *sniper, bunker, troops, mine, storm, cave, avalanche, bear*). Although there may be some broad semantic connectedness between some of those attractors (military threats and natural threats), it is clearly the case that some are artifacts, whereas others are natural kinds; some are sentient, others are not, and so on. The semantic category of these objects is certainly not narrowly defined, and therefore this collection of attractors is not expected to be tightly clustered. As shown in figure 7.5B, when the dynamical system is projected into this region of state space, roughly equidistant from each of these attractors, it is not impressively close to any single one of them. Thus, the system is in a location in state space that will involve a bit of time before it can settle into the right attractor when the ambiguous word is presented. And any probe words related to the two different meanings of *mine* that enter the system early on as a measure of semantic priming will not exhibit radically different settling times into their attractors, because neither attractor is especially closer than the other.

Spoken Word Recognition

In many lexical ambiguity studies, the ambiguous words are presented visually. Because eye movement measures of visual word recognition suggest that the letters in most words tend to be processed more or less simultaneously (see Rayner, 1998), there may not be very much in the way of temporal dynamics for how the sublexical components of written words are processed. However, in *spoken* word recognition, the individual parts of a word (the phonemes) are received by the sensory apparatus more or less one at a time. Therefore, even apparently unambiguous words, like *candle*, are temporarily and dynamically ambiguous as they unfold over time (e.g., Grosjean, 1980; Marslen-Wilson, 1987; Marslen-Wilson & Welsh, 1978; McClelland & Elman, 1986). Just as with completely ambiguous words, this temporary ambiguity leads to brief partial activation of multiple lexical representations. Marslen-Wilson's (1987) cohort theory proposed that as the acoustic-phonetic input for a word begins, it activates all the lexical representations that begin with that input, for example, *candle, candy, candid, candelabra*. This set of activated lexical items is called the cohort. As further acoustic-phonetic input is received, some of the lexical items in the cohort are ruled out and omitted. Eventually, but often before the end of the spoken word, the cohort is winnowed down to only one lexical item. Cross-modal priming studies, much like those described in the previous section, have shown supporting evidence for the cohort theory (e.g., Cutler, 1995; Gaskell & Marslen-Wilson, 2002; Zwitserlood, 1989).

Rather than relying solely on faster reaction times to semantically related probe words as evidence for partial activation of a cohort member, additional compelling evidence for partial activation of multiple lexical items can come from motor output aimed at real objects that correspond to the competing lexical representations. Eye movement behavior is a motor output that is fast, ballistic, largely resistant to strategic control, and especially sensitive to partially active representations.

Spivey-Knowlton, Sedivy, Eberhard, and Tanenhaus (1994) first reported cohort effects in eye movement patterns by using a headband-mounted eye tracker that allowed subjects to move around naturally and follow spoken instructions to manipulate real objects. While wearing the eye tracker, participants sat in front of a table with a central fixation cross and various objects on it, for example, a transparent bag of candy, a fork, a pincushion, and a pair of scissors. With a display such as that, the participant was instructed to pick up the candy. On about one-fourth of the trials, the participants looked at one of the other objects (about equally likely for each of the three) for about 250 milliseconds, and then to the candy to pick it up. On the other three-fourths of the trials, the participant looked immediately to the candy, on an average of 150 milliseconds after the end of the word *candy*, and then began reaching for it. Note that it takes about 200 milliseconds for the motor programming of an eye movement (Matin, Shao, & Boff, 1993). Thus in this kind of visual context, listeners were frequently recognizing the word *candy*, and initiating the motor programming for moving the eyes to the candy, *before the word was even finished being said!* This could happen because the visual context contained only one object whose name sounded anything like the first couple sounds in *candy*.

What if the visual context contained another object whose name had similar initial phonemes? In another condition, we replaced the pincushion with a candle, and delivered the exact same instruction: "Pick up the candy." Now, on about a third of the trials, the participants looked at something other than the candy initially, and over two-thirds of those "mistake" eye movements were to the *candle*, not the fork or the scissors. This is exactly what one would predict if partway through hearing the word, probabilistic representations of multiple words (for *candy* and for *candle*) were partially active, and eye movements could occasionally be triggered by these only moderately high activation levels. Notably, when the participant was later debriefed and told, "When you were instructed to pick up the candy, you briefly looked at the candle," he or she would often respond incredulously with "No, I didn't."

Figure 7.6 shows the proportion of trials at each time slice (averaged over several different target objects, dozens of trials, and a dozen subjects) in which the eyes were looking at the various objects as the target word unfolded over time, in the "competitor-absent" condition, that is, when no object in the

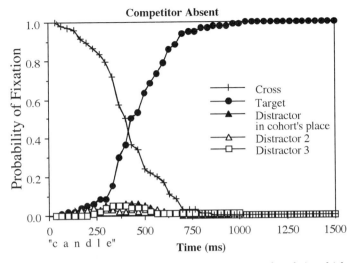

Figure 7.6. Cohort competitor absent: Proportion of trials in which participants were fixating each object as the spoken target word unfolded in time (e.g., "candle," lasting approximately 300 ms).

display had a name with similar phonology to the spoken target word. As time proceeded, participants were less likely to be looking at the central cross that they started out fixating and more likely to be looking at the target object. The distractor objects received very few fixations.

In contrast, figure 7.7 shows the same measure for the "competitor-present" condition, in which an unrelated distractor object had been replaced by a cohort competitor object. Just as in the competitor-absent condition, the probability of the participant looking at the central cross steadily decreased, and the probability of looking at the target steadily increased. However, the probability of looking at the cohort object (e.g., the candy, when instructed to "pick up the candle") rose just as quickly as the probability of looking at the target object for a period of about 200 milliseconds around the tail end of the spoken word. And even when the two curves diverge, the proportion of fixations of the cohort object still persist for a few hundred milliseconds. This salience of the cohort object conspicuously attracting eye movements is indicative of the competing lexical representation being partially active during and perhaps shortly after delivery of the spoken word. Figure 7.8 superimposes the two target fixation probability curves from the cohort absent condition and the cohort present condition. Note how the presence of the cohort object delays eye movements to the target object.

Headband-mounted eye tracking studies like this have demonstrated the continuous uptake of acoustic-phonetic input and resulting lexical competition effects using computer-displayed objects (Allopenna et al., 1998), using artificial lexicons (Magnuson et al., 2003b), with young children (Fernald,

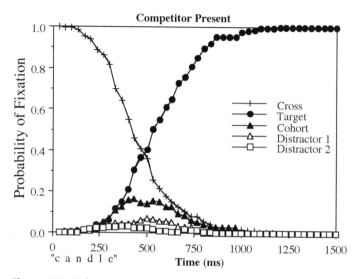

Figure 7.7. Cohort competitor present: Proportion of trials in which participants were fixating each object as the spoken target word unfolded in time (e.g., "candle," lasting approximately 300 ms). Note how participants' eyes briefly fixated the cohort object (filled triangles) on a substantial proportion of trials between about 300 and 700 ms after word onset.

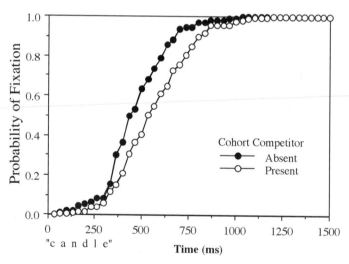

Figure 7.8. The rising curves for eyes fixating the target object over time, from figures 7.6 and 7.7, overlaid on one another to show the effects of visual context.

Swingley, & Pinto, 2001), and even across two languages in bilingual participants (Marian & Spivey, 2003a, 2003b; Spivey & Marian, 1999). In terms of a state space containing attractors for lexical items, these findings can be described as the state of the listener traversing regions of her mental state space that are more proximal to the target word and the cohort word (when the visual context supports it) as the spoken word begins. Then as the latter portion of the spoken word is being uttered, the state of the listener gravitates away from the cohort and only toward the actual spoken word. The filled circles curve and the filled triangles curve in figure 7.7 can be likened to proximity functions reporting how close the listener's state is to those attractors over time (recall figure 2.12).

Marslen-Wilson's (1987) cohort theory naturally predicts findings like these, and McClelland and Elman's (1986) TRACE model can quantitatively simulate them.[10] In the TRACE connectionist model (inspired by the interactive-activation framework of McClelland & Rumelhart, 1981), a layer of phonetic feature nodes is externally fed activation as a spoken word unfolds over time. These phonetic feature nodes then spread their activation to appropriate phoneme nodes in the middle layer of the network, which then spread their activation to appropriate lexical nodes at the top layer of the network. Importantly, both the lexical layer and the phoneme layer also send feedback to their preceding layers. Thus, as this localist attractor network receives phonetic feature activation corresponding to a word being heard, the system gradually settles toward exhibiting activation for the lexical nodes that are consistent with the speech input. In this way, TRACE can explicitly implement the cohort effect described in the cohort theory. However, this attractor network makes a divergent prediction as well. Because TRACE has only positive connections between layers (and only inhibitory connections within layers), it does not prevent and will in fact induce the activation of lexical items that rhyme with the actual word being spoken. Therefore, TRACE predicts that when instructed to "pick up the candle," a person should conspicuously fixate a *handle* in the display—whereas the standard version of the cohort theory would not predict this. Indeed, TRACE's prediction holds true. Listeners will briefly fixate an object whose name rhymes with the spoken word more so than unrelated control objects (Allopenna et al., 1998).

Discrete Functions Underlying Smooth Curves?

It is worth noting that the curves in figures 7.6 and 7.7 are averaged over many trials and many subjects. Therefore, the actual activation of lexical representations over time in an individual instance could in principle be discrete and symbolic—with just the timing of the inflections in the step functions varying from trial to trial. When one averages many discrete step functions that are slightly time-shifted relative to each other, the result can often be a surprisingly smooth, continuous curve. This is, of course, precisely how these eye movement data and these simulations come up with smooth curves. Saccades to objects (and simulated saccades to objects) are extremely fast, ballistic, practically discrete responses. The key issue is whether these early discrete motor outputs constitute *the first time* that the graded, multifarious, distributed pattern of neural activation has "had its wave collapsed," as it were. Or was the temporary ambiguity in the perceptual signal converted into a discrete cognitive symbol internally at some point, and it is that 100% confident symbol that generated the eye movement?

In principle, a listener could hear part of the word *candle* and occasionally initially perceive it wholly and confidently (albeit incorrectly) as *candy*, and that would be why the eyes initially look at the candy on some trials. If the timing of these effects varied from trial to trial and from listener to listener, then when the results of such discrete mental phenomena were averaged, you could get smooth curves that would mislead you into thinking that the mental dynamics were smooth. That said, this account needs a story for how the listener then quickly realizes (usually about a quarter of a second later) that the spoken word was actually *candle* and that he or she is currently fixating the wrong object and should make a saccade to the candle in the display to correctly carry out the instruction. Such a story for explaining this pattern of corrective eye movements could be reasonably workable. However, there is another pattern of errant eye movements that shows up regularly in these experiments that could make an account based on the discrete toggling between symbolic lexical activations somewhat hard to swallow. These experiments always have a fair number of trials in which the listener first fixates the correct target object, then a quarter second later fixates the cohort object, then a quarter second later fixates the target object again and picks it up. It seems as though a story based on a toggling between discrete binary lexical activations would have to bend over backward to accommodate such eye movement patterns. Why would a discrete logical process of spoken word recognition allow such a stochastic skittering between alternating confident representations of a spoken word?

In a normalized recurrence simulation with TRACE lexical activations as input, this particular skittering eye movement pattern can simply be the result of a very early (and mostly lucky) sample from the distribution in the visual nodes driving the eyes to fixate the target object, followed about 10 time steps later by a still rather early (and, this time, unlucky) sample from the visual nodes driving the eyes to fixate the cohort object. Another 10 time steps later, the eyes are ready to move again, and by this time, the target object is the only one with noticeable activation in the visual nodes.

Thus, on careful examination, the standard criticism of averaged smooth curves having discrete functions underlying them may not be as damning as it first appears. The discrete functions in question are saccades, which cannot help but be discrete under most circumstances. But underlying them is a temporally dynamic and graded pattern of multiple partially active representations for potential saccade targets (see Gold & Shadlen, 2000).

Localist Attractor Simulations of Spoken Word Recognition

Allopenna et al. (1998) showed that the activations of the lexical nodes in TRACE closely mimic the probability-of-fixation functions from these eye tracking experiments (e.g., figures 7.6 and 7.7), as long as the simulation examines only the lexical nodes corresponding to the names of the objects present in the display, and the activations are scaled by an exponent to adjust separation, normalized against each other by the Luce choice rule (Luce, 1959), and finally scaled by the ratio of the current maximum activation over the greatest asymptotic activation achieved during the simulated input for a given target referent. However, limiting examination of the TRACE lexical nodes a priori to only the four words that correspond to objects present in a display on any one trial runs the risk of characterizing these findings as due to a kind of artificial word selection from a working memory buffer of prepared lexical items, rather than as evidence pertaining to natural word recognition in a visual context. As the same kinds of eye movement results have been found with very brief previews of the display (Tanenhaus et al., 2000), and lexical frequency effects modulate these probability-of-fixation curves as well (Dahan, Magnuson, & Tanenhaus, 2001), it seems unlikely that the results are due to a laboratory-induced strategy of word selection from a buffer. Therefore, a simulation that does not summarily exclude lexical items that correspond to objects not currently present in a display and one that also simulates the selection of saccade targets might provide a richer linking hypothesis between the observed discrete eye movements and the inferred graded lexical activations.

A larger TRACE model, with all experimentally relevant lexical items included, can be used if the raw, unaltered, lexical activations from TRACE are fed into a normalized recurrence localist attractor network that allows idealized visual nodes to do the gradual winnowing of all possible lexical activations down to only those that correspond to objects present in the visual display (Spivey-Knowlton & Allopenna, 1997). Figure 7.9 shows the normalized recurrence network, with all 14 TRACE lexical activations being added to its lexical layer at every competition cycle (corresponding to 25 milliseconds). To simulate the human data, this model was run several times with each target stimulus (*candle, candy, doll, dolphin, penny, pencil, car, carton*) with its cohort object absent and with it present, and the results were averaged in the same way as was done with the human data.

As a time step in TRACE typically corresponds to about a dozen milliseconds (see Allopenna et al., 1998), TRACE's lexical activations were averaged over two time steps before being added to the lexical layer of the normalized recurrence network. At the beginning of a cycle of competition, the current

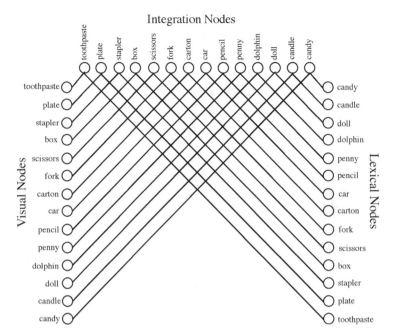

Figure 7.9. Normalized recurrence network for simulating the real-time integration of spoken words and visual objects.

TRACE activations were added to the lexical layer's current activation, then lexical and visual layers were normalized, then they summed at the integration layer, then the integration layer was normalized, and finally the multiplicative feedback from the integration nodes was added to the lexical and visual nodes.[11]

In the visual layer of the normalized recurrence network, only the four nodes corresponding to visibly present objects were active and equally so. Thus, the indirect cross-talk between the visual layer and the lexical layer affected only those nodes whose referents were present in the display. Having the simulated eye movements generated by sampling from the probabilistic distribution of activation over the visual nodes (where only the nodes corresponding to visually present objects will ever exceed zero activation) ensured that the model only predicted eye movements to objects that were present, never to partially active concepts that were partly supported by the speech input but not present in the visual display. This sampling from the visual nodes was triggered by a dynamic criterion that became more and more lax as time went by (a kind of saccade deadline). The rate of decrement for this dynamic criterion varied randomly from trial to trial, between 0.001 per time step and 0.07 per time step. Once this gradually decreasing activation criterion was exceeded, a biased random selection, based on the probabilistic activations of the nodes, was made to determine which object was targeted for a saccade. To approximate oculomotor programming time (e.g., Matin et al., 1993), as well as

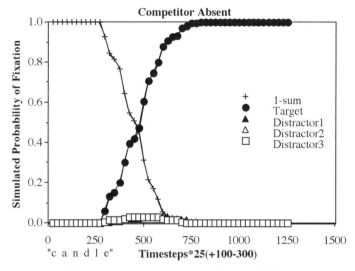

Figure 7.10. Normalized recurrence simulation (with TRACE input, and some random jitter in saccade latency from 100 to 300 ms) roughly mimics the human data from figure 7.6.

variation in oculomotor readiness (Fischer & Weber, 1993; Klein & Pontefract, 1994; Reuter-Lorenz, Hughes, & Fendrich, 1991), the simulated saccade was launched 4 to 12 time steps later (the equivalent of 100–300 milliseconds). For simplicity, the saccade itself was treated as instantaneous.

This biased random selection of a saccade target from the probabilistic distribution in the visual vector is generally necessary for the model to make any errors at all. Moreover, it is theoretically motivated by computational work on eye movement latencies, suggesting that some form of random component is necessary leading up to the decision process of an eye movement (Carpenter, 1999; Leach & Carpenter, 2001; see also Ratcliff, 1980; Ratcliff, Carpenter, & Reddi, 2001). To model corrective saccades that follow fixations of incorrect objects, a second eye movement was resampled from the distribution in the visual nodes 10 time steps after the first eye movement (the equivalent of 250 milliseconds later).

Figures 7.10 and 7.11 show results from the simulation, averaged over 10 runs of each of the eight spoken targets, when the cohort object was absent and when it was present. Note the close match between these plots and the human data in figures 7.6 and 7.7. Figure 7.12 superimposes the simulated fixation probability curve for the target-absent condition on that for the target-present condition. The plot shows that the presence of the cohort competitor delays the simulated eye movements to the target object in a manner similar to that observed with the human data (figure 7.8).

Now that we have a simulation that mimics the basic human data rather well, we can examine its internal processes to get a handle on how it does its job—and thus better articulate some guesses as to how the human mind

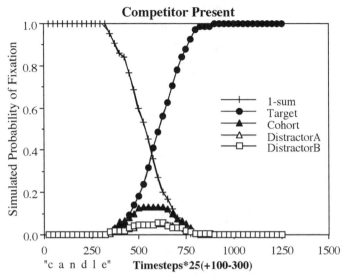

Figure 7.11. Normalized recurrence simulation also roughly mimics the human data from figure 7.7.

might be integrating language and vision in real time. Because the model uses localist representations, examining their activations over time is quite easy. For example, figure 7.13 shows the normalized activations of the lexical nodes over time, as a result of additive TRACE input as well as cumulative feedback from the integration nodes, when the speech input was "candle" and the

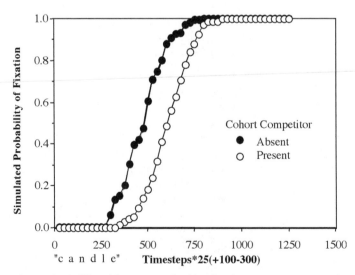

Figure 7.12. The rising curves for simulated eye movements to the target object over time, from figures 7.10 and 7.11, overlaid on one another to show the effects of visual context—as also seen in figure 7.8.

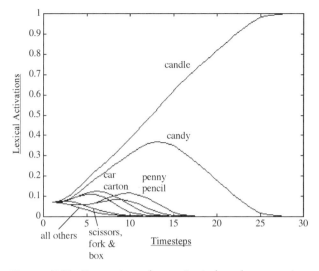

Figure 7.13. Competitor absent: Lexical nodes over time inside normalized recurrence.

cohort competitor was absent from the display (e.g., only the *candle, scissors, fork,* and *box* visual nodes had nonzero activation). Notice how the lexical activation curves for /candle/ and for /candy/ are both rising during the first dozen cycles of competition, because those first few phonemes of speech input are identical for /candle/ and for /candy/. However, as early as time step 2, they are already rising at different rates. This early separation in activation is due entirely to the indirect cross-talk from the visual layer positively biasing the /candle/ lexical node (because the corresponding visual node is active) and not the /candy/ lexical node (because that object is absent). Figure 7.14 shows the normalized activations of the visual nodes over time in the same simulation, in which indirect cross-talk from the lexical layer clearly causes the *candle* visual node to take over the probability distribution. (Of course, the normalized integration nodes are simply an average of these lexical and visual activations at each point in time.)

When the cohort object is present (e.g., a *candy* in the display when the spoken word is "candle"), the lexical activations over time exhibit a different pattern (figure 7.15). Most noticeably, the "candy" lexical node reaches greater activation and does so for a longer period of time than in the cohort-absent condition (figure 7.13). Thus, the model demonstrates how a cohort lexical representation's interference with the recognition of a spoken word could be exacerbated by probabilistic biases spreading from the visual modality. Similarly, the activations of the visual nodes in the competitor-present condition (figure 7.16) also exhibit the salience of the cohort object, *candy*, as a result of the partial phonological overlap influencing visual attention.

An important observation about how this integrated model allows visual representations to influence lexical representations, is that it is *not the case* that

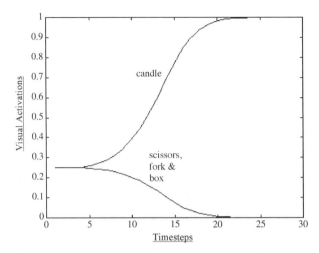

Figure 7.14. Competitor absent: Visual nodes from normalized recurrence, acting as a kind of object-based salience map over time for guiding eye movements.

a potential cohort lexical representation does not get active at all when its referent is absent from the visual input. The lexical representation for "candy" still accrues some activation and still competes with the target word "candle," even when the *candy* is not present in the display. Thus, in the competitor-absent condition, if one were to transform lexical activations directly into curves of eye position over time, it would make the peculiar prediction that the eyes should spend some time fixating an object that is not there. By integrating

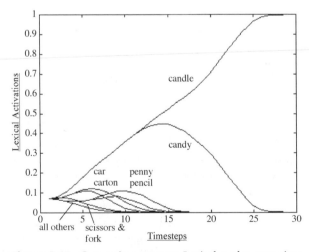

Figure 7.15. Competitor present: Lexical nodes over time inside normalized recurrence.

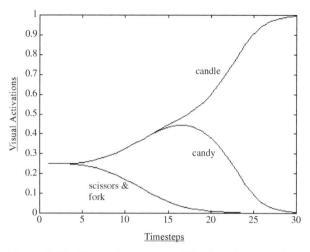

Figure 7.16. Competitor present: Visual nodes over time inside normalized recurrence.

normalized recurrence with TRACE, one can see how probabilistic visual and lexical representations can exert graded bidirectional influences on one another, while allowing partial activation of cohort lexical items when their corresponding objects are absent and not predicting eye movements to them.

To explicitly examine the graded effect of the visual nodes on the lexical nodes, figure 7.17 plots the activation of the target lexical node when the cohort object is present versus absent. This juxtaposition highlights how the

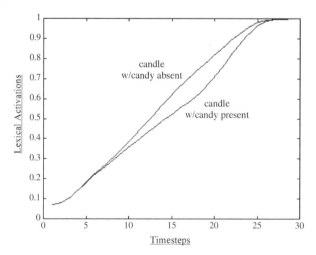

Figure 7.17. Overlaid lexical activation curves for the target word from the competitor absent condition (figure 7.13) and the competitor present condition (figure 7.15).

contextual biasing of lexical activations is a gradual process that—although it takes place simultaneously with the processing of afferent speech input—will often reveal its influence in rather subtle ways (see Kawamoto, 1993). The subtlety of these influences can sometimes mislead theorists into postulating an early stage of processing that is unaffected by context. However, dynamical simulations like this one, as well as Kawamoto's (1993) Boltzmann machine simulation of lexical ambiguity resolution, demonstrate that delays in the visibility of a contextual bias do not necessarily imply an architectural delay built into the design of the processing system.

Language Comprehension Is a "Hungry" Process

The very idea that the subsystems in the brain that participate in language processing would go out of their way to delay the use of certain information sources, for even brief periods of time, strikes most people as rather non-sensical. It is only after repeated exposure to the digital computer metaphor of the mind, numerous box-and-arrow diagrams of cognitive processes, and eloquent prose on the virtues of modular cognitive architectures, that the idea can even begin to sound plausible. Perhaps some of the idea's popularity in cognitive science owes to it initially feeling so surprising and counterintuitive. However, the more we measure these online processes in real time, and the more we understand the anatomical connections between neural subsystems, the more we see that part of the reason *strong modularity* (and its architectural delays in information transmission) initially appears so counterintuitive is because, put simply, it's wrong.

But describing a dynamic mind in a way that exudes the apparent precision and explication afforded by the modular reverse-engineering framework turns out to be difficult. Drawing wavy partially overlapping clouds with lots of bidirectional arrows connecting them is not really an improvement over the pristine box-and-arrow diagrams. When I was an undergraduate working on my senior thesis with Ray Gibbs, I had this vague idea of language comprehension being active not passive (see Bransford, Barclay & Franks's 1972 "constructive" rather than "interpretive" approach to language comprehension). The notion was not developed enough at the time to be describable or even imageable, but it was compelling for me nonetheless, and it motivated my research interests. Rather than an equation, an acronym, or a box-and-arrow diagram, the notion was more of a sense impression in which the system doing the language comprehension was moving forward and voraciously gobbling up words in the environment, rather than sitting still and having the words fed to it by a conveyor belt. Language comprehension is best conceptualized as an eager biological process—rather than a passive mechanical one—*pursuing* interpretations instead of waiting for them to be spoon fed. Language comprehension is not at all like a string of beads being delivered to the listener one bead at a time. It is more like a whale swimming steadily through a school of krill, continuously and ravenously consuming the content of its environment. It is a "hungry" process.

This hungry process that proactively—almost greedily—absorbs environmental stimulation, is not just forward-looking in terms of information acquisition; it is also forward-looking in *time*. The continuous mind is not content to accept the input it has received up to time t as its lot in life. It imagines, anticipates, and predicts what input it may acquire at time $t + 1$, $t + 2$, and further—it's that hungry!

A great many theorists have postulated an important role for prediction or anticipation of future perceptual inputs in general (e.g., Bruner, Goodnow, & Austin, 1951; Craik, 1943; Dewey, 1896; Grossberg, 1980; Jordan, 1999; Neisser, 1976; Rosen, 1985; Solomonoff, 1978, just to name a few). Some form of sensory anticipation is a commonly employed explanatory construct in a wide range of psychological research, including perceptual-motor processing (e.g., Blakemore, Wolpert, & Frith, 1998; Jordan & Rumelhart, 1992; Wolpert & Kawato, 1998), visual perception (e.g., Duhamel, Colby, & Goldberg, 1992; Freyd, 1987; Wexler, Kosslyn, & Berthoz, 1998), music perception (e.g., Boltz, 1993; Narmour, 1990; Schellenberg, 1997), and even classical conditioning (Bouton, 2004; Tolman, 1937) and Hebbian learning (Abbot & Blum, 1996). So why should things be any different with language processing?

In fact, online prediction of linguistic input turns out to be an extremely powerful tool for language learning (e.g., Cleeremans, Servan-Schrieber, & McClelland, 1989; Elman, 1990, 1991; Rohde & Plaut, 1999; Roy & Mukherjee, 2005; Schütze, 1994; Spivey-Knowlton & Saffran, 1995). It is a tool that can actually free the field of language acquisition from a logical trap that it set for itself decades ago. The language acquisition literature has been caught in this trap ever since Gold (1967) proved the necessity of negative evidence for language identification in the limit, and analyses of child–parent interaction transcripts kept coming up with little or no corrective feedback for a child's grammatical errors (e.g., the "poverty of the stimulus" argument; Brown, 1964; Gibson & Wexler, 1994; Marcus, 1993; Morgan, Bonamo, & Travis, 1995; Niyogi & Berwick, 1996; but see Bohannon, MacWhinney, & Snow, 1990; Bohannon & Stanowicz, 1988; Moerk, 1990). If no environmental negative evidence means no error signal, then language cannot be learned and therefore must be innate. This syllogism really is regularly sold in that simplistic a manner. But it turns out, as long as the learner is using some form of predictive processing, the absence of environmental negative evidence *does not* imply the absence of an error signal. And so, as occasionally noted in small rebellion caucuses in the back alleys of the language acquisition field, the argument based on "poverty of the stimulus" is more accurately an argument based on "poverty of the imagination."

Of course, self-consciously predicting a single particular next word after each current word while listening to a spoken sentence would be an unrealistic (and unfair) version of this predictive processing account of language comprehension and learning. All the system would really need to take advantage of sensory anticipation would be some form of continuously generated distributed lexical/syntactic priming (e.g., Sereno, 1991) during real-time exposure to linguistic input. With several different bets on the table for what lexical classes might come next in the speech stream, the learner can simply listen to find out which bet won to calculate its error signal. If the system is employing probabilistic representations, and it increments the probability of the predicted linguistic element that was indeed just experienced, this necessarily means that this bit of increased probability has to come from somewhere. In general, it comes from all the other nonzero predictions that were just made and just proven wrong. Hence, the repeatedly failed predictions of a hypothesized grammatical relationship allow the learner to greatly decrement the probability of that relationship, and thus learn from the conspicuous absence of particular data (Spivey-Knowlton & Saffran, 1995). Negative evidence from the environment is not needed in such a situation, because the predictive learner generates his or her own negative evidence. These anticipations can be based on phonotactics (Gow, 2001), lexical statistics (Elman, 1990), verb argument structure preferences (Spivey-Knowlton & Sedivy, 1995), and even discourse-based expectations (Spivey-Knowlton, 1992). If the mind relies on multifarious predictions such as this, perhaps it is only natural that it would eat, breathe, and sleep probabilistic representations, as suggested by the continuity of mind.

This naked opportunism in the use of information not only applies to the continuous uptake and anticipation of sensory input, but also to the sharing of representations between internal subsystems. The mind's coupled subsystems promiscuously share their neural patterns with one another. Results from the studies discussed in this chapter generally point to an account of real-time language comprehension that integrates lexical, syntactic, semantic, discourse, visual, and even situational variables *continuously*. In light of these findings, language comprehension no longer looks like the functioning of a digital computer, with subprocessors waiting until they complete a symbolic representation before sending it to the next subprocessor. Partial, incomplete information (in the form of probabilistic biases) seems to be shared continuously between different formats of representation. It simply cannot be the case that partially active symbols compete until one discretely wins and *only that discrete representation* is passed on to later stages for rule-based computations (see Anderson & Lebiere, 1998; Budiu & Anderson, 2004; Stevenson, 1994). Such hybrid accounts of perceptual-and-cognitive processing are perhaps useful stopgaps in the interim, so that functioning models can be designed.

However, everything that we have learned from neuroscience, from neural population codes to rich anatomical connectivity, tells us that neural subsystems do not hold back their signals to other subsystems until they are discrete and narrowly defined. The multifarious pattern of dynamically competing partially active representations continuously flows (or cascades, McClelland, 1979) from one subsystem to another and back. Activation of partial patterns of spiking neurons flows between neural areas just as readily as activation of succinct coherent patterns. That is, if neuron A in subsystem X projects to neuron B in subsystem Y, then neuron A's action potentials will travel to neuron B regardless of whether neuron A is accompanied by *many* of its partners in a population code or by only a *few*. Hence, subsystem Y gets continuously updated on the progress of the competition between multiple partially coherent population codes in subsystem X. It does *not* merely find out about the winner. Such a scenario foretells a rather short life span for theories that pretend that cognition is comprised of discrete binary symbols being passed from one computational module to another.

Continuous Trajectories Through a Neurolinguistic State Space

In this last section of this chapter on language, I will illustrate a kind of cartoon depiction of how to think about the continuous fluidity with which language is processed. The concept is framed within a particular focus on what the brain might be doing during language comprehension. However, I must first acknowledge that language is much bigger than "the comprehension processes of the brain." Language involves speech production and statistical learning processes that result from the individual language user being embedded in an environment containing other language users as well as linguistic conventions that take on a life of their own in any given culture. For example, my undergraduate thesis advisor, Ray Gibbs, once lost his patience with my wording choices, and barked at me, "Michael, language is not processed by *language processors*, it's processed by *people!*" Then, about 10 years later, my graduate student Stanka Fitneva said to me, after getting exasperated with my pooh-poohing of social psychology approaches to language processing, "News flash, Michael, language is a *social* phenomenon!" I try very hard not to forget these admonitions, because it is all too easy to slip into the mindset of dealing *only* with idealized representations/attractors in the hypothetical state space of *a brain*. A neural state space is a very useful starting point for understanding how a core subcomponent of real-time language processing works. But, as discussed at the beginning of this chapter (and also in chapter 11), there are multiple time scales at which communicative signals are processed by brains, by people, by cultures, by species. And it would be naive to think that the places where we've chosen to cleave these time scales apart, for ease of analysis, will be divisions that actually render these levels of analysis independent of one another.

With that caveat firmly lodged in our collective craw, let's get on with visualizing an idealized linguistic trajectory through a mental state space. Humor me now and say out loud, in an appropriately chiding manner, "Spivey waxed philosophical." That sentence took two to three seconds to say, and would probably take two to three seconds for a listener to understand. However, despite it clearly being an event stretched out in time, sentences are often treated as though they are static, whole things with no temporal properties whatsoever. Theoretical linguistics regularly draws static upside-down tree structures that illustrate the grammatical branching of the noun phrase and the verb phrase of such a sentence, and then the nested branching of the verb and adverb within that verb phrase. That kind of static illustration is typically intended to be an abstractly isomorphic proxy for a representation that a person has in their brain once they've understood such a sentence. The meaning of the sentence is often treated similarly, as symbols in the head that are accessed and placed in some kind of attended processing arena that resembles all too much a Cartesian theater, with the lone audience member being dangerously close to a homunculus (whose mind may have its own theater and homunculus, ad infinitum).

If we step away from the theoretical perspectives that rely so much on static representational objects in the mind and focus on the observation that a sentence's production and its comprehension take place over a period of time, we can look for an alternative and more neurally plausible account for how a spoken sentence is understood. While a person hears a sentence, it is obviously not the case that their brain is doing nothing until the sentence is finished and then it constructs some static representation. As the sentence is unfolding in time, the listener's brain is undergoing changes in its patterns of neural activation that are significantly driven by this environmental auditory input. If we describe these averaged firing rates of many neurons as locations in a neural state space (see chapter 2), then the changes over time comprise a continuous trajectory through the state space. Thus, the understanding of a sentence is here conceived of as an *event* in the mind, not an *object* (see also Slobin, 1996).

If some of the dimensions that one could construct in this state space are largely phonetic, others are largely semantic, and still others largely syntactic, one can imagine regions in the state space (which correspond to a cluster of similar patterns of neural activation) "belonging" to particular words (see Elman, 1991). When a word is properly understood, it means that the listener's brain has achieved a pattern of neural activation that during some brief period of time, maps roughly onto that region in state space. Hence, the understanding of a sentence would involve having this moving average of neural firing rates changing over time such that it corresponds to a continuous trajectory through the state space, traveling from one word's region to another and to another (figure 7.18A). As the locations visited in state space are the result of a moving average of the neural firing rates, the trajectory would necessarily traverse through intermediate regions of state space that do not significantly belong to any word. That is, because the patterns of neural activation cannot instantaneously shift from one pattern to another, the state of the system in the state space cannot teleport from one word to another.[12]

So the internal mental representation of a sentence is not a *thing* but a *process*. As figure 7.18A shows, the understanding of the sentence is the trajectory itself, and this trajectory continuously moves through state space over the course of the two or three seconds it took to say the sentence. Now, even if one

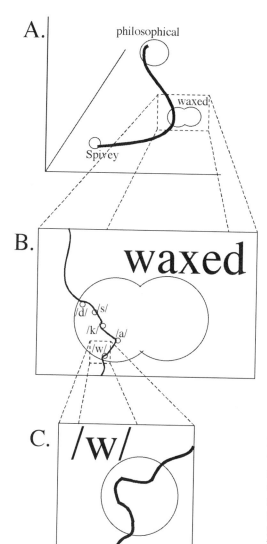

Figure 7.18. Zoomings-in of a highly idealized linguistic state space, to emphasize the spatio-temporal continuity of spoken language comprehension. (Note that there have to be hidden dimensions not depicted in this two-dimensional cartoon, so that for example, the phonemes in *waxed* do not live exclusively inside *that* word's attractor basin.)

relinquishes the idea that a sentence is a static object in the mind, one might still argue that the encircled regions depicted in figure 7.18A can be interpreted as static things corresponding to the individual words. Maybe sentences aren't things in the mind, but words are, right?

Wrong. The results from spoken word recognition experiments described in this chapter indicate a continuous accrual of acoustic-phonetic input. That is, just like with sentences, over the course of the few hundred milliseconds that it takes to say a word, the brain is not passively waiting until the end of the word before it starts processing the input. It processes *partial* acoustic-phonetic input, and therefore must be engaging in partial representational patterns that are initially slightly consistent with multiple different words. Crucially, this continuous movement through state space is still evident even during the lifetime of an individual spoken word. Figure 7.18B zooms in on the region corresponding to the word *waxed* and idealistically illustrates how even this process is temporally dynamic and continuous in time. Recognizing a spoken word does not involve visiting and resting at the corresponding location in state space. It involves constant change in neural patterning, as the first few phonemes push the system in a somewhat ambiguous direction in state space, later phonemes redirect the system toward a more specific region, and by the time that specific region is reached, the next spoken word is already coming!

Once again, the idealizations necessary to make this cartoon demonstration interpretable (i.e., the encircled regions corresponding to labeled representational objects) can lead one to mistakenly conclude, "All right, maybe words aren't static objects, but at least those phonemes inside the word's region are objects. The system visits one, then visits the next, etc., and eventually a spoken word is understood." Wrong again. Recall from chapter 6 that categorical speech perception, at a time scale of dozens of milliseconds for the acoustic-phonetic input, exhibits continuous temporal dynamics (McMurray et al., 2003). Hence, as shown in figure 7.18C, the visitation of a phoneme region in state space is also best illustrated as a continuous trajectory even at that tiny time scale.

Whether you're looking at a time scale of seconds (as in panel A), tenths of seconds (panel B), or hundredths of seconds (panel C), there is no point in time when the mental trajectory through state space, which is propelled by a combination of environmental sensory input and goal-oriented expectations, stops and stands still. It is always in motion. The patterns of neural activation in the brain are in perpetual flux. An important consequence of this temporal continuity of mind is that there can be no mediating states (e.g., Dietrich & Markman, 2003), because states require stasis. However, these dynamic patterns, or continuous processes, can certainly be thought of as mediational and perhaps even representational, in a somewhat nonstandard way. But they are not states, and therefore cannot be static symbols that are discretely separable from one another in time or in representational space. What this means is that language is not a string of symbols whose grammatical relationships are encoded by discrete hierarchical structures in an encapsulated linguistic module. Language, like the rest of perception and cognition, is a continuous trajectory through a high-dimensional state space that combines phonetic, semantic, and syntactic constraints for understanding with perceptual and motor constraints for continuously converting this developing understanding into successful bodily interaction with the environment (see Barsalou, 1999; Chambers, Tanenhaus, & Magnuson, 2004; Glenberg & Kaschak, 2002; Matlock, Ramscar, & Boroditsky, 2005; Richardson et al., 2003; Richardson, Spivey, & Cheung, 2001).

8

Temporal Dynamics in Visual Perception

It should be obvious by now that this minute inflow of stimulus energy does not consist of discrete inputs—that stimulation does not consist of stimuli. The flow is continuous. There are, of course, episodes in the flow, but these are nested within one another and cannot be cut up into elementary units. Stimulation is not momentary.

—J. J. Gibson

The Ideal (i.e., Motionless) Observer

In the previous chapter on language, it might seem natural and obvious that the continuous delivery of speech input is a case where continuous temporal dynamics would be prominent in the resulting perceptual-cognitive processing. In contrast, *visual* input is often conceptualized as arriving on its sensory apparatus, the retina, in the form of a single static parallel exposure of the entire visual scene. As presaged by J. J. Gibson, and gradually rediscovered in the past 10 years or so, this is simply not true. This chapter walks through several examples of how visual perception is just as temporally dynamic as language processing and other cognitive skills.

The past 40 years of research in vision were dominated by theoretical frameworks and accompanying methodologies that too frequently limited themselves to isolated visual stimuli presented to immobilized observers—drawing selected insights from Gibson (1958, 1979) but never quite embracing his philosophy (see Nakayama, 1994, for a review). Interestingly, this limited purview of types of visual stimulation allowed research in visual perception to become the one place where the computer engineering mentality in cognitive science has been most rigorously and successfully applied to the mind. Whereas traditional cognitive psychology rarely got beyond Marr's (1982) computational level of drawing boxes and arrows, early research in vision developed explicit linear systems mathematical accounts of perception at Marr's algorithmic level. Linear systems theory has enabled rigorous first approximations of a wide range of early visual processing phenomena (Cornsweet, 1970; Julesz, 1971; Watson, 1986, 1992; see also Adelson & Bergen, 1991), including space perception (Graham, 1989), lightness perception (Gilchrist, 1988), color perception (Wandell, 1993), and motion perception (Sperling & Lu, 1998). Many of the early results from single-cell recording in the visual cortex of anesthetized primates and cats were consistent with these linear feedforward accounts of visual feature analyzers (e.g., Hubel & Weisel, 1959; Lennie, 1980; Movshon et al., 1986).

But the devil is in the details. Marr's (1982) lowest level, the implementational one, involving neural hardware, is where all the good intentions developed at the computational and algorithmic levels simply fall apart. This tripartite hierarchy, which perhaps depends too much on a unidirectional predication, is significantly compromised when the brain is considered as a complex dynamical system (McClamrock, 1991). The existence of a rich connectivity of lateral projections *within* visual cortical areas (Gilbert, 1998; Wilson & Wilkinson, 1997), as well as the many recurrent synaptic projections *between* various cortical areas (e.g., Churchland & Sejnowski, 1992; Douglas et al., 1995) and the integral role of frequent eye movements during visual perception (Bridgeman, van der Heijden, & Velichkovsky, 1994; Findlay & Gilchrist, 2003), together cause serious problems for feedforward linear systems accounts of vision (and of the rest of perception and cognition, for that matter).

As long as vision scientists limited their psychophysical measurements to isolated responses to isolated (and highly simplified) stimuli, and their neurophysiological measurements to anesthetized animals, the temporal dynamics and recurrent feedback inherent in normal everyday goal-directed visual perception could be ignored, and linear systems analysis was able to make impressive strides in fitting laboratory data. However, as discussed in chapter 5, the accumulation of neurophysiological and psychophysical evidence for visual attention influencing low-level visual processes has led the field away from those neat and tidy linear systems theories of vision and toward a more nonlinear recurrent dynamical framework (e.g., Churchland, Ramachandran, & Sejnowski, 1994; Damasio, 1989; Desimone & Duncan, 1995; Heeger et al., 2001; Martinez et al., 1999; Moran & Desimone, 1984; Motter, 1993; Shulman, 1992; Spivey & Spirn, 2000).

Moreover, as noted by Ballard (1989), computer vision researchers who had followed psychologists down their linear systems information-processing pathway to vision eventually found themselves at an impasse. As it turns out, artificial intelligence is making more progress with its new emphasis on dynamic *processing of actions* as the core of cognition (e.g., Bajcsy & Goldberg, 1984; Beer, 1989; Brooks, 1991, 1995) than it ever did with its traditional emphasis on static representation of knowledge (e.g., Banerji, 1980; Hunt, 1975; Lenat, 1995). When this dynamical systems perspective on visual perception is expanded to include not only processes of the human brain but also processes of the human body and the environment, as advocated by Gibson (1979; see also Turvey, 1977), it becomes clear that many cognitive operations span the boundary between brain and body as well as the boundary between body and environment (see Ballard et al., 1997; Kirsh, 1995; O'Regan, 1992; O'Regan & Noë, 2001). See chapter 11 for further discussion.

The Ecologically Valid Moving Observer

The only nondynamic retinal images in the world are ones concocted in the cognitive psychologist's laboratory, where an experimental trial often consists of a static image presented on a computer screen while the participant is instructed to maintain eye fixation on a central dot. Not only do ecologically valid stimulus environments generally include dynamic visual environments, they also tend to include a moving observer who allows herself to make eye movements. Admittedly, saccadic eye movements provide a rather staccato series of static images to the eyes, with perceptual processing being suppressed during the saccade itself (Matin, 1974; although processing is not entirely eliminated, see Bridgeman & Fisher, 1990). But the process of *directing* those saccades involves some time-sensitive nonlinear neural interactions.

For example, Duhamel, Colby, and Goldberg (1992) have shown that visual neurons in the parietal cortex will reorient their retinal receptive fields about 50 milliseconds before an eye movement takes place. Parietal cortex and oculomotor nuclei appear to seamlessly coordinate their interface with the visual field with respect to the destination of an impending saccade, such that a parietal cell dynamically repositions its receptive field[1] to receive afferent input from the region of the visual field that *will be* its appropriate receptive field once this impending saccade is completed! A neural mechanism like this may be exactly what is responsible for the behavioral effects that are described as an anticipatory movement of spatial attention that precedes an eye movement (e.g., Henderson, 1993; Hoffman, 1998). Findings like these, as well as a wide array of others (e.g., Cavanaugh, Bair, & Movshon, 2002a, 2002b; Gallant, Connor, & Van Essen, 1998; Vinje & Gallant, 2002; see also Rao & Ballard, 1999), have contributed to the traditional concept of a visual receptive field that is purely feedforward and nondynamic becoming relabeled as a "*classical* receptive field"—meaning "importantly wrong under certain circumstances," as in classical physics and classical logic. Even in early regions of visual cortex, the area of the retina to which a neuron responds turns out to be much larger (often referred to as a nonclassical receptive field) when the animal is purposefully interacting with its environment than when the animal is slowly dying on a slab with its eyelids propped open. Go figure.

Moreover, in a naturally moving observer, saccades are accompanied by at least as many pursuit eye movements, tracking a moving object in the environment, or maintaining fixation on an object during self-motion.[2] During these pursuit and fixational pursuit eye movements, everywhere on the retina but the fovea itself is exposed to a great deal of mathematically complex continuous movement of the environment (Cutting, 1996; Gibson, 1977). This kind of naturalistic retinal input is far more continuously dynamic than the typical cognitive psychologist's experiment would have you expect. Whether you're talking about the shift from anesthetized animals to awake behaving animals in electrophysiology research (e.g., Motter, 1993), or the shift from nonmoving observers to interactive participants in cognitive psychology experiments (e.g., Ballard, Hayhoe, & Pelz, 1995; Tanenhaus et al., 1995), or the shift from abstract meaningless features to functionally relevant features in concepts and categorization research (e.g., Markman & Ross, 2003), there is a definite trend in the cognitive and neural sciences toward collecting data from subjects that are interacting with their environment in a manner that is at least somewhat ecologically valid. And this trend needs to be encouraged.

Nonetheless, even during a single eye fixation of a static visual scene while not moving, there are some important temporal dynamics inherent in what the brain does with that visual input. An instantaneously presented visual stimulus, with no eye or body movement taking place, sets off an interesting temporally dynamic internal process in perception. In this chapter, I describe a number of findings and demonstrations of cascaded accrual of activation during visual processing. In the same way that recognizing a spoken word involves a continuous trajectory through state space, in which cognitive expectations meet face to face with perceptual input, so does recognizing a single object and mapping a visual percept onto oculomotor output, and finding a target object amid a clutter of distractor objects.

Toy Simulation as Transparent Demonstration

To make the point clear about how the gradual forming of high-level visual representations may influence lower level visual representations through feedback connections, let's start with a simple demonstration. The Kanisza triangle (figure 8.1), for example, shows how an incomplete majority of perceptual evidence for a familiar shape—the upright triangle in the image—can nonetheless result in a relatively complete percept of the shape's full set of contours. Despite the sides of the triangle having no luminance contrast defining any actual contour on the page, it looks as if there are subtle contours there. In fact, neurons in primary visual cortex, area V1, respond to such illusory contours even though they are not receiving any afferent luminance contrast input (Grosof, Shapley, & Hawken, 1993). It is generally believed that this is the result of complex lateral interactions within visual layers as well as recurrent feedback between visual areas (e.g., Gilbert, 1998; Grossberg, Mingolla, & Ross, 1997; Pessoa & De Weerd, 2003). A somewhat playful—but not entirely inaccurate—way to think of it is in terms of areas of extrastriate cortex that are responsible for object recognition initially representing the afferent visual input as "almost a triangle," and then sending feedback to earlier areas of visual cortex, telling them that they think they might be perceiving a triangle. Orientation-sensitive contour-detecting cells that are accustomed to participating in that triangle percept—but were not initially activated by the

Figure 8.1. The Kanizsa triangle's white upright triangle exhibits illusory contours.

afferent input, because their receptive fields are on the blank regions of the Kanizsa triangle stimulus—gradually accumulate feedback signals and lateral signals that convince them to become active and thus "hallucinate a contour" exactly where a *genuine* triangle would have had one anyway. In fact, one of the consequences of these pattern-completing neural connections, resulting from extensive perceptual learning, is that we occasionally see what we *expect* to see even when it's not there (see Seitz et al., 2005).

If feedback projections in the visual system are used for this kind of process (e.g., Churchland & Sejnowksi, 1992; Di Lollo, Enns, & Rensink, 2000; Douglas et al., 1995; Grossberg et al., 1997), what in the world would make one think that feedback projections in other areas of the brain that figure prominently in higher order cognition (e.g., hippocampus, parietal cortex, prefrontal and frontal cortex) aren't also used for this kind of dynamic pattern completion? In general, continuous feedback from confident high-level representations down to uncertain or noisy low-level representations is exactly the pattern completion process, discussed in chapter 1, that causes the phonemic restoration effect (Warren, 1970), where a nonspeech sound replacing a phoneme in the middle of a spoken word is nonetheless perceived as the appropriate phoneme. It also causes the McGurk effect (McGurk & MacDonald, 1976), where visual perception of mouth movements strongly influences speech perception. Indeed, some form of this multilevel recurrent pattern completion may even be what determines effects seen with people's changing beliefs and attitudes, the resolution of cognitive dissonance, and even the maintenance of inconsistent beliefs (see Shastri, 1999). The feedback pathways that allow cognitive expectations to modulate the processing of perceptual input not only enable such context effects, they also lead to the very kind of nonlinear temporally dynamic settling processes that are discussed throughout this book.

TⱯE
CⱯT

Figure 8.2. The ambiguously shaped middle letter is readily resolved by the lexical context.

Another visual demonstration of dynamics and feedback in perceptual information transmission, with global visual context influencing local feature-based processing, comes from Neisser's (1967; see also Rumelhart & McClelland, 1986) classic discussion of how the same ambiguous letter in figure 8.2 is so readily seen as an H in the upper word and so readily seen as an A in the lower word. Here, I will walk through a simple simulation of how letter-based information at early layers of a network can affect gradual recognition of a word at a later layer of the network, which can then send feedback to influence the recognition of letters in the early layer of the network.

For normalized recurrence to model how a letter is perceived differently in different lexical contexts, it must have a vector for letters and a vector for words. And for the competition algorithm to recurrently cycle and sharpen the probability distributions over different words, the probabilistic support that each letter provides for a given word must be intermediately converted into a word-supporter vector. Figure 8.3 shows a simple normalized recurrence network with added input vectors for the first, second, and third letters of three-letter words (bidirectional weights between letter nodes and appropriate word supporter nodes are set at 0.01).

By turning on only the C node in the first letter vector, only the T node in the third letter vector, and *both* the A and H nodes in the second letter vector, with each vector then being normalized to sum to 1.0, the network demonstrates how the word can be easily recognized despite ambiguous orthographic input. Note how the CAT node's activation in figure 8.4A rises over time while the other nodes decline. More important, the cyclic feedback in the network allows the simulation to demonstrate how the perfectly ambiguous middle letter itself can, in that context, become perceived as more of an A than an H (See appendix for details and code on this simple normalized recurrence simulation.)

As the CAT word node becomes substantially more active than the competing word nodes, it sends more feedback to its three corresponding nodes in

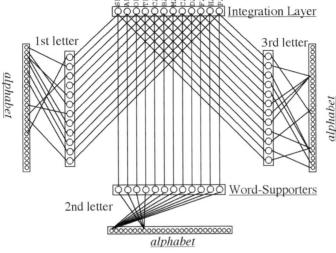

Figure 8.3. A normalized recurrence localist attractor network for simulating lexical context effects on letter resolution.

the word-supporting vectors. And as those particularly active word-supporting nodes send feedback to their corresponding letters, the probability distribution in the second letter vector begins to skew toward the A node and away from the H node (figure 8.4B). This general process of recurrent multilevel pattern

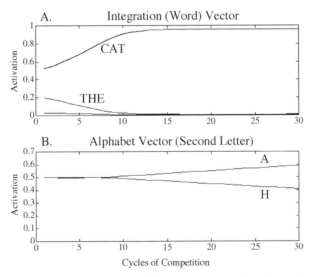

Figure 8.4. A: Activation of the lexical nodes for the word "C?T," with that ambiguous second letter; B: Multilayer feedback from the lexical layer eventually influences activation of the letter nodes to cause that second letter to "look" more like an A than an H.

completion may be how, when you cover up the lower word, that middle letter in figure 8.3 does, indeed, somehow appear substantially H-like. When you cover up the upper word, that same middle letter looks reasonably A-like.

In fact, this implemented network bears a striking resemblance to Selfridge's (1959) pandemonium model, in which many abstract lower level demons call out their votes to a smaller number of higher level demons, who then tabulate and call out those results accordingly to the next level of fewer still demons. The key difference that this kind of localist attractor network exhibits is that the emerging consensus among the higher level demons actually filters down via feedback channels to gradually sway the lower level demons' opinions. As with most complex dynamical systems that employ feedback, the higher level patterns are both *a result of* and *an influence on* the lower level patterns. This temporally drawn-out circular causality shows up when multiple subcomponents of a system gradually coalesce into a coherent global form over time partly because the subcomponents want that form, and partly because the coherent whole wants that form. This kind of autocatalysis can be seen in a wide range of complex adaptive systems (Holland, 1995), such as chemical processes (Prigogine & Stengers, 1984), insect behavior (Bonadeau, Dorigo, & Theraulaz, 1999), traffic patterns (Resnick, 1997), stock trading (Strogatz, 2003), clothing fashion (Braham, 1997), and even during the visual recognition of a single object (Deco & Lee, 2002).

Recognizing a Single Object

As vision is a modality in which we share much in common with nonhuman primates, it has been studied in depth with neurophysiologically invasive real-time measures that richly illustrate the temporal dynamics of the resulting perceptual-cognitive processing. Vision research abounds with examples of temporal continuity in real-time perception. The gradual settling (or pattern completion) of a neuronal population code, over the course of hundreds of milliseconds, is a common way to think about how the visual system recognizes objects and faces. Compelling visualizations of the continuous manner in which sensory input gradually produces a percept can easily be found in visual neuroscience. Recall the discussion of Rolls and Tovee (1995), from chapter 1 (figure 1.6), in which they recorded from multiple neurons in the inferotemporal cortex of the macaque monkey and found that it takes a few hundred milliseconds for the right population of cells to achieve their appropriate firing rates for fully identifying a fixated object or face. As the cells begin depolarizing in response to the features of a recognizable visual stimulus, the population code reaches about 50% of its full resonant activity after just the first 70 milliseconds. The remaining 50% of the information to be encoded by that population code (measured in bits) accumulates over the course of a few hundred milliseconds more. When you look at the right time scale for perception and cognition, that is, hundreds of milliseconds, there's nothing instantaneous about it at all. There are no meaningful instants; there is only process.

Perrett, Oram, and Ashbridge (1998) report additional support for gradual accumulation of neuronal evidence in face recognition with images rotated in depth. When a face or object is partly rotated away from a canonical or frontal view, recognition or matching will generally take longer as a function of how far it is rotated (e.g., Cooper & Shepard, 1973; Jolicoeur, 1985; Shepard & Metzler, 1971). The increase in response time as a function of stimulus rotation is sometimes quite linear, suggesting that some form of neural analog computation may be doing something functionally isomorphic to actually rotating a 3D representation of the object in real time until it is in an orientation that is appropriate for the recognition or matching task (Shepard, 2001; but see Hecht, 2001; Kubovy & Epstein, 2001).

Perrett et al. (1998) describe recordings from cells in the monkey temporal cortex while the monkey viewed frontal, three-quarter profile, profile, and quarter profile schematic faces. When the cumulative number of action potentials are simply plotted over time, these curves rise at different rates as a function of how canonical the face orientation was. Figure 8.5 illustrates the continuous nonlinear rise in accumulated neuronal spikes over the course of several hundred milliseconds as the monkey recognizes the face. Similar to the results of Rolls and Tovee (1995), these curves reach their half-height relatively early on, yet still spend several hundred milliseconds gradually approaching their respective asymptotes (except for the back-of-head view, which asymptotes rather low within a few hundred milliseconds).

Thus even the mere process of recognizing a single object carries with it a temporal continuity in its representational form that makes it ideal for description in terms of a nonlinear trajectory through a high-dimensional state space. Outside of the laboratory, in complex visual environments, with saccadic eye movements occurring two to four times per second, and with

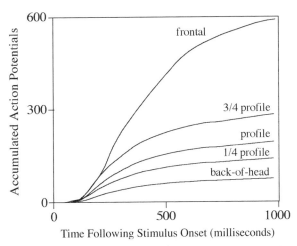

Figure 8.5. Sigmoidal accumulation of neuronal spikes for various face orientations (adapted from Perrett et al., 1998).

body movement taking place as well, these graded representations of visual objects whose images get projected onto those retinas (i.e., partially active neural population codes that would take several hundreds of milliseconds to fully reach asymptote) must surely be the norm, rather than the exception.

Perceptual Decisions

A particularly impressive example of continuous temporal dynamics in visual processing being coupled with continuous temporal dynamics in motor processing comes from work by Gold and Shadlen (2000) examining decision processes in the frontal eye field (FEF) of the macaque monkey. A common task in visual psychophysics involves presenting a display of quasi-randomly moving dots and instructing the subject to judge the majority direction of motion exhibited by the dots. As the experimenter increases the proportion of dots that move in a roughly consistent direction, the perception of a coherent direction of flow amid the dots becomes more apparent (Britten et al., 1992). Figure 8.6 shows two simple examples of dynamic random dot displays, with only 10 dots for ease of depiction. In panel A, 7 of the 10 dots are moving in the same leftward direction, making it rather easy to discern the direction of coherent motion. In panel B, only 4 of the 10 dots are moving in the same rightward direction, making it relatively difficult to perceive the direction of coherent motion.

Gold and Shadlen (2000) presented displays like this to monkeys and trained them to indicate the perceived direction of dot flow, on offset of the stimulus, by making an eye movement to a leftward peripheral location or a rightward one. Then they found a region of FEF in which electrical micro-stimulation evoked an involuntary saccade that was perpendicular to the two voluntary response saccades (upward in figure 8.7). On some of the direction-of-flow judgment trials, this region of FEF was microstimulated immediately after the moving dot display disappeared, that is, exactly when the monkey was supposed to produce a voluntary eye movement (to the left or right

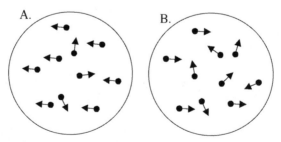

Figure 8.6. Simplified examples of moving dot patterns with 70% coherent leftward motion (A), and 40% coherent rightward motion (B).

response box) that would indicate his decision regarding the perceived direction of flow of the dots.

Perhaps not surprisingly, the evoked involuntary upward saccade was executed first, and a corrective saccade typically redirected the eyes to the voluntarily chosen response box. However, the evoked saccade was not bereft of influence from the evolving perceptual decision. In fact, when the percentage of coherent motion was greater and (more important, for my temporal continuity argument) when the viewing time was longer, more perceptual evidence apparently accrued to induce greater deviation of that initial involuntary saccade slightly in the direction of the voluntary response. Figure 8.7 shows the visual display that followed the dynamic random dot display. In this idealized example, 51% of the dots in the dot display coherently moved leftward (a rather easy perceptual decision), and then the evoked upward saccade was triggered after either 100, 200, or 300 milliseconds of exposure to the moving dot display. With more time to perceive the dynamic random dot display, the evoked saccade acted more like a combination of the evoked upward saccade and the voluntary leftward saccade.

Essentially, by incrementally increasing viewing time, the experimenters could observe the gradual increase in strength or confidence of the perceptual decision over time, as indicated by the degree to which that voluntary decision leaked into the execution of FEF-microstimulated evoked saccade. Thus, the population of cells that—once some of them were microstimulated—produced the *evoked* saccade were already somewhere in the process of settling on a pattern of activation that would produce the *voluntary* response saccade. If the microstimulation took place very early on in this decision process, rather

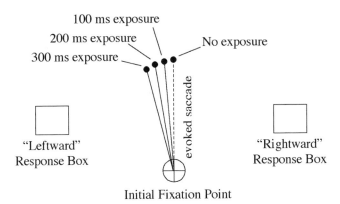

Figure 8.7. Schematic example of greater and greater deviation in the *evoked* saccade toward the direction of the *voluntary* saccade after varying amounts of time for the motor system to accumulate perceptual evidence (at high motion strength, 51%) for a "motion leftward" response. The dashed line shows the pure evoked saccade in the control condition (see Gold & Shadlen, 2000).

little effect of the voluntary response would be apparent in the evoked saccade, but if the microstimulation took place later on, a significant amount of the voluntary eye movement would be apparent in the evoked saccade. These results suggest that decision processes themselves may be coextensive with the gradual settling of partially active and competing neural representations in motor areas of cortex (Gold & Shadlen, 2000, 2001; Schall, 2000; see also Georgopoulos, 1995).

Visual Search Phenomena

The same kind of gradual accumulation of perceptual evidence can be observed when multiple objects are competing for attention during visual search. The field of visual search has generally been driven by two opposing perspectives on attention. The *serial-processing* perspective claims that the observer allocates attentional resources wholly and discretely to individual objects, one at a time (e.g., Treisman & Gelade, 1980; Treisman, 1988). This view is expressed in Wilhelm Wundt's introspection that "one can turn the inner point of sight successively to the various parts of the inner field of view. At the same time, one can narrow it or broaden it, unlike the point of sight of the external eye, whereby its brightness alternately increases and decreases. Strictly speaking it is thus not a point, but a field of somewhat variable extent" (Wundt, 1903, p. 334, translation by Bruce Bridgeman). The *parallel-processing* perspective claims that attention is best characterized as comprised of partially active representations of objects simultaneously competing for probabilistic mappings onto motor output (e.g., Desimone & Duncan, 1995; Mounts & Tomaselli, 2005; Reynolds & Desimone, 2001; see also Godijin & Theeuwes, 2002; Keysers & Perrett, 2002). This more probabilistic view is expressed in Sir William Hamilton's observation that "the greater the number of objects to which our consciousness is simultaneously extended, the smaller is the intensity with which it is able to consider each" (Hamilton, 1859, p. 164).

In the visual search paradigm, the subject is presented with a display of multiple objects and must respond as to whether a prespecified target is present or absent. When the target object differs from all the distractor objects by a single feature (or perceptual dimension), subjects' response times are not affected by the number of distractors in the display (called the set size). Subjectively, the target seems to "pop out."[3] See figure 8.8A. However, when the target object differs from some distractors along one feature and from other distractors along another feature (figure 8.8B), subjects' response times increase quite linearly with set size (e.g., Treisman & Gelade, 1980; Treisman, 1988; Wolfe, 1994, 1998). In addition to linear slopes with set size, this conjunction of features also causes an approximately 1 : 2 slope ratio for target-present versus target-absent trials (e.g., Treisman & Gelade, 1980). See figure 8.9. This fits nicely with a serial search account because when the target is present, one should expect to have to apply the attentional spotlight to about half of the

■ = red   ▨ = green

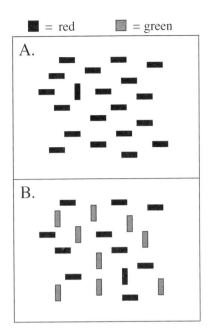

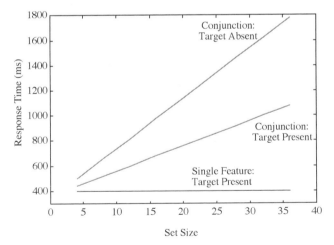

Figure 8.8. A: A single-feature search for a red vertical bar amid red horizontal bars; B: a conjunction search for a red vertical bar amid red horizontal bars and green vertical bars.

Figure 8.9. The three basic effects of visual search: (1) Single feature pop out, idealized as 0 ms/item; (2) linear increase in conjunction search response time as a function of set size; and (3) the 1:2 ratio of target-present slope to target-absent slope for conjunction search. Target-present conjunction search is idealized here as 20 ms/item, and target-absent conjunction search is idealized as 40 ms/item.

objects before stumbling onto the target, whereas when the target is absent, one should have to apply the spotlight to all of the objects before confirming that the target is absent.

These three phenomena (pop out, linear slope for conjunction search, and 1 : 2 present/absent slope ratio for conjunction search) have been interpreted as evidence for the feature integration theory of attention (Treisman, 1988; Treisman & Gelade, 1980). In this theory, features are initially, "preattentively," extracted in parallel across the visual field and represented on separate feature maps. Thus, a target that differs from the distractors by a single feature will have a solitary point of activation in that feature map, and thus pop out. However, in a conjunction search, a second, attentional stage of processing is necessary to bind the two target features by combining the separate feature maps onto a master map. This attentional stage implements a spotlight of attention (Eriksen & Yeh, 1985; Hurlbert & Poggio, 1985; Posner, Snyder, & Davidson, 1980; but see Driver & Baylis, 1989) that serially checks objects in the display for their match to the prespecified target description.

However, several studies have discovered particular conjunctions of features that do not produce steeply sloped response time functions by set size (McLeod, Driver, & Crisp, 1988; Nakayama & Silverman, 1986; Theeuwes & Kooi, 1994). Moreover, it has been argued that steeply sloped response time functions may not even reflect serial processing of objects in the first place. Rather, probabilistic models based on signal-to-noise ratio can accommodate many visual search phenomena (Eckstein, 1998; Palmer, Verghese, & Pavel, 2000; see also McElree & Carrasco, 1999). Overall, a wide range of studies have suggested that the distinction between putatively serial and parallel search functions is continuous rather than discrete and should be considered extremes on a continuum of search efficiency (Duncan & Humphreys, 1989; Nakayama & Joseph, 1998; Olds, Cowan, & Joliceur, 2000a, 2000b, 2000c; van der Heijden, 1996a; Wolfe, 1998).

Rather than these different ranges of response time by set size slopes being the result of fundamentally different search processes (i.e., a parallel processor or a serial processor), it has been suggested that they emerge from a single process, perhaps determined by the relative salience of the target and the distractors (e.g., Dosher, Han, & Lu, 2004; Duncan & Humphreys, 1989; Eckstein, 1998; McElree & Carrasco, 1999; Palmer, Verghese, & Pavel, 2000; Wolfe, 1998; see also Mounts & Tomaselli, 2005). For example, Wolfe (1998) performed a meta-analysis on almost a million conjunction search and single-feature search trials and was unable to find any evidence for bimodality in the distribution of response time by set size slopes (but see Haslam, Porter, & Rothschild, 2001). As a result, the visual search literature has taken to using the rather noncommittal terms *efficient* and *inefficient* search in place of the dichotomy of parallel and serial search. Although certainly vague and nonexplanatory, the terms *efficient search* and *inefficient search* more readily accommodate the notion of a continuum between these extremes,[4] rather than the now dubious categorical distinction between two putatively independent search mechanisms.

One of the more compelling results to argue against the independent functioning of a parallel preattentive stage of visual search and a later serial attentional stage comes from visual search displays that are temporally dynamic. For example, Olds et al. (2000a, 2000b, 2000c; see also Watson & Humphreys, 1997) presented visual search displays in the form of single-feature pop-out displays for very brief periods of time (in some conditions, less than 100 milliseconds) before changing them to conjunction-search displays. Although participants did not report experiencing a pop-out, and their response times were not as fast as with pure pop-out displays, they did nonetheless show some graded facilitation in response times due to the very brief period of time during which the display had only single-feature distractors. Olds and colleagues described this effect as a partial pop-out process assisting the conjunction search process and called it "search assistance."

A similar progressive delivery of search stimuli was explored by Spivey, Tyler, Eberhard, and Tanenhaus (2001; see also Tyler & Spivey, 2001), except they presented the target identity incrementally, rather than the search display. When participants were informed of the target's features by a spoken target query (e.g., "Is there a red vertical bar?") while the conjunction search display was concurrently visible, they produced response time by set size slopes in the neighborhood of about 5 milliseconds per item, instead of 15 or 20. Although the exact process by which this incremental linguistic input turns an inefficient search into an efficient one is still under investigation (Gibson, Eberhard, & Bryant, 2005; Reali et al., in press), it could very well be due to the continuous processing of spoken language transferring its gradually accumulated information to the visual search process in real time. If the participant is viewing a conjunction display like the one in figure 8.8B, then on hearing just "Is there a red—," he or she may already be able to begin a search process based on that first-heard adjective. Of course, this initial search process would be based solely on one feature, redness, and thus may take place in a rather parallel fashion. Then, a few hundred milliseconds later, as the second adjective is being heard, some of the distractors have already been somewhat excluded from the rest of the search process because they lack the first-mentioned feature—a bit like Olds et al.'s (2000a, 2000b) notion of search assistance. Importantly, this explanation demands considerably richer and more continuous interaction between the language system and the visual system than typically acknowledged (see chapter 5).

Based on results like these, it appears that rather than a collection of individual feature maps simply outputting a pop-out signal or a "must conjoin" signal to a master map for serial attentional search, some form of graded or probabilistic information is continuously "cascaded" (McClelland, 1979) from the *parallel* feature maps to some *serial-like* search process. In one theoretical framework, it has been argued that information from the feature maps can guide the attention-based serial search (Huebner, 2001; Wolfe, Cave, & Franzel, 1989; Wolfe, 1992a).

Visual Search Modeling

Moving even farther away from the traditional distinction between a parallel preattentive stage of processing and a serial attentional mechanism, Desimone and Duncan (1995; Reynolds & Desimone, 2001; see also Keysers & Perrett, 2002) describe a theory of biased competition in which multiple representations of objects are simultaneously partially active and compete for the privilege of driving motor output (e.g., pressing the target-present button, naming an object, reaching to grasp an attended object, or even turning to shoot the computer-generated avatar of your opponent in a video game). Experimenter instructions, goal-oriented plans, and contextual constraints provide the top-down bias for this competition process (e.g., Awh, Matsukura, & Serences, 2003).

The following localist attractor network simulations serve as a kind of mid-level generic implementation of a biased competition account of visual search. Some more complex and neurally explicit network models have been designed to handle specific sets of visual search tasks and phenomena (e.g., Cave, 1999; Cave & Wolfe, 1990; Godijn & Theeuwes, 2002; Grossberg, Mingolla, & Ross, 1994; Humphreys & Müller, 1993; Koch & Ullman, 1985; Phaf, van der Heijden, & Hudson, 1990; Sandon, 1990). And more abstract mathematical accounts, based on signal detection theory and information theory, have also fit a range of visual search data (e.g., Eckstein, 1998; Eckstein et al., 2000; McElree & Carrasco, 1999; Palmer, 1995; Tsotsos, 1990). The more explicit neural network implementations tend to carry with them a substantial number of architectural assumptions and adjustable parameters, whereas the static equation accounts tend to gloss over the temporal dynamics of the process of search. These normalized recurrence simulations of visual search lack the neural explicitness of the network models and the mathematical elegance of the models inspired by signal detection theory. Instead, they combine the transparency of the equation-based models with the temporal dynamics of the network models. They function as a conceptual bridge between those two different kinds of models, whereby one can envision a theoretical framework for biased competition during visual search that can exist at multiple levels of description. For purposes of simplicity, the simulations I report here—in which many object representations compete against each other and one finally wins—will be limited to target-present trials. Although there are many different ideas about what cognitive processes may be involved in deciding that the target is absent on any given trial, it is probably safe to say that it does *not* involve a process of one object representation eventually winning a probabilistic competition.[5]

Simulation 1: The Basics

In this first simulation, one feature vector represents the likelihood of each object being the target based solely on it exhibiting the target property of *redness,* and the other feature vector represents the likelihood of each object being the target based solely on it exhibiting the target property of *verticalness.* The integration vector serves as a measure of each object's overall likelihood of being the target. Figure 8.10 shows a schematic diagram of this normalized recurrence network with input values corresponding to a target-present conjunction search for a red vertical bar with a set size of seven (i.e., one red vertical, three red nonverticals, and three nonred verticals).

As with other normalized recurrence simulations here, within each cycle of competition, the two feature vectors are normalized, then averaged at the integration layer,[6] and the integration vector then sends pointwise multiplicative cumulative feedback to those feature vectors. As cycles of competition continue, the integration node corresponding to the target object (exhibiting both redness and verticalness) increases in activation while the other nodes decrease in activation. Competition continues until an integration node exceeds a 0.95 activation criterion. The conjunction search simulation involves setting node 1 at 1.0 activation in both feature vectors, because it is the target, exhibiting both redness and verticalness. Also, a nonoverlapping half of the remaining nodes, in each vector, are set at 1.0 activation, as they each exhibit one and only one target feature. Thus, for a set size of eight, the starting activations for the feature

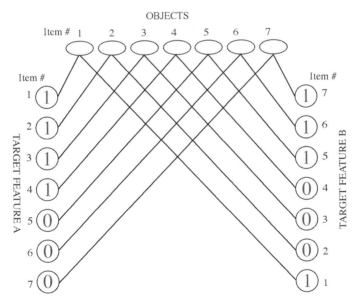

Figure 8.10. Diagram of the normalized recurrence localist attractor network as applied to visual search for a conjunction target. The number of nodes in the network need not be related to the set size, as only those nodes whose objects exhibit the relevant target feature will ever have nonzero activation. For example, the same network with 36 nodes in each vector can be used for set sizes of 1–36.

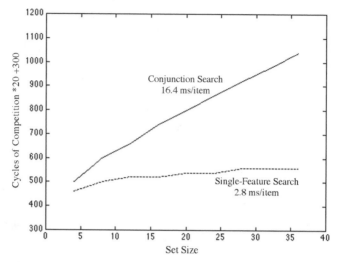

Figure 8.11. Normalized recurrence results for visual search simulation 1: the basics.

vectors would be [1 1 1 1 0 0 0 0] for the redness vector, and [1 0 0 0 1 1 1 1] for the verticalness vector. See the appendix for example MATLAB code.

Across set sizes of 4 to 36, in steps of four, this normalized recurrence competition algorithm produces an almost perfectly linear slope of settling time as a function of set size for standard conjunction search; $r^2 = 0.995$.[7] If one treats each time step as equivalent to 20 milliseconds and adds 300 milliseconds for baseline perceptual-motor delays, one sees response times that are highly typical of conjunction search tasks, and a response time by set size slope of 16.4 milliseconds per item. Of course, the simulation can also produce a nearly flat (2.8 milliseconds per item) search function for single-feature pop-out displays as well—where the starting activations would look like [1 0 0 0 0 0 0 0] and [1 1 1 1 1 1 1 1]. See figure 8.11. This first basic result, out of such a simple localist attractor network, is noteworthy. One of the field's landmark findings that has traditionally been taken as evidence for a serial fixed-duration template matching of each object one at a time, that is, linearly increasing search functions, is exactly mimicked by a parallel competitive architecture where the only capacity limitations are that its representations are forced to share a probability density function.

Initially, it is not necessarily obvious why normalized recurrence should produce this linear increase in search time as a function of set size. The activations of the different vectors certainly change quite nonlinearly over time. See figure 8.12. It should be noted that this linear increase in settling time holds true as long as the criterion for stopping competition is set anywhere above 0.5. (Importantly, this means the model is not really ready to deal with displays that have multiple targets; e.g., Ward & McClelland, 1989).

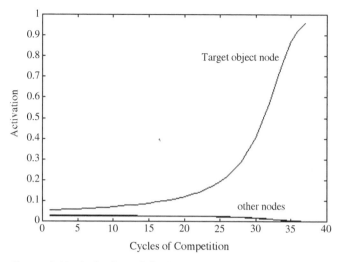

Figure 8.12. Activation of the integration vector over time in a normalized recurrence simulation of a target-present 36-item conjunction search.

Part of understanding how this unassuming little localist attractor network produces this linear increase in settling time involves comparing the starting activations at different set sizes with the rate at which the winning node accrues activation over time. As set size increases linearly, the initial activation of the target object's integration node decreases nonlinearly. Additionally, as competition takes place within a given trial, that target integration node's activation value increases nonlinearly over time. In fact, this nonlinear increase over time exactly compensates for the nonlinear differences in starting activation across set size. For example, as shown in figure 8.13, competition increases the target integration node's activation with an asymmetric sigmoid function over time. Thus, although the initial activation values vary nonlinearly with set size (i.e., 0.415, 0.225, 0.155, 0.118, 0.095, for set sizes 4, 8, 12, 16, and 20), their nonlinear rise over time causes them to achieve a criterion of activation at approximately linear intervals in time (Spivey-Knowlton, 1996). In a sense, two nonlinearities make a linearity.

One can think of this activation curve over time as a hill that the target object representation has to climb to win the competition. The further away from the top that it starts out, naturally, the longer it will take to reach the top. Figure 8.14 depicts a generic version of this activation hill, with dots showing where the target integration node starts, with different set sizes. The nonlinear decrease in starting activation as set size increase is due to the normalization. But note how, as set size increases from 4 to 8 to 12 and so on, the smaller decreases in starting activation actually push the dot back (horizontally leftward) by a relatively fixed amount of added time (as indicated by the dashed lines).

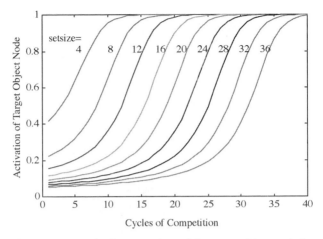

Figure 8.13. Activation over time of the target object node in the integration vector for all set sizes. Once the curves exceed 0.5 activation, they are generally evenly spaced apart from one another in competition cycles, thus producing the linear increase in response time across set size.

The key observation from this simulation is the fact that the representations of the various objects are all processed simultaneously; their activations updated in tandem. Despite this parallel processing of all object representations, the network produces linearly increasing settling times, as a function of set size, which for a long time were commonly interpreted as evidence for serial processing. Thus the simulation stands as an existence proof that linear functions can

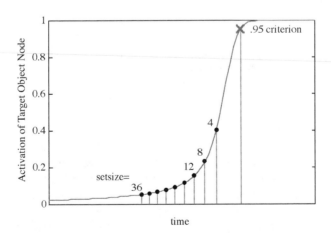

Figure 8.14. Target node starting activations and their temporal distance from reaching criterion (see text for details).

come out of a system in which multiple partially active representations are competing simultaneously, and an object's targethood gradually emerges over the course of hundreds of milliseconds during visual search.

Simulation 2: Target-Distractor Similarity

One of the fundamental predictions that a probabilistic competitive account of visual search has to make is that graded similarity between distractor and target will modulate the efficiency of the search (see Duncan & Humphreys, 1989). Given the same set size, distractors that are highly similar to the target should compete strongly and therefore increase response times, whereas distractors that are less similar to the target should compete only weakly and thus decrease response times. Therefore, this account predicts a range of search functions from very steep to nearly flat and everywhere in between—in conjunction search displays as well as in single-feature displays (e.g., Bauer, Cowan, & Jolicoeur, 1996; D'Zmura, 1991; Olds et al., 2000a, 2000b, 2000c).

In the high-similarity condition, the feature vectors for a single-feature search, where the target might be a red vertical bar and the distractors pink (instead of green) vertical bars, would look like the following for a set size of eight: redness = [1 0.5 0.5 0.5 0.5 0.5 0.5 0.5], verticalness = [1 1 1 1 1 1 1 1]. This simulation also included a high-similarity conjunction search in which the target was a red vertical bar and the distractors were red diagonals and pink verticals, for example, redness = [1 1 1 1 0.5 0.5 0.5 0.5], verticalness = [1 0.5 0.5 0.5 1 1 1 1]. Figure 8.15 (dashed line) shows how increased similarity between target and distractors dramatically increased the slope for a single-feature search (from 2.8 milliseconds per item to 24.75 milliseconds

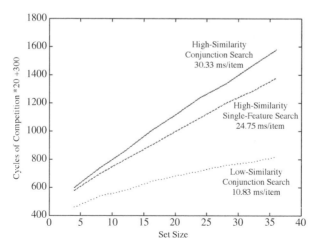

Figure 8.15. Normalized recurrence simulation results for simulation 2: target-distractor similarity.

per item). Such a steep slope is comparable to what D'Zmura (1991) and Bauer et al. (1996) found when the target color was not linearly separable from the distractor colors (in CIELUV color space; Robertson, 1977). The high-similarity manipulation for the conjunction search also increased its corresponding response time by set size slope (from 16.4 milliseconds per item to 30.33 milliseconds per item). See the solid line in figure 8.15. Additionally, the slopes in both cases were highly linear; $r^2 > 0.99$.

Similarity between target and distractors can also be *decreased* by, for example, replacing red distractors with pink ones in the conjunction search display; that is, a red vertical target amid green verticals and pink horizontals. In such a simulation, the starting values for the feature vectors, in a set size of eight, would look like: redness = [1 0 0 0 0.5 0.5 0.5 0.5], verticalness = [1 1 1 1 0 0 0 0]. In this low-similarity conjunction search condition (also shown in figure 8.15, dotted line), search slopes decreased to 10.83 milliseconds per item, compared to the standard conjunction search's 16.4 milliseconds per item (recall figure 8.11). Again, the slope was highly linear; $r^2 = 0.98$.

Simulation 2 demonstrates that with the normalized recurrence competition algorithm, conjunction searches (as well as feature searches) are capable of a wide range of response time by set size slopes. As target-distractor similarity increases, search becomes less efficient (steeper response time slopes). As target-distractor similarity decreases, search becomes more efficient (shallower response time slopes). The past results and current simulations suggest that visual search phenomena are best described via a *continuum* of search efficiency (Duncan & Humphreys, 1989), rather than via a discrete distinction between parallel (sensory) processing and serial (attentional) processing (Treisman, 1988).

Simulation 3: Distractor-Distractor Similarity

In addition to target-distractor similarity, it has also been found that similarity between distractors themselves affects search efficiency (Duncan & Humphreys, 1989; Humphreys, Quinlan, & Riddoch, 1989), as well as eye movement patterns during search (Shen, Reingold, & Pomplun, 2000, 2003). Duncan and Humphreys (1989, 1992) have argued that features can produce a spreading suppression, such that when many distractors exhibit the same feature, they suppress one another, allowing the target to be detected more quickly. Some have explored this type of phenomena as a texture segmentation process (e.g., Rieth & Sireteanu, 1994; Wolfe, 1992b) or a spatial/featural grouping process (e.g., Braithwaite, Humphreys, & Hodsoll, 2003; Gilchrist et al., 1997). Essentially, if a red vertical target is immersed in a clump of mostly red horizontals and only a few green verticals, a large patch of red horizontals can wind up being perceived as a kind of background wallpaper pattern, as it were, and filtered out en masse. Thus, even in a conjunction search, if the distractors are sufficiently homogenous, the search function can be nearly flat (Egeth, Virzi, & Garbart, 1984; Humphreys et al., 1989).

In the normalized recurrence competition algorithm, this spreading suppression referred to by Duncan and Humphreys (1989, 1992) is a natural consequence of initial feature normalization. If a majority of the distractors exhibit the same feature (e.g., redness = [1 0 0 1 1 1 1 1]), each of these featural activations is then divided by a larger number. Of course, the target item's feature node is also divided by this large number. However, this means that the target item has fewer competitors along the other feature (e.g., verticalness = [1 1 1 0 0 0 0 0]) and gets divided by a smaller number. The result is that in the object array, the target starts out with higher activation and with weaker competitors (integration = [0.25 0.17 0.17 0.08 0.08 0.08 0.08 0.08]) than if there were a roughly equal number of the two types of distractors (integration = [0.225 0.125 0.125 0.125 0.1 0.1 0.1 0.1]).

The first demonstration in simulation 3 is of a conjunction search in which the majority (about three-fourths) of the distractors were identical, instead of being equally composed of the two types of distractors, as in the previous simulations. For example, a red vertical target might be surrounded mostly by red horizontals and by only a few green verticals. (In all of the demonstrations for simulation 3, the coding of the display always included at least one green vertical.) With this type of input, normalized recurrence produced a search function (14.25 milliseconds per item; see figure 8.16) that was shallower than that of a conjunction search with equally distributed distractors (recall figure 8.11). Again, the slope was quite linear; $r^2 > 0.99$.

With even greater homogeneity of distractors, the search slope approached the flat function characteristic of pop out. When seven-eighths of the distractors

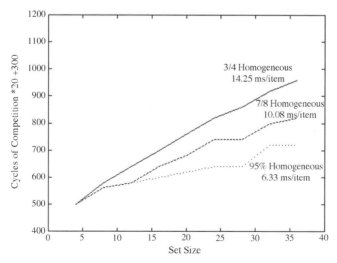

Figure 8.16. Normalized recurrence simulation results for simulation 3: distractor-distractor similarity.

were identical, the model took the equivalent of 10.08 milliseconds per item to find the target (figure 8.16, dashed line). With 95% homogeneity of distractors—where only set sizes 32 and 36 have more than one green vertical—the model took 6.33 milliseconds per item (figure 8.16, dotted line). Although the search slope for the seven-eighths homogenous display was still highly linear ($r^2 = 0.98$), the slope for the 95% homogeneity condition was slightly less so ($r^2 = 0.94$).

Simulation 3 corroborates the importance of distractor-distractor similarity (e.g., Duncan & Humphreys, 1989; Humphreys et al., 1989). When the distractors are more or less homogenous, a kind of spreading suppression causes them to interfere less with the target's salience, as if the homogenous distractors were being grouped and rejected in one fell swoop (Humphreys & Müller, 1993). Normalized recurrence implements this spreading suppression as a natural result of the representations in any one feature vector being forced to share a probability density function.

The Search Surface

Together, simulations 2 and 3 demonstrate the interplay between target-distractor similarity and distractor-distractor similarity. Whereas greater target-distractor similarity makes visual search *less* efficient, greater distractor-distractor similarity makes it *more* efficient. In fact, Duncan and Humphreys (1989; see also Duncan, 1989) suggested exactly this relationship between these two types of similarity, and they even sketched a three-dimensional surface plot of how these two similarity measures might affect response time by set size slopes. Figure 8.17A shows a re-creation of their hypothesized search surface, whereby greater degrees of just target-distractor similarity or of just distractor-distractor dissimilarity do not especially increase response time by set size slopes, but greater degrees of both do produce significant increases in slopes.

By conducting further simulations like those in the previous sections, for a total of 20 response time by set size slopes across the different similarity conditions, normalized recurrence can fill out the missing points in its own version of this predicted search surface (figure 8.17B). In panel B, distractor homogeneity (based on simulation 3) serves as a rough equivalent to Duncan and Humphrey's (1989) notion of distractor-distractor similarity in panel A. For target-distractor similarity in panel B, "very low" refers to conditions where both types of distractors share only one feature in common with the target, and even then it's not a perfect match of that feature (e.g., search for a red vertical amid pink horizontals and green diagonals). Low target-distractor similarity refers to conditions where one type of distractor shares one feature perfectly with the target, and the other type shares only one partially matching feature (e.g., search for a red vertical amid red horizontals and green diagonals). Standard target-distractor similarity is, of course, the usual case where

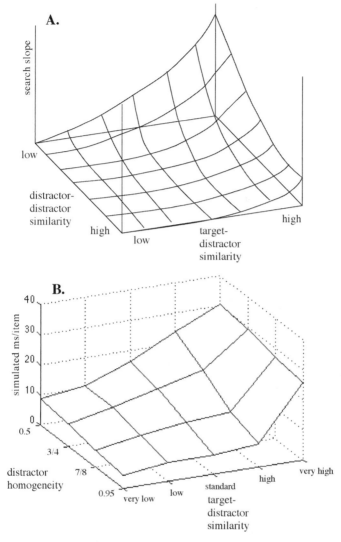

Figure 8.17. A: Theoretical search surface depicting effects of similarity on response time by set size slopes (Duncan & Humphreys, 1989). B: Normalized recurrence's approximation of that search surface (see text for details).

each distractor shares exactly one feature perfectly with the target (e.g., search for a red vertical amid red horizontals and green verticals). High target-distractor similarity is when one type of distractor shares one feature perfectly and one feature partially with the target, whereas the other type of distractor is standard (e.g., search for a red vertical amid red diagonals and green verticals). Finally, what I am calling very high target-distractor similarity refers to an experimental condition rarely explored in the visual search literature, where both types of distractors share one feature perfectly with the target and one feature partially (e.g., search for a red vertical amid red diagonals and pink verticals). As can be seen in figure 8.17A, Duncan and Humphreys hypothesized that distractor-distractor similarity would have almost no effect when target-distractor similarity is low, and would have its largest effect when target-distractor similarity is high. The simulation results in panel B generally concur with this, but add that with *very high* target-distractor similarity homogeneity of distractors should go back to having little effect.

Overall, the encouraging thing about this collection of simulations is that despite this localist attractor network being frightfully simple, it elegantly and intuitively handles the basic findings of visual search phenomena, as well as these modulations of search efficiency caused by similarity manipulations. Without adjusting any parameters—other than merely selecting 0.5 activation for similar features—this high-level implementation of a biased competition kind of process (Desimone & Duncan, 1995) naturally simulates a variety of visual search phenomena. Importantly, for my purposes in this book, these simulations permit a concrete visualization of what is meant by multiple representations being simultaneously partially active and competing with one another over time (figure 8.12) to produce a nonlinear trajectory in mental state space (which, in laboratory tasks that require one response per trial, eventually settles into one attractor basin).

What this little localist attractor network in its current incarnations does not handle is spatiotopic effects, such as eccentricity and spatial grouping, because the model does not have spatial proximity encoded. All objects, in all the vectors, are essentially treated as equally near one another in these simulations. Nonetheless, the general algorithm—as is—elegantly handles effects of similarity, as just demonstrated, as well as search asymmetries (Treisman & Gormican, 1988), triple conjunctions (Quinlan & Humphreys, 1987), and search assistance (Olds et al., 2000a, 2000b, 2000c). A minor modification to the algorithm allows it to simulate Spivey et al.'s (2001) linguistic modulation of visual search efficiency (see Reali, Spivey, Tyler, & Terranova, in press). But rather than continue to belabor this generic simulation of visual search response times in further excruciating detail, perhaps this would be a good time to bring this chapter to a close and try to sum up.

Visual Perception Is a Hungry Process

This chapter's brief tour through a handful of selected observations in visual processing highlights findings that are highly supportive of a general view of perception, cognition, and action in which partially active mental representations compete over time until one (or in some cases an amalgam of more than one) wins the privilege to execute its associated motor output. The temporal continuity inherent in these representations changing over time is reminiscent of a number of well-known findings in cognitive psychology. For example, Shepard and Metzler's (1971) mental rotation findings, where the time it takes to recognize a rotated object is linearly related to how far it would need to be rotated to be in its upright orientation, is a paragon example of a smooth spatiotemporally contiguous alteration of some form of internal representation. Similarly, Kosslyn, Ball, and Reiser's (1978) mental scanning experiments, where the time taken to move one's focus of attention in a mental image from one location to another is metrically related to the relative distances being moved, hints at a general observation that real-time changes of mental content involve continuous trajectories in state space, rather than discrete instantaneous teleportations from one symbolic location in state space to another.

Importantly, these trajectories through a visual-processing state space do not merely consist of a string of previous locations and a current location. They also tend to include a kind of anticipatory impetus for where in state space they are likely to go next. For example, Freyd (1987) has argued that representational transitions are more important than representational states and has shown evidence for this in terms of what she calls "representational momentum." When a moving stimulus on a computer screen stops and the screen goes blank, observers routinely report the last viewed location/position of the stimulus as slightly beyond where it was actually last seen. It is as though the visual system's anticipation of what it will perceive next becomes part of what it "thinks" it genuinely sees. Indeed, some vision researchers have proposed that feedback projections in cortex may be responsible for anticipatory perception (e.g., Kosslyn, 1994; Rao & Ballard, 1999; Thomas, 1999; see also Neisser, 1976) and that it may solve a number of computational problems in perceptual learning (Poggio et al., 2004; Jordan & Rumelhart, 1992; see also Elman, 1991; Sutton & Barto, 1981). The point here is that whether the visual system is adjusting its receptive fields in anticipation of an upcoming eye movement, recognizing a face, deciding on what oculomotor signal to send to the eye muscles, or searching among a cluttered array for a target object, the population code corresponding to the representation that will be the winner of the competition—and thus get to drive behavior (or even just constitute an internal monolog)—spends a considerable amount of time *approaching that status* and rather little time *enjoying it.* The perceptual-cognitive system is better described by how it gets to various places in state space, rather than by where those places are.

The emphasis on winning the privilege to drive behavior underscores an important distinction between two often opposing traditions in visual science: representation-based and action-based approaches to visual perception. A great deal of cognitive psychology and visual psychophysics has focused, perhaps too much, on what neural computations are involved in converting an image on the retina into an internal interpretation of the visual scene (e.g., Biederman, 2000; Edelman & Intrator, 2003; Hummel, 2003; Marr, 1982; Treisman, 1996). This tradition has often treated the purpose of vision as though it were solely to perform this conversion of a two-dimensional retinal image into a three-dimensional mental model. The job of converting the mind's percepts into the mind's selected motor outputs is treated as though it should be handled by a separate field. Even disregarding the recursive homunculus problems that such an approach may invite (i.e., how does the little man inside the head, in between perception and action, make sense out of that reconstructed internalized mental model of the world?), it seems clear that the millions of years of natural selection that shaped the mammalian visual apparatus never really cared a whit about internalized mental models. Natural selection cares about behavioral results, not the fidelity of internalized renditions of scenes. Therefore, although internal mental models certainly may exist in some form as a useful means to an end, they surely are not the purpose of vision. When our proverbial caveman ancestor detected an alligator in the reeds, it wasn't just impressive "shape from shading" (e.g., Atick, Griffin, & Redlich, 1996; Kingdom, 2003; Ramachandran, 1988) that allowed him to make it home alive to make more babies with his cavewife. Fancy internal representation would merely allow him to think, "Oh, I recognize that animal. That's the bastard who ate my brother." It was mapping those visual processes onto the right *motor output*, that is, running, that allowed him to further propagate his genes that night.[8]

Action-based approaches to vision and visual attention (e.g., Allport, 1989; Gibson, 1979; Hommel et al., 2001; Müsseler, van der Heijden, & Kerzel, 2004; O'Regan & Noë, 2001; Tucker & Ellis, 1998; Turvey & Carello, 1986; van der Heijden, 1996a, 1996b; see also Milner & Goodale, 1995) don't stop with some fancy "internal representation." That's only half the job. (Or, by some accounts, not even part of the job at all.) A general overarching version of the arguments put forward by these various perspectives is that the recognition of an object is crucially connected to the activation of potential motor patterns defining how the organism might *interact with that object*—not how it might sit back and appreciate the object's contours, surfaces, textures, and colors. Gibson called these potential motor patterns "affordances."

More recently, Ellis and Tucker (2000) have been developing the concept of micro-affordances as physical properties of liftable objects that afford motor interaction by the human body, especially handles. In their examination of the role of micro-affordances during object perception, they have shown that reaction times for simple perceptual judgments about whether the object is right-side up or upside down are subtly affected by whether the object's handle is on the left or right side (from the perspective of the observer) and whether the left or right hand is executing the button-press response (Tucker & Ellis, 1998). Their claim is that because part of recognizing an object (even a computer-screen image of an object that one obviously couldn't really physically manipulate with one's hands) involves partial activation of the motor actions one might execute to interact with it, for example, grasping its handle with the hand on the appropriate side, even just the pressing of a response button is slightly facilitated when that hand is the one that would have been involved in taking advantage of that micro-affordance.

In fact, Shepard & Metzler's (1971) mental rotation results are recapitulated in a motor version of the task, where populations of neurons that act as distributed representations of hand movements in particular directions exhibit the gradual continuous transition from biasing one movement direction to eventually biasing (and executing) another movement direction, during the time course of the mental rotation (Georgopoulos et al., 1989). Even relatively static internally generated mental images, which are known to activate some of the same visual cortical areas used for perception of afferent visual input (Kosslyn & Thompson, 2003), appear to elicit eye movements (around a blank screen) that are similar to those elicited by viewing that actual image (Brandt & Stark, 1997; see also Demarais & Cohen, 1998; Laeng & Teodorescu, 2002; Spivey & Geng, 2001)—as Donald Hebb (1968) predicted long ago.

A similar prominence for the role of motor processing in perception is seen in research related to mirror neurons (e.g., Meltzoff & Prinz, 2002; Stamenov & Gallese, 2002; see also Knoblich et al., 2005). Mirror neurons are cells in the precentral region of motor cortex (area F5) that respond equally to the animal *executing* a particular motor action and to *perceiving* another animal producing the same motor action. Interestingly, this "action-execution-observation matching system" (Avikainen, Kulomaki, & Hari, 1999) appears to be selective to biologically plausible actions. For example, Stevens and colleagues (2000) presented participants with apparent motion displays of arm movement, flashed at rates that make the motion either biologically plausible or not, and fMRI scans revealed motor and parietal cortices to be active only during the perception of biologically plausible arm motion. Thus, one could argue that part of visually recognizing another's actions involves some degree of internally simulating one's own (successful) execution of those same actions.

There is an anticipatory quality here to the way imagined action seems to accompany visual perception in so many circumstances. It looks as though an important part of how we visually recognize other people's actions is to induce partial activation of the motor representations that we might use to imitate those actions. Similarly, an important part of how we visually recognize objects is to induce partial activation of the motor actions we might execute to interact with that object. That is, a crucial component of visually recognizing an object involves partially activating neural patterns for how one's effectors (e.g., arms, legs, speech apparatus, even eyes) might manipulate it. It's a bit like a forward model of perceptual-motor performance (e.g., Jordan & Rumelhart, 1992; Kawato, 1996; see chapter 9) that's in self-train mode all the time (Dayan et al., 1995).

If we think of visual perception as a continuous trajectory through a high-dimensional state space, then each freeze-frame of a visual mental state is best characterized not only by a particular location in that state space and perhaps some residual activation of the immediately previous locations, but also by some kind of momentum vector describing the general direction it wants to go next. Where in state space the trajectory actually winds up going will be determined by a combination of forces brought on by actual afferent sensory inputs as well as forces brought on by expectations of sensory inputs and of potential motor outputs. Based on findings like those discussed in this chapter, visual perception—much like language comprehension (chapter 7)— looks like a dynamical system that opportunistically takes the information it needs and integrates it promiscuously, rather than being a computational device that passively receives information and processes it in a feedforward linear systems manner. With the help of anticipatory feedback processes, visual perception continuously pursues its interpretations rather than waiting to be given them. And thus, I like to call it a hungry process.

9

Temporal Dynamics in Action

But the point which needs to be understood (as it is well understood by Piaget) is that the importance of the body is in the *genesis* of intelligence and not in its eventual practice. . . . By the time he is an adult, a person's intelligence depends on him possessing a body only in the obvious sense that his body contains the mechanisms in which intelligence is realized and provides the means for perception, locomotion, etc. To claim otherwise is to suggest that a person who is paralyzed has lost his intelligence!
—Zenon Pylyshyn

Where Can a Cognitive Psychologist
Get a Little Action Around Here?

To be sure, the hypothesized role of one's physical embodiment in cognition is not so extreme that embodiment theorists would be forced to conclude, as Pylyshyn (1974, p. 69) taunted, that a paralyzed person would no longer have a mind. But it is perhaps reasonable to suspect that some very basic bodily constraints do influence how we perceive and conceptualize our worlds. For example, a very tall person who is accustomed to having to duck through doorways certainly must have slightly different perceptual-motor routines for indoor navigation than people of average height. Perhaps this alters the way they distribute their visual attention as they locomote, as well as their conceptualization of 3D spatial layout and their use of affordances (Warren & Whang, 1987; see also Bhalla & Proffitt, 1999). If the way that one's body interacts with the world can influence the way that one's brain conceptualizes the world (e.g., Barsalou, 1999; Brooks, 1995; Clark, 1997; Glenberg, 1997; Varela, Thompson, & Rosch, 1992), then we should actually expect differently abled body types and differently trained motor cortices to be accompanied by slightly differently functioning cognitive processes. Indeed, over the past several years, Pylyshyn's somewhat bold assertion has gradually been softened into a quite reasonable empirical question.

Far from being the encapsulated caboose at the end of a linear feedforward train of boxes going from perception to cognition to action, motor movement does appear to play a powerful role in much of perception and cognition. For example, the dorsal visual stream, including parietal cortex, appears to encode not just where objects are in the visual field but also how our hands and arms might interact with those objects (e.g., Jacob & Jeannerod, 2003; Milner & Goodale, 1995). In fact, the shape of a person's hand while they manually respond to visual images in an object categorization task affects their response times as a function of the graspability of that object with that hand shape. Tucker and Ellis (2001) had participants categorize visual images of objects as natural or manufactured, either by squeezing a response handle with a full-hand power grasp in one condition, or by pinching a response manipulandum with thumb-and-forefinger precision grasp in the other condition. When people were responding to the natural/manufactured task with a power grasp, larger objects (that afforded a power grasp for lifting) were categorized more quickly. When they were responding with a precision grasp, smaller objects (that afforded a precision grasp for lifting) were categorized more quickly. Thus, far from computing amodal symbolic representations of taxonomic class inclusion, the way traditional artificial intelligence would do for such a task, the process of cognitively determining the category membership of these objects was recruiting current manual grasping parameters and their match or mismatch to the affordances of that object to carry out the categorization task. (See also Wohlschläger & Wohlschläger, 1998, for related findings with mental rotation and hand movement.)

As mentioned briefly in the previous chapter, mirror neurons in cortical area F5 become relevant to this discussion, as these cells appear to represent both the production and the perception of particular motor actions (Decety & Grèzes, 1999; Gallese et al., 1996). The idea of a common code for the perception and production of actions has a history in ideomotor theory (Greenwald, 1970), in the motor theory of speech (Liberman & Mattingly, 1985; Liberman & Whalen, 2000), and the theory of event coding (Hommel et al., 2001). In this general framework, an important component of recognizing someone else's actions or utterances is knowing how one would produce those actions or utterances oneself. Likewise, an important component of knowing how to produce the motor output one intends to produce is knowing what tactile feedback one's effectors/limbs should receive during the action, what one's limbs should look like when successfully producing that action, as well as what end-result changes to one's environmental layout should be perceivable after the action has been successfully completed. In such an arrangement, where *sensory* and *motor* processes are so closely interwoven, the *cognitive* middle man gets sandwiched so tightly that he no longer functions like the meat between two slices of bread but more like a thin cheese spread that soaks into both sides.

As an example of the role played by the body in perceptual-cognitive judgments, when anticipating where a thrown object might land, we naturally recruit our own body schema and motor kinematics to construct the perceptual simulation. Knoblich and Flach (2001; see also Repp & Knoblich, 2004, for related findings with pianists) had participants throw darts at a dartboard and later showed them video clips of themselves and others throwing these darts (from a side view perspective). Without being allowed to see the trajectory of the dart itself, only the dynamics of the arm movement (and in some conditions the body as well), participants were asked to predict whether each thrown dart would land in the upper third, middle, or lower third of the dartboard. Participants were reliably better at making these predictions when they were watching video clips of themselves than when they were watching video clips of others. Thus, even though these participants had never before watched themselves (from a third-person perspective) throw darts, their perceptual anticipation of action effects (such as where the dart would land) was more accurate when the observed movement had been produced by the same system now performing the perceptual simulation.

The importance of one's own sensory-motor routines for judgments about observed motor movements becomes especially relevant for the challenge delivered by Pylyshyn that began this chapter. Consider the cases of two individuals whose somatosensory input across the entire surface of the body (except the head) has been eliminated due to a degenerative neural disease when they were young. They are the only two such patients in the world. These gentlemen can walk, very slowly and carefully, purely due to the fact that they can watch when each foot lands and looks stable, and then can command the next leg to step and find stable footing. They get no tactile or proprioceptive feedback from their limbs as to whether the foot is evenly supported, whether the weight that is being put on it is evenly balanced, or whether their fingers have adequately grasped a drinking glass before lifting it. They must rely entirely on visual feedback to tell them these things. Here are two persons whose somatosensory-motor feedback loops have been inactive for many years. Does this significant limitation in their degree of embodiment impair their ability to make cognitive judgments (or construct perceptual simulations) regarding someone else interacting physically with their environment?

Bosbach and colleagues (2005) gave these two patients the task of watching an actor lift a box and judging whether the box is heavy or light depending on the actor's posture and limb dynamics. For this simple task, these two deafferented patients did as well as nonimpaired control participants. But what about when the actor occasionally lifted the box in a manner suggesting that he had been deceived as to the weight of the box? We all know what it's like to lift a juice carton that is emptier than we thought or more full than we thought. Are the postural and limb dynamics in such a case readily perceivable by an observer? Well, control participants were quite good at this task. And if you side with Pylyshyn in his quote, you might expect a low-level sensory deficit, such as that experienced by these two deafferented patients, to have little effect on such a high-level cognitive task as guessing whether someone has been deceived. Bosbach et al. found that these two patients performed far worse on this task than the control participants. Thus, it would appear that one's own perceptual-motor routines do indeed play a significant role in cognitively simulating the mental state of someone else interacting with their environment.

In fact, far subtler deviations in sensory-motor experience can influence people's cognitive processes while viewing other peoples' motor movements

(Calvo-Merino et al., 2005; see also Hamilton, Wolpert, & Frith, 2004). When ballet dancers watch other ballet dancers, or when capoeira dancers watch other capoeira dancers, they exhibit activation in the mirror neuron region. Thus, while simply watching the dancers, they seem to be generating their own motor simulations of the movements being carried out. However, when ballet dancers watch capoeira, or when capoeira dancers watch ballet, this mirror system is not active. And this is not due solely to amount of visual exposure. Female ballet dancers, who are of course visually exposed to a great deal of male ballet movements but do not include many of them in their own movement repertoire, also *do not* show activation of the mirror system when watching male ballet dancers (Calvo-Merino et al., 2005).

Even relatively high-level linguistic and conceptual representations appear to be deeply rooted in perceptual-motor components (e.g., Barsalou, 2002; Mandler, 1992; Zwaan et al., 2004). For example, activation of motor cortex can result from even just hearing an action verb (Hauk & Pulvermüller, 2004; Pulvermüller, 1999; Tettamanti et al., 2005) or looking at a tool (Chao & Martin, 2000). When children are applying learned names to novel objects, they use the (vertical or horizontal) spatial orientation of their motoric interaction with the original object to guide their generalization for the new object (Smith, 2005). Thus, they appear to associate a vertical or horizontal extent to the object's identity (see also Richardson et al., 2003). Notably, this only works when the child herself moves the object in the specified orientation, not when she merely observes the experimenter moving the object in that orientation.

In fact, even the comprehension of a sentence about movement can be affected by the direction of the motoric response being used. Glenberg and Kaschak (2002) had participants push or pull a lever to respond to sentences that described away-from-self or toward-self events, and they found a reliable stimulus-response compatibility effect such that participants were faster to push (and slower to pull) the lever in response to sentences about away-from-self events and faster to pull (and slower to push) the lever in response to sentences about toward-self events. Perhaps not surprisingly—given the flexibility afforded by the mirror system—the representation of self, with respect to push and pull responses, can even be dislodged from the body and simulated as elsewhere (by presenting the participant's own name on the computer screen) to induce a spatial stimulus-response compatibility effect that treats the *external* location as though it were the self (Markman & Brendl, 2005). Evidently, the spatial effects of sensorimotor processes in cognitive tasks may at times be mediated by higher level conceptual representations of the sensorimotor relationships and not necessarily solely by the original raw sensorimotor activation patterns themselves (see Boroditzky & Ramscar, 2002). Thus, rather than eliminating higher level conceptual representations altogether, the proper goal of embodiment theories is perhaps better described as emphasizing the continuous spatiotemporal and sensorimotor character of these higher level conceptual representations.

Any one of these findings on its own could easily be accommodated by a traditional information-processing account of cognition in which a vestigial, largely epiphenomenal connection is hypothesized between the relevant amodal cognitive symbol and the motor process involved in the experimental task. This growing collection of findings together, however, would require so many post hoc vestigial connections as to make this amodal symbolic model of cognition positively unwieldy, if not downright scientifically irresponsible. The vestigial connections would end up doing more work in accounting for the human data than the core symbolic model would. In contrast, a theory of cognition in which embodied cognitive representations emerge from perceptual-motor interactions (e.g., Barsalou, 1999; Glenberg, 1997; Hommel et al., 2001; Mandler, 1992) naturally predicts these kinds of findings already.

Given even just this brief sampling of the accumulating evidence for actions, prepared actions, and simulated actions exhibiting significant influences on our real-time cognitive processing, it seems incumbent on all cognitive scientists to begin paying some attention to how motor movement works in general and on the constraints that the body's physical and motoric embodiment place on how our minds function (see Ballard et al., 1997; Seitz, 2000). Although a significant portion of traditional cognitive science has chosen to turn a blind eye to the research going on in motor movement, this voluntary ignorance is now giving way to genuine curiosity in the possible broad generality of the theoretical developments taking place in that field. There was a time when a cognitive psychologist who recorded reaction times, verbal protocols, or card-sorting results could get away with saying things like, "I'm not measuring motor output, I'm measuring cognition." As if pressing a button for a reaction time, speaking aloud about one's intuitions, or sorting cards into groups did not necessarily involve motor output.

The majority of the experimental methodologies in cognitive psychology actually involve recording motor output and inferring the internal representations that may have led to that motor output. However, many cognitive psychologists have become so inured to those inferences that they take them for granted and slip into a mindset of blindly assuming that their measures somehow directly tap cognitive processes in a way that could not possibly be influenced by properties of the motor system. As more evidence accrues for embodied perceptual-motor routines determining much of cognition, the time of ignoring motor action because one is "a cognitive psychologist" is rapidly fading.

Dynamical Systems Accounts of Motor Movement

When you open your door to embodied cognition, you have to be ready for ecological psychology to come into your house as well. As you expand your definition of "mental activity" beyond the brain to include the rest of the body, you find yourself on a very slippery slope that takes you right to including the body's inextricable biomechanical interaction with the environment as part and parcel to your definition of *mental activity*. Motor movement research is perhaps the strongest place where dynamical approaches to the mind and the ecological framework in psychology have been cooperating rather healthily for the past 20 years. This is a vast field and, in hopes to pique rather than sate the interest of the cognitive psychologist, I only scratch the surface here.

One of the more exciting aspects of specifically studying motor output is that it tends to more readily avail itself to continuous measures, compared to the typical experimental measures used in perception and cognition (see chapter 3). Rather than simply acquiring one data point after presenting a stimulus and eliciting a response, such as a reaction time or an accuracy evaluation at the end of a time-delimited perceptual-motor event, continuous measures of motor output can reveal the ongoing properties of the continuous perceptual-motor process. Postural sway, for example, is something that we all do while standing or sitting upright. We usually don't notice it, but it's always there. A number of scientists have capitalized on this natural continuous motor output as a uniquely informative data emission from the dynamical system that is body-and-mind. Researchers have documented how fluctuating visual input rhythmically drives fluctuating postural sway in adults (e.g., Warren, Kay, & Yilmaz, 1996) as well as in infants (e.g., Bertenthal, Boker, & Xu, 2000), and how different visual tasks will modulate postural sway in different ways (Stoffregen et al., 2000). Studies of the effects of proprioceptive input from oscillation of the surface on which the feet are standing reveal distinct modes of compensatory sway that recruit their own degrees of freedom at different rates of oscillation (Ko, Challis, & Newell, 2001). Recurrence analysis of postural sway over time indicates that anteroposterior sway and mediolateral sway are independent (but mutually compensating) of one another during a laser-pointing task (Balasubramaniam, Riley, & Turvey, 2000). An important lesson emerging from much of this work is that postural control appears to be a blend of deterministic and stochastic processes (Riley, Balasubramaniam, & Turvey, 1999) and that other perceptual-motor phenomena may also be advantageously examined by utilizing the variability inherent in behavior, rather than dismissing it as uninformative noise (see Riley & Turvey, 2002; Van Orden, Holden, & Turvey, 2003).

The scientific elegance of this kind of work comes from the idea of applying concretely observable biomechanical principles to the examination of perception-action loops (Bertenthal, 1990), without the need to infer unobservable representational symbols that are putatively computed by a modular central executive. For example, Barac-Cikoja and Turvey (1991, 1993) gave participants rods to rattle between two distant unseen and unheard blocks and instructed them to estimate the size of the aperture between the blocks. Take a minute to imagine doing this task. You can't see the blocks, you can't hear the taps, and you don't know how long the rod is or how far away the blocks are. It's a pretty hard task! When perceived size was plotted as a function of actual size, quite linear but nonoverlapping curves were observed for conditions with different distances and rod lengths. With short distances, perceived aperture size was close to actual size, but with longer distances, its range was substantially compacted. Thus, mapping actual size to perceived size is a many-valued function not easily lending itself to a universal equation. However, equation 9.1 proved to be a single-valued function that accounted for 98% of the variance in the entire data set.

$$\lambda = \sin(\alpha/2) \times [1 - (2a/b) + (a/p)] \qquad (9.1)$$

In equation 9.1, α is the angle through which the rod moves, a is the distance from the fixed point of rotation (i.e., the wrist) to the rod's center of mass, b is the distance from the wrist to the rod's point of contact, and p is the center of percussion. Thus, taking into account the dynamical system of a few rod-and-wrist dimensions, combined with the rod's motion in space, turned out to be sufficient to describe the range of accurate and inaccurate perceptions of aperture size resulting from dynamic touch. And all this without needing to calculate afferent somatosensory input or efferent muscle forces, and most important, without needing to postulate perceptual inference mechanisms of any kind. The simple mechanics of the arm-and-rod dynamical system can, on their own, account for the perceptual phenomena.

The goal of discovering collective variables that can serve as single-valued functions of behavior is also evident in the work of Kelso and colleagues on interlimb rhythmic coordination (e.g., Haken, Kelso, & Bunz, 1985; Kelso, 1995; Kelso, Scholz, & Shöner, 1986). This work requires a shift of emphasis from descriptions of state space, as I often use in this book, to descriptions of phase space. Recall the logistic map, from chapter 4, where figures 4.4–7 each depicted cyclic transitions in the state space (along the y-axis) as a function of time (along the x-axis) for an individual run of the system. Figure 4.8, by contrast, depicted a value related to phase space (along the y-axis) as a function of control space (along the x-axis) observed over many runs of the system. The y-axis in figure 4.8 showed the regions of state space that get visited in a cyclic fashion when the system's control variable (η) is set such that the system's behavior is static, periodic, or quasi-periodic. Plotting the behavior of the system that way, phase space as a function of a control parameter can sometimes allow one to detect large structural patterns in the data more readily than simply looking at raw state space over time (as in figures 4.4–7).

In one of Kelso's (1995) many interlimb rhythmic coordination experiments, participants were instructed to rhythmically move their two index fingers while keeping them straight and without moving the rest of the hands, in antiphase with respect to one another (i.e., the first lumbricalis muscle on the left hand must contract to pull the left index finger *toward* that hand's palm, and the first dorsal interosseus muscle on the right hand must pull the right index finger *away* from that hand's palm, and then they reverse simultaneously). This is done in time with a metronome. Thus enters the control parameter, center stage. When the metronome rate, ω_c, is set at slow to moderate

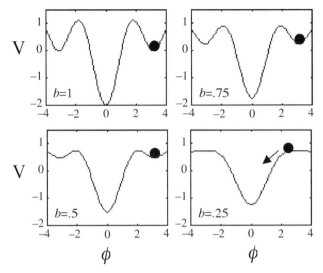

Figure 9.1. Phase space attractor manifolds for different parameter values of *b* in equation 9.1. The black ball stands for the state of the oscillatory system, in antiphase until *b* drops to 0.25, at which point the system gravitates to an in-phase pattern of coordination dynamics.

frequencies, participants are reasonably good at maintaining the antiphase finger movement. However, when that coupling frequency reaches a critical value, participants tend to slip into in-phase movement of their fingers (i.e., away from their respective palms at the same time, and then toward their respective palms at the same time). Equation 9.2 describes an energy landscape, *V*, as a function of finger oscillation phase difference, ϕ, with $\phi = 0$ being in-phase movement and $\phi = \pm\pi$ being antiphase movement. Changes in the coupling frequency, ω_c, produce changes in the energy landscape resulting in different strengths of phase attractor basins.

$$V(\phi) = \Delta\omega\phi - a\cos(\phi) - b\cos(2\phi) \qquad (9.2)$$

In equation 9.2, $\Delta\omega$ is the difference in frequency between the two fingers/oscillators, and *a* and *b* are coefficients that determine the stability of the antiphase and in-phase attractors. As the coupling frequency, ω_c, increases, the ratio of *b* to *a* is made to decrease. Figure 9.1 shows this energy landscape with coefficient *a* fixed at 1.0, and *b* being manipulated, because the *b*/*a* ratio is crucial. Also, $\Delta\omega = 0$, assuming that the two fingers/oscillators are matched in frequency, thus making the energy landscape symmetric across its positive and negative sides of ϕ. In figure 9.1, as the value of *b*/*a* ratio is reduced, the stability of the antiphase attractor basins are likewise reduced. The black circle indicates the state of the system, maintaining antiphase movement while

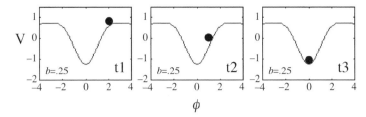

Figure 9.2. When the system in figure 9.1 carries out its switch from antiphase coordination to in-phase coordination, fine-grain time steps could, in principle, reveal a continuous transition in which the system spends some brief portion of time in phase relationships that are somewhere in between antiphase and in-phase.

$b > 0.25$. However, when b/a reaches $1/4$, as in the bottom right panel of figure 9.1, the antiphase energy wells vanish, and the system naturally gravitates to the remaining in-phase energy well.

Think of the panels in figure 9.2 as representing time slices ($t1$, $t2$, $t3$) of the system's actual phase difference (the black circle's position along the x-axis) immediately after the coupling frequency of the metronome, ω_c, has achieved a rate that no longer accommodates antiphase finger movement. The point I want to make with figure 9.2, and why it differs slightly from other renditions of the same phenomena (Kelso, 1995), is that although the switch from antiphase to in-phase is relatively sudden, it is not instantaneous. In traveling from one attractor in phase space to another, the system must at least briefly instantiate versions of itself that do not easily fall into the prespecified categories. The somewhat abrupt but nonetheless continuous trajectory in phase space that takes the system from one stable phasic pattern to another reveals the kind of ineffable blending of multiple identifiable states that is so ubiquitous to perception, action, and cognition—and yet so fundamentally ignored by most of cognitive science. (This is not unlike the regions of unstable chaotic behavior exhibited by the logistic map in between the regions of stable periodic behavior; see figure 4.8 in chapter 4). It is the small but nonzero amount of time spent *in between* energy wells in a phase space such as this— not quite adhering to one limit cycle or any other—that makes discrete logical symbolic accounts of mind and behavior so transparently and problematically oversimplified.

Dynamical Coordination Beyond One's Body

Kelso's (1995) beloved limb oscillation task can even be extended to show coordination dynamics taking place between organisms (Schmidt, Carello, & Turvey, 1990) in much the same way that it takes place between areas of a single brain (Bressler & Kelso, 2001). For example, following Kelso's numerous demonstrations of an involuntary phase change in limb coordination tasks (from antiphase flexion to in-phase flexion), Schmidt et al. (1990) demonstrated that the same involuntary phase change occurs when two different people carry out the two-limb coordination (i.e., one limb from each person)—as long as they can see each other's movements, of course. I regularly conduct this demonstration in my Introduction to Cognitive Science course, with two students recruited on the spot to come up on stage and perform the limb oscillation task in front of the other 300+ students, and it works every time. Two students sit next to each other on a table with their legs dangling. They tuck their inside legs under the table and swing their outside legs (e.g., left person's left leg and right person's right leg) left and right, pivoting from the knee, both leftward and then both rightward in antiphase motion. As my faux metronome tapping increases in rate, they invariably slip into in-phase motion, with both legs moving toward each other and then away from each other in synchrony. Thus, the same control parameter appears to have the same effects on the phase space manifold that describes the coordinated behavior, regardless of whether that phase space is devoted to one person or spanning the behavior of two people. It kind of makes you wonder whether the theoretical purview of psychology should really be "the brain in the context of its inputs and outputs," or perhaps instead "behavior in the context of other behavers and environmental constraints" (see chapter 11).

Another form of coordination of actions shows up in the Simon effect, where the compatibility between stimulus and response can produce interference and enhancement effects—as revealed by slowed or speeded reaction times. For example, let's say your right hand is supposed to press a button for a green stimulus and your left hand is supposed to press a different button for a red stimulus, but some of the colored stimuli happen to be shaped as arrows pointing left or right. The direction of the arrow is irrelevant to your task, but it nonetheless affects your reaction time. If a green arrow is pointing right, then your right hand's correct response is faster than the control condition, and if a green arrow is pointing left, then your right hand's correct response is slower than the control condition (e.g., Kornblum, Hasbroucq, & Osman, 1990; Simon, 1990). If you change this two-choice condition to a "go–no go" condition, where you only have to care about green stimuli and pressing the right button when green is presented and not pressing it when a different color is presented, you no longer see the compatibility effect. But what if one person is controlling the right button (for green stimuli) and another person, sitting to their left, is controlling the left button (for red stimuli)? In this group-based go–no go condition, the compatibility effect, where an irrelevant spatial dimension influences reaction time, comes back (Sebanz, Knoblich, & Prinz, 2003; Sebanz et al., 2006). That is, when the right-side person responds to a green stimulus, they are slower if the stimulus points toward the left side than if its direction is neutral—but only when there is an actual person next to them whose job is to work that left button! Somehow, the fact that there is another person there taking care of the alternative action produces some form of response competition that slows reaction time in a fashion similar to what happens within a person.

Now let's look at a task that requires even closer time locking of coordination and anticipation of a partner's actions. Knoblich and Jordan (2003) gave participants a dot-tracking task in which the objective was to keep a circle encompassing a dot that moved from left to right and back again several times across the computer screen. The circle's movement was controlled by one button that incremented leftward velocity and another button that incremented rightward velocity. The crucial manipulation was whether a single individual controlled both buttons or whether two separate individuals each controlled one button. After half an hour or so of this task, individuals and groups both showed improvement in overall performance as well as in the use of anticipatory braking (e.g., pressing the leftward velocity button as the rightward moving dot and circle approached the right edge of the screen). Thus, an improvement of action coordination was taking place not just across the two hands of an individual but also across two individuals. Interestingly, in a condition where the groups received distinctive auditory feedback for each partner's button presses, overall performance and anticipatory braking were eventually as good across two people as in the single-individual condition. That is, the actions of the two participants were sufficiently coupled that their performance in this task was indistinguishable from that of a single individual.

Resonant dynamics between two people can emerge even when they are not explicitly instructed to cooperate in a joint motor task. For example, when two people are standing on their own postural sway plates and conversing with one another on solving a puzzle, recurrence quantification analysis reveals that the phase space of their sway patterns over time exhibits numerous regions of cross-recurrence or resonance (Shockley, Santana, & Fowler, 2003). When the same two people are separately conversing with different people, this cross-recurrence in their sway is substantially reduced. Thus, a little bit like more readily visible forms of implicit behavioral mimicry (such as leg crossing and arm crossing, see Chartrand & Bargh, 1999; Lakin & Chartrand, 2003; see also Meltzoff & Prinz, 2002), the recurrent postural sway patterns of two mutual conversants appear to get entrained to one another.

Limb swinging, button pressing, and posture swaying are not the only dynamic motor behaviors that get coupled as two people interact. Using a categorical adaptation of recurrence quantification analysis, Dale and Spivey (2006) found that children and their caregivers exhibit cross-recurrence in their lexical and syntactic word choices when they converse. Similar to syntactic priming in language processing with adults (Balcetis & Dale, 2005; Bock, 1986; Branigan, Pickering, & Cleland, 2000; Pickering & Garrod, 2004), child and caregiver seem to entrain one another's language use within the minute-by-minute time scale of a conversation. Extending that categorical adaptation of recurrence quantification analysis to eye fixations of particular objects, Richardson and Dale (2005) found that when a listener comprehends well a story about six people he's looking at, his eye movement sequences to those six faces exhibit substantial cross-recurrence with those of the speaker (who is also looking at the same arrangement of six faces). And when a listener's eye movement patterns are exhibiting little cross-recurrence with those of the speaker, that listener tends to do poorly on comprehension tests. Thus, the degree to which two people's eye movement patterns are entrained with one another during a conversation about a particular visual array, on the second-by-second time scale of several sentences, plays an important role in how well they understand each other.

But people do not only get dynamically entrained to other people. On the time scale of days, a person's circadian rhythms get dynamically entrained to the light (and feeding) patterns in their environment (Nakao et al., 2002). On the time scale of hundreds of milliseconds, a person's rhythm perception gets dynamically entrained to the music in their environment (Large & Palmer, 2002; McAuley & Jones, 2003). Whenever oscillators get physically near each other—be they pendulum clocks, fireflies, menstrual cycles, or even occupied rocking chairs—they tend to naturally fall into synchrony and function as one system (Strogatz, 2003; see also Goodman et al., 2005). People are no different.

Consider the unusual case of induced alien limb phenomenon or "the rubber hand illusion." When unseen tactile input to one's hand (tapping and stroking) is tightly correlated over time with the visual input of a rubber hand being tapped and stroked in corresponding locations, the rubber hand can become compellingly perceived as being a part of the person's own body (e.g., Botvinick & Cohen, 1998; Ramachandran & Hirstein, 1998). Essentially, a key manner by which the brain determines that an observed hand belongs to it is by recognizing synchrony in the patterns of sensory input over time from different sensory systems (as well as correlations between planned actions and those sensory inputs; see Wegner, Sparrow, & Winerman, 2004).

What I'm describing here is a form of embodiment that goes beyond the body. To further demonstrate the flexibility of the neural representations used for this kind of visual, tactile, and proprioceptive encoding of the body's posture and limb positions, Maravita and Iriki (2004) found that visual/somatosensory receptive fields in the premotor cortex can extend the body schema beyond the actual body itself to include handheld tools as though they were part of the body. This extended body schema coding is a remarkably concrete manifestation of the brain expanding its own definition of self to include inanimate objects in the immediate environment. Thus, when Ramachandran (Ramachandran & Blakeslee, 1998) waxes poetic about his sports car, feeling like it is "a part of him," he's not just being metaphorical. When I'm shooting well at the pool table and it feels like I am "at one" with the pool cue and the table and the balls (that little microcosm of determinism), I'm not just being metaphorical. There's some neurophysiological verity to these impressions!

The incorporation of tools into one's body schema introduces a profound blurring of the line between *embodiment* (where the body's sensors and effectors help perform the processes of cognition; see Barsalou, 1999; Brooks, 1995) and *embeddedness* (where the objects and spaces in the surrounding environment also help perform the processes of cognition; see Haugeland, 1995; Kirsh, 1995). Sometimes manufactured objects, that are strictly speaking external to the body, can become some of our body's sensors and effectors (Clark, 2003). This is precisely why inviting embodiment into your theory of cognition naturally and unavoidably brings along with it ecological psychology.

The lesson from these kinds of findings is that when any two physically separate systems become dynamically coupled and function as one system, smooth coordination resulting from action anticipation (as well as interference resulting from irrelevant stimulus features that have dimensional overlap with the available responses) can arise between the two subsystems. The growing psychological research on joint action coordination and related areas is showing that this coordination and interference can be functionally equivalent regardless of whether the subsystems that determine the movements are located within one person or are distributed across two persons—and even when one of them is not a person at all.

Continuous Motor Dynamics Reveal
Continuous Mental Dynamics

Coordination dynamics, which typically involve rhythmic motor movements and focus on the phase space (e.g., figure 9.1), are not the only kind of motoric dynamics that can reveal continuity in the mind. *State space* dynamics of motor movement can also be informative for understanding how cognition can be advantageously described as a continuous trajectory through an attractor landscape. Recall from chapter 8 Gold and Shadlen's (2000) amalgam of two simultaneous saccade commands producing a kind of blend of those two saccade directions in two-dimensional visual space. That work shows how the continuous accumulation of information for a perceptual decision is not just something that happens in some encapsulated cognitive system, which then, once it's settled on a unique selected response, shunts that single command to the motor system for execution. This continuous flow of information from perceptual subsystems to cognitive subsystems cascades into motor subsystems as well (see Coles, Gratton, & Donchin, 1988; Miller, Riehle, & Requin, 1992; Shin & Rosenbaum, 2002). With feedforward and feedback projections between these brain areas, motor subsystems are therefore participating in the dynamic process of decision making just as much as perceptual and cognitive subsystems are.

Coarticulation in speech production (and even in sign language finger spelling; Jerde, Söchting, & Flanders, 2003) is another concrete example of a kind of motor output that blends two incompatible motor commands. Certain transitions between phonemes actually require the speech apparatus to move from one configuration to a very different one more quickly than is physically possible (or at least more quickly than that particular apparatus has been calibrated for). As a result, the system compromises and produces phonemes that are strictly speaking poor examples of those phonemes, by actuating the articulators in ways that put them slightly near where they need to be for the previous phoneme or the next phoneme (or even farther). Thus, if one imagined each idealized phoneme representation as being a graded fuzzy basin of attraction in the state space of speech articulation parameters, then producing a spoken word that had coarticulation of some of the phonemes would be equivalent to following a trajectory in that space that traveled *near* each appropriate attractor in the proper sequence (recall figure 7.18B). However, the extent to which it missed each attractor would be in the directions of the previous and/or next phoneme regions, thereby causing the assimilation of some of the temporally neighboring phonemic features with each current phoneme's production.

Thus, although the outcome of an action often needs to be rather discrete (e.g., your eyes need to eventually settle on the object of your goal, your speech apparatus needs to utter something that is recognizable by your listener, your hammer needs to land on the nail with each swing), the dynamic *process* of getting to that outcome can take a variety of forms. Hidden in that variation are clues regarding the dynamic perceptual/cognitive processes that are associated with that action. The manner in which the motor output is executed on the way toward its endpoint—not the action outcome itself—is where variability in the motor movement can reveal multifarious dynamic patterns of cognitive representation.

Allow me to describe a simple concrete example. Coles and colleagues (1985) gave participants two response handles (dynamometers) that recorded the timing and force of the squeeze performed on them. One handle was to be used for responding to one type of target stimulus, and the other handle was for responding to another type of target stimulus. On some trials, the target stimulus for, say, the left handle was surrounded by irrelevant stimuli that actually corresponded to a right-handle response. On these trials, the left-handle response was delayed (not surprisingly). However, what might be surprising is that those trials also exhibited a significant graded increase in force applied to the *right handle*, when compared to noncompetition control trials. That is, the response competition typically purported to take place in those kinds of trials did not appear to be something that was resolved in a cognitive stage and then a single lateralized movement command was issued to the motor system (albeit delayed due to the competition). Rather, the two alternative responses, squeezing left handle and squeezing right handle, were both still partially active and competing even in motor areas of the brain (as suggested by their event-related potential evidence), even in the electrical activity in the participants' arm muscles (as shown by their electromyography evidence), and even in the actual force that was physically applied to the handles.

Not long after that, Abrams and Balota (1991) reported a study in which they gave participants a lexical decision task (i.e., "is this a word or a nonword?") and had them respond with a leftward movement of a slide-bar for nonword responses, and with a rightward movement for word responses.

Higher frequency words elicited not only faster initiation of the right-hand movement but also greater force and acceleration of the overall sliding movement. (For in-depth discussion of the theoretical consequences of these kinds of findings, see Balota & Abrams, 1995; Mattes, Ulrich, & Miller, 2002; and Ulrich, Mattes, & Miller, 1999.) As pointed out in chapter 3, finding a point in time where a response is initiated (such as a button-press reaction time or a saccade latency) may be the most popular measure in cognitive psychology, but it is only one of a handful of potentially interesting variables.

Consider the eye movement patterns elicited in the spoken word recognition tasks described in chapter 7. When instructed to pick up the candle, a quarter of the trials actually revealed the listener looking first at a bag of candy (because the initial acoustic-phonetic patterns for those two words share a great deal in common) and then fixating the candle and reaching out to grasp it. By averaging trials together, with discrete fixations of this or that object at different periods of time, one can approximate the central tendencies of the group data, and produce graded curves of the proportion of trials in which the candy and the candle were being fixated at each time slice during and after the spoken word (figure 7.7).

Although the smooth curves are suggestive of a gradual accumulation of activation and continuous competition between lexical alternatives, the fact remains that the actual motor outputs from which those curves arise are unambiguous ballistic saccades to the candy, or to the candle, or to one of the other objects. If saccades weren't so remarkably ballistic (see Doyle & Walker, 2001, for mild exceptions), then maybe one could detect a sizable curvature of the saccade in the direction of the candy even though the eye movement didn't actually stop until it landed on the candle. Evidence like that would make a powerful case for the gradual fluctuation of simultaneously active lexical representations competing over time as a spoken word is being heard, and for such competition leaking into the motor system even during the execution of the motor output.

As it turns out, such curvatures in movement trajectory, indicating competition between two potential action targets, are in fact detectable in certain reaching movements (Goodale et al., 1986; Tipper et al., 1997). If two reaching targets have not quite been completely adjudicated among but the reaching movement has already begun, the trajectory of the hand will show graded attraction in the direction of the competing target before it finally turns and stops at the chosen target. Now imagine how cool it would be if, in one of your experiment-running software packages, you could simply click a box in a menu window that would make it record the x and y coordinates of the mouse while the participant moved the cursor to click on, say, the picture of the candy or the picture of the candle. It would be like the poor man's eye tracker. It would be as though the experimental task was performing some dimensionality-reduction statistic on the immense neural state space of the participant's brain and projecting his or her continuous mental trajectory onto a two-dimensional rendition in which the external objects themselves were the attractors and the record of the mouse movement was an actual emission of the mental trajectory (not unlike the two-dimensional state-space trajectories in figures 3.4, 4.14, and 6.3).

PsyScope (Cohen et al., 1993) has exactly that box in one of its menu windows.[1] Spivey, Grosjean, and Knoblich (2005) clicked that box. We recorded the streaming x, y coordinates of participants' mouse movements while they were instructed to click a start box at the bottom of the screen and then click a candle or a candy at the top of the screen, or a candy versus a pickle (control condition), or a pickle versus a picture, and so on. The continuous graded deflection toward the cohort competitor object was strikingly evident in the movement trajectories. Although skeletal movements tend to be initiated a few hundred milliseconds after the relevant eye movement, the trade-off for that loss in immediacy is that you now have 60 samples per second telling you where the effector in question is located relative to the alternative objects—instead of 3–4 samples per second when recording eye fixations and saccades.

Figure 9.3 shows the averaged trajectory for cohort-present trials and the averaged trajectory for control (cohort-absent) trials. Participants did occasionally click the wrong object—a bit like making an initial saccade to the

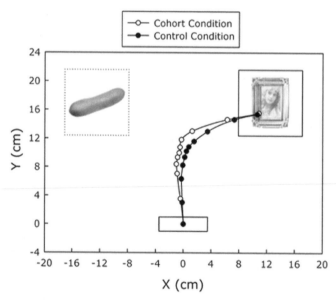

Figure 9.3. The averaged computer mouse trajectory for cohort-present trials (in open circles at every 10th normalized time step) show significant deviation toward the cohort object (a pickle in this case) when instructed to click the picture. In conditions where a control object (such as a candle) replaced the pickle, there was less curvature in the mouse movement (filled circles at every 10th normalized time step). (Reprinted from Spivey, Grosjean, & Knoblich, 2005.)

wrong object—but those trials were excluded from these data. Only trials in which the participant clicked the correct object were included in these averaged trajectories. Yet the cohort-present averaged trajectory for these right-target trials shows a statistically significant leftward deflection along the x-axis, compared to the control trajectory, for more than 80% of its duration. Thus it appears that as the arm and hand were executing the movement to have the computer mouse cursor settle on the picture, as instructed, the acoustic-phonetic similarity between *picture* and *pickle* caused the movement trajectory to travel partly in the direction of the pickle. (One concern might be that because the movement instruction was delivered auditorily, participants may have actually just been strategically moving straight upward until they heard enough of the instruction to start turning left or right. Such an account would conflict with our claim that two language-related attractors were simultaneously "pulling" the motor movement in their respective directions. However, the same kinds of effects are seen with instantaneous presentation of the stimulus that initiates movement. Dale, Kehoe, and Spivey [in press] show similar trajectory curvatures with taxonomic classification of typical and atypical animals when a picture or the written name of the animal is presented). This new methodology provides a compelling visual record of the spatial and temporal continuity with which attractor landscape effects can seep from the domain of cognitively competing representations to a concomitant motor command.

Action Is a Hungry Process

The mind is not a sequence of computational processors that each patiently await their next input. It is not merely a series of static filters through which the environmental stimulation passes, with some informational properties getting caught and staying while others continue through unnoticed. These integrated subcomponents of mind, which too often get mistaken for such static filters, are constantly proactively preparing for a particular set of anticipated next inputs—not passively waiting for whatever the world decides to give them. Motor subsystems are no different.

Indeed, it could very well be that motor action is the most obvious and ubiquitous arena in which anticipation and prediction drive real-time processing. We make motor predictions all the time. We predict perceptual-motor routines in ourselves and in others. We anticipate the perceptual results of our actions, of others' actions, and even of gravity's effects on objects. We even predict other people's intentions.

Forward models of perceptual-motor learning (e.g., Haruno, Wolpert, & Kawato, 2001; Jordan & Rumelhart, 1992) rely on predictions like this. With a forward model, a system that does not receive training or explicit instruction in how to produce a particular action can nonetheless experiment with a variety of motor outputs, compare their perceived results with their expected results, estimate the inverse dynamics of its motor system, and thereby learn how to control its motor output in a way that reliably produces the intended action. Consider the game of darts. If your first-ever throw of the dart results in piercing a hole in the wall just above the dartboard, you probably have little understanding of exactly which muscle forces need to be altered to prevent that from happening again. But you can certainly try producing a very different pattern of muscle forces the next time and find out where the dart lands then. Let's say the dart pierces a hole in the wall just to the left of the dartboard this time. Now if the desired result is to see the dart land in the bull's eye, then you already have three perceptual results in mind (one of which has only been imagined so far), and two of them have known motor activation patterns associated with them. And somewhere in the state space of your perceptual-motor dynamics is a detectable degree of isomorphism between the two-dimensional range of perceptual results and the high-dimensional range of muscle forces, joint angles, and manual release times. Therefore, the two-dimensional triangulation between the two observed dart landings and the third desired dart landing can be mapped onto an estimated multidimensional triangulation between those two stored movement patterns in the motor dynamics manifold and a third candidate next movement pattern, whose predicted perceptual result will be a bull's eye. When that perceptual result is not a bull's eye—and, believe me, your third-ever dart throw will *not* be a bull's eye—the difference between where you expected the dart to land (given those motor parameters) and where the dart actually landed (based on the perceptual parameters) can once again give the learner some information for how to adjust the motor parameters next time to get closer to the bull's eye. Of course, the isomorphism between the manifold of perceptual results and the manifold of motor outputs is a rather complex and nonlinear one in a very high-dimensional state space. So it will probably take you more than three or four throws of the dart to learn to reliably hit the bull's eye.

As mentioned in other chapters, this kind of predictive processing can be found in all kinds of discussions of learning. Even classical conditioning now relies on a notion of the conditioned stimulus producing an expectation for the unconditioned stimulus (e.g., Bouton, 2004; Rescorla & Wagner, 1972; Tolman, 1937). After all, why else would forward conditioning be so broadly successful (Pavlov's bell preceding the food) while backward conditioning is almost never effective (the food preceding the bell)? But even after learning has become asymptotic in a subsystem, predictive processing is still widely prevalent in its real-time processing. Anticipation is not only good for learning, it is good for coordination of one's behaviors with the constraints of the environment and the behaviors of other organisms in that environment.

Let's look first at the time scale of tens of milliseconds. Take smooth pursuit eye movements, for example. These eye movements exhibit predictive vectors based on expectations of where/when the foveated moving visual stimulus is likely to go (e.g., Boman & Hotson, 1992; Fukushima, 2003; Kowler & Steinman, 1979), thus they often *lead* the stimulus rather than follow it.

Rhythmic finger-tapping tasks routinely elicit anticipatory taps that precede the auditory signal by a few dozen milliseconds (e.g., Franek et al., 1987; Repp, 2003b). Finally, as mentioned earlier, anticipatory coarticulation during speech production causes us to move our speech articulators in ways that are partially consistent with the upcoming speech sounds and partially inconsistent with the speech sound currently being produced. For example, we purse our lips for the /u/ sound in *choose* before we even begin the /ch/. Compare it to *chain*. You'll find you don't purse your lips as much for the /ch/ in that word. With respect to the ubiquity of predictive processing, it is noteworthy that this kind of anticipatory coarticulation appears to be far more prevalent than perseverative coarticulation (see Guenther, 1995; Katz et al., 1990; West, 1999), where phonetic features of previous speech sounds linger into currently produced speech sounds.

At a time scale of hundreds of milliseconds, one can observe infants making anticipatory saccadic eye movements to regions of space that they expect will soon contain an attractive object (e.g., Haith & McCarty, 1990; Richardson & Kirkham, 2004). A bit like the case with coarticulation, anticipatory speech errors (e.g., saying "prupid president") tend to outnumber perseverative speech errors (e.g., "stupid stesident") by a ratio of nearly 3 : 1 (see Dell, Burger, & Svec, 1997; Garnham et al., 1981). Even piano playing tends to show subtly different finger kinematics on the note preceding a departure between two melodies (Engel, Flanders, & Söchting, 1997).

At the time scale of seconds, perceptual-motor anticipations can have consequences for quite high-level cognitive phenomena. For example, Blakemore and Frith (2003) review a wide variety of evidence indicating that accurate predictions of sensory consequences of movement are used to identify actions as self-generated, leading to a sense of self, whereas inaccurate or absent predictions suggest that the action was not self-generated.[2] And of course, we all have everyday experiences where we find ourselves anticipating another's intentions. Imagine you're at a restaurant, the food has just arrived, someone is still telling a long-winded story, and you notice one of your party hasn't started eating but is instead looking expectantly back and forth between the speaker and a saltshaker that is out of their reach. You reach out, lift the saltshaker, and make eye contact with the person, and they smile and nod. Prediction accomplished. We predictively simulate our own actions as well, especially when mentally exploring possible ways to do something that we've never done before. Even just preparing to slice a rare, oddly shaped vegetable for the first time, you may grasp it with one hand, rest the knife edge along one of its awkwardly curved axes, and imagine the result of carving from there. Suddenly your internal physics simulation reveals your finger getting cut. You find yourself wincing from the pain, even though the knife hasn't actually moved yet.

This quick sampling of examples from speech production, eye movements, finger movements, and so on just serves to highlight the wide-ranging importance of dynamic patterns of activity that lean forward in time, if you will.

Successful actions depend on the organism's ability to couple those movements with the environment, and the environment is often dynamic itself, so anticipating those changing environmental constraints is crucial. Therefore, the dynamic interaction between our perceptual and motor areas of the brain, as well as the dynamic interaction between our sensory and biomechanical interfaces with the world, from which emerges this thing we call *action*, must be a hungry process indeed.

In sum, just as real-time categorization, language, and vision appear to be characterized by continuous trajectories in a state space (often with a kind of future-minded momentum of their own), so is motor output well described by a temporally dynamic change of state (and steady phase, for rhythmic movements) that not only helps entrain different perceptual/cognitive processes with one another toward the goal of driving coherent motor output but also entrains the organism with its environment. Action representations play such a powerful role in perception and cognition—as evinced by the embodied cognition findings discussed at the beginning of this chapter, and as suggested by the many bidirectional neural projections between motor and perceptual areas—that they really and truly should not be conceived of as "the stuff that happens after cognition." Dynamic patterns of behavior and of neural activations in motor-related brain areas should be treated as contemporaries (in every sense of the word) of perceptual and cognitive patterns: on the same level, on the same playing field, in the same mind.

10

Temporal Dynamics in Reasoning

Now, man actually finds in himself a power which distinguishes
him from all other things—and even from himself so far as he is
affected by objects. This power is *reason*. … Because of this, a
rational being must regard himself *qua intelligence* (and
accordingly not on the side of his lower faculties) as belonging to
the intelligible world, not to the sensible one.
—Immanuel Kant (translated by Seidler, 1986)

I am two with nature.
—Woody Allen

The Old Dualism

If the previous chapters have instilled in the reader some sense of appreciation
for cognition being composed of rather than separate from the "lower faculties" of sensory and motor processing, then I hope Kant's quote strikes the
reader as somewhat chilling. Kant's argument is an appeal to one's intuition—
and a compelling one to be sure—that one's mind is separate from one's body.
Despite the numerous experimental results described in the previous chapter,
documenting a fundamental role of the body's action in cognition, it is
nonetheless tempting sometimes to feel as though our minds live in a kind
of ivory tower inside our bodies. And a great deal of research in psychology
has treated high-level cognition, such as reasoning and problem solving, as
though it were carried out by just such an ivory tower, using discrete rules and
computations that are completely unrelated to and independent of the causal
processes that perform the functions of perception, action, and the rest of the
body. In fact, Kant suggested that the sensible world of sensation, perception,
and action, or *Sinnenwelt*, could perhaps be described with the natural laws of
biology, chemistry and physics, but the intelligible world, or *Verstandeswelt*,
functions via "laws, which being independent of nature, are not empirical but
have their ground in reason alone." It is exactly this rationalist perspective that
encourages some cognitive scientists to adhere, even today, to an extreme
functionalist view of the mind (teetering on the edge of Cartesian dualism) in
which the mind somehow supervenes on the processes of brain and body
without actually being informatively described by them—because a mind
supposedly uses nonnomic representations whose relations to their referents

are not dictated by natural laws (Dietrich & Markman, 2003; Fodor, 1986; see also Epstein, 1993; Wallis, 1992). In fact, it has even been suggested that we humans are innately predisposed to think about our selves in this dualistic fashion of separating mind from body (Bloom, 2004).

A number of theorists criticize this lingering dualism—which permeates cognitive science implicitly and sometimes explicitly—on the grounds that it imposes artificial boundaries between scientific disciplines, it ignores reams of evidence for mental processes being understood via neural processes, and it flouts Occam's razor (e.g., Churchland, 1989; Dennett, 1991; Kim, 1998; Polger, 2004; Smart, 1959; Streeck, 2003). However, even among cognitive scientists who accept the materialist, antidualist view of mind, there is often a search for a smaller form of dualism, one that may be equally deserving of the same criticisms: the dualism of continuous perception and symbolic cognition. This putative distinction between certain parts of the mind that function via some form of distributed analog computation and other parts of the mind that function via some form of discrete digital computation has part of its root structure in the history of artificial intelligence. The idea that reasoning and complex thought are conducted via symbolic representations and logical rules was given considerable cachet by a number of early successes that implemented rule-and-symbol cognitive architectures. For example, conversation programs, such as Weizenbaum's (1966) ELIZA and Winograd's (1972) SHRDLU, provided impressive demonstrations of artificial systems carrying out somewhat natural conversations with humans, at least about particular narrow topics. Automated theorem proving in symbolic logic helped cement the physical symbol systems hypothesis (Newell & Simon, 1976). Gigantic predicate calculus databases made impressive attempts at representing commonsense knowledge (Lenat, 1982). Myriad chess programs, such as that running on IBM's Deep Blue supercomputer, still use powerful decision-tree search algorithms, augmented by hand-coded heuristics, to regularly beat chess experts.[1]

Early achievements like those convinced many researchers in the cognitive sciences to believe that when people participate in naturalistic conversations, or reason about alternative chess moves, or solve problems in any complex task, they are using computational modules with formal logical rules and discrete representations, just like those inside the artificial intelligence algorithms (see Newell, 1990, for a review). As a result, throughout the 1970s and 1980s, theories of the human mind abounded with an encapsulated rule-based module for just about every perceptual process and cognitive computation that anyone could think of (see chapter 5). However, in the 1990s, as neuroscience and neural network theory began to accrue more compelling evidence for recurrent feedback and interaction between neural subsystems and for distributed representations inside them, work in artificial intelligence similarly began to find its new successes with interactive subsystems instead of independent modules (e.g., Ballard, 1997), with fuzzy logical representations instead of discrete symbols (e.g., Kosko, 1993), with statistical contingencies instead of formal logical rules (e.g., Charniak, 1993), and with ecological coordination between a CPU, its effectors and sensors, and its environment (e.g., Brooks, 1999). Now with the symbolic reputation of artificial intelligence rapidly fading, the question with respect to human cognition still manages to linger nonetheless: Do the continuous interactive patterns of neural activity in perceptual and motor areas of the brain need to be supplemented with some form of internal discrete logical computation to produce complex human reasoning?

This chapter will discuss several research areas in high-level cognition where discrete symbolic representations have been proposed as necessary accompaniments to continuous graded patterns of neural activity. In some of these areas, symbolic rule-based systems are indeed still the best game in town for describing human reasoning, but in others, continuous temporally dynamic accounts of thought are producing intriguing results. Comparing dynamical accounts versus symbolic accounts of general intelligence might be like comparing apples versus oranges. Perhaps they are not compatible enough for comparison. Unlike the cases for categorization, language, vision, and action in the previous four chapters, the promise of a dynamical systems framework adequately accommodating the bulk of the phenomena in high-level cognition is so far largely unfulfilled. It is not yet clear whether this is due to there actually being some delineated separation somewhere in the brain between perceptual-and-motor cortices that use graded partially overlapping population codes and cognitive cortices that use rules and symbols, or whether this is simply due to there still being comparatively little research on dynamical accounts of problem solving and reasoning (but see, for example, Guastello, 1998; Hoffman, 1997; Read & Montoya, 1999; Roe, Townsend, & Busemeyer, 2001; Thagard, 1989; Van Overwalle & Van Rooy, 2001). What *is* clear is that contrary to the attitude that I cop throughout most of this book, reasoning and problem solving may very well be the one area of cognition where the rule-and-symbol framework has not yet run its course, and some further useful advances may still be coming from this approach for a little longer. Therefore, this chapter is as much a brief congratulatory recounting of a few places where rule-and-symbol systems are still enjoying some supremacy as it is a rough speculative battle plan of the places on which the dynamical ranks will soon march.

Veja Du-alism All Over Again

Quite a few researchers have followed Kant (and William James and others) in suggesting that the mind somehow encodes the contingencies in its environment via two completely different coexisting formats of representation: graded statistical patterns and formal rules. Sloman (1996) compiled an excellent review of evidence in favor of not just the coexistence of an associative system and a rule-based system but also cases where mutually exclusive beliefs were simultaneously held by experimental participants: one the result of the associative system and the other the result of the rule-based system (but see Gigerenzer & Regier, 1996). Sloman also suggested that the two systems can interact during learning and thus are not encapsulated from one another (Ross, 1989; see also Mathews et al., 1989). However, the mechanistic account of this kind of hybrid system is under considerable debate. It is not exactly clear how neural circuitry can implement graded statistical processing for one situation and then turn around and implement formal logical rules for another.

In designing computational implementations of such hybrid systems, one popular solution has been to build the associative part with a distributed neural network that has *graded* activations and connection strengths and build the rule-based part with a localist network that has *binary* activations and connection strengths (Erikson & Kruschke, 1998, 2002; Hummel & Holyoak, 2003; Sun, 2002; see also Hinton, 1991). In some of these models, a third gating network determines which part gets to exert its output for any given problem instance (Erikson & Kruschke, 1998, 2002). Another way to implement this kind of dualism between (a) continuous activation or graded salience of representations and (b) discrete rule-based operations that are performed on those representations is to build a hybrid model that uses a production system to posit and connect symbols, but these symbols sometimes have simultaneously partially active mutually exclusive alternatives that are quantitatively compared, or compete against each other, until one is discretely selected (e.g., Anderson & Lebiere, 1998; Jurafsky, 1996; Stevenson, 1994).

In general, when two incompatible computational frameworks appear to have mutually compensatory strengths and weakness, it is perhaps just a little too easy to blithely combine the two types of mechanisms in your theory and claim that the two somehow share the mind. For example, striking differences between regular and irregular past tense verbs have compelled some researchers to suggest that there may be one system in the brain devoted to the regular verbs and a separate neural module devoted to the irregular verbs (e.g., Jaeger et al., 1996; Marcus, 1995; Pinker, 1991; Pinker & Ullman, 2002). However, a host of experiments and model simulations has been showing that rulelike past tenses and irregular past tenses are probably processed by a single associative system that is capable of simultaneously encoding strong regularities amid weak statistical patterns (e.g., Joanisse, 2004; McClelland & Patterson, 2002; Plunkett & Juola, 1999; Plunkett & Marchman, 1993; Ramscar, 2002; Rumelhart & McClelland, 1986b). Similar claims were made in favor of a dual-route system for reading aloud (mapping orthography to phonology) with regard to words that have rule-following pronunciations, such as *mint*, *hint*, and *flint*, versus irregularly pronounced words, such as *pint* (e.g., Coltheart, 2000; Rastle & Coltheart, 1999; Roberts et al., 2003). Just like the case with past tense verbs, numerous experiments and model simulations strongly suggest that this dissociation can be accommodated within one connectionist system (e.g., Harm & Seidenberg, 2004; Jared, McRae, & Seidenberg, 1990; Plaut et al., 1996; Seidenberg & McClelland, 1989; Taraban & McClelland, 1987).

Even higher level abstractions in mental activity, such as concepts, analogies, and social cognition—which were traditionally described in terms of discrete rules—have recently been accounted for by distributed dynamical models. For example, Rogers and McClelland (2004) recount numerous simulations and tests of a connectionist model of conceptual representation that fits experimental data from cognitive psychology, developmental psychology, and even handles phenomena purported to only be accommodated by a rule-based component (e.g., Carey, 1985; Keil, 1989; see also Gärdenfors, 2003). And models of how people understand analogies have traditionally relied on discrete symbols and rules (Hofstadter & Mitchell, 1994), distributed representations combined by logical rules (Hummel & Holyoak, 2003), or symbolic representations combined by graded constraint-satisfaction algorithms (Holyoak & Thagard, 2002). However, considerable success has been achieved with a model that uses continuous patterns of representation and processing all the way down. Eliasmith and Thagard's (2001) neural network, Drama, combines distributed representation with graded mapping via holographic reduced representations (see Borsellino & Poggio, 1973; Plate, 1994), which are similar to tensor products (Smolensky, 1988b, 1995) but can limit themselves to a fixed number of dimensions.

Loss aversion in decision making, where people will make clearly suboptimal choices to avoid low-probability or low-value losses (Tversky & Kahneman, 1991), is another example from complex cognition that has conventionally been described via rules and heuristics rather than continuous distributed patterns. However, neural networks and dynamical systems simulations have begun to provide a graded neurally plausible account of loss aversion (Roe, Busemeyer, & Townsend, 2001; Usher & McClelland 2004; see also Busemeyer et al., 2005). Even cognitive dissonance, where conflict between mutually exclusive beliefs is resolved by modifying the representation of one of the beliefs (e.g., Festinger 1957; Lepper, 1973; Steele, 1988), is being modeled with connectionist neural networks (Shultz & Lepper, 1996; Van Overwalle & Jordens, 2002).

Another potential solution for accommodating the observation that some cognitive phenomena seem to exhibit both continuous dynamics and rulelike behavior is to design a model that has an early stage that uses graded activations of competing localist representations which then feeds into a later stage that uses binary activations of the winning representations and performs logical operations on them (Anderson & Lebiere, 1998). Anderson's ACT-R framework is based on a long-standing tradition of treating perception as a continuous processing system whose dynamics are closely linked to the activity of actual neural ensembles and cognition as a separate rule-governed system whose binary computations are best described in an ideal form that is abstracted from the actual neuronal dynamics. At the level of neural systems—not their connectivity, ensembles, or dynamics—candidate cortical regions for the computational subcomponents of ACT-R are already being identified (Anderson et al., 2004). Thus, there are those would argue that after simulating some perceptual-cognitive phenomena with a collection of computational modules based on ideas of computing theory, we are now on the verge of finding the components of the brain that correspond to those very same postulated computational subsystems.

The concept of taking graded neuronal dynamics and converting them into discrete symbols is at the core of many debates in cognitive science, between those accustomed to using the computer as a metaphor for the mind and those who wish to use the brain as the mind's primary reference point. This putative dynamic-to-discrete conversion is hand-built in a variety of ways in various models of cognition, but there may in fact be a useful mathematical home for this general idea, called symbolic dynamics. Take ACT-R (Anderson & Lebiere, 1998), for example. In its front end, it uses multiple partially active symbols continuously competing with one another until one finally wins. This early graded competition stage shares properties in common with the normalized recurrence localist attractor network (Spivey & Tanenhaus, 1998; Spivey et al., 2002a). Thus in this first stage of the system, ACT-R implements something equivalent to a continuous trajectory in the state space where the dimensions are the relevant competing symbols. When the state of the system finally settles toward a corner of the space, a single symbol has won, and that symbol is discretely emitted from the continuous system into a rule-based production system for cognitive computations. This discretizing of the continuous trajectory in state space, into symbols to be used by a formal logical process, implements something closely related to what complex systems scientists call symbolic dynamics (see Crutchfield, 1994; Devaney, 2003; see also chapter 4). Of the many possible futures of this long-standing debate between symbolic and dynamic cognition, the mathematics of symbolic dynamics may very well be the only one that holds a consensual resolution. Until then, continuous statistical systems (e.g., dynamical and network models) versus discrete rule-based systems will continue to be the apples and oranges of cognitive science, treated almost as if they cannot be adjudicated among.

From Apples and Oranges to Symbolic Dynamics

In the physical sciences, the times when consensually agreed-on progress has been made in adjudicating between competing theories has usually been when those theories (a) are applied to a common set of phenomena, and (b) employ a common format of explication (e.g., the same basic equation, but with certain parameters present or absent). As most symbolic representationalists have essentially conceded that perception and action are handled by graded partially overlapping distributed patterns of neural activation, the common set of phenomena where the most fair contest will be able to take place between symbolic and dynamic accounts of mind is high-level cognition. As for the common format of explication, this may be a little trickier to recognize and develop. Before getting to that, allow me to illustrate what I think is the key distinction between a symbolic framework of high-level cognition and a dynamical account of the same.

For cases of complex reasoning and problem solving, it seems fair to assume that no matter what theoretical framework you happen to advocate, some form of discretization of the cognitive process will have to be imposed at some point in the perception-action loop—if for no other reason than the simple fact that we will need to use language to describe the phenomena to one another. The question is whether that discretization happens only in between the motor movement and its action effects on the environment or also in between the neural processes of perception and action (Dietrich & Markman, 2003). The continuity of mind thesis places this discretization only in between the motor action itself and its effects on the problem-solving environment. At the level of real-time perception and action, motor output can be quite graded and continuous, but descriptions of the changes made to the environment as a result of that motor output are often quite discrete. For example, the arm's actual movement trajectory when hammering a nail is never perfectly repeated, but its effects on the environment can be well described (for the purposes of building something out of wood) as either hitting the nail or not. Similarly, your arm trajectory while reaching for a candle, which happens to be near a bag of candy, can exhibit graded competition at the time scale of dozens of milliseconds, but at the time scale of seconds, only one object is actually grasped and lit aflame. Moving a bishop to a location on the chessboard where it can threaten your opponent's pawn, rather than to a nearby location where it would have checked your opponent's king, involves some rather continuous and perhaps wavering arm movements and may even have involved simultaneous conflicting partially active movement commands in motor cortex. But at the level of description relevant for game play, one and only one thing took place—and you probably should have put the king in check instead.

For ease of understanding, figure 10.1 depicts idealized separations in the perception-action loop that could be conceived of as dynamic or symbolic for the two competing theoretical frameworks. Note that unlike real-time perception and action, in the case of reasoning and problem solving, the problem space is typically presented to the human in a rather static and nondynamic form. The only changes to the problem space come from actions, or imagined actions, that the person carries out. And these changes typically move the state of the problem to a new stationary location in that problem space. The problem itself often has little or no continuous temporal dynamics of its own. In that sense, the presentation of the problem can be thought of as discrete, and actions carried out on the problem can be thought of as discrete. However, the question at hand is whether the person's mind employs discrete symbolic representations during its real-time cognitive negotiation of the problem. The continuity of mind thesis would have it that the brain and body's real-time processes never employ genuinely discrete symbolic representations, because distributed populations of neurons and continuous muscle movements can't

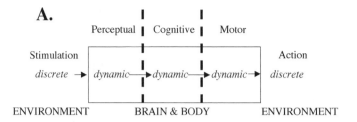

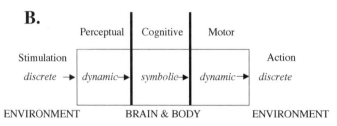

Figure 10.1. At the time scale of reasoning and problem solving, where changes in the environment might be conceived of as discrete, the continuity of mind thesis (A) still assumes dynamical cognitive processes, whereas the symbolic framework (B) posits an intermediate mental stage in which discrete symbols are operated on by logical rules.

quite do that. The only conversion of dynamic patterns into symbolic components (figure 10.1A) happens when motor output exacts discrete observable changes to the environment.[2]

The classical symbolic account (figure 10.1B), however, proposes that there is also a system in the brain that converts dynamic patterns into discrete symbolic *internal* representations (see Marcus, 2001). It is not entirely clear how the symbolicists would have a cognitive area of the brain implement a bona fide formal logical symbol, because neural activation patterns are never static in time, but it could perhaps be conducted via individual "grandmother cells" (see Lettvin, 1995; Rose, 1996) or via extremely reliable limit cycles in state space that correspond to highly stable locations in phase space (Atmanspacher & beim Graben, in press; Yamaguchi & Shimizu, 1994; see also Kuhn & Cruse, 2005; O'Brien & Opie, 1999a, for discussion of stable distributed representations). The neurophysiological evidence in motor movement research (e.g., Georgopoulos, 1995; Gold & Shadlen, 2000) requires this account to then reconvert those symbols back into distributed dynamic patterns in the motor cortices, as that is what is found there. Thus, the symbolic view of the mind is like "a kind of sandwich in which [distributed] perception and action hold a classical centre in place" (Hurley, 1998b, p. 4). Then, of course, those dynamic motor commands are converted yet again—this time into actions that at the time scale of reasoning and problem solving perform discrete changes to the environment.

Now that I've outlined a hopefully agreeable description of this pair of minimally contrasting architectures, I can describe the "common format of explication" that future research in high-level cognition might fruitfully use to consensually adjudicate between theories that propose an internal symbolization of the brain's continuous dynamics and theories that propose only an external discretization of them. The mathematical arena of symbolic dynamics (e.g., Crutchfield, 1994; Devaney, 2003; Goertzel, 1998; Shalizi & Albers, 2002; see also Cleeremans et al., 1989; Tabor, 2002; and chapter 4 for related discussions) has exactly the ingredients for building systems that implement continuous temporal dynamics in a high-dimensional state space (of perception and of action), and can convert that continuous trajectory into an emitted string of formal logical symbols for describing external action effects in a problem-solving environment and perhaps also for describing internal cognitive states.[3]

In the limit, symbolic dynamics actually shows us that the symbolic account and the dynamical account can be perfectly compatible with one another. It is known that a string of symbols emitted from a dynamical system via generating partitions "yields approximately complete and precise descriptions of the system" (beim Graben, 2004, p. 47). Generating partitions are thresholds in the dynamical system's state or phase space that can be defined to arbitrary precision for identifying individual points in that space, such that each unique trajectory corresponds to a unique resultant string of symbols. Perfect placement of these generating partitions requires already knowing the continuous map of the dynamical system in the first place, but there are statistical methods for approximating these placements (e.g., Davidchack et al., 2000; Kennel & Buhl, 2003). Properly placed generating partitions allow the derived symbolic dynamics to be topologically equivalent to the original continuous dynamics (beim Graben, 2004; Kitchens, 1998; Shalizi & Albers, 2002). However, there is no general method for finding true generating partitions, and they are notoriously difficult to find in dynamical systems of greater than two dimensions (Kennel & Buhl, 2003), and they only work for deterministic dynamical systems (Crutchfield & Packard, 1983). Therefore, much of the practical applicability of symbolic dynamics may lie in iteratively refined approximations of generating partitions, rather than true generating partitions. For example, nongenerating partitions in symbolic dynamics have been used for describing the phase space of bimanual rhythmic coordination (Engbert et al., 1998) of heart rate variability (Kurths et al., 1995), and language processing (Andrews, 2001).

However, with even slightly misplaced partitions, the threshold-crossing method for emitting symbol strings from continuous systems with non-generating partitions can very easily introduce severe compounded misrepresentations of the original continuous dynamics, that is, grammatical errors in the symbol strings (Bollt et al., 2000, 2001). This means that the symbolic account of high-level cognition (figure 10.1B) has to be ready for serious errors to be brought in by the analog-to-digital conversions taking place—and not just those performance errors from motor dynamics being discretized into action effects but also something akin to competence errors from the perceptual dynamics being discretized into cognitive symbols. Ironically, it is the dynamical account of high-level cognition (figure 10.1A), with its analog-to-digital conversion taking place only at motor output, that can rightfully describe its grammatical errors as due purely to performance parameters, not competence.

The mathematics of symbolic dynamics could quite constructively pose as the level playing field on which both dynamical theories and symbolic theories of the mind could participate in a fair scientific contest (see Dale & Spivey, 2005), rather than being the incommensurate apples and oranges of cognitive science. However, a symbolicist will instantly recognize that when using symbolic dynamics as the common format of explication, his or her theoretical framework is already starting at a disadvantage with regard to parsimony. Compared to the dynamical approach, the symbolic approach posits more analog-to-digital (and digital-to-analog) conversions in the processing of mental activity—but at least they are of the same general mathematical nature in both approaches. For example, in the case of the symbolic cognition framework (figure 10.1B), not only must continuously dynamic patterns in the perceptual stage be converted into a string of symbols for the rule-based cognitive stage, but those symbols must then be reconverted back into a continuous high-dimensional trajectory for the motor stage, perhaps in a manner similar to state space reconstruction (e.g., Andrews, 2001; Sauer, Yorke, & Casdagli, 1991; Takens, 1981). And then, in both theoretical frameworks, the continuous dynamic patterns in the motor subsystem are converted, via symbolic dynamics, into discretely labeled action-based changes in the problem-solving environment. In this way, to provide a full description of high-level cognition, I suspect that both dynamical and symbolic accounts will need to employ some form of symbolic dynamics. Therein will be the common set of phenomena (e.g., problem solving and reasoning) fit by models that use a common format of explication (symbolic dynamics), which will finally allow the debate between symbolic and dynamical theories of mind to proceed in a resolvable fashion (Dale & Spivey, 2005).

Insight Problem Solving

One strikingly discrete-seeming cognitive phenomenon that poses a particular challenge to continuous descriptions of cognition is creative insight during problem solving. To describe what insight problems are, I begin by telling you what they are not. Most math problems, mechanical reasoning problems, and a variety of straightforward puzzles are typically called noninsight problems, because as the solver works on the problem, she has a sense of gradually getting closer to the correct solution. In fact, when participants provide regular reports of warmth ratings as they progress through the problem, noninsight problems elicit rather accurate subjective estimates of how close one is to achieving the solution. Insight problems, by contrast, elicit warmth ratings that have no correlation whatsoever with how much longer the person has to go before reaching the solution. And solvers of insight problems often reach an impasse, where they report being completely stymied and out of ideas. (In most insight problem-solving experiments, the majority of the participants never find the solution—not without hints, anyway.) While struggling with this impasse, they flail about with seemingly random ideas for a while, and the few participants that do manage to discover the solution burst out with an "Aha! I got it!" In these "Aha!" moments, they report feeling as though the solution came to them suddenly, out of nowhere—that is, not like a sigmoid curve over time (figure 4.1) but like a genuine step function (figure 4.3).

One such insight problem is Karl Duncker's (1945) candle-mounting problem, which purportedly measures a person's functional fixedness (the degree to which they treat objects as having fixed unalterable functions). Imagine you have, on a table in front of you, a candle, a box of tacks, and a book of matches (figure 10.2), and you are given the task of mounting the candle on the wall using only what's on the table. Many people struggle for some time with Byzantine wall sconce architectures of matches and tacks, and then find themselves having to "restructure their representation of the problem" and of the resources at hand, to find the solution (Fleck & Weisberg, 2004; see also Knoblich et al., 1999). Some of them figure out the solution, and some do not. Interestingly, five-year-olds, who may be less limited by functional fixedness, perform better on this task than do six- and seven-year-olds (German & Defeyter, 2000). If you haven't already read about this problem before, have you figured out the solution yet? If so, did it "suddenly pop" into your mind?

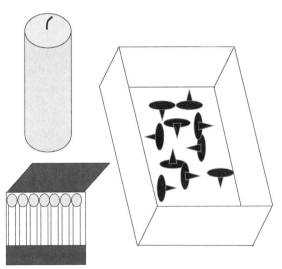

Figure 10.2. Materials for Duncker's candle-mounting problem: candle, matches, and cardboard box of tacks.

I spend a bit of time on insight problem solving here because this topic is an area where the much-touted instantaneity of the problem solution popping into one's mind poses as a striking discontinuity in cognition that contrasts sharply with my continuity of mind thesis. However, I will argue that this striking discontinuity is more a property of people's attempts to describe their subjective experience than a property of the actual cognitive processes themselves. The "suddenly out of nowhere" impression that has been branded on insight problem solving is due largely to experimental participants having poor introspective access to their cognitive processes (see Nisbett & Wilson, 1977) and to psychologists relying on off-line measures of subjective report.[4] As I will show, the process of insight problem solving actually has a number of introspectively inaccessible gradual precursors to that "Aha!" moment. Some of these precursors are rooted in perceptual-motor processes, not cognitive ones.

For example, more than 40 years ago, and less than 20 years after Duncker's (1945) book, a young Sam Glucksberg (1964) carefully watched participants as they attempted to solve Duncker's candle problem with the actual objects in front of them. He recorded how many times they touched the cardboard box of tacks (which solves the problem by being emptied and tacked to the wall as the mounting platform itself), and found that participants who solved the problem happened to touch the box, well before their "Aha!" moment, more times than those who did not solve the problem. This suggests that before their subjectively instantaneous discovery of the box as the solution, something inside their nervous system was paying a little extra attention to the box. Moreover, right before that "Aha!" moment, the object that these participants had most recently touched was always the box—*and in most cases that touch had been adventitious and nonpurposeful*. It is almost as if the participant's hands suspected that the box would be useful, in and of itself, before the participant himself knew!

A related example of perceptual-motor subsystems partially suspecting the correct solution to an insight problem, long before the explicit language subsystems have managed to verbalize it to themselves, comes from a study by Betsy Grant and myself (Grant & Spivey, 2003). We recorded participants' eye movements while they attempted to solve a diagram-based version of Duncker's (1945) classic tumor-and-lasers radiation problem. "Given a human being with an inoperable stomach tumor, and lasers which destroy organic tissue at sufficient intensity, how can one cure the person with these lasers and, at the same time, avoid harming the healthy tissue that surrounds the tumor?" A schematic diagram was provided, composed simply of a filled oval, representing the tumor, with a circumscribing oval representing the stomach lining (which must not be injured). Nothing else in Duncker's problem description was depicted in the schematic diagram. Because this problem is a very difficult insight problem, only a third of the participants (Cornell University undergraduates) solved it without needing hints—and that's a relatively high proportion compared to studies at other universities. Although the eye movement patterns were very similar for successful and unsuccessful solvers, one difference stood out. During the 30 seconds before encountering their "Aha!" moment, successful solvers tended to look at the stomach lining, the circumscribing oval, more than unsuccessful solvers did (during the corresponding 30 seconds just before they gave up and requested a hint). A bit like Glucksberg's (1964) successful candle problem solvers idly touching the box before discovering its usefulness, our successful solvers were making frequent eye movements inward toward the tumor and back outward again, stopping regularly on the stomach lining, almost *sketching* the solution (of multiple incident lasers) with their scan path. We used this observation to try to influence participants' cognitive performance by manipulating the perceptual salience of components of the diagram.

In a second experiment, the schematic diagram was animated (with a single pixel increase in diameter pulsating at 3 Hz) to subtly increase the perceptual salience of the stomach lining in one condition or the tumor in another condition. A control condition had no animation. In the control and pulsating tumor conditions, one third of the participants solved the problem without hints, as expected. However, in the pulsating stomach lining condition, *two-thirds* of the participants solved the problem without hints! Grant and Spivey (2003) hypothesized that the increased perceptual salience of the stomach lining helped elicit patterns of eye movements and attention that were conducive to developing a perceptual simulation (Barsalou, 1999) of the correct solution, involving multiple weak lasers passing through the stomach lining at different locations and converging their energies at the tumor. In this case, a perceptual-motor process—an eye movement pattern characterized by saccades into and back out of the stomach region, including a conspicuous proportion of fixations of stomach lining itself—seemed to be playing an important role in high-level cognition and was evident in successful solvers' behavior *before* they had discovered the solution.

It has been argued that long before a person has that "Aha!" moment with an insight problem, incremental implicit cognitive processes, possibly in the form of spreading activation, may be continuously guiding them toward the solution (Bowers, Farvolden, & Mermigis, 1995; Bowers et al., 1990; see also Ashby, Valentin, & Turken, 2002). To test for evidence of partial activation of an insight, Bowers et al. (1990) presented participants with a pair of remote-associate word triplets.[5] One of them would have a coherent solution and the other would not. (For example, "What one word makes a compound with the words *still*, *pages*, and *music*?" and "What one word makes a compound with the words *playing*, *credit*, and *report*?") Participants were asked to find the solution to the coherent triplet that actually has a solution, and barring that, at least guess which word triplet has a solution at all. In trials where participants could not find the solution to the coherent word triplet, they could still nonetheless identify, more often than not, which triplet had a solution. Thus, some kind of implicit knowledge was brewing in there, a subtle suspicion that *playing/credit/report* somehow was more likely to be the triplet that had a coherent solution—even when that coherent solution itself was not forthcoming. In fact, using the same kind of remote associates task, Bowden and Beeman (1998) have recorded word naming latencies to reveal significant priming for the *undiscovered* correct answers to remote associate problems, such as "What one word makes a compound with the words *back, step,* and *screen?*"

Further evidence for implicit processing of insight comes from sleep consolidation research. After some initial exposure to a cognitive task that contains a hidden rule, eight hours of normal sleep can facilitate discovery of the hidden rule better than eight hours of wakefulness (Wagner et al., 2004; see also Mazzarello, 2000). This is likely due to a process of memory consolidation and restructuring of task representations that occurs during sleep (e.g., Maquet, 2001; Wilson & McNaughton, 1994; see also Hinton et al., 1995). During sleep, or a similar "mental incubation" period, it appears that something implicit is taking place that sets the stage for a representational change in the problem space when the task is faced once again after waking. Thus, far from being an event of *fiat lux*, instantaneous illumination from out of nowhere, insight during problem solving actually has implicit cognitive processes that are continuously "chewing on" the conceptual rearrangement necessary for solving the problem, long before the participant experiences that sudden awareness of the correct solution (for a review, see Knoblich, Öllinger, & Spivey, 2005).

Shape and Movement in an Attractor Landscape

Rather little in the way of dynamical modeling has been applied to insight problem solving so far (but see Ashby et al., 2002). However, given the graded continuous processing that may be underlying insight problem solving, future dynamical modeling of these phenomena may prove extremely elucidating. Much of the promise in dynamical systems approaches to cognition is in their ability to recast old theoretical problems in a new shape and examine the temporal continuity that is underlying the apparently symbolic. In many cases, this recasting may melt away certain aspects of long-debated distinctions that have stalemated the field. For example, the battle between exemplar-based models of implicit conceptual representation (e.g., Brooks, 1978; Medin & Schaffer, 1978; Nosofsky & Zaki, 2002; see also Heit & Barslaou, 1996) and prototype-based models of the same phenomena (e.g., Minda & Smith, 2001; Posner & Keele, 1968) continues to rage in the literature (Brooks, 2005). This despite the distinct possibility that both exemplar and prototype simulations are overfitting their data at this point (Olsson, Wennerholm, & Lyxzen, 2004) and that a third, nonparametric and procedural alternative may be more appropriate (Ashby & Waldron, 1999).

This distinction between exemplars and prototypes can begin to look decidedly different when placed in a neurally inspired dynamical systems framework.

Let's assume that recognizing an object (as being mostly a member of a particular concept that you have learned) consists of your neural population codes approaching a semi-stable pattern of activation that is similar to the patterns of activation achieved for similarly categorized objects. If this is true, then one could in principle define an attractor landscape that mathematically described how those patterns of neural activity cluster (and subcluster) near each other in state space and how similar patterns may gravitate toward those learned patterns. If this attractor landscape had several narrow nonoverlapping basins for each previous experience with an object that was categorized the same, it might look something like the idealized depiction in figure 10.3. This would be a straw man dynamical version of the exemplar-based model. Such a state space manifold would have some difficulty generalizing the concept label to many novel objects that find themselves eliciting patterns of neural activation that are on the flat portion of the manifold in between the tiny attractor basins.

In contrast, an extreme version of a prototype-based model in attractor terms would look something like figure 10.4. The smooth interpolation seen across this basin of attraction elegantly includes all relevant objects, whether they've been experienced or not. In fact, the nadir of the basin, the "best" example of the concept, does not even need to correspond to any object that has actually been experienced. It is the prototype. Mountains of empirical data have been published in support of both exemplar and prototype theories (e.g., Hintzman, 1986; Medin & Smith, 1984; Minda & Smith, 2002; Olsson et al., 2004; Stanton, Nosofsky, & Zaki, 2002), therefore some form of representational medium that could flexibly elicit both kinds of phenomena would be ideal.

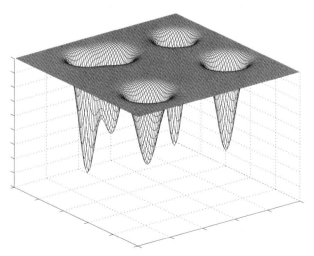

Figure 10.3. A hypothetical attractor landscape consistent with an exemplar model of categorization.

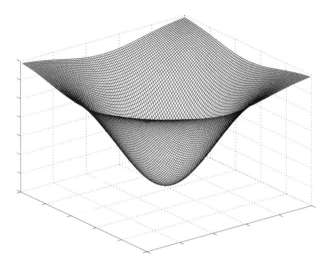

Figure 10.4. A hypothetical attractor landscape consistent with
a prototype model of categorization.

Although attempts to simultaneously account for exemplar and prototype phenomena with traditional rule-based approaches generally require the
stipulation of separate modules (e.g., Nosofsky, Palmeri, & McKinley, 1994),
an attractor landscape describing the dynamical tendencies of neural activation patterns can blend the two theories quite naturally and parsimoniously.
This idea combines the clustering and subclustering seen in the distributed
representational state space of static connectionist networks (e.g., Elman,
1990; McClelland & Rogers, 2003; Schyns, 1991) with the temporal dynamics
of the settling process seen in fully recurrent networks (e.g., Hinton &
Shallice, 1991; McRae, de Sa, & Seidenberg, 1997). The attractor landscape in
figure 10.5, with small attractors inside a large one, maintains the individual
item variation from exemplar theory and also preserves the generalizability of
prototype theory—even including a best-fit case (at the deepest portion of the
basin) that does not correspond to any experienced object. It may not be a
very pretty attractor basin, but it's what's on the inside that counts. This is, of
course, not a functioning model of categorization but merely a speculative
visual illustration (in a paltry three dimensions, at that) of the flexibility
inherent in attractor landscapes that can potentially accommodate seemingly
conflicting theoretical mechanisms.

Another visualizable insight from the dynamical systems framework can
be gleaned from applying the dynamic attractor landscape idea to similarity
judgments. Almost 30 years ago, Amos Tversky (1977) offered his discrete
feature list account (the contrast model) of similarity as a replacement for geometric state space accounts of similarity (e.g., Shepard, 1964, 2001). His evidence in support for a feature list account was that state space proximity as a
measure of similarity fails to account for asymmetries in similarity judgments

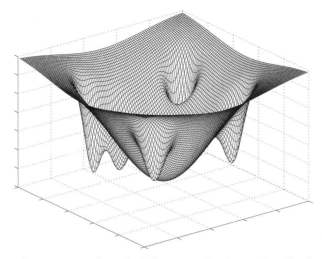

Figure 10.5. A hypothetical attractor landscape that blends prototype and exemplar accounts.

(but see Holman, 1978; Krumhansl, 1978; Nosofksy, 1991). For example, acceptability ratings of statements such as "Korea is like China" were reliably higher than acceptability ratings of statements such as "China is like Korea." Therefore, people somehow conceive of Korea as being more similar to China than China is to Korea. Intuitively, the reader can probably agree with this asymmetry in the similarity of Korea to China versus China to Korea.[6] But if the two countries are represented as locations in a semantic state space, with Euclidean proximity being equivalent to their similarity, then there shouldn't be any asymmetry at all. In that semantic state space, China is exactly as close to Korea as Korea is to China.

However, if the multidimensional similarity space is not treated merely as a static arena in which one measures distances but instead as a dynamic medium in which thought itself is a trajectory from one attractor basin to the next, then asymmetric similarities begin to make a bit of sense. Some trajectories are smoother, faster, and easier than others and thus may elicit higher acceptability ratings. Thus, if an experimental participant hears or reads "Korea" first, then "is like China," they are first projected to the Korea attractor basin in semantic space and must travel to the China attractor basin (figure 10.6A). Traversing from an attractor that is weak (due to low salience or relative importance) to an attractor that is strong will be quick and effortless. However, traversing from an attractor that is strong to one that is weak (i.e., "China is like Korea") will require a fair bit of time for the strong basin to give way, as the unfolding meaning of the sentence changes the shape of the manifold to allow the state of the system to move to the other attractor. As figure 10.6B shows, by the end of the sentence, the Korea attractor is trying to pull the state of the system to itself, but because the China attractor was so large to begin with, it

A.

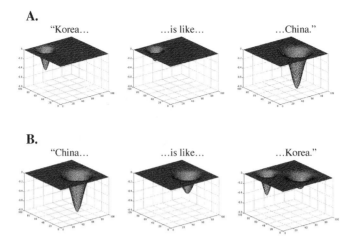

Figure 10.6. Panel A shows the changing attractor landscape for understanding "Korea is like China," where the more frequent and salient China attractor would pull the system quickly into completing its left-to-right trajectory. Panel B shows the changing attractor landscape for "China is like Korea," where the less frequent and salient Korea attractor has some difficulty competing with the China attractor and thus the right-to-left trajectory might be problematic or deemed somewhat infelicitous.

has not quite given way yet. By paying attention to the temporal dynamics of stimulus delivery in this task and plotting comprehension as a continuous trajectory in an attractor landscape, asymmetric similarity effects can actually be seen as a perfectly natural result of representing concepts as locations in a dynamic state space.

Probabilistic Mind, Not Probabilistic Reasoning

Probabilistic reasoning is another place where feature lists and rulelike heuristics have been proffered as the actual mechanisms of reasoning (see Gilovich, Griffin, & Kahneman, 2002; Kahneman, Slovic, & Tversky, 1982), rather than probabilistic dynamic representations. It is certainly the case that many aspects of the transition from stimulation to perception do in fact adhere to genuine probability theory (see Kersten, 1991; Knill, 1998; Rao, Olshausen, & Lewicki, 2002). However, as that stimulation-to-perception transition becomes more complex, involving richer time-dependent stimulus environments and more in-depth cognitive processing, the opportunities for contaminating those implicit probabilities with explicit strategies and heuristics become numerous. There are a number of experimental demonstrations of people reasoning in ways that do not adhere to the actual probabilities of the environment. Therefore, a continuous probabilistic account of mental activity will need to be prepared to accommodate explicit judgments and decisions that somehow violate Bayesian probability.

For example, Tversky and Kahneman's (1983) conjunction fallacy displays a shocking mistreatment of probability theory in people's intuitive judgments. They had participants read a vignette about a woman named Linda who is intelligent, outspoken, and concerned with issues of discrimination and social justice, among other things, and then asked them to rank several statements about her in order of their probability. One of the statements, "Linda is a bank teller and an activist in the feminist movement," was, in set theoretic terms, a subset of another of the statements, "Linda is a bank teller." As the former statement is the conjunction of the latter proposition and an additional proposition, probability theory would multiply the probabilities of those two propositions to calculate the probability of the conjoined statement. Therefore, the former statement can never be of higher probability than the latter. Yet most participants—including some with training in statistics—rate the former (conjunction) statement with higher probability than the latter statement (Tversky & Kahneman, 1983; Zizzo, 2003; see also Fisk & Pidgeon, 1997). Although some of this error in judgment may be due to participants misinterpreting the latter statement as implying Linda is conspicuously *not* a feminist (Bonini, Tentori, & Osherson, 2004), it is interesting to note that this conjunction fallacy behavior goes away when the problem is posed in terms of frequencies rather than probabilities (Cosmides & Tooby, 1996; Gigerenzer, 1994).

An even more worrisome example of people's poor reasoning about probabilities is base-rate neglect. Imagine that a woman is getting a test for a form of cancer that occurs in 1 in 10,000 people. Further imagine that this particular test has a 100% hit rate (therefore, 0% miss rate) and a 99% correct rejection rate (therefore, a mere 1% false positive rate). If this woman's test result is positive, what is the probability that she actually has this cancer? People regularly make huge overestimations of the probability that such a person in this situation actually has the disease in question (e.g., Kahneman & Tversky, 1973; Tversky & Kahneman, 1980; but see also Birnbaum, 1983; Koehler, 1993). Because the probability of a false positive is only 0.01, people often conclude that the probability that this woman has cancer is 0.99. In fact, the probability that this person has cancer, according to Bayesian statistics, can be calculated at 0.0099. This is quite a bit higher than the 1-in-10,000 base rate, by two orders of magnitude in fact, but perhaps not reason enough to say good-bye to loved ones already.

As Gigerenzer and Hoffrage (1995) point out, this counterintuitive probabilistic calculation is much easier to understand when framed in terms of frequencies. If the doctors performed this test on a randomly selected population of 10,000 people, the one person with this cancer would get a positive test result, and of the remaining 9,999 people who did not have this cancer, 1% of them would also get positive test results—but they'd be *false* positives. That's 99.99 people with false positives; we'll call it 100. So out of these 101 people with positive test results, only one of them actually has the cancer in question. Therefore, each of them has a 1-in-101 chance ($p = 0.0099$) of being that poor soul. Sadly, even trained doctors exhibit this same kind of base-rate neglect and grossly overestimate the probability of cancer in these word problems (Eddy, 1982; Wallsten, 1981).[7] Although some have claimed that this error in probabilistic reasoning is due to heuristics that produce systematic rule-based errors in these circumstances (Tversky & Kahneman, 1980), others have suggested that the format of representation of the problem is the culprit and that describing the problem in terms of frequencies is more ecologically valid, engaging our reasoning skills in a manner more suited to their normal everyday use (Gigerenzer & Hoffrage, 1995). Interestingly, neural network models can, without the use of any rule or heuristic, exhibit the kind of base-rate neglect that humans exhibit (e.g., Gluck & Bower, 1988; Kruschke, 1992; but see Lewandowsky, 1995; Shanks, 1990).

Perhaps it is not surprising that people are bad at diagnosing patients based on something complex like Bayesian statistics and probability values with multiple decimal places. You might think that faulty probabilistic reasoning wouldn't rear its ugly head with something as simple as flipping a coin. But it does. Ask people without any training in statistics if they think that with coin flips after four tails in a row, a heads is more likely than a tails, and most of them will answer "yes." This is called the gambler's fallacy. As long as it's a fair coin, and the person flipping it isn't cheating somehow, the probabilities associated with each coin flip are independent of one another. This means that it doesn't matter how many tails have come up in a row in the past, the odds for each new coin flip are 50/50 for heads or tails.

Think of it this way: If you were planning on flipping a coin five times, and you wanted to figure out the probability, in advance, of flipping exactly four tails and then a heads, it would simply be that 0.5 probability of correctly predicting each coin flip, but compounded five times in a row, or $0.5^5 = .03125$. Now, what would be the probability, in advance, of flipping exactly five tails in a row? Simply 0.5^5 as well. The only difference between those two little time series is the last coin flip, and they have the same probability. Therefore, four tails being followed by another tails is no less likely than four tails being followed by a heads.[8]

Yet the probabilities of something as innocent as a time series of coin flips is a surprisingly difficult thing to teach people to reason correctly about. You can get them to repeat back to you that "these probabilities are independent," but getting them to behave in ways that respect that fact is another thing altogether. Take for example the prolific mathematician Jean d'Alembert, who, during the development of probability theory in the eighteenth century, claimed that the probability of getting at least one heads on two coin flips was actually two-thirds rather than three-fourths (see Weatherford, 1982). His reasoning was that because you would stop flipping if you got heads on the first flip, this meant that there were actually only *three* possible results: H, HT, and TT (instead of all four HH, HT, TH, and TT). As two of those three possible results contain a heads, d'Alembert concluded that the probability of at least one heads on two coin flips was two-thirds. He was, of course, completely wrong. And I must admit, I find it profoundly shocking that an academic with his status would make such bold claims about how a mathematical process works without empirically trying the process out himself, don't you? I mean, how hard could it have been for d'Alembert to spend an afternoon recording the results of a few hundred bouts of two flips of a coin and see if his prediction of two-thirds of them having at least one heads was true?[9]

Related to this point, the act of seeking disconfirmatory evidence (and not just confirmatory evidence) is another important aspect in reasoning about uncertainty that is notoriously difficult to teach people. When reasoning about probabilities, people tend to seek confirmatory information and ignore potentially disconfirming information (Gilovich, 1991; Wason & Johnson-Laird, 1972). This "confirmation bias" appears to be at the heart of why about 80% of people fail at the Wason card selection task (Evans, 1982; Wason, 1966; Wason & Shapiro, 1971). Imagine having four cards lying face down, with the first of them showing an A, the second showing a T, the third showing a 6, and the fourth showing a 3. See figure 10.7. Now, the experimenter tells you that there is a rule for how these cards are made, and it is this: "All cards with vowels on one side must have even numbers on the other side." And your task is to test this rule by flipping over two and only two cards. Which two do you flip over?

Flipping the A card is obvious, and most people do that. Ignoring the T card is also obvious, and very few people flip it over. Most people feel at least tempted to flip the 6 card to see whether it does indeed have a vowel on its other side. But that would be wrong. The truth is, the rule never said anything about the cards with consonants. Maybe half of them have even numbers on their other side and the other half of them have odd numbers. So flipping over the 6 card won't actually test the rule. Finding a vowel would perhaps be moderately encouraging confirmatory evidence, but finding a consonant wouldn't mean anything with regard to testing the rule. Flipping over the 3 card is what will test the rule. This checks for disconfirmatory information. If there's a vowel on its other side, then you know the rule has been violated. The fact that people usually flip the 6 card instead of the 3 card suggests that they are biased more toward acquiring confirmatory evidence than disconfirmatory evidence.

Figure 10.7. Card display for the Wason task, where the rule is "All vowels must have even numbers on the other side of the card." Which *two* cards should you flip to properly test this rule?

Interestingly, a number of studies have examined variations on this task and found improved performance when the task involves a more ecologically valid and personally relevant scenario (Johnson-Laird, Legrenzi, & Legrenzi, 1972). For example, when the cards indicate alcoholic or nonalcoholic drinks and ages that are of drinking age or not, and the rule is "If someone is drinking alcohol, then they better be 21+," undergraduate students' performance increases dramatically (Griggs & Cox, 1982). In general, when the Wason card selection task is put in the context of a social contract, where a cheater is to be detected, participants perform better on the task (Cosmides, 1989). When participants are working on a version of the Wason card selection task that has implications for their own life span, they perform substantially better than students working on a version whose early death implications were not personally relevant (Dawson, Gilovich, & Regan, 2002).

The point being made with this litany of probabilistic reasoning tasks is that reasoning about uncertainty is impaired when people are trying to use probabilities that have little do with their own daily lives. But when they use frequencies and other ecologically valid formats of problem representation, all of a sudden their performance adheres to probability theory rather well. Thus, although people's explicit use of probability theory is clearly very flawed, their minds can still work in ways that are at least implicitly quite consistent with probability. There's just something about when graded fuzzy ideas get converted into verbalized axioms, which the person tries to use in an explicit fashion, that seems to cause those articulated heuristics to be in conflict with the person's underlying natural frequentistic competence, and thus they become quite faulty.

Think Not of p, But of $1 - p$

As demonstrated by the Wason card selection task, paying attention only to the probability of confirming the result you want, p, is at the core of many failures in human reasoning. When you instead focus on $1 - p$, the probability of *anything but* what you have in mind, you can actually perform calculations that will provide some impressive predictive power. Take the game of roulette as a concrete example. If there are 34 numbers on the roulette wheel, and you put your money on number 23, your probability of winning is 1 in 34. Easy. But what is the probability of winning at least once during 10 tries? It's certainly not 10 in 34, that would imply that on your 34th try you would be *guaranteed* to win, and that on your 35th try you would somehow have a >1.0 probability of winning. Any time your math produces a probability that is greater than 1.0 or less than 0, you should check your math. Probability summation over time (Watson, 1979) is a convenient and surprisingly easy way to calculate this probability. The key is in focusing on $1 - p$, not on p. Probability doesn't allow you to do much with p for this circumstance, but what you *can* do is calculate the probability of not winning even once during these 10 spins of the roulette wheel. That's simply a 33 in 34 chance that is multiplied by itself 10 times. Now all you have to do is subtract that value from 1, and you have the probability, p, that you will not lose on all 10 of those spins, and hence will win at least once: $p = 1 - (33/34)^{10} = 0.258$.

The function in figure 10.8 shows this probability rising nonlinearly, on a logarithmic x-axis, as a person bets on 23 again and again in roulette. This kind of sigmoid curve should look familiar at this point in this book. Interestingly, the curve shows that on the 34th spin of the roulette wheel, the probability of 23 coming up would just barely exceed 0.63212055882856, or $1 - 1/e$. This means that if 100 people played roulette this way at 100 different tables, about 63 of them would win on or before their 34th spin. Figure 10.9 is a frequency distribution showing how many of these 100 players would have their first win within 1–10 spins, 11–20 spins, and so on. Note how this frequency distribution is almost a mirror image of the previous sigmoid curve in figure 10.8.

With any base probability of $1/n$, the probability of that event occurring at least once during a bout of attempts exceeds that magic number, $1 - 1/e$, on the nth attempt. For example, the probability of accurately guessing—at least once—what you are about to roll on a six-sided die exceeds 0.632 on the sixth roll. The probability of guessing what card is on the bottom of a shuffled deck exceeds 0.632 on the 52nd try. Somewhat less encouragingly, the probability of winning a state lottery exceeds 0.632 around the 10 or 20 millionth try (depending on how many numbers there are to choose from). Thus, with higher probability events (such as guessing the face of a rolled die), the curve and its intersection of the dashed lines in figure 10.8 would simply be shifted leftward on the time scale; with lower probability events (such as winning a state lottery), it would be shifted rightward.

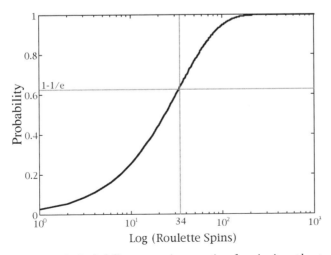

Figure 10.8. Probability summation over time for winning at least once during many sequential spins of a 34-slot roulette wheel.

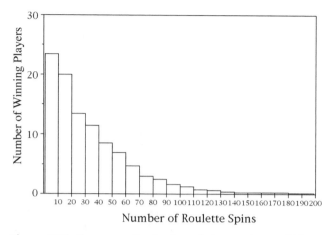

Figure 10.9. Frequency distribution of players who would have their first win during their first 10 spins, or between their 11th and 20th spins, or between their 21st and 30th spins, and so on.

Another case where attending to $1 - p$ is important is in the Monty Hall problem. Derived from Monty Hall's *Let's Make a Deal* game show from the 1970s, this problem involves three doors, behind one of which is a "brand-new car!" Behind each of the other two doors is a goat, or something similarly unexciting. The game host invites you to pick one of the doors—which (unless you are psychic) will be a random guess as to which one has the car behind it. Then, once you've chosen a door, he opens one of the other doors to reveal a goat munching on some hay. (The host knows where the car is, and his constraints are that the door he opens cannot be the door you've chosen, nor can it be the door that has the car.) Now that you've seen one of the doors opened and revealing a goat, the host turns to you and asks whether you want to *stay* with the door you first chose or *switch* to the other remaining closed door. The correct answer to that question is trickier than it might seem. The way in which people try to deal with the Monty Hall problem has been studied by a number of psychologists and statisticians for some time now (e.g., Gilovich, Medvec, & Chen, 1995; Granberg & Brown, 1995; Selvin, 1975; for reviews, see Burns & Wieth, 2004; Krauss & Wang, 2003).

This intriguing problem of probabilistic reasoning was popularized by Marilyn vos Savant (1990) in *Parade Magazine*, where she explained that the probabilistically most advantageous solution is to *switch*. This solution seems quite counterintuitive at first.[10] Most people's initial (erroneous) intuition is that after one of the doors has been opened, the probabilities are 50/50 for the car being behind your chosen door or behind the remaining unopened door. In fact, vos Savant received numerous angry letters telling her that her "switch" strategy was wrong—some of them even came from mathematics professors!

The key to understanding this counterintuitive solution is twofold. First, you must keep in mind that your initial door selection was probably wrong. If the probability that you chose correctly at the beginning (p) is 0.33, then $1 - p = 0.67$. This latter probability, that the door you've initially chosen is likely wrong, does not (indeed, *cannot*) change during the course of the game. Second, the host's selection of which door to open is not random. He cannot open your chosen door, nor can he open the door with the car. This means that in the event that your chosen door is not the door with the car (and this is a pretty likely event: $1 - p = 0.67$), then there is only one door that the host can select to open: the only unchosen door that does not have the car. In such a circumstance (and don't forget that this *is* the most likely circumstance), once the host has opened a door with a goat behind it, that one unchosen and unopened door remaining definitely contains the car, and so you should definitely switch. Stated another way, because there is only a 0.33 probability that your first choice was correct, there is therefore only a 0.33 probability that switching will lose you the car.

As Gigerenzer and Hoffrage (1995) have suggested for probabilistic reasoning in general, it may be the case that the correct solution to the Monty Hall problem is easier to understand when framed in *frequentistic* terms instead of probabilistic terms. That is, what if you were told to imagine playing the game 30,000 times, and given frequentistic math questions that pumped your intuitions about how many times the car would be behind each door and how many times staying or switching in those various circumstances would win you the car? In three experiments with over 250 participants, Aaron and Spivey (1998) compared this frequency-based version of the problem to the standard probability-based version (with corresponding probabilistic math questions about the probability of the car being behind each door and the probability that staying or switching would win the car). We found that participants performed reliably better on the mathematics questions when the problem was framed in terms of frequencies rather than probabilities. However, with regard to their ultimate choice of whether they would choose to stay or switch on a single round of the game, only a marginally greater percentage of participants in the frequency condition chose to switch (28%) compared to those in the probability condition (19%). Thus, even with the problem described in frequentistic terms, and even with leading questions regarding how many times the car would be won or lost in various circumstances, we still had 72% of the participants making the wrong choice when they got to that final point in the questionnaire. Perhaps, as suggested by work with the Wason card selection task (Griggs & Cox, 1982; Johnson-Laird et al., 1972), what it comes down to is that conducting the experiment in an abstracted questionnaire format just doesn't make it real enough for participants.

Sanford and Sanford (2005) actually had individual participants play a physically demonstrated interactive 3D version of the Monty Hall problem— using a coin and a bunch of upside-down cups. After the participant made their initial choice of a cup, the experimenter physically removed a different

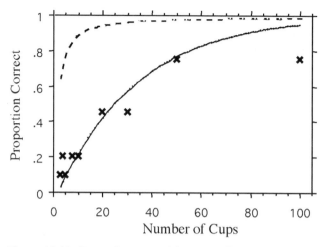

Figure 10.10. Proportion correct (choosing to "switch") in Sanford and Sanford's (2005) cups-and-coin version of the Monty Hall problem (x's). The top-most dashed curve is the actual probability that switching will win. The lower exponential curve, roughly fitting the data, comes from probability summation over time: $1 - (1 - p)^{(\text{cups}-2)}$, where $p = 0.03$.

cup, revealing no coin. With a total of three cups, only 2 out of 20 participants chose to switch. However, other groups of 20 participants each played a version of the game with 4, 5, 8, 10, 20, 30, 50, or 100 cups. After making their initial cup selection, participants sat and watched while the experimenter removed as many cups as needed for there to be only two cups remaining: their chosen cup and one other. (Note that the odds of a switch decision winning you the coin increase dramatically with more and more cups, from 3/4 with 4 cups to 99/100 with 100 cups.) In these additional experimental conditions, the proportion of participants deciding to switch was 20%, 10%, 20%, 20%, 45%, 45%, 75%, and 75%, respectively. When you read those percentages in the text like this, they may seem a rather awkward stair-step sequence. However, when plotted on a graph, they actually conform reasonably lawfully to an exponential function. And probability summation over time (Watson, 1979) may, once again, have exactly the exponential we're looking for.

Imagine that each time a participant watches a cup getting removed, there is some probability, let's say $p = 0.03$, that it will explicitly occur to her that the host's cup-removal process may not be entirely random and that this fact has important consequences for her decision to stay or switch. Probability summation over time allows us to compound that probability with each cup removal, but it requires that we use $1 - p$, instead of p. The probability of the participant *not* experiencing that insight on a given cup removal, 0.97, can be iteratively multiplied by itself every time she witnesses a cup getting removed (as long as we take the simplifying assumption that each cup removal's chance at triggering such an insight is independent of every other one). Thus, the total number of cups (minus the two that do not get removed) can be an exponent on the $1 - p$ figure. When the resulting calculation is subtracted from 1, we now have the probability that the participant will experience that insight sometime during the temporally drawn-out cup-removal process. Figure 10.10 plots Sanford and Sanford's (2005) results, along with this incredibly simple exponential function which fits the data surprisingly well; $r^2 = 0.95$. The smooth curve fitting the data in figure 10.10, reminiscent of many information-accumulation curves shown throughout this book (e.g., figures 1.6, 3.2, 6.16, 8.5), is the result of a probabilistic process by which insight for a difficult problem gradually accrues over time. The fact that it accounts for 95% of the variance in the human data suggests that it may be a reasonably adequate account of the phenomenon.[11]

Reasoning Is a Hungry Process

There is something of a tradition in the cognitive sciences of treating categorization, language comprehension, visual perception, and motor movement (chapters 6–9) as though they were bottom-up, stimulus-driven processes. Therefore, arguing for anticipatory processes in those phenomena requires a fair bit of ammunition from the literature. In the case of high-level cognition, however, it hardly needs to be said that reasoning is dependent on anticipatory processes. Anyone who has ever made a well-thought-out move in a game of chess, prepared a holiday meal for several people, or planned a vacation knows that reasoning involves imagining future events. Higher-order cognition is certainly the one place where anticipatory processes are uncontroversial. Thinking people make plans. And these plans often have an impressively discrete quality to them, reminiscent of symbolic logic. When you ask a little boy what he plans to be when he grows up, he doesn't answer with "I expect to be a cowboy with 0.3 probability, an astronaut with 0.2 probability, and a fireman with 0.5 probability." The kid just says, "I'm gonna be a fireman." That's what plans often look and feel like: rules and symbols.

This intuitive characterization may make it somewhat difficult for dynamical systems models of high-level cognition to accommodate long-range planning of this sort. However, as these models gradually move more into the realm of high-level cognition, the conceptual scale of the attractor basins may be able to gradually increase to simulate the more abstracted content. Instead of the attractors in the state space being phonemes (Indrebo, Povinelli, & Johnson, 2006), or words (Elman, 1995), or objects (Deco, Rolls, & Horwitz, 2004), or concepts (McRae, 2004), they could perhaps become strategies, goals, and drives (van der Maas, 1998). As always, the trajectory in this state space would have an anticipatory momentum all its own, making it what I call a hungry process. For example, this anticipatory momentum can even be seen in the real-time measurement of emotional expectations.

Chung and colleagues (1996) recorded ERPs of participants who were induced into pessimistic or optimistic moods to see if these moods could alter their immediate expectations of little vignettes ending with good or bad outcomes. A person who is in a pessimistic mood exhibits an N400 (i.e., a wave peak indicative of an expectation violation) for good outcomes and not for bad outcomes. A person who is in an optimistic mood exhibits a reversed differentiation between these outcomes. Thus, in dynamical cognition terms, one could say that your emotional mood can contribute to the direction of your anticipatory momentum in conceptual state space.

On the Future of Symbolic High-Level Cognition

This chapter has provided only a very brief sampling of the huge body of literature on high-level cognition—a teaser, as it were. To some cognitive scientists, this literature is at the core of what gets called cognitive science. Unfortunately, it is quite rare for this core set of phenomena to be studied with real-time methodologies that can reveal their temporal dynamics. This makes for a paucity of the kind of evidence that could distinguish between symbolic and dynamic theories. Proper adjudication between symbolic and dynamic approaches to high-level cognition will likely require future work that focuses more on the real-time temporal dynamics of reasoning, conceptual representation, and problem solving and whether there is indeed some internal cognitive stage in which these dynamics are discretized in time and in representational space (and then redynamicized for graded continuous action commands in motor cortex).

With comparatively more real-time data in the research areas of motor movement, visual perception, language processing, and even categorization, the dynamical systems movement in cognitive science has had enough grist for the mill to begin making a compelling case in those areas. In high-level cognition, however, it has barely scratched the surface and will need a great deal more development to compete with the rule-and-symbol framework. As Dietrich and Markman (2003) suggest, 50 years of development for the symbolic paradigm in cognitive science is not actually that long by scientific standards, and perhaps the dynamicist's disillusionment with symbolic cognition may just be a sign of juvenile impatience. Then again, it may turn out that the computer metaphor of the mind is a fundamentally flawed guide for understanding how the mind works (Dreyfus, 1972; van Gelder, 1998; see also Fodor, 2000), and that's precisely why it hasn't succeeded yet.

At the time of this writing, the dynamical movement in the cognitive sciences must acknowledge that for the case of high-level cognition, such as reasoning, analogy making, problem solving, and playing strategic games, rule-and-symbol systems have accumulated the most successes in their half-century of scientific development. The distributed and dynamical approach to the mind, in its 20 or so years of activity, has focused more on successes in accounting for perceptual-motor phenomena. So it has a long way to go to catch up. It is not yet clear whether there just may be certain mental processes that are not well described by continuous dynamical systems and that may always be better accommodated by discrete symbolic systems. However, I will say this: In the past, when advocates of symbolic cognition have drawn lines in the sand that separate continuous perception from discrete cognition (or discrete cognition from continuous action), they have watched in disbelief as dynamical-minded theories and data resolutely stepped over those lines. Each time, these symbolicists then changed their story and labeled that newly occupied territory as "just part of perception, not really part of cognition," while drawing a new line in the sand—this time a little closer to their own feet. Time and time again, each new line in the sand was crossed by the dynamical framework. More aspects of the mind that were once thought of as symbolic (or at least thought of as best described by symbolic abstraction) have been taken over, on the one side by continuous perception-based accounts and on the other side by continuous motor-based accounts. Perhaps this constant shrinking of their island of symbols will eventually stop, as continuous dynamical descriptions of cognitive phenomena finally wash up against some firm bedrock that forms the core of highly complex mental processes like reasoning and problem solving. . . . And then again, perhaps not.

These things happen. One day you run everything, and the next day you run like a dog.

—*Hunter S. Thompson*

11

Uniting and Freeing the Mind

By their very nature, open systems require going outside a system, going from a smaller system to a larger one to understand its behaviors. Stated another way, openness means that even a complete understanding of internal parts and subsystems cannot, of itself, account for what happens when a system is open.
—Robert Rosen

A human being is a part of the whole called by us universe, a part limited in time and space. He experiences himself, his thoughts and feelings as something separated from the rest, a kind of optical delusion of his consciousness. This delusion is a kind of prison for us, restricting us to our personal desires and to affection for a few persons nearest to us. Our task must be to free ourselves from this prison by widening our circle of compassion to embrace all living creatures and the whole of nature in its beauty.
—Albert Einstein

Mind Inside Brain, or Brain Inside Mind?

The cognitive and neural sciences have spent more than a few decades relying on the mantra of "dividing and conquering the mind" to understand it. Although this tactic was useful at one time and resulted in some important early advances, such advances are fewer and farther between now and definitely less certain. Perhaps it is time to stop dividing and conquering the mind, and instead start uniting and freeing it.

Cognitive science's proclivity for carving up mental activity into individuated boxes that are devoted to seemingly independent categories of thought and behavior and assigning mutually exclusive names to those putative modules, has clearly led the field astray (see Farah, 1994; Haxby et al., 2001; Inui & McClelland, 1996; Sarter, Berntson, & Cacioppo, 1996; Uttal, 2001; Van Orden, Jansen op de haar, & Bosman, 1997). With so much evidence in support of continuous dynamical and richly interactive processing within and between cognitive subsystems that are loosely specialized for different domains of mental processing (e.g., chapters 5, 6, 7, and 8; see also Churchland, Ramachandran, & Sejnowski, 1994; Damasio, 1989; Spivey et al., 2001; Tanenhaus et al., 1995), the borders between things like word recognition and object recognition can start to blur. Even the borders between language and vision, or between cognition and perception, become somewhat vague and fuzzy. In fact, as we begin to acknowledge that each of these subsystems is an open system, which behooves us to zoom out the microscope and examine the larger system in which it is embedded, we eventually run into that seemingly obvious (but nonetheless historically disputed) border between the organism and its environment. On further scrutiny, does that border become vague and fuzzy as well? When one attempts to define what mental activity is, does it straddle even *that* fuzzy border? Hurley (1998b, p. 3) posed the question especially eloquently when she noted that "if internal relations can qualify as [representational] vehicles, why not external relations? Given a continuous complex dynamic system of reciprocal causal relations between organism and environment, what in principle stops the spread? The idea that vehicles might go external takes the notion of distributed processing to its logical extreme."

Humor me a bit while I go out on this limb here: It just might be that your mind is bigger than your brain. This is not because you have an ethereal soul that influences your brain via the pineal gland, as proposed in Descartes's dualism, but because your external physical environment contains information that you can *perceptually* access as quickly and directly as you can *cognitively* access information from internal memory. One might even say, what is in your immediate physical environment is "part of what you know," even when you're not looking directly at it. For example, do you know what time it is? If looking at your watch is about as quick as (perhaps quicker than) recalling from memory what time it was 30 seconds ago when you last looked at your watch and involves functionally quite similar processes (e.g., content-addressable memory), then perhaps both processes can constitute "accessing your knowledge of the time." And where that knowledge resides is not only in your brain but also on your wrist.

In this chapter, I describe a range of experimental demonstrations of ways in which people tend to rely on the external environment to store information for them rather than storing it all in their brains. On the surface, the phenomenon that I report—use of deictic pointers or spatial indices—may appear intriguing, but not necessarily revolutionary. At a deeper level, however, this constellation of findings hints at the potential upheaval of some very old and cherished assumptions in cognitive science: a mindset that philosophers have called internalism (Segal, 2000; see also Putnam, 1975).

Internalism Versus Externalism

Internalism holds that the contents of the mind at any one point in time can be fully accounted for by a description of the state of the brain. A full description of the state of the brain eludes current technology, but it is noteworthy that an internalist account of mental content rules out any need for reference to the organism's environment in this description of mental content.

Thus, although philosophy will never be able to provide a full account of mental content (because it will not be the field that produces a full description of a brain state), an internalist philosopher will at least tell us where *not* to look for one. The environment contains stimuli that influence the organism, and the environment undergoes changes due to that organism's actions, but the environment is not part of that organism's mind (see Newell, 1990). According to internalism, the mind and the environment are separate.

Perhaps it should not be surprising that so many people accept internalism, at first glance, as a foregone conclusion. Lakoff (1987, 1997) provides a number of naturally occurring linguistic examples of people taking for granted the conceptual metaphor "the mind is a container." For example, people talk of "taking in" a movie or a book, being "full of ideas," or, sadly, being "empty-headed." If the mind is indeed a container, then it must have discrete boundaries delineating what is inside and what is outside, and in the case of the human mind, the skull seems to be the best box for the job.

However, it might surprise most cognitive psychologists that the majority of philosophers of mind are, in fact, not internalists but externalists. That's right. The contemporary version of the discipline that *invented* theorization about how the mind works—without which cognitive psychology would surely not exist—generally leans toward an account of mind that many cognitive psychologists have not even heard about. Although the internalist conception of mental states may initially seem intuitively obvious, such intuitions can be severely challenged by Putnam's (1975) Twin Earth thought experiment. Imagine that there's an alternative universe, and in this universe there's a terrestrial planet just like Earth, called Twin Earth. On this planet lives a man who is exactly like Gary from our Earth. We'll call him Twin Gary. In this thought experiment, imagine that Twin Gary interacts with a fluid he calls "water" in just the same way that Gary on Earth interacts with a fluid he calls "water," but the two fluids actually have very different chemical structures (H_2O on Earth, but XYZ on Twin Earth) and thus are fundamentally different things. So what happens when our Gary visits Twin Earth to go swimming with Twin Gary, and they exclaim in unison, "Gosh, I like swimming in this water?" If you feel as though their respective mental states are not quite identical, because Gary's mental state involves an incorrect reference to XYZ as though it were Earth water, then you are predicating a mental state on the truth value of a relationship that crosses the organism–environment barrier. That is, you are using aspects of the environment to define Gary's mental state, and therefore—like it or not—you're an externalist.

There are many criticisms of this thought experiment. For starters, given that Earth humans are comprised of at least 60% H_2O, and therefore Twin Earth humans would probably be comprised of at least 60% XYZ, Gary and Twin Gary can obviously not be perfect twins (Segal, 2000). But even disregarding that, it might not be too unintuitive to imagine that Gary's mental state is simply incorrect or delusional because it refers to XYZ as though it were H_2O. The fact that we can see Gary's mental state as incorrect is made possible by *our* reference to the environment, not *his*. Perhaps Gary's brain state, despite being delusional, is exactly the same as Twin Gary's brain state. In this case, if you prefer to think of a mental state as equivalent to a brain state, then Putnam's (1975) thought experiment has not succeeded in challenging your internalist perspective at all.

Like this discussion, much of the debate between externalism and internalism has employed variations on such Twin Earth thought experiments to test for a relatively static inclusion of the environment in determining the truth value of belief states (e.g., Fodor, 1980; Segal, 2000; Wilson, 1994). In contrast, a recent version of externalism that focuses rigorously on the immediate participatory role of the environment (in addition to brain and body, of course) in constructing mind has been called active externalism (Clark & Chalmers, 1998). This perspective marshals demonstrations from self-organized artificial intelligence (Beer, 1989; Brooks, 1991; Steels & Brooks, 1995), demonstrations from connectionism and dynamical systems theory (Thelen & Smith, 1994), observations of situated action (Greeno, 1998; Suchman, 1987), of collective action (Hutchins, 1995), and collective intelligence (Lévy, 1997), as well as a few thought experiments (Wilson, 1994), to argue for the importance of "cognitive properties of systems that are larger than an individual" (Hutchins, 1995; for review, see Clark, 2001; Wilson, 2002). Haugeland (1995) has dubbed it an "embodied and embedded" account of mind. Not only does the central nervous system's *embodiment* in a particular biological vehicle with particular sensors and effectors pose as a crucial expansion of the old-fashioned concept of mind-as-just-brain, but that brain–body dyad's *embedding* in a particular environment makes the whole system a richly interactive brain-body-environment triad.

Although the case for an embodied and embedded mind is compelling for some (e.g., McClamrock, 1995; Ross, 1997; see also Shaw & Turvey, 1999; Turvey & Shaw, 1999), with its robot implementations, computer simulations, natural observations, and thought experiments, the one thing this literature has been short on is controlled laboratory experimentation. Importantly, as some of the most devoted (and sometimes unwitting) customers of the mind-as-just-brain assumption, cognitive psychologists have found it easy to ignore this new embodied and embedded perspective precisely because it has lacked controlled experimental results. Therefore, a great deal of contemporary cognitive psychology has gone about its merry way assuming internalism, as though there were no alternative—completely unaware that some powerful challenges to this perspective do indeed exist.

The intuition that a complete description of mental activity will come solely from properties of the organism's central nervous system is so strong that it has successfully resisted quite a few attempts to dispel it. Not only has the internalist perspective survived the recent critiques of contemporary philosophers such as Putnam (1975), Haugeland (1995), Hurley (1998a), and Clark (2001), but decades ago it survived Dewey (1896), Le Bon (1916), Ryle (1949), Merleau-Ponty (1962), and Gibson (1966) as well, just to name a few.

Cognitive Psychology's Tacit Internalism

As one example manifestation of this internalist perspective in psychology, a popular framework for theories of visual perception, the spatiotopic fusion hypothesis critiqued by Irwin (1993), assumes that the successive retinal images that are acquired in between saccadic eye movements are metrically combined to construct and store an internal representation of the external visual world inside the brain (see Marr, 1982). This kind of approach is at the core of a representational theory of mind. An understanding of the external visual world is proposed not to emerge from the continuous dynamic inter-action of the organism with its environment (e.g., Gibson, 1979), but rather to be computed by static knowledge representations stored somewhere in the brain. This assumption of an "internal screen" (O'Regan, 1992) on which is projected an image of the external visual world for the perusal of some central executive has—despite its obvious homunculus problems—driven a great deal of research in visual psychophysics, visual neuroscience, visual cognition, as well as computer vision. Numerous theories have been constructed to account for the problem of how such noisy, illusion-prone, ballistic optical devices as the eyes can avail the construction of a contiguous metrically accu-rate internally represented 3D model of the visual environment (for a review, see O'Regan, 1992). O'Regan (1992) notes that over the years several researchers have proposed not to solve this problem but instead to dissolve it (e.g., Gibson, 1950; Haber, 1983; Turvey, 1977; see also Bridgeman, van der Heijden, & Velichkovsky, 1994; Bridgeman, 2002). If we do not have a contiguous met-rically accurate internally represented 3D model of the visual environment in our brains, then there is no need to figure out how our eyes and visual systems build one (and perhaps computer vision should stop trying things that way too; see Ballard, 1989; Churchland, Ramachandran, & Sejnowksi, 1994). O'Regan (1992) suggests that rather than visual perception being a passive process of accumulating retinal images from which to build an internal 3D model, "seeing constitutes an active process of probing the external environ-ment as though it were a continuously available external memory . . . if we so much as faintly ask ourselves some question about the environment, an answer is immediately provided by the sensory information on the retina, possibly rendered available by an eye movement" (p. 484). Not unlike the externalist philosophers, O'Regan and Noë (2001) claim that "activity in inter-nal representations does not generate the experience of seeing. The outside world serves as its own, external, representation" (p. 939).

If it is the case that relatively little of the external visual environment is actually internalized, then logically, unexpected changes in the visual environment should go unnoticed. For example, one should be able to change the color, location, and other properties as well—even the very presence—of large objects in a complex scene and have it frequently go unnoticed. This, however, clashes sharply with our intuition that we are continuously aware of the complete contents of the visual scene laid out before our eyes. This logical but counterintuitive prediction of

O'Regan's (1992) brand of visual externalism led directly to the recent cottage industry of change blindness research (for a review, see Simons, 2000).

Abrupt changes in a display will typically attract attention immediately if they take place during an uninterrupted eye fixation (e.g., Yantis & Jonides, 1990). However, it turns out that a range of minor ocular and attentional disturbances are sufficient to mask this ability. If the image flickers briefly during the scene change, participants rarely notice the change (Rensink, O'Regan, & Clark, 1997). If the scene is briefly overlaid by a few blobs, or "mud splashes," flashed on the screen during the change—without occluding the region that changes—participants rarely detect the change (O'Regan, Rensink, & Clark, 1999). If the scene change takes place during a saccade, it is likely to go unnoticed (Grimes, 1996; McConkie & Currie, 1996). And if the scene change takes place during a blink, it is rarely detected (O'Regan et al., 2000). In fact, even if the eyes were fixating within a degree of the object to be changed, right before the blink, when the eyelids open back up, and the object has changed, participants notice the change only 40% of the time (O'Regan et al., 2000).

This kind of phenomenon is not new, of course. In fact, decades ago *Highlights* magazine for kids had a game involving two line drawings of a cluttered scene in which there were subtle differences, and the goal was to find the differences between the two images. It was no simple task. Allow me to demonstrate. Figures 11.1 and 11.2 show two photographs of the same scene, slightly altered. (This scene was obviously *not* taken from an issue of *Highlights*.) Count how many looks back and forth it takes to find any differences.

As you eventually noticed, figure 11.2 has a wine bottle in place of figure 11.1's vermouth bottle. This is no trivial difference; you'd really know what I mean if you've ever run out of vermouth and tried to make a martini with wine instead. But it probably took you a little while to find it, didn't it? Can you find any other differences? As is the case with most change blindness effects, once you've noticed the difference, it seems so obvious that it's hard to imagine how you could have missed it for so long.

Change blindness also works in dynamic, real-world scenarios. For example, inspired by a gag from the old *Candid Camera* television show, Simons and Levin (1998) had a confederate accost passersby on the Cornell University campus and ask for directions on a map. Midway through the conversation, two young men carrying a door walked between the confederate and the passerby. The confederate and one of the door carriers exchanged places, and the door carrier took up the conversation as if nothing unusual had happened. Only about half the time did the passerby notice that the person he was talking to had changed!

The dramatic effects observed in change blindness experiments provide compelling support for an externalist claim that the locus of perception is as much in the environment itself as it is in the organism interacting with that environment (e.g., Noë, Pessoa, & Thompson, 2000). This is not to say that nothing about the environment is stored internally. As the reports show, semantically relevant scene changes are often detected more than 50% of the

Figure 11.1. A photograph of the fixings for a small martini party. As in the typical "change blindness" experiment, there are some subtle differences between this and figure 11.2 that may take a little while to detect. See how many you can find.

Figure 11.2. Note subtle differences between this photograph and photograph in figure 11.1.

time (e.g., Hollingworth & Henderson, 2002; Hollingworth, Williams, & Henderson, 2001). For example, when the location of an object changes the set of navigational affordances in a scene, such as suddenly adding an obstructing airplane on a pilot's runway, such a change is detected about 75% of the time (Haines, 1991). Moreover, implicit measures of perception, such as fixation duration, often reveal greater change detection than that seen with explicit verbal report (Hayhoe, 2000). Thus, certain attended aspects of the scene are stored in internal memory, and when those aspects are altered in the scene, the mismatch between internal and external representations is detected at least somewhere in the visual system. This point will become especially important in the later discussion of exactly how visual properties that are not stored internally can be accurately indexed and accessed from the external environment, via internally stored semantic tags for the index.

Thinking Outside the Brain

If the external environment is even just occasionally relied on as a source of visual memory, one can ask whether it is possible in those circumstances to purposefully take advantage of and optimize that external memory. In fact, Kirsh (1995; see also Kirsh & Maglio, 1994) cites numerous real-world examples of people doing exactly that. Kirsh (1995) makes the observation that we physically "jig" our environment with physical constraints that structure and optimize our interaction with it. For example, when moving into a new house, deciding what utensils, dishes, and pans to put in which kitchen drawers and cabinets is often done with imagined plans of when and where the various accoutrements will be needed during cooking and cleaning. When arranging one's office desk, the computer, the telephone, the stapler, the tape dispenser, in and out boxes, and so on are all placed in locations that the user expects will maximize their coordinated and sequential use. Similarly, a colleague of mine, who worries that he paces too much while lecturing, deliberately places chairs, overhead projectors, and so on, blocking the way of the most natural pacing routes. In fact, many Montessori (1917/1946) math-learning techniques exploit a child's early knowledge of spatial properties/constraints to jig their educational tools and implements in ways that scaffold and accelerate learning. These are all examples of physically jigging one's environment so that accessibility and restriction of various objects and actions is optimally timed for successful behavior and learning. This means that information is being built into the environment, and thus that information will not always need to be cognitively represented. In a way, a properly jigged work environment can be counted on to do some of the thinking for you.

Additionally, Kirsh (1995) notes that one way of informationally jigging an environment is to "seed" it with attention-getting cues. For example, to help you remember to bring a book to school, you might place the book next to the front door inside your house. Also, many people have specific wall hooks or dishes near the front door where they keep their keys. Thus, the knowledge that one's keys will be needed when leaving the house need not be an active component of the cognitive plan to go to the store because that knowledge is built into the environment to become perceptually salient at just the right time. In these kinds of circumstances, we've externalized (offloaded, if you will) information onto our environment, thereby freeing up internal processing capacity, and thus certain crucial bits of information that are necessary for complex behavior are provided not by neural-based memory representations but by the environment itself, on a need-to-know basis (see Scaife & Rogers, 1996). In fact, one might say, having an intelligent environment is just as important as having an intelligent brain.

Deictic Pointers in Space

In the next sections, I will outline several examples of the bidirectional interaction between the environment and cognition, examples of salient external information triggering internal processes, as well as internally generated information being linked back to external objects and locations. In fact, we humans have quite a penchant for externalizing our internal information. Of course, we communicate to others by linguistic means (speaking and writing) as well as nonlinguistic means (hand gestures, facial expressions, prosody, etc.). For example, during communication, people often gesture in ways that help depict an object being described (Streeck, 2002), locate referents in a discourse space (McNeill, 2005), or even assist in the conceptualization of complex explanations (Alibali, Kita, & Young, 2000).

But we also find ways to externalize our internal information in noncommunicative situations. We recite phone numbers out loud to ourselves so that the environment can deliver the information to our ears, doubling the phonological loop. We make lists of things to do and of groceries to buy. Some of us talk to ourselves. Some of us even write on our hands. We write down appointments on calendars. We occasionally point a finger at an object when we're silently reminding ourselves to do something with it. And sometimes when we imagine things, our eyes virtually paint our imagery on the world.

In a headband-mounted eye tracking experiment, Spivey and Geng (2001, experiment 1; see also Spivey et al., 2000) recorded participants' eye movements while they listened to spoken descriptions of spatiotemporally dynamic scenes and faced a large white projection screen that took up most of their visual field. For example, "Imagine that you are standing across the street from a 40-story apartment building. At the bottom there is a doorman in blue. *On the 10th floor, a woman is hanging her laundry out the window. On the 29th floor, two kids are sitting on the fire escape smoking cigarettes. On the very top floor, two people are screaming.*" While listening to the italicized portion of this passage, participants made reliably more upward saccades than in any other direction. Corresponding biases in spontaneous saccade directions were also observed for a downward story, as well as for leftward and rightward stories. Thus, while looking at ostensibly nothing, listeners' eyes were doing something similar to what they would have done if the scene being described were actually right there before them. Instead of relying solely on an internal "visuospatial sketchpad" (Baddeley, 1986) on which to illustrate their mental model of the scene being described, participants also recruited the external environment as an additional canvas on which to depict the spatial layout of the imagined scene.

Although eye movements may not be required for vivid imagery (Hale & Simpson, 1970; but see Ruggieri, 1999), it does appear that they often naturally accompany it (e.g., Antrobus, Antrobus, & Singer, 1964; Brandt & Stark, 1997; Demarais & Cohen, 1998; Neisser, 1967; see also Hebb, 1968). But what is it that the eyes are trying to do in these circumstances? Obviously, it is not the case that the eyes themselves can actually externally record this internal information. When the eyes move upward from the imagined 10th floor of the apartment building to the imagined 29th floor, no physical mark is left behind on the external location in the environment that was proxying for that 10th floor.

Rather than a physical mark, perhaps what they "leave behind" is a deictic pointer, or spatial index. According to Ballard and colleagues (1997; see also Agre & Chapman, 1987; Pylyshyn, 1989, 2001), deictic pointers can be used in visuomotor routines to conserve the use of working memory. Instead of storing all the detailed properties of an object internally, one can simply store an address, or pointer, for the object's location in the environment—perhaps via a pattern of activation on an attentional/oculomotor salience map in parietal cortex (e.g., Duhamel, Colby, & Goldberg, 1992), along with a spatial memory salience map in prefrontal cortex (e.g., Chafee & Goldman-Rakic, 1998, 2000; Goldman-Rakic, 1993). If this spatial pointer is associated with some kind of coarse semantic information, for example, a pattern of activation in one of the language cortices, auditory cortex, or even visual cortex, then the spatial pointer can be triggered when sensory input activates that semantic information. Such pointers allow the organism to perceptually access relevant properties of the external world when they are needed (rather than storing them all in memory).

In the case of Spivey & Geng's (2001) eye movements during imagery, a few pointers allocated on a blank projection screen will obviously not reference any external visual properties, but they can still provide perceptual-motor information about the relative spatial locations of the *internal* content associated with the pointers. If one is initially thinking about *x* (e.g., the 10th floor) and then transitions to thinking about *y* (e.g., the 29th floor), then storing in working memory the relation *above* (*y, x*) may not be necessary if the eye movements, and their allocation of spatial indices, have embodied that spatial relationship already (see Pylyshyn, 1989). In this way, a low-level motor process, such as eye movements, can actually do some of the work involved in the high-level cognitive act of visual imagery.

Although it is the address in the pointer that allows one to rely on the external environment to store information, the *semantic tags* for the pointer are also a very important ingredient in this recipe. The internally represented semantic tags that accompany a spatial pointer could be something as simple as a sound that is associated with a visual object that frequents a particular location in space. It could be the experimenter-induced task-relevant designation of *target.* It could be rich information such as "the doorman in blue at the bottom of the 40-story apartment building." Or it could be a reminder of what to do with the objects in the pointer's location: "Pick up these car keys as you leave the house because it will make starting the car much easier." A pointer/reminder must have some internal content attached to it indicating what it's for, so that one can know when and how to use it (e.g., Chun & Nakayama, 2000; Guynn, McDaniel, & Einstein, 1998). Otherwise, you wind up like Ernie on *Sesame Street* trying to explain to Bert why he has a string tied around his finger when he can't remember what it was that the string was supposed to remind him about. A pointer with no internal information attached to it is useless.

Deictic Pointers to Objects

To illustrate the use of such spatial indices in visual attention, Pylyshyn introduced a multiple object tracking task (e.g., Pylyshyn & Storm, 1988; Scholl & Pylyshyn, 1999). In this task, participants view an initial display of indistinguishable discs or squares of which a subset flash several times to indicate that they are the targets. Then all the objects begin to move in pseudo-random directions across the screen, and the participant's task is to keep track of the handful of target discs while maintaining central fixation. Participants can successfully track up to about four or five such targets, but if there are more than that, they begin to make errors. As participants must maintain central fixation throughout this task, these spatial indices are clearly being allocated and updated extrafoveally.

In another experimental paradigm that demonstrates the use of spatial indices in natural visuomotor processing, Ballard, Hayhoe, and Pelz (1995) recorded participants' eye movements during a block-pattern copying task, with a model pattern, a resource of blocks, and a workspace in which to copy the model. In this kind of framework, eye position serves the function of allocating spatial pointers for working memory, in which a pointer stores an *address* in spatial coordinates along with little more than a few *semantic tags* for when and why to use the pointer. For example, a pointer's address might be something like "the block just to the right of the top-leftmost block in the model," and its semantic tag might be "the block I am working on now." Thus, if the participant has just finished placing the previous block in the incomplete block pattern in the workspace, then this pointer can guide the eyes to this new block in the model block pattern to access and store its color. With the color of this block now stored internally, the eyes can then move to the resource space, containing many blocks of various colors, and search for a block of the same color. Once that new block is picked up, to put it in the appropriate location in the workspace, one needs to know its position relative to the other blocks in the incomplete block pattern. As the pointer's address itself may make reference to blocks that have not yet been placed in the workspace, the eyes must once again call up this pointer allocated to "the block just to the right of the top-leftmost block in the model" and perceptually access its spatial relationships with the adjacent blocks. With this new information stored in working memory, the eyes can move down to the workspace for placement of the new block. The pointer with the tag "the block I am working on now" must then relinquish its current address and find a new one elsewhere on the model block pattern and begin the process all over again. This sequence of fixating the model, then the resource, then back to the model, before finally looking at the workspace for block placement was indeed the modal pattern of eye movements observed in Ballard et al.'s (1995) experiments.

But what happens if the external information referred to by these spatial indices changes? According to the framework, one should expect the person copying the block pattern not to notice when a block changes color, except under those circumstances in which the process is at a stage where the visual property that's been changed is the one currently being stored in working memory. This is, indeed, exactly what happens (Hayhoe, 2000; Hayhoe, Bensinger, & Ballard, 1998). If a few deictic pointers have been allocated to particular objects or regions of space, and the current task activates a semantic tag belonging to one of those pointers, the system will automatically seek the address associated with that pointer—fixate the indexed object or location—and perceptually access the external information at that address. If neither the pointer's tags nor working memory contain information that conflict with this externally accessed information, then naturally any change that took place in that external information will go undetected. The newly accessed visual properties will be trusted as if they had been that way all along.

Deictic Pointers to Absent Objects

Interestingly, accessing a pointer when its semantic information is activated is so automatic that it can even happen when the object to which it was originally allocated is no longer present at all. In Spivey and Geng's (2001) second experiment, they presented four different shapes of varying colors, tilted 15 degrees leftward or rightward, in the four quadrants of the screen. Participants were instructed to look at the object in each quadrant and then back to a central fixation cross. One of the four shapes then disappeared and participants were asked to recall either its color or its direction of tilt. On as many as 50% of the trials, as they formulated their answer, participants spontaneously fixated the empty quadrant that used to contain the shape being queried—despite the fact that they could easily determine in peripheral vision that the object was no longer there. Participants rarely looked at the other remaining shapes. This is exactly what one should expect if observers are employing pointers to rely on the external world to store object properties in addition to what is stored in the pointers' semantic tags themselves and in working memory. The task calls on the shape's name (e.g., diamond), which activates the pointer with that tag, and queries a property of that shape (e.g., color). If the pointer's tag does not include the attribute (e.g., green), then the pointer's address to the external environment is the next obvious resource. A relatively automatic eye movement to that address verifies that the queried information is absent from the external environment. At this point, internal working memory is the only resort. On the trials where participants fixated the empty quadrant, as well as on the trials where they did not fixate it, the same information resource, internal working memory, is used to answer the question. Thus, one should actually *not* expect a difference in memory accuracy between trials in which the empty quadrant was fixated and those in which it was not. And that is, indeed, what Spivey and Geng (2001, experiment 2) found.

Spivey and Geng (2001) concluded that because there is no improvement of memory, the eye movement to the empty quadrant does not appear to be an attempt to recruit visual surroundings to encourage a context-dependent improvement of memory. Nor is it a deliberate, strategic, attempt to answer the question by looking at the queried object because participants can easily tell from peripheral vision, as well as from previous trials, that the object is not there. Rather, the eye movement to the empty quadrant is an automatic attempt by an embodied working memory system to access the contents of a pointer's address in the external environment. Just as in the change blindness studies, this embodied working memory system does not know that the content in that external location has been removed until it accesses the pointer with that address. Although it is possible to attend to and access these pointers without eye movements when the task instructions require it (Pylyshyn & Storm, 1988), a wide range of research indicates that eye movements naturally follow such allocations of attention (e.g., Ballard et al., 1997; Corbetta & Shulman, 1999; Henderson, 1993; Hoffman, 1998; Tanenhaus et al., 1995).

Welcome to Hollywood Squares

Perhaps it is not surprising that an embodied working memory system, relying on pointers that reference visual objects, elicits eye movements to the addresses of those pointers when the system is trying to access memory of visual properties. But what about when the content associated with that pointer is not visual but auditory? In a series of experiments referred to as Hollywood Squares because the task somewhat resembles the television game show, Richardson and Spivey (2000) presented four talking heads in sequence, in the four quadrants of the screen, each reciting an arbitrary fact and then disappearing (e.g., "Shakespeare's first plays were historical dramas. His last play was *The Tempest*."). With the display completely blank except for the lines delineating the four empty quadrants, a voice from the computer delivered a statement concerning one of the four recited facts, and participants were instructed to verify the statement as true or false (e.g., "Shakespeare's first play was *The Tempest*.").

While formulating their answer, participants were twice as likely to fixate the quadrant that previously contained the talking head that had recited the relevant fact than any other quadrant. Despite the fact that the queried information was delivered auditorily, and therefore cannot possibly be visually accessed via a fixation, something about that location drew eye movements during recall. Richardson and Spivey (2000) suggested that spatial indices had been allocated to the four quadrants to aid in sorting and separating the events that took place in them. Thus, when a semantic tag of one of those pointers was called on (e.g., Shakespeare), attempts to access the relevant information were made both from the pointer's address in the external environment and from internal working memory. As before with Spivey and Geng's (2001) findings, because the external environment no longer contained the queried information, internal working memory was the sole determinant of memory accuracy. Therefore, verification accuracy was the same on trials that did have fixations of the queried quadrant as on trials that did not.

Richardson and Spivey (2000, experiment 2) replicated these results using four identical spinning crosses in the quadrants during delivery of the facts, instead of the talking heads. Participants seemed perfectly happy to allocate pointers to the four facts in those four locations, even when spatial location was the only visual property that distinguished the pointers. Moreover, in the tracking condition (Richardson & Spivey, 2000, experiment 5), participants viewed the grid through a virtual window in the center of the screen. Behind this mask, the grid moved, bringing a quadrant to the center of the screen for fact presentation. Then, during the question phase, the mask was removed. Even in this case, when the spinning crosses had all been viewed in the center of the computer screen, and the relative locations of the quadrants implied by translation, participants continued to treat the quadrant associated with the queried fact as conspicuously worthy of overt attention. In fact, even if the crosses appear in empty squares that move around the screen following fact delivery, participants spontaneously fixate the square associated with the fact being verified (Richardson & Kirkham, 2004, experiment 1). Thus, once applied, a deictic pointer—even one that attempts to index auditorily delivered semantic information—can dynamically follow the moving object to which it was allocated (e.g., Scholl & Pylyshyn, 1999; see also Tipper & Behrmann, 1996).

It actually should not be surprising that an embodied working memory system using deictic pointers would attempt to index information from events that are over and done with. The pointer doesn't know that the sought-after information at its address is long gone precisely because it has offloaded that knowledge onto the environment—it wouldn't be a pointer otherwise. These findings demonstrate the robustness and automaticity with which spatial indices are relied on to employ the body's environment as a sort of notice board of virtual sticky notes that complement our internal memory.

Cross-Cutting the Internal and External

Spatial indices that connect internal neural patterns to external environmental patterns appear to be employed not just in low- and mid-level perception, such as perceptual-motor routines (Hayhoe, 2000) visual working memory (Ballard et al., 1995) and visual imagery (Spivey & Geng, 2001) but also in higher level cognition, such as reading (see Kennedy, 1992; Weger, 2005), spatial memory for semantic information (Richardson & Spivey, 2000), and even problem solving (Grant & Spivey, 2003; see chapter 10). Based on these findings, I suggest that the objects of thought, the very things on which mental processes directly operate, are not always inside the brain (e.g., Hutchins, 1995; O'Regan & Noë, 2001; see also Dretske, 1997). The cognitive processing that gives rise to mental experience may be something whose functioning cuts across the superficial physical boundaries between brain, body, and environment.

And those boundaries are, indeed, superficial. Even trying to localize them can quickly turn into an arbitrary decision process, fraught with subjective bias. Take, for example, a continuous environmental sound that travels into the ear and produces the mental experience of audition. The sound waves outside of the auditory canal seem naturally definable as external to the body and brain, but what about the same vibrations in pressure inside the auditory canal? Then, those vibrations in air pressure mechanically exert a deterministic causal influence on the vibration of the tympanic membrane. Is that where we cross the boundary from phenomena that belong to the external environment to phenomena that belong to the internal mental activity of the organism? The tympanic membrane, hammer, anvil, and stirrup then amplify the vibration through the liquid media in the cochlea, displacing the hair cells there. Have we crossed the boundary into internal mental phenomena now? Next, the hair cells transduce their mechanical deformation into electrochemical signals. Is this where the physical suddenly and discretely becomes mental? Admittedly, sensory transduction is very impressive, but it is well understood as a systematic biophysical and biochemical process, certainly not mysterious or magical. Suddenly adding electrically charged chemicals to a process does not, on the face it, straightforwardly add mental experience to it. Besides, we are certainly not introspectively aware of the early sensory patterns of sound representation at the level of the hair cells, and indeed many scientists would argue that the mental experience of audition takes place at much later cortical stages of the auditory system. Clearly, when following a substantially deterministic causal chain of events that appears to transition from external to internal, localizing the discrete point at which external physical events belonging to the environment become internal mental events belonging to the organism or to the mind is extremely difficult, if not impossible.

Perhaps one can say that the brain is more or less separable from the environment if one ignores very real problems with exactly where to draw even that separation (see Jarvilehto, 1998). However, according to externalism, one cannot say that the *mind* is separable from its environment. For example, when the environment is removed, under sensory deprivation, the coherence of mind clearly begins to dissolve. Thought becomes disorganized, imperfect perceptual simulations of an environment result in bizarre hallucinations, and eventually delusions take over (Hebb, 1961; Lilly, 1956; Robertson, 1961). Similarly, during REM sleep, the brain constructs less than perfect perceptual simulations that take the place of genuine sensory input, and most people can remember doing things and making decisions in nonlucid dreams that they would never intentionally do or make in real life. The dream mind, with its altered simulated environment, is thus an altered mind. There can be no such thing as a *core* mind that exists independently of the organism's environment, because that fraction of mind that is contributed by the central nervous system does not on its own resemble what we mean when we say "mind." The brain is like an ingredient in a baking recipe, whose contribution—though essential to the result—involves such a complex chemical transformation with the other ingredients that its original individual properties are almost unrecognizable in the end product. An individual's personal (seemingly internally generated) sense of *intention* actually self-organizes across multiple coupled time scales from a combination of evolutionary, biological, cultural, parental, and social constraints (e.g., Gibbs, 1999; Juarerro, 1999; Van Orden & Holden, 2002), not the least of which is—for evidence admissible to the court of cognitive psychology, anyway—experimenter instructions.

In this view, mind becomes something not completely dependent on the body, although certainly not completely independent of it either. Rather, mind appears to be an emergent property that arises among the interactions of a brain, its body, and the surrounding environment—which, interestingly, often includes other brains and bodies. Multiple brains, bodies, and environmental properties will often interact and function in a manner that most decidedly *does* resemble what we mean when we say "mind," as seen in collaborative task performance, mimicry, and other examples of social embodiment and embeddedness (e.g., Barsalou et al., 2004; Hutchins, 1995; Knoblich & Jordan, 2003; Schmidt, Carello, & Turvey, 1990; Sebanz, Knoblich, & Prinz, 2003; Spurrett, 2003; Stary & Stumptner, 1992).

What Does Such a Mind Look Like?

But what does such a nonbrain-based mind look like? The mind, to an externalist, must be a rather graded entity, like a fuzzy set (Zadeh, 1965). In fuzzy set theory, the inclusion of members in a set is graded rather than all or none. A fuzzy set is often depicted as something like a probability distribution, with a mode and tails that gradually approach zero (see chapter 6). Fuzzy set theory is useful to an externalist because determining the discrete boundary in the external environment where things suddenly go from being part of the mind to being not part of the mind is arguably impossible. Instead, one can hypothesize graded membership of external objects and events to the set of *mental contents*, gradually falling off with greater distance and with more mediated causes (see Clark & Chalmers, 1998).

According to this version of externalism, the fuzzy set for your mental contents would include your brain, your body, as well as objects in the environment, and partially overlapping—at multiple spatial scales—with other mindlike fuzzy sets. Figure 11.3 presents an idealized sketch of this fuzzy set. The small oval in the middle of the diagram represents the classical set of your brain contents. Things inside that Venn diagram are part of your brain. Things outside it are not. The circumscribing oval represents the classical set of your body contents. Things inside that Venn diagram are part of your body. Things outside it are not. The fuzzy set of mental contents subsumes these two sets, and extends somewhat beyond them in x- and y-space. The third dimension of height in the diagram indicates degree of membership.

Importantly, the fuzzy set of mental contents includes to varying degrees not just physical material in the present (such as a brain, a body, and other objects in the immediate environment) but also causal forces in that fuzzy set's history. As one traces back the causal forces of the environment's role in determining the set of mental contents, one must include—with some nonzero degree of membership—social influences accrued over days, parental

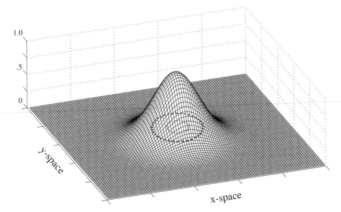

Figure 11.3. Along two spatial dimensions (x and y) the classical set of body contents (larger circle) circumscribes the classical set of brain contents (smaller circle). However, according to externalism, the fuzzy set of mental contents subsumes them both, as well as some of the properties of the surrounding environment, with a distribution function indicating degree of set membership (z-axis). Nonspatial dimensions that are likely to be relevant, such as semantic features and causal forces, are not depicted.

influences accrued over decades, cultural influences accrued over centuries, and evolutionary influences accrued over many millennia.

Thus, the temporal dynamics of these fuzzy minds/sets become crucial for their accurate description—especially when one considers what happens as one fuzzy mind/set interacts with others over time. Figure 11.4A presents a schematic depiction of three bodies (and brains), like the one in figure 11.3, moving in space as a function of time. Only one spatial dimension is shown so that the second dimension, time, can be easily graphed. In figure 11.4A, two

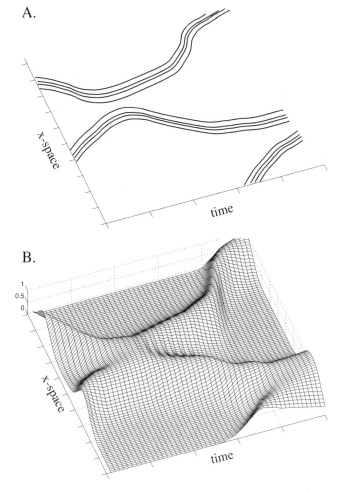

Figure 11.4. Using only one of the spatial dimensions from figure 11.3, and adding a temporal dimension, panel A presents spatial trajectories of three bodies interacting over time. In panel B, the probabilistic distributions intended to characterize the minds of those bodies do more than interact, they merge into one another at times.

bodies travel near one another for a period of time, then they diverge, and one of them begins traveling near a different body. Because time is fractal, or self-similar, in this framework, the scale of the temporal dimension for these interactions could be just about anything. The bodies could be interacting over the course of minutes (going from one hallway conversation to another), over the course of hours (going from one meeting to another), over the course of weeks or years or decades (going from one friendship/relationship to another).

For a fuzzy externalist, the depiction of these trajectories looks importantly different when they are defined over how the minds interact instead of how the bodies interact. Note in figure 11.4B how the fuzzy set distributions merge as they approach each other. When two bodies are particularly close in space (and presumably close in other nondepicted semantic dimensions), the envelope of their distributions approaches having one mode instead of two. This demonstration offers a portrayal of how multiple different brains can cohere to such a degree that they function, at least to some extent, as though they were one mind: a "shared manifold of intersubjectivity" (Gallese, 2003; see also Sonnenwald & Pierce's, 2000, interwoven situational awareness). The findings described in this chapter suggest that many of the interfacing links that maintain this shared manifold are the spatial indices that connect bundles of information in one brain to bundles of information in other brains via bundles of information in the environment.

Ramifications and Speculations

With this considerable dependence on external information for its function, the mind is perhaps best measured by its capabilities rather than its capacities—by its processing, not its putative representations (see Jones & Smith, 1993; see also Pirolli & Card, 1999). To borrow a common adage, a mind should be judged by what it does, not by what it has. Crucially, the mind's capabilities and processing are inextricably linked to the organism's continuous and dynamic interaction with the environment. According to active externalism, it is that very interaction between organism and environment from which "mind" emerges.

A wide adoption of this externalist concept of mind would have profound and far-reaching consequences for society. Much more than just reshaping the theories and experimental methods of cognitive psychology and cognitive science, externalism legitimates the concepts of distributed cognition (Hinsz, Tindale, & Vollrath, 1997; Jonasse, 1995; Nowak, Vallacher, & Burnstein, 1998), transactive memory systems (Wegner, 1995; Weldon, 2001), intersubjectivity manifolds (Gallese, 2003), and the collective mind (Yoo & Kanawattanachai, 2001). Moreover, externalism promises new and different applied understandings of social behavior, group decision making, and even personal relationships (e.g., Hutchins, 1995; Larson et al., 1998; Pedersen & Larsen, 2001). For example, when you spend time with a group from a different demographic background, you don't just wind up *acting* like someone else, you *are* someone else. For a couple to "be one" becomes more than a pleasing metaphor, it becomes a scientifically viable statement of fact (see Hollingshead, 1998; Wegner, Erber, & Raymond, 1991). Externalism also has implications for treatments of culture, explaining how a tradition or fashion or sociological pattern might literally "have a mind of its own" (Cole & Engeström, 1997). Indeed, a serious reexamination of the concept of individual responsibility instigated by externalism would shake the very foundations of Western legal theory, shifting much of the focus of reform from individual criminals to the criminogenic conditions that create them (Haney, 2002).

Finally, and most important of all, a sincere espousing of externalism radically alters one's phenomenological sense of self. For example, all of the previous chapters in this book have tended to encourage the reader to think like a dynamical connectionist and conceive of the brain as an interactive dynamical system that enacts mind. While you are replacing your computer metaphor of the mind with a dynamical systems account of the mind, you might be tempted to imagine your mind as a kind of floating ball that moves around in the high-dimensional neural state space of the brain. What you have to be careful about, however, is conceiving of your self as the equivalent of a little homunculus sitting on that ball going along for the ride. You are not a little homunculus. You are not even the ball. *You are the trajectory.*

As the primary message of this entire book, I think this is an important realization that focuses emphasis on the continuous past, present, and (anticipated) future of the dynamical mind. The mind is not a container of knowledge objects. It is not that static. The mind is a process composed of many interactive subprocesses. The trajectory that the state of the brain travels, in its neural state space, is continuous in both space and time. In this treatment of mind, there are no discretely delineated periods of time or regions of state space in which a symbolic unchanging representation could reside.

However, the radical amendment proposed by the present chapter is that this "trajectory through neural state space" account of the mind is still incomplete. If you widen your scope just enough to examine that neural dynamical system as embedded inside a larger dynamical system comprising the environment and other organisms, then the self is no longer conceived of as an ivory tower in the skull and can be understood as an amalgam of interweaving influences from both internal and external sources. That is, the dimensions that define your mental trajectory are not only neural firing rates but also biomechanical variables that constrain how your body interfaces with the environment, as well as information-bearing properties of that environment itself. This larger dynamical system describes the range of trajectories exhibited by that brain-*cum*-environment process. And the prevailing argument throughout this chapter has been that the embedding of that neural dynamical subsystem inside the larger environmental dynamical system prevents them from being categorically separable. Given that, now ask yourself the following question: Even in this larger nondecomposable dynamical system comprising organism and environment, is it still the case that "*I* am the trajectory?" Perhaps the answer to that question, somehow, is "yes."

> *Well, maybe it's like Casy says. A fella ain't got a soul of his own, just a little piece of a big soul—the one big soul that belongs to everybody. . . . I'll be everywhere—wherever you can look. Wherever there's a fight so hungry people can eat, I'll be there. Wherever there's a cop beatin' up a guy, I'll be there. I'll be in the way guys yell when they're mad. I'll be in the way kids laugh when they're hungry and they know supper's ready. And when the people are eating the stuff they raise, and living in the houses they build—I'll be there too.*
>
> —Henry Fonda (*as Tom Joad in* Grapes of Wrath)

12

Dynamical (Self-)Consciousness?

Perhaps the immobility of the things around us is forced upon
them by our conviction that they are themselves and not anything
else, and by the immobility of our convictions.
—Marcel Proust

See this? This is *this*. This ain't something else. *This* is *this*.
—Robert DeNiro

Mindful of Continuity

In the movie *The Deer Hunter*, Robert DeNiro's character was trying to convey
to one of his more careless hunting partners that the world is not fuzzy, blurry,
and full of slippery gray areas that tolerate slop and error; that the world can
indeed be carved into discrete, rigid, nonoverlapping categories that do not
suffer fools. The immobility of his conviction is palpable when he delivers this
cryptic statement in reference to a bullet held between his thumb and index
finger. Intuitively, it seems that such a formal logical world would be safe, predictable, and definable. Every communication between conversants would be
flawless. Every perception would be perfectly repeatable from observation to
observation, as well as from observer to observer. And every scientific description could be based in discrete Boolean logic.

Unfortunately, such a world would also be dangerously inflexible, not to
mention downright boring. We know that we do not live in such a world precisely because communications always lose some information during transfer
(from a sender to a receiver), perceptions are never perfectly repeatable, and a
number of sciences have already been forced to employ complex dynamical
and/or probabilistic mathematical descriptive formats. The physical world in
which we live has an ontological graded continuity stretching across the vast
majority of epistemological categories that one wishes to impose on it.
Perhaps the most important thing to acknowledge with regard to our relationship with this continuous world is that our minds are not separate from it. Just
as a key understanding in contemporary physics is that a physical phenomenon is not independent of the observational process that records it, a crucial

understanding in psychology must be that our own observational processes are not independent of the physical phenomena that we observe. For example, when we watch a bride and groom dance, it is not the case that the dancers produce an event that plays out exactly the same way regardless of whether they are being watched. The observers clearly influence that physical process. And of course, the visual and auditory patterns of the dance clearly influence the observers' brains. Thus, a cyclic interplay ensues between the observers and the observed that changes *both* parties. They become one system instead of two. When we (seemingly passively) perceive the "outside world," we unavoidably interact with that world, whether we want to or not. As a result, our perceptual process becomes part of that world, not just part of our brains (see O'Regan & Nöe, 2001).

Importantly, this spatial continuity between mind and environment is accompanied by a temporal continuity between one perception and the next, between one thought and the next. When you introspect about how your mind works, what you *think* you're thinking is just the tip of the iceberg. Or perhaps more fitting with a continuity approach to psychology, what you think you're thinking is a lot like the collinear but unconnected exposed stitches on the outside of a hand-sewn hem: each stitch looks like a separate individual unit, but of course they are actually just the visible portions of one continuous thread. For example, when you are reading this sentence, it might feel like you are experiencing one thought, or concept, and then another and then another. Not so. According to the continuity of mind thesis, that introspective impression of one discrete mental state after another is an illusion caused largely by the discreteness of the semantic labels we use in our internal monologue and by the discreteness of some of our goal-directed motor output. Our actions on the world around us and our unspoken narration to ourselves sometimes appear to be composed of separable units, particularly as we automatically apply linguistic labels to certain regions of mental state space. However, the mental activity that produces those actions and self-narration is not composed of separable units. This mental activity is one continuous trajectory through a state space containing graded attractor basins that often correspond to the apparent units, but this trajectory rarely dwells near any one attractor for long, and indeed spends most of its time in transit, in between labeled regions. Thus, although you might feel as though you think p and then q and then r, what you're actually thinking during that period is *mostly p and partly q*, then *partly p, partly q*, and perhaps *a bit of m and x*, then *mostly q and partly r*, and so on. This temporal contiguity in thought has profound implications not just for the cognitive sciences but for everyday life as well.

The genuine continuousness of thought—in the face of apparent intermittent pieces of thoughts, and in direct opposition to the symbol-processing mind-as-computer metaphor—has been the leitmotif running throughout this book. Together, we have explored this temporal continuity in several popular cottage industries in cognitive psychology, including categorization, language, vision, action, and even reasoning. Now, here we are discussing introspection.

Yes, that is correct. Indeed, here do I stand before you, compelled, for better or worse, to end with what has become the obligatory chapter on consciousness for books like this. I suppose, after all, the continuity of mind thesis may have some interesting consequences for the notion of consciousness, for those who care about such things. Note, however, that nothing in the preceding chapters hinges on the speculations that I will propound in this chapter. If you find my musings on consciousness objectionable, feel free to pay them very little attention. That's what I do. The strengths of this final chapter are not in its philosophical rigor, but in its casual approach to getting the reader to think about what the continuity of mind has to say about your everyday mental life—and it has some nifty illustrations, too.

I have no intention of slogging through a comprehensive literature review of how philosophers and psychologists have debated over the notion of consciousness. There are entire books where one can find scholastically responsible treatments like that, such as Blackmore (2003), Dietrich and Hardcastle (2005), Gray (2004), Kim (1998), Koch (2004), and Polger (2004), among many others. Perhaps more constructively, this chapter can be treated as a guide to thinking about ways the continuity of mind has implications for our everyday thoughts and experiences—irrespective of whatever consciousness truly is. As an Internet blogger who covered my research recently put it, "Even if this new study is right, what will it change for us? Will you wake up different tomorrow morning?" Parts of this chapter just might convince you that you will. I know I did.

Laying Siege to the Ivory Tower of Consciousness

The first potential implication—and a rather controversial one—that the continuity of mind might have for consciousness is that it may actually be irrelevant, unnecessary, or even nonexistent. If the entire perception-action loop (including linguistic reports of conscious experience) can be re-created, in principle, with a deterministic attractor landscape exhibiting complex dynamics, then what exactly would a notion of consciousness add to that explanation? Let's take a concrete experimental example. When Kolers and Brewster (1985) had participants tap their fingers to visual and auditory rhythms, and they subtly shifted the phase of those rhythms, participants' tapping often smoothly accommodated the phase shift without the participants reporting that they were aware of the phase shift. Thus, a dynamical account of a person's entrainment with the environment gives a more accurate account of their perceptual-motor functioning than their verbal protocol does. It is interesting, no doubt, that their conscious report did something different than their actual behavior. But in understanding how humans process perceptual input and produce motor output, that is, the key observables we scientists have at our disposal, the inaccurate subjective report is perhaps little more than a curiosity. As cognitive scientists, we should be more focused on what people are *actually* doing than on what they *think* they're doing. Put another way, if conscious awareness is unnecessary for the maintenance of dynamically entrained performance of an organism coping in its environment, is it really necessary as a topic of scientific study?

Part of an answer to that question may be reached by picking apart some definitions of consciousness. Clearly bucking the philosophical tradition of inventing new and abstruse terminology in the treatment of consciousness, Chalmers (1996) carved up the issue into the "easy problems" of consciousness and the "hard problem" of consciousness. According to Chalmers, the easy problems include things like language processing, visual perception, memory, and especially introspection, or "self-consciousness." By neophytes and laypersons, self-consciousness is routinely mistaken for what consciousness is supposed to refer to. Thinking about the thoughts you just had, self-consciousness, belongs to Chalmers's easy problems because it can more or less be implemented simply by looping the language subsystem back onto itself (or perhaps some form of nonlinguistic self-evaluative subsystem; see Bermudez, 1998). Self-consciousness is not the hard problem that consciousness is, because consciousness refers to the instantaneous (not rehashed) awareness that we supposedly experience *before* we can tell ourselves what it felt like. This "zeroth-order consciousness," if you will, is like a diving catch made in an untelevised college football game. The radio announcer, the referees, the coaches, and even the players involved will all have their own personal reports about whether the ball hit the ground before or after the receiver had control of it. Those reports are like the secondhand interpretations that self-consciousness constructs after a conscious event has taken place. But the event itself, the catching of the ball (perhaps with, perhaps without, the help of the turf), is gone forever. It cannot be reanalyzed or replicated in its original form. We will never know what *really* happened.

Yet Chalmers (1996) is rather optimistic about the science of consciousness eventually knowing what happens during pure zeroth-order consciousness, or perhaps even discovering the fundamental physical element that imbues people with consciousness, and adding it to the periodic table. This position smacks wet with the flavor of early vitalists, who argued that living plants and animals possessed life because they contained some as yet unidentified molecule that instilled them with the capacity for self-replication. (And we all know what happened to that theory.) However, more problematic than a half-hearted speculation about the presence/absence of a fundamental physical element for consciousness, Chalmers's definition of pure consciousness may actually define it right out of scientific measurability. It is this definition with which my point most directly takes issue.[1]

The hard problem of consciousness rests on a personal phenomenology that cannot be intersubjectively observed. That is, by the time a team of laboratory researchers have collected data that may speak to the conscious experience of an experimental participant, that measurement will have been contaminated by the participants' *self*-consciousness. Even just answering the experimenter's question about whether you were consciously aware of a recent percept or an action requires a self-conscious introspection that can significantly alter the answer to such a question.[2] But wait, it gets worse. Conscious experience, in its pure form, is not only *inter*subjectively unobservable, it is *subjectively* unobservable. By the time an individual can mentally record for herself what her conscious experience was like, she's already slipped into the process of self-consciousness. This mental recording process involves memory and interpretive introspection, trying its best to preserve the purity of the original data, but contamination is unavoidable every time. Once you try to give some type of report of your immediate conscious experience, even just to yourself, your use of discrete linguistic labels inevitably misrepresents the original sense. Thus, the very data that the hard problem claims exist and must be accounted for scientifically—a set of zeroth-order, uncontaminated, conscious impressions—by definition cannot be made available to scientific inquiry. Perhaps instead of the hard problem of consciousness, Chalmers should have called it the impossible problem of consciousness. Now, if the hard problem of consciousness defines itself out of feasibility, then all that remains are the easy problems of consciousness. And, believe me, those easy problems are quite hard enough, thank you very much.

One of those easy problems, working memory, is a process that so ineluctably mediates our sense of consciousness that some researchers have essentially equated consciousness with the way working memory allows you to "hold things in your mind" (Courtney et al., 1998). For example, the only time that I ever feel as though I may have a sense of consciousness—and I suspect this is true for other people as well—is when I stop what I'm thinking and self-reflect on what I was thinking a second ago, and on who or what was doing that thinking. Thus, my only evidence that I may have a consciousness is filtered through memory. My only accessible record of consciousness seems to be composed of a continuous monologue made up of incomplete sentences that are filled in by some form of visual/auditory/motor imagery. If that's all there is to consciousness, turning the perception-action loop so tightly in on itself that the brain structures involved talk to themselves, then all of a sudden consciousness begins to sound a bit more like one of Chalmers's easy problems. And thus, "What is consciousness?" can once again be considered a scientifically viable question, but it is no longer definable as something over and above the normal perceptual, motor, and memory processes of the brain interacting with its environment.

Firmly placing the immediate experience of consciousness in the backseat of neuronal descriptions of the mind is the fact that neural correlates of action preparation appear to precede the reportable conscious intent to act. The point in time where people can associate the awareness of a conscious intent to perform a spontaneous action, while watching a clock, has been shown to lag behind the readiness potential observed in ERP measures associated with performing that action (see Haggard, 2005; Libet, 1985). Thus, the brain is already preparing to formulate an action before the time at which the person can report being self-aware of that intended action. Moreover, Dennett (1991) spends considerable time explaining the fact that self-conscious reflection on one's conscious states is unavoidably revisionist, due to memory processes employed in recounting mental experience—whether we're talking about a few hundred milliseconds ago or several seconds ago. But you must keep in mind (pardon the pun) that memory is not the accessing of old things in the mind. As I've stated before, there are no real "things" in the mind. It would be hard for memory to be as exquisitely reconstructive as it is (e.g., Bartlett, 1932; Hasher & Griffin, 1978; Neisser & Harsch, 1992), if it merely involved selecting old chestnuts from a box and rolling them around in your homunculus's hand. Memory, like categorization and language and vision, is perhaps better described as a process of revisiting patterns of neural activation (and sequences of such patterns) over time. This revisitation involves a pattern completion process that can often deviate from the original or veridical pattern. There is no chestnut. When engaged in memory (working or long-term, it doesn't matter), the mind attempts to reinstate much of what it was doing when the remembered event was first being experienced.[3] Any obvious gaps in this reinstantiation are seamlessly filled in by automatic confabulation. When examining working memory's part in consciousness, this reconstruction and confabulation plays a key role in making the original conscious experience scientifically inaccessible. As you introspect about what you were consciously experiencing a few seconds ago, you convert it into far more concrete and explicit propositions and images than it was originally composed of. The original fuzzy inarticulate blur that is our instantaneous immediate untranslated experience—spending much of its time in between identifiable attractor basins—is extremely difficult for a linguistically categorized "folk psychology" to capture. What you actually have on your mental laboratory's dissection table at that point is not pure consciousness but self-consciousness—which I suppose is reasonably interesting in its own right anyway (see Bermudez, 1998).

Self-consciousness has detectable effects on behavior. For example, the *presence* of internally oriented self-consciousness can interfere with motor performance (Wulf, McNevin, & Shea, 2001), as when you are trying to teach someone how to drive a manual transmission and your own self-examination of what your normally automatic arm and leg movements are doing causes you to slip up and grind the gears. The absence of self-consciousness can lead you to drive all the way home from work (while daydreaming and thus leaving no memory of the trip itself) when you had intended to stop at the grocery store on the way. Self-consciousness is not the result of some mysterious force outside the realm of our normal brain- and environment-based cognitive processing, and perhaps that is why Chalmers (1996) considers it an easy problem. This means that self-consciousness can influence cognition and behavior in a natural physical manner, which is more than can be said for a zeroth-order consciousness that somehow exists in this world but does not function via normal causal processes, like some kind of epiphenomenal red-headed stepchild of cognition, locked in the basement and kept away from the rest of the mind.

I say "epiphenomenal" because the natural physical processes that implement self-consciousness, such as self-evaluative or linguistic subsystems in the brain, looping their output back onto themselves as input, could quite possibly be responsible for producing all the evidence that we've ever witnessed for people being "conscious" (see Huxley, 1902). In fact, it is quite startling, when you think about it, that the only evidence that anyone is actually experiencing a pure consciousness, that is, that they are "aware" of sensory experiences (or qualia), rather than simply mapping those sensory inputs onto sets of potential motor outputs, is that they *tell you* they are. Well, let me be the first to break with that tradition and offer an opposing piece of evidence. I do not experience a zeroth-order pure consciousness. I am an anaqualiac (Churchland, 1998). Whenever I do feel like I might be experiencing pure consciousness, I ask myself whether the definition of self-consciousness is perhaps more applicable, and the answer is invariably "yes" (see Lycan, 1996; Wegner, 2002). When I occasionally feel like I have a conscious self, I strongly suspect that I am merely falling prey to the seductive tacit language game of "me and my mind," that implicit Cartesian-theater mindset that allows people to say things like "when I think about *x*." However, when you are thinking about *x*, there is no "you" separate from the "thinking about *x*." When you are thinking about *x*, the "thinking about *x*" *is what you are.* This means that when talking about internal mental activity, there is no observer separate from the observed. The internal observing act is all there is. Thus, there can be no experience of qualia because there is no experiencer separate from the qualia being experienced. The dynamic neural patterns in association cortices (which might get called qualia), occurring in between sensory stimulation and motor execution, are not being *experienced* by you, they *are a core part of* you. To quote Daniel Dennett (1993) quoting Ivan Fox, "a quale thrown into that gap falls right through."

I recognize that without buying into the rich history of intricate terminology that philosophers of mind have developed for discussions of consciousness and qualia, these claims that I am making may have a difficult time fitting into their ways of understanding. But I hope that readers who are outside of that tradition can glean some comprehension from this argument that will help them avoid the implicit dualism that plagues much of the cognitive and neural sciences. As for you philosophers of mind, take this: I am a "zombie." Or perhaps more accurately, I am one of Moody's (1994) "zombie scientists." As described by a number of philosophers of mind (e.g., Block, 1978; Chalmers, 1996; Kirk, 1974), the zombie brain and body, and their interaction with the environment, function in the normal ways that allow a person to behave like an intentional being. However, the zombie does not have, over and above those complex dynamical processes, any experience of qualia.[4] That's me. I realize that this is a startling admission that may cause some readers to feel uneasy, but surely you've noticed how some people just *seem* a little less conscious than others. (In fact, I know some computer programs that seem more conscious than certain people; see Spivey, 2000.) All joking aside, I am convinced that the "me" that is hunched over this laptop computer right now is most definitely not a Kantian reasoning self in an ivory tower in my brain. That "me" is my entire body coupled with the environment in which it is situated. Try as I might, I simply cannot construct for myself a version of the notion of qualia that does not (at least implicitly) invoke the empirically implausible and theoretically problematic Cartesian theater framework. And therefore, I must reject it.

Throughout this book I have argued that mental activity is best described as a continuous trajectory in mental state space that flirts with various attractor basins as the manifold changes over time. Note that portions of this trajectory may be more or less epistemically identifiable or permitting of labels. These explicit labeling events probably form much of what feels like consciousness. Critically, if imbuing portions of this trajectory with the gift of consciousness and denying it to other portions does not actually change the path it travels by one iota, then, much like Thomas Huxley (1902), I am not sure I see the usefulness of the distinction.[5]

Das Seelenleben der Zombies

Before becoming the father of psychophysics, Gustav Fechner wrote a book titled *Das Seelenleben der Pflanzen,* or *The Mental Life of Plants.* That's right, the man who was chiefly responsible for helping psychology turn the corner toward scientific, methodological, and quantitative rigor was a rabid panpsychist who believed that everything had a consciousness and that philosophical materialism was evil. Although I suspect that plants may actually have rather uneventful mental lives, I can say from personal experience that zombies have perfectly healthy and happy mental lives—and all without Chalmers's mysterious brand of pure consciousness. A zombie, such as myself, engages in self-consciousness reasonably frequently and can therefore manufacture reports on his or her mental processes in exactly the same way that putatively conscious people do. That is why, until I told you that I was a zombie, you probably never would have guessed it (at least I hope not).

My mental life is composed of a continuous trajectory through an attractor landscape that approaches regions in space that correspond to relatively nameable constructs such as various concepts, visual objects, and words (see also Atmanspacher, 2004). If we were to look at a visual-processing subspace of my mind or a planned-action subspace when its trajectory gets especially close to a particular point attractor, the label for that attractor (not necessarily a linguistic label but at least a unique identity pattern) may be more readily transmitted to other subspaces (especially the linguistic subspace, in the case of humans), and the result is that this animal feels conscious of that visual object or that intended action. This description portrays the feeling of consciousness as something very much akin to symbolic dynamics. But when the trajectory merely flirts with an attractor and has its traversal subtly perturbed by that attractor, the identity pattern for that attractor may not be strongly transmitted to other subspaces. Thus the mental trajectory is routinely influenced by attractors that never reach conscious reportability. Under such circumstances, would you, as a scientist, rather have access to the original continuous trajectory or just see the string of outputted symbols?

For epistemological and pragmatic reasons, the cognitive and neural sciences may occasionally need some "thinglike" labeled entity to refer to when discussing mental activity whether or not it is described as conscious. Without some overidealized construct of bounded entities in the mind, discussions of the distributed patterns that actually make up mental content could end up requiring reference to large vectors of averaged neuronal spike rates. Would it really be an improvement for us to prohibit people from saying, "This person is thinking about the concept *dog*," and instead force them to say, "This person is thinking about [0.322 0.674 0.438 0.216 0.439 0.892 0.341 0.435 0.237 0.654 0.527 0.085 0.332 0.689 0.982 0.372]"?

One way to ease the tension between these two extreme ways of referring to mental content might be to look at the spatiotemporally graded structure of attractorlike regions in the high-dimensional manifold of the mind. We can perhaps satisfy both of these cravings—for thinglike entities that can be easily referred to, and for acknowledging the continuous nature of the trajectory—by imposing soft partitions on the early portion and on the later portion of the collection of trajectory records that visited a given attractor. Figure 12.1A shows a simplified rendition (in a mere three dimensions) of a demarcated region in state space that might function like a conceptual representation. (The succinct partitioning of the inside of the concept as separate from the outside of the concept is an arbitrary setting used purely for ease in communication. The actual cluster of different senses/uses of that concept would be distributed in a gradually sparser perimeter surrounding the centroid of the concept.) If the brain state were to visit that region and sit there statically—like settling on a point attractor in an unchanging attractor landscape or instantiating a discrete symbol and holding it in mind—then this format of representation would be sufficient to describe mental content. However, in our normal everyday cognitive experiences, we never sit there statically. When we think about some concept, it is because a previous concept is bringing us to the current one, and the current one is likewise launching us to the next. This is true whether we're talking about producing one phoneme followed by another and another, or hearing one word followed by another and another, or moving your eyes from one object in a complex scene to another and another, or going through the complex set of actions of making your lunch on a Saturday afternoon. As pragmatically useful as it is to have some discretely bounded object in your inventory of mental contents that allows you to refer to it as though it were separate from other bounded objects, it can be a profoundly misleading oversimplification.

Figure 12.1B illustrates some example records of trajectories that traveled through said location in state space. Although this framework is intended to work for any kind of mental attractor space, describing it in terms of word attractors in a language space may be the easiest introduction. If the location in question is the concept for the verb *eat*, for example, then sometimes the trajectory will be coming from the location associated with yourself, or the location associated with your spouse, as when you're thinking about where the two of you might go for dinner tonight. Other times the trajectory may be entering the *eat* region from the direction of the *cat* region of space, as when you're feeding your cat. Still other times, on its way to the *eat* attractor, the trajectory may be coming from a location belonging to a fictional character in a novel you are reading. And the specific location that is entered, within the region in question, is subtly different depending on that preceding context (Elman, 2004). That is, the different nouns that act as the agent of the *eating* event cause slightly different gradations in the sense of *eat* that gets visited.

Importantly, the dynamics of the attractor landscape are such that when an attractor is visited, it warps into a repellor, so that the trajectory keeps on going through and can thus approach the next concept. On its way out of the

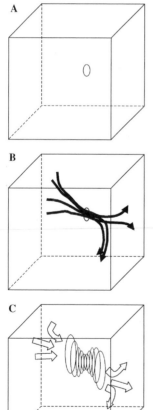

Figure 12.1. Panel A shows a location in state space that might be associated with a concept, and Panel B shows some example trajectories that have passed through that location. Panel C sketches the average entranceways and exitways of those trajectories to depict a spatiotemporally contextualized version of that concept.

eat location, sometimes the trajectory might go in the direction of pasta, tuna, or fried green tomatoes. In fact, as it exits the *eat* region, the trajectory may even occasionally go in the direction of inedible things, as when someone is being metaphorical or insulting.

All these various potential pasts and potential futures for the concept of *eat* play an important role in making the concept what it is. Therefore, figure 12.1C can be seen as a rough sketch of what the concept looks like when its incoming entranceways and outgoing exitways are included in its boundaries. This depicts the spatiotemporal distribution of most of the trajectories that pass through this location in space. Thus, an integral part of knowing what *eat* means involves knowing what kinds of words are the agents of *eating* events and also what kinds of words are the direct objects of *eating* events (McRae, Ferreti, & Amyote, 1997).

These idealized demarcations form wasp-waisted tubes, or spatiotemporal hourglasses, in mental space that outline the typical range of contextual pasts that immediately precede an attractor visitation as well as the typical range of anticipated futures that follow that attractor visitation. A little bit like the past light cone and future light cone associated with an event in astrophysics, what is depicted in figure 12.2 (a smoother version of the rough sketch in figure 12.1C) is a contextual past cone and an anticipated future

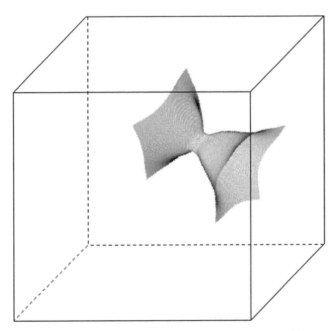

Figure 12.2. A smoother portrayal of the spatiotemporal hourglass in figure 12.1C. This wasp-waisted tube in state space illustrates the typical contextual pasts and anticipated futures that accompany any given concept or word.

cone that represent the set of likely directions in state space that a trajectory came from and is going to when it visits a particular attractor (which turns into a repellor once visited).

I understand that the thirst for "things" in the mind is strong. Therefore, I offer these spatiotemporal hourglasses in hopes to slake that thirst while still robustly acknowledging that these "things" are not separated from one another and are in fact nothing more than averages of conspicuous clusterings of trajectory records. In much the same way that ecological psychologists allow themselves to refer to organism and environment as different nouns, while still intending that the their proper description requires a conjoined space of mutual parameters, the wasp-waisted tube in figure 12.2 is how I allow myself to refer to different concepts with different nouns for ease of description, when in fact I intend that their proper treatment require a spatio-temporal format that emphasizes their continuous temporal blending with one another, as the trajectory of thought snakes its way through mental state space. These spatiotemporal hourglasses are "representationlike" in that they are each individually enumerable and uniquely nameable (if artificially so). However, they are also *not* representationlike in that they do not require that a read-out be performed by some central executive interpreter—that is, they are not really "representing something to someone." The continuous trajectory is what the mind is doing, and these hourglasses are merely regions in state space that happen to have been visited frequently enough to have relatively explicit conceptual identities associated with them, which are useful for the observing scientist.

Figure 12.2 is what a spatiotemporally contextualized concept looks like. Thousands of these hourglasses in mental state space is what I contend a zombie's mind is made of. This is what *my* mind is made of. And this is what I think *your* mind is made of. When your mental trajectory thoroughly visits one of these hourglasses, its identity becomes explicitly reportable, and thus feels like what we call a conscious experience. But the moniker of "conscious" does not alter the path of the trajectory, and thus is essentially irrelevant to my purposes for the continuity of mind. (Flanagan, 1991, calls this *conscious inessentialism*.) You may add your own magic of consciousness on top of this account, if you must, but do it on your own time—and at your own risk.

If Free Will Did Not Exist, It Would Be Necessary to Invent It

A particularly nasty bugbear that often stows away on the good ship *Consciousness* is the notion of free will. As scientifically problematic as it is to champion the existence of a construct like pure consciousness, whose definition makes it epiphenomenal and unmeasurable, imagine championing the existence of a construct like free will, which happily violates everything physics has learned about how the universe works! The common notion of free will is basically conceived of as a psychological effect that had no preexisting cause.

For example, when you're playing chess and you make a move that gets your king out of check, rather than some other kind of move, you are *not* exercising free will in that circumstance. The rules require that you get your king out of check before making any other moves. So the rules *caused* you to defer the other moves that you had been considering. But when you're trying to decide between taking your opponent's pawn or sacrificing a piece to set a trap, the consternation and eventual selection among those two choices will often feel like what people refer to when they use the term *free will.* You may feel as though your choice of move was solely your own, based on a nondecomposable hunch, rather than on your experience and training with the strategies of the game.

It seems that we usually experience this personal sense of free will when we find ourselves choosing among options on which we weren't initially sure how we would decide. However, the readiness potential observed in ERPs shows that the brain is preparing such choices several hundred milliseconds before they are consciously reportable (Haggard, 2005; Libet, 1985). Therefore, it looks as though nonfreely willed garden-variety neural processes are actually responsible for these apparently freely willed choices. Wegner (2002) recounts a variety of psychological and neurological findings indicating that this disconnect, between the *actual deterministic causes* of our decisions and the *illusory* fiat lux of our decisions, is due to processes by which the mind interprets itself after the fact: essentially the self-consciousness to which I've been referring.

But could a truly free will have existed in the first place? When it comes down to it, a causal force that is known as free will, that is, "free" because it is not predetermined and "willed" because it is not random, would actually make for a very strange bedfellow with the other causal forces known to science (see Bridgeman, 2003; Pereboom, 2001). After all, conventional physics suggests that there are two general kinds of forces in the universe: (1) random fluctuation, with no preexisting cause, typically observed at the spatial scales of electrons, quarks, bosons, and so on, and (2) deterministic cause and effect, typically observed at the spatial scales of molecules, apples, trees, mountains, stars, planets, and so on. (Emergent properties, such as self-organization in complex nonlinear systems, do not necessarily belong to a separate kind of force because deterministic processes are perfectly capable of producing them; see Solow, 2000.) It is not at all clear what form a third kind of force would take if it were to exist and call itself free will. It would not be caused by prior determinants, nor would it be random when it comes out of nowhere. Pray tell, how exactly would it work?

For the vast majority of free will advocates, the randomness introduced at the subatomic level by quantum mechanics just won't cut it. It is not the kind of effect without a cause that they have in mind. They want the willed decision to belong entirely to the individual person, not to deterministic causes and not to randomness. It's as if they want you to believe that an inexplicable cosmological big bang (with no preexisting causal forces) is going off in your brain every time you make a freely willed decision. For example, Kant said that the will is "a kind of causality belonging to living beings so far as they are rational. Freedom would then be the property this causality has of being able to work independently of determination by alien causes." Although perhaps not impossible, this scenario portrays a world in which human minds are uniquely capable of nonrandomly flouting causality on a regular basis. I can understand humans feeling tempted to think that humans are that universally special, but I suspect their legacy, like those of the trilobites and the dinosaurs, will eventually prove otherwise.

The very idea that there might be a part of the mind that can make decisions that are not causally traceable and also not random should actually chill you to the bone. An unconstrained variable like free will compromises science at its core. Everywhere that free will goes, it scorches the theoretical terrain, leaving it bereft of any scientific testability. Perhaps it is no surprise that theorists who use homuncular phrasings like "central executive" and "an internal cognizer that thinks about things" tend to also believe in modularity. After all, if a freely willed and scientifically impenetrable homunculus is making untraceable decisions, then those decisions had better not be deeply influencing every cognitive and perceptual process that goes on, because then all those processes would likewise be contaminated by an uncontrollable variable and thus immune to scientific discovery. As long as the perceptual and cognitive processes of interest are informationally encapsulated from this central executive, then they can be studied systematically and successfully. If they are interactive and thus become contaminated by the influence of an unpredictable and unmodelable variable like free will, via feedback signals from the central executive, then they are doomed to remain in shadow, unilluminated by science. What it comes down to is this: If you believe in free will and you believe in the promise of cognitive science, then you *have to* be a modularist. However, as the empirical evidence against modularity accumulates (see chapter 5), this conjunction of beliefs becomes untenable. I trust readers to perform their own modus tollens and struggle with the alternative conclusions on their own time. A full discussion of the forced choice between free will versus the promise of cognitive science is not within the scope of this book. As for myself, for what it's worth, I choose the promise of cognitive science.

But all this begs the question of why people *feel* like they have free will. One way in which something could feel very much like free will and still allow the mind to function along with the rest of the universe, is if the sense and observation of apparent free will were indeed actually the result of random processes in the brain. For example, random selection among a few optimal escape movements has been seen in fish (Domenici & Blake, 1993). And prey animals have been observed to scan for predators at random temporal intervals, with a Poisson-like distribution (Bertram, 1980; Caraco, 1982; Scannell, Roberts, & Lazarus, 2001). In fact, for some time now, it has been recognized that randomized behavior can, under some circumstances, be the optimal competitive strategy (Von Neumann & Morgenstern, 1947). Note also that foraging animals appear to produce flight lengths while searching for food that are random with an inverse square power law distribution (Viswanathan et al., 1999). Similarly, while humans are visually searching a complex display, the lengths of their saccadic eye movements vary with a $1/f$ power law distribution, but the locations of their fixations are distributed like a Brownian noise function (Aks, Zelinsky, & Sprott, 2002). In fact, eye movements have been an important source of inspiration for hypothesizing the existence of random processes in cognition. For example, Carpenter (1999, 2004) notes how the rate of increase in neuronal firing frequency (in the frontal eye fields) is correlated with saccadic reaction time, and this rate of increase appears randomly distributed across trials in a similar manner as saccadic reaction times are randomly distributed across trials (see also Hanes & Schall, 1996; Schall, 1995). There is evidence for intrinsic neural noise in sensory transduction and in neural transmission in sensory cortices (e.g., Shadlen & Newsome, 1994). Interestingly, the infant retina exhibits nine times as much intrinsic neural noise as the adult retina (Skoczenski & Norcia, 1998). There are, in fact, circumstances where such intrinsic neural noise may actually be advantageous for pattern completion (or resonance) and even for learning (e.g., Hennig et al., 2002; Mato, 1999; Rappel & Karma 1996; for a review of stochastic resonance, see Ward, 2002). However, Carpenter's (1999, 2004) specific suggestion with regard to his eye movement evidence is that over and above this sensory noise, there may be some degree of randomness injected in the timing of response selection in the motor and frontal cortices. It may be this particular random component that gives humans the impression that they and others exhibit free will in their choices and actions.

But what about the underlying mechanism of such neural noise? Some have speculated (e.g., Jibu et al., 1994; Penrose, 1994; Stapp, 1993) that the microtubules, receptor sites, and transmitter ions in neuronal membranes are small enough that quantum subatomic randomness could perhaps influence their likelihood of action potentials (for a review, see Atmanspacher, 2004). For example, the Heisenberg uncertainty distribution surrounding the destination of a calcium ion inside an axon terminal (as it makes its long journey toward a trigger site, which will release a neurotransmitter vesicle into the synaptic cleft) is a few hundred picometers, near the size of the trigger site itself (Stapp, 1999). Thus, the calcium ion is reminiscent of our friendly Schrödinger's cat from chapter 1 in that before the completion of its journey has had a chance to produce observable consequences in the rest of the network, the distributed destination of this ion can be mathematically described as having both *actuated* the trigger site and *missed* it—and quantum randomness mediates which of those fates is realized. However, if the observable consequences that comprise mental activity (e.g., percepts and concepts) are themselves self-organizing neuronal population codes composed of dozens or hundreds or perhaps even thousands of neurons (Noë & Thompson, 2004), then it would require some elaborately orchestrated "spooky action at a distance" (on a far grander scale than envisioned in Bell's theorem, perhaps even warranting the phrase "*Byzantine* action at a distance") for enough quantum-perturbed calcium ions in enough separate neurons to coordinate their stochastic influences in unison such that they significantly alter which population code comes to fruition. In other words, just as the random quantum effects involved in a tennis ball bouncing generally average each other out to produce no sum influence on the ball's classical mechanical behavior, so might the random quantum effects across a population of neurons average out to produce no sum influence on their behavior. It is perhaps more plausible that the apparently random noise observed in neuronal firing rates is actually the chaotic unpredictability that emerges from a deterministic complex recurrent system (Scott, 1996; Usher, Stemmler, & Olami, 1995), a bit like the logistic map when its parameter is set at 4.0 (Ulam & Von Neumann, 1947; see also chapter 4).

That said, one of the reasons that people argue for the existence of personal free will (of the nondeterministic and nonrandom kind) has nothing at all to do with its mechanistic explanation and everything to do with its supposed functional consequences for society. They posit that free will had better exist, or else people will run wild in the streets raping and pillaging with impunity on the rationalization that they cannot be held responsible for their behavior. I must admit, I have never understood how this argument can hold any water at all. The argument is as bankrupt as Fodor's (1983) claim that the mind had better be modular, or we'll never understand how it works. The universe knows whether free will exists (and whether the mind is modular), and I'm quite sure that it cares not one whit about whether we will misuse (or be able to grasp) that truth. In other words, our supposedly dire epistemological need for the ontological facts of the matter to be a certain way so that we may behave fairly (or even understand them) cannot possibly play a role in determining how those facts of the matter actually turn out. For example, the mind is probably not very modular (see chapter 5), and that probably *does* mean that we'll never understand it quite as clearly as we would have if it had been modular. Live with it. Because free will postulates a third type of unique causal force—apart from randomness and determinism (with its concomitant emergent properties)—that has no preexisting causes of its own, thus failing to adhere to the core tenets of how we've come to understand the universe, free will probably does not exist. Live with it.

But the nonexistence of free will is in no way a license to commit crimes. Only a child would argue such. One must recognize that all smoothly functioning societies will have deterministically evolved such that punitive and rehabilitative measures are applied to the causes of antisocial behavior, whether it's theft, rape, murder, or whatever—regardless of anyone's ideas about free will. Societies that did not develop such measures simply did not survive the process of cultural evolution. These punitive and rehabilitative measures are needed to prevent the destructive behavior, in general, from happening again. When the causes of the destructive behavior can be reliably traced to someone other than the actual perpetrator—as in hypothetical cases of someone being forced at gunpoint to commit a crime—the punitive measures would naturally be applied to that other someone. When a parent's raising of their child, who is still a minor, looks as if it is partly responsible for causing the child to commit a crime, many cultures do indeed hold that parent at least partly accountable for the crime.[6] An individual is a dynamic turbulent funnel for thousands of causal forces that at many different time scales determine that individual's behavior. (In fact, in the huge state space made of social, cultural, and evolutionary dimensions, a person might look a lot like the wasp-waisted tube in figure 12.2.) In a rough analogy to a nonlinear multiple regression analysis (with many interaction terms), some of those identified causal forces may account for a statistically significant proportion of the variance in that individual's behavior. When that happens, applying some of the punitive and rehabilitative measures to those identifiable significant preexisting causal forces, instead of to the perpetrator, is the smartest thing to do because it carries with it the possibility of preventing hundreds or thousands of other individuals from being negatively influenced in the future by those same causal forces (see Haney, 2002; Honderich, 1988). Thus, pretending that an individual has free will, and is therefore solely responsible for his or her actions, can actually be a socially inefficient way to mete out justice.

When one asks the scientific question of "what causes this person, or this people, to conduct these crimes?"—and when the political climate encouraged by a nation's government allows one to ask such a question—it quickly becomes clear that people do not commit crimes for no reason. They may have justified or unjustified reasons, but there are always reasons. If a person's culture has trained him to devalue life, and especially if his mentors have encouraged him to hate another culture, the deterministic result of such a learning environment is that you often produce a mind that is willing and capable of theft, rape, and murder. That person did not ask to be raised in that environment. That person did not ask to be born with an impressionable intellect. So is that individual really the best place to apply all the punitive and/or rehabilitative measures? If a person's upbringing taught him to attempt to solve problems with violence or deception, is it his fault that he was born into that environment? If a person is genetically predisposed to acting in a generally violent manner, is it his fault that he was born with those genes?

In a sense, the bastardized quote from Voltaire that heads this section of the chapter is true. Without the ontological existence of free will, it becomes necessary for societies to pretend that it exists to make up for the epistemological failures involved in attempting to track down all the myriad forces that cause a person to act in socially harmful ways. It is often easier and more pragmatic to simply treat the individual as if he or she is the sole source of the causal chain that produced the criminal behavior. Note, however, that pretending free will exists so that you have an easy place to apply punitive and rehabilitative measures does not make it actually exist. From a scientific standpoint, it still makes absolutely no sense to insert a causeless effect like free will into a theory of dynamic processes that already promises to account for all of the data via deterministic (albeit nonlinear, complex, and overflowing with emergent phenomena) forces and perhaps the occasional stochastic nudge.

Vehicles All the Way Down

Having far too glibly dispensed with the notions of pure consciousness and free will, we can now move on to giving short shrift to another rhetorical challenge that philosophers of mind have posed with regard to mental life and consciousness. In attempting to stave off eliminative reductionism, where mental states are reducible to brain states (e.g., Bickle, 1998; Churchland, 1984; Kim, 1998), philosophers introduced the vehicle/content distinction as a way to discriminate between the physical matter that implements mental activity and the intrinsic informational qualities of that mental activity.[7]

Informal discussions of the vehicle/content distinction have occasionally leaned on the layperson's conception of the difference between computer hardware and software. However, this analogy has at least two major problems. First, the standard philosophical position on the vehicle/content distinction assumes that the content is dependent on (though not fully reducible to) the vehicle, and the vehicle is not dependent on the content. But when you manipulate computer software, the resulting structure of the hardware is dependent on the new structure of your software (i.e., when you rewrite a line of code and save the program on some storage medium, that storage medium has been forced to change its physical magnetic or optical properties). Thus, although the vehicle/content distinction is commonly thought to involve a one-way dependence, the hardware/software distinction appears to involve a two-way dependence. The second problem with the hardware/software analogy involves the fact that it is terribly easy to find places where the boundary between hardware and software becomes difficult to discern. For example, when you savagely rip the plastic casing off of a 3.5-inch diskette and closely examine the actual floppy disc inside, you can begin to come to terms with the fact that the software on that disc is not merely *dependent on* the pattern of magnetic fields across microscopic regions of the disc, the software *is* the pattern of magnetic fields across microscopic regions of the disc. If you were to swipe a magnet over a portion of the disc, the swath of destruction wreaked across the pattern of magnetic fields would bear a lawful correspondence to the swath of destruction wreaked on the machine language that underlies whatever programming language was originally used to write the software. Therefore, the idea that hardware and software are completely independent levels of description does not really hold as firmly as people often think.

The assumed one-way dependence of the vehicle/content distinction is due to its adherents covering their tracks to make sure that they cannot be accused of full-on Cartesian dualism. For example, when I work on changing my language use around my child (so that I don't get a neighbor mother knocking on my door and complaining about how my three-year-old son taught her three-year-old daughter to use profanity), there is a sense in which I might be reprogramming my biocomputer (Lilly, 1967). But to claim that this reprogramming was instigated by my mind, without the initial participation of my brain, would sound mystically dualistic. Therefore, functionalists who embrace the vehicle/content distinction would argue that all the matter-based causal processing involved in that reprogramming is instigated and performed by my brain, but the level of description of *the mind* (where abstract formal rules determine which words get produced as a result of discrete cognitive interpretations of sensory inputs) is independent of how that brain functions. So what they're saying is that the mind is causally dependent on the brain, but descriptively independent of it.

When they invoke Putnam's (1975; see also Fodor, 1975) multiple realizability argument, it can begin to sound like they have a pretty good case. The multiple realizability argument goes a little something like this: Assume we all have the same psychological experience of pain, and then examine the physical substrate that implements that psychological experience. The exact pattern of neural excitation in your brain when you experience pain is undoubtedly subtly different from the pattern of neural excitation in my brain when I experience pain. Moreover, if we are treating pain as a psychological category of broad usefulness, it might be safe to assume that other kinds of animals also experience this category of psychological experience, and some such animals have dramatically different brain structures and even completely different types of nerves for transmitting avoidance signals in the presence of harmful stimulation. If you impute to other humans and to these other animals the same functional category of pain as you claim for yourself, then you have a clear case of the same psychological entity being realized by multiple non-overlapping physical implementations. Under such circumstances, it is arguable that reducing a human's pain or a mollusk's pain down to their respective underlying physical processes is less informative than staying at the level of a functionalist description—a little like a computer program—of how pain generally works.

If you were sitting on the fence about this issue before that paragraph, it's possible that you were nudged toward one side. I hope it didn't hurt. But now let's see if I can nudge you the other way, toward the materialists. Ask yourself the following: Do *your* experience of pain and *my* experience of pain truly belong together in a formal nondecomposable indistinguishable equivalence class? Is it really the case that if you looked closely at our respective reaction times, eye movements, heart rates, and the temporal dynamics of our galvanic skin response and electromyograph output (heck, go ahead and include our verbal protocols, if you want), you would still be comfortable inferring that the two different experiences of pain were functionally identical? Because if you think there may be some subtle differences at the psychological level of description between your experience of pain (or happiness, or hunger, or lust) and mine, then the multiple realizability argument loses ground on its very first assumption: that the *same type of psychological entity* is being realized by different physical implementations. That is, when implemented by subtly different physical manifestations, the cognitive results may not be exactly the same psychological entities either—but they may cluster in roughly isomorphic ways.

Let's say you don't like pain, but you hear that I am a teensy bit of a masochist. So when you experience a moderate amount of physical pain, it's entirely unpleasant for you, but when I experience an equivalent amount of pain, it's mixed with just a teaspoon of pleasure.[8] In neural state space, when one compares the spatial relationship between *your* neural patterns for pain and for pleasure to the spatial relationship between *my* neural patterns for pain and for pleasure, one might find that my patterns are little closer together than yours. That would be a first step toward revealing an isomorphy between how instances of psychological pain experience vary around a psychological prototype and how instances of neural pain patterns cluster in a corresponding fashion around a broad region of neural state space (which includes all relevant neurophysiological dimensions for all pain-feeling animals). Thus, it might be described as there being multiple different types of pain and multiple corresponding types of physical implementations of that pain. Under such circumstances, it would be abundantly clear that reducing your pain, or my pain, or a mollusk's pain, down to the neural level of description would be wonderfully informative for understanding what pain is all about.

But perhaps the biggest problem with the vehicle/content distinction is that it implies some form of read-out being performed on the content, and leaves unexplained exactly *who* is doing the read-out. Whether it's a conceptual level of content being read off of the nonconceptual level (Byrne, 2003; Gunther, 2003), or a personal level of content being read off of a subpersonal level (Dennett, 1991; Hurley, 1998b; Millikan, 1993), assuming a strict distinction between information and matter can risk leading one right into the homunculus problem, where a little man in the head winds up mysteriously doing all the work that the theory was supposed to do. In fact, a number of researchers (e.g., Damasio, 1992; Dennett, 1991, 1993; Rosenthal, 1993; Streeck, 2003) have pointed out that an implicit Cartesian theater can easily sneak its way into a theory of mental activity when it conceives of symbolic content being received and processed by some central executive.[9] If allowed to continue spreading implicitly, this pandemic of "homunculitis" (Monsell & Driver, 2000) could threaten to permanently poison the entire discipline.

In the continuity of mind framework that I am proposing here, the closest thing to a read-out that ever takes place is when one vehicle (a pattern of neural activation or a biomechanical process) alters/influences another such vehicle. But this requires no interpretation of content; it merely requires that causal forces be implemented from the first vehicle to the second. The second vehicle does not need to perform a read-out of the first vehicle's meaning with regard to it, any more than the eight ball has to perform a read-out of my cue ball's meaning when it gets hit by it and knocked into the corner pocket. If a theoretical description of this network of vehicles continuously influencing one another manages to map perception to action to the environment and back around to perception again (and also produce internal loops that involve language areas, for self-consciousness), then why would you need the concept of content residing inside those vehicles in the first place? The process will have been explained with no need for any notion of content, nor for a Cartesian reader of said content. This decentralized view of the mind—where control (or intention) is not generated from some unitary internal homuncular source but instead is a dynamic emergent property of a brain, its body, and the environment in which it is embedded—is gaining ground in cognitive science (e.g., Churchland, 1996; Hommel, Daum, & Kluwe, 2004; Metzinger, 2003; Van Orden & Holden, 2002; Wegner, 2002).

Note, however, that this proposal is a bit different from Churchland's (1981) eliminative materialism because I'm not saying that mind is nothing more than brain. In fact, I'm not really even saying that mind is nothing more than brain, body, and environment. Saying it that way fails to put sufficient emphasis on the temporal dynamics that are so crucial for making the mind what it is. A static freeze-frame of brain, body, and environment is not mind-like. The continuous trajectory that describes their coupled state changes is what is mindlike.

In this view, you are no different from the information that you feel like you are processing. The "you" that feels like it is answering the questions when you introspect and self-reflect (as well as the you that feels like it is *asking* those questions) is made up of the same informational medium that the rest of the world is made up of. Dynamic patterns of spatiotemporal relationships between elements of physical matter are what compose processes (that we often refer to as things) in the world, and those same kinds of patterns are also what compose your mind—because when it comes down to it, your mind is just another process in the world, like any other. In philosophy of mind terminology, what I am suggesting is that there are no vehicles that are separate from their content, and no content that is separate from its vehicle. Your mind is not a processor built from stuff that is independent of the dynamic information it processes. The apparent process*or* and the process*ed* are part of the same collection of dynamic patterns, and they can even seem to trade roles at times. What this means is that strictly speaking, there is no objectively identifiable input and output in describing how the mind works (although these are convenient terms to use for rough descriptions). Your mind is not a hierarchical set of sequential and parallel filters that sift through the sense data from the world, performing transformations of and computations on those data to produce an interpretation of that world. What good is an interpretation of the world if it's not leading to action on the world? And what good is a theory if it punts when it comes to determining how that interpretation leads to action? That computer-inspired metaphor for the mind has officially outlasted its usefulness (and perhaps outused its lastfulness). Your mind is part and parcel with the data of the world, not a separate thing that processes those data.

So by heading this section with the phrase "vehicles all the way down," I am of course alluding to the famous (and quite possibly apocryphal) story of a noted professor (in some versions it's Bertrand Russell, in others it's William James, in still others it's Carl Sagan) lecturing on the origins of the planet Earth. After describing how the Earth is spherical and orbiting the sun in space, an old lady in the audience tells him that he's wrong, and that the Earth is actually flat and resting on the back of a turtle. "Okay," responds the professor, "but what is supporting the turtle?" "Very clever, young man," the lady retorts, "but I have an answer to your question. It's turtles all the way down." In a similar way (though a smidgen more scientifically viable), the mind may be vehicles all the way down, from behavior to brains to neurons to microtubules to quarks, and so on. And it might just be that at no point is any one of those levels getting its "content" interpreted off of it.

Writing About Talking About Thinking About Thinking

Introspective self-consciousness, the process that I contend produces the mistaken impression that we have a pure immediate consciousness (and in some cases, the illusion of free will), need not be conceived of as the reading of some content off of a vehicle. Rather, it can actually be conceived of as just another motor plan like any other. A self-referential internal monologue—where you might say to yourself something like, "Gosh, I sure *feel* like I'm conscious. What is Spivey's problem, anyway?"—is nothing more than (partially) prepared speech that is simply not executed. It is not a special kind of higher order thought that functions differently from the rest of everyday perception and cognition (Rosenthal, 2000). These self-conscious thoughts are due to the language subsystem receiving its biased updates of the meandering, looping, and loop-de-looping mental trajectory and converting it (or collapsing its distributed wave function) into individual words and phrases. The manual motor subsystem has its own set of biased updates of that trajectory's whereabouts. As does the oculomotor subsystem and the ambulation subsystem. All of the action subsystems (e.g., for speaking, reaching, looking, walking, etc.) have their own peculiar slant on how they deal with their incoming signals, as well as their own internal recurrent processes. That slant exaggerates some dimensions of the mental state space and minimizes others, so that when each of these action subsystems tries to convert its perspective on the trajectory into a motor plan, these different motor plans can occasionally be wildly incommensurate with one another. What's more, the timing of that conversion, as well as any stochastic components in the conversion process, probably vary as well. So the same mental trajectory (or evolving understanding of the situational context and how it accommodates one's goals) can get collapsed into different kinds of motor actions from the different action subsystems. This is part of how blindsight patients can be linguistically unable to report awareness of a visual stimulus and yet their selection of that stimulus is above chance performance (Lamme, 2001). This is how a verbal report task can fall prey to a visual illusion while a similar pointing task can maintain accurate performance (Bridgeman, 1991). This is how one can erroneously look at the peppershaker, then make a corrective saccade to the saltshaker, accidentally call it "the sugar," and reach perfectly for the right thing, all in less than a second.

This is also how people can say one thing, do another, and not think they're lying.[10] Different motor outputs collapse the wave function at different times and with different stochastic parameters, so they can often provide conflicting evidence on what the same mental trajectory was doing. Importantly, for the discussion at hand, psychologists have been aware for quite some time that explicit verbal report of one's own mental processes is highly unreliable (e.g., Bem, 1967; Nisbett & Wilson, 1977), whereas implicit measures tend to be more honest indicators. Relying on verbal reports as a measure of cognitive processing (e.g., Carruthers, 2002; Ericsson & Simon, 1993; Hurlburt, 1990) can be spectacularly misleading because they are late, slow, and prone to confabulation. Think of the language subsystem like a cultural informant, telling the anthropologist what goes on in the village. Sometimes he's right, sometimes he's mistaken, and sometimes he's even purposely deceitful (see Dean & Whyte, 1958).

A self-conscious mental inventory is not only problematic for the experimenter, it can be problematic for the person doing it. Self-indulgent verbose introspection (which might feel like responsible detail-oriented self-awareness) can wind up interfering with accurate or successful performance of a task. The unintentional confabulation that results from rich introspection about what one thinks one has been thinking can drastically misrepresent and misguide one's decision processes. For example, Wilson and Schooler (1991) had people rate the quality of several strawberry jams, half of whom were instructed to provide detailed introspective reports about their gustatory perceptions along with their ratings and half of whom were told simply to provide a rating without any other details. The people in the nonintrospecting condition produced ratings of the jams that corresponded significantly better (than the introspectors) with industry expert ratings of those jams. Moreover, eyewitness identification of a criminal in a lineup is more likely to be accurate when the witness is unable to provide an introspective explanation of how they know the person they've picked out is indeed the perpetrator (Dunning & Stern, 1994). When eyewitnesses provide in-depth details about how they are comparing features of the different faces in the lineup, they often end up fingering an innocent person (Wells, 1984). Finally, providing a running verbal protocol of one's thought processes while trying to solve an insight problem (see chapter 10 for examples of such problems) actually interferes with the person's ability to find the solution (Schooler, Ohlsson, & Brooks, 1993).

While I am criticizing introspection as a method, allow me to in the same breath tell you what I think happens in my own mind when I engage in "inner speech" with the intent of having it organize my thoughts. When I try to post-examine my internal monologue, I find that the first few words of a sentence often ring clear in my head like a well-trained newscaster's voice, and the next several are somewhat vague or poorly enunciated, and the last few words of the sentence are often left off entirely, because I've completed the thought for myself by then and finishing the linguistic version is unnecessary.[11] One can think of this in terms of a state space trajectory that gets especially close to certain word regions and then only moderately close to others. In a somewhat similar framework, Botvinick and Plaut (2004) have plotted the changes in activation patterns of the hidden layer in a simple recurrent network to reveal the global similarity, as well as the subtle differences, between sequential procedures like making coffee and making tea. When multidimensional scaling is applied to the hidden node activations over time, the trajectories can show subtle nuances in how context and noise affect action plans and subplans. Interestingly, subplans inside the larger action plan often manifest as small internal loops in the middle of the trajectory.

A mental trajectory of inner speech during performance of a task like playing racquetball might look something like those in figure 12.3. All four mental trajectories are geared toward getting the same action performed, hitting the racquetball, but some get it done faster and smoother than others. The longest and most circuitous trajectory, #1 (solid line), where I say to myself the full sentence, "I must get to the ball," would clearly not permit efficient racquetball performance, as it is far too discursive an excursion. I simply wouldn't get to the ball in time if I told myself what to do in complete sentences. Trajectory #2 (long dash line) streamlines this excursion somewhat by producing an internal sentence similar to the ones that comic book superheroes

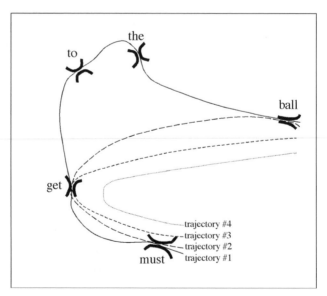

Figure 12.3. Trajectories in a linguistic portion of mental state space that might be traversed while playing racquetball. Smoother and less discursive versions of this trajectory are depicted from #1 to #4. (See text for details.)

use when they talk to themselves in stressful situations: "Must get ball." With more practice at the game, and streamlining of the perceptual-motor and cognitive processes, one might hear only the main verb in one's head, "get," as in trajectory #3 (short dash line). With still more practice, the real-time coupling of my perceptual-motor system with the dynamic environmental patterns of the ball (and court and opponent) produce mental trajectories that are quite smooth, efficient, and wordless. Trajectory #4 (dotted line) shows a thought pattern that would probably be called nonlinguistic by most people, although it is clear that it has some almost linguistic structure to its path. In terms of "discrete mentalese," not a word is spoken. But in terms of a "continuous mentalese," trajectory #4 speaks volumes.

Toward a Continuity Psychology?

In this final section of the final chapter, I might be tempted to indulge my more rancorous instincts one more time. If I were to get up on my Fodor-brand barbed-wire soapbox, you might hear me say something like the following:

> The modular rule-and-symbol-based information-processing framework has misled the cognitive and neural sciences for too long. Dynamic, ecological, and connectionist approaches outstrip this outdated perspective in every worthwhile arena of cognitive study. Those who continue to dig their heels in to protect this obsolete theoretical position are infidels who put the defense of their own bodies of work above the communal advancement of knowledge. We must declare a jihad against the computer metaphor of the mind! The unemployment lines will flow with the graduate students of the nonbelievers!

However, inflammatory rhetoric like that would be unfair, egregious, offputting, and even irresponsible of me. So I won't say that. I will instead take the high road and note that the field genuinely wouldn't be as advanced as it is today if the cognitive revolution of the 1960s hadn't happened. It was a necessary swing of the pendulum that brought psychology out of a rut and invited several other disciplines over for dinner and conversation. But now the pendulum is swinging back, and not just along that one dimension. Thankfully, the force of this pendulum has reduced since that last apex, and the middle ground that will responsibly and in measured tones integrate the right aspects of various frameworks is only a few small oscillations away. I submit that the cognitive and neural sciences are currently witnessing a gradual transition from the traditional information-processing framework to more dynamical, ecological, and neural network–oriented frameworks. During this gradual transition, we may expect to see an increase in hybrid theories that successfully combine discrete representational structures with continuous and probabilistic processes, and symbolic dynamics may play an important role in this transitional phase. But a steady diet of dynamic equations (Kelso, 1995), attractor networks (Amit, 1989), and principles of self-organization (Van Orden, Holden, & Turvey, 2003) will strengthen the bones of the dynamical systems approach and it will grow to become the dominating theoretical framework. With increased cooperation between dynamicists and connectionists (e.g., Churchland & Sejnowski, 1992; Smolensky, 1988a; Spencer & Thelen, 2003; see also Eliasmith, 1996), patterns of neural activity that mediate between sensory stimulation and motor movement will continue to be sought after as the mechanistic level of explanation, and equations that fit organism–environment coupling phenomena will continue to accompany them as the covering law level of explanation (see Bechtel, 1998).

As continuous formats of description begin to do more explaining than is provided by the discrete rule-based descriptions for areas like visual perception, language comprehension, and memory, they will likely supplant the latter approach. In contrast, areas of cognition that rely heavily on discrete action effects in the environment, such as problem solving and reasoning, will be greatly enriched by the development of continuous theoretical accounts that underlie the discrete symbolic description, but they may never be fully dominated by those continuous accounts. That is, some areas in cognitive science may be forced to allow continuous and discrete formats for describing mental activity to coexist indefinitely. The dynamical systems framework will add much to the study of problem solving and reasoning that the information-processing framework is unable to provide, but it is unlikely to evict that venerable tenant.

Now, before I end this tirade of a book, I should offer one last disclaimer. I have not been completely honest with you. To gradually guide cognitive psychologists away from the computer metaphor of mind, this book has focused a bit too much on continuous trajectories in a neuronal state space. As cognitive psychologists tend to be implicit internalists (see Segal, 2000), I felt it necessary to apply most of my pressure on prying loose the assumption of stable symbolic internal representations. First, a reader must be shown the strengths of conceiving of mental activity as continuous change in neuronal population codes, rather than as a string of nonoverlapping symbols. Then, and only then, will the reader be ready to open her mind to continuous trajectories in an ecological state space that includes brain, body, and environment (arguably, the more common purview of dynamical systems approaches to cognition). The movement toward conceiving of mind as a continuous trajectory in a neuronal state space is an important intermediate step that a cognitive psychologist must first become comfortable with before continuing on to a fully ecological dynamical account of perception, cognition, and action. One of the goals of these last two chapters has been to prepare the reader with just a little momentum for making that continuation in the future. By recognizing that your mind is made of the same stuff that the physical environment is made of, and that it doesn't do things that violate physics, you can begin to understand how the proper level of analysis might be ecological (including neural, biomechanical, and environmental processes) rather than solely brain-based. A little bit like at the end of a horror movie, when some small piece of the monster remains and the camera angle hints at a sequel (probably to be shot by a different director), I hope the reader has a sneaking suspicion that their trajectory away from modular discrete stage-based descriptions of mind and toward something else entirely is not over.

In my final comment, I'd like to bring your attention back to figure 12.3. In the context of thinking about how much explaining will be done by discrete symbolic accounts of cognition and by dynamic distributed accounts of cognition, the diagram in figure 12.3 has some thought-provoking properties. Note how, when plotted in two dimensions, the spatiotemporal hourglasses for the word regions in figure 12.3 look a bit like the symbol for a bridge on a map. This is actually a useful way to think of such attractorlike tubes in state space, because it treats them not as destinations or regions of interest in their own right as much as passageways from one territory to the next. In fact, a wide variety of cognitive models have a history of treating their static symbols or stable states as secondary in importance to the *transitions* between those symbols or states, for example, Wickelfeatures (Wickelgren, 1969), Markov chains (Kemeny & Snell, 1976), and basically every dynamical system model ever used. In this way, maybe cognitive psychology has had it all wrong, and words, objects, and concepts are not really the *regions of interest* after all, but are instead the *modes of transport* to the regions of interest. Maybe the real regions of interest are the vast uncharted nondemarcated nuance-rich areas of mental state space where an unspoken continuous coupling between brain, body, and environment can take place unhindered by partitions and symbols.

In the body of the world, they say, there is a soul and you are that. But we have ways within each other that will never be said by anyone.
—Jelaluddin Rumi

Appendix: MATLAB Code for Several Normalized Recurrence Simulations

The normalized recurrence competition algorithm is a simple enough and generic enough localist attractor network that it can be implemented in just a few lines of code. This appendix provides some example bits of code from some of the simulations described in the book. They are intended to make it easy for the reader to copy, alter, and experiment with the algorithm.

Chapter 4: Generic Normalized Recurrence

```
%normrec: a simple generic version based on three constraints
%competing over three alternative interpretations (using four
%stimulus items).
%inelegantly written by Michael Spivey

clear
clf
numalt=3; %number of alternative interpretations competing

Aw=.333; %Weight of constraint A
Bw=.333; %Weight of constraint B
Cw=.333; %Weight of constraint C

%4 stimuli with their A-based biases for the three alternatives
Abiases=[3 5 2; 2 5 3; 1 5 2; 4 3 2];
%4 stimuli with their B-based biases for the three alternatives
Bbiases=[1 1 1; 1 4 5; 3 2 5; 6 2 1];
%4 stimuli with their C-based biases for the three alternatives
```

```
Cbiases=[32 21 48; 20 26 40; 19 19 19; 12 14 19];
%Since the values will get normalized within each vector,
%scales need not match across bias-types in these matrices.

for item=1:4,
  Avec=Abiases(item,:); %collects biases for appropriate items
  Bvec=Bbiases(item,:);
  Cvec=Cbiases(item,:);
  t=0; %resets counter
  integvec=zeros(1,numalt); %resets integration vector to
  zeros
  integacts=zeros(1,numalt); %resets stored activation values

  %dynamic criterion prevents indefinite stalemate
  while max(integvec)<1-(t*.01),
    t=t+1;  %increment time

    %normalize feature vectors
    Avec=Avec/sum(Avec);
    Bvec=Bvec/sum(Bvec);
    Cvec=Cvec/sum(Cvec);

    %recalculate integvec (non-cumulative)
    integvec=Aw*Avec+Bw*Bvec+Cw*Cvec;

    %store integ activations
    integacts(t,:)=integvec;

    %if weights did not sum to 1.0,
    %one would need to normalize integvec here
    %as follows: integvec=integvec/sum(integvec);

    %cumulative multiplicative feedback
    Avec=Avec+integvec.*Avec;
    Bvec=Bvec+integvec.*Bvec;
    Cvec=Cvec+integvec.*Cvec;

  end

subplot(4,1,item)
plot(integacts)
title('Integ Activations Over Time')
axis([0 20 0 1])
hold on

Interps(item,:)=integvec;
RTs(item)=t;

end
hold off
%Activation pattern once criterion was reached, for the
%four items
```

```
Interps

%Time to reach dynamic criterion, for the four items
RTs
```

Chapter 4: Simulation of Beer Selection

```
%beers: a normalized recurrence simulation
%of the beer selection process.
%inelegantly written by Michael Spivey
clear
clf
%Vector elements stand for PabstBR, SamAdams, Guinness,
%Franziskaner, in that order
flavor=[.1 .2 .3 .4]; %flavor ratings
afford=[.33 .29 .23 .15]; %affordability ratings
wf=.25; %weight for flavor vector
wa=.75; %weight for affordability vector

%for simplicity, dynamic criterion not used here
for t=1:30,

  %normalize feature vectors
  flavor=flavor/sum(flavor);
  afford=afford/sum(afford);
  %store values
  flav(t,:)=flavor;
  aff(t,:)=afford;

  %recalculate integration vector (non-cumulative)
  integ=wf*flavor+wa*afford;
  %if weights did not sum to 1.0,
  %one would need to normalize integvec here
  %as follows: integ=integ/sum(integ);

  %store values
  beers(t,:)=integ;

  %cumulative multiplicative feedback
  flavor=flavor+integ.*flavor;
  afford=afford+integ.*afford;

end
subplot (4,1,1), plot(beers), title ('integ');
subplot(4,1,2), plot(flav), title ('flavor');
subplot(4,1,3), plot(aff), title ('affordability');

P=beers(:,1); %extract PBR values for potential scatterplot
S=beers(:,2); %extract SamAdams values for potential scatterplot
G=beers(:,3); %extract Guinness values for potential scatterplot
F=beers(:,4); %extract Franzie values for potential scatterplot
subplot (4,1,4)
```

```
scatter(P, S, 32, 'k')
axis([0 1 0 1])
axis square
xlabel('Pabst')
ylabel('Sam Adams')
title('Beer-space')
```

Chapter 6: Simulation of Taxonomic Class Categorization

```
%animals: a normalized recurrence simulation
%of taxonomic class categorization.
%inelegantly written by Michael Spivey
clear
clf
%Feature values are currently set for PLATYPUS
limbs=[0 1 0 1];%fins legs wings legs
environ=[1 1 0 1];%water land sky land
blood=[0 1 1 0]; %cold warm warm cold
breath=[0 1 1 1]; %water air air air
birth=[1 0 1 1];%eggs live eggs eggs

categ=[0 0 0 0];%fish mammal bird reptile

%for simplicity, dynamic criterion not used here
for t=1:40,
  %normalize feature values
  limbs=limbs/sum(limbs);
  environ=environ/sum(environ);
  blood=blood/sum(blood);
  breath=breath/sum(breath);
  birth=birth/sum(birth);

  %recalculate integration vector (non-cumulative)
  %each feature's weight is simply 1.0
  categ=limbs+environ+blood+breath+birth;
  %normalize integration vector, since weights do not sum
  %to 1.0
  categ=categ/sum(categ);
  %store values
  acts(t,:)=categ;

  %cumulative multiplicative feedback
  limbs=limbs+categ.*limbs;
  environ=environ+categ.*environ;
  blood=blood+categ.*blood;
  breath=breath+categ.*breath;
  birth=birth+categ.*birth;
end
'fish   mammal  bird   reptile'
categ
subplot(2,1,1)
plot(acts) %activations over time
```

```
axis ([0 30 0 1])
subplot(2,1,2)
F=acts(:,1);
M=acts(:,2);
B=acts(:,3);
R=acts(:,4);
scatter(M, R, 32, 'k') %trajectory plot
axis([0 1 0 1])
axis square
xlabel('mammal')
ylabel('reptile')
title('PLATYPUS')
```

Chapter 8: Simulation of Ambiguous Letter Resolution

```
%thecat: an unusual version of a normalized recurrence simulation
%that has differential weight matrices connecting the various
%layers instead of one-to-one connections between corresponding
%nodes.
%Simulates word-level feedback resolving ambiguous letter
%perception.
%clumsily written by Michael Spivey
clear
clf
t=0;
settled=0;
%create all the vectors
letter1=zeros(1,26);
letter2=zeros(1,26);
letter3=zeros(1,26);
L1Integ=zeros(1,12);
L2Integ=zeros(1,12);
L3Integ=zeros(1,12);
WInteg=zeros(1,12);
s=.01;

%create weight matrices
%(read word labels vertically)
%S A O T C B M C D F H P (1st letter)
%H H H H A A A A A A A A (2nd letter)
%E A M E T T T B D D T L (3rd letter)
w1=...
[0 s 0 0 0 0 0 0 0 0 0 0;
 0 0 0 0 0 s 0 0 0 0 0 0;
 0 0 0 0 s 0 0 s 0 0 0 0;
 0 0 0 0 0 0 0 0 s 0 0 0;
 0 0 0 0 0 0 0 0 0 0 0 0;
 0 0 0 0 0 0 0 0 0 s 0 0;
 0 0 0 0 0 0 0 0 0 0 0 0;
 0 0 0 0 0 0 0 0 0 0 s 0;
 0 0 0 0 0 0 0 0 0 0 0 0;
 0 0 0 0 0 0 0 0 0 0 0 0;
```

```
0 0 0 0 0 0 0 0 0 0 0 0;
0 0 0 0 0 0 0 0 0 0 0 0;
0 0 0 0 0 0 s 0 0 0 0 0;
0 0 0 0 0 0 0 0 0 0 0 0;
0 0 s 0 0 0 0 0 0 0 0 0;
0 0 0 0 0 0 0 0 0 0 0 s;
0 0 0 0 0 0 0 0 0 0 0 0;
0 0 0 0 0 0 0 0 0 0 0 0;
0 0 0 0 0 0 0 0 0 0 0 0;
0 0 0 s 0 0 0 0 0 0 0 0;
0 0 0 0 0 0 0 0 0 0 0 0;
0 0 0 0 0 0 0 0 0 0 0 0;
0 0 0 0 0 0 0 0 0 0 0 0;
0 0 0 0 0 0 0 0 0 0 0 0;
0 0 0 0 0 0 0 0 0 0 0 0;
0 0 0 0 0 0 0 0 0 0 0 0];

%S A O T C B M C D F H P
%H H H H A A A A A A A A
%E A M E T T T B D D T L
w2=...
[0 0 0 0 s s s s s s s s;
0 0 0 0 0 0 0 0 0 0 0 0;
0 0 0 0 0 0 0 0 0 0 0 0;
0 0 0 0 0 0 0 0 0 0 0 0;
0 0 0 0 0 0 0 0 0 0 0 0;
0 0 0 0 0 0 0 0 0 0 0 0;
0 0 0 0 0 0 0 0 0 0 0 0;
s s s s 0 0 0 0 0 0 0 0;
0 0 0 0 0 0 0 0 0 0 0 0;
0 0 0 0 0 0 0 0 0 0 0 0;
0 0 0 0 0 0 0 0 0 0 0 0;
0 0 0 0 0 0 0 0 0 0 0 0;
0 0 0 0 0 0 0 0 0 0 0 0;
0 0 0 0 0 0 0 0 0 0 0 0;
0 0 0 0 0 0 0 0 0 0 0 0;
0 0 0 0 0 0 0 0 0 0 0 0;
0 0 0 0 0 0 0 0 0 0 0 0;
0 0 0 0 0 0 0 0 0 0 0 0;
0 0 0 0 0 0 0 0 0 0 0 0;
0 0 0 0 0 0 0 0 0 0 0 0;
0 0 0 0 0 0 0 0 0 0 0 0;
0 0 0 0 0 0 0 0 0 0 0 0;
0 0 0 0 0 0 0 0 0 0 0 0;
0 0 0 0 0 0 0 0 0 0 0 0;
0 0 0 0 0 0 0 0 0 0 0 0;
0 0 0 0 0 0 0 0 0 0 0 0];

%S A O T C B M C D F H P
%H H H H A A A A A A A A
%E A M E T T T B D D T L
w3=...
[0 s 0 0 0 0 0 0 0 0 0 0;
0 0 0 0 0 0 0 s 0 0 0 0;
```

```
0 0 0 0 0 0 0 0 0 0 0 0 0;
0 0 0 0 0 0 0 0 s s 0 0;
s 0 0 s 0 0 0 0 0 0 0 0;
0 0 0 0 0 0 0 0 0 0 0 0;
0 0 0 0 0 0 0 0 0 0 0 0;
0 0 0 0 0 0 0 0 0 0 0 0;
0 0 0 0 0 0 0 0 0 0 0 0;
0 0 0 0 0 0 0 0 0 0 0 0;
0 0 0 0 0 0 0 0 0 0 0 0;
0 0 0 0 0 0 0 0 0 0 0 s;
0 0 s 0 0 0 0 0 0 0 0 0;
0 0 0 0 0 0 0 0 0 0 0 0;
0 0 0 0 0 0 0 0 0 0 0 0;
0 0 0 0 0 0 0 0 0 0 0 0;
0 0 0 0 0 0 0 0 0 0 0 0;
0 0 0 0 0 0 0 0 0 0 0 0;
0 0 0 0 0 0 0 0 0 0 0 0;
0 0 0 0 s s s 0 0 0 s 0;
0 0 0 0 0 0 0 0 0 0 0 0;
0 0 0 0 0 0 0 0 0 0 0 0;
0 0 0 0 0 0 0 0 0 0 0 0;
0 0 0 0 0 0 0 0 0 0 0 0;
0 0 0 0 0 0 0 0 0 0 0 0;
0 0 0 0 0 0 0 0 0 0 0 0];

%input is set for "T", ambiguous A/H character, and "E".
letter1(20)=1;%index3=C,index20=T
letter2(1)=1;%index1=A
letter2(8)=1;%index8=H
letter3(5)=1;%indeax5=E,index20=T

for t=1:30,

  %normalize letter vectors
  letter1=letter1/sum(letter1);
  letter2=letter2/sum(letter2);
  letter3=letter3/sum(letter3);

  %store letter vectors over time
  Let1(t,:)=letter1;
  Let2(t,:)=letter2;
  Let3(t,:)=letter3;

  %calculate word-supporters (cumulative)
  L1Integ=L1Integ+letter1*(w1);
  L2Integ=L2Integ+letter2*(w2);
  L3Integ=L3Integ+letter3*(w3);

  %normalize word-supporters
  L1Integ=L1Integ/sum(L1Integ);
  L2Integ=L2Integ/sum(L2Integ);
  L3Integ=L3Integ/sum(L3Integ);
  %calculate word layer (non-cumulative)
  WInteg=L1Integ+L2Integ+L3Integ;
```

```
%normalize word layer
WInteg=WInteg/sum(WInteg);
%when a word node reaches .9, record how long it took
if and((max(WInteg)>.9), (settled==0)),
  'Word Level Settling Time'
  t
  settled=1;
end

%store word vector over time
Words(t,:)=WInteg;

%cumulative multiplicative feedback to word-supporters
L1Integ=L1Integ+WInteg.*L1Integ;
L2Integ=L2Integ+WInteg.*L2Integ;
L3Integ=L3Integ+WInteg.*L3Integ;

%re-normalize word-supporters before computing
%next multiplicative feedback
L1Integ=L1Integ/sum(L1Integ);
L2Integ=L2Integ/sum(L2Integ);
L3Integ=L3Integ/sum(L3Integ);

%cumulative multiplicative feedback to letters
letter1=letter1+(L1Integ)*w1';
letter2=letter2+(L2Integ)*w2';
letter3=letter3+(L3Integ)*w3';

end
subplot(2,1,1),
plot(Words) %activations of word vector over time
subplot(2,1,2),
plot(Let2) %activations of second-letter vector over time
```

Chapter 8: Simulation of Visual Search

```
%vissearch: a normalized recurrence simulation of reaction time
%during conjunction search for a red vertical target
%amidst red horizontals and green verticals.
%inelegantly written by Michael Spivey
clear
clf
setsizes=0;

for ss=4:4:36, %setsizes 4, 8, 12, etc.
  setsizes=setsizes+1;
  t=0;
  integ=zeros(1,ss);
  %Red vec with half of the distractors being red
  red=[1 zeros(1, ss/2-1) (ones(1, ss/2))];
```

```
%Vertical vec with the other half of distractors being
%vertical
vert=[1 ones(1, ss/2-1) zeros(1, ss/2)];

%static criterion of .95 activation used to terminate
%competition
while max(integ)<.95,
  t=t+1;

  %normalize feature vectors
  red=red/sum(red);
  vert=vert/sum(vert);

  %recalculate integration vector (non-cumulative)
  %feature weights are each 1.0
  integ=red+vert;

  %normalize integ vector, since weights do not sum
  %to 1.0
  integ=integ/sum(integ);

  %cumulative multiplicative feedback
  red=red+integ.*red;
  vert=vert+integ.*vert;

  end

  %Reaction time = 300 ms + 20 ms per competition cycle
  rts(setsizes)=t*20+300;
end
plot([4:4:36], rts) %Reaction time as a function of set size
axis([0 40 0 1200])
ylabel('RT')
xlabel('Set Size')
```

Notes

Notes to Chapter 1

1. In fact, it is the act of looking inside the box that collapses this wave function, of the cat being partly dead and partly alive, into a randomly determined discrete unitary state of being *either* dead *or* alive. But this random wave-collapsing part of the story is only relevant to discussions of consciousness in chapter 12.

2. Of course, this is not to say that the Copenhagen interpretation of quantum mechanics is a happily accepted and parsimoniously integrated theory in physics. Indeed, the incompatibility of quantum theory and relativity theory has vexed physicists for many decades. For an excellent treatment of this conflict, and of the possible resolution offered by superstring theory, read Greene (2000), if you haven't already.

3. Properties of objects, such as overall shape, appear to be represented by population codes as well, in visual area V4 (Pasupathy & Connor, 2002).

4. Of equal importance but less relevant to the upcoming demonstrations, is second-order stability, or metastability. A system may never actually be even close to a fixed stable state, yet some of its possible trajectories may become so frequently traveled that they become stable *patterns* of continuous change in state.

5. In fact, some of the theoretical arguments for the existence of genuinely discrete, symbolic mental representations (e.g., Dietrich & Markman, 2003; Marcus, 2001) could be satisfied by placing partitions in the state space and assigning labels to the partitions. When the state of a dynamic system moves around inside a labeled partition, partition-based measurement of that system will make it appear as though the system is in stasis, when in fact it is not (see "symbolic dynamics" in chapters 2 and 4).

Notes to Chapter 2

1. At the subatomic spatial scale, time is thought to progress in unit increments that correspond to the duration it would take a photon to traverse the Planck length (roughly 1.6×10^{-35} meters) at 186,282 miles a second. That duration is about 10^{-43} seconds. However, I would suggest that for the purposes of describing neural process at the spatial scale of about 10^{-6} meters, 29 orders of magnitude larger than the Planck length, time is best treated as continuous.

2. By associating linguistic labels to the mental states here, I refer to the cognitive scientist's attempt to categorize the mental state, not to the cognitive system itself using language per se to identify its mental states. Thus, for example, a dog could have a mental state of *being hungry* (or even of *recognizing Grandma*) for which the observing scientist might use that linguistic label, but of course the dog is unlikely to be using a linguistic label. Moreover, unfortunately, I doubt a dog will ever be in the mental state of grasping the continuity of mind thesis.

Notes to Chapter 3

1. Not to mention the fact that there is a 500–1,000-millisecond hemodynamic response time that varies from region to region as a function of the richness of vasculature there. Then there's the theoretical problems with treating an active area as though it were the module devoted to the task at hand (see Sarter, Berntson, & Cacioppo, 1996; Uttal, 2001).

2. However, one can avoid the forced interruption of ongoing processing by grouping normal responses into those that happen to be fast, medium, or slow, to compare early and late preferences and accuracies (e.g., Fox, 1984; Lamberts, 2000; Miller & Dexter, 1988).

3. Repetitive pulses delivered in quick succession (e.g., a 50 Hz bout of these pulses for a second or more) can cause seizures (Bernabeu et al., 2004).

4. At this point, you may be wondering why some waves are positive and some are negative. Don't ask.

5. A more continuous treatment of the EEG signal will be discussed in a later section of this chapter.

6. See Boas et al. (2001) for discussion of noninvasive laser-optical methods that continuously record changes in blood oxygen level in human brains.

7. MEG can, of course, also be used in this nonevent-related fashion as well.

8. See also the electromagnetic articulometer system developed by Perkell et al. (1992).

9. There are also claims from a clinical- and sales-oriented system, called neuro linguistic programming, that an observer can tell whether someone is recalling visual or auditory memories—or even whether they are lying—by watching the directions of their eye movements. Do yourself a favor and put that nonsense out of your mind immediately. Scientific tests of these claims have systematically produced insignificant results (Baddeley & Predebon, 1991; Salas, de Groot, & Spanos, 1989; Thomason, Arbuckle, & Cady, 1980).

10. There also are various types of time-series analyses of scan paths that can test for particular eye movement sequences (e.g., Brandt & Stark, 1997; Richardson & Dale, 2005).

11. Brennan (2004) describes using a similar record of mouse cursor proximity (to a target location) during interactive conversation and cooperative task performance, revealing the real-time interplay between spoken language processing and motor movement.

12. On potential concern for this upward, then curved movement might be that participants could be strategically moving straight upward and then at earlier or later points in time turning left or right. Under this account, differential curvatures in the movement trajectories (between conditions) would not be due to differential spatial attraction toward the competing response option, but would instead be due to a blending of one upward motor command and one (early or late) sideways motor command. However, this alternative explanation is obviated by the recent finding that with instantaneous stimulus presentation (using pictures or written words), even the very *first x, y* transitions already show differential angles as a function of the strength of the competing response option (Dale, Kehoe, & Spivey, in press).

Notes to Chapter 4

1. It should be noted that the logistic function is not the only way to produce a sigmoid curve. For example, gain functions work as well: $y = 0.5 * (1 + \tan h(G * x))$, where G determines the slope (Amit, 1989).

2. Of course, each set of weight changes needs to be tiny on any given training iteration to avoid "unlearning" previously learned patterns.

3. The distinction between descriptive and explanatory theories has been used before to take an illusory high ground to better reject competing theories, but that is not the intent here. One can always transmogrify any putatively explanatory theory into a descriptive one by simply asking how its assumptions came into being. Thus, the descriptiveness of gravity equations is not justification for rejecting them but merely encouragement for being persistent at eventually developing an explanation for gravity's effects.

Notes to Chapter 5

1. In fact, Neisser himself has suggested that "information processing models of the classical kind, built on and tested by laboratory reaction-time experiments, may go the way of Ptolemaic epicycles" (Neisser, 1997).

2. Even with the 40 Hz oscillations occasionally observed in groups of neurons (Singer, 1999), the synchrony is only approximate, and it is not at all clear whether such phase-locking serves a functional purpose or is merely a nonfunctional side effect of recurrent processes (Shadlen and Movshon, 1999).

3. For example, if the sliding window for the moving average of neuronal activation in the global state space was one millisecond wide (and all neurons were somehow in perfect lockstep at the microsecond time scale), then each activation in this space would essentially be 0 or 1. In such a case, the trajectory in this system would be a series of teleportations to various corners in the state space.

4. One way to preserve some semblance of the modularity perspective might be to acknowledge continuous flow of information between subsystems but still insist that the subsystems use domain-specific representational formats which require agile

"interface modules" for their interaction (Jackendoff, 2002), such as a language-to-vision converter and a vision-to-language converter. However, the solution to the modularity hypothesis going bankrupt should probably not be to add more modules. That would be like paying off your overdrafted credit cards with new, higher interest credit cards.

5. Curiously, despite these cross-modal interactions among visual, auditory, and tactile inputs, statistical sequence learning may not transfer from any of these modalities to the other (Conway & Christiansen, 2005).

Notes to Chapter 6

1. Similarly, one might ask, at what point do the plucked hairs collecting on the floor become a "heap?"

2. See Love (2005), for a model that sets thresholds for a stimulus being granted its own category. And see Goldstone, Lippa, and Shiffrin (2001) for evidence that exemplars themselves move closer to one another in state space when they are identified as belonging to the *same* category, while the category label itself is explicitly used for separating exemplars that are identified as belonging to *different* categories.

3. In fact, in this rather small and oversimplified simulation, because the principal limbs and environment feature vectors for a bat uniquely support the bird category, and only the birth mode feature vector uniquely supports the mammal category, there actually winds up being more overall support for incorrectly categorizing a bat as a bird (asymptote at 0.8) than as a mammal (asymptote at 0.2). Expansion of the model to include more features and more classes would eradicate this error.

4. For example, the cup that is in the second column and fourth row of the matrix in figure 6.7 would be entered into the model, prior to normalization, as 2 wide (and thus 8 narrow) and 4 short (and thus 6 tall).

5. I should note that I am not implying that categorization tasks are artificial or unlike normal everyday life. A major point of the continuity of mind thesis is that everyday life very frequently *requires* a discretized response. But the discrete response is not proof that the internal cognitive processing is not continuous. For example, if you wanted someone to pass you a bowl, you wouldn't say, "Please pass me a concave object with an aspect ratio between 2 and 4." You would say, "Please pass me a bowl." Indeed, it is the very ubiquity of everyday situations that *do* require discretization of how we act on our perceptions that often tricks us into concluding that we think in categories.

6. For example, the bowl that is in the seventh column (width) and ninth row (shortness) of the matrix in figure 6.7 would be entered into the model, prior to normalization, as *width* = [0.17 0.29 0.45 0.64 0.82 0.95 1.0 0.95 0.82 0.64] and *height* = [0.95 1.0 0.95 0.82 0.64 0.45 0.29 0.17 0.09 0.04]. If only a single node is activated in each input vector (instead of this Gaussian distribution), the model performs approximately the same, except that the diagonal identification function (figure 6.13) is slightly more jagged throughout.

7. In information theory (Shannon & Weaver, 1949), the standard mathematical approach is to use the logarithm (base 2) of probabilities—and taking the logarithm of a 0 is not recommended.

Notes to Chapter 7

1. "I could care less" is clearly not intended to be ironic or sarcastic, because the speech intonation is quite variable from one use to another—there is not one stereotyped ironic or sarcastic form of the utterance. Besides, you can ask the speaker if he means it ironically, and he'll say, "No. I said I could care less, and I meant it!"

2. In *spoken* language, the future tense marking use of "be going to" is quite possibly in the process of developing its own separate lexical item: "be *gonna*" (i.e., one either says "I'm going to the store" or "I'm *gonna* drive to the store", never "I'm *gonna* the store"). In fact, nowadays, it's not uncommon to hear someone say "I'm *gonna go* to the store in a few minutes." If someone had said something like that back in the 18th century, they probably would have been criticized for being redundant or even "bastardizing the English language!"

3. This is easy enough to try for yourself by simply listening to a talk radio program and trying to shadow a speaker as quickly as possible. With some practice, you can approach the short latency exhibited by Marslen-Wilson's subjects, and you will probably start making some very interesting errors. However, you may need to record yourself and the radio program, as you may not even notice your errors when you make them.

4. Unless, of course, one has in their mental lexicon the noun *barnfell*. In such a case, the sentence merely describes a single event in which a horse races past the communal living house that the University of Rochester linguistics graduate students in the early 1990s dubbed "the Barnfell."

5. In fact, these and similar constraints also combine to determine how people deal with impending linguistic ambiguity during language *production*, where the time course of their integration is under considerable debate (e.g., Ferreira & Dell, 2000; Horton & Keysar, 1996; Nadig & Sedivy, 2002; Schober, 1993).

6. These kinds of referential contexts have often been shown to reduce the magnitude of garden path effects in syntactic ambiguity resolution studies (Altmann & Steedman, 1988; Altmann et al., 1992; Crain & Steedman, 1985), but there was some criticism about whether they can actually eliminate garden path effects (Clifton & Ferreira, 1989). As long as the contextual influence could be interpreted as an efficient and fast repair of a syntactic-heuristic-induced garden path, then syntax could still be viewed as an early modular stage of processing that was impervious to contextual guidance (Frazier, 1995; Rayner, Garrod, & Perfetti, 1992).

7. Importantly, to match the actual experimental results, the simulation must be run individually for each stimulus item, and then those competition durations must be averaged for each critical sentence region, just like with the human data. Due to the nonlinear temporal dynamics of normalized recurrence, if one instead averages all the stimulus constraints into one amalgam stimulus, and runs that one stimulus through the model, the results will be quite different and not particularly interpretable.

8. These values are typical for transitive verbs and close to the mean for the verbs used by Spivey and Tanenhaus (1998).

9. In fact, sentence processing can even be affected by apparent partial activation of locally coherent but syntactically *impermissible* versions of a construction (Tabor, Galantucci, & Richardson, 2004).

10. A version of Elman's (1990) simple recurrent network can simulate these findings as well (Magnuson et al., 2003b; see also Gaskell & Marslen-Wilson, 2002; Grossberg & Myers, 2000; Luce et al., 2000).

11. Ideally, the lexical nodes in normalized recurrence would be the exact same nodes as in TRACE, and thus visual cross-talk that gently modulates those lexical nodes could trickle all the way back to the phoneme and phonetic feature layers of TRACE. But that is for future work.

12. That said, it may well be that *reading* is a slightly more staccato, stop-and-start, dynamical process (like that depicted in figure 7.3, and in Elman, 1991, and Tabor & Tanenhaus, 1999) than *spoken* language comprehension (as depicted here), because during reading the eyes tend to fixate near the center of a word and the letters to the left and right of fixation appear to be processed roughly simultaneously and then the eyes jump to the next word and process it essentially in parallel (see Rayner, 1998).

Notes to Chapter 8

1. See Olshausen, Anderson, and Van Essen (1993) for a related computational model of dynamic receptive fields.

2. In fact, the neural signals for executing saccades and pursuit eye movements are richly coordinated with one another (Gardner & Lisberger, 2002).

3. However, the subjective phenomena of pop out may still occur with displays that produce a statistically reliable (albeit small) linear increase in response time with set size (Bridgeman & Aiken, 1994).

4. There was a period during which serial-like search was being renamed "difficult search" and parallel-like search was being renamed "easy search." This has more recently been converted into efficient and inefficient—with the apparent assumption that these new terms are somehow less circular than *difficult* and *easy*.

5. One possibility is that the system has some kind of running estimate, perhaps using probability summation over time (Watson, 1979), for the probability that the target should have been found by now. When that probability gets sufficiently high, for example, $1 - 1/e = 0.632$, but the target still has not been found, then the system concludes that the target is absent (Spivey-Knowlton, 1996).

6. The Bayesian approach to this feedforward integration process would be to multiply these probabilities and then normalize them, but with binary feature vectors that would of course eliminate any temporal dynamics, as the target integration node would achieve 1.0 activation on the first time step.

7. Moreover, it is clearly not simply operating within a linear portion of an otherwise nonlinear function. All the way to a set size of 300, in steps of 10, the slope function produced by normalized recurrence is perfectly linear, $r^2 = 1.0$.

8. I chose a hypothetical alligator here, instead of the more commonly used example of a saber-toothed tiger, because deciding even really quickly on the right motor output, when facing a saber-toothed tiger, probably wouldn't make much of a difference.

Notes to Chapter 9

1. See also the application Director (Macromedia), and several smaller software packages devoted solely to recording mouse coordinates (e.g., Tension Software's Point Recorder).

2. In fact, this could explain why we can't tickle ourselves, because there are no surprises when we automatically anticipate the somatosensory input that should result from our own finger movements on our own skin (Blakemore, Wolpert, & Frith, 2000).

Notes to Chapter 10

1. Although Tesauro's (1989, 1994) distributed neural network, TD-Gammon, has enjoyed considerable success at winning backgammon tournaments, the game of chess is still best played by discrete logical algorithms.

2. Note that this has the interesting result of including discrete environmental components (although certainly not "representations") in my description of the brain-body-environment triad—for the time scale of problem steps or game moves anyway, not for the time scale of actual motor movements. I prefer to assume that the locations and states of physical objects in the world (at the molar, superatomic, level of description) are generally consensually identifiable and discrete, and I also prefer to include the environment (along with brain and body) in my definition of mind, so I am thus forced to include these discrete environmental components in my conceptualization of mind—for the time scale in question, that is. What this amounts to is that, in a high-dimensional state space that describes how a mind conducts complex reasoning or problem solving, some of the dimensions (the environmental ones) might only use their extreme values, 0 and 1.

3. In fact, in defending discrete representations in cognition, Dietrich and Markman (2003) essentially describe the basic concept of symbolic dynamics, without referring to it by name, in their fourth argument (their discussion of figure 3).

4. In fact, verbalizing one's thought processes while trying to solve insight problems can sometimes interfere with one's ability to find the solution (Schooler, Ohlsson, & Brooks, 1993).

5. This is sometimes called a compound remote associates problem, but that doesn't make for a very good acronym.

6. Of course, this example was used in the 1970s when China was perhaps more prominent in U.S. news than Korea. A safer example for the present day might be "Ecuador is like Mexico" versus "Mexico is like Ecuador."

7. Of course, this ignores the fact that in a medical doctor's experience, people undergoing cancer tests are usually not randomly selected from the population. They are often visiting the clinic because of some symptoms of illness. Preexisting risk factors such as these make the actual calculation of the probabilities significantly more complicated than has been depicted here.

8. If it still feels intuitively frustrating, make like a frequentist and try the Monte Carlo method (closely related to the bootstrap method in statistics; Efron & Tibshirani, 1993). Write a computer program that randomly flips a two-sided coin 100,000 times and save the time-series output of heads and tails. Then, compute a search for every case of four tails in a row, and count how many of those cases are immediately followed by another tails, and how many are immediately followed by a heads. The two counts will *each* be pretty close to 3,125.

9. Chalk up another piece of evidence for the fact that although experimental data can be hard to interpret without theories, theories can be downright misleading without experimental data.

10. However, it is easily verified. Play the game 100 times with switching every time, and then play the game 100 times with staying every time. I promise that you will win the car about twice as often with the switching strategy. This could be called Monte Carloing the Monty Hall problem.

11. Note that the exponential curve is a bit optimistic for the 100-cup condition. One potential solution for this might be to multiply the equation by a scalar, perhaps 0.8 (and slightly increase p), to impose a < 1 asymptote on the curve.

Notes to Chapter 12

1. I do not wish to claim that no form of awareness exists, as that could indeed be "ludicrous and insane" (see Searle, 1992). However, the minds of scientifically inclined researchers should weigh heavy with the knowledge that each and every report of a sensory impression or qualia is first filtered through self-awareness and/or linguistic processes. Therefore, although many people report experiencing them, no single qualia has itself ever been *consensually* observed. As a result, we might consider treating those self-awareness and linguistic processes as *the phenomena of interest*, and not merely as filters through which some putative measure of pure consciousness is extruded.

2. For example, neuroimaging studies of what the brain is doing during "conscious experience" compared to "nonconscious experience" (e.g., Crick & Koch, 1998; Raichle, 1998; Taylor, 1999; see also Revonsuo, 2001) are actually demonstrating correlations between particular brain activity and the later reportability of conscious experience, which is more the purview of self-consciousness rather than pure consciousness.

3. Ryle (1949, p. 72) puts it this way: "A person picturing his nursery is, in a certain way, like that person seeing his nursery, but the similarity does not consist in his really looking at a real likeness of his nursery, but in his seeming to see his nursery itself, when he is not really seeing it. He is not being a spectator of a resemblance of his nursery, but he is resembling a spectator of his nursery."

4. Note, however, that by admitting that I am a zombie, I am deviating somewhat from being a proper zombie, because proper zombies are supposed to be indistinguishable from normal people (see Dennett, 1995)—and believe me, normal people do not admit to being zombies.

5. Ironically, Searle (1992, p. 71) uses this same basic point, when discussing conscious robots and nonconscious robots producing identical behaviors, to bring attention to the other side of the coin: that "as far as the ontology of consciousness is concerned, behavior is simply irrelevant." However, it is unclear whether he makes an exception for the behavior of claiming to be conscious, which, after all, is the only empirical evidence we have that supports the existence of consciousness in the first place.

6. Obviously, seeking preexisting causes could in principle continue going back and back all the way to the big bang. But a middle ground of distributing the punitive and rehabilitative measures among the perpetrator and a few statistically reliable preexisting causal forces should not be impossible to find.

7. The distinction has also been used as an all too convenient excuse to avoid reading neuroscience research.

8. In fact, there does seem to be a pretty wide array of subtle psychological modulations to people's emotional/visceral responses to pain. Some people's pain is

accompanied by nausea. Some people's pain is mixed with sadness or anger. In fact, I know someone who says she doesn't really know the difference between a sharp pain and a dull pain! (She has a master's degree in rhetoric and communications, so she's not stupid or illiterate.)

9. Sometimes it's not so implicit. For example, O'Brien and Opie (1999b), among others, have espoused what they call Cartesian materialism.

10. This is a little like a president implementing new laws for restricting industrial pollution that actually impose far *weaker* constraints than the already existing but largely unenforced legislation, and then calling it the Clear Skies Initiative.

11. In fact, one of the smartest people I know actually converses with people that way sometimes. With lots of practice, you can understand her most of the time.

Bibliography

Aaron, E., & Spivey, M. (1998). Frequency vs. probability formats: Framing the three doors problem. *Proceedings of the Twentieth Annual Conference of the Cognitive Science Society* (pp. 13–18). Mahwah, N.J.: Lawrence Erlbaum.

Abbott, L., & Blum, K. (1996). Functional significance of long-term potentiation for sequence learning and prediction. *Cerebral Cortex, 6*, 406–416.

Abrams, R., & Balota, D. (1991). Mental chronometry: Beyond reaction time. *Psychological Science, 2*, 153–157.

Adelson, E., & Bergen, J. (1991). The plenoptic function and the elements of early vision. In M. Landy & J. Movshon (Eds.), *Computational models of visual processing* (pp. 3–20). Cambridge, Mass.: MIT Press.

Agre, P. E., & Chapman, D. (1987). Pengi: An implementation of a theory of activity. *Proceedings of the 6th National Conference on Artificial Intelligence* (pp. 268–272). San Mateo, Calif.: Morgan Kaufmann.

Aks, D., Zelinsky, G., & Sprott, J. (2002). Memory across eye-movements: 1/f dynamic in visual search. *Nonlinear Dynamics, Psychology, and Life Sciences, 6*, 1–25.

Aleksander, I. (1973). Random logic nets: Stability and adaptation. *International Journal of Man Machine Studies, 5*, 115–131.

Alibali, M. W., Kita, S., & Young, A. J. (2000). Gesture and the process of speech production: We think, therefore we gesture. *Language and Cognitive Processes, 15*, 593–613.

Allman, J., Miezen, F., & McGuinness, E. (1985). Stimulus specific responses from beyond the classical receptive field: Neurophysiological mechanisms for local-global comparisons in visual neurons. *Annual Review of Neuroscience, 8*, 407–430.

Allopenna, P. D., Magnuson, J. S., & Tanenhaus, M. K. (1998). Tracking the time course of spoken word recognition using eye movements: Evidence for continuous mapping models. *Journal of Memory and Language, 38*, 419–439.

Allport, A. (1989). Visual attention. In M. Posner (Ed.), *Foundations of cognitive science* (pp. 631–682). Cambridge, Mass.: MIT Press.

Altmann, G., & Kamide, Y. (2004). Now you see it, now you don't: Mediating the mapping between language and the visual world. In J. Henderson & F. Ferreira (Eds.), *The interface of language, vision, and action: Eye movements and the visual world.* New York: Psychology Press.

Altmann, G., Garnham, A., & Dennis, Y. (1992). Avoiding the garden-path: Eye movements in context. *Journal of Memory and Language, 31,* 685–712.

Altmann, G., Garnham, A., & Henstra, J. (1994). Effects of syntax in human sentence parsing: Evidence against a structure-based proposal mechanism. *Journal of Experimental Psychology: Learning, Memory, and Cognition, 20,* 209–216.

Altmann, G., & Steedman, M. (1988). Interaction with context during human sentence processing. *Cognition, 30,* 191–238.

Amit, D. (1989). *Modeling brain function: The world of attractor neural networks.* New York: Cambridge University Press.

Anderson, J. A., Siverstein, J., Ritz, S., & Jones, R. (1977). Distinctive features, categorical perception, and probability learning: Some applications of a neural model. *Psychological Review, 84,* 413–451.

Anderson, J. R. (1983). A spreading activation theory of memory. *Journal of Verbal Learning and Verbal Behavior, 22,* 261–295.

Anderson, J. R., Bothell, D., & Douglass, S. (2004). Eye movements do not reflect retrieval processes: Limits of the eye-mind hypothesis. *Psychological Science, 15,* 225–231.

Anderson, J. R., & Bower, G. (1971). On an associative trace for sentence memory. *Journal of Verbal Learning and Verbal Behavior, 10,* 673–680.

Anderson, J. R., & Bower, G. (1972). Configural properties in sentence memory. *Journal of Verbal Learning and Verbal Behavior, 11,* 594–605.

Anderson, J. R., & Lebiere, C. (1998). *The atomic components of thought.* Mahwah, N.J.: Lawrence Erlbaum.

Anderson, J. R., Qin, Y., Stenger, V., & Carter, C. (2004). The relationship of three cortical regions to an information-processing model. *Journal of Cognitive Neuroscience, 16,* 637–653.

Anderson, N. (1964). Test for number-averaging behavior. *Psychonomic Science, 1,* 191–192.

Anderson, N. (1996). *A functional theory of cognition.* Hillsdale, N.J.: Lawrence Erlbaum.

Andrews, M. (2001). Processing and recognition of symbol sequences. In J. Moore & K. Stenning (Eds.), *Proceedings of the 23rd Annual Conference of the Cognitive Science Society* (pp. 61–65). Mahwah, N.J.: Lawrence Erlbaum.

Andrews, M. (2003). Language learning and nonlinear dynamical systems. Unpublished Ph.D. dissertation, Cornell University.

Antrobus, J., Antrobus, J., & Singer, J. (1964). Eye movements accompanying daydreaming, visual imagery, and thought suppression. *Journal of Abnormal and Social Psychology, 69,* 244–252.

Ashby, F., Valentin, V., & Turken, A. (2002). The effects of positive affect and arousal on working memory and executive attention: Neurobiology and computational models. In S. Moore & M. Oaksford (Eds.), *Emotional cognition: From brain to behaviour* (pp. 245–287). Amsterdam: John Benjamins.

Ashby, F., & Waldron, E. (1999). On the nature of implicit categorization. *Psychonomic Bulletin and Review, 6,* 363–378.

Aslin, R., Jusczyk, P., & Pisoni, D. (1998). Speech and auditory processing during infancy: Constraints on and precursors to language. In W. Damon (Ed.), *Handbook of child psychology, vol. 2: Cognition, perception, and language* (pp. 147–198). New York: Wiley.

Atick, J., Griffin, P., & Redlich, A. (1996). Statistical approach to shape and shading: Reconstruction of three-dimensional face surfaces from single two-dimensional images. *Neural Computation, 8,* 1321–1340.

Atmanspacher, H., (2004). Quantum theory and consciousness: An overview with selected examples. *Discrete Dynamics, 8,* 51–73.

Atmanspacher, H., & beim Graben, P. (in press). Contextual emergence of mental states from neurodynamics. *Chaos and Complexity Letters.*

Avikainen, S., Kulomaki, T., & Hari, R. (1999). Normal movement reading in Asperger subjects. *Neuroreport: An International Journal for Rapid Communication of Neuroscience Research, 10,* 3467–3470.

Awh, E., Matsukura, M., & Serences, J. (2003). Top-down control over biased competition during covert spatial orienting. *Journal of Experimental Psychology: Human Perception and Performance, 29,* 52–63.

Baas, J., Kenemans, J., & Mangun, G. (2002). Selective attention to spatial frequency: An ERP and source localization analysis. *Clinical Neurophysiology, 113,* 1840–1854.

Babiloni, C., Babiloni, F., Carducci, F., Cincotti, F., Del Percio, C., Hallett, M., Kelso, A., Moretti, D., Liepert, J., & Rossini, P. (2003). Shall I move my right or my left hand? An EEG study in frequency and time domains. *Journal of Psychophysiology, 17,* 69–86.

Baddeley, A. (1986). *Working memory.* Oxford: Oxford University Press.

Baddeley, M., & Predebon, J. (1991). "Do the eyes have it?": A test of neurolinguistic programming's eye-movement hypothesis. *Australian Journal of Clinical Hypnotherapy and Hypnosis, 12,* 1–23.

Bajcsy, R., & Goldberg, K. (1984). Active touch and robot perception. *Cognition and Brain Theory, 7,* 199–216.

Bak, P. (1996). *How nature works: The science of self-organized criticality.* New York: Springer-Verlag.

Balasubramaniam, R., Riley, M., & Turvey, M. (2000). Specificity of postural sway to the demands of a precision task. *Gait & Posture, 9,* 65–78.

Balcetis, E., & Dale, R. (2005). Shades of the chameleon: Social influences on syntactic mimicry. *Proceedings of the 27th Annual Meeting of the Cognitive Science Society* (pp. 184–189). Mahwah, N.J.: Lawrence Erlbaum.

Ballard, D. (1989). Behavioral constraints on animate vision. *Image and Vision Computing, 7,* 3–9.

Ballard, D. (1997). *An introduction to natural computation.* Cambridge, Mass.: MIT Press.

Ballard, D., Hayhoe, M., & Pelz, J. (1995). Memory representations in natural tasks. *Journal of Cognitive Neuroscience, 7,* 66–80.

Ballard, D., Hayhoe, M., Pook, P., & Rao, R. (1997). Deictic codes for the embodiment of cognition. *Behavioral and Brain Sciences, 20,* 723–767.

Balota, D., & Abrams, R. (1995). Mental chronometry: Beyond onset latencies in the lexical decision task. *Journal of Experimental Psychology: Learning, Memory, and Cognition, 21,* 1289–1302.

Banerji, R. (1980). *Artificial intelligence: A theoretical approach.* New York: Elsevier Science.

Barac-Cikoja, D., & Turvey, M. (1991). Perceiving aperture size by striking. *Journal of Experimental Psychology: Human Perception and Performance, 17*, 330–346.

Barac-Cikoja, D., & Turvey, M. (1993). Haptically perceiving size at a distance. *Journal of Experimental Psychology: General, 122*, 347–370.

Barber, M., Clark, J., & Anderson, C. (2003). Neural representation of probabilistic information. *Neural Computation, 15*, 1843–1846.

Barclay, J. (1973). The role of comprehension in remembering sentences. *Cognitive Psychology, 4*, 229–254.

Barlow, H. (1972). Single units and sensation: A neuron doctrine for perceptual psychology? *Perception, 1*(4), 371–394.

Barsalou, L. (1991). Deriving categories to achieve goals. In G. Bower (Ed.), *The psychology of learning and motivation: Advances in research and theory, vol. 27* (pp. 1–64). San Diego, Calif.: Academic Press.

Barsalou, L. (1999). Perceptual symbol systems. *Behavioral and Brain Sciences, 22*, 577–660.

Barsalou, L. (2002). Being there conceptually: Simulating categories in preparation for situated action. In N. Stein, P. Bauer, & M. Rabinowitz (Eds.), *Representation, memory, and development: Essays in honor of Jean Mandler*. Mahwah, N.J.: Lawrence Erlbaum.

Barsalou, L. (2003). Situated simulation in the human conceptual system. *Language and Cognitive Processes, 18*, 513–562.

Barsalou, L., Niedenthal, P., Barbey, A., & Ruppert, J. (2003). Social embodiment. In B. H. Ross (Ed.), *The psychology of learning and motivation, vol. 43*. San Diego, Calif.: Academic Press.

Bartlett, F. (1932). *Remembering: A study in experimental and social psychology*. Oxford: Macmillan.

Bastian, A., Schöner, G., & Riehle, A. (2003). Preshaping and continuous evolution of motor cortical representations during movement preparation. *European Journal of Neuroscience, 18*, 2047–2058.

Batali, J. (1998). Computational simulations of the emergence of grammar. In J. Hurford, M. Studdert-Kennedy, & C. Knight (Eds.), *Approaches to the evolution of language: Social and cognitive bases*. Cambridge: Cambridge University Press.

Bates, E., & Dick, F. (2002). Language, gesture, and the developing brain. *Developmental Psychology, 40*, 293–310.

Bates, E., & MacWhinney, B. (1989). Functionalism and the competition model. In B. MacWhinney & E. Bates (Eds.), *The cross-linguistic study of sentence processing* (pp. 3–73). New York: Cambridge University Press.

Bauer, B., Jolicoeur, P., & Cowan, W. (1996). Visual search for colour targets that are or are not linearly separable from distractors. *Vision Research, 36*, 1439–1465.

Bayes, T. (1763/1958). Studies in the history of probability and statistics: IX. Thomas Bayes's essay "Towards solving a problem in the doctrine of chances." *Biometrika, 45*, 296–315.

Baylis, G., & Rolls, E. (1987). Responses of neurons in the inferior temporal cortex in short term and serial recognition memory tasks. *Experimental Brain Research, 65*, 614–622.

Beale, J., & Keil, F. (1995). Categorical effects in the perception of faces. *Cognition, 57*, 217–239.

Beatty, J. (1982). Task-evoked pupillary responses, processing load, and the structure of processing resources. *Psychological Bulletin, 91*, 276–292.

Bechtel, W. (1998). Representations and cognitive explanations: Assessing the dynamicist's challenge in cognitive science. *Cognitive Science, 22*, 295–318.

Bechtel, W. (2003). Modules, brain parts, and evolutionary psychology. In S. Scher & F. Rauscher (Eds.), *Evolutionary psychology: Alternative approaches* (pp. 211–227). Dordrecht, Netherlands: Kluwer Academic.

Bechtel, W., & Abrahamsen, A. (2002). *Connectionism and the mind: Parallel processing, dynamics, and evolution in networks* (2nd ed.). Malden, Mass.: Blackwell.

Bednar, J., & Miikkulainen, R. (2000). Tilt aftereffects in a self-organizing model of the primary visual cortex. *Neural Computation, 12*, 1721–1740.

Beek, P., & van Wieringen, P. (1994). Perspectives on the relation between information and dynamics: An epilogue. *Human Movement Science, 13*, 519–533.

Beer, R. (1989). *Intelligence as adaptive behavior.* New York: Academic Press.

Beer, R. (1995). On the dynamics of small continuous-time recurrent neural networks. *Adaptive Behavior, 3*, 471–511.

Beer, R. (1996). Toward the evolution of dynamical neural networks for minimally cognitive behavior. In P. Maes, M. Mataric, J. Meyer, J. Pollack, & S. Wilson (Eds.), *From animals to animats 4: Proceedings of the 4th International Conference on Simulation of Adaptive Behavior* (pp. 393–401). Cambridge, Mass.: MIT Press.

Beer, R. (2000). Dynamical approaches to cognitive science. *Trends in Cognitive Sciences, 4*, 91–99.

Behrmann, M., Geng, J., & Shomstein, S. (2004). Parietal cortex and attention. *Current Opinion in Neurobiology, 14*, 212–217.

beim Graben, P. (2004). Incompatible implementations of physical symbol systems. *Mind and Matter, 2*, 29–51.

beim Graben, P., Saddy, J., Schlesewsky, M., & Kurths, J. (2000). Symbolic dynamics of event-related potentials. *Physical Review E, 62*, 5518–5541.

Bem, D. (1967). Self-perception: An alternative interpretation of cognitive dissonance phenomena. *Psychological Review, 74*, 183–200.

Ben-Nun, Y. (1986). The use of pupillometry in the study of on-line verbal processing: Evidence for depths of processing. *Brain and Language, 28*, 1–11.

Berlin, B., & Kay, P. (1969). *Basic color terms.* Berkeley: University of California Press.

Bermudez, J. (1998). *The paradox of self-consciousness.* Cambridge, Mass.: MIT Press.

Bernabeu, M., Orient, F., Tormos, J., & Pascual-Leone, A. (2004). Seizure induced by fast repetitive transcranial magnetic stimulation. *Clinical Neurophysiology, 115*, 1714–1715.

Bertelson, P., & Radeau, M. (1981). Cross-modal bias and perceptual fusion with auditory-visual spatial discordance. *Perception and Psychophysics, 29*, 578–584.

Bertenthal, B. (1990). Application of biomechanical principles to the study of perception and action. In B. Bertenthal & H. Bloch (Eds.), *Sensory-motor organizations and development in infancy and early childhood* (pp. 243–260). New York: Kluwer Academic/Plenum.

Bertenthal, B., Boker, S., & Xu, M. (2000). Analysis of the perception-action cycle of visually induced postural sway in 9-month-old sitting infants. *Infant Behavior and Development, 23*, 299–315.

Bertram, B. (1980). Vigilance and group size in ostriches. *Animal Behavior, 28*, 2278–2286.

Bever, T. (1970). The cognitive basis for linguistic structures. In J. Hayes (Ed.), *Cognition and the development of language.* New York: Wiley.

Bever, T., & Hurtig, R. (1975). Detection of nonlinguistic stimulus is poorest at the end of a clause. *Journal of Psycholinguistic Research, 4*, 1–7.

Bhalla, M. & Proffitt, D. R. (1999). Visual-motor recalibration in geographical slant perception. *Journal of Experimental Psychology: Human Perception and performance, 25*, 1076–1096.

Bickle, J. (1998). *Psychoneural reductionism: The new wave.* Cambridge, Mass.: MIT Press.

Biederman, I. (2000). Recognition by components: A theory of human image understanding. In S. Yantis (Ed.), *Visual perception: Essential readings* (pp. 320–340). Philadelphia: Psychology Press.

Billock, V., de Guzman, G., & Kelso, J. (2001). Fractal time and 1/f spectra in dynamic images and human vision. *Physica D, 148*, 136–146.

Binder, K., Duffy, S., & Rayner, K. (2001). The effects of thematic fit and discourse context on syntactic ambiguity resolution. *Journal of Memory and Language, 44*, 297–324.

Birnbaum, M. (1983). Base rates in Bayesian inference: Signal detection analysis of the cab problem. *American Journal of Psychology, 96*, 85–94.

Blackmore, S. (2003). *Consciousness: An introduction.* Oxford: Oxford University Press.

Blakemore, C., & Campbell, F. (1969). On the existence of neurons in the human visual system selectively sensitive to the orientation and size of retinal images. *Journal of Physiology, 203*, 237–260.

Blakemore, S., & Frith, C. (2003). Self-awareness and action. *Current Opinion in Neurobiology, 13*, 219–224.

Blakemore, S., Wolpert, D., & Frith, C. (1998). Central cancellation of self-produced tickle sensation. *Nature Neuroscience, 1*, 635–640.

Blakemore, S., Wolpert, D., & Frith, C. (2000). Why can't you tickle yourself? *Neuroreport: An International Journal for Rapid Communication of Neuroscience Research, 11*, R11–R16.

Block, N. (1978). Troubles with functionalism. In W. Savage (Ed.), *Perception and cognition, Minnesota Studies in the Philosophy of Science*, vol. 9. Minneapolis: University of Minnesota Press.

Bloom, P. (2004). *Descartes' baby: How the science of child development explains what makes us human.* New York: Basic Books.

Boas, D., Gaudette, T., Strangman, G., Cheng, X., Marota, J., & Mandeville, J. (2001). The accuracy of near infrared spectroscopy and imaging during focal changes in cerebral hemodynamics. *Neuroimage, 13*, 76–90.

Bock, J. (1986). Syntactic persistence in language production. *Cognitive Psychology, 18*, 355–387.

Bohannon, J., MacWhinney, B., & Snow, C. (1990). No negative evidence revisited: Beyond learnability or who has to prove what to whom. *Developmental Psychology, 26*, 221–226.

Bohannon, J., & Stanowicz, L. (1988). The issue of negative evidence: Adult responses to children's language errors. *Developmental Psychology, 24*, 684–689.

Bohte, S. (2004). The evidence for neural information processing with precise spike-times: A survey. *Natural Computing, 3*, 195–206.

Bollt, E., Stanford, T., Lai, Y., & Zyczkowski, K. (2000). Validity of threshold crossing analysis of symbolic dynamics from chaotic time series. *Physical Review Letters, 85*, 3524–3527.

Bollt, E., Stanford, T., Lai, Y., & Zyczkowski, K. (2001). What symbolic dynamics do we get with a misplaced partition? On the validity of threshold crossings analysis of chaotic time-series. *Physica D, 154*, 259–286.

Boltz, M. (1993). The generation of temporal and melodic expectancies during musical listening. *Perception and Psychophysics, 53*, 585–600.

Boman, D. K., & Hotson, J. R. (1992). Predictive smooth pursuit eye movements near abrupt changes in motion direction. *Vision Research, 32,* 675–689.

Bonadeau, E., Dorigo, M., & Theraulaz, G. (1999). *Swarm intelligence: From natural to artificial systems.* London: Oxford University Press.

Bonanno, C., & Menconi, G. (2002). Computational information for the logistic map at the chaos threshold. *Discrete and Continuous Dynamical Systems—Series B, 2,* 415–431.

Bonini, N., Tentori, K., & Osherson, D. (2004). A different conjunction fallacy. *Mind and Language, 19,* 199–210.

Bonner, J. (1980). *The evolution of culture in animals.* Princeton, N.J.: Princeton University Press.

Bornstein, M., & Korda, N. (1984). Discrimination and matching within and between hues measured by reaction times: Some implications for categorical perception and levels of information processing. *Psychological Research, 46,* 207–222.

Bornstein, M., & Korda, N. (1985). Identification and adaptation of hue: Parallels in the operation of mechanisms that underlie categorical perception in vision and in audition. *Psychological Research, 47,* 1–17.

Boroditsky, L. (2001). Does language shape thought? Mandarin and English speakers' conceptions of time. *Cognitive Psychology, 43,* 1–22.

Boroditzky, L., & Ramscar, M. (2002). The roles of body and mind in abstract thought. *Psychological Science, 13,* 185–189.

Borsellino, A., & Poggio, T. (1973). Convolution and correlation algebras. *Kybernetik, 13,* 113–122.

Bosbach, S., Cole, J., Prinz, W., & Knoblich, G. (2005). Inferring another's expectation from action: The role of peripheral sensation. *Nature Neuroscience, 8,* 1295–1297.

Botvinick, M., & Cohen, J. (1998). Rubber hands "feel" touch that eyes see. *Nature, 391,* 756.

Botvinick, M., & Plaut, D. (2004). Doing without schema hierarchies: A recurrent connectionist approach to normal and impaired routine sequential action. *Psychological Review, 111,* 395–429.

Bouton, M. (2004). Context and behavioral processes in extinction. *Learning and Memory, 11,* 485–494.

Bowden, E., & Beeman, M. (1998). Getting the right idea: Semantic activation in the right hemisphere may help solve insight problems. *Psychological Science, 6,* 435–440.

Bowers, J. (2002). Challenging the widespread assumption that connectionism and distributed representations go hand-in-hand. *Cognitive Psychology, 45,* 413–445.

Bowers, K., Farvolden, P., & Mermigis, L. (1995). Intuitive antecedents of insight. In S. Smith, T. Ward, & R. Finke (Eds.), *The creative cognition approach.* Cambridge, Mass.: MIT Press.

Bowers, K., Regehr, G., Balthazard, C., & Parker, K. (1990). Intuition in the context of discovery. *Cognitive Psychology, 22,* 72–110.

Boynton, R. (1960). Theory of color vision. *Journal of the Optical Society of America, 50,* 929–944.

Bradshaw, J. (1968). Pupillary changes and reaction time with varied stimulus uncertainty. *Psychonomic Science, 13,* 69–70.

Braham, P. (1997). Fashion: Unpacking a cultural production. In P. du Gay (Ed.), *Production of culture/cultures of production* (pp. 119–175). Thousand Oaks, Calif.: Sage.

Braitenberg, V. (1977). *On the texture of brains: An introduction to the neuroanatomy for the cybernetically minded* (translation of *Gehirngespinste*). New York: Springer-Verlag.

Braithwaite, J., Humphreys, G., & Hodsoll, J. (2003). Color grouping in space and time: Evidence from negative color-based carryover effects in preview search. *Journal of Experimental Psychology: Human Perception and Performance, 29,* 758–778.

Brandt, S., & Stark, L. (1997). Spontaneous eye movements during visual imagery reflect the content of the visual scene. *Journal of Cognitive Neuroscience, 9,* 27–38.

Branigan, H., Pickering, M., & Cleland, A. (2000). Syntactic co-ordination in dialogue. *Cognition, 75,* B13–B25.

Bransford, J., Barclay, J., & Franks, J. (1972). Sentence memory: A constructive versus interpretive approach. *Cognitive Psychology, 3,* 193–209.

Bransford, J., & Johnson, M. (1972). Contextual prerequisites for understanding: Some investigations of comprehension and recall. *Journal of Verbal Learning and Verbal Behavior, 11,* 717–726.

Brefczynski, J., & DeYoe, E. (1999). A physiological correlate of the "spotlight" of visual attention. *Nature Neuroscience, 2,* 370–374.

Brennan, S. (2004). How conversation is shaped by visual and spoken evidence. In J. Trueswell & M. Tanenhaus (Eds.), *Approaches to studying world-situated language use: Bridging the language-as-product and language-as-action traditions* (pp. 95–129). Cambridge, Mass.: MIT Press.

Bressler, S., & Kelso, J. (2001). Cortical coordination dynamics and cognition. *Trends in Cognitive Sciences, 5,* 26–36.

Bridgeman, B. (1991). Complementary cognitive and motor image processing. In G. Obrecht & L. Stark (Eds.), *Presbyopia research: From molecular biology to visual adaptation* (pp. 189–198). New York: Plenum Press.

Bridgeman, B. (2002). The grand illusion and petit illusions: Interactions of perception and sensory coding. *Journal of Consciousness Studies, 9,* 29–34.

Bridgeman, B. (2003). Is mental life possible without the will? A review of Daniel M. Wegner's *The Illusion of Conscious Will*. *Psyche: An Interdisciplinary Journal of Research in Consciousness, 9.*

Bridgeman, B., & Aiken, W. (1994). Attentional "popout" and parallel search are separate phenomena. *Investigative Ophthalmology & Visual Science, 35,* 1623.

Bridgeman, B., & Fisher, B. (1990). Saccadic suppression of displacement is strongest in central vision. *Perception, 19,* 103–111.

Bridgeman, B., van der Hejiden, A., & Velichkovsky, B. (1994). A theory of visual stability across saccadic eye movements. *Behavioral and Brain Sciences, 17,* 247–292.

Bridle, J. (1990). Alpha-nets: A recurrent "neural" network architecture with a hidden Markov model interpretation. *Speech Communication, 9,* 83–92.

Britt, M., Perfetti, C., Garrod, S., & Rayner, K. (1992). Parsing in discourse: Context effects and their limits. *Journal of Memory and Language, 31,* 293–314.

Britten, K., Shadlen, M., Newsome, W., & Movshon, J. (1992). The analysis of visual motion: a comparison of neuronal and psychophysical performance. *Journal of Neuroscience, 12,* 4745–4767.

Broadbent, D. (1958). *Perception and communication*. New York: Pergamon Press.

Broadbent, D. (1987). Simple models for experimentable situations. In P. Morris (Ed.), *Modelling cognition.* Chichester: Wiley.

Brooks, L. (1978). Nonanalytic concept formation and memory for instances. In E. Rosch & B. Lloyd (Eds.), *Cognition and categorization* (pp. 169–211). Hillsdale, N.J.: Lawrence Erlbaum.

Brooks, L. (2005). The blossoms and the weeds. *Canadian Journal of Experimental Psychology, 59,* 62–74.

Brooks, R. (1991). Intelligence without representation. *Artificial Intelligence, 47,* 139–159.

Brooks, R. (1995). Intelligence without reason. In L. Steels & R. Brooks (Eds.), *The artificial life route to artificial intelligence: Building embodied, situated agents* (pp. 25–81). Hillsdale, N.J.: Lawrence Erlbaum.

Brooks, R. (1999). *Cambrian intelligence: The early history of the new AI.* Cambridge, Mass.: MIT Press.

Brown, G., Hulme, C., & Dalloz, P. (1996). Modelling human memory: Connectionism and convolution. *British Journal of Mathematical and Statistical Psychology, 49,* 1–24.

Brown, R. (1964). Three processes in the child's acquisition of syntax. *Harvard Educational Review, 34,* 133–151.

Browne, A. (2002). Representation and extrapolation in multilayer perceptions. *Neural Computation, 14,* 1739–1754.

Brownell, H., & Caramazza, A. (1978). Categorizing with overlapping categories. *Memory and Cognition, 6,* 481–490.

Bruner, J., Goodnow, J., & Austin, G. (1956). *A study of thinking.* Oxford: Wiley.

Brunswick, E. (1955). *The conceptual framework of psychology.* Chicago: University of Chicago Press.

Buchel, C., Price, C., Frackowiak, R., & Friston, K. (1998). Different activation patterns in the visual cortex of late and congenitally blind subjects. *Brain, 121,* 409–419.

Budiu, R., & Anderson, J. R. (2004). Interpretation-based processing: A unified theory of semantic sentence comprehension. *Cognitive Science, 28,* 1–44.

Bugmann, G. (1992). The neuronal computation time. In I. Alexander & J. Taylor (Eds.), *Artificial neural networks II* (pp. 861–864). Brighton, U.K.: Elsevier, Proc. of ICANN'92.

Burnod, Y., & Korn, H. (1989). Consequences of stochastic release of neurotransmitters for network computation in the central nervous system. *Proceedings of the National Academy of Sciences of the USA, 86,* 352–356.

Burns, B., & Weith, M. (2004). The collider principle in causal reasoning: Why the Monty Hall dilemma is so hard. *Journal of Experimental Psychology: General, 133,* 434–449.

Burton, M. (1994). Learning new faces in an interactive activation and competition model. *Visual Cognition, 1,* 313–348.

Busemeyer, J., Townsend, J., Diederich, A., & Barkan, R. (2005). Contrast effects of loss aversion? Comment on Usher and McClelland (2004). *Psychological Review, 112,* 253–255.

Buswell, G. (1935). *How people look at pictures: A study of the psychology and perception in art.* Oxford: University of Chicago Press.

Byrne, A. (2003). Consciousness and nonconceptual content. *Philosophical Studies, 113,* 261–274.

Cacioppo, J., Martzke, J., Petty, R., & Tassinary, L. (1988). Specific forms of facial EMG response index emotions during an interview: From Darwin to the continuous flow hypothesis of affect-laden information processing. *Journal of Personality and Social Psychology, 54,* 592–604.

Calvert, G. (2001). Crossmodal processing in the human brain: Insights from functional neuroimaging studies. *Cerebral Cortex, 11,* 110–1123.

Calvert, G., Bullmore, E., Brammer, M., Campbell, R., Williams, S., McGuire, P., Woodruff, P., Iversen, S., & David, A. (1997). Activation of auditory cortex during silent lipreading. *Science, 276,* 593–596.

Calvo-Merino, B., Glaser, D., Grèzes, J., Passingham, R., & Haggard, P. (2005). Action observation and acquired motor skills: An fMRI study with expert dancers. *Cerebral Cortex, 15,* 1243–1249.

Cangelosi, A., & Parisi, D. (1998). The emergence of a "language" in an evolving population of neural networks. *Connection Science: Journal of Neural Computing, Artificial Intelligence and Cognitive Research, 10,* 83–97.

Cangelosi, A., & Parisi, D. (Eds.) (2002). *Simulating the evolution of language.* New York: Springer-Verlag.

Caraco, T. (1982). Flock size and the organization of behavioral sequences in juncos. *Condor, 84,* 101–105.

Carandini, M. (2000). Visual cortex: Fatigue and adaptation. *Current Biology, 10,* R605–R607.

Carandini, M., & Heeger, D. (1994). Summation and division by neurons in primate visual cortex. *Science, 264,* 1333–1336.

Carandini, M., Heeger, D., & Movshon, J. (1997). Linearity and normalization in simple cells of the macaque primary visual cortex. *Journal of Neuroscience, 17,* 8621–8644.

Carandini, M., Heeger, D., & Senn, W. (2002). A synaptic explanation of suppression in visual cortex. *Journal of Neuroscience, 22,* 10053–10065.

Carey, S. (1985). *Conceptual change in childhood.* Cambridge, Mass.: MIT Press.

Carpenter, R. (1999). A neural mechanism that randomizes behavior. *Journal of Consciousness Studies, 6,* 13–22.

Carpenter, R. (2004). The saccadic system: A neurological microcosm. *Advances in Clinical Neuroscience and Rehabilitation, 4,* 6–8.

Carruthers, P. (2002). The cognitive functions of language. *Behavioral and Brain Sciences, 25,* 657–674.

Casey, M. (1996). The dynamics of discrete time computation with application to recurrent neural networks and finite state machine extraction. *Neural Computation, 8,* 1135–1178.

Cavanagh, P. (1988). Pathways in early vision. In Z. Pylyshyn (Ed.), *Computational processes in human vision: An interdisciplinary perspective* (pp. 254–289). Norwood, N.J.: Ablex.

Cavanaugh, J., Bair, W., & Movshon, J. (2002a). Nature and interaction of signals from the receptive field center and surround in macaque V1 neurons. *Journal of Neurophysiology, 88,* 2530–2546.

Cavanaugh, J., Bair, W., & Movshon, J. (2002b). Selectivity and spatial distribution of signals from the receptive surround in macaque V1 neurons. *Journal of Neurophysiology, 88,* 2547–2556.

Cave, K. (1999). The FeatureGate model of visual selection. *Psychological Research, 62,* 182–194.

Cave, K., & Wolfe, J. (1990). Modeling the role of parallel processing in visual search. *Cognitive Psychology, 22,* 225–271.

Chafee, M., & Goldman-Rakic, P. (1998). Matching patterns of activity in primate prefrontal area 8a and parietal area 7ip neurons during a spatial working memory task. *Journal of Neurophysiology, 79,* 2919–2940.

Chafee, M., & Goldman-Rakic, P. (2000). Inactivation of parietal and prefrontal cortex reveals interdependence of neural activity during memory-guided saccades. *Journal of Neurophysiology, 83,* 1550–1566.

Chalmers, D. (1996). *The conscious mind: In search of a fundamental theory.* New York: Oxford University Press.

Chambers, C., Tanenhaus, M., & Magnuson, J. (2004). Actions and affordances in syntactic ambiguity resolution. *Journal of Experimental Psychology: Learning, Memory and Cognition, 30,* 687–696.

Chao, L., & Martin, A. (2000). Representation of manipulable man-made objects in the dorsal stream. *Neuroimage, 12,* 478–484.

Charniak, E. (1993). *Statistical language learning.* Cambridge, Mass.: MIT Press.

Chartrand, T., & Bargh, J. (1999). The chameleon effect: The perception-behavior link and social interaction. *Journal of Personality and Social Psychology, 76,* 893–910.

Chater, N., & Ganis, G. (1991). Double dissociation and isolable cognitive processes. *Proceedings of the 13th Annual Meeting of the Cognitive Science Society* (pp. 668–672). Hillsdale, N.J.: Lawrence Erlbaum.

Chaudhuri, A. (1990). Modulation of the motion aftereffect by selective attention. *Nature, 344,* 60–62.

Chialvo, D. (2004). Critical brain networks. *Physica A, 340,* 756–765.

Chistovich, L. (1960). Classification of rapidly repeated speech sounds. *Akusticheskii Zhurnal, 6,* 392–398.

Chomsky, N. (1957). *Syntactic structures.* Oxford: Mouton.

Chomsky, N. (1959). A review of B. F. Skinner's *Verbal Behavior. Language, 35,* 26–58.

Christiansen, M., Allen, J., & Seidenberg, M. (1998). Learning to segment speech using multiple cues: A connectionist model. *Language and Cognitive Processes, 13,* 221–268.

Christiansen, M., & Chater, N. (1999). Toward a connectionist model of recursion in human linguistic performance. *Cognitive Science, 23,* 157–205.

Christiansen, M., & Chater, N. (Eds.) (2001). Connectionist psycholinguistics. Westport, Conn.: Ablex.

Christiansen, M., & Dale, R. (2003). Language evolution and change. In M. Arbib (Ed.), *Handbook of brain theory and neural networks* (2nd ed.). Cambridge, Mass.: MIT Press.

Christiansen, M., & Dale, R. (2004). The role of learning and development in language evolution: A connectionist perspective. In K. Oller, D. Griebel, & K. Plunkett (Eds.), *The evolution of communication systems: A comparative approach* (pp. 90–109). Cambridge, Mass.: MIT Press.

Christiansen, M., & Kirby, S. (2003). *Language evolution.* Oxford: Oxford University Press.

Chun, M., & Nakayama, K. (2000). On the functional role of implicit visual memory for the adaptive deployment of attention across scenes. *Visual Cognition, 7,* 65–81.

Chung, G., Tucker, D., West, P., Potts, G., Liotti, M., Luu, P., & Hartry, A. (1996). Emotional expectancy: Brain electrical activity associated with an emotional bias in interpreting life events. *Psychophysiology, 33,* 218–233.

Churchland, P. M. (1981). Eliminative materialism and propositional attitudes. *Journal of Philosophy, 78,* 67–90.

Churchland, P. M. (1984). *Matter and consciousness: A contemporary introduction to the philosophy of mind.* Cambridge, Mass.: MIT Press.

Churchland, P. M. (1989). *A neurocomputational perspective: The nature of mind and the structure of science.* Cambridge, Mass.: MIT Press.

Churchland, P. M. (1996). *The engine of reason, the seat of the soul: A philosophical journey into the brain.* Cambridge, Mass.: MIT Press.

Churchland, P. M., & Churchland, P. S. (1998). *On the contrary: Critical essays, 1987–1997.* Cambridge, Mass.: MIT Press.

Churchland, P. S. (1998). Brainshy: Nonneural theories of conscious experience. In S. Hameroff, A. Kaszniak, & A. Scott (Eds.), *Toward a Science of Consciousness II* (pp. 109–124). Cambridge, Mass.: MIT Press.

Churchland, P. S., Ramachandran, V., & Sejnowski, T. (1994). A critique of pure vision. In C. Koch & J. Davis (Eds.), *Large-scale neuronal theories of the brain.* Cambridge, Mass.: MIT Press.

Churchland, P. S., & Sejnowski, T. (1992). *The computational brain.* Cambridge, Mass.: MIT Press.

Clark, A. (1993). *Associative engines: Connectionism, concepts, and representational change.* Cambridge, Mass.: MIT Press.

Clark, A. (1997). *Being there: Putting brain, body and world together again.* Cambridge, Mass.: MIT Press.

Clark, A. (2001). Reasons, robots and the extended mind. *Mind and Language, 16,* 121–145.

Clark, A. (2003). *Natural-born cyborgs: Minds, technologies, and the future of human intelligence.* New York: Oxford University Press.

Clark, A., & Chalmers, D. (1998). The extended mind. *Analysis, 58,* 7–19.

Clark, H., & Carlson, T. (1982). Hearers and speech acts. *Language, 58,* 332–373.

Cleeremans, A., Servan-Schreiber, D., & McClelland, J. (1989). Finite state automata and simple recurrent networks. *Neural Computation, 1,* 372–381.

Clifford, C., Spehar, B., Solomon, S., Martin, P., & Zaidi, Q. (2003). Interactions between color and luminance in the perception of orientation. *Journal of Vision, 3,* 106–115.

Clifton, C., & Ferreira, F. (1989). Ambiguity in context. *Language and Cognitive Processes, 4,* SI77–SI103.

Cohen, J., Dunbar, K., & McClelland, J. (1990). On the control of automatic processes: A parallel distributed processing account of the Stroop effect. *Psychological Review, 97,* 332–361.

Cohen, J., MacWhinney, B., Flatt, M., & Provost, J. (1993). PsyScope: An interactive graphic system for designing and controlling experiments in the psychology laboratory using Macintosh computers. *Behavior Research Methods, Instruments, and Computers, 25,* 257–271.

Cole, M., & Engeström, Y. (1997). A cultural historical approach to distributed cognition. In S. Gavriel (Ed.), *Distributed cognitions: Psychological and educational considerations* (pp. 1–46). New York: Cambridge University Press.

Coles, M., Gratton, G., & Donchin, E. (1988). Detecting early communication: Using measures of movement-related potentials to illuminate human information processing. *Biological Psychology, 26,* 69–89.

Coles, M., Gratton, G., Bashore, T., Eriksen, C., & Donchin, E. (1985). A psychophysiological investigation of the continuous flow model of human information processing. *Journal of Experimental Psychology: Human Perception and Performance, 11,* 529–553.

Coltheart, M. (2000). Dual routes from print to speech and dual routes from print to meaning: Some theoretical issues. In A. Kennedy, R. Radach, J. Pynte, & D. Heller (Eds.), *Reading as a perceptual process* (pp. 475–490). Amsterdam: North-Holland/Elsevier Science.

Constantine-Paton, M., & Law, M. (1978). Eye-specific termination bands in tecta of three-eyed frogs. *Science, 202,* 639–641.

Conway, C., & Christiansen, M. (2005). Modality-constrained statistical learning of tactile, visual, and auditory sequences. *Journal of Experimental Psychology: Learning, Memory, and Cognition, 31,* 24–39.

Cooper, D. (1999). *Linguistic attractors: The cognitive dynamics of language acquisition and change.* Amsterdam: John Benjamins.

Cooper, E., Biederman, I., & Hummel, J. (1992). Metric invariance in object recognition: A review and further evidence. *Canadian Journal of Psychology, 46*(2), 191–214.

Cooper, L., & Shepard, R. (1973). The time required to prepare for a rotated stimulus. *Memory and Cognition, 1,* 246–250.

Corbetta, M. (1998). Functional anatomy of visual attention in the human brain: Studies with positron emission tomography. In R. Parasuraman (Ed.), *The attentive brain* (pp. 95–122). Cambridge, Mass.: MIT Press.

Corbetta, M., & Shulman, G. (1999). Human cortical mechanisms of visual attention during orienting and search. In G. Humphreys & J. Duncan (Eds.), *Attention, space, and action: Studies in cognitive neuroscience* (pp. 183–198). London: Oxford University Press.

Cornsweet, T. (1970). *Visual perception.* Oxford: Academic Press.

Cosmides, L. (1989). The logic of social exchange: Has natural selection shaped how humans reason? Studies with the Wason selection task. *Cognition, 31,* 187–276.

Cosmides, L., & Tooby, J. (1994). Origins of domain specificity: The evolution of functional organization. In L. Hischfeld & S. Gelman (Eds.), *Mapping the mind: Domain specificity in cognition and culture* (pp. 85–116). New York: Cambridge University Press.

Cosmides, L., & Tooby, J. (1996). Are humans good intuitive statisticians after all? Rethinking some conclusions from the literature on judgment under uncertainty. *Cognition, 58,* 1–73.

Cottrell, G. (1989). *A connectionist approach to word sense disambiguation.* London: Pitman.

Courtney, S., Petit, L., Haxby, J., & Ungerleider, L. (1998). The role of prefrontal cortex in working memory: Examining the contents of consciousness. *Philosophical Transactions of the Royal Society of London B: Biological Sciences, 353,* 1819–1828.

Craik, K. (1943). *The nature of explanation.* Oxford: Oxford University Press, Macmillan.

Crain, S., & Steedman, M. (1985). On not being led up the garden path. In D. Dowty, L. Karttunen, & A. Zwicky (Eds.), *Natural language parsing.* Cambridge: Cambridge University Press.

Cree, G., McRae, K., & McNorgan, C. (1999). An attractor model of lexical conceptual processing: Simulating semantic priming. *Cognitive Science, 23,* 371–414.

Crick, F., & Koch, C. (1998). Consciousness and neuroscience. *Cerebral Cortex, 8,* 97–107.

Crundall, D. (2005). The integration of top-down and bottom up factors in visual search during driving. In G. Underwood (Ed.), *Cognitive processes in eye guidance.* Oxford: Oxford University Press.

Crutchfield, J. (1994). The calculi of emergence: Computation, dynamics, and induction. *Physica D, 75,* 11–54.

Crutchfield, J., & Packard, N. (1983). Symbolic dynamics of noisy chaos. *Physica D, 7,* 201–223.

Culicover, P., & Nowak, A. (2003). *Dynamical grammar.* New York: Oxford University Press.

Cutler, A. (1995a). Spoken word recognition and production. In J. Miller & P. Eimas (Eds.), *Speech, language, and communication. Handbook of perception and cognition* (2nd ed.), Vol. 11 (pp. 97–136). San Diego, Calif.: Academic Press.

Cutting, J. (1996). Wayfinding from multiple sources of local information in retinal flow. *Journal of Experimental Psychology: Human Perception and Performance, 22,* 1299–1313.

Cutting, J. (2000). Accuracy, scope, and flexibility of models. *Journal of Mathematical Psychology, 44,* 3–19.

Cutting, J., Bruno, N., Brady, N., & Moore, C. (1992). Selectivity, scope, and simplicity of models: A lesson from fitting judgments of perceived depth. *Journal of Experimental Psychology: General, 121,* 262–270.

Cutting, J., & Rosner, B. (1974). Categories and boundaries in speech and music. *Perception and Psychophysics, 16,* 564–570.

Cutzu, F. & Tsotsos, J. (2003). The selective tuning model of attention: psychophysical evidence for a suppressive annulus around an attended item. *Vision Research, 43,* 205–219.

Dahan, D., Magnuson, J., & Tanenhaus, M. (2001). Time course of frequency effects in spoken-word recognition: Evidence from eye movements. *Cognitive Psychology, 42,* 317–367.

Dailey, M., Cottrell, G., Padgett, C., & Adolphs, R. (2002). EMPATH: A neural network that categorizes facial expressions. *Journal of Cognitive Neuroscience, 14,* 1158–1173.

Dale, C., West, C., Eade, J., Rito-Palomares, M., & Lyddiatt, A. (1999). Studies on the physical and compositional changes in collapsing beer foam. *Chemical Engineering Journal, 72,* 83–89.

Dale, R., Kehoe, C., & Spivey, M. (in press). Graded motor responses in the time course of categorizing atypical exemplars. *Memory and Cognition.*

Dale, R., & Spivey, M. (2005). From apples and oranges to symbolic dynamics: A framework for conciliating notions of cognitive representation. *Journal of Experimental and Theoretical Artificial Intelligence, 17,* 317–342.

Dale, R., & Spivey, M. (2006). Unraveling the dyad: Using recurrence analysis to explore patterns of syntactic coordination between children and caregivers in conversation. *Language Learning, 56,* 391–430.

Damasio, A. (1989). The brain binds entities and events by multiregional activation from convergence zones. *Neural Computation, 1,* 123–132.

Damasio, A. (1992). The selfless consciousness. *Behavioral and Brain Sciences, 15,* 208–209.

Damasio, A., & Damasio, H. (1994). Cortical systems for retrieval of concrete knowledge: The convergence zone framework. In C. Koch & J. Davis (Eds.), *Large-scale neuronal theories of the brain: Computational neuroscience.* Cambridge, Mass.: MIT Press.

Damper, R., & Harnad, S. (2000). Neural network models of categorical perception. *Perception and Psychophysics, 62,* 843–867.

Davidchack, R., Lai, Y., Bollt, E., & Dhamala, M. (2000). Estimating generating partitions of chaotic systems by unstable periodic orbits. *Physical Review E, 61*, 1353–1356.

Davies, B. (1999). *Exploring chaos: Theory and experiment.* Boulder, Colo.: Westview Press.

Dawkins, R. (1976). *The selfish gene.* New York: Oxford University Press.

Dawson, E., Gilovich, T., & Regan, D. (2002). Motivated reasoning and performance on the Wason selection task. *Personality and Social Psychology Bulletin, 28*, 1379–1387.

Dayan, P., & Abbott, L. (2005). *Theoretical neuroscience.* Cambridge, Mass.: MIT Press.

Dayan, P., Hinton, G., Neal, R., & Zemel, R. (1995). The Helmholtz machine. *Neural Computation, 7*, 889–904.

Dean, J., & Whyte, W. (1958). How do you know if the informant is telling the truth? *Human Organization, 17*, 34–38.

Decety, J., & Grèzes, J. (1999). Neural mechanisms subserving the perception of human actions. *Trends in Cognitive Sciences, 3*, 172–178.

Deco, G., & Lee, T. (2002). A unified model of spatial and object attention based on inter-cortical biased competition. *Neurocomputing: An International Journal, 44–46*, 775–781.

Deco, G., Rolls, E., & Horwitz, B. (2004). "What" and "where" in visual working memory: A computational neurodynamical perspective for integrating fMRI and single-neuron data. *Journal of Cognitive Neuroscience, 16*, 683–701.

DeFrance, J., Sands, S., Schweitzer, F., Ginsberg, L., & Sharma, J. (1997). Age-related changes in cognitive ERPs of attenuation. *Brain Topography, 9*, 283–293.

Delabarre, E. (1898). A method of recording eye-movements. *American Journal of Psychology, 9*, 572–574.

Dell, G. (1986). A spreading-activation theory of retrieval in sentence production. *Psychological Review, 93*, 283–321.

Dell, G., Burger, L., & Svec, W. (1997). Language production and serial order: A functional analysis and a model. *Psychological Review, 104*, 123–147.

Dell, G., & Reich, P. (1981). Stages in sentence production: An analysis of speech error data. *Journal of Verbal Learning and Verbal Behavior, 20*, 611–629.

Demarais, A., & Cohen, B. (1998). Evidence for image scanning eye movements during transitive inference. *Biological Psychology, 49*, 229–247.

DeMaris, D. (2000). Attention, depth gestalts, and spatially extended chaos in the perception of ambiguous figures. In D. Levine & V. Brown (Eds.), *Oscillations in neural systems: The international neural networks society series.* Mahwah, N.J.: Lawrence Erlbaum.

Dennett, D. (1991). *Consciousness explained.* Boston: Little, Brown.

Dennett, D. (1993). The message is: There is no *medium*: Reply to Jackson, Rosenthal, Shoemaker & Tye. *Philosophy & Phenomenological Research, 53*, 889–931.

Dennett, D. (1995). The unimagined preposterousness of zombies: Commentary on T. Moody, O. Flanagan, & T. Polger. *Journal of Consciousness Studies, 2*, 322–326.

Desimone, R., & Duncan, J. (1995). Neural mechanisms of selective visual attention. *Annual Review of Neuroscience, 18*, 193–222.

de'Sperati, C. (2003). Precise oculomotor correlates of visuospatial mental rotation and circular motion imagery. *Journal of Cognitive Neuroscience, 15*, 1244–1259.

Devaney, D. (2003). *An introduction to chaotic dynamical systems* (2nd ed.). Boulder, Colo.: Westview Press.

Devlin, J., Gonnerman, L., Andersen, E., & Seidenberg, M. (1998). Category-specific semantic deficits in focal and widespread brain damage: A computational account. *Journal of Cognitive Neuroscience, 10,* 77–94.

Dewey, J. (1896). The reflex arc concept in psychology. *Psychological Review, 3,* 357–370.

Diefendorf, A., & Dodge, R. (1908). An experimental study of the ocular reactions of the insane from photographic records. *Brain, 31,* 451–492.

Dietrich, E., & Hardcastle, V. (2005). *Sisyphus's boulder: Consciousness and the limits of the knowable.* Amsterdam: John Benjamins.

Dietrich, E., & Markman, A. (2003). Discrete thoughts: Why cognition must use discrete representations. *Mind and Language, 18,* 95–119.

Dill, M., & Edelman, S. (2001). Imperfect invariance to object translation in the discrimination of complex shapes. *Perception, 30*(6), 707–724.

Di Lollo, V., Enns, J., & Rensink, R. (2000). Competition for consciousness among visual events: The psychophysics of reentrant visual pathways. *Journal of Experimental Psychology: General, 129,* 481–507.

Dobkins, K., & Anderson, C. (2002). Color-based motion processing is stronger in infants than in adults. *Psychological Science, 13,* 76–80.

Dollaghan, C. (1985). Child meets word: "Fast mapping" in preschool children. *Journal of Speech and Hearing Research, 28,* 449–454.

Domenici, P., & Blake, R. (1993). Escape trajectories in angelfish (*Pterophyllum eimekei*). *Journal of Experimental Biology, 177,* 253–272.

Donchin, E., Gratton, G., Dupree, D., & Coles, M. (1988). After a rash action: Latency and amplitude of the P300 following fast guesses. In G. Galbraith, M. Kietzman, & E. Donchin (Eds.), *Neurophysiology and psychophysiology: Experimental and clinical applications* (pp. 173–188). Hillsdale, N.J.: Lawrence Erlbaum.

Donders, F. (1868/1969). On the speed of mental processes (translated by W. Koster). *Acta Psychologica, 30,* 412–431.

Dorman, M. (1974). Auditory evoked potential correlates of speech sound discrimination. *Perception and Psychophysics, 15,* 215–220.

Dosher, B. (1976). The retrieval of sentences from memory: A speed-accuracy study. *Cognitive Psychology, 8,* 291–310.

Dosher, B., Han, S., & Lu, Z. (2004). Parallel processing in visual search asymmetry. *Journal of Experimental Psychology: Human Perception and Performance, 30,* 3–27.

Douglas, R., Koch, C., Mahowald, M., Martin, K., & Suarez, H. (1995). Recurrent excitation in neocortical circuits. *Science, 269,* 981–985.

Doyle, M., & Walker, R. (2001). Curved saccade trajectories: Voluntary and reflexive saccades curve away from irrelevant distractors. *Experimental Brain Research, 139,* 333–344.

Dragoi, V., Sharma, J., & Sur, M. (2000). Adaptation-induced plasticity of orientation tuning in primary visual cortex. *Neuron, 28,* 287–298.

Dretske, F. (1997). *Naturalizing the mind.* Cambridge, Mass.: MIT Press.

Dreyfus, H. (1972). *What computers can't do: A critique of artificial reason.* New York: Harper & Row.

Driver, J., & Baylis, G. (1989). Movement and visual attention: The spotlight metaphor breaks down. *Journal of Experimental Psychology: Human Perception and Performance, 15,* 448–456.

Driver, J., & Spence, C. (1998). Crossmodal attention. *Current Opinion in Neurobiology, 8,* 245–253.

Duhamel, J., Colby, C., & Goldberg, M. (1992). The updating of the representation of visual space in parietal cortex by intended eye movements. *Science, 255,* 90–92.

Duncan, J. (1989). Boundary conditions on parallel processing in human vision. *Perception, 18,* 457–469.

Duncan, J., & Humphreys, G. (1989). Visual search and stimulus similarity. *Psychological Review, 96,* 433–458.

Duncan, J., & Humphreys, G. (1992). Beyond the search surface: Visual search and attentional engagement. *Journal of Experimental Psychology: Human Perception and Performance, 18,* 578–588.

Duncker, K. (1945). On problem solving. *Psychological Monographs,* 58(5, whole no. 270).

Dunlap, G., & Hurtig, R. (1981). Effects of clausal structure and word frequency in sentence processing. *Journal of Psycholinguistic Research, 10,* 313–326.

Dunning, D., & Stern, L. (1994). Distinguishing accurate from inaccurate eyewitness identifications via inquiries about decision processes. *Journal of Personality and Social Psychology, 67,* 818–835.

Durgin, F. H. (2002). The Tinkerbell effect: Motion perception and illusion. *Journal of Consciousness Studies, 9,* 88–101.

D'Zmura, M. (1991). Color in visual search. *Vision Research, 31,* 951–966.

Eberhard, K., Spivey-Knowlton, M., Sedivy, J., & Tanenhaus, M. (1995). Eye movements as a window into real-time spoken language comprehension in natural contexts. *Journal of Psycholinguistic Research, 24,* 409–436.

Eckstein, M. (1998). The lower visual search efficiency for conjunctions is due to noise and not serial attentional processing. *Psychological Science, 9,* 111–118.

Eckstein, M., Thomas, J., Palmer, J., & Shimozaki, S. (2000). A signal detection model predicts the effects of set size on visual search accuracy for feature, conjunction, triple conjunction, and disjunction displays. *Perception and Psychophysics, 62,* 425–451.

Eddy, D. (1982). Probabilistic reasoning in clinical medicine: Problems and opportunities. In D. Kahneman, P. Slovic, & A. Tversky (Eds.), *Judgment under uncertainty: Heuristics and biases* (pp. 249–267). Cambridge: Cambridge University Press.

Edelman, S. (1998). Representation is representation of similarities. *Behavioral and Brain Sciences, 21,* 449–498.

Edelman, S. (1999). *Representation and recognition in vision.* Cambridge, Mass.: MIT Press.

Edelman, S. (2002). Multidimensional space: The final frontier. *Nature Neuroscience, 5,* 1252–1254.

Edelman, S., & Intrator, N. (2003). Towards structural systematicity in distributed, statistically bound visual representations. *Cognitive Science, 27,* 73–109.

Efron, B., & Tibshirani, R. (1993). *An introduction to the bootstrap.* New York: Chapman & Hall.

Egeth, H., Virzi, R., & Garbart, H. (1984). Searching for conjunctively defined targets. *Journal of Experimental Psychology: Human Perception and Performance, 10,* 32–39.

Eimas, P., & Corbit, J. (1973). Selective adaptation of a linguistic feature detector. *Cognitive Psychology, 4,* 99–109.

Eimer, M. (1998). Mechanisms of visuospatial attention: Evidence from event-related potentials. *Visual Cognition, 5,* 257–286.

Eimer, M., & Schröger, E. (1998). ERP effects of intermodal attention and cross-modal links in spatial attention. *Psychophysiology, 35,* 313–327.

Eimer, M., Van Velzen, J., & Driver, J. (2002). Cross-modal interactions between audition, touch, and vision in endogenous spatial attention: ERP evidence on preparatory states and sensory modulations. *Journal of Cognitive Neuroscience, 14,* 254–271.

Eliasmith, C. (1996). The third contender: A critical examination of the dynamicist theory of cognition. *Philosophical Psychology, 9,* 441–463.

Eliasmith, C., & Thagard, P. (2001). Integrating structure and meaning: A distributed model of analogical mapping. *Cognitive Science, 25,* 245–286.

Ellis, R., & Tucker, M. (2000). Micro-affordance: The potentiation of components of action by seen objects. *British Journal of Psychology, 91,* 451–471.

Elman, J. (1990). Finding structure in time. *Cognitive Science, 14,* 179–211.

Elman, J. (1991). Distributed representations, simple recurrent networks, and grammatical structure. *Machine Learning, 7,* 195–224.

Elman, J. (1995). Language as a dynamical system. In R. Prot & T. van Gelder (Eds.), *Mind as motion: Explorations in the dynamics of cognition* (pp. 195–223). Cambridge, Mass.: MIT Press.

Elman, J. (2004). An alternative view of the mental lexicon. *Trends in Cognitive Sciences, 8,* 301–306.

Elman, J., Bates, E., Johnson, M., Karmiloff-Smith, A., Parisi, D., & Plunkett, K. (1996). *Rethinking innateness: A connectionist perspective on development.* Cambridge, Mass.: MIT Press.

Elman, J., & McClelland, J. (1988). Cognitive penetration of the mechanisms of perception: Compensation for coarticulation of lexically restored phonemes. *Journal of Memory and Language, 27,* 143–165.

Engbert, R., Scheffczyk, C., Krampe, R., Kurths, J., & Kliegl, R. (1998). Symbolic dynamics of bimanual production of polyrhythms. In H. Kantz, J. Kurths, & G. Mayer-Kress (Eds.), *Nonlinear analysis of physiological data.* Berlin: Springer-Verlag.

Engel, A., Moll, C., Fried, I., & Ojemann, G. (2005). Invasive recordings from the human brain: Clinical insights and beyond. *Nature Reviews Neuroscience, 6,* 35–47.

Engel, K., Flanders, M., & Söchting, J. (1997). Anticipatory and sequential motor control in piano playing. *Experimental Brain Research, 113,* 189–199.

Engel, S., Rumelhart, D., Wandell, B., Lee, A., Glover, G., Chichilnisky, E., & Shadlen, M. (1994). fMRI of human visual cortex. *Nature, 369,* 525.

Enns, J., Di Lollo, V. (2002). What competition? *Trends in Cognitive Sciences, 6,* 118.

Epstein, R. (1982). A note on the mythological character of categorization research in psychology. *The Journal of Mind and Behavior, 3,* 161–170.

Epstein, R., & Kanwisher, N. (1998). A cortical representation of the local visual environment. *Nature, 392,* 598–601.

Epstein, W. (1993). The representational framework in perceptual theory. *Perception and Psychophysics, 53,* 704–709.

Erickson, M., & Kruschke, J. (1998). Rules and exemplars in category learning. *Journal of Experimental Psychology: General, 127,* 107–140.

Erickson, M., & Kruschke, J. (2002). Rule-based extrapolation in perceptual categorization. *Psychonomic Bulletin and Review, 9,* 160–168.

Ericsson, K., & Simon, H. (1993). *Protocol analysis: Verbal reports as data* (rev. ed.). Cambridge, Mass.: MIT Press.

Eriksen, C., & Schultz, D. (1979). Information processing in visual search: A continuous flow conception and experimental results. *Perception and Psychophysics, 25,* 249–263.

Eriksen, C., & Yeh, Y. (1985). Allocation of attention in the visual field. *Journal of Experimental Psychology: Human Perception and Performance, 11*, 583–597.

Erlhagen, W., & Schöner, G. (2002). Dynamic field theory of movement preparation. *Psychological Review, 109*, 545–572.

Evans, J. (1982). *The psychology of deductive reasoning.* London: Routledge & Kegan Paul.

Fairhall, A., Lewen, G., Bialek, W., & de Ruyter van Steveninck, R. (2001). Efficiency and ambiguity in an adaptive neural code. *Nature, 412*, 787–792.

Farah, M. (1994). Neuropsychological inference with an interactive brain: A critique of the "locality" assumption. *Behavioral and Brain Sciences, 17*, 43–104.

Farne, A., Roy, A., Giraux, P., Dubernard, J., & Sirigu, A. (2002). Face and hand, not both: Perceptual correlates of reafferentation in a former amputee. *Current Biology, 12*, 1342–1346.

Farrar, W., & Kawamoto, A. (1993). The return of "visiting relatives": Pragmatic effects in sentence processing. *Quarterly Journal of Experimental Psychology: Human Experimental Psychology, 46A*, 463–487.

Feigenbaum, M. (1978). Quantitative universality for a class of nonlinear transformations. *Journal of Statistical Physics, 19*, 25–52.

Felleman, D., & Van Essen, D. (1991). Distributed hierarchical processing in primate cerebral cortex. *Cerebral Cortex, 1*, 1–47.

Fernald, A., Swingley, D., & Pinto, J. (2001). When half a word is enough: Infants can recognize spoken words using partial phonetic information. *Child Development, 72*, 1003–1015.

Ferreira, F., & Clifton, C. (1986). The independence of syntactic processing. *Journal of Memory and Language, 25*, 348–368.

Ferreira, F., Bailey, K., & Ferraro, V. (2002). Good-enough representations in language comprehension. *Current Directions in Psychological Science, 11*, 11–15.

Ferreira, V., & Dell, G. (2000). Effect of ambiguity and lexical availability on syntactic and lexical production. *Cognitive Psychology, 40*, 296–340.

Festinger, L. (1957). *A theory of cognitive dissonance.* Stanford, Calif.: Stanford University Press.

Fiebach, C., Vos, S., & Friederici, A. (2004). Neural correlates of syntactic ambiguity in sentence comprehension for low and high span readers. *Journal of Cognitive Neuroscience, 16*, 1562–1575.

Field, D., Hayes, A., & Hess, R. (1993). Contour integration by the human visual system: Evidence for a local "association field." *Vision Research, 33*, 173–193.

Findlay, J., & Gilchrist, I. (2003). *Active vision: The psychology of looking and seeing.* Oxford: Oxford University Press.

Fine, K. (1975). Vagueness, truth and logic. *Synthese, 30*, 265–300.

Fischer, B., & Weber, H. (1993). Express saccades and visual attention. *Behavioral and Brain Sciences, 16*, 553–610.

Fisher, B., & Pylyshyn, Z. (1994). The cognitive architecture of bimodal event perception: A commentary and addendum to Radeau (1994). *Cahiers de Psychologie Cognitive/Current Psychology of Cognition, 13*, 92–96.

Fisk, J., & Pidgeon, N. (1997). The conjunction fallacy: The case for the existence of competing heuristic strategies. *British Journal of Psychology, 88*, 1–27.

Fitneva, S., & Spivey, M. (2004). Context and language processing: The effect of authorship. In J. Trueswell & M. Tanenhaus (Eds.), *World situated language use: Psycholinguistic, linguistic and computational perspectives on bridging the product and action traditions.* Cambridge, Mass.: MIT Press.

Fitts, P. (1954). The information capacity of the human motor system in controlling the amplitude of movement. *Journal of Experimental Psychology, 47*, 381–391.

Fitzgibbon, S., Pope, K., Mackenzie, L., Clark, C., & Willoughby, J. (2004). Cognitive tasks augment gamma EEG power. *Clinical Neurophysiology, 115*, 1802–1809.

Fitzpatrick, P., Carello, C., & Turvey, M.T. (1994). Eigen values of the inertia tensor and exteroception by the "muscular sense." *Neuroscience, 60*, 551–568.

Flanagan, O. (1991). *The science of mind* (2nd ed.). Cambridge, Mass.: MIT Press.

Fleck, J., & Weisberg, R. (2004). The use of verbal protocols as data: An analysis of insight in the candle problem. *Memory and Cognition, 32*, 990–1006.

Fodor, J. (1975). *The language of thought.* New York: Thomas Y. Crowell.

Fodor, J. (1980). Methodological solipsism considered as a research strategy in cognition psychology. *Behavioral and Brain Sciences, 3*, 63–109.

Fodor, J. (1983). *The modularity of mind: An essay on faculty psychology.* Cambridge, Mass.: MIT Press.

Fodor, J. (1986). Why paramecia don't have mental representations. *Midwest Studies in Philosophy, 10*, 3–23.

Fodor, J. (1998). *Concepts: Where cognitive science went wrong.* New York: Clarendon Press/Oxford University Press.

Fodor, J. (2000). *The mind doesn't work that way: The scope and limits of computational psychology.* Cambridge, Mass.: MIT Press.

Fodor, J., & Lepore, E. (1996). What can't be evaluated can't be evaluated, and it can't be supervalued either. *Journal of Philosophy, 93*, 516–536.

Fodor, J., & Pylyshyn, Z. (1981). How direct is visual perception? Some reflections on Gibson's "ecological approach." *Cognition, 9*, 139–196.

Fodor, J., & Pylyshyn, Z. (1995). Connectionism and cognitive architecture: A critical analysis. In G. Macdonald & C. Macdonald (Eds.), *Connectionism: Debates on psychological explanation, Vol. 2* (pp. 90–163). Malden, Mass.: Blackwell.

Ford, M., Bresnan, J., & Kaplan, R. (1982). A competence-based theory of syntactic closure. In J. Bresnan (Ed.), *The mental representation of grammatical relations.* Cambridge, Mass.: MIT Press.

Fox, R. (1984). Effect of lexical status on phonetic categorization. *Journal of Experimental Psychology: Human Perception and Performance, 10*, 526–540.

Francis, W., & Kucera, H. (1982). *Frequency analysis of English usage: Lexicon and grammar.* Boston: Houghton Mifflin.

Franek, M., Radil, T., Indra, M., & Lansky, P. (1987). Following complex rhythmical acoustical patterns by tapping. *International Journal of Psychophysiology, 5*, 187–192.

Frazier, L. (1995). Constraint satisfaction as a theory of sentence processing. *Journal of Psycholinguistic Research, 24*, 437–468.

Frazier, L. (1998). Getting there (slowly). *Journal of Psycholinguistic Research, 27*, 123–146.

Frazier, L., & Clifton, C. (1989). Comprehension of sluiced sentences. *Language and Cognitive Processes, 13*, 499–520.

Frazier, L., & Fodor, J. (1978). The sausage machine: A new two-stage parsing model. *Cognition, 6*, 291–325.

Frazier, L., & Rayner, K. (1987). Resolution of syntactic category ambiguities: Eye movements in parsing lexically ambiguous sentences. *Journal of Memory and Language, 26*, 505–526.

Frege, G. (1903/1964). *The basic laws of arithmetic.* Berkeley: University of California Press.

Freyd, J. (1987). Dynamic mental representations. *Psychological Review, 94*, 427–438.

Fridlund, A., & Cacioppo, J. (1986). Guidelines for human electromyographic research. *Psychophysiology, 23*, 567–589.

Fukushima, K. (2003). Frontal cortical control of smooth-pursuit. *Current Opinion in Neurobiology, 13*, 647–654.

Gallant, J., Connor, C., & Van Essen, D. (1998). Neural activity in areas V1, V2 and V4 during free viewing of natural scenes compared to controlled viewing. *Neuroreport: An International Journal of the Rapid Communication of Research in Neuroscience, 9*, 85–89.

Gallese, V. (2003). The manifold nature of interpersonal relations: The quest for a common mechanism. *Philosophical Transactions of the Royal Society of London B: Biological Sciences, 358*, 517–528.

Gallese, V., Fadigo, L., Fogassi, L., & Rizzolatti, G. (1996). Action recognition in the premotor cortex. *Brain, 119*, 593–609.

Gandhi, S., Heeger, D., & Boynton, G. (1999). Spatial attention in human primary visual cortex. *Proceedings of the National Academy of Sciences of the USA, 96*, 3314–3319.

Gärdenfors, P. (2003). *How homo became sapiens: On the evolution of thinking*. Oxford: Oxford University Press.

Gardner, J., & Lisberger, S. (2002). Serial linkage of target selection for orienting and tracking eye movements. *Nature Neuroscience, 5*, 892–899.

Garnham, A., Shillock, R., Brown, G., Mill, A., & Cutler, A. (1981). Slips of the tongue in the London-Lund corpus of spontaneous conversation. *Linguistics, 19*, 805–817.

Gaskell, M., & Marslen-Wilson, W. (2002). Representation and competition in the perception of spoken words. *Cognitive Psychology, 45*, 220–266.

Gauthier, I., & Logothetis, N. K. (2000). Is face recognition not so unique after all? *Cognitive Neuropsychology, 17*, 125–142.

Gauthier, I, & Tarr, M. J. (1997). Orientation priming of novel shapes in the context of viewpoint-dependent recognition. *Perception, 26*(1), 51–73.

Gaveau, V., Martin, C., Prablanc, O., Pélisson, D., Urquizar, C., & Desmurget, M. (2003). Online modification of saccadic eye movements by retinal signals. *Neuroreport, 14*, 875–878.

Georgopoulos, A. (1995). Motor cortex and cognitive processing. In M. Gazzaniga (Ed.), *The cognitive neurosciences* (pp. 507–517). Cambridge, Mass.: MIT Press.

Georgopoulos, A., Kalaska, J., Caminiti, R., & Massey, J. (1982). On the relations between the direction of two-dimensional arm movements and cell discharge in primate motor cortex. *Journal of Neuroscience, 2*, 1527–1537.

Georgopoulos, A., Lurito, J., Petrides, M., Schwartz, A., & Massey, J. (1989). Mental rotation of the neuronal population vector. *Science, 243*, 234–236.

German, T., & Defeyter, M. (2000). Immunity to functional fixedness in young children. *Psychonomic Bulletin and Review, 7*, 707–712.

Gernsbacher, M. (1990). *Language comprehension as structure building*. Hillsdale, N.J.: Lawrence Erlbaum.

Gibbs, R. (1999). *Intentions in the experience of meaning*. New York: Cambridge University Press.

Gibson, B., Eberhard, K., & Bryant, T. (2005). Linguistically mediated visual search: The critical role of speech rate. *Psychonomic Bulletin and Review, 12*, 276–281.

Gibson, E., & Wexler, K. (1994). Triggers. *Linguistic Inquiry, 25*, 407–454.

Gibson, J. (1933). Adaptation, after-effect and contrast in the perception of curved lines. *Journal of Experimental Psychology, 16,* 1–31.

Gibson, J. (1950). *The perception of the visual world.* Oxford: Houghton Mifflin.

Gibson, J. (1958). Visually controlled locomotion and visual orientation in animals. *British Journal of Psychology, 49,* 182–194.

Gibson, J. (1966). *The senses considered as perceptual systems.* Oxford: Houghton Mifflin.

Gibson, J. (1977). On the analysis of change in the optic array. *Scandinavian Journal of Psychology, 18,* 161–163.

Gibson, J. (1979). *The ecological approach to visual perception.* Boston: Houghton Mifflin.

Gigerenzer, G. (1994). Why the distinction between single-event probabilities and frequencies is important for psychology (and vice versa). In G. Wright & P. Ayton (Eds.), *Subjective probability* (pp. 129–161). Oxford: Wiley.

Gigerenzer, G., & Hoffrage, U. (1995). How to improve Bayesian reasoning without instruction: Frequency formats. *Psychological Review, 102,* 684–704.

Gigerenzer, G., & Regier, T. (1996). How do we tell an association from a rule? Comment on Sloman (1996). *Psychological Bulletin, 119,* 23–26.

Gilbert, C. (1983). Microcircuitry of the visual cortex. *Annual Review of Neuroscience, 6,* 217–247.

Gilbert, C. (1998). Adult cortical dynamics. *Physiological Reviews, 78,* 467–485.

Gilchrist, A. (1988). Lightness contrast and failures of constancy: A common explanation. *Perception and Psychophysics, 43,* 415–424.

Gilchrist, I., Humphreys, G., Riddoch, M., & Neumann, H. (1997). Luminance and edge information in grouping: A study using visual search. *Journal of Experimental Psychology: Human Perception and Performance, 23,* 464–480.

Gilden, D. (2001). Cognitive emissions of 1/f noise. *Psychological Review, 108,* 33–56.

Gilovich, T. (1991). *How we know what isn't so: The fallibility of human reason in everyday life.* New York: Free Press.

Gilovich, T., Griffin, D., & Kahneman, D. (Eds.) (2002). *Heuristics and biases: The psychology of intuitive judgment.* New York: Cambridge University Press.

Gilovich, T., Medvec, V., & Chen, S. (1995). Commission, omission, and dissonance reduction: Coping with regret in the "Monty Hall" problem. *Personality and Social Psychology Bulletin, 21,* 182–190.

Glass, A., & Meany, P. (1978). Evidence for two kinds of low-typical instances in a categorization task. *Memory and Cognition, 6,* 622–628.

Glenberg, A. (1997). What memory is for. *Behavioral and Brain Sciences, 20,* 1–55.

Glenberg, A., & Kaschak, M. (2002). Grounding language in action. *Psychonomic Bulletin and Review, 9,* 558–565.

Glendinning, P. (1994). *Stability, instability and chaos: An introduction to the theory of nonlinear differential equations.* Cambridge: Cambridge University Press.

Gluck, M., & Bower, G. (1988). From conditioning to category learning: An adaptive network model. *Journal of Experimental Psychology: General, 117,* 227–247.

Glucksberg, S. (1964). Functional fixedness: Problem solution as a function of observing responses. *Psychonomic Science, 1,* 117–118.

Godijn, R., & Theeuwes, J. (2002). Programming of endogenous and exogenous saccades: Evidence for a competitive integration model. *Journal of Experimental Psychology: Human Perception and Performance, 28,* 1039–1054.

Goertzel, B. (1998). Learning the language of mind: Symbolic dynamics for modeling adaptive behavior. In C. Wynne & J. Staddon (Eds.), *Models of action: Mechanisms for adaptive behavior* (pp. 1–27). Mahwah, N.J.: Lawrence Erlbaum.

Gold, E. (1967). Language identification in the limit. *Information and Control, 10,* 447–474.

Gold, J., & Shadlen, M. (2000). Representation of a perceptual decision in developing oculomotor commands. *Nature, 404,* 390–394.

Gold, J., & Shadlen, M. (2001). Neural computations that underlie decisions about sensory stimuli. *Trends in Cognitive Sciences, 5,* 10–16.

Goldfield, B., & Reznick, S. (1990). Early lexical acquisition: Rate, content, and the vocabulary spurt. *Journal of Child Language, 17,* 171–183.

Goldman-Rakic, P. (1993). Working memory and the mind. In *Mind and brain: Readings from Scientific American magazine* (pp. 67–77). New York: Freeman/Times Books/Henry Holt.

Goldstone, R. L., Lippa, Y., & Shiffrin, R. M. (2001). Altering object representations through category learning. *Cognition, 78,* 27–43.

Goodale, M., Pélisson, D., & Prablanc, C. (1986). Large adjustments in visually guided reaching do not depend on vision of the hand or perception of target displacement. *Nature, 320,* 748–750.

Goodman, J., Isenhower, R., Marsh, K., Schmidt, R., & Richardson, M. (2005). The interpersonal phase entrainment of rocking chair movements. In H. Heft & K. Marsh (Eds.), *Studies in perception and action VIII* (pp. 49–53). Mahwah, N.J.: Lawrence Erlbaum.

Goswami, A. (1990). Consciousness in quantum physics and the mind/body problem. *Journal of Mind and Behavior, 11,* 75–96.

Gow, D. (2001). Assimilation and anticipation in continuous spoken word recognition. *Journal of Memory and Language, 45,* 133–139.

Graham, N. (1989). *Visual pattern analyzers.* New York: Oxford University Press.

Grainger, J., & Jacobs, A. (Eds.) (1998). *Localist connectionist approaches to human cognition.* Mahwah, N.J.: Lawrence Erlbaum.

Grainger, J., & Jacobs, A. (1999). Temporal integration of information in orthographic priming. *Visual Cognition, 6,* 461–492.

Granberg, D., & Brown, T. (1995). The Monty Hall dilemma. *Personality and Social Psychology Bulletin, 21,* 711–723.

Grant, E., & Spivey, M. (2003). Eye movements and problems solving: Guiding attention guides thought. *Psychological Science, 14,* 462–466.

Gray, J. (2004). *Consciousness: Creeping up on the hard problem.* Oxford: Oxford University Press.

Green, D., & Swets, J. (1966). *Signal detection theory and psychophysics.* New York: Wiley.

Green, M., & Mitchell, D. (2006). Absence of real evidence against competition during syntactic ambiguity resolution. *Journal of Memory and Language, 55,* 1–17.

Greene, B. (2000). *The elegant universe: Superstrings, hidden dimensions, and the quest for the ultimate theory.* New York: Norton.

Greeno, J. (1989). A perspective on thinking. *American Psychologist, 44,* 134–141.

Greeno, J. (1998). The situativity of knowing, learning, and research. *American Psychologist, 53,* 5–26.

Greenwald, A. (1970). A choice reaction time test of ideomotor theory. *Journal of Experimental Psychology, 86,* 20–25.

Griffin, Z., & Bock, K. (2000). What the eyes say about speaking. *Psychological Science, 11,* 274–279.

Griggs, R., & Cox, J. (1982). The elusive thematic-materials effect in Wason's selection task. *British Journal of Psychology, 73,* 407–420.

Grimes, J. (1996). On the failure to detect changes in scenes across saccades. In K. Akins (Ed.), *Perception: Vancouver studies in cognitive science* (pp. 89–110). Oxford: Oxford University Press.

Grinvald, A. (1984). Real-time optical imaging of neuronal activity. *Trends in Neuroscience, 7*, 143–150.

Grinvald, A. (1992). Optical imaging of architecture and function in the living brain sheds new light on cortical mechanisms underlying visual perception. *Brain Topography, 5*, 71–75.

Grosjean, F. (1980). Spoken word recognition processes and the gating paradigm. *Perception and Psychophysics, 28*, 267–283.

Grosof, D., Shapley, R., & Hawken, M. (1993). Macaque V1 neurons can signal "illusory" contours. *Nature, 365*, 550–552.

Grossberg, S. (1980). How does a brain build a cognitive code? *Psychological Review, 87*, 1–51.

Grossberg, S., Mingolla, E., & Ross, W. (1994). A neural theory of attentive visual search: Interactions of boundary, surface, spatial, and object representations. *Psychological Review, 101*, 470–489.

Grossberg, S., Mingolla, E., & Ross, W. (1997). Visual brain and visual perception: How does the cortex do perceptual grouping? *Trends in Neurosciences, 20*, 106–111.

Grossberg, S., & Myers, C. (2000). The resonant dynamics of speech perception: Interword integration and duration-dependent backward effects. *Psychological Review, 107*, 735–767.

Guastello, S. (1998). Creative problem solving groups at the edge of chaos. *Journal of Creative Behavior, 32*, 38–57.

Guenther, F. (1995). Speech sound acquisition, coarticulation, and rate effects in a neural network model of speech production. *Psychological Review, 102*, 594–621.

Gumperz, J., & Levinson, S. (1996). *Rethinking linguistic relativity.* New York: Cambridge University Press.

Gunther, Y. (Ed.) (2003). *Essays on nonconceptual content.* Cambridge, Mass.: MIT Press.

Gupta, G. (1992). Shaping of mind. *Pharmacopsychoecologia, 5*, 47–56.

Guynn, M., McDaniel, M., & Einstein, G. (1998). Prospective memory: When reminders fail. *Memory and Cognition, 26*, 287–298.

Haack, S. (1979). Do we need "fuzzy logic?" *International Journal of Man-Machine Studies, 11*, 432–445.

Haber, R. (1983). The impending demise of the icon: A critique of the concept of iconic storage in visual information processing. *Behavioral and Brain Sciences, 6*, 1–54.

Haggard, P. (2005). Conscious intention and motor cognition. *Trends in Cognitive Sciences, 9*, 290–295.

Hagoort, P. (2003). Interplay between syntax and semantics during sentence comprehension: ERP effects of combining syntactic and semantic violations. *Journal of Cognitive Neuroscience, 15*, 883–899.

Haines, R. F. (1991). A breakdown in simultaneous information processing. In G. Obrecht & L. Stark (Eds.), *Presbyopia research: From molecular biology to visual adaptation* (pp. 171–176). New York: Plenum Press.

Haith, M., & McCarty, M. (1990). Stability of visual expectations at 3.0 months of age. *Developmental Psychology, 26*, 68–74.

Haken, H., Kelso, J., & Bunz, H. (1985). A theoretical model of phase transitions in human hand movements. *Biological Cybernetics, 51,* 347–356.

Hale, S., & Simpson, H. (1970). Effects of eye movements on the rate of discovery and the vividness of visual images. *Perception and Psychophysics, 9,* 242–246.

Hamilton, A., Wolpert, D., & Frith, U. (2004). Your own action influences how you perceive another person's action. *Current Biology, 14,* 493–498.

Hamilton, W. (1859). *Lectures on metaphysics and logic, Vol. 1.* Boston: Gould and Lincoln.

Hanes, D., & Schall, J. (1996). Neural control of voluntary movement initiation. *Science, 274,* 427–430.

Haney, C. (2002). Making law modern: Toward a contextual model of justice. *Psychology, Public Policy, and Law, 8,* 3–63.

Hanson, S., Matsuka, T., & Haxby, J. (2004). Combinatoric codes in ventral medial temporal lobes for objects: Is there a face area? *NeuroImage, 23,* 156–166.

Hanson, S., & Negishi, M. (2002). On the emergence of rules in neural networks. *Neural Computation, 14,* 2245–2268.

Hare, M., & Elman, J. (1995). Learning and morphological change. *Cognition, 56,* 61–98.

Hari, R., & Antervo, A. (1982). Comparison of magneto- and electroencephalographic techniques in event-related response research: A brief history. *Scandinavian Journal of Psychology, Suppl 1,* 170–174.

Harm, M., & Seidenberg, M. (2004). Computing the meanings of words in reading: Cooperative division of labor between visual and phonological processes. *Psychological Review, 111,* 662–720.

Harnad, S. (Ed.) (1987). *Categorical perception: The groundwork of cognition.* New York: Cambridge University Press.

Harnad, S. (1993). Grounding symbols in the analog world with neural nets. *Think, 2,* 12–78.

Haruno, M., Wolpert, D., & Kawato, M. (2001). MOSAIC model for sensorimotor learning and control. *Neural Computation, 13,* 2201–2220.

Hasher, L., & Griffin, M. (1978). Reconstructive and reproductive processes in memory. *Journal of Experimental Psychology: Human Learning and Memory, 4,* 318–330.

Haslam, N., Porter, M., & Rothschild, L. (2001). Visual search: Efficiency continuum or distinct processes? *Psychonomic Bulletin and Review, 8,* 742–746.

Haugeland, J. (1995). Mind embodied and embedded. In Y. Houng & J. Ho (Eds.), *Mind and cognition.* Taipei: Academia Sinica.

Hauk, O., & Pulvermüller, F. (2004). Neurophysiological distinction of action words in the fronto-central cortex. *Human Brain Mapping, 21,* 191–201.

Hausdorff, J., & Peng, C. (1996). Multiscaled randomness: A possible source of 1/f noise in biology. *Physical Review E, 54,* 2154–2157.

Hauser, M., Chomsky, N., & Fitch, W. (2002). The faculty of language: What is it, who has it, and how did it evolve? *Science, 298,* 1569–1579.

Haxby, J., Gobbini, M., Furey, M., Ishai, A., Schouten, J., & Pietrini, P. (2001). Distributed and overlapping representations of faces and objects in ventral temporal cortex. *Science, 293,* 2425–2430.

Hayhoe, M. (2000). Vision using routines: A functional account of vision. *Visual Cognition, 7,* 43–64.

Hayhoe, M., Bensinger, D., & Ballard, D. (1998). Task constraints in visual working memory. *Vision Research, 38,* 125–137.

Hebb, D. (1949). *The organization of behavior: A neuropsychological theory.* Oxford: Wiley.

Hebb, D. (1961). Sensory deprivation: Facts in search of a theory. Discussion. *Journal of Nervous and Mental Disease, 132,* 40–43.

Hebb, D. (1968). Concerning imagery. *Psychological Review, 75,* 466–477.

Hecht, H. (2001). Regularities of the physical world and the absence of their internalization. *Behavioral and Brain Sciences, 24,* 608–617.

Heeger, D., Boynton, G., Demb, J., Seidemann, E., & Newsome, W. (1999). Motion opponency in visual cortex. *Journal of Neuroscience, 19,* 7162–7174.

Heeger, D., Gandhi, S., Huk, A., & Boynton, G. (2001). Neuronal correlates of attention in human visual cortex. In C. Koch, J. Braun, & J. Davis (Eds.), *Visual attention and cortical circuits* (pp. 25–47). Cambridge, Mass.: MIT Press.

Hegarty, M. (1992). Mental animation: Inferring motion from static displays of mechanical systems. *Journal of Experimental Psychology: Learning, Memory, and Cognition, 18,* 1084–1102.

Heider, E. (1972). Universals in color naming and memory. *Journal of Experimental Psychology, 93,* 10–20.

Heit, E., & Barsalou, L. (1996). The instantiation principle in natural categories. *Memory, 4,* 413–451.

Henderson, J. (1993). Visual attention and saccadic eye movements. In G. d'Ydewalle & J. Van Rensbergen (Eds.), *Perception and cognition: Advances in eye movement research* (pp. 37–50). Amsterdam: North-Holland/Elsevier Science.

Hennig, M., Kerscher, N., Funke, K., & Wörgötter, F. (2002). Stochastic resonance in visual cortical neurons: Does the eye-tremor actually improve visual acuity? *Neurocomputing: An International Journal, 44–46,* 115–120.

Hesslow, G. (2002). Conscious thought as simulation of behaviour and perception. *Trends in Cognitive Sciences, 6,* 242–247.

Hillis, A. E., & Caramazza, A. (1991). Category-specific naming and comprehension impairment: A double dissociation. *Brain, 114,* 2081–2094.

Hillyard, S., & Kutas, M. (1983). Electrophysiology of cognitive processing. *Annual Review of Psychology, 34,* 33–61.

Hillyard, S., Simpson, G., Woods, D., Van Voorhis, S., & Münte, T. (1984). Event-related brain potentials and selective attention to different modalities. In F. Reinoso-Suarez (Ed.), *Cortical integration* (pp. 395–414). New York: Raven Press.

Hinsz, V., Tindale, R., & Vollrath, D. (1997). The emerging conceptualization of groups as information processes. *Psychological Bulletin, 121,* 43–64.

Hinton, G. (1981). Implementing semantic networks in parallel hardware. In G. Hinton & J. Anderson (Eds.), *Parallel models of associative memory.* Hillsdale, N.J.: Lawrence Erlbaum.

Hinton G. (Ed.) (1991). *Connectionist symbol processing.* Cambridge, Mass.: MIT Press.

Hinton, G., Dayan, P., Frey, B., & Neal, R. (1995). The wake-sleep algorithm for unsupervised neural networks. *Science, 268,* 1158–1161.

Hinton, G., McClelland, J., & Rumelhart, D. (1986). Distributed representations. In D. Rumelhart & J. McClelland (Eds.), *Parallel distributed processing, Vol. 1.* Cambridge, Mass.: MIT Press.

Hinton, G., Plaut, D., & Shallice, T. (1993). Simulating brain damage. *Scientific American, 296,* 76–82.

Hinton, G., & Shallice, T. (1991). Lesioning an attractor network: Investigations of acquired dyslexia. *Psychological Review, 98,* 74–95.

Hintzman, D. (1986). "Schema abstraction" in a multiple-trace memory model. *Psychological Review*, *93*, 411–428.

Hintzman, D. (1993). Twenty-five years of learning and memory: Was the cognitive revolution a mistake? In D. Meyer & S. Kornblum (Eds.), *Attention and performance 14: Synergies in experimental psychology, artificial intelligence, and cognitive neuroscience*. Cambridge, Mass.: MIT Press.

Hintzman, D. L. (1991). Why are formal models useful in psychology? In W. Hockley & S. Lewandowsky (Eds.), *Relating theory and data: Essays on human memory in honor of Bennet B. Murdock* (pp. 39–56). Hillsdale, N.J.: Lawrence Erlbaum.

Hock, H., Kelso, J., & Schöner, G. (1993). Bistability and hysteresis in the organization of apparent motion patterns. *Journal of Experimental Psychology: Human Perception and Performance*, *19*(1), 63–80.

Hoffman, J. (1998). Visual attention and eye movements. In H. Pashler (Ed.), *Attention* (pp. 119–153). Hove, England: Psychology Press.

Hoffman, W. (1997). Mind and the geometry of systems. In S. O'Naullain, P. McKevitt, & E. Mac Aogain (Eds.), *Two sciences of mind: Readings in cognitive science and consciousness* (pp. 459–483). Amsterdam: John Benjamins.

Hofstadter, D., & Mitchell, M. (1994). The Copycat project: A model of mental fluidity and analogy-making. In K. Holyoak & J. Barnden (Eds.), *Advances in connectionist and neural computation theory, Vol. 2: Analogical connections* (pp. 31–112). Norwood, N.J.: Ablex.

Holland, J. (1995). *Hidden order: How adaptation builds complexity*. Reading, Mass.: Addison-Wesley.

Hollingshead, A. (1998). Retrieval processes in transactive memory systems. *Journal of Personality and Social Psychology*, *74*, 659–671.

Hollingworth, A., & Henderson, J. (2002). Accurate visual memory for previously attended objects in natural scenes. *Journal of Experimental Psychology: Human Perception and Performance*, *28*, 113–136.

Hollingworth, A., Williams, C., & Henderson, J. (2001). To see and remember: Visually specific information is retained in memory from previously attended objects in natural scenes. *Psychonomic Bulletin and Review*, *8*, 761–768.

Holman, E. (1978). Completely nonmetric multidimensional scaling. *Journal of Mathematical Psychology*, *18*, 39–51.

Holt, L. (2005). Temporally nonadjacent nonlinguistic sounds affect speech categorization. *Psychological Science*, *16*, 305–312.

Holyoak, K., & Thagard, P. (2002). Analogical mapping by constraint satisfaction. In T. Polk & C. Seifert (Eds.), *Cognitive modeling* (pp. 849–909). Cambridge, Mass.: MIT Press.

Hommel, B., Daum, I., & Kluwe, R. (2004). Exorcizing the homunculus, phase two: Editors' introduction. *Acta Psychologica*, *115*, 99–104.

Hommel, B., Müsseler, J., Aschersleben, G., & Prinz, W. (2001). The theory of event coding (TEC): A framework for perception and action planning. *Behavioral and Brain Sciences*, *24*, 849–937.

Honderich, T. (1988). *A theory of determinism: The mind, neuroscience, and life-hopes*. Oxford: Clarendon Press.

Hopf, J., Vogel, E., Woodman, G., Heinze, H., & Luck, S. (2002). Localizing visual discrimination processes in time and space. *Journal of Neurophysiology*, *88*, 2088–2095.

Hopfield, J. (1982). Neural networks and physical systems with emergent collective computational abilities. *Proceedings of the National Academy of Sciences of the USA, 79*, 2554–2588.

Hopfield, J. (1984). Neurons with graded response have collective computational properties like those of two-state neurons. *Proceedings of the National Academy of Sciences of the USA, 81*, 3088–3092.

Horgan, T., & Tienson, J. (1996). *Connectionism and the philosophy of psychology.* Cambridge, Mass.: MIT Press.

Horton, W., & Keysar, B. (1996). When do speakers take into account common ground? *Cognition, 59*, 91–117.

Howard, I., & Templeton, W. (1966). *Human spatial orientation.* Oxford: Wiley.

Hubel, D., & Weisel, T. (1959). Receptive fields of single neurons in the cat's striate cortex. *Journal of Physiology, 148*, 574–591.

Huber, D., & O'Reilly, R. (2003). Persistence and accommodation in short-term priming and other perceptual paradigms: Temporal segregation through synaptic depression. *Cognitive Science, 27*, 403–430.

Huebner, R. (2001). A formal version of the guided search (GS2) model. *Perception and Psychophysics, 63*, 945–951.

Huey, E. (1898). Preliminary experiments in the physiology and psychology of reading. *American Journal of Psychology, 9*, 575–586.

Hummel, J. (2003). "Effective systematicity" in, "effective systematicity" out: A reply to Edelman and Intrator (2003). *Cognitive Science, 27*, 327–329.

Hummel, J., & Holyoak, K. (2003). A symbolic-connectionist theory of relational inference and generalization. *Psychological Review, 110*, 220–264.

Humphreys, G., & Müller, H. (1993). SEarch via Recursive Rejection (SERR): A connectionist model of visual search. *Cognitive Psychology, 25*, 43–110.

Humphreys, G., Quinlan, P., & Riddoch, M. (1989). Grouping processes in visual search: Effects with single- and combined-feature targets. *Journal of Experimental Psychology: General, 118*, 258–279.

Hunt, E. (1975). *Artificial intelligence.* Orlando, Fla.: Academic Press.

Hurlbert, A., & Poggio, T. (1985). Spotlight on attention. *Trends in Neurosciences, 8*, 309–311.

Hurlburt, R. (1990). *Emotions, personality, and psychotherapy.* New York: Plenum Press.

Hurley, S. (1998a). *Consciousness in action.* Cambridge, Mass.: Harvard University Press.

Hurley, S. (1998b). Vehicles, contents, conceptual structures, and externalism. *Analysis, 58*, 1–6.

Hutchins, E. (1995). *Cognition in the wild.* Cambridge, Mass.: MIT Press.

Huxley, T. (1902). *Methods and results.* New York: Appleton.

Hyde, D. (1997). From heaps and gaps to heaps and gluts. *Mind, 106*, 641–660.

Imai, M., & Gentner, D. (1997). A cross-linguistic study of early word meaning: Universal ontology and linguistic influence. *Cognition, 62*, 169–200.

Indrebo, K., Povinelli, R., & Johnson, M. (2006). Sub-banded reconstructed phase spaces for speech recognition. *Speech Communication, 48.*

Inui, T., & McClelland, J. (Eds.) (1996). *Attention and performance 16: Information integration in perception and communication.* Cambridge, Mass: MIT Press.

Irwin, D. (1993). Perceiving an integrated visual world. In D. Meyer & S. Kornblum (Eds.), *Attention and performance 14: Synergies in experimental psychology, artificial intelligence, cognitive neuroscience* (pp. 121–142). Cambridge, Mass.: MIT Press.

Ito, M., & Gilbert, C. (1999). Attention modulates contextual influences in the primary visual cortex of alert monkeys. *Neuron, 22,* 593–604.

Itti, L., & Koch, C. (2001). Computational modeling of visual attention. *Nature Reviews Neuroscience, 2,* 194–203.

Jackendoff, R. (2002). *Foundations of language: Brain, meaning, grammar, evolution.* New York: Oxford University Press.

Jacob, P., & Jeannerod, M. (2003). *Ways of seeing: The scope and limits of visual cognition.* Oxford: Oxford University Press.

Jacobovits, L. (1967). Semantic satiation and cognitive dynamics. *Journal of Special Education, 2*(1), 35–44.

Jacobs, A., & Grainger, J. (1994). Models of visual word recognition: Sampling the state of the art. *Journal of Experimental Psychology: Human Perception and Performance, 20,* 1311–1334.

Jacobs, R., Jordan, M., & Barto, A. (1991). Task decomposition through competition in a modular connectionist architecture: The what and where vision tasks. *Cognitive Science, 15,* 219–250.

Jaeger, J., Lockwood, A., Kremmerer, D., Van Valin, R., Jr., Murphy, B., & Khalak, H. (1996). A positron emission tomographic study of regular and irregular verb morphology in English. *Language, 72,* 451–497.

Jancke, D., Chavane, F., Naaman, S., & Grinvald, A. (2004). Imaging cortical correlates of illusion in early visual cortex. *Nature, 428,* 423–426.

Jared, D., McRae, K., & Seidenberg, M. (1990). The basis of consistency effects in word naming. *Journal of Memory and Language, 29,* 687–715.

Jarvilehto, T. (1998). The theory of the organism environment system: I. Description of the theory. *Integrative Physiological and Behavioral Science, 33,* 321–334.

Jeannerod, M. (1996). Reaching and grasping. Parallel specification of visuomotor channels. In S. Keele & H. Heuer (Eds.), *Handbook of perception and action, Vol. 2: Motor skills* (pp. 405–460). San Diego, Calif.: Academic Press.

Jeannerod, M. (2003). Simulation of action as a unifying concept for motor cognition. In S. Johnson-Frey (Ed.), *Taking action: Cognitive neuroscience perspectives on intentional acts* (pp. 139–163). Cambridge, Mass.: MIT Press.

Jennings, J. (1992). Is it important that the mind is in a body? Inhibition and the heart. *Psychophysiology, 29,* 369–383.

Jerde, T., Söchting, J., & Flanders, M. (2003). Coarticulation in fluent fingerspelling. *Journal of Neuroscience, 23,* 2383–2393.

Jibu, M., Hagan, S., Hameroff, S., Pribram, K., & Yasue, K. (1994). Quantum optical coherence in microtubules: Implications for brain function. *Biosystems, 32,* 195–209.

Jirsa, V., & Kelso, J. (2005). The excitator as a minimal model for the coordination dynamics of discrete and rhythmic movement generation. *Journal of Motor Behavior, 37,* 35–51.

Joanisse, M. (2004). Specific language impairments in children: Phonology, semantics, and the English past tense. *Current Directions in Psychological Science, 13,* 156–160.

Joanisse, M., & Seidenberg, M. (1999). Impairments in verb morphology after brain injury: A connectionist model. *Proceedings of the National Academy of Sciences of the USA, 96,* 7592–7597.

Johnson, E., Hawken, M., & Shapley, R. (2001). The spatial transformation of color in the primary visual cortex of the macaque monkey. *Nature Neuroscience, 4,* 409–416.

Johnson-Laird, P., Legrenzi, P., & Legrenzi, M. (1972). Reasoning and a sense of reality. *British Journal of Psychology*, *63*, 395–400.

Jolicoeur, P. (1985). The time to name disoriented natural objects. *Memory and Cognition*, *13*, 289–303.

Jonasse, R. (1995). Collectively seeing the wind: Distributed cognition in smoke-jumping. *Mind, Culture, and Activity*, *2*, 81–101.

Jones, G. (1982). Stacks not fuzzy sets: An ordinal basis for prototype theory of concepts. *Cognition*, *12*, 281–290.

Jones, S., & Smith, L. (1993). The place of perception in children's concepts. *Cognitive Development*, *8*, 113–139.

Jordan, J. (1999). Recasting Dewey's critique of the reflex-arc concept via a theory of anticipatory consciousness: Implications for theories of perception. In J. Jordan (Ed.), *Modeling consciousness across the disciplines* (pp. 65–94). Lanham, Md.: University Press of America.

Jordan, M., & Rumelhart, D. (1992). Forward models: Supervised learning with a distal teacher. *Cognitive Science*, *16*, 307–354.

Josiassen, R., Shagass, C., Roemer, R., Slepner, S., & Czartorysky, B. (1990). *International Journal of Psychophysiology*, *9*, 139–149.

Juarrero, A. (1999). *Dynamics in action*. Cambridge, Mass.: MIT Press.

Julesz, B. (1971). *Foundations of cyclopean perception*. Oxford: University of Chicago Press.

Jurafsky, D. (1996). A probabilistic model of lexical and syntactic access and disambiguation. *Cognitive Science*, *20*, 137–194.

Jurafsky, D. (2002). Probabilistic modeling in psycholinguistics: Linguistic comprehension and production. In R. Bod, J. Hay, & S. Jannedy (Eds.), *Probabilistic linguistics*. Cambridge, Mass.: MIT Press.

Just, M., & Carpenter, P. (1993). The intensity dimension of thought: Pupillometric indices of sentence processing. *Canadian Journal of Experimental Psychology*, *47*, 310–339.

Kahneman, D., Slovic, P., & Tversky, A. (Eds.) (1982). *Judgment under uncertainty: Heuristics and biases*. New York: Cambridge University Press.

Kahneman, D., Tursky, B., Shapiro, D., & Crider, A. (1969). Pupillary, heart rate, and skin resistance changes during a mental task. *Journal of Experimental Psychology*, *79*, 164–167.

Kahneman, D., & Tversky, A. (1973). On the psychology of prediction. *Psychological Review*, *80*, 237–251.

Kako, E., & Wagner, L. (2001). The semantics of syntactic structures. *Trends in Cognitive Sciences*, *5*, 102–108.

Kambe, G., Rayner, K., & Duffy, S. (2001). Global context effects on processing lexically ambiguous words: Evidence from eye fixations. *Memory and Cognition*, *29*, 363–372.

Kant, I. (1785/1996). *The metaphysics of morals*. New York: Cambridge University Press.

Karatekin, C. (2004). Development of attentional allocation in the dual task paradigm. *International Journal of Psychophysiology*, *52*, 7–21.

Karmiloff-Smith, A. (1992). *Beyond modularity: A developmental perspective on cognitive science*. Cambridge, Mass.: MIT Press.

Katz, W., Machetanz, J., Orth, U., & Schönle, P. (1990). A kinematic analysis of anticipatory coarticulation in the speech of anterior aphasic subjects using electromagnetic articulography. *Brain and Language*, *28*, 555–575.

Kawamoto, A. (1993). Nonlinear dynamics in the resolution of lexical ambiguity: A parallel distributed processing account. *Journal of Memory and Language, 32,* 474–516.

Kawamoto, A., & Anderson, J. (1985). A neural network model of multi-stable perception. *Acta Psychologica, 59,* 35–56.

Kawato, M. (1996). Bidirectional theory approach to integration. In J. McClelland & T. Inui (Eds.), *Attention and performance 16: Information integration in perception and communication* (pp. 335–367). Cambridge, Mass.: MIT Press.

Kay, P., & Kempton, W. (1984). What is the Sapir-Whorf hypothesis? *American Anthropologist, 86,* 65–79.

Keil, F. (1989). *Concepts, kinds, and cognitive development.* Cambridge, Mass.: MIT Press.

Kelso, J. (1981). On the oscillatory basis of movement. *Bulletin of the Psychonomic Society, 18,* 63.

Kelso, J. (1984). Phase transitions and critical behavior in human bimanual coordination. *American Journal of Physiology: Regulatory, Integrative and Comparative, 15,* 1000–1004.

Kelso, J. (1995). *Dynamic patterns: The self-organization of brain and behavior.* Cambridge, Mass.: MIT Press.

Kelso, J. A. S., Tuller, B., & Harris, K. S. (1983). A dynamic pattern perspective on the control and coordination of movement. In P. F. MacNeilage (Ed.), *The production of speech* (pp. 137–173). New York: Springer-Verlag.

Kelso, J., Del-Colle, J., & Schöner, G. (1990). Action-perception as a pattern formation process. In M. Jeannerod (Ed.), *Attention and performance 13: Motor representation and control* (pp. 139–169). Hillsdale, N.J.: Lawrence Erlbaum.

Kelso, J., & Jeka, J. (1992). Symmetry breaking dynamics of human multilimb coordination. *Journal of Experimental Psychology: Human Perception and Performance, 18,* 645–668.

Kelso, J., Scholz, J., & Schöner, G. (1986). Nonequilibrium phase transitions in coordinated biological motion: Critical fluctuations. *Physics Letters A, 118,* 279–284.

Kemeny, J., & Snell, J. (1976). *Finite Markov chains.* New York: Springer-Verlag.

Kennedy, A. (1992). The spatial coding hypothesis. In K. Rayner (Ed.), *Eye movements and visual cognition: Scene perception and reading* (pp. 379–396). New York: Springer-Verlag.

Kennel, M., & Buhl, M. (2003). Estimating good discrete partitions from observed data: Symbolic false nearest neighbors. *Physical Review Letters, 91,* 084102.

Kersten, D. (1991). Transparency and the cooperative computation of scene attributes. In M. Landy & A. Movshon (Eds.), *Computational models of visual processing* (pp. 209–228). Cambridge, Mass.: MIT Press.

Keysers, C., & Perrett, D. (2002). Visual masking and RSVP reveal neural competition. *Trends in Cognitive Sciences, 6,* 120–125.

Killeen, P. (1989). Behavior as a trajectory through a field of attractors. In J. Brink, C. Burawa, & C. Haden (Eds.), *The computer and the brain.* New York: North-Holland.

Kim, J. (1998). *Mind in a physical world: An essay on the mind-body problem and mental causation.* Cambridge: Cambridge University Press.

Kim, M., Kim, J., & Kwon, J. (2001). The effect of immediate and delayed word repetition on event-related potential in a continuous recognition task. *Cognitive Brain Research, 11,* 387–396.

Kim, U., & McCormick, D. (1998). The functional influence of burst and ionic firing mode on synaptic interactions in the thalamus. *Journal of Neuroscience, 18,* 9500–9516.

Kimball, J. (1973). Seven principles of surface structure parsing in natural language. *Cognition, 2,* 15–47.

Kinchla, R. (1974). Detecting target elements in multielement arrays: A confusability model. *Perception & Psychophysics, 15,* 149–158.

King, A. (1999). Sensory experience and the formation of a computational map of auditory space in the brain. *BioEssays, 21,* 900–911.

King, A., Hutchings, M., Moore, D., & Blakemore, C. (1988). Developmental plasticity in the visual and auditory representations in the mammalian superior colliculus. *Nature, 332,* 73–76.

Kingdom, F. (2003). Color brings relief to human vision. *Nature Neuroscience, 6,* 641–645.

Kingsbury, M., & Finlay, B. (2001). The cortex in multidimensional space: Where do cortical areas come from? *Developmental Science, 4,* 125–156.

Kirk, R. (1974). Zombies v. materialists. *Proceedings of the Aristotelian Society, 48,* 135–152.

Kirsh, D. (1995). The intelligent use of space. *Artificial Intelligence, 73,* 31–68.

Kirsh, D., & Maglio, P. (1994). On distinguishing epistemic from pragmatic action. *Cognitive Science, 18,* 513–549.

Kiss, G. (1972). Long-term memory: A state-space approach. *British Journal of Psychology, 63,* 327–341.

Kitchens, B. (1998). *Symbolic dynamics: One-sided, two-sided and countable state Markov shifts.* Berlin: Springer-Verlag.

Klein, R., & Pontefract, A. (1994). Does oculomotor readiness mediate cognitive control of visual attention? Revised! In M. Moscovitch & C. Umilta (Eds.), *Attention and performance 15: Conscious and nonconscious information processing* (pp. 333–350). Cambridge, Mass.: MIT Press.

Kleinberg, J. (2000). Navigation in a small world. *Nature, 406,* 845.

Kluender, K., Keith, R., Diehl, R., & Killeen, P. (1987). Japanese quail can learn phonetic categories. *Science, 237,* 1195–1197.

Knill, D. (1998). Surface orientation from texture: Ideal observers, generic observers and the information content of texture cues. *Vision Research, 38,* 1655–1682.

Knoblich, G., & Flach, R. (2001). Predicting the effects of actions: Interactions of perception and action. *Psychological Science, 12,* 467–472.

Knoblich, G., & Jordan, J. (2003). Action coordination in groups and individuals: Learning anticipatory control. *Journal of Experimental Psychology: Learning, Memory, and Cognition, 29,* 1006–1016.

Knoblich, G., Ohlsson, S., Haider, H., & Rhenius, D. (1999). Constraint relaxation and chunk decomposition in insight problem solving. *Journal of Experimental Psychology: Learning, Memory, and Cognition, 25,* 1534–1555.

Knoblich, G., Öllinger, M., & Spivey, M. (2005). Tracking the eyes to obtain insight into insight problem solving. In G. Underwood (Ed.), *Cognitive processes in eye guidance.* Oxford: Oxford University Press.

Knoblich, G., Thornton, I., Grosjean, M., & Shiffrar, M. (Eds.) (2005). *The human body: Perception from the inside out.* New York: Oxford University Press.

Knudsen, E., & Knudsen, P. (1989). Vision calibrates sound localization in developing barn owls. *Journal of Neuroscience, 9,* 3306–3313.

Ko, Y., Challis, J., & Newell, K. (2001). Postural coordination patterns as a function of dynamics of the support surface. *Human Movement Science, 20,* 737–764.

Koch, C. (2004). *The quest for consciousness: A neurobiological approach.* Englewood, Colo.: Roberts.

Koch, C., & Ullman, S. (1985). Shifts in selective visual attention: Towards the underlying neural circuitry. *Human Neurobiology, 4,* 219–227.

Koehler, J. (1993). The base rate fallacy myth. *Psycoloquy, 4*(49).

Köhler, W. (1922/1938). Physical gestalten. In W. Ellis (Ed. & Trans.), *A source book of gestalt psychology* (pp. 17–54). London: Routledge & Kegan Paul.

Köhler, W., & Wallach, H. (1944). Figural aftereffects; an investigation of visual processes. *Proceedings of the American Philosophical Society, 88,* 269–357.

Kolers, P., & Brewster, J. (1985). Rhythms and responses. *Journal of Experimental Psychology: Human Perception and Performance, 11,* 150–167.

Kornblum, S., Hasbroucq, T., & Osman, A. (1990). Dimensional overlap: Cognitive basis for stimulus-response compatibility: A model and taxonomy. *Psychological Review, 97,* 253–270.

Kosko, B. (1993). *Fuzzy thinking: The new science of fuzzy logic.* New York: Hyperion/Disney Books.

Kosslyn, S. (1994). *Image and brain: The resolution of the imagery debate.* Cambridge, Mass.: MIT Press.

Kosslyn, S., Ball, T., & Reiser, B. (1978). Visual images preserve metric spatial information: Evidence from studies of image scanning. *Journal of Experimental Psychology: Human Perception and Performance, 4,* 47–60.

Kosslyn, S., & Thompson, W. (2003). When is early visual cortex activated during visual mental imagery? *Psychological Bulletin, 129,* 723–746.

Kowler, E., Anderson, E., Dosher, B., & Blaser, E. (1995). The role of attention in the programming of saccades. *Vision Research, 35,* 1897–1916.

Kowler, E., & Steinman, R. (1979). The effect of expectations on slow oculomotor control: I. Periodic target steps. *Vision Research, 19,* 619–632.

Krauss, S., & Wang, X. (2003). The psychology of the Monty Hall problem: Discovering psychological mechanisms for solving a tenacious brain teaser. *Journal of Experimental Psychology: General, 132,* 3–22.

Krumhansl, C. (1978). Concerning the applicability of geometric models to similarity data: The interrelationship between similarity and spatial density. *Psychological Review, 85,* 445–463.

Kruschke, J. K. (1992). ALCOVE: An exemplar-based connectionist model of category learning. *Psychological Review, 99,* 22–44.

Kubovy, M., & Epstein, W. (2001). Internalization: A metaphor we can live without. *Behavioral and Brain Sciences, 24,* 618–625.

Kugler, P., & Turvey, M. (1987). *Information, natural law, and the self-assembly of rhythmic movement.* Hillsdale, N.J.: Lawrence Erlbaum.

Kuhl, P., & Miller, J. (1975). Speech perception by the chinchilla: Voiced-voiceless distinction in alveolar plosive consonants. *Science, 190,* 69–72.

Kuhn, S., & Cruse, H. (2005). Static mental representations in recurrent neural networks for the control of dynamic behavioural sequences. *Connection Science, 17,* 343–360.

Kurths, J., Voss, A., Saparin, P., Witt, A., Kleiner, H., & Wessel, N. (1995). Quantitative analysis of heart rate variability. *Chaos, 5,* 88–94.

Kutas, M., & Federmeier, K. (1998). Minding the body. *Psychophysiology, 35,* 135–150.

Kutas, M., & Hillyard, S. (1980). Reading senseless sentences: Brain potentials reflect semantic incongruity. *Science, 207,* 203–205.

Kutas, M., & Hillyard, S. (1984). Brain potentials during reading reflect word expectancy and semantic association. *Nature, 307,* 161–163.

Labov, W. (1973). The boundaries of words and their meanings. In C. Bailey & R. Shuy (Eds.), *New ways of analyzing variations in English.* Washington, D.C.: Georgetown University Press.

Laeng, B., & Teodorescu, D. (2002). Eye scanpaths during visual imagery reenact those of perception of the same visual scene. *Cognitive Science, 26,* 207–231.

Lakin, J., & Chartrand, T. (2003). Using nonconscious behavioral mimicry to create affiliation and rapport. *Psychological Science, 14,* 334–339.

Lakoff, G. (1987). *Women, fire, and dangerous things: What categories reveal about the mind.* Chicago: University of Chicago Press.

Lakoff, G. (1997). The internal structure of the self. In U. Neisser & D. Jopling (Eds.), *The conceptual self in context: Culture, experience, self-understanding* (pp. 92–113). New York: Cambridge University Press.

Lambert, W. E., & Jakobovits, L. A. (1960). Verbal satiation and changes in the intensity of meaning. *Journal of Experimental Psychology, 60,* 376–383.

Lamberts, K. (1995). Categorization under time pressure. *Journal of Experimental Psychology: General, 124,* 161–180.

Lamberts, K. (1998). The time course of categorization. *Journal of Experimental Psychology: Learning, Memory, and Cognition, 24,* 695–711.

Lamberts, K. (2000). Information-accumulation theory of speeded categorization. *Psychological Review, 107,* 227–260.

Lamme, V. (2001). Blindsight: The role of feedforward and feedback corticocortical connections. *Acta Psychologica, 107,* 209–228.

Lamme, V., & Roelfsema, P. (2000). The distinct modes of vision offered by feedforward and recurrent processing. *Trends in Neuroscience, 23,* 571–579.

Land, M., & Lee, D. (1994). Where do we look when we steer? *Nature, 369,* 742–744.

Landauer, T. K., & Dumais, S. T. (1997). A solution to Plato's problem: The latent semantic analysis theory of acquisition, induction, and representation of knowledge. *Psychological Review, 104,* 211–240.

Large, E., Fink, P., & Kelso, J. (2002). Tracking simple and complex sequences. *Psychological Research/Psychologische Forschung, 66,* 3–17.

Large, E., & Palmer, C. (2002). Perceiving temporal regularity in music. *Cognitive Science, 26,* 1–37.

Larson, J., Christensen, C., Franz, T., & Abbott, A. (1998). Diagnosing groups: The pooling, management, and impact of shared and unshared case information in team based medical decision making. *Journal of Personality and Social Psychology, 75,* 93–108.

Lashley, K. (1950). In search of the engram. *Symposia of the Society for Experimental Biology, 4,* 454–482.

Lashley, K. (1951). The problem of serial order in behavior. In L. Jeffress (Ed.), *Cerebral mechanisms in behavior.* New York: Wiley.

Law, M., & Constantine-Paton, M. (1981). Anatomy and physiology of experimentally produced striped tecta. *Journal of Neuroscience, 1,* 741–759.

Le Bon, G. (1916). *The crowd, a study of the popular mind.* London: T. F. Unwin.

Leach, J., & Carpenter, R. (2001). Saccadic choice with asynchronous targets: Evidence for independent randomization. *Vision Research, 41,* 3437–3445.

Leahy, R. (1992). Scripts in cognitive therapy: The systemic perspective. *Journal of Cognitive Psychotherapy, 5,* 291–304.

Leike, A. (2002). Demonstration of the exponential decay law using beer froth. *European Journal of Physics, 23,* 21–26.

Lenat, D. (1982). The nature of heuristics. *Artificial Intelligence, 19,* 189–249.

Lenat, D. (1995). CYC: A large-scale investment in knowledge infrastructure. *Communications of the ACM, 38,* 32–38.

Lennie, P. (1980). Parallel visual pathways: A review. *Vision Research, 20,* 561–594.

Lennie, P. (1984). Recent developments in the physiology of color vision. *Trends in Neurosciences, 7,* 243–248.

Lepper, M. (1973). Dissonance, self-perception, and honesty in children. *Journal of Personality and Social Psychology, 25,* 65–74.

Lettvin, J. (1995). J Y Lettvin on grandmother cells. In M. Gazzaniga (Ed.), *The cognitive neurosciences* (pp. 434–435). Cambridge, Mass.: MIT Press.

Lévy, P. (1997). *Collective intelligence: Mankind's emerging world in cyberspace.* New York: Plenum Press.

Lewandowsky, S. (1995). Base-rate neglect in ALCOVE: A critical reevaluation. *Psychological Review, 102,* 185–191.

Liberman, A. (1982). On finding that speech is special. *American Psychologist, 37,* 148–167.

Liberman, A., Harris, K., Hoffman, H., & Griffith, B. (1957). The discrimination of speech sounds within and across phoneme boundaries. *Journal of Experimental Psychology, 53,* 358–368.

Liberman, A., Harris, K., Kinney, J., & Lane, H. (1961). The discrimination of relative onset-time of the components of certain speech and nonspeech patterns. *Journal of Experimental Psychology, 61,* 379–388.

Liberman, A., & Mattingly, I. (1985). The motor theory of speech perception revised. *Cognition, 21,* 1–36.

Liberman, A., & Whalen, D. (2000). On the relation of speech to language. *Trends in Cognitive Sciences, 4,* 187–196.

Libet, B. (1985). Unconscious cerebral initiative and the role of conscious will in voluntary action. *Behavioral and Brain Sciences, 8,* 529–566.

Lilly, J. (1956). Mental effects of reduction of ordinary levels of physical stimuli on intact, healthy persons. *Psychiatric Research Reports, 5,* 1–9.

Lilly, J. (1967). *Programming and metaprogramming in the human biocomputer.* New York: Julian Press.

Lin, E., & Murphy, G. (1997). Effects of background knowledge on object categorization and part detection. *Journal of Experimental Psychology: Human Perception and Performance, 23,* 1153–1169.

Little, W., & Shaw, G. (1975). A statistical theory of short and long term memory. *Behavioral Biology, 14,* 115–133.

Livingston, K., Andrews, J., & Harnad, S. (1998). Categorical perception effects induced by category learning. *Journal of Experimental Psychology: Learning, Memory, and Cognition, 24,* 732–753.

Livingstone, M., & Hubel, D. (1988). Segregation of form, color, movement, and depth: Anatomy, physiology, and perception. *Science, 240,* 740–749.

Lockwood, M., Brown, H., Butterfield, J., Deutsch, D., Loewer, B., Papineau, D., & Saunders, S. (1996). Symposium: The "many minds" interpretation of quantum theory. *British Journal for the Philosophy of Science, 47,* 159–248.

Love, B. (2005). Environment and goals jointly direct category acquisition. *Current Directions in Psychological Science, 14*, 195–199.

Love, B., Medin, D., & Gureckis, T. (2004). SUSTAIN: A network model of category learning. *Psychological Review, 111*, 309–332.

Luce, P., Goldinger, S., Auer, E., & Vitevitch, M. (2000). Phonetic priming, neighborhood activation, and PARSYN. *Perception and Psychophysics, 62*, 615–625.

Luce, R. (1959). *Individual choice behavior: A theoretical analysis.* New York: Wiley.

Lukatela, G., Lukatela, K., & Turvey, M. T. (1993). Further evidence for phonological constraints on visual lexical access: Towed primes FROG. *Perception and Psychophysics, 53*(5), 461–466.

Lund, K., & Burgess, C. (1996). Producing high-dimensional semantic spaces from lexical co-occurrence. *Behavior Research Methods: Instruments and Computers, 28*(2), 203–208.

Lycan, W. (1996). *Consciousness and experience.* Cambridge, Mass.: MIT Press.

Lynch, J., Mountcastle, V., Talbot, W., & Yin, T. (1977). Parietal lobe mechanisms for directed visual attention. *Journal of Neurophysiology, 40*, 362–389.

Maass, W. (1997). Networks of spiking neurons: The third generation of neural network models. *Neural Networks, 10*, 1659–1671.

Maass, W., Natschläger, T., & Markram, H. (2002). Real-time computing without stable states: A new framework for neural computation based on perturbations. *Neural Computation, 14.*

Macaluso, E., Frith, C., & Driver, J. (2000). Modulation of human visual cortex by crossmodal spatial attention. *Science, 289*, 1206–1208.

MacDonald, M., Pearlmutter, N., & Seidenberg, M. (1994). The lexical nature of syntactic ambiguity resolution. *Psychological Review, 101*, 676–703.

Machina, K. (1976). Truth, belief, and vagueness. *Journal of Philosophical Logic, 5*, 47–48.

MacWhinney, B. (Ed.) (1999). *The emergence of language.* Mahwah, N.J.: Lawrence Erlbaum.

Maffei, L., Fiorentini, A., & Bisti, S. (1973). Neural correlate of perceptual adaptation to gratings. *Science, 182*, 1036–1038.

Magnuson, J., McMurray, B., Tanenhaus, M., & Aslin, R. (2003a). Lexical effects on compensation for coarticulation: The ghost of Christmash past. *Cognitive Science, 27*, 285–298.

Magnuson, J., Tanenhaus, M., Aslin, R., & Dahan, D. (2003b). The time course of spoken word learning and recognition: Studies with artificial lexicons. *Journal of Experimental Psychology: General, 132*, 202–227.

Mandelbrot, B. (1999). *Multifractals and 1/f noise: Wild self-affinity in physics (1963–1976).* New York: Springer-Verlag.

Mandler, J. (1992). How to build a baby: II. Conceptual primitives. *Psychological Review, 99*, 587–604.

Mangun, G., & Hillyard, S. (1988). Event-related brain potentials and perceptual sensitivity during visual selective attention. *Psychophysiology, 25*, 467.

Mann, V., & Repp, B. (1980). Influence of vocalic context on perception of the [sh]-[s] distinction. *Perception & Psychophysics, 28*, 213–228.

Manneville, P. (1980). Intermittency, self-similarity and 1/f spectrum in dissipative dynamical systems. *Journal de Physique, 41*, 1235–1243.

Maquet, P. (2001). The role of sleep in learning and memory. *Science, 294*, 1048–1052.

Maravita, A., & Iriki, A. (2004). Tools for the body (schema). *Trends in Cognitive Sciences, 8*, 79–86.

Marcus, G. (1993). Negative evidence in language acquisition. *Cognition, 46,* 53–85.

Marcus, G. (1995). The acquisition of the English past tense in children and multilayered connectionist networks. *Cognition, 56,* 271–279.

Marcus, G. (2001). *The algebraic mind: Integrating connectionism and cognitive science.* Cambridge, Mass.: MIT Press.

Marcus, G., Pinker, S., Ullman, M., Hollander, M., Rosen, T., & Xu, F. (1992). Overregularization in language acquisition. *Monographs of the Society for Research in Child Development, 57,* i–182.

Marcus, G., Vouloumanos, A., & Sag, I. (2003). Does Broca's play by the rules? *Nature Neuroscience, 6,* 651–652.

Marian, V., & Spivey, M. (2003a). Bilingual and monolingual processing of competing lexical items. *Applied Psycholinguistics, 24,* 173–193.

Marian, V., & Spivey, M. (2003b). Competing activation in bilingual language processing: Within- and between-language competition. *Bilingualism: Language and Cognition, 6,* 97–115.

Markman, A., & Brendl, C. (2005). Constraining theories of embodied cognition. *Psychological Science, 16,* 6–10.

Markman, A., & Dietrich, E. (2000). In defense of representation. *Cognitive Psychology, 40,* 138–171.

Markman, A., & Ross, B. (2003). Category use and category learning. *Psychological Bulletin, 129,* 592–613.

Marks, L. (1978). *The unity of the senses: Interrelations among the modalities.* New York: Academic Press.

Markson, L., & Bloom, P. (1997). Evidence against a dedicated system for word learning in children. *Nature, 385,* 813–815.

Marr, D. (1982). *Vision: A computational investigation into the human representation and processing of visual information.* New York: W. H. Freeman.

Marslen-Wilson, W. (1973). Linguistic structure and speech shadowing at very short latencies. *Nature, 244,* 522–523.

Marslen-Wilson, W. (1975). Sentence perception as an interactive parallel process. *Science, 189,* 226–228.

Marslen-Wilson, W. (1987). Functional parallelism in spoken word recognition. *Cognition, 25,* 71–102.

Marslen-Wilson, W., & Welsh, A. (1978). Processing interactions and lexical access during word recognition in continuous speech. *Cognitive Psychology, 19,* 29–63.

Martin, C., Vu, H., Kellas, G., & Metcalf, K. (1999). Strength of discourse context as a determinant of the subordinate bias effect. *Quarterly Journal of Experimental Psychology: Human Experimental Psychology, 52A,* 813–839.

Martinez, A., Anillo, V., Sereno, M., Frank, L., Buxton, R., Dubowitz, D. Wong, E., Hinrichs, H., Heinze, H., & Hillyard, S. (1999). Involvement of striate and extrastriate visual cortical areas in special attention. *Nature Neuroscience, 2,* 364–369.

Mason, M. (1941). Changes in the galvanic skin response accompanying reports of changes in meaning during oral repetition. *Journal of General Psychology, 25,* 353–401.

Massaro, D. (1987). *Speech perception by ear and eye: A paradigm for psychological inquiry.* Hillsdale, N.J.: Lawrence Erlbaum.

Massaro, D. (1989). *Experimental psychology: An information processing approach.* San Diego, Calif.: Harcourt Brace Jovanovich.

Massaro, D. (1997). *Perceiving talking faces: From speech perception to a behavioral principle.* Cambridge, Mass.: MIT Press.

Massaro, D. (1999). Speechreading: Illusion or window into pattern recognition. *Trends in Cognitive Sciences, 3,* 310–317.

Massaro, D., & Cohen, M. (1983). Categorical or continuous speech perception: A new test. *Speech Communication, 2,* 15–35.

Masson, M. (1991). A distributed memory model of context effects in word identification. In D. Benser (Ed.), *Basic processes in reading: Visual word recognition* (pp. 233–263). Hillsdale, N.J.: Lawrence Erlbaum.

Mathews, R., Buss, R., Stanley, W., Blanchard-Fields, F., Cho, J., & Druhan, B. (1989). Role of implicit and explicit processes in learning from examples: A synergistic effect. *Journal of Experimental Psychology: Learning, Memory, and Cognition, 15,* 1083–1100.

Matin, E. (1974). Saccadic suppression: A review and an analysis. *Psychological Bulletin, 81,* 899–917.

Matin, E., Shao, K., & Boff, K. (1993). Saccadic overhead: Information-processing time with and without saccades. *Perception and Psychophysics, 53,* 372–380.

Matlock, T., Ramscar, M., & Boroditsky, L. (2005). The experiential link between spatial and temporal language. *Cognitive Science, 29,* 655–664.

Mato, G. (1999). Stochastic resonance using noise generated by a network. *Physical Review E, 59,* 33–39.

Mattes, S., Ulrich, R., & Miller, J. (2002). Response force in RT tasks: Isolating effects of stimulus probability and response probability. *Visual Cognition, 9,* 477–501.

Mazzarello, P. (2000). What dreams may come? *Nature, 408,* 523.

McAuley, J., & Jones, M. (2003). Modeling effects of rhythmic context on perceived duration: A comparison of interval and entrainment approaches to short-interval timing. *Journal of Experimental Psychology: Human Perception and Performance, 29,* 1102–1125.

McClamrock, R. (1991). Marr's three levels: A re-evaluation. *Minds and Machines, 1,* 185–196.

McClamrock, R. (1995). *Existential cognition: computational minds in the world.* Chicago: University of Chicago Press.

McClelland, J. (1979). On the time relations of mental processes: An examination of systems of processes in cascade. *Psychological Review, 86,* 287–330.

McClelland, J., & Elman, J. (1986). The TRACE model of speech perception. *Cognitive Psychology, 18,* 1–86.

McClelland, J., & Patterson, K. (2002). Rules or connections in past-tense inflections: What does the evidence rule out? *Trends in Cognitive Sciences, 6,* 465–472.

McClelland, J., & Rogers, T. (2003). The parallel distributed processing approach to semantic cognition. *Nature Reviews Neuroscience, 4,* 310–322.

McClelland, J., & Rumelhart, D. (1981). An interactive activation model of context effects in letter perception: Part 1. An account of basic findings. *Psychological Review, 88,* 375–407.

McCollough, C. (1965). Color adaptation of edge-detectors in the human visual system. *Science, 149,* 1115–1116.

McConkie, G., & Currie, C. (1996). Visual stability across saccades while viewing complex pictures. *Journal of Experimental Psychology: Human Perception and Performance, 22,* 563–581.

McDonald, J., & Ward, L. (2000). Involuntary listening aids seeing: Evidence from human electrophysiology. *Psychological Science, 11*, 167–171.

McElree, B., & Carrasco, M. (1999). The temporal dynamics of visual search: Evidence for parallel processing in feature and conjunction searches. *Journal of Experimental Psychology: Human Perception and Performance, 25*, 1517–1539.

McElree, B., & Griffith, T. (1995). Syntactic and thematic processing in sentence comprehension: Evidence for a temporal dissociation. *Journal of Experimental Psychology: Learning, Memory, and Cognition, 21*, 134–157.

McElree, B., & Griffith, T. (1998). Structural and lexical constraints on filling gaps during sentence comprehension: A time-course analysis. *Journal of Experimental Psychology: Learning, Memory, and Cognition, 24*, 432–460.

McGurk, H., & MacDonald, J. (1976). Hearing lips and seeing voices. *Nature, 264*, 746–748.

McLeod, P., Driver, J., & Crisp, J. (1988). Visual search for a conjunction of movement and form is parallel. *Nature, 332*, 154–155.

McMurray, B., & Spivey, M. (1999). The categorical perception of consonants: The interaction of learning and processing. *Proceedings of the Chicago Linguistic Society.*

McMurray, B., Tanenhaus, M., & Aslin, R. (2002). Gradient effects of within-category phonetic variation on lexical access. *Cognition, 86*, B33–B42.

McMurray, B., Tanenhaus, M., Aslin, R., & Spivey, M. (2003). Probabilistic constraint satisfaction at the lexical/phonetic interface: Evidence for gradient effects of within-category VOT on lexical access. *Journal of Psycholinguistic Research, 32*, 77–97.

McNeil, D. (2005). *Gesture and thought.* Chicago: University of Chicago Press.

McRae, K. (2004). Semantic memory: Some insights from feature-based connectionist attractor networks. In B. Ross (Ed.), *The psychology of learning and motivation: Advances in research and theory, Vol. 45* (pp. 41–86). San Diego, Calif.: Elsevier Academic Press.

McRae, K., Cree, G., Westmacott, R., & de Sa, V. (1999). Further evidence for feature correlations in semantic memory. *Canadian Journal of Experimental Psychology, 53*, 360–373.

McRae, K., de Sa, V., & Seidenberg, M. (1997). On the nature and scope of featural representations of word meaning. *Journal of Experimental Psychology: General, 126*, 99–130.

McRae, K., Ferretti, T., & Amyote, L. (1997). Thematic roles as verb-specific concepts. *Language and Cognitive Processes, 12*, 137–176.

McRae, K., Spivey-Knowlton, M., & Tanenhaus, M. (1998). Modeling the effects of thematic fit (and other constraints) in on-line sentence comprehension. *Journal of Memory and Language, 37*, 283–312.

Medin, D., & Schaffer, M. (1978). Context theory of classification learning. *Psychological Review, 85*, 207–238.

Medin, D., & Smith, E. E. (1981). Strategies and classification learning. *Journal of Experimental Psychology: Human Learning and Memory, 7*, 241–253.

Medin, D., & Smith, E. E. (1984). Concepts and concept formation. *Annual Review of Psychology, 35*, 113–138.

Meltzoff, A., & Prinz, W. (Eds.) (2002). *The imitative mind: Development, evolution, and brain bases.* New York: Cambridge University Press.

Meredith, M. (2002). On the neuronal basis for multisensory convergence: A brief overview. *Cognitive Brain Research, 14*, 31–40.

Merleau-Ponty, M. (1962). *The phenomenology of perception.* New York: Humanities Press.

Merzenich, M., Nelson, R., Stryker, M., Cynader, M., Schoppmann, A., & Zook, J. (1984). Somatosensory cortical map changes following digit amputation in adult monkeys. *Journal of Comparative Neurology, 224,* 591–605.

Metzinger, T. (2003). *Being no one: The self-model theory of subjectivity.* Cambridge, Mass.: MIT Press.

Meyer, D. E., Irwin, D. E., Osman, A. M., & Kounios, J. (1988). The dynamics of cognition and action: Mental processes inferred from speed-accuracy decomposition. *Psychological Review, 95,* 183–237.

Miller, G., & McKean, K. (1964). A chronometric study of some relations between sentences. *Quarterly Journal of Experimental Psychology, 16,* 197–308.

Miller, J. (1982). Discrete versus continuous stage models of human information processing: In search of partial output. *Journal of Experimental Psychology: Human Perception and Performance, 8,* 273–296.

Miller, J. (1988). Discrete and continuous models of human information processing: Theoretical distinctions and empirical results. *Acta Psychologica, 67,* 191–257.

Miller, J., & Dexter, E. (1988). Effects of speaking rate and lexical status on phonetic perception. *Journal of Experimental Psychology: Human Perception and Performance, 14,* 369–378.

Miller, J., Riehle, A., & Requin, J. (1992). Effects of preliminary perceptual output on neuronal activity of the primary motor cortex. *Journal of Experimental Psychology: Human Perception and Performance, 18,* 1121–1138.

Millikan, R. (1993). Content and vehicle. In N. Eilan, R. McCarthy, & B. Brewer (Eds.), *Spatial representation* (pp. 256–268). Malden, Mass.: Blackwell.

Milner, A., & Goodale, M. (1995). *The visual brain in action.* London: Oxford University Press.

Minda, J., & Smith, J. D. (2001). Prototypes in category learning: The effects of category size, category structure, and stimulus complexity. *Journal of Experimental Psychology: Learning, Memory, and Cognition, 27,* 775–799.

Minda, J., & Smith, J. D. (2002). Comparing prototype-based and exemplar-based accounts of category learning and attentional allocation. *Journal of Experimental Psychology: Learning, Memory, and Cognition, 28,* 275–292.

Mitchell, D., Corley, M., & Garnham, A. (1992). Effects of context in human sentence parsing: Evidence against a discourse-based proposal mechanism. *Journal of Experimental Psychology: Learning, Memory and Cognition, 18,* 69–88.

Mitchell, D., & Holmes, V. (1985). The role of specific information about the verb in parsing sentences with local structural ambiguity. *Journal of Memory and Language, 24,* 542–559.

Moerk, E. (1990). Three-term contingency patterns in motherchild verbal interactions during first-language acquisition. *Journal of the Experimental Analysis of Behavior, 54,* 293–305.

Molfese, D. (1987). Electrophysiological indices of categorical perception for speech. In S. Harnard (Ed.), *Categorical perception: The groundwork of cognition* (pp. 421–443). New York: Cambridge University Press.

Møller, P., & Hurlbert, A. (1997). Interactions between colour and motion in image segmentation. *Current Biology, 7,* 105–111.

Monsell, S., & Driver, J. (Eds.) (2000). *Control of cognitive processes: Attention and performance 18.* Cambridge, Mass.: MIT Press.

Montessori, M. (1917). *Spontaneous activity in education* (translated by F. Simmonds). New York: Frederick A. Stokes.

Moody, T. (1994). Conversations with zombies. *Journal of Consciousness Studies, 1,* 196–200.

Moran, J., & Desimone, R. (1984). Selective attention gates visual processing in the extrastriate cortex. *Science, 229,* 782–784.

Morgan, J., Bonamo, K., & Travis, L. (1995). Negative evidence on negative evidence. *Developmental Psychology, 31,* 180–197.

Morrison, L. (1984). *Integration in thought and behavior: A neuropsychological theory.* New York: Harbor.

Motter, B. (1993). Focal attention produces spatially selective processing in visual cortical areas V1, V2, and V4 in the presence of competing stimuli. *Journal of Neurophysiology, 70,* 909–919.

Mounts, J. (2000). Evidence for suppressive mechanisms in attentional selection: Feature singletons produce inhibitory surrounds. *Perception & Psychophysics, 62,* 969–983.

Mounts, J., & Tomaselli, R. (2005). Competition for representation is mediated by relative attentional salience. *Acta Psychologica, 118,* 261–275.

Movshon, J., Adelson, E., Gizzi, M., & Newsome, W. (1986). The analysis of moving visual patterns. *Experimental Brain Research, 11,* 117–152.

Movshon, J., Thompson, I., & Tolhurst, D. (1978). Receptive field organization of complex cells in the cat's striate cortex. *Journal of Physiology, 283,* 79–99.

Müller, K., Aschersleben, G., Koch, R., Freund, H., & Prinz, W. (1999). Action timing in an isochronous tapping task. Evidence from behavioral studies and neuroimaging. In G. Aschersleben, T. Bachman, & J. Müsseler (Eds.), *Cognitive contributions to the perception of spatial and temporal events* (pp. 233–250). Amsterdam: North Holland/Elsevier Science.

Munhall, K., & Vatikiotis-Bateson, E. (1998). The moving face during speech communication. In R. Campbell, B. Dodd, & D. Burnham (Eds.), *Hearing by eye, Part 2: The psychology of speechreading and audiovisual speech.* London: Taylor & Francis, Psychology Press.

Musha, T. (1985). Biological information and 1/f fluctuations. *Japanese Journal of Applied Physics, 54,* 429–435.

Müsseler, J., van der Heijden, A., & Kerzel, D. (2004). *Visual space perception and action.* Hove, England: Psychology Press.

Nadig, A., & Sedivy, J. (2002). Evidence of perspective-taking constraints in children's on-line reference resolution. *Psychological Science, 13,* 329–336.

Nakao, M., Yamamoto, K., Honma, K., Hashimoto, S., Honma, S., Katayama, N., & Yamamoto, M. (2002). A phase dynamics model of human circadian rhythms. *Journal of Biological Rhythms, 17,* 476–489.

Nakayama, K. (1994). James J. Gibson: An appreciation. *Psychological Review, 101,* 329–335.

Nakayama, K., & Joseph, J. (1998). Attention, pattern recognition, and pop-out visual search. In R. Parasuraman (Ed.), *The attentive brain* (pp. 279–298). Cambridge, Mass.: MIT Press.

Nakayama, K., & Silverman, G. (1986). Serial and parallel processing of visual feature conjunctions. *Nature, 320,* 264–265.

Narmour, E. (1990). *The analysis and cognition of basic melodic structures: The implication-realization model.* Chicago: University of Chicago Press.

Navon, D. (1984). Resources—a theoretical soup stone? *Psychological Review, 91,* 216–234.

Nazzi, T., & Bertoncini, J. (2003). Before and after the vocabulary spurt: Two modes of word acquisition? *Developmental Science, 6,* 136–142.

Nederhouser, M., & Spivey, M. (2004). Eye-tracking and simulating the temporal dynamics of categorization. *Proceedings of the 24th Annual Conference of the Cognitive Science Society.* Mahwah, N.J.: Erlbaum.

Neely, J. (1977). Semantic priming and retrieval from lexical memory: Roles of inhibitionless spreading activation and limited-capacity attention. *Journal of Experimental Psychology: General, 106*(3), 226–254.

Neisser, U. (1967). *Cognitive psychology.* East Norwalk, Conn.: Appleton-Century-Crofts.

Neisser, U. (1976). *Cognition and reality: Principles and implications of cognitive psychology.* San Francisco: W. H. Freeman.

Neisser, U. (1994). Self-perception and self-knowledge. *Psyke and Logos, 15,* 392–407.

Neisser, U. (1997). The future of cognitive science: An ecological analysis. In C. Erneling & D. Johnson (Eds.), *The future of the cognitive revolution* (pp. 247–260). London: Oxford University Press.

Neisser, U., & Harsch, N. (1992). Phantom flashbulbs: False recollections of hearing the news about Challenger. In E. Winograd & U. Neisser (Eds.), *Affect and accuracy in recall: Studies of "flashbulb" memories* (pp. 9–31). New York: Cambridge University Press.

Nelken, I., Bizley, J., Nodal, F., Ahmed, B., Schnupp, J., & King, A. (2004). Large-scale organization of ferret auditory cortex revealed using continuous acquisition of intrinsic optical signals. *Journal of Neurophysiology, 92,* 2574–2588.

Newell, A. (1990). *Unified theories of cognition.* Cambridge, Mass.: Harvard University Press.

Newell, A., Shaw, J. C., & Simon, H. A. (1958). Elements of a theory of human problem solving. *Psychological Review, 65,* 151–166.

Newell, A., & Simon, H. (1976). Computer science as empirical inquiry: Symbols and search. *Communications of the ACM, 19,* 113–126.

Newell, F., & Bültoff, H. (2002). Categorical perception of familiar objects. *Cognition, 85,* 113–143.

Newell, K., Liu, Y., & Mayer-Kress, G. (2001). Time scales in motor learning and development. *Psychological Review, 108,* 57–82.

Newsome, W., & Paré, E. (1988). A selective impairment of motion perception following lesions of the middle temporal visual area (MT). *Journal of Neuroscience, 8,* 2201–2211.

Nisbett, R., & Wilson, T. (1977). Telling more than we can know: Verbal reports on mental processes. *Psychological Review, 84,* 231–259.

Niyogi, P., & Berwick, R. (1996). A language learning model for finite parameter spaces. *Cognition, 61,* 161–193.

Noë, A., Pessoa, L., & Thompson, E. (2000). Beyond the grand illusion: What change blindness really teaches us about vision. *Visual Cognition, 7,* 93–106.

Noë, A., & Thompson, E. (2004). Are there neural correlates of consciousness? *Journal of Consciousness Studies, 11,* 3–28.

Noguchi, Y., Inui, K., & Kakigi, R. (2004). Temporal dynamics of neural adaptation effect in the human visual ventral stream. *Journal of Neuroscience, 24,* 6283–6290.

Nosofsky, R. (1991). Stimulus bias, asymmetric similarity, and classification. *Cognitive Psychology, 23,* 94–140.

Nosofsky, R., & Alfonso-Reese, L. (1999). Effects of similarity and practice on speeded classification response times and accuracies: Further tests of an exemplar-retrieval model. *Memory and Cognition, 27,* 78–93.

Nosofsky, R., & Palmeri, T. (1998). A rule-plus-exception model for classifying objects in continuous-dimension spaces. *Psychonomic Bulletin and Review, 5,* 345–369.

Nosofsky, R., Palmeri, T., & McKinley, S. (1994). Rule-plus-exception model of classification learning. *Psychological Review, 101,* 53–79.

Nosofsky, R., & Zaki, S. (2002). Exemplar and prototype models revisited: Response strategies, selective attention, and stimulus generation. *Journal of Experimental Psychology: Learning, Memory, and Cognition, 28,* 924–940.

Nowak, A., Vallacher, R. R., & Burnstein, E. (1998). Computational social psychology: A neural network approach to interpersonal dynamics. In W. Liebrand & A. Nowak (Eds.), *Computer modeling of social processes* (pp. 97–125). London: Sage.

Nowak, M., Komarova, N., & Niyogi, P. (2002). Computational and evolutionary aspects of language. *Nature, 417,* 611–617.

Nowak, M., Plotkin, J., & Jansen, V. (2000). The evolution of syntactic communication. *Nature, 404,* 495–498.

O'Brien, G., & Opie, J. (1999a). A connectionist theory of phenomenal experience. *Behavioral and Brain Sciences, 22,* 127–148.

O'Brien, G., & Opie, J. (1999b). A defense of Cartesian materialism. *Philosophy and Phenomenological Research, 59,* 939–963.

Oden, G. (1981). A fuzzy propositional model of concept structure and use: A case study in object identification. In G. W. Lasker (Ed.), *Applied systems and cybernetics, Vol. 6* (pp. 2890–2897). Elmsford, N.Y.: Pergamon Press.

Ojemann, G., Creutzfeldt, O., Lettich, E., & Haglund, M. (1988). Neuronal activity in human lateral temporal cortex related to short-term verbal memory, naming and reading. *Brain, 111,* 1383–1403.

Olds, E., Cowan, W., & Jolicoeur, P. (2000a). The time-course of pop-out search. *Vision Research, 40,* 891–912.

Olds, E., Cowan, W., & Jolicoeur, P. (2000b). Partial orientation pop-out helps difficult search for orientation. *Perception and Psychophysics, 62,* 1341–1347.

Olds, E., Cowan, W., & Jolicoeur, P. (2000c). Tracking visual search over space and time. *Psychonomic Bulletin and Review, 7,* 292–300.

Oliphant, M. (1999). The learning barrier: Moving from innate to learned systems of communication. *Adaptive Behavior, 7,* 371–384.

Olshausen, B., Anderson, C., & Van Essen, D. (1993). A neurobiological model of visual attention and invariant pattern recognition based on dynamic routing of information. *Journal of Neuroscience, 12,* 4700–4719.

Olshausen, B., & Field, D. (2004). Sparse coding of sensory inputs. *Current Opinion in Neurobiology, 14,* 481–487.

Olsson, H., Wennerholm, P., & Lyxzen, U. (2004). Exemplars, prototypes, and the flexibility of classification models. *Journal of Experimental Psychology: Learning, Memory, and Cognition, 30,* 936–941.

Orbach, J., Ehrlich, D., & Heath, H. A. (1963). Reversibility of the necker cube: I. An examination of the concept of "satiation of orientation." *Perceptual and Motor Skills, 17*(2), 439–458.

O'Regan, J. (1992). Solving the "real" mysteries of visual perception: The world as an outside memory. *Canadian Journal of Psychology, 46,* 461–488.

O'Regan, J., & Noë, A. (2001). A sensorimotor account of vision and visual consciousness. *Behavioral and Brain Sciences, 24,* 939–1031.

O'Regan, J., Deubel, H., Clark, J., & Rensink, R. (2000). Picture changes during blinks: Looking without seeing and seeing without looking. *Visual Cognition, 7,* 191–211.

O'Regan, J., Rensink, R., & Clark, J. (1999). Change-blindness as a result of "mudsplashes." *Nature, 398,* 34.

O'Reilly, R., & Munakata, Y. (2000). *Computational explorations in cognitive neuroscience: Understanding the mind by simulating the brain.* Cambridge, Mass.: MIT Press.

Osgood, C., Suci, G., & Tennenbaum, P. (1957). *The measurement of meaning.* Champaign: University of Illinois Press.

Osherson, D., & Smith, E. (1981). On the adequacy of prototype theory as a theory of concepts. *Cognition, 9,* 25–58.

Osherson, D., & Smith, E. (1982). Gradedness and conceptual combination. *Cognition, 12,* 299–318.

Osterhout, L., & Holcomb, P. (1992). Event-related brain potentials elicited by syntactic anomaly. *Journal of Memory and Language, 31,* 785–806.

Pagano, C., & Turvey, M. T. (1993). Perceiving by dynamic touch the distances reachable with irregular objects. *Ecological Psychology, 5,* 125–151.

Page, M. (2000). Connectionist modeling in psychology: A localist manifesto. *Behavioral and Brain Sciences, 23,* 443–512.

Pallas, S., & Sur, M. (1993). Visual projections induced into the auditory pathway of ferrets: II. Corticocortical connections of visually-driven primary auditory cortex (AI). *Journal of Computational Neurology, 337,* 317–333.

Palm, G. (1982). *Neural assemblies: An alternative approach to artificial intelligence.* Berlin: Springer-Verlag.

Palmer, J. (1995). Attention in visual search: Distinguishing four causes of a set-size effect. *Current Directions in Psychological Science, 4,* 118–123.

Palmer, J., Verghese, P., & Pavel, M. (2000). The psychophysics of visual search. *Vision Research, 40,* 1227–1268.

Palmeri, T., & Gauthier, I. (2004). Visual object understanding. *Nature Reviews Neuroscience, 5,* 291–303.

Paninski, L., Fellows, M., Hatsopoulos, N., & Donoghue, J. (2004). Spatiotemporal tuning of motor cortical neurons for hand position and velocity. *Journal of Neurophysiology, 91,* 515–532.

Parker, A., & Newsome, W. (1998). Sense and the single neuron: Probing the physiology of perception. *Annual Review of Neuroscience, 21,* 227–277.

Parkhurst, D., Law, K., & Niebur, E. (2002). Modeling the role of salience in the allocation of overt visual attention. *Vision Research, 42,* 107–123.

Pasternak, T., & Merigan, W. (1994). Motion perception following lesions of the superior temporal sulcus in the monkey. *Cerebral Cortex, 4,* 247–259.

Pasupathy, A., & Connor, C. E. (2002). Population coding of shape in area V4. *Nature Neuroscience, 5,* 1332–1338.

Pearlmutter, B. A. (1989). Learning state space trajectories in recurrent neural networks. *Neural Computation, 1,* 263–269.

Pearlmutter, B. A. (1995). Gradient calculation for dynamic recurrent neural networks: A survey. *IEEE Transactions on Neural Networks, 6,* 1212–1228.

Pecher, D., Zeelenberg, R., & Barsalou, L. (2003). Verifying different-modality properties for concepts produces switching costs. *Psychological Science, 14,* 119–124.

Pedersen, M., & Larsen, M. (2001). Distributed knowledge management based on product state models: The case of decision support in health care administration. *Decision Support Systems, 31,* 139–158.

Penrose, R. (1994). *Shadows of the mind: A search for the missing science of consciousness.* New York: Oxford University Press.

Pereboom, D. (2001). *Living without free will.* New York: Cambridge University Press.

Perkell, J., Cohen, M., Svirsky, M., Matthies, M., Garabieta, I., & Jackson, M. (1992). Electromagnetic midsagittal articulometer systems for transducing speech articulatory movements. *Journal of the Acoustical Society of America, 92,* 3078–3096.

Perrett, D., Oram, M., & Ashbridge, E. (1998). Evidence accumulation in cell populations responsive to faces: An account of generalization of recognition without mental transformations. *Cognition, 67,* 111–145.

Pessoa, L., & De Weerd, P. (Eds.) (2003). *Filling-in: From perceptual completion to cortical reorganization.* London: Oxford University Press.

Phaf, R., van der Heijden, A., & Hudson, P. (1990). SLAM: A connectionist model for attention in visual selection tasks. *Cognitive Psychology, 22,* 273–341.

Pickering, M., & Garrod, S. (2004). Toward a mechanistic psychology of dialogue. *Behavioral and Brain Sciences, 27,* 169–226.

Picton, T., Bentin, S., Berg, P., Donchin, E., Hillyard, S., Johnson, R., Miller, G., Ritter, W., Ruchkin, D., Rugg, M., & Taylor, M. (2000). Guidelines for using human event-related potentials to study cognition: Recording standards and publication criteria. *Psychophysiology, 37,* 127–152.

Pilling, M., Wiggett, A., Özgen, E., & Davies, I. (2003). Is color "categorical perception" really perceptual? *Memory and Cognition, 31,* 538–551.

Pinker, S. (1991). Rules of language. *Science, 253,* 530–535.

Pinker, S. (1994). *The language instinct.* New York: William Morrow.

Pinker, S. (1999). *Words and rules: The ingredients of language.* New York: Basic Books.

Pinker, S., & Bloom, P. (1990). Natural language and natural selection. *Behavioral and Brain Sciences, 13,* 707–784.

Pinker, S., & Prince, A. (1988). On language and connectionism: Analysis of a parallel distributed processing model of language acquisition. *Cognition, 28,* 73–193.

Pinker, S., & Ullman, M. (2002). The past and future of the past tense. *Trends in Cognitive Sciences, 6,* 456–463.

Pirolli, P., & Card, S. (1999). Information foraging. *Psychological Review, 106,* 643–675.

Pisoni, D., & Tash, J. (1974). Reaction times to comparisons within and across phonetic categories. *Perception and Psychophysics, 15,* 285–290.

Pitt, M., & McQueen, J. (1998). Is compensation for coarticulation mediated by the lexicon? *Journal of Memory and Language, 39,* 347–370.

Pitt, M., & Myung, I. (2002). When a good fit can be bad. *Trends in Cognitive Sciences, 6,* 421–425.

Pitt, M., Myung, I., & Zhang, S. (2002). Toward a method of selecting among computational models of cognition. *Psychological Review, 109,* 472–491.

Plate, T. (1994). Estimating structural similarity by vector dot-products of Holographic Reduced Representations. In J. Cowan, G. Tesauro, & J. Alspector (Eds.), *Advances in Neural Information Processing Systems 6 (NIPS*93)* (pp. 1109–1116). San Mateo, Calif.: Morgan Kaufmann.

Plaut, D. (1995). Double dissociation without modularity: Evidence from connectionist neuropsychology. *Journal of Clinical and Experimental Neuropsychology, 17,* 291–321.

Plaut, D., McClelland, J., Seidenberg, M., & Patterson, K. (1996). Understanding normal and impaired word reading: Computational principles in quasi-regular domains. *Psychological Review, 103,* 56–115.

Plunkett, K., & Juola, P. (1999). A connectionist model of English past tense and plural morphology. *Cognitive Science, 23,* 463–490.

Plunkett, K., & Marchman, V. (1993). From rote learning to system building: Acquiring verb morphology in children and connectionist nets. *Cognition, 48,* 21–69.

Plunkett, K., & Marchman, V. (1996). Learning from a connectionist model of the acquisition of the English past tense. *Cognition, 61,* 299–308.

Poggio, T., Rifkin, R., Mukherjee, S., & Niyogi, P. (2004). General conditions for predictivity in learning theory. *Nature, 428,* 419–422.

Poincare, H. (1906). Les mathematiques et la logique. *Revue de Metaphysique et de Morale, 14,* 294–317.

Polger, T. (2004). *Natural minds.* Cambridge, Mass.: MIT Press.

Polking, J. C. (1995). *Ordinary differential equations: Using MATLAB.* New Jersey: Prentice Hall.

Pollard, C., & Sag, I. (1994). *Head-driven phrase structure grammar.* Chicago: University of Chicago Press.

Port, R. (2002). The dynamical systems hypothesis in cognitive science. *Encyclopedia of cognitive science.* London: Macmillan.

Port, R., & van Gelder, T. (Eds.) (1995). *Mind as motion: Explorations in the dynamics of cognition.* Cambridge, Mass.: MIT Press.

Posner, M., & Cohen, Y. (1984). Components of visual orienting. In H. Bouma & D. Bowhuis (Eds.), *Attention and performance X.* Hillsdale, N.J.: Lawrence Erlbaum.

Posner, M., & Keele, S. (1968). On the genesis of abstract ideas. *Journal of Experimental Psychology, 77,* 353–363.

Posner, M., Snyder, C., & Davidson, B. (1980). Attention and the detection of signals. *Journal of Experimental Psychology: General, 109,* 160–174.

Potter, M. C. (1976). Short-term conceptual memory for pictures. *Journal of Experimental Psychology: Human Learning and Memory, 2*(5), 509–522.

Potter, M. C. (1993). Very short-term conceptual memory. *Memory and Cognition, 21*(2), 156–161.

Pouget, A., Dayan, P., & Zemel, R. (2000). Inference and computation with population codes. *Annual Review of Neuroscience, 26,* 381–410.

Pratt, R. (1970). Cognitive processing of uncertainty: Its effect on pupillary dilation and preference ratings. *Perception and Psychophysics, 8,* 193–198.

Pressing, J. (1999). The referential dynamics of cognition and action. *Psychological Review, 106,* 714–747.

Prigogine, I., & Stengers, I. (1984). *Order out of chaos.* New York: Bantam Books.

Prinz, J. (2002). *Furnishing the mind: Concepts and their perceptual basis.* Cambridge, Mass.: MIT Press.

Proctor, R. (1986). Response bias, criteria settings, and the fast-same phenomenon: A reply to Ratcliff. *Psychological Review, 93,* 473–477.

Pulvermüller, F. (1999). Words in the brain's language. *Behavioral and Brain Sciences, 22,* 253–279.

Putnam, H. (1975). The meaning of "meaning." In K. Gunderson (Ed.), *Language, mind and knowledge: Minnesota studies in philosophy of science, Vol. 7.* Minneapolis: University of Minnesota Press.

Pylyshyn, Z. (1974). Minds, machines and phenomenology: Some reflections on Dreyfus' "What computers can't do." *International Journal of Cognitve Psychology, 3*, 57–77.

Pylyshyn, Z. (1984). *Computation and cognition: Toward a foundation for cognitive science.* Cambridge, Mass.: MIT Press.

Pylyshyn, Z. (1989). The role of location indexes in spatial perception: A sketch of the FINST spatial index model. *Cognition, 32*, 65–97.

Pylyshyn, Z. (2001). Visual indexes, preconceptual objects, and situated vision. *Cognition, 80*, 127–158.

Pylyshyn, Z., & Storm, R. (1988). Tracking multiple independent targets: Evidence for a parallel tracking mechanism. *Spatial Vision, 3*, 179–197.

Quinlan, P., & Humphreys, G. (1987). Visual search for targets defined by combinations of color, shape, and size: An examination of the task constraints on feature and conjunction searches. *Perception and Psychophysics, 41*, 455–472.

Raichle, M. (1998). The neural correlates of consciousness: An analysis of cognitive skill learning. *Philosophical Transactions of the Royal Society of London B: Biological Sciences, 353*, 1889–1901.

Ramachandran, V. (1988). Perception of shape from shading. *Nature, 331*, 163–166.

Ramachandran, V., & Blakeslee, S. (1998). *Phantoms in the brain: Probing the mysteries of the human mind.* New York: William Morrow.

Ramachandran, V., & Hirstein, W. (1998). The perception of phantom limbs: The D. O. Hebb lecture. *Brain, 121*, 1603–1630.

Ramscar, M. (2002). The role of meaning in inflection: Why the past tense does not require a rule. *Cognitive Psychology, 45*, 45–94.

Rao, R., & Ballard, D. (1997). Dynamic model of visual recognition predicts neural response properties in the visual cortex. *Neural Computation, 9*, 721–763.

Rao, R., & Ballard, D. (1999). Predictive coding in the visual cortex: A functional interpretation of some extra-classical receptive-field effects. *Nature Neuroscience, 2*, 79–87.

Rao, R., Olshausen, B., & Lewicki, M. (Eds.) (2002). *Probabilistic models of the brain: Perception and neural function.* Cambridge, Mass.: MIT Press.

Rappel, W., & Karma, A. (1996). Noise induced coherence in neural networks and excitable elements. *Physical Review Letters, 77*, 3256.

Rastle, K., & Coltheart, M. (1999). Lexical and nonlexical phonological priming in reading aloud. *Journal of Experimental Psychology: Human Perception and Performance, 25*, 461–481.

Ratcliff, R. (1979). Group reaction time distributions and an analysis of distribution statistics. *Psychological Bulletin, 86*, 446–461.

Ratcliff, R. (1980). A note on modeling accumulation of information when the rate of accumulation changes over time. *Journal of Mathematical Psychology, 21*, 178–184.

Ratcliff, R. (1981). A theory of order relations in perceptual matching. *Psychological Review, 88*, 552–572.

Ratcliff, R. (1985). Theoretical interpretations if the speed and accuracy of positive and negative responses. *Psychological Review, 92*, 212–225.

Ratcliff, R. (1987). More on the speed and accuracy of positive and negative responses. *Psychological Review, 94*, 277–280.

Ratcliff, R. (1988). Continuous versus discrete information processing: Modeling accumulation of partial information. *Psychological Review, 95*, 238–255.

Ratcliff, R. (2002). A diffusion model account of response time and accuracy in a brightness discrimination task: Fitting real data and failing to fit fake but plausible data. *Psychonomic Bulletin and Review, 9,* 278–291.

Ratcliff, R., Carpenter, R., & Reddi, B. (2001). Putting noise into neurophysiological models of simple decision making. *Nature Neuroscience, 4,* 336–337.

Rayner, K. (1978). Eye movements in reading and information processing. *Psychological Bulletin, 85,* 618–660.

Rayner, K. (1998). Eye movements in reading and information processing: 20 years of research. *Psychological Bulletin, 124,* 372–422.

Rayner, K., Binder, K., & Duffy, S. (1999). Contextual strength and the subordinate bias effect: Comment on Martin, Vu, Kellas, and Metcalf. *Quarterly Journal of Experimental Psychology: Human Experimental Psychology, 52A,* 841–852.

Rayner, K., Carlson, M., & Frazier, L. (1983). The interaction of syntax and semantics during sentence processing: Eye movements in the analysis of semantically biased sentences. *Journal of Verbal Learning and Verbal Behavior, 22,* 358–374.

Rayner, K., Garrod, S., & Perfetti, C. (1992). Discourse influences during parsing are delayed. *Cognition, 45,* 109–139.

Read, S., & Montoya, J. (1999). An autoassociative model of causal reasoning and causal learning: Reply to Van Overwalle's (1998) critique of Read and Marcus-Newhall (1993). *Journal of Personality and Social Psychology, 76,* 728–742.

Reali, F., Spivey, M., Tyler, M., & Terranova, J. (in press). Inefficient conjunction search made efficient by concurrent spoken delivery of target identity. *Perception and Psychophysics.*

Reed, A. (1973). Speed-accuracy trade-off in recognition memory. *Science, 181,* 574–576.

Reed, E., & Jones, R. (Eds.) (1982). *Reasons for realism: Selected essays of James J. Gibson.* Hillsdale, N.J.: Lawrence Erlbaum.

Rehder, B., & Hoffman, A. (2005). Eyetracking and selective attention in category learning. *Cognitive Psychology, 51,* 1–41.

Reingold, E., & Charness, N. (2005). Perception in chess: Evidence from eye movements. In G. Underwood (Ed.), *Cognitive processes in eye guidance.* Oxford: Oxford University Press.

Rensink, R., O'Regan, J., & Clark, J. (1997). To see or not to see: The need for attention to perceive changes in scenes. *Psychological Science, 8,* 368–373.

Repp, B. (2003a). Rate limits in sensorimotor synchronization with auditory and visual sequences: The synchronization threshold and the benefits and costs of interval subdivision. *Journal of Motor Behavior, 35,* 355–370.

Repp, B. (2003b). Phase attraction in sensorimotor synchronization with auditory sequences: Effects of single and periodic distractors on synchronization accuracy. *Journal of Experimental Psychology: Human Perception and Performance, 29,* 290–309.

Repp, B., & Knoblich, G. (2004). Perceiving action identity: How pianists recognize their own performances. *Psychological Science, 15,* 604–609.

Repp, B., & Penel, A. (2004). Rhythmic movement is attracted more strongly to auditory than to visual rhythms. *Psychological Research, 68,* 252–270.

Rescorla, R., & Wagner, A. (1972). A theory of Pavlovian conditioning: Variations in the effectiveness of reinforcement and nonreinforcement. In A. Black & W. Prokasy (Eds.), *Classical conditioning II: Current research and theory* (pp. 64–99). New York: Appleton-Century-Crofts.

Resnick, M. (1997). *Turtles, termites, and traffic jams: Explorations in massively parallel microworlds.* Cambridge, Mass.: MIT Press.

Reuter-Lorenz, P., Hughes, H., & Fendrich, R. (1991). The reduction of saccadic latency by prior offset of the fixation point: An analysis of the "gap effect." *Perception and Psychophysics, 49,* 167–175.

Revonsuo, A. (2001). Can functional brain imaging discover consciousness in the brain? *Journal of Consciousness Studies, 8,* 3–23.

Reynolds, J., & Desimone, R. (2001). Neural mechanisms of attentional selection. In J. Braun, C. Koch, & J. Davis (Eds.), *Visual attention and cortical circuits* (pp. 121–135). Cambridge, Mass.: MIT Press.

Richardson, D., & Dale, R. (2005). Looking to understand: The coupling between speakers' and listeners' eye movements and its relationship to discourse comprehension. *Cognitive Science, 29,* 1045–1060.

Richardson, D., & Kirkham, N. (2004). Multi-modal events and moving locations: Eye movements of adults and 6-month-olds reveal dynamic spatial indexing. *Journal of Experimental Psychology: General, 133,* 46–62.

Richardson, D., & Spivey, M. (2000). Representation, space and Hollywood Squares: Looking at things that aren't there anymore. *Cognition, 76,* 269–295.

Richardson, D., & Spivey, M. (2004). Eye tracking: Characteristics and methods. In G. Wnek & G. Bowlin (Eds.), *Encyclopedia of biomaterials and biomedical engineering.* New York: Marcel Dekker.

Richardson, D., Spivey, M., Barsalou, L., & McRae, K. (2003). Spatial representations activated during real-time comprehension of verbs. *Cognitive Science, 27,* 767–780.

Richardson, D., Spivey, M., & Cheung, J. (2001). Motor representations in memory and mental models. *Proceedings of the 23rd Annual Conference of the Cognitive Science Society* (pp. 839–844). Mahwah, N.J.: Lawrence Erlbaum.

Rieth, C., & Sireteanu, R. (1994). Texture segmentation and visual search based on orientation contrast: An infant study with the familiarization-novelty preference method. *Infant Behavior and Development, 17,* 359–369.

Riley, M., Balasubramaniam, R., & Turvey, M. (1999). Recurrence quantification analysis of postural fluctuations. *Gait & Posture, 11,* 12–24.

Riley, M., & Turvey, M. (2002). Variability and determinism in motor behavior. *Journal of Motor Behavior, 34,* 99–125.

Rips, L., Shoben, E., & Smith, E. (1973). Semantic distance and the verification of semantic relations. *Journal of Verbal Learning and Verbal Behavior, 12,* 1–20.

Rissanen, J. (1978). Modeling by the shortest data description. *Automatica, 14,* 465–471.

Roberson, D., & Davidoff, J. (2000). The categorical perception of colors and facial expressions: The effect of verbal interference. *Memory and Cognition, 28,* 977–986.

Roberson, D., Davies, I., & Davidoff, J. (2000). Color categories are not universal: Replications and new evidence from a stone-age culture. *Journal of Experimental Psychology: General, 129,* 369–398.

Roberts, M., Rastle, K., Coltheart, M., & Besner, D. (2003). When parallel processing in visual word recognition is not enough: New evidence from naming. *Psychonomic Bulletin and Review, 10,* 405–414.

Roberts, S., & Pashler, H. (2000). How persuasive is a good fit? A comment on theory testing. *Psychological Review, 107,* 358–367.

Robertson, A. (1977). The CIE 1976 color-difference formulae. *Color Research and Application, 2,* 7–11.

Robertson, M. (1961). Theoretical implications of sensory deprivation. *Psychological Record, 11*, 33–42.

Robinson, C. (1998). *Dynamical systems: Stability, symbolic dynamics, and chaos* (2nd ed.). Boca Raton, Fla.: CRC Press.

Rodriguez, P., Wiles, J., & Elman, J. (1999). A recurrent neural network that learns to count. *Connection Science: Journal of Neural Computing, Artificial Intelligence and Cognitive Research, 11*, 5–40.

Roe, R., Busemeyer, J., & Townsend, J. (2001). Multialternative decision field theory: A dynamic connectionist model of decision making. *Psychological Review, 108*, 370–392.

Rogers, R. (1994). Magnetoencephalographic imaging of cognitive processes. In R. Thatcher, M. Hallett, T. Zeffiro, E. John, & M. Huerto (Eds.), *Functional neuroimaging: Technical foundations* (pp. 289–297). San Diego: Academic Press.

Rogers, T., & McClelland, J. (2004). *Semantic cognition: A parallel distributed processing approach.* Cambridge, Mass.: MIT Press.

Rohde, D., & Plaut, D. (1999). Language acquisition in the absence of explicit negative evidence: How important is starting small? *Cognition, 72*, 67–109.

Rolls, E., & Tovee, M. (1995). Sparseness of the neuronal representation of stimuli in the primate temporal visual cortex. *Journal of Neurophysiology, 73*, 713–726.

Rosch, E. (1973). Natural categories. *Cognitive Psychology, 4*, 328–350.

Rosch, E., Simpson, C., & Miller, R. (1976). Structural bases of typicality effects. *Journal of Experimental Psychology: Human Perception and Performance, 2*, 491–502.

Rose, D. (1996). Some reflections on (or by?) grandmother cells. *Perception, 25*, 881–886.

Rosen, R. (1985). *Anticipatory systems.* New York: Pergamon Press.

Rosen, R. (2000). *Essays on life itself.* New York: Columbia University Press.

Rosenblatt, F. (1961). *Principles of neurodynamics: Perceptrons and the theory of brain mechanisms.* Buffalo, N.Y.: Cornell Aeronautical Laboratory.

Rosenthal, D. (1993). Higher-order thoughts and appendage theory of consciousness. *Philosophical Psychology, 6*, 155–167.

Rosenthal, D. (2000). Metacognition and higher-order thoughts. *Consciousness and Cognition, 9*, 231–242.

Ross, B. (1989). Remindings in learning and instruction. In S. Vosniadou & A. Ortony (Eds.), *Similarity and analogical reasoning* (pp. 438–469). Cambridge: Cambridge University Press.

Ross, D. (1997). Critical notice of Ron McClamrock: *Existential cognition. Canadian Journal of Philosophy, 27*, 271–284.

Roy, D., & Mukherjee, N. (2005). Towards situated speech understanding: Visual context priming of language models. *Computer Speech and Language, 19*, 227–248.

Rozenblit, L., Spivey, M., & Wojslawowicz, J. (2002). Mechanical reasoning about gear-and-belt systems: Do eye movements predict performance? In M. Anderson, B. Meyer, & P. Olivier (Eds.), *Diagrammatic representation and reasoning* (pp. 223–240). Berlin: Springer-Verlag.

Rudolph, K., & Pasternak, T. (1999). Transient and permanent deficits in motion perception after lesions of cortical areas MT and MST in the macaque monkey. *Cerebral Cortex, 9*, 90–100.

Rugg, M., & Coles, M. (1995). The ERP and cognitive psychology: Conceptual issues. In M. Rugg & M. Coles (Eds.), *Electrophysiology of mind: Event-related brain potentials and cognition* (pp. 27–39). London: Oxford University Press.

Ruggieri, V. (1999). The running horse stops: The hypothetical role of the eyes in imagery of movement. *Perceptual and Motor Skills, 89,* 1088–1092.

Rumelhart, D. (1970). A multicomponent theory of perception of briefly exposed visual displays. *Journal of Mathematical Psychology, 7,* 191.

Rumelhart, D. (1977). Toward an interactive model of reading. In S. Dornic (Ed.), *Attention and performance 6.* Hillsdale, N.J.: Lawrence Erlbaum.

Rumelhart, D., Hinton, G., & Williams, R. (1986). Learning representations by back-propagating errors. *Nature, 323,* 533–536.

Rumelhart, D., & McClelland, J. (1982). An interactive activation model of context effects in letter perception: Part 2. The contextual enhancement effect and some tests and extensions of the model. *Psychological Review, 89,* 60–94.

Rumelhart, D., & McClelland, J. (1986a). *Parallel distributed processing: Explorations in the microstructure of cognition, Volumes 1 & 2. Cambridge,* Mass.: MIT Press.

Rumelhart, D., & McClelland, J. (1986b). On learning the past tenses of English verbs. In D. Rumelhart, J. McClelland, & the PDP Research Group, *Parallel distributed processing: Explorations in the microstructure of cognition, Vol. 2.* Cambridge, Mass.: MIT Press.

Rumelhart, D., & Todd, P. (1993). Learning and connectionist representations. In D. Meyer & S. Kornblum (Eds.), *Attention and performance 14: Synergies in experimental psychology, artificial intelligence, and cognitive neuroscience.* Cambridge, Mass.: MIT Press.

Ruppertsberg, A., Wuerger, S., & Bertamini, M. (2003). The chromatic input of global motion perception. *Visual Neuroscience, 20,* 421–428.

Russell, B. (1903). *Principles of mathematics.* Cambridge: Cambridge University Press.

Russell, B. (1906). Les mathematiques et la logique. *Revue de Metaphysique et de Morale, 14,* 627–650.

Ryle, G. (1949). *The concept of mind.* New York: Barnes & Noble.

Sadato, N., Pascual-Leone, A., Grafman, J., Ibanez, V., Deiber, M., Dold, G., & Hallett, M. (1996). Activation of the primary visual cortex by Braille reading in blind subjects. *Nature, 380,* 526–528.

Saffran, J., Newport, E., & Aslin, R. (1996). Word segmentation: The role of distributed cues. *Journal of Memory and Language, 35,* 606–621.

Sailor, K., & Shoben, E. (1996). The role of categorical information in processing relational attributes. *Memory and Cognition, 24,* 756–765.

Salas, J., de Groot, H., & Spanos, N. (1989). Neuro-linguistic programming and hypnotic responding: An empirical evaluation. *Journal of Mental Imagery, 13,* 79–89.

Sandon, P. (1990). Simulating visual attention. *Journal of Cognitive Neuroscience, 2,* 213–231.

Sanford, A. J., & Sanford, A. J. S. (2005). *Brute force and ignorance: Changing the odds in the Monty Hall task.* Unpublished manuscript.

Sarter, M., Berntson, G., & Cacioppo, J. (1996). Brain imaging and cognitive neuroscience: Toward strong inference in attributing function to structure. *American Psychologist, 51,* 13–21.

Sasai, M., Ohmine, I., & Ramaswamy, R. (1992). Long time fluctuations of liquid water: 1/f spectrum of energy fluctuations in hydrogen-bond network rearrangement dynamics. *Journal of Chemical Physics, 96,* 3045–3053.

Saslow, M. G. (1967) Effects of components of displacement-step stimuli upon latency of saccadic eye movements. *Journal of the Optical Society of America, 57,* 1024–1029.

Sathian, K., Zangaladze, A., Hoffman, J., & Grafton, S. (1997). Feeling with the mind's eye. *Neuroreport: An International Journal for the Rapid Communication of Research in Neuroscience, 8,* 3877–3881.

Sauer, T., Yorke, J., & Casdagli, M. (1991). Embedology. *Journal of Statistical Physics, 65,* 579–616.

Savage-Rumbaugh, E. (1987). Communication, symbolic communication, and language: A reply to Seidenberg and Pettito. *Journal of Experimental Psychology: General,* 116, 288–292.

Scaife, M., & Rogers, Y. (1996). External cognition: How do graphical representations work? *International Journal of Human-Computer Studies, 45,* 185–213.

Scannell, J., Roberts, G., & Lazarus, J. (2001). Prey scan at random to evade observant predators. *Proceedings of the Royal Society of London B: Biological Sciences, 268,* 541–547.

Schall, J. (1995). Neural basis of saccade target selection. *Reviews in the Neurosciences, 6,* 63–85.

Schall, J. (2000). Decision making: From sensory evidence to a motor command. *Current Biology, 10,* R404–R406.

Scheinerman, E. R. (1995). *Invitation to dynamical systems.* New Jersey: Prentice Hall.

Schellenberg, E. (1997). Simplifying the implication-realization model of melodic expectancy. *Music Perception, 14,* 295–318.

Schluroff, M. (1982). Pupil responses to grammatical complexity of sentences. *Brain and Language, 17,* 133–145.

Schluroff, M. (1986). Pupillary responses to syntactic ambiguity of sentences. *Brain and Language, 27,* 322–344.

Schluter, N., Rushworth, M., Passingham, R., & Mills, K. (1998). Temporary interference in human lateral premotor cortex suggests dominance for the selection of movements: A study using transcranial magnetic stimulation. *Brain, 121,* 785–799.

Schmidt, R., Carello, C., & Turvey, M. (1990). Phase transitions and critical fluctuations in the visual coordination of rhythmic movements between people. *Journal of Experimental Psychology: Human Perception and Performance, 16,* 227–247.

Schober, M. (1993). Spatial perspective-taking in conversion. *Cognition, 47,* 1–24.

Scholl, B., & Pylyshyn, Z. (1999). Tracking multiple items through occlusion: Clues to visual objecthood. *Cognitive Psychology, 38,* 259–290.

Schöner, G. (2002). Timing, clocks and dynamical systems. *Brain and Cognition, 48,* 31–51.

Schooler, J., Ohlsson, S., & Brooks, K. (1993). Thoughts beyond words: When language overshadows insight. *Journal of Experimental Psychology, 122,* 166–183.

Schrödinger, E. (1935). Die gegenwärtige Situation in der Quantenmechanik. *Naturwissenschaft, 23,* 807–812, 823–828, 844–849.

Schrödinger, E. (1944). *What is life? The physical aspect of the living cell.* Cambridge: Cambridge University Press.

Schutze, H. (1993). Word space. In S. Hanson, J. Cowan, & L. Giles (Eds.), *Advances in neural information processing systems 5.* San Mateo, Calif.: Morgan Kaufmann.

Schutze, H. (1994). A connectionist model of verb subcategorization. *Proceedings of the 16th Annual Conference of the Cognitive Science Society* (pp. 784–788). Hillsdale, N.J.: Lawrence Erlbaum.

Schwarz, N. (1998). Warmer and more social: Recent developments in cognitive social psychology. *Annual Review of Sociology, 24,* 239–264.

Schyns, P. (1991). A modular neural network model of concept acquisition. *Cognitive Science, 15,* 461–508.

Scott, A. (1996). On quantum theories of the mind. *Journal of Consciousness Studies, 3,* 484–491.

Searle, J. (1992). *The rediscovery of the mind.* Cambridge, Mass.: MIT Press.

Sebanz, N., Knoblich, G., & Prinz, W. (2003). Representing others' actions: Just like one's own? *Cognition, 88,* B11–B21.

Sebanz, N., Knoblich, G., Prinz, W., & Wascher, E. (2006). Twin peaks: An ERP study of action planning and control in coacting individuals. *Journal of Cognitive Neuroscience, 18,* 859–870.

Segal, G. (2000). *A slim book about narrow content.* Cambridge, Mass.: MIT Press.

Seidenberg, M. (1993). Connectionist models and cognitive theory. *Psychological Science, 4,* 228–235.

Seidenberg, M. (1997). Language acquisition and use: Learning and applying probabilistic constraints. *Science, 275,* 1599–1603.

Seidenberg, M., & McClelland, J. (1989). A distributed, developmental model of word recognition and naming. *Psychological Review, 96,* 523–568.

Seidenberg, M., & Pettito, L. (1987). Communication, symbolic communication, and language in child and chimpanzee: Comment on Savage-Rumbaugh, McDonald, Sevcik, Hopkins, and Rupert (1986). *Journal of Experimental Psychology: General, 116,* 279–287.

Seidler, V. (1986). *Kant, respect and injustice: The limits of liberal moral theory.* London: Routledge & Kegan Paul.

Seitz, A. R., Nanez, J. E., Holloway, S. R., Koyama, S., & Watanabe, T. (2005). Seeing what is not there shows the costs of perceptual learning. *Proceedings of the National Academy of Sciences of the USA, 102,* 9080–9085.

Seitz, J. (2000). The bodily basis of thought. *New Ideas in Psychology, 18,* 23–40.

Sekuler, R., & Pantle, A. (1967). A model for after-effects of seen movement. *Vision Research, 7,* 427–439.

Sekuler, R., Sekuler, A., & Lau, R. (1997). Sound alters visual motion perception. *Nature, 385,* 308.

Selfridge, O. (1959). Pandemonium: A paradigm for learning. In *Symposium on the mechanization of thought processes* (pp. 511–527). London: H. M. Stationary Office.

Selvin, S. (1975). On the Monty Hall problem (Letter to the editor). *American Statistician, 29,* 134.

Sengpiel, F., Godecke, I., Stawinski, P., Hubener, M., Lowel, S., & Bonhoeffer, T. (1998). Intrinsic and environmental factors in the development of functional maps in cat visual cortex. *Neuropharmacology, 37,* 607–621.

Sereno, J. (1991). Graphemic, associative, and syntactic priming effects at a brief stimulus onset asynchrony in lexical decision and naming. *Journal of Experimental Psychology: Learning, Memory, and Cognition, 17,* 459–477.

Servos, P., & Goodale, M. (1995). Preserved visual imagery in visual form agnosia. *Neuropsychologia, 33,* 1383–1394.

Severance, E., & Washburn, M. F. (1907). Minor studies from the psychological laboratory of Vassar College: The loss of associative power in words after long fixation. *American Journal of Psychology, 18*(2), 182–186.

Shadlen, M., & Movshon, J. (1999). Synchrony unbound: A critical evaluation of the temporal binding hypothesis. *Neuron, 24,* 67–77.

Shadlen, M., & Newsome, W. (1994). Noise, neural codes and cortical organization. *Current Opinion in Neurobiology, 4,* 569–579.

Shalizi, C., & Albers, D. (2002). Symbolic dynamics for discrete adaptive games. Unpublished manuscript.

Shams, L., Kamitani, Y., & Shimojo, S. (2000). What you see is what you hear. *Nature, 408,* 788.

Shanks, D. (1990). Connectionism and human learning: Critique of Gluck and Bower (1988). *Journal of Experimental Psychology: General, 119,* 101–104.

Shannon, C., & Weaver, W. (1949). *The mathematical theory of communication.* Urbana: University of Illinois Press.

Sharma, J., Angelucci, A., & Sur, M. (2000). Induction of visual orientation modules in auditory cortex. *Nature, 404,* 841–847.

Shastri, L. (1999). Advances in SHRUTI—a neurally motivated model of relational knowledge representation and rapid inference using temporal synchrony. *Applied Intelligence, 11,* 78–108.

Shaw, R., & Turvey, M. (1999). Ecological foundations of cognition: II. Degrees of freedom and conserved quantities in animal-environment systems. *Journal of Consciousness Studies, 6,* 111–123.

Shen, J., Reingold, E. M., & Pomplun, M. (2000). Distractor ratio influences patterns of eye movements during visual search. *Perception, 29,* 241–250.

Shen, J., Reingold, E. M., & Pomplun, M. (2003). Guidance of eye movements during conjunctive visual search: The distractor-ratio effect. *Canadian Journal of Experimental Psychology, 57,* 76–96.

Shepard, R. (1962). The analysis of proximities: Multidimensional scaling with an unknown distance function: Part I. *Psychometric Society, 27,* 125–140.

Shepard, R. (1964). Attention and the metric structure of the stimulus space. *Journal of Mathematical Psychology, 1,* 54–87.

Shepard, R. (2001). Perceptual-cognitive universals as reflections of the world. *Behavioral and Brain Sciences, 24,* 581–601.

Shepard, R., & Metzler, J. (1971). Mental rotation of three dimensional objects. *Science, 171,* 701–703.

Shin, J., & Rosenbaum, D. (2002). Reaching while calculating: Scheduling of cognitive and perceptual-motor processes. *Journal of Experimental Psychology: General, 131,* 206–219.

Shockley, K., Santana, M., & Fowler, C. (2003). Mutual interpersonal postural constraints are involved in cooperative conversation. *Journal of Experimental Psychology: Human Perception and Performance, 29,* 326–332.

Shulman, G. (1992). Attentional modulation of a figural aftereffect. *Perception, 21,* 7–19.

Shultz, T., & Lepper, M. (1996). Cognitive dissonance reduction as constraint satisfaction. *Psychological Review, 103,* 219–240.

Siegler, R., & Crowley, K. (1991). The microgenetic method: A direct means for studying cognitive development. *American Psychologist, 46,* 606–620.

Simon, J. (1990). The effects of an irrelevant directional cue on human information processing. In R. Proctor & T. Reeve (Eds.), *Stimulus-response compatibility: An integrated perspective* (pp. 31–86). Amsterdam: North-Holland.

Simons, D. (2000). Current approaches to change blindness. *Visual Cognition, 7,* 1–15.

Simons, D., & Levin, D. (1998). Failure to detect changes to people during a real world interaction. *Psychonomic Bulletin and Review, 5,* 644–649.

Simos, P., Diehl, R., Breier, J., Molis, M., Zouridakis, G., & Papanicolaou, A. (1998). MEG correlates of categorical perception of a voice onset time continuum in humans. *Cognitive Brain Research, 7*, 215–219.

Singer, W. (1999). Neuronal synchrony: A versatile code for the definition of relations? *Neuron, 24*, 49–65.

Skoczenski, A., & Norcia, A. (1998). Neural noise limitations on infant visual sensitivity. *Nature, 391*, 697–700.

Slobin, D. (1997). The origins of grammaticizable notions: Beyond the individual mind. In D. Slobin (Ed.), *The crosslinguistic study of language acquisition, Vol. 5: Expanding the contexts* (pp. 265–323). Mahwah, N.J.: Lawrence Erlbaum.

Sloman, S. (1996). The empirical case for two systems of reasoning. *Psychological Bulletin, 119*, 3–22.

Sloman, S. (1998). Categorical inference is not a tree: The myth of inheritance hierarchies. *Cognitive Psychology, 35*, 1–33.

Smart, J. (1959). Sensations and brain processes. *Philosophical Review, 68*, 141–156.

Smith, E. (1978). Theories of semantic memory. In W. Estes (Ed.), *Handbook of learning and cognitive processes* (pp. 1–56). Hillsdale, N.J.: Lawrence Erlbaum.

Smith, L. B. (2006). Action alters shape categories. *Cognitive Science, 29*, 665–679.

Smith, L. B., & Samuelson, L. (2003). Different is good: Connectionism and dynamic systems theory are complimentary emergentist approaches to development. *Developmental Science, 6*, 434–439.

Smith, L. C., & Klein, R. (1990). Evidence for semantic satiation: Repeating a category slows subsequent semantic processing. *Journal of Experimental Psychology: Learning, Memory, and Cognition, 16*, 852–861.

Smolensky, P. (1988a). On the proper treatment of connectionism. *Behavioral and Brain Sciences, 11*, 1–74.

Smolensky, P. (1988b). Analysis of distributed representation of constituent connectionist systems. *Proceedings of the First IEEE Conference on Neural Information Processing Systems* (pp. 730–739).

Smolensky, P. (1995). Connectionism, constituency and the language of thought. In C. Macdonald & G. Macdonald (Eds.), *Connectionism: Debates on psychological explanation, Vol. 2* (pp. 164–198). Malden, Mass.: Blackwell.

Snedeker, J., & Trueswell. J. (2004). The developing constraints on parsing decisions: The role of lexical-biases and referential scenes in child and adult sentence processing. *Cognitive Psychology, 49*, 238–299.

Softky, W. (1996). Fine analog coding minimizes information transmission. *Neural Networks, 9*, 15–24.

Solomon, K., & Barsalou, L. (2004). Perceptual simulation in property verification. *Memory and Cognition, 32*, 244–259.

Solomonoff, R. (1978). Complexity-based induction systems: Comparisons and convergence theorems. *IEEE Transactions on Information Theory, 24*, 422–432.

Solow, D. (2000). On the challenge of developing a formal mathematical theory for establishing emergence in complex systems. *Complexity, 6*, 49–52.

Sonnenwald, D. H., & Pierce, L. G. (2000). Information behavior in dynamic group work contexts: Interwoven situational awareness, dense social networks and contested collaboration in command and control. *Information Processing and Management, 36*, 461–479.

Sparks, D., Holland, R., & Guthrie, B. (1976). Size and distribution of movement fields in the monkey. *Brain Research, 113*, 21–34.

Spence, C., & Driver, J. (Eds.) (2004). *Crossmodal space and crossmodal attention.* Oxford: Oxford University Press.

Spence, C., Lloyd, D., McGlone, F., Nicholls, M., & Driver, J. (2000). Inhibition of return is supramodal: A demonstration between all possible pairings of vision, touch and audition. *Experimental Brain Research, 134,* 42–48.

Spence, C., McDonald, J., & Driver, J. (2004). Exogenous spatial-cuing studies of human crossmodal attention and multisensory integration. In C. Spence & J. Driver (Eds.), *Crossmodal space and crossmodal attention* (pp. 277–320). Oxford: Oxford University Press.

Spencer, J., & Schöner, G. (2003). Bridging the representational gap in the dynamic systems approach to development. *Developmental Science, 6*(4), 392–412.

Spencer, J., & Thelen, E. (2003). Introduction to the special issue: Why this question and why now? *Developmental Science, 6,* 375–377.

Sperling, G., & Lu, Z. (1998). A systems analysis of visual motion perception. In T. Watanabe (Ed.), *High-level motion processing: Computational, neurobiological, and psychophysical perspectives* (pp. 153–183). Cambridge, Mass.: MIT Press.

Spillman, L., & Werner, J. (1996). Long-range interactions in visual perception. *Trends in Neuroscience, 19,* 428–434.

Spivey, M. (2000). Turning the tables on the Turing test: The Spivey test. *Connection Science, 12,* 91–94.

Spivey, M., & Dale, R. (2004). On the continuity of mind: Toward a dynamical account of cognition. In B. Ross (Ed.), *The Psychology of learning and motivation,* Vol. 45 (pp. 87–142). San Diego, Calif.: Elsevier.

Spivey, M., Fitneva, S., Tabor, W., & Ajmani, S. (2002a). The time course of information integration in sentence processing. In P. Merlo & S. Stevenson (Eds.), *The lexical basis of sentence processing: Formal, computational, and experimental issues* (pp. 207–232). Amsterdam: John Benjamins.

Spivey, M., & Geng, J. (2001). Oculomotor mechanisms activated by imagery and memory: Eye movements to absent objects. *Psychological Research, 65,* 235–241.

Spivey, M., Grosjean, M., & Knoblich, G. (2005). Continuous attraction toward phonological competitors. *Proceedings of the National Academy of Sciences of the USA, 102,* 10393–10398.

Spivey, M., & Marian, V. (1999). Crosstalk between native and second languages: Partial activation of an irrelevant lexicon. *Psychological Science, 10,* 281–284.

Spivey, M., Richardson, D., & Fitneva, S. (2004). Thinking outside the brain: Spatial indices to linguistic and visual information. In J. Henderson & F. Ferreira (Eds.), *The interface of vision, language and action* (pp. 161–189). New York: Psychology Press.

Spivey, M., & Spirn, M. (2000). Selective visual attention modulates the direct tilt after-effect. *Perception and Psychophysics, 62,* 1525–1533.

Spivey, M., & Tanenhaus, M. (1998). Syntactic ambiguity resolution in discourse: Modeling the effects of referential context and lexical frequency. *Journal of Experimental Psychology: Learning, Memory, and Cognition, 24,* 1521–1543.

Spivey, M., Tanenhaus, M., Eberhard, K., & Sedivy, J. (2002b). Eye movements and spoken language comprehension: Effects of visual context on syntactic ambiguity resolution. *Cognitive Psychology, 45,* 447–481.

Spivey, M., Tyler, M., Eberhard, K., & Tanenhaus, M. (2001). Linguistically mediated visual search. *Psychological Science, 12,* 282–286.

Spivey, M., Tyler, M., Richardson, D., & Young, E. (2000). Eye movements during comprehension of spoken scene descriptions. *Proceedings of the 22nd Annual*

Conference of the Cognitive Science Society (pp. 487–492). Mahwah, N.J.: Lawrence Erlbaum.

Spivey-Knowlton, M. (1992). Another context effect in sentence processing: Implications for the principle of referential support. *Proceedings of the 14th Annual Conference of the Cognitive Science Society* (pp. 486–491). Hillsdale, N.J.: Lawrence Erlbaum.

Spivey-Knowlton, M. (1994). Quantitative predictions from a constraint-based theory of syntactic ambiguity resolution. In M. Mozer, J. Elman, P. Smolensky, D. Touretzky, & A. Weigand (Eds.), *Proceedings of the 1993 Connectionist Models Summer School.* Hillsdale, N.J.: Lawrence Erlbaum.

Spivey-Knowlton, M. (1996). Integration of visual and linguistic information: Human data and model simulations. Doctoral dissertation, University of Rochester, Rochester, N.Y.

Spivey-Knowlton, M., & Allopenna, P. (1997). A computational account of the integration of linguistic and visual information during spoken word recognition. *Proceedings of the Computational Psycholinguistics Conference.* Berkeley, Calif.

Spivey-Knowlton, M., & Saffran, J. (1995). Inducing a grammar without an explicit teacher: Incremental distributed prediction feedback. *Proceedings of the 17th Annual Conference of the Cognitive Science Society.* Hillsdale, N.J.: Lawrence Erlbaum.

Spivey-Knowlton, M., & Sedivy, J. (1995). Resolving attachment ambiguities with multiple constraints. *Cognition, 55,* 227–267.

Spivey-Knowlton, M., Sedivy, J., Eberhard, K., & Tanenhaus, M. (1994). Psycholinguistic study of the interaction between language and vision. *Proceedings of the 12th National Conference on Artificial Intelligence: Workshop on the Integration of Natural Language and Vision Processing* (pp. 189–192). Menlo Park, Calif.: AAAI Press.

Spivey-Knowlton, M., Trueswell, J., & Tanenhaus, M. (1993). Context effects in syntactic ambiguity resolution: Discourse and semantic influences in parsing reduced relatives. *Canadian Journal of Experimental Psychology, 47,* 276–309.

Sporns, O., Chialvo, D., Kaiser, M., & Hilgetag, C. (2004). Organization, development and function of complex brain networks. *Trends in Cognitive Sciences, 8,* 418–426.

Spurrett, D. (2003). Why think that cognition is distributed? *AlterNation, 10,* 292–306.

St. John, M. (1992). The story gestalt: A model of knowledge-intensive processes in text comprehension. *Cognitive Science, 16,* 271–306.

Stamenov, M., & Gallese, V. (Eds.) (2002). *Mirror neurons and the evolution of brain and language.* Amsterdam: John Benjamins.

Stanton, R., Nosofsky, R., & Zaki, S. (2002). Comparisons between exemplar similarity and mixed prototype models using a linearly separable category structure. *Memory and Cognition, 30,* 934–944.

Stapp, H. (1993). *Mind, matter, and quantum mechanics.* New York: Springer-Verlag.

Stapp, H. (1999). Attention, intention, and will in quantum physics. *Journal of Consciousness Studies, 6,* 143–164.

Stary, C., & Stumptner, M. (1992). Representing organizational changes in distributed problem solving environments. *IEEE Transactions on Systems, Man, and Cybernetics, 22,* 1168–1177.

Steele, C. (1988). The psychology of self-affirmation: Sustaining the integrity of the self. In L. Berkowitz (Ed.), *Advances in experimental social psychology, Vol. 21: Social psychological studies of the self: Perspectives and programs* (pp. 261–302). San Diego: Academic Press.

Steels, L., & Brooks, R. (1995). (Eds.) *The artificial life route to artificial intelligence: Building embodied, situated agents*. Hillsdale, N.J.: Lawrence Erlbaum.

Stein, B., & Meredith, M. (1993). *The merging of the senses*. Cambridge, Mass.: MIT Press.

Steinschneider, M., Schroeder, C., Arezzo, J., & Vaughan, H. (1995). Physiologic correlates of the voice onset time boundary in primary auditory cortex (A1) of the awake monkey: Temporal response patterns. *Brain and Language, 48,* 326–340.

Sternberg, S. (1969). The discovery of processing stages: Extensions of Donders' method. *Acta Psychologica, 30,* 276–315.

Stettler, D., Das, A., Bennett, J., & Gilbert, C. (2002). Lateral connectivity and contextual interactions in macaque primary visual cortex. *Neuron, 36,* 739–750.

Stevens, J., Fonlupt, P., Shiffrar, M., & Decety, J. (2000). New aspects of motion perception: Selective neural encoding of apparent human movements. *Neuroreport: An International Journal for Rapid Communication of Neuroscience Research, 11,* 109–115.

Stevenson, S. (1994). Competition and recency in a hybrid network model of syntactic disambiguation. *Journal of Psycholinguistic Research, 23,* 295–322.

Stoffregen, T., Pagulayan, R., Bardy, B., & Hettinger, L. (2000). Modulating postural control to facilitate visual performance. *Human Movement Science, 19,* 203–220.

Stone, G., & Van Orden, G. (1989). Are words represented by nodes? *Memory and Cognition, 17,* 511–524.

Streeck, J. (2003). The body taken for granted: Lingering dualism in research on social interaction. In P. Glenn, C. LeBaron, & J. Mandelbaum (Eds.), *Studies in language and social interaction* (pp. 427–440). Mahwah, N.J.: Lawrence Erlbaum.

Strogatz, S. (1994). *Nonlinear dynamics and chaos: With applications in physics, biology, chemistry, and engineering (studies in nonlinearity)*. New York: Perseus Publishing.

Strogatz, S. (2003). *Sync: The emerging science of spontaneous order*. New York: Hyperion.

Suchman, L. (1987). *Plans and situated actions: The problem of human-machine communication*. New York: Cambridge University Press.

Sun, R. (2002). *Duality of the mind: A bottom up approach toward cognition*. Mahwah, N.J.: Lawrence Erlbaum.

Sutton, R. S., & Barto, A. G. (1981). Toward a modern theory of adaptive networks: expectation and prediction. *Psychological Review, 88,* 135–170.

Swick, D., Kutas, M., & Neville, H. (1994). Localizing the neural generators of event-related brain potentials. In A. Kertesz (Ed.), *Localization and neuroimaging in neuropsychology* (pp. 73–121). San Diego: Academic Press.

Swinney, D. (1979). Lexical access during sentence comprehension: (Re)consideration of context effects. *Journal of Verbal Learning and Verbal Behavior, 18,* 645–659.

Tabor, W. (1995). Lexical change as nonlinear interpolation. *Proceedings of the 17th Annual Conference of the Cognitive Science Society* (pp. 242–247). Hillsdale, N.J.: Lawrence Erlbaum.

Tabor, W. (2002). The value of symbolic computation. *Ecological Psychology, 14,* 21–51.

Tabor, W., Galantucci, B., & Richardson, D. (2004). Effects of merely local syntactic coherence on sentence processing. *Journal of Memory and Language, 50,* 355–370.

Tabor, W., Juliano, C., & Tanenhaus, M. K. (1997). Parsing in a dynamical system: An attractor-based account of the interaction of lexical and structural constraints in sentence processing. *Language and Cognitive Processes, 12,* 211–271.

Tabor, W., & Tanenhaus, M. (1999). Dynamical models of sentence processing. *Cognitive Science, 23,* 491–515.

Tabossi, P., Colombo, L., & Job, R. (1987). Accessing lexical ambiguity: Effects of context and dominance. *Psychological Research, 49,* 161–167.

Tabossi, P., Spivey-Knowlton, M., McRae, K., & Tanenhaus, M. (1994). Semantic effects on syntactic ambiguity resolution: Evidence for a constraint-based resolution process. In M. Morris & C. Umilta (Eds.), *Attention and performance 15: Conscious and nonconscious information processing* (pp. 589–615). Cambridge, Mass.: MIT Press.

Takens, F. (1981). Detecting strange attractors in turbulence. In D. Rand & L. Young (Eds.), *Lecture notes in mathematics, Vol. 898: Dynamical systems and turbulence* (pp. 366–381). Berlin: Springer-Verlag.

Tallal, P., Galaburda, A., Llinás, R., & von Euler, C. (Eds.) (1993). *Temporal information processing in the nervous system: Special reference to dyslexia and dysphasia.* New York: New York Academy of Sciences.

Tanaka, K. (1996). Representation of visual features of objects in the inferotemporal cortex. *Neural Networks, 9,* 1459–1475.

Tanaka, K. (1997). Mechanisms of visual object recognition: Monkey and human studies. *Current Opinion in Neurobiology, 7,* 523–529.

Tanenhaus, M., Leiman, J., & Seidenberg, M. (1979). Evidence for multiple stages in the processing of ambiguous words in syntactic contexts. *Journal of Verbal Learning and Verbal Behavior, 18,* 427–440.

Tanenhaus, M., Magnuson, J., Dahan, D., & Chambers, C. (2000). Eye movements and lexical access in spoken-language comprehension: Evaluating a linking hypothesis between fixations and linguistic processing. *Journal of Psycholinguistic Research, 29,* 557–580.

Tanenhaus, M., Spivey-Knowlton, M., Eberhard, K., & Sedivy, J. (1995). Integration of visual and linguistic information during spoken language comprehension. *Science, 268,* 1632–1634.

Tanenhaus, M., Spivey-Knowlton, M., & Hanna, J. (2000). Modeling thematic and discourse context effects with a multiple constraints approach: Implications for the architecture of the language comprehension system. In M. Crocker, C. Clifton, & M. Pickering (Eds.), *Architectures and mechanisms for language processing* (pp. 90–118). New York: Cambridge University Press.

Tanenhaus, M., & Trueswell, J. (1995). Sentence comprehension. In J. Miller & P. Eimas (Eds.), *Handbook of cognition and perception.* New York: Academic Press.

Taraban, R., & McClelland, J. (1987). Conspiracy effects in word pronunciation. *Journal of Memory and Language, 26,* 608–631.

Taylor, J. (1999). *The race for consciousness.* Cambridge, Mass.: MIT Press.

Tesauro, G. (1989). Neurogammon wins computer Olympiad. *Neural Computation, 1,* 321–323.

Tesauro, G. (1994). TD-Gammon, a self-teaching backgammon program, achieves master-level play. *Neural Computation, 6,* 215–219.

Tettamanti, M., Buccino, G., Saccuman, M., Gallese, V., Danna, M., Scifo, P., Fazio, F., Rizzolatti, G., Cappa, S., & Perani, D. (2005). Listening to action-related sentences activates fronto-parietal motor circuits. *Journal of Cognitive Neuroscience, 17,* 273–281.

Thagard, P. (1989). Explanatory coherence. *Behavioral and Brain Sciences, 12,* 435–502.

Theeuwes, J., & Kooi, F. (1994). Parallel search for a conjunction of contrast polarity and shape. *Vision Research, 34,* 3013–3016.

Theeuwes, J., Olivers, C., & Chizk, C. (2005). Remembering a location makes the eyes curve away. *Psychological Science, 16,* 196–199.

Thelen, E. (1995). Motor development: A new synthesis. *American Psychologist, 50,* 79–95.

Thelen, E., & Smith, L. (1994). *A dynamic systems approach to the development of cognition and action.* Cambridge, Mass.: MIT Press.

Thomas, N. (1999). Are theories of imagery theories of imagination? An active perception approach to conscious mental content. *Cognitive Science, 23,* 207–245.

Thomason, T., Arbuckle, T., & Cady, D. (1980). Test of the eye-movement hypothesis of neurolinguistic programming. *Perceptual and Motor Skills, 51,* 230.

Thompson-Schill, S., D'Esposito, M., & Kan, I. (1999). Effects of repetition and competition on activity in left prefrontal cortex during word generation. *Neuron, 23,* 513–522.

Tinker, M. (1928). Eye movement duration, pause duration, and reading time. *Psychological Review, 35,* 385–397.

Tipper, S., & Behrmann, M. (1996). Object centered not scene based visual neglect. *Journal of Experimental Psychology: Human Perception and Performance, 22,* 1261–1278.

Tipper, S., Howard, L., & Jackson, S. (1997). Selective reaching to grasp: Evidence for distractor interference effects. *Visual Cognition, 4,* 1–38.

Toiviainen, P., & Snyder, J. (2003). Tapping to Bach: Resonance-based modeling of pulse. *Music Perception, 21,* 43–80.

Tolman, E. (1937). The acquisition of string-pulling by rats—Conditioned response or sign-gestalt? *Psychological Review, 44,* 195–211.

Townsend, D., & Bever, T. (1978). Interclause relations and clausal processing. *Journal of Verbal Learning and Verbal Behavior, 17,* 509–521.

Tranel, D., & Damasio, A. (1988). Non-conscious face recognition in patients with face agnosia. *Behavioural Brain Research, 30,* 235–249.

Trappenberg, T. (2002). *Fundamentals of computational neuroscience.* New York: Oxford University Press.

Treisman, A. (1964). Selective attention in man. *British Medical Bulletin, 20,* 12–16.

Treisman, A. (1988). Features and objects: The Fourteenth Bartlett Memorial Lecture. *Quarterly Journal of Experimental Psychology, 40A,* 201–237.

Treisman, A. (1996). Selection for perception for selection for action. *Visual Cognition, 3,* 353–357.

Treisman, A., & Gelade, G. (1980). A feature integration theory of attention. *Cognitive Psychology, 12,* 97–136.

Treisman, A., & Gormican, S. (1988). Feature analysis in early vision: Evidence from search asymmetries. *Psychological Review, 95,* 15–48.

Treue, S., & Martinez-Trujillo, J. (1999). Feature-based attention influences motion processing gain in macaque visual cortex. *Nature, 399,* 575–579.

Trueswell, J., & Hayhoe, M. (1993). Surface segmentation mechanisms and motion perception. *Vision Research, 33,* 313–328.

Trueswell, J., & Kim, A. (1998). How to prune a garden path by nipping it in the bud: Fast priming of verb argument structure. *Journal of Memory and Language, 39*(1), 102–123.

Trueswell, J., Sekerina, I., & Logrip, L. (1999). The kidergarten-path effect: Studying on-lien sentence processing in young children. *Cognition, 73,* 89–134.

Trueswell, J., Tanenhaus, M., & Garnsey, S. (1994). Semantic influences on parsing: Use of thematic role information in syntactic disambiguation. *Journal of Memory and Language, 33,* 285–318.

Trueswell, J., Tanenhaus, M., & Kello, C. (1993). Verb-specific constraints in sentence processing: Separating effects of lexical preference from garden-paths. *Journal of Experimental Psychology: Learning, Memory, and Cognition, 19*, 528–553.

Tsotsos, J. (1990). Analyzing vision at the complexity level. *Behavioral and Brain Sciences, 13*, 423–469.

Tucker, M., & Ellis, R. (1998). On the relations between seen objects and components of potential actions. *Journal of Experimental Psychology: Human Perception and Performance, 24*, 830–846.

Tucker, M., & Ellis, R. (2001). The potentiation of grasp types during visual object categorization. *Visual Cognition, 8*, 769–800.

Tuller, B., Case, P., Ding, M., & Kelso, J. A. (1994). The nonlinear dynamics of speech categorization. *Journal of Experimental Psychology: Human Perception and Performance, 20*, 3–16.

Tuller, B., Ding, M., & Kelso, J. A. (1997). Fractal timing of verbal transforms. *Perception, 26*(7), 913–928.

Tuller, B., Kelso, J. S., & Harris, K. S. (1982). Interarticulator phasing as an index of temporal regularity in speech. *Journal of Experimental Psychology: Human Perception and Performance, 8*(3), 460–472.

Turvey, M. (1973). On peripheral and central processes in vision: Inferences from an information-processing analysis of masking with patterned stimuli. *Psychological Review, 80*, 1–52.

Turvey, M. (1977). Contrasting orientations to the theory of visual information processing. *Psychological Review, 84*, 67–88.

Turvey, M. (2004). Impredicativity, dynamics, and the perception-action divide. In V. Jirsa & J. Kelso (Eds.), *Coordination dynamics: Issues and trends, Vol. 1: Applied complex systems* (pp. 1–20). New York: Springer-Verlag.

Turvey, M., & Carello, C. (1986). The ecological approach to perceiving-acting: A pictorial essay. *Acta Psychologica, 63*, 133–155.

Turvey, M., & Carello, C. (1995). Some dynamical themes in perception and action. In R. Port & T. van Gelder (Eds.), *Mind as motion: Explorations in the dynamics of cognition* (pp. 373–401). Cambridge, Mass.: MIT Press.

Turvey, M., & Shaw, R. (1999). Ecological foundations of cognition: I. Symmetry and specificity of animal-environment systems. *Journal of Consciousness Studies, 6*, 111–123.

Tversky, A. (1977). Features of similarity. *Psychological Review, 84*, 327–352.

Tversky, A., & Kahneman, D. (1980). Causal schemata in judgments under uncertainty. In M. Fishbein (Ed.), *Progress in social psychology* (pp. 49–72). Hillsdale, N.J.: Lawrence Erlbaum.

Tversky, A., & Kahneman, D. (1983). Extensional versus intuitive reasoning: The conjunction fallacy in probability judgment. *Psychological Review, 90*, 293–315.

Tversky, A., & Kahneman, D. (1991). Loss aversion in riskless choice: A reference-dependent model. *Quarterly Journal of Economics, 106*, 1039–1061.

Tyler, L., & Marslen-Wilson, W. (1977). The on-line effects of semantic context on syntactic processing. *Journal of Verbal Learning and Verbal Behavior, 16*, 683–692.

Tyler, M., & Spivey, M. (2001). Spoken language comprehension improves the efficiency of visual search. *Proceedings of the 23rd Annual Conference of the Cognitive Science Society*. Mahwah, N.J.: Lawrence Erlbaum.

Ulam, S., & Von Neumann, J. (1947). On combination of stochastic and deterministic processes. *Bulletin of the American Mathematical Society, 53*, 1120.

Ulrich, R., Mattes, S., & Miller, J. (1999). Donders's assumption of pure insertion: An evaluation on the basis of response dynamics. *Acta Psychologica, 102,* 43–75.

Underwood, J. (2005). Novice and expert performance with a dynamic control task: Scanpaths during a computer game. In G. Underwood (Ed.), *Cognitive processes in eye guidance.* Oxford: Oxford University Press.

Usher, M., & McClelland, J. (2001). The time course of perceptual choice: The leaky, competing accumulator model. *Psychological Review, 108,* 550–592.

Usher, M., & McClelland, J. (2004). Loss aversion and inhibition in dynamical models of multialternative choice. *Psychological Review, 111,* 757–769.

Usher, M., Stemmler, M., & Olami, Z. (1995). Dynamic pattern formation leads to 1/f noise in neural populations. *Physical Review Letters, 74,* 326–329.

Uttal, W. (2001). *The new phrenology: The limits of localizing cognitive processes in the brain.* Cambridge, Mass.: MIT Press.

Valian, V., & Wales, R. (1976). What's what: Talkers help listeners hear and understand by clarifying sentential relations. *Cognition, 4,* 155–176.

Van Berkum, J., Brown, C., & Hagoort, P. (1999). Early referential context effects in sentence processing: Evidence from event-related brain potentials. *Journal of Memory and Language, 41,* 147–182.

Van der Heijden, A. (1996a). Two stages in visual information processing and visual perception? *Visual Cognition, 3,* 325–353.

Van der Heijden, A. (1996b). Perception for selection, selection for action, and action for perception. *Visual Cognition, 3,* 357–361.

Van der Maas, H. (1998). The dynamical and statistical properties of cognitive strategies: Relations between strategies, attractors, and latent classes. In K. Newel & P. Molenaar (Eds.), *Applications of nonlinear dynamics to developmental process modeling* (pp. 161–176). Mahwah, N.J.: Lawrence Erlbaum.

Van Gelder, T. (1998). The dynamical hypothesis in cognitive science. *Behavioral and Brain Sciences, 21,* 615–665.

Van Gompel, R., Pickering, M., & Traxler, M. (2001). Reanalysis in sentence processing: Evidence against current constraint-based and two-stage models. *Journal of Memory and Language, 45,* 225–258.

Van Gompel, R. P. G., Pickering, M .J., Pearson, J., & Liversedge, S. P. (2005). Evidence against competition during syntactic ambiguity resolution. *Journal of Memory and Language, 52,* 284–307.

Van Heuven, W., Dijkstra, T., Grainger, J., & Schriefers, H. (2001). Shared neighborhood effects in masked orthographic priming. *Psychonomic Bulletin and Review, 8,* 96–101.

Van Leeuwen, C., Steyvers, M., & Nooter, M. (1997). Stability and intermittency in large-scale coupled oscillator models for perceptual segmentation. *Journal of Mathematical Psychology, 41,* 319–344.

Van Orden, G., & Holden, J. (2002). Intentional contents and self-control. *Ecological Psychology, 14,* 87–109.

Van Orden, G., Holden, J., & Turvey, M. (2003). Self-organization of cognitive performance. *Journal of Experimental Psychology: General, 132,* 331–350.

Van Orden, G., Holden, J., & Turvey, M. (2005). Human cognition and 1/f scaling. *Journal of Experimental Psychology: General, 134,* 117–123.

Van Orden, G., Jansen op de Haar, M., & Bosman, A. (1997). Complex dynamic systems also predict dissociations, but they do not reduce to autonomous components. *Cognitive Neuropsychology, 14,* 131–165.

Van Orden, G., Moreno, M., & Holden, J. (2003). A proper metaphysics for cognitive performance. *Nonlinear Dynamics, Psychology, and Life Sciences, 7*, 49–60.

Van Overwalle, F., & Jordens, K. (2002). An adaptive connectionist model of cognitive dissonance. *Personality and Social Psychology Review, 6*, 204–231.

Van Overwalle, F., & Van Rooy, D. (2001). How one cause discounts or augments another: A connectionist account of causal competition. *Personality and Social Psychology Bulletin, 27*, 1613–1626.

Van Rullen, R., & Thorpe, S. (2001). Is it a bird? Is it a plane? Ultra-rapid categorization of natural and artificial objects. *Perception, 30*, 655–668.

Van Zandt, T. (2000). How to fit a response time distribution. *Psychonomic Bulletin and Review, 7*, 424–465.

Van Zandt, T. (2002). Analysis of response time distributions. In J. Wixted & H. Pashler (Eds.), *Stevens' handbook of experimental psychology* (3rd ed.), *Vol. 4: Methodology in experimental psychology* (pp. 461–516). New York: Wiley.

Varela, F., Thompson, J., & Rosch, E. (1992). *The embodied mind: Human cognition and experience*. Cambridge, Mass.: MIT Press.

Verney, S., Granholm, E., & Dionisio, D. (2001). Pupillary responses and processing resources on the visual backward masking task. *Psychophysiology, 38*, 76–83.

Vinje, W., & Gallant, J. (2002). Natural stimulation of the nonclassical receptive field increases information transmission efficiency in V1. *Journal of Neuroscience, 22*, 2904–2915.

Viswanathan, G., Buldyrev, S., Havlin, S., da Luz, M., Raposo, E., & Stanley, H. (1999). Optimizing the success of random searches. *Nature, 401*, 911–914.

Viviani, P. (1990). Eye movements in visual search: Cognitive, perceptual and motor control aspects. In E. Kowler (Ed.), *Eye movements and their role in visual and cognitive processes* (pp. 353–393). Amsterdam: Elsevier Science.

Von Melchner, L., Pallas, S., & Sur, M. (2000). Visual behavior mediated by retinal projections directed to the auditory pathway. *Nature, 404*, 871–876.

Von Neumann, J., & Morgenstern, O. (1947). *Theory of games and economic behavior* (2nd ed.). Princeton, N.J.: Princeton University Press.

Vos Savant, M. (1990, September 9). Ask Marilyn. *Parade*, 15.

Voss, R., & Clarke, J. (1975). 1/f noise in music and speech. *Nature, 258*, 317–318.

Vroomen, J., Bertelson, P., & de Gelder, B. (2001). The ventriloquist effect does not depend on the direction of automatic visual attention. *Perception and Psychophysics, 63*, 651–659.

Vu, H., & Kellas, G. (1999). Contextual strength and the subordinate bias effect: Reply to Rayner, Binder, and Duffy. *Quarterly Journal of Experimental Psychology: Human Experimental Psychology, 52A*, 853–855.

Vu, H., Kellas, G., & Paul, S. (1998). Sources of sentence constraint on lexical ambiguity resolution. *Memory and Cognition, 26*, 979–1001.

Wagenmakers, E., Farrell, S., & Ratcliff, R. (2005). Human cognition and a pile of sand: A discussion on serial correlations and self-organized criticality. *Journal of Experimental Psychology: General, 134*, 108–116.

Wagner, U., Gais, S., Haider, H., Verleger, R., & Born, J. (2004). Sleep inspires insight. *Nature, 427*, 352–355.

Wallach, H., & Slaughter, V. (1988). Viewing direction and pictorial representation. *Perception and Psychophysics, 43*, 79–82.

Wallenstein, G., Nash, A., & Kelso, J. (1995). Frequency and phase characteristics of slow cortical potentials preceding bimanual coordination. *Electroencephalography and Clinical Neurophysiology, 94,* 50–59.

Wallis, C. (1992). Asymmetric dependence and mental representation. *Psycoloquy, 3.*

Wallsten, T. (1981). Physician and medical student bias in evaluating diagnostic information. *Medical Decision Making, 1,* 145–164.

Walsh, V., & Pascual-Leone, A. (2003). *Transcranial magnetic stimulation: A neurochronometrics of mind.* Cambridge, Mass.: MIT Press.

Walsh, V., & Rushworth, M. (1999). A primer of magnetic stimulation as a tool for neuropsychology. *Neuropsychologia, 37,* 125–135.

Wandell, B. (1993). Color appearance: The effects of illumination and spatial resolution. *Proceedings of the National Academy of Sciences of the USA, 90,* 9778–9784.

Ward, L. (2002). *Dynamical cognitive science.* Cambridge, Mass.: MIT Press.

Ward, R., & McClelland, J. (1989). Conjunctive search for one and two identical targets. *Journal of Experimental Psychology: Human Perception and Performance, 15,* 664–672.

Warren, R. (1970). Perceptual restoration of missing speech sounds. *Science, 167,* 392–393.

Warren, W. (1998). Visually controlled locomotion: 40 years later. *Ecological Psychology, 10,* 177–219.

Warren, W., Kay, B., & Yilmaz, E. (1996). Visual control of posture during walking: Functional specificity. *Journal of Experimental Psychology: Human Perception and Performance, 22,* 818–838.

Warren, W. H., & Whang, S. (1987). Visual guidance of walking through apertures: Body-scaled information for affordances. *Journal of Experimental Psychology: Human Perception and Performance, 13,* 371–383.

Wason, P. (1966). Reasoning. In B. Foss (Ed.), *New horizons in psychology* (pp. 135–151). Harmondsworth, U.K.: Penguin Books.

Wason, P., & Johnson-Laird, P. (1972). *Psychology of reasoning: Structure and content.* Oxford: Harvard University Press.

Wason, P., & Shapiro, D. (1971). Natural and contrived experience in a reasoning problem. *Quarterly Journal of Experimental Psychology, 23,* 63–71.

Watson, A. (1979). Probability summation over time. *Vision Research, 19,* 515–522.

Watson, A. (1986). Apparent motion occurs only between similar spatial frequencies. *Vision Research, 26,* 1727–1730.

Watson, A. (1992). Transfer of contrast sensitivity in linear visual networks. *Visual Neuroscience, 8,* 65–76.

Watson, D., & Humphreys, G. (1997). Visual marking: Prioritizing selection for new objects by top-down attentional inhibition of old objects. *Psychological Review, 104,* 90–122.

Watts, D., & Strogatz, S. (1998). Collective dynamics of 'small-world' networks. *Nature, 393,* 440–442.

Weatherford, R. (1982). *Philosophical foundations of probability theory.* London: Routledge & Kegan Paul.

Webb, B., Tinsley, C., Barraclough, N., Easton, A., Parker, A., & Derrington, A. (2002). Feedback from V1 and inhibition from beyond the classical receptive field modulates the responses of neurons in the primate lateral geniculate nucleus. *Visual Neuroscience, 19,* 583–592.

Weger, U. (2005). *Spatial and linguistic control of eye movements during reading.* Ph.D. dissertation, State University of New York, Binghamton.

Wegner, D. (1995). A computer network model of human transactive memory. *Social Cognition, 13,* 319–339.

Wegner, D. (2002). *The illusion of conscious will.* Cambridge, Mass.: MIT Press.

Wegner, D., Erber, R., & Raymond, P. (1991). Transactive memory in close relationships. *Journal of Personality and Social Psychology, 61,* 923–929.

Wegner, D., Sparrow, B., & Winerman, L. (2004). Vicarious agency: Experiencing control over the movements of others. *Journal of Personality and Social Psychology, 86,* 838–848.

Weizenbaum, J. (1966). ELIZA—A computer program for the study of natural language communication between man and machine. *Communications of the ACM, 9,* 36–45.

Welch, R., & Warren, D. (1986). Intersensory interactions. In K. Boff, L. Kaufman, & J. Thomas (Eds.), *Handbook of perception and human performance, Vol. 1: Sensory processes and perception* (pp. 1–36). New York: Wiley.

Weldon, M. (2001). Remembering as a social process. In D. Medin (Ed.), *The psychology of learning and motivation: Advances in research and theory, Vol. 40* (pp. 67–120). San Diego: Academic Press.

Wells, G. (1984). The psychology of lineup identifications. *Journal of Applied Social Psychology, 14,* 89–103.

West, P. (1999). The extent of coarticulation of English liquids: An acoustic and articulatory study. *Proceedings of the 14th International Congress of Phonetic Sciences, 3,* 1901–1904.

Wexler, K., & Culicover, P. (1980). *Formal principles of language acquisition.* Cambridge, Mass.: MIT Press.

Wexler, M., Kosslyn, S., & Berthoz, A. (1998). Motor processes in mental rotation. *Cognition, 68,* 77–94.

Whaley, C. (1979). Predictive analysis vs segmentational analysis in sentence perception. *Journal of Psycholinguistic Research, 8,* 523–542.

Whorf, B. (1956). *Language, thought, and reality: Selected writings* (ed. by J. Carroll). Cambridge, Mass.: MIT Press.

Wickelgren, W. (1969). Context-sensitive coding, associative memory, and serial order in (speech) behavior. *Psychological Review, 76,* 1–15.

Wilkinson, K., Dube, W., & McIlvane, W. (1996). A crossdisciplinary perspective on studies of rapid word mapping in psycholinguistics and behavior analysis. *Developmental Review, 16,* 125–148.

Williams, R. J., & Zipser, D. (1989). A learning algorithm for continually running fully recurrent neural networks. *Neural Computation, 1,* 270–280.

Williamson, T. (1994). *Vagueness.* London: Routledge.

Wilson, H., & Wilkinson, F. (1997). Evolving concepts of spatial channels in vision: From independence to nonlinear interactions. *Perception, 26,* 939–960.

Wilson, M. (2002). Six views of embodied cognition. *Psychonomic Bulletin and Review, 9,* 625–636.

Wilson, M. A., & McNaughton, B. (1993). Dynamics of the hippocampal ensemble code for space. *Science, 261,* 1055–1058.

Wilson, M. A., & McNaughton, B. (1994). Reactivation of hippocampal ensemble memories during sleep. *Science, 265,* 676–679.

Wilson, R. (1994). Wide computationalism. *Mind, 103,* 351–372.

Wilson, T., & Schooler, J. (1991). Thinking too much: Introspection can reduce the quality of preferences and decisions. *Journal of Personality and Social Psychology, 60,* 181–192.

Winograd, T. (1972). *Understanding natural language.* Oxford: Academic Press.

Wohlschläger, A., & Wohlschläger, A. (1998). Mental and manual rotation. *Journal of Experimental Psychology: Human Perception and Performance, 24,* 397–412.

Wolfe, J. (1992a). The parallel guidance of visual attention. *Current Directions in Psychological Science, 1,* 124–128.

Wolfe, J. (1992b). "Effortless" texture segmentation and "parallel" visual search are not the same thing. *Vision Research, 32,* 757–763.

Wolfe, J. (1994). Visual search in continuous, naturalistic stimuli. *Vision Research, 34,* 1187–1195.

Wolfe, J. (1998). What can 1 million trials tell us about visual search? *Psychological Science, 9,* 33–39.

Wolfe, J., Cave, K., & Franzel, S. (1989). Guided search: An alternative to the feature integration model for visual search. *Journal of Experimental Psychology: Human Perception and Performance, 15,* 419–433.

Wolpert, D., & Kawato, M. (1998). Multiple paired forward and inverse models for motor control. *Neural Networks, 11,* 1317–1329.

Wulf, G., McNevin, N., & Shea, C. (2001). The automaticity of complex motor skill learning as a function of attentional focus. *Journal of Experimental Psychology A: Human Experimental Psychology, 54,* 1143–1154.

Wundt, W. (1903). *Physiologische psychologie* (5th ed.) Vol. 3. Leipzig: Engelmann.

Yamaguchi, Y., & Shimizu, H. (1994). Pattern recognition with figure-ground separation by generation of coherent oscillations. *Neural Networks, 7,* 49–63.

Yantis, S., & Jonides, J. (1990). Abrupt visual onsets and selective attention: Voluntary versus automatic allocation. *Journal of Experimental Psychology: Human Perception and Performance, 16,* 121–134.

Yarbus, A. (1967). *Eye movements and vision* (trans. by Basil Haigh). New York: Plenum Press.

Yoo, Y., & Kanawattanachai, P. (2001). Developments of transactive memory systems and collective mind in virtual teams. *International Journal of Organizational Analysis, 9,* 187–208.

Young, M., & Yamane, S. (1992). Sparse population coding of faces in the infero-temporal cortex. *Science, 256,* 1327–1331.

Zadeh, L. (1965). Fuzzy sets. *Information and Control, 8,* 338–353.

Zadeh, L. (Ed.) (1975). *Fuzzy sets and their applications to cognitive and decision processes.* New York: Academic Press.

Zangaladze, A., Epstein, C., Grafton, S., & Sathian, K. (1999). Involvement of visual cortex in tactile discrimination of orientation. *Nature, 401,* 587–590.

Zeki, S. (1993). *A vision of the brain.* Malden, Mass.: Blackwell Scientific.

Zemel, R., Dayan, P., & Pouget, A. (1998). Probabilistic interpretation of population codes. *Neural Computation, 10,* 403–430.

Zemel, R., & Mozer, M. (2001). Localist attractor networks. *Neural Computation, 13,* 1045–1064.

Zizzo, D. (2003). Verbal and behavioral learning in a probability compounding task. *Theory and Decision, 54,* 287–314.

Zohar, D. (1995). A quantum mechanical model of consciousness and the emergence of "I." *Minds and Machines, 5,* 597–560.

Zwaan, R., Madden, C., Yaxley, R., & Aveyard, M. (2004). Moving words: Dynamic representations in language comprehension. *Cognitive Science, 28,* 611–619.

Zwitserlood, P. (1989). The locus of the effects of sentential-semantic context in spoken-word processing. *Cognition, 32,* 25–64.

Index

The letter *f* following a page number refers to a figure on that page.